lonely planet

Iceland

AF060036

The Westfjords
p220

North Iceland
p249

West Iceland
p191

The Highlands
p327

East Iceland
p302

REYKJAVÍK
p42

Southwest Iceland & the Golden Circle
p99

Southeast Iceland
p162

Eygló Svala Arnarsdóttir, Alexis Averbuck,
Jade Bremner, Mary Fitzpatrick, Anthony Ham

Vatnajökull (p166)

CONTENTS

Plan Your Trip

The Journey Begins Here........4
Iceland Map................................6
Our Picks......................................8
Regions & Cities 20
Itineraries................................. 22
When to Go 30
Get Prepared............................ 32
The Food Scene 34
The Outdoors........................... 36

The Guide

Rejkjavík.....................................42
Find Your Way 44
Plan Your Days...................... 46
Historic Miðborg................... 48
Laugavegur 62
Vesturbær &
the Old Harbour 74
Laugardalur & Hlíðar..........84
Kópavogur
& Hafnarfjörður 91

Southwest Iceland &
the Golden Circle................. 99
Find Your Way 100
Plan Your Time......................102
Reykjanes Peninsula...... 104

Vesturdalur (p290)

The Golden Circle.............. 116
Beyond the
Golden Circle......................129
Hvolsvöllur..........................136
Beyond Hvolsvöllur..........143
Vík..153
Beyond Vík..........................158

Southeast Iceland.............. 162
Find Your Way 164
Plan Your Time....................165
Skaftafell..............................166
Beyond Skaftafell 172
Jökulsárlón & Around..... 178
Höfn & Around...................185

West Iceland 191
Find Your Way 192
Plan Your Time....................193
Borgarnes 194
Beyond Borgarnes............198
Stykkishólmur....................205
Beyond Stykkishólmur...209
Snæfellsnes
Peninsula.............................. 213

The Westfjords.................... 220
Find Your Way 222
Plan Your Time.................... 224
Arnarfjörður........................ 226
Beyond Arnarfjörður........ 231
Ísafjörður............................. 236
Beyond Ísafjörður 240
Hólmavík............................. 244

North Iceland 249
Find Your Way 250
Plan Your Time....................252
Skagafjörður 254
Beyond Skagafjörður...... 261
Akureyri............................... 266
Beyond Akureyri............... 275
Húsavík 280
Beyond Húsavík................284
Jökulsárgljúfur
Canyon.................................288
Melrakkaslétta
Peninsula............................ 294
Beyond
Melrakkaslétta 298

East Iceland........................ 302
Find Your Way 304
Plan Your Time.................. 305
Fljótsdalur.......................... 306
Beyond Fljótsdalur..........310
Seyðisfjörður 316
Beyond Seyðisfjörður.....319

The Highlands.....................327
Find Your Way 328
Plan Your Time....................329
Kjölur Route 330
Sprengisandur Route 335
Askja Route 339

Toolkit

Arriving 350
Getting Around 351
Money.....................................352
Accommodation................353
Family Travel......................354
Health & Safe Travel 355
Food, Drink & Nightlife 356
Responsible Travel 358
LGBTIQ+ Travellers 360
Accessible Travel 361
Take Care of Iceland..........362
Nuts & Bolts.........................363
Language..............................364

Storybook

A History of Iceland
in 15 Places........................368
Meet the Icelanders..........372
Iceland Minus the Ice 374
Life under Fire....................377
Iceland's Pop-Rock
Juggernaut 380

Icelandic horses, Fjallabak Nature Reserve (p146)

ICELAND
THE JOURNEY BEGINS HERE

Growing up in Akureyri, I met a tourist at the harbour one autumn day. She had just arrived by cruise ship and was absorbing her surroundings with an expression of stunned disbelief. 'Do you live here?' she asked. A little hesitant, I agreed, because I was about to move abroad for college. 'You are so lucky!' she proclaimed and walked on. Suddenly, I saw my hometown in a new light. Stately houses on a slope, surrounded by fiery foliage, and the gleaming Eyjafjörður fjord framed by towering mountains.

We have a saying here, '*glöggt er gests augað*', or 'sharp is the guest's eye'. Visitors have truly made us appreciate our own country more. Untouched multicoloured landscapes, vast moss-covered lava fields, peculiar rock formations, thundering waterfalls, rich birdlife, fresh seafood and hot springs. Many of Iceland's natural phenomena exist in other countries, too. But nowhere else is nature so diverse in such a compact area.

Eygló Svala Arnarsdóttir

@eyglosvala

Eygló has written for Iceland Review, Kinfolk Travel *and* Lonely Planet, *among other travel publications, and children's books about Krummi, inspired by her travels.*

My favourite experience is feeling true horse power when riding in fast and smooth *tölt* (gait) along a soft dirt path in the peaceful countryside (p309).

WHO GOES WHERE

Our writers and experts choose the places which, for them, define Iceland.

The highlands around **Askja** (pictured; p339) crack open my heart with their beauty. Undulating crater rows give way to iridescent volcanic pools and hidden oases, green with life. And the crater itself, with its magenta rocks and snow-studded rim, reminds me of how vast and grand this earth is – a magnificent world to be protected and revered.

Alexis Averbuck
alexisaverbuck.com

Alexis paints and writes about her adventures for Lonely Planet, National Geographic UK and other international outlets. Alexis wrote the Reykjavík and Southwest Iceland & the Golden Circle chapters.

It's hard to beat the **Westfjords Way** (pictured; p227) – an empty stretch of tarmac that zigzags around beautiful fjords, through dramatic mountain passes and long tunnels almost impossibly carved out of rock. It connects adventurous road-trippers to waterfalls, hot pools, expansive beaches and more – yet few of Iceland's visitors make it here.

Jade Bremner
@jadeob

Jade has authored more than 60 Lonely Planet books and has edited sections for a number of major media outlets. Jade wrote the West Iceland and The Westfjords chapters.

North Iceland's **Arctic Coast Way** (pictured Hvítserkur; p262) is the journey of a lifetime, with its remote coastal villages, bird-filled headlands and unhindered views of the sky. Travelling here brings one spectacular vista after another – snow-covered mountains tumbling down into icy fjords, dramatic waterfalls, soaring gannets, cliffsides filled with nesting puffins and, everywhere, the sea.

Mary Fitzpatrick
@MaryFitzTravel

Mary is a professional travel writer who seeks out the world's remote and beautiful corners. She has travelled extensively in Iceland and wrote the Akureyri and North Iceland chapters.

Every time I climb up over the mountains from Egilsstaðir and down to **Seyðisfjörður** (pictured; p316), I can almost hear the earth exhale. Almost as far as you can get from Reykjavík without falling into the sea, this stunning village – with its storybook blue church, thriving art scene and great food – wraps around a narrow harbour and inspires in me a feeling of never wanting to leave.

Anthony Ham
anthonyham.com, @AnthonyHamWrite

Anthony has travelled the world to research and write nearly 200 guidebooks for Lonely Planet. He has written two books of narrative non-fiction. Anthony wrote the Southeast Iceland and The Highlands chapters.

Húsavík
Spot blue whales off the north coast (p280)

Akureyri
View the Northern Lights (p272)

Jökulsárlón
See glistening icebergs and a diamond beach (p178)

DRIVE THE RING ROAD

This is one of the world's most iconic road trips. The 1322km Rte 1 loops around Iceland, passing through most of the country's towns and villages. In a single journey, the Ring Road can lead from the quirky northern capital of Reykjavík through the remote Arctic Coast Way, along zigzagging fjords and to coastal fishing towns. Enjoy views of jagged cliffs, towering rock formations and black-sand beaches on the way.

Visit Charming Towns

Iceland is proof the most charming things can come in small packages. There's no better way to experience the island's small towns (pictured Seyðisfjörður; p316) than this road trip.

Enjoy Epic Scenery

From the dramatic Tröllaskagi peninsula (pictured; p275) to long coastal stretches, rugged fjords and black-sand beaches, you'll find it all along this route.

Summer & Winter

Winter weather and road closures could force you to alter your itinerary. Travel in the summer for long stretches of daylight; perfect for driving remote roads.

Kirkjufell (p211)

BEST ROAD-TRIP STOP EXPERIENCES

Get a close-up view of ❶ **Kirkjufell**, an iconic pyramid-shaped mountain on the Snæfellsnes Peninsula. (p211)

Take in views of picturesque ❷ **Lake Mývatn**. Go birdwatching, soak in a geothermal lagoon and check out the rare Skútustaðagígar pseudocraters. (p284)

Look for gigantic blue whales on a whale-watching tour off the coast of ❸ **Húsavík**. (p280)

Marvel at magnificent rock formations near Reynisfjara beach. Hike the ❹ **Dyrhólaey peninsula** to take in sweeping views of black-sand beaches and towering basalt columns. (p153)

Follow the rainbow street in ❺ **Seyðisfjörður** to the blue church and find a cosy cafe for lunch. (p316)

EXPLORE VOLCANOES

Volcano tourism has exploded in popularity in recent years as the Reykjanes Peninsula has produced a steady number of mesmerising eruptions that have captured the world's attention. Visitors can hike eruption zones, fly over fresh lava fields and descend to the floor of an inactive volcano not far from Reykjavík. Explore the colourful craters that volcanic eruptions leave behind. Or walk through the long tunnels carved out by boiling lava thousands of years ago.

Hike an Eruption Zone

Hike fresh lava fields around the Fagradalsfjall (pictured; p110) volcano system on the Reykjanes Peninsula to see the effects of recent eruptions. Several companies offer guided tours.

Fly Over an Eruption

Depending on your timing, you may be able to fly over a volcanic eruption (pictured Fagradalsfjall; p110) on a helicopter tour and see bubbling, flowing lava.

Explore Colourful Calderas

Experience the striking craters that volcanic eruptions leave behind by embarking on a challenging hike of the Askja caldera or an easy walk around Kerið crater.

FROM LEFT: ALEKSANDRA TOKARZ/SHUTTERSTOCK, IMAGEBANKAU/SHUTTERSTOCK, EDGARS KARKLIS/SHUTTERSTOCK

Víti crater (p343)

BEST VOLCANIC EXPERIENCES

Hike through newly formed lava fields from the 2021–23 eruptions of ❶ **Fagradalsfjall** and **Litli-Hrútur** on the Reykjanes Peninsula. (p110)

Descend to the floor of ❷ **Þríhnúkagígur** volcano to make your own journey to the centre of the Earth. (p93)

Take an hour-long hike around the lake in ❸ **Víti crater** in the Krafla volcanic area near Lake Mývatn. (p343)

Walk to the top of ❹ **Eldfell** volcano, which formed in the 1973 eruption in Vestmannaeyjar, and visit Eldheimar museum. (p147)

Brace for a bumpy highlands drive to reach the immense ❺ **Askja** caldera with its sapphire blue lake. (p343)

ENJOY THE WATER

Fire and ice may get most of the attention, but Iceland is also a country of water. Pristine lakes and rivers are teeming with fish. There are a couple of suitable areas for kayaking on the South Coast, and there's an under-the-radar beach at the southern edge of Reykjavík that's become a haven for sea swimmers. A fissure between tectonic plates allows for swimming between continents, while river-rafting adventures, geothermal lagoons and epic waterfalls are plentiful.

River Rafting

If you're a beginner, go rafting down the welcoming Hvitá (pictured; p123) or West Glacial rivers. If you're looking for more of an adventure, take on the East Glacial River.

Sea Swimming

The water surrounding Iceland is cold all year, and there aren't many places to jump in. Nauthólsvík Geothermal Beach (pictured; p89) is your best bet for sea swimming.

Fishing

Fish pristine lakes and rivers for Arctic char, Atlantic salmon and trout. Or go sea angling to fish for cod, haddock, rockfish and pollock.

Silfra fissure (p122)

BEST WATER EXPERIENCES

Dive into the glacial water of the ❶ **Silfra fissure**, the only place in the world where it's possible to swim between continents. (p122)

Go rafting down the beginner-friendly ❷ **Hvítá river** in South Iceland, taking in the views as you cut through Gullfoss Canyon. (p123)

Take a more adventurous river-rafting adventure on the ❸ **East Glacial River** in North Iceland, where even experienced rafters may feel challenged. (p260)

Fish for giant trout and salmon on the ❹ **Tungufljót river**. You'll find the best fishing conditions in spring and autumn, and equipment is available to rent. (p125)

Settle into a kayak and head out from ❺ **Klettsvík Bay** in search of puffins off the coast of Vestmannaeyjar. (p147)

ANIMAL ENCOUNTERS

From small and sturdy horses and cute and clownish puffins to behemoth blue whales and playful dolphins, there's lots of wildlife in Iceland. And you don't have to worry about any of it trying to eat you. The country has no large predators, which makes it a haven for migrating birds. You don't have to be on the lookout for snakes or spiders, and you're not likely to encounter a polar bear.

Go Whale Watching

Whales are frequently spotted off the coast of Iceland. Humpback (pictured) and minke whales are most common, but blue whales have also been seen near Húsavík.

Look for Puffins

Look for puffins between May and August on Lundey island (pictured; p81) off Reykjavík, on Tjörnes Peninsula on the northern coast, on Heimaey in Vestmannaeyjar, or in Borgarfjörður Eystri in the East.

Ride Horses

Icelandic horses are smaller than the average horse and have five gaits instead of the typical three. They're friendly and fun to ride, even for beginners.

Puffins, Heimaey (p147)

BEST BIRDWATCHING EXPERIENCES

Take a boat tour from Reykjavík's Old Harbour to ❶ **Akurey**, **Engey** or **Lundey**, where thousands of puffin pairs nest each summer. (p81)

See Arctic terns form a summer colony around the ❷ **Grótta Lighthouse** and keep an eye out for the seals that occasionally come to visit. (p83)

Look for gyrfalcons hunting near ❸ **Lake Mývatn**, and check out the variety of ducks that call the lake home. (p284)

Head to ❹ **Látrabjarg** in the Westfjords to see puffins, razorbills, white-tailed eagles and more. (p234)

Follow the coastal path to Stórhöfði, a mountain peak at the southern edge of ❺ **Heimaey** that's home to a large puffin colony during the summer. (p147)

Northern Lights, Þingvellir National Park (p120)

CHASE NORTHERN LIGHTS

Iceland is far enough north that it's almost in the Arctic Circle, and winters are marked by long, dark nights. This combination makes Iceland one of the best places in the world for viewing the Northern Lights: the magical green aurora that can take over clear skies when there's increased solar activity (see forecasts on *en.vedur.is*).

When to Go

The best time to visit for the Northern Lights is between mid-September and early April when darkness can stretch for up to 20 hours a night.

Where to Go

Head to dark places with minimal light pollution from things like street lights. Also look for clear skies or breaks in the clouds where lights can peek through.

BEST NORTHERN LIGHTS EXPERIENCES

Head to ❶ **Þingvellir National Park** to watch the Northern Lights over the birthplace of modern democracy. (p120)

Drive out to Garður lighthouse on ❷ **Reykjanes Peninsula** for an unobstructed view of the ocean and, hopefully, the Northern Lights. (p114)

Chase the Northern Lights around ❸ **Akureyri**; for example from Hlíðarfjall ski resort, just 100km from the Arctic Circle. (p272)

Take a boat tour from Reykjavík's Old Harbour or walk out to Grótta on ❹ **Seltjarnarnes peninsula** to see the Northern Lights near the capital. (p83)

See the Northern Lights over a towering waterfall at ❺ **Mígandifoss Viewpoint** on the Troll Peninsula. (p264)

GEOTHERMAL SPA DAYS

Icelandic water is some of the purest and cleanest in the world. And Icelanders have turned enjoying this natural resource into an art and a science. The Blue Lagoon is just the beginning. From sprawling lagoon complexes with multi-step bath rituals to tiny secluded natural pools, you'll find a variety of geothermal facilities across the country.

BEST GEOTHERMAL EXPERIENCES

Feel the rich silica mud between your toes as you wade into the ❶ **Blue Lagoon** to soak in its iconic blue geothermal water. (p104)

Indulge in the seven-step bath ritual at the ❷ **Sky Lagoon** and give yourself plenty of time to soak in its warm lagoon overlooking the water. (p91)

Escape the crowds and save some krónur by visiting the not-so-secret ❸ **Secret Lagoon** on the Golden Circle. (p127)

Enjoy a truly magical north-coast experience at ❹ **Forest Lagoon**, where forest bathing meets Icelandic spa culture. (p268)

Relax in the ❺ **GeoSea** geothermal sea baths while enjoying endless Atlantic Ocean views. (p283)

Famous Spas

These sprawling spa complexes tap into Iceland's crystal-clear geothermal water and take things up a notch with bath rituals, massages and more (pictured Blue Lagoon; p104).

Hidden Gems

Spending a lot of money isn't your only option. Lots of tiny geothermal pools are scattered across Iceland and cost a fraction of the price (pictured Sky Lagoon; p91).

Local Pools

Icelanders take swimming seriously and some public pools are closer to what foreign visitors may call waterparks, but with hot tubs. Visiting is a cultural experience.

FROM LEFT: PALMI GUDMUNDSSON/SHUTTERSTOCK, RENATA TY/SHUTTERSTOCK

EXPLORE EPIC GLACIERS

Iceland is home to an estimated 400 glaciers that cover approximately 11% of this island nation. This is a country where majestic glacial views are everywhere, and memories are just waiting to be made. Vatnajökull is Iceland's largest and best-known glacier, but it's just one of many majestic ice caps offering unforgettable adventures on – or inside – ice. Go snowmobiling on Langjökull, venture into Vatnajökull's Crystal Ice Cave, sail the Jökulsárlón lagoon or traverse the ice at Sólheimajökull.

Snowmobile Across Ice Caps

There really is nothing like snowmobiling across a magnificent glacier (pictured Langjökull; p129). Suit up for the adventure of a lifetime.

Journey into Ice Caves

Visit during winter to explore natural ice caves (pictured Katla Ice Cave; p151). A human-made ice cave within Langjökull is open year-round.

Hike a Glacier

There's nothing quite like walking on ice, and there's no better place to do it than these magical blue and white spaces.

Jökulsárlón glacier lagoon (p180)

BEST GLACIAL EXPERIENCES

Sail among magnificent icebergs on a ❶ **Jökulsárlón** glacier lagoon boat tour. (p180)

Feel like you're flying across the moon on a snowmobile ride across ❷ **Langjökull**, Iceland's second largest ice cap. (p129)

Hike across ❸ **Falljökull** glacier on a tour from Skaftafell to walk around magical ice formations and through winding crevasses. (p168)

Head inside the ❹ **Katla Ice Cave** to tour an elaborate palace of black and blue ice that opened to visitors in 2016 and is in a constant state of evolution. (p151)

Take a guided glacial hike across remote Kverkfjöll to the ❺ **Hveradalir geothermal area**, a colourful oasis of steam in the highlands. (p333)

REGIONS & CITIES

Find the places that tick all your boxes.

The Westfjords

OFFBEAT ICELAND

This mountainous peninsula is sparsely populated, even by Icelandic standards. Snow and ice close the roads along the narrow fjords that define the coastline for several months each year. Travel during the summer when road conditions are best to take in the spectacular scenery in this remote region.

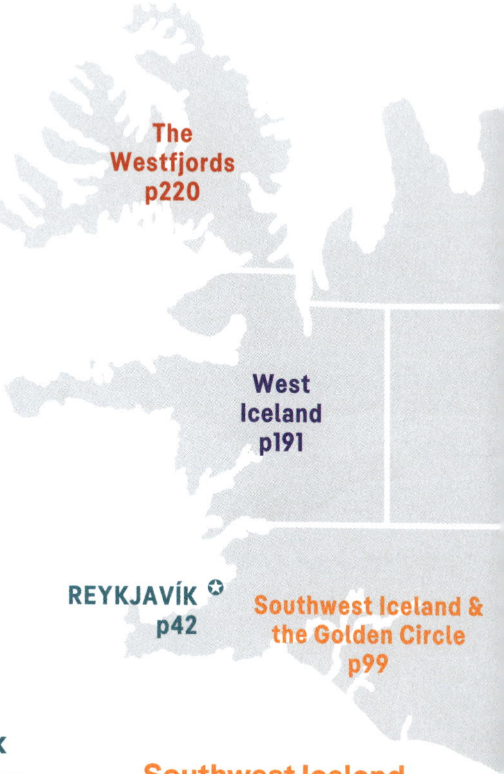

West Iceland

STUNNING VOLCANIC AND GLACIAL TERRAIN AND WILD COASTLINES

West Iceland is a short drive from Reykjavík but feels like a different world. This geographically diverse area is home to volcanoes, waterfalls and Langjökull, Iceland's second-largest glacier. This is a popular destination for snowmobiling and exploring ice tunnels. It's also home to the scenic Snæfellsnes Peninsula.

Reykjavík

DYNAMIC CAPITAL FULL OF SURPRISES

Iceland's national capital is also its cultural capital. This is the heart of the Icelandic art, music and nightlife scenes. Come for Michelin-star dining, vintage shopping and all-night parties under the midnight sun. Stay to hike, fish and eat your way around the world, all without leaving the city.

Southwest Iceland & the Golden Circle

VOLCANO, GLACIER AND BLACK-SAND ADVENTURES

With charming small towns, magnificent natural wonders and frequent volcanic eruptions, it's no surprise this region is Iceland's biggest draw. Soak in geothermal lagoons. Explore a rugged coastline shaped by volcanic activity and an otherworldly interior where lava fields meet bubbling hot springs, rivers and waterfalls.

The Westfjords p220

West Iceland p191

REYKJAVÍK p42

Southwest Iceland & the Golden Circle p99

North Iceland

ICELAND'S ARCTIC STRONGHOLD

There are few better places for viewing the Northern Lights or experiencing the midnight sun than this region at the edge of the Arctic Circle. This remote area hosts the Arctic Open golf tournament during the summer and is a popular ski destination during the winter.

North Iceland p249

East Iceland

AS FAR FROM REYKJAVÍK AS POSSIBLE

This sparsely populated area is popular for skiing during the winter and a haven for artists and musicians in summer. Charming fishing towns surround picturesque natural harbours. Narrow fjords define a jagged coastline often dotted with puffins and seals, and herds of wild reindeer live in the mountains.

The Highlands p327

East Iceland p302

Southeast Iceland p162

The Highlands

RUGGED, RAW, WILD ICELANDIC INTERIOR

This vast uninhabitable area – only accessible between June and September – is as off-the-beaten path as it gets. There are no towns, hotels or fancy restaurants here, just hiking huts, majestic glaciers and unbelievable landscapes. Navigating the rough gravel roads leading into the highlands requires a 4WD.

Southeast Iceland

RAW GLACIAL BEAUTY, CHARMING HAMLETS

This region of Iceland puts the ice in the 'land of fire and ice'. It's best known for Vatnajökull, the country's largest glacier, and Jökulsárlón, a glacial lagoon whose majestic icebergs crash-land onto a black-sand beach, glittering like diamonds as they settle.

Hraunfossar falls (p201)

ITINERARIES

Reykjavík & the Southwest

Allow: 5 days **Distance:** 670km

Iceland is small enough to pack a lot into even a short trip. Base yourself in Reykjavík for easy access to Iceland's top natural wonders. Explore magnificent waterfalls, hot springs and lava fields by day, and spend the evenings meandering the streets of Iceland's lively capital.

❶ REYKJAVÍK ⏱ 1 DAY

The walkable **city centre** (pictured; p48) is filled with gourmet restaurants, one-of-a-kind boutiques and public art, and serves as a good base for day trips. Dive into Icelandic history at the **Settlement Exhibition** (p54) or the **Árbær Open Air Museum** (p89), catch a show at the **Harpa concert hall** (p56) and enjoy a Michelin-worthy meal (**Óx** and **Dill** (p59) have stars – book ahead).

❷ THE GOLDEN CIRCLE ⏱ 1 DAY

From Reykjavík, take yourself on a day tour of Iceland's top three sights – **Þingvellir National Park** (p120), **Gullfoss** (p126) and the **Geysir geothermal area** (p124). Rent a car or join one of several guided Golden Circle tours. Explore ancient bishopric **Skálholt** (p125), **Laugarvatn Fontana** (p117) baths, **Kerið crater** (pictured; p128), and tomato and horse farm Friðheimar. Drive through **Hveragerði** (p130) on the way back to Reykjavík.

❸ LANGJÖKULL GLACIER ⏱ 1 DAY

Leave Reykjavík early for a full day of adventure on Langjökull (pictured; p129), Iceland's second-largest glacier. Book a tour to ride a massive eight-wheel monster truck across the ice. Spend an hour wandering the world's longest human-made ice tunnel with a guide. Stop at **Hraunfossar** and **Barnafoss falls** (p201) and **Reykholt** (p200) to look at saga author Snorri Sturluson's pool on the way back through Borgarfjörður.

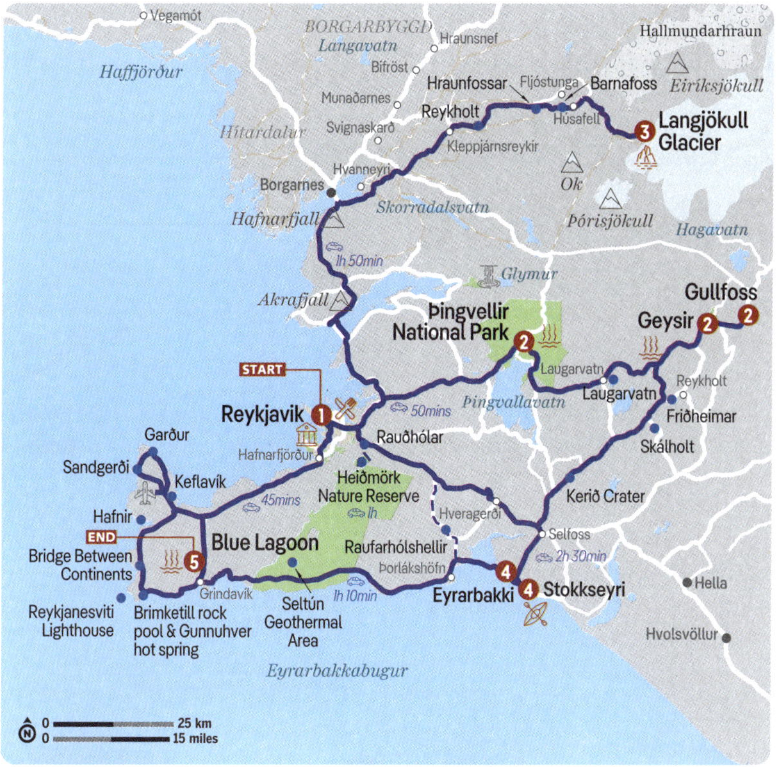

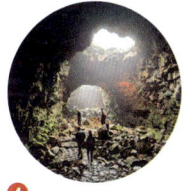

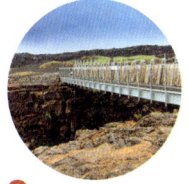

4 STOKKSEYRI & EYRARBAKKI ⏱ 1 DAY

Drive through **Hveragerði** (p130) and **Selfoss** (p132) to neighbouring coastal towns Stokkseyri (p134) and Eyrarbakki (p134), kayak in calm water canals, stroll past beautifully restored houses, learn about local history and myths in quirky museums, and eat delicious seafood. Explore **Raufarhólshellir** (pictured; p133), one of the country's longest lava tunnels, on Rte 39, which leads back to Reykjavík. Before entering town, stop by **Rauðhólar** (p92), red lava hills, and for a walk in **Heiðmörk Nature Reserve** (p92).

Detour: *Explore the colourful* ***Seltún geothermal area*** *(p112) and take Rte 42 back instead.*

FROM LEFT: TEREZA TOTHOVA/SHUTTERSTOCK, PETER ZAMOROWSKI/SHUTTERSTOCK

5 REYKJANES & THE BLUE LAGOON ⏱ 1 DAY

Before taking off, explore Reykjanes Peninsula (p104). Book an early slot at the Blue Lagoon (p104), then carry on towards **Grindavík** (p110) – both might close due to volcanic activity. Rte 425 takes you to **Brimketill rock pool** (p113), **Gunnuhver hot spring** (p113) and **Reykjanesviti Lighthouse** (p113), and onwards to the **Bridge Between Continents** (pictured; p114). Drive past quiet seaside hamlet Hafnir and either around the peninsula on Rte 45 through villages **Sandgerði** (p114) and **Garður** (p114), or take Rte 44 to **Keflavík** (p115), home to the Icelandic Museum of Rock 'n' Roll.

ITINERARIES

South Coast Adventure

Allow: 6 days **Distance:** 932km

Six days is enough time to get to know Iceland's South Coast without feeling rushed. Check out a glacial lagoon. Ride horses on the beach. Go paragliding, hiking or chasing waterfalls. Eat farm-to-table meals. Try hot springs bread. Soak in a lagoon. Go inside a volcano, and make memories you'll never forget.

❶ HVERAGERÐI & SELFOSS
⏱ 1 DAY

Leave Reykjavík early for Hveragerði (p130). Allow 2½ hours for hiking **Reykjadalur geothermal valley** (pictured; p130) and bathing in the hot river. For an adrenaline rush, try the longest zipline in Iceland. Stop by Gróðurhúsið (p130) food hall for a lovely meal or an ice cream. Continue to **Selfoss** (p132) and walk through the town centre with reconstructed historical buildings.

FROM LEFT: MATTHEW MICAH WRIGHT/GETTY IMAGES, TRAVELWILD/SHUTTERSTOCK, HEATHER CARSWELL/LONELY PLANET

❷ CAVES & WATERFALLS
⏱ 1 DAY

Just before Hella, take a tour of human-made caves (p142). Continue to **Seljalandsfoss** (p139), and walk behind the veil of water. Walk an hour on to Gljúfrabúi, another fall, hidden in a gorge. The 60m high **Skógafoss** (pictured; p149) awaits. Walk to the top of the falls, then visit the turf farm at Skógar museum. En route to Vík, drive up to **Sólheimajökull** (p150) glacial tongue – or book a tour and hike it.

⤴ *Detour:* After Seljalandsfoss, take Rte 242 to Seljavellir and walk for 20 minutes to **Seljavallalaug pool** (p140).

❸ VÍK ⏱ 1 DAY

Use Vík (p153) as your home base for exploring this stretch of the South Coast. The village is known for black-sand beach Reynisfjara (pictured; p155), the distinct Reynisdrangar sea stack and a fairy-tale church. Activities include paragliding and ziplining, and horseriding on the beach. It's also home to award-winning **LavaShow** (p79).

PLAN YOUR TRIP ITINERARIES

❹ KATLA GEOPARK ⏱ 1 DAY

From Vík, head out on an off-road adventure on a super-Jeep tour of Katla Geopark (pictured; p150). Take a journey deep into the Katla Ice Cave. Go ice climbing, or snowmobiling across Mýrdalsjökull glacier. You'll need a specially modified vehicle to access these areas. These aren't available for rent, so you'll need to sign up for a guided tour.

❺ JÖKULSÁRLÓN ⏱ 1 DAY

Take a day trip from Vík to see the glittering icebergs that have washed up at **Fellsfjara** (Diamond Beach; p181). Marvel at the glorious blue Jökulsárlón glacial lagoon (pictured; p180) and take a boat tour to get up close to the giant chunks of ice – white, striped and brilliant blue. Look out for seals that swim between the icebergs.

🔸 Detour: *Stop at **Fjaðrárgljúfur** canyon (p151) on your way back to Vík. It looks like a serpent carved into the earth and is well worth the detour.*

❻ VESTMANNAEYJAR ⏱ 1 DAY

Have an early breakfast in Vík and head west on Rte 1 – drive to **Landeyjahöfn** (p143) and take the ferry to Vestmannaeyjar (p147) to look for puffins (pictured) and visit the Eldheimar Museum. Take the ferry back and stop in Selfoss at the **Old Dairy** (p133) food hall for dinner on your way to Keflavík International Airport.

Vatnajökull glacier (p166)

ITINERARIES

Full Circle

Allow: 7 days **Distance:** 1500km

This itinerary will take you around the entire country in a week. From artsy Reykjavík past the treasures of the West and North, to a whale haven and narrow fjords, glacial wonders and black-sand beaches, you can experience every scene and season as you circle the country, even if you don't have a lot of time.

❶ REYKJAVÍK ⏱ 1 DAY

Spend your first night in Reykjavík (p42) preparing for an unforgettable trip on Rte 1, the scenic Ring Road that loops around Iceland. Unwind in the **Sky Lagoon** (pictured; p91) after a long flight. Browse stores and galleries, visit curious museums, have a fancy meal, langoustine soup or simple hot dog or for dinner, and set out on the road trip of a lifetime after breakfast.

❷ BORGARFJÖRÐUR & THE NORTHWEST ⏱ 1 DAY

Just north of Bifröst in Borgarfjörður lies **Grábrók** (pictured; p198) crater. Walk to its rim and enjoy the view of lava fields. Continue to **Blönduós** (p261) and drop by the seasonal Textile Museum for a look at the Icelandic national costume. Enjoy a three-course New Nordic dinner at **Brimslóð Atelier** (p258), or an Ethiopian dinner at **Teni** (p258).

🢂 *Detour: Take part in the **Arctic Coast Way** (p262), Rte 711 from Hvammstangi, for **Hvítserkur sea stack** (p263) and fortress Borgarvirki.*

❸ AKUREYRI & HÚSAVÍK ⏱ 1 DAY

Wander the charming streets of Akureyri (pictured; p266) and walk the steps to the church that overlooks it. Have a stroll in beautiful botanical garden **Lystigarður** (p269) and enjoy a cup of coffee at a cosy cafe. Continue to Húsavík (p280) with a stop at **Goðafoss** (p287) waterfall. Book a whale-watching tour and prepare to be charmed by humpbacks, other whales and dolphins. Keep an eye out for the rare giant blue whale.

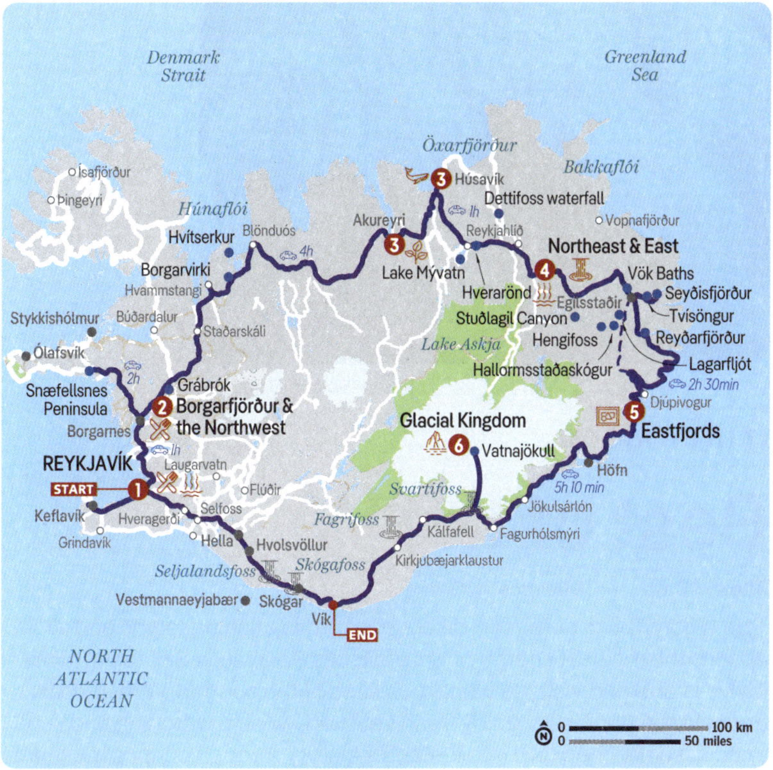

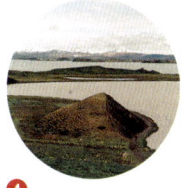

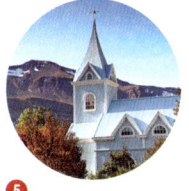

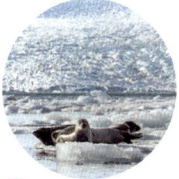

4 NORTHEAST & EAST
1 DAY

Take Rte 87 to **Mývatn** (pictured; p284), a marvel of a lake, then brave the sulphur smell of the fumaroles at **Hverarönd** (p286). From Rte 1, take a turn on Rte 862 for **Dettifoss** (p288), Europe's most powerful waterfall. Continue on Rte 1 to Egilsstaðir via Stuðlagil river canyon and soak in **Vök Baths** (p312) before moving on to **Seyðisfjörður** (p316).

Detour: *Drive around* ***Lake Lagarfljót*** *(p309) on Rte 391 for Hengifoss waterfall and Hallormsstaðaskógur.*

5 EASTFJORDS
1 DAY

Follow the rainbow path to Seyðisfjörður's **charming blue church** (pictured; p316). Walk up to Tvísöngur sound sculpture and check out the latest exhibit in Skaftfell. Continue to **Reyðarfjörður** (p321) with a stop in Sesam bakery, then continue your drive through friendly Eastfjords towns, at the foot of rugged mountains. Stop in **Djúpivogur** (p314) to check out 34 granite egg sculptures, representing the birds that nest there, before heading for **Höfn** (p185).

6 GLACIAL KINGDOM
1 DAY

Wake up to epic views of **Vatnajökull glacier** (p166), or better yet, book a tour to explore it by super-Jeep, snowmobile or on foot (see *visitvatnajokull.is*). Remember to try langoustine, the local delicacy, before setting out for **Jökulsárlón** (pictured; p178), where seals swim among the glistening icebergs. Drive on to **Vík** (p153) as you bid the glacial kingdom farewell.

FROM LEFT: DANIEL DORSA/LONELY PLANET, MATT MUNRO/LONELY PLANET, CARLOS GMOYO/SHUTTERSTOCK

Waterfall Dynjandi (p226)

ITINERARIES

Best of the West

Allow: 5 Days **Distance:** 1100km

Tour a fjord full of surprises, discover charming fishing towns and absorb the magical energy of Snæfellsnes Peninsula. Sail to the most idyllic island and visit the wondrous sites of the southern Westfjords. Encircle the peninsula, enjoy fresh seafood, wildlife watching and special soaks, then dive into Iceland's history through curious museums.

❶ HVALFJÖRÐUR ⏱ 1 DAY

Book a morning swim at **Hvammsvík Hot Springs** (p199) and drive from Reykjavík to Hvalfjörður (p199) on Rte 47. Continue into the fjord for the three- to four-hour steep hike to **Glymur** (pictured; p202), Iceland's second-highest waterfall (the path can be dangerous in winter), or opt for an easier walk to the other side of the valley to admire it from a distance. Visit the **War & Peace Museum** (p200) to learn more about Iceland's role in WWII.

❷ SNÆFELLSNES PENINSULA ⏱ 1 DAY

From **Borgarnes** (p194), continue to Snæfellsnes (p215) and stop at Lýsulaugar, green algae baths. Rte 547 leads to hamlets Hellnar and Arnarstapi and Djúpalónssandur beach, known for their rock formations. Drive around the peninsula to view pyramid mountain **Kirkjufell** (pictured; p211) by Grundarfjörður, then feast on seafood in **Stykkishólmur** (p205).

🔖 *Book ahead and allow more time for tours of* ***Vatnshellir lava tube*** *(p217) or* ***Snæfellsjökull glacier*** *(p217).*

❸ FLATEY & SOUTHERN WESTFJORDS ⏱ 1 DAY

Take the ferry to Brjánslækur via idyllic Flatey Island (p209). In the southern Westfjords, take Rte 62 towards Patreksfjörður and then Rte 612 to **Látrabjarg Bird Cliffs** (pictured; p234), Iceland's westernmost point. Enjoy panoramic views and an up-close look of puffins (May–August; avoid the edges). Stop at **Rauðisandur** (p231), a reddish sand beach, for a stroll, on the way to Patreksfjörður.

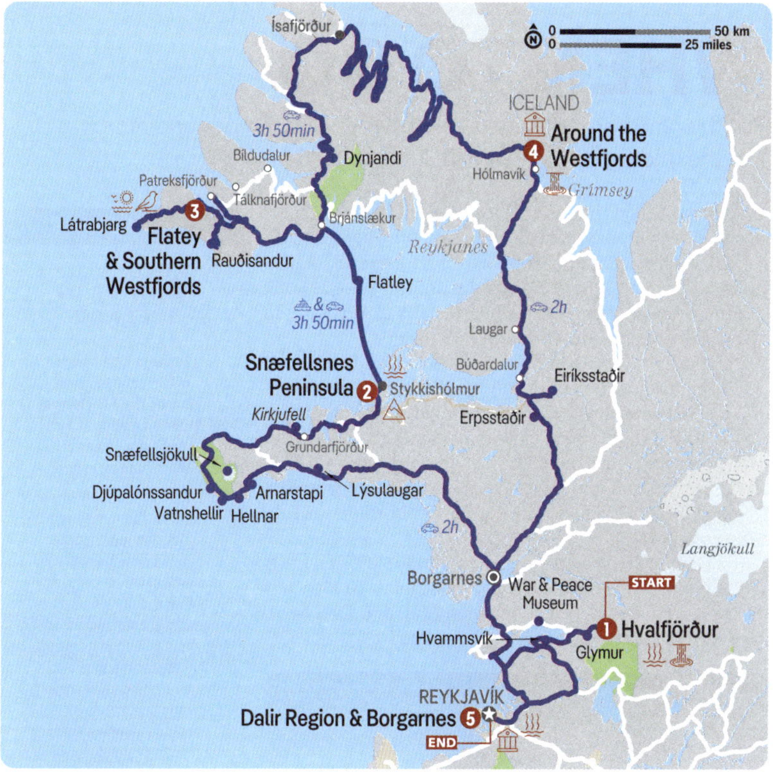

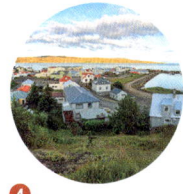

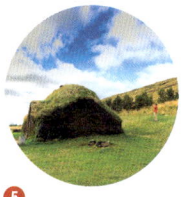

AROUND THE WESTFJORDS 1 DAY

Head towards tiered waterfall **Dynjandi** (p226) on Rte 63 via villages Tálknafjörður and Bíldudalur. Move on to **Ísafjörður** (p236) for a seafood lunch at Tjöruhúsið and a stroll in the old village. Up next is the long and winding drive in and out the fjords in **Ísafjarðardjúp** (p240), eventually leading to **Hólmavík** (pictured; p244). Get spooked at the Museum of Icelandic Sorcery and Witchcraft.

DALIR REGION & BORGARNES 1 DAY

Head southwards on Rte 61 and dive into Viking history. In Laugar, bathe in **Guðrúnarlaug** (p210), the reconstructed pool of Laxdæla's heroine. Pass through Búðardalur, then turn on Rte 586 to visit **Eiríksstaðir** (pictured; p210), replica of Eiríkur Rauði's (Erik the Red's) longhouse. Rte 60 leads past **Erpsstaðir creamery** (p210), perfect for a sweet treat. Continue to Rte 1 for Borgarnes and the **Settlement Centre** (p195), dedicated to the settlement of Iceland and Egill Skallagrímsson.

FROM LEFT: BILL KENNEDY/SHUTTERSTOCK, JANNHUIZENGA/GETTY IMAGES

WHEN TO GO

For the Northern Lights, travel between September and March. For the midnight sun, travel in June or July.

It's always a good time to visit Iceland, but you can expect a very different experience depending on when you go.

Long nights offer ample opportunity for taking in dazzling Northern Lights displays during the winter. Long summer days are perfect for lengthy hikes, revelling in the streets and taking in midnight sunsets.

Iceland has four distinct seasons. If a full Ring Road trip or multiday hikes in the highlands, are on your agenda, travel between July and September when mountain roads are usually open, days are long and the winter thaw has passed. For puffins, travel between mid-May and early August. Ski areas are generally open from December to April. You'll find the best conditions in February and March.

You can go whale watching, snowmobiling, glacier hiking and horse riding year-round. November to March is best for ice caving. Travel between May and October if you want to take a Jökulsárlón boat tour.

⊛ I LIVE HERE

SUMMER IN ICELAND

Jewells Chambers is the founder and host of the All Things Iceland podcast and YouTube channel. @allthingsiceland

This is the season when Iceland's enchanting landscapes, from cascading waterfalls to verdant moss-covered valleys, truly shine. The midnight sun, adorable puffins, hiking in gorgeous mountain ranges and rejuvenating soaks in hot springs late into the bright evenings all make visiting at this time of year a unique and amazing experience.

PREPARE FOR EVERYTHING

There's only one predictable thing about the Icelandic weather: it's unpredictable. Be prepared to experience four seasons in a single day and for dramatic changes in wind, rain and winter weather, especially in the countryside and mountains.

Kirkjufell (p211) in summer

Weather Through the Year: Reykjavík

JANUARY	FEBRUARY	MARCH	APRIL	MAY	JUNE
Avg. daytime max: **3.1°C**	Avg. daytime max: **3.3°C**	Avg. daytime max: **4°C**	Avg. daytime max: **6.8°C**	Avg. daytime max: **9.8°C**	Avg. daytime max: **12.7°C**
Days of rainfall: 15	Days of rainfall: 14	Days of rainfall: 14	Days of rainfall: 11	Days of rainfall: 10	Days of rainfall: 9

MILD WINTERS & CHILLY SUMMERS

This country's name may be Iceland, but don't let that fool you. Because of the Gulf Stream, winters here are milder than you might imagine, with average temperatures around freezing. Icelandic summers are pleasant, but you'll want to bring a light jacket.

Summer Festivals Galore

Summer is festival season in Iceland. **Fisherman's Day** (p257) honours Iceland's 'heroes of the sea' with family-friendly events, funny fish exhibits and pillow fights on the plank across the country. **June**

Akureyri Art Summer (p257) is celebrated with diverse happenings, musical events, art exhibitions, art performances, workshops and craft markets throughout the North Iceland capital. **June–July**

The **National Festival** (p149) in Vestmannaeyjar draws thousands of visitors for a long-weekend campout. It includes outdoor concerts, a bonfire, singalong, and a light show symbolising volcanic flames. **August**

Reykjavík Culture Night (p58), held in celebration of the capital's anniversary, starts early with the Reykjavík Marathon, continuing with performances, exhibitions, homemade waffles and other treats, culminating in a grand concert and fireworks. **August**

Eclectic Music Festivals

Iceland Airwaves (p59) is the biggest music event on the Icelandic calendar. The four-day multi-genre music festival features hundreds of bands from around the world. Held at venues across Reykjavik, it includes a conference with talks on the music business, Icelandic films and more. **November**

Free music festival **Aldrei fór ég suður** (p238) is held in Ísafjörður in the Westfjords at Easter with performances by local acts and nationally famous musicians, newcomers and veterans of all genres. **March or April**

There are only 800 tickets sold for the **Bræðslan** music festival in Borgarfjörður Eystri (p319), but don't let this party's size fool you. This exclusive festival hosts intimate performances from some of the biggest names in music. **Late July**

The **Reykjavík Jazz festival** (p59) celebrates everything from contemporary jazz and gospel music to Latin jazz and big bands. **August**

⊕ I LIVE HERE

COSY WINTERS

Anna Lisa Terrazas is a native Icelander living and working in Reykjavík.

I love the winter months. They are cosy with lots of candlelit nights. People go downhill skiing, cross-country skiing and snowmobiling. There are geothermal pools where you can be outside and still stay warm. And of course, there's the chance to see the Northern Lights. I spend winter wearing cosy sweaters, and around March I like being able to feel and see the days growing longer.

Blue Lagoon (p104)

RARE THUNDERSTORMS

Thunderstorms are rare in Iceland, which sees maybe a handful of them each year. Those that do occur typically happen during the summer and are usually caused by warm-air masses coming up from Europe.

JULY	AUGUST	SEPTEMBER	OCTOBER	NOVEMBER	DECEMBER
Avg. daytime max: 14.6°C	Avg. daytime max: 13.9°C	Avg. daytime max: 11.1°C	Avg. daytime max: 7.5°C	Avg. daytime max: 4.5°C	Avg. daytime max: 3.3°C
Days of rainfall: 10	Days of rainfall: 11	Days of rainfall: 15	Days of rainfall: 13	Days of rainfall: 13	Days of rainfall: 14

Birdwatching from ferry to Heimaey (147)

GET PREPARED FOR ICELAND

Useful things to load in your bag, your ears and your brain.

Clothes

Layers The weather in Iceland is unpredictable, and layering is your best strategy regardless of when you're travelling. Pack a lightweight puffer jacket and sturdy waterproof hiking boots for summer travel. Choose waterproof trousers over jeans for hiking, and leave the vest tops, sandals and shorts at home – you won't need them, even in July.

Winter gear Winter weather is milder than you might expect, with temperatures rarely dipping below freezing. Pack snow pants, snow boots, a warm coat, gloves, a hat and thermal base layers. Excursion operators provide heavy winter gear for activities like snowmobiling and glacial hiking, but bundle up for aurora expeditions.

Manners

Always shower before getting into a pool or sauna. Don't wear your shoes or socks into the locker room.

Tipping is not required but may be appreciated where businesses put out tip jars.

Take shoes off when entering someone's home.

When camping, only use designated areas.

Casual vs formal Icelanders dress casually, so you can leave the heels, sport coats and formalwear behind.

Jackets A rain jacket is always a good idea.

READ

The Sagas of Icelanders (1997) A collection of medieval Icelandic literary treasures, stories of love, hate and adventure.

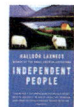

Independent People (Halldór Laxness; 1934–35) Classic novel on the woes of farmers past, filled with humour and drama.

Burial Rites (Hannah Kent; 2013) Historical novel featuring the gruesome fate of Agnes Magnúsdóttir, a servant accused of murder.

The Little Book of the Icelanders (Alda Sigmundsdóttir; 2014) Insights into the quirks of Icelandic culture through 50 miniature essays.

Words

Icelandic is a Germanic language of the same family as German, English and the Scandinavian languages (excluding Finnish). It stems from Old Norse and has changed remarkably little since the Saga Age. Words and names take on different forms due to declension and some include the special characters 'eth' (ð) and 'thorn' (þ).

Most Icelanders speak English, and many of the people who work in the tourist industry are migrant workers, so you can get by without understanding much of the native language. However, Icelanders do appreciate it when visitors make an effort to learn some words.

Here are a few helpful words and phrases:
Halló (hah-lo) 'Hello'
Góðan daginn (go-thah-n die-in) 'Good day'
Vinsamlegast (vin-saam-leh-gast) 'Please'
Takk (tak) 'Thank you'
Já (y-ow) 'Yes'
Nei (neigh) 'No'
Bless (bles) 'Goodbye'
Hvar er...? (kva-r-eh-r) 'Where is...?'
Klósett (k-low-seht) 'Toilet'
Hvað kostar þetta? (hvahth kost-ar thet-ta) 'How much does this cost?'
Ég tala ekki íslensku (yeh tah-la ekkee ees-len-skew) 'I don't speak Icelandic.'
Skál (sk-owl) 'Cheers'

Here are a few tips:
- The Icelandic 'j' sounds like the English 'y'.
- The character 'Þ' is pronounced 'th' like 'think'.
- The character 'Ð/ð' is pronounced 'th' like 'the'.
- 'Reykjavík' is pronounced 'Rayk-yah-veek'.
- 'Rs' get rolled.

WATCH

Noi the Albino (Dagur Kári; 2003) Set in Bolungarvík; features the trials and tribunals of teenage outsider Nói.

Game of Thrones (2012; pictured) Some of Iceland's most stunning sites appear in the fantasy series.

The Secret Life of Walter Mitty (Ben Stiller; 2013) Features places such as Seyðisfjörður, Stykkishólmur, Höfn and Skógafoss.

Children of Nature (Friðrik Þór Friðriksson; 1991) Oscar-nominated love story about an elderly couple escaping the retirement home.

Trapped (Baltasar Kormákur; 2015) Murder mystery series set in Siglufjörður, a remote fishing town cut off by snowstorm.

LISTEN

Debut (Björk;1993) Featuring a variety of styles, this album propelled Iceland's most famous singer-songwriter to stardom.

My Head Is an Animal (Of Monsters and Men; 2011) The album, which contains hipster hit 'Little Talks', vaulted this Icelandic folk rock band to global fame.

Ágætis byrjun (Sigur Rós; 1999) The breakthrough album of Icelandic post-rock band Sigur Rós with tracks such as 'Svefn-g-englar' and 'Viðrar vel til loftárása'.

Haglél (Mugison; 2011) The Icelandic blues-rocker's most successful album to date, sung part in praise of Icelandic nature, most notably 'Stingum af'.

Arctic char

THE FOOD SCENE

Don't be fooled. There's far more to the Icelandic food scene than fish, meat and potatoes.

The Icelandic food scene has come a long way. While the traditional fermented and dried foods of the past can still be found in shops and on some restaurant menus, freshly caught fish, delicious gamey lamb and creamy *skyr* (yoghurt-like dessert) are staples of the modern diet.

Icelandic food is some of the freshest and purest in the world. Rye, barley and wheat are preferred grains. The North Atlantic provides an abundance of fish, mussels and scallops. Geothermal energy allows farmers to grow a variety of vegetables year-round.

Traditional Foods

For many years, people here had to make the most of what they had and make it last through long, harsh winters. Salt and fermentation were key to extending the shelf life of the food that was available, and eating every part of every creature became the norm. Dishes like *harðfiskur* (a dried fish snack), *svið* (a boiled sheep's head cut in half) and *hákarl* (fermented shark) were common. Horse was – and occasionally remains – on the menu. Icelandic rye bread, sometimes cooked over a hot spring, accompanied meals. This *hverabrauð* is still available today.

Modern Icelandic Cuisine

Iceland's culinary star has been on the rise. Michelin-star chefs whip up creative tasting menus featuring farm-fresh ingredients and unforgettable fine-dining experiences. Casual cafes and coffee shops dot Reykjavík and are spreading across the Icelandic countryside.

Modern Icelandic cuisine is farm-to-table dining at its best. Most restaurants serve freshly caught fish of the day and locally grown vegetables and berries. High-end dining is just part of what Iceland has to offer. Its casual foods are some of its most memorable. Have farm-fresh ice cream at a dairy. Try cake made with fresh *skyr*. Or stop for a famous Bæjarins Beztu (p59) lamb hot dog, a local staple that's won over visitors from around the world.

Beer & Liquor

Beer was illegal in Iceland until 1989, but you can now find quality craft breweries across the country. Beer is also sold at government liquor stores. Icelandic beer is made with Icelandic water, giving these lagers, pilsners, pale ales and stouts an exceptional taste.

Iceland is also the home of a growing distillery business. It's best known for Reyka, a small-batch producer that finishes its vodka in coastal Borgarnes. Several distilleries are located in the southwest and produce spirits including gin, rum, whisky and Brennivín (caraway-flavoured schnapps).

Local Specialities

Fresh from the Water

Atlantic cod Lean flaky fish that's a staple of the Icelandic diet.

Arctic char Restaurant menu staple, sometimes caught wild, but also raised in aquafarms.

Wolffish Meaty white fish with a sweet taste and crab-like texture.

Langoustine Small lobster that's fished off the southern coast. Often served in soup.

Haddock Versatile white fish with a fine texture and delicate flakiness.

Fresh from the Farm

Lamb Free-roaming sheep graze on wild herbs and grasses, making Icelandic lamb especially tender and flavourful.

Beef High-quality, grass-fed local meat, free of hormones and antibiotics.

Tomatoes Greenhouse-grown with glacier water, Icelandic tomatoes are flavourful and pesticide-free.

Snacks & Sweets

Harðfiskur A traditional dried fish snack often eaten with butter.

Pönnukökur Similar to a sweet crepe, often with jam and whipped cream.

Laufabrauð A leaf-shaped flatbread eaten during the holiday season.

Kleinur Fried twisted doughnuts flavoured with vanilla or cardamom.

Dare to Try

Hákarl Fermented shark often with a shot of Brennivín.

Svið A boiled half of a sheep's head with potatoes or turnips.

Hrútspungar Sour ram testicles in gelatine eaten as a pâté.

Hreindýr Wild reindeer, gamey meat served in finer restaurants.

Hrossakjöt Horse meat, usually served as steak or in stews.

Kleinur

FOOD FESTIVALS

Food & Fun (p58) Held in Reykjavík each March, this is Iceland's premier food festival. It brings chefs from around the world to Iceland, challenging them to create affordably priced gourmet menus using only Icelandic ingredients over the course of a week-long competition.

Þorrablót (p58) This February food festival is a celebration of Iceland's pagan history. Traditional feasts include dried fish, boiled sheep's head, dung-smoked lamb and pickled ram's testicles.

Great Forest Day (p311) Held in Hallormsstaðaskógur near Egilsstaðir around Midsummer's Day in June, serving meat roasted over open fire, *lummur* (small Icelandic pancakes) and other treats.

Humarhátíð (p186) Höfn is the lobster capital of Iceland, and it celebrates its bounty with a festival each June. Try delicious Icelandic lobster while experiencing an authentic small-town festival.

THE YEAR IN FOOD

SPRING

Have an Easter feast of lamb, fish, potatoes and vegetables and a *skyr* cake topped with chocolate eggs. Brown-trout and sea-trout fishing begin in April, with prime season between July and October.

SUMMER

June brings candy floss and Icelandic-flag-themed sweets for Iceland Day, and the start of salmon season. Berry season can start any time from late July to the end of August.

AUTUMN

Icelandic lobster (langoustine) fishing begins in April and tapers off in September. You'll also find the freshest lamb as flocks will have spent their summers eating wild herbs and grasses.

WINTER

Enjoy Christmas meals of savoury smoked lamb and vegetables and warm bowls of soup and stew. Or feast on traditional Viking fare during the Þorrablót festival in February.

Skógá River (p149)

THE OUTDOORS

With spectacular scenery, excellent infrastructure and an endless list of things to do, you may never want to go inside.

The best things in Iceland are outdoors. Prepare for stunning mountains, gargantuan glaciers, expansive lava fields and beautiful black-sand beaches along a rugged coast. Iceland is known for its spectacular natural beauty, and there's no shortage of ways to experience it. Hike a glacier or explore an ice cave. Go snowmobiling, skiing, snowboarding or mountain biking. Spend your days hiking and fishing and your evenings enjoying candlelit campsite dinners. Whatever you choose, you'll find endless waterfalls and stunning views.

Walking & Hiking

From the smooth path along the Reykjavík waterfront to the emerald kingdom that is the Þórsmörk Valley, you'll find countless adventures on foot here. Iceland's towering mountains, calm valleys, rugged coastlines and endless waterfalls are made for hiking. You'll find easy trails across the country as well as difficult mountain treks to challenge even the most experienced hikers.

The Fagradalsfjall volcano has taken off as a hiking destination thanks to several recent eruptions. You'll also find well-marked and well-maintained trails in national parks, along rugged coastlines and through idyllic valleys. The Laugavegur and Fimmvörðuháls trails are two of Iceland's most popular. Laugavegur offers experienced hikers an unforgettable journey through caramel-coloured dunes and the

---

Adrenaline Adventures

PARAGLIDING
Soar over Vík's black-sand beaches and the magnificent **Reynisdrangar** (p155) rock formations off Iceland's southern coast.

SKIING & SNOWBOARDING
Ski or snowboard down jagged mountain peaks towards the sea at **Siglufjörður** (p276) on the Troll Peninsula.

SCUBA DIVING & SNORKELLING
Dive into the **Silfra fissure** (p122), the only place in the world where you can swim between tectonic plates.

> **FAMILY ADVENTURES**
>
> **Bundle up and bring your warmest hats** because you'll find Iceland's best family adventures outdoors. Ride precious Icelandic horses across **Þingvellir National Park** (p120) or on a **beach** (p155) near Vík.
> **Head out for an unforgettable whale-watching tour** from **Reykjavík's Old Harbour** (p80), or take children 14 and older on a kayak tour in search of **puffins** (p147) off the coast of Vestmannaeyjar.
> **Chase waterfalls** across the South Coast and beyond.
> **Traverse wild topography** on a snowmobile, ATV or mountain bike.
> **Take memorable family hikes**, soak in idyllic lagoons and have candlelit dinners in caves. Go fishing, enjoy local pools that feel like waterparks or set out to see the **Northern Lights** (p272). No one's getting bored here.

Icelandic desert. Fimmvörðuháls follows a trail of waterfalls leading from Skógafoss to Þórsmörk.

Cycling

The Ring Road is a popular route for visitors looking for an Icelandic cycling adventure. It's paved throughout and passes through most major towns, but there are no designated bike lanes. Outside of Reykjavík, the two-lane Rte 1 sometimes narrows to one lane. You'll need to be comfortable sharing roads with vehicles as well as the occasional sheep or horse.

This ride is best tackled during the summer when campsites are open, road conditions are at their best and there's ample daylight for long rides. Be prepared for rain, especially in June and July, and the occasional summer snow. Cyclists are not allowed to pass through the Hvalfjörður Tunnel, but cycling the fjord is a far more scenic experience. Cyclists will also need to switch to local paths in Reykjavík.

Mountain biking is growing in popularity but trails are limited because of the delicate ecosystems they'd have to pass through. You'll find some pristine sections of singletrack in places like Þórsmörk, and welcoming trails such as Laugavegur and those in the Reykjadalur Valley. It's often acceptable for mountain bikers to use existing sheep trails. Tour operators in Reykjavík (Icebike Adventures) and Húsavík (Mountain Bike Húsavík) offer scenic rides and heli-biking.

> **BEST SPOTS**
>
> For the best outdoor spots, see the map on p38.

Cycling in West Iceland (p191)

Resources

Safetravel.is is the official source for driving tips and safety alerts, and *road.is* has the latest information on road conditions and the weather. *Fi.is* provides information on cabins and mountain huts for hikers, and has a list of hiking trails with estimated difficulty levels.

RIVER RAFTING	SNOWMOBILING	GLACIER HIKING	ICE CAVING
White-water raft the **Hvítá river** (p123), which carves its way through Gullfoss Canyon and is suitable for beginners.	Zoom across magnificent **Langjökull glacier** (p129) on a snowmobile. Crisscross this snowy expanse while enjoying pristine mountain views.	Hike across the marble-like blue and black ice of **Sólheimajökull glacier** (p150). Walk across a volcanic ash field along the way.	Venture inside the wild blue and black ice caves at the **Katla volcano** (p151).

ACTION AREAS

Where to find Iceland's best outdoor activities.

Walking/Hiking
1. Mt Esja (p199)
2. Laugavegurinn (p144)
3. Fimmvörðuháls (p149)
4. Þórsmörk (p143)
5. Canyon Trail (Dettifoss to Ásbyrgi; p292)
6. Glymur waterfall (p202)
7. Skaftafell (p166)

Cycling

1. Svalvogar Circuit (p227)
2. Westfjords Way (p227)
3. Hlíðarfjall Bike Park (p271)
4. Reykjanes Peninsula (p104)
5. Reykjavík (p42)

Skiing/Snowboarding

1. Siglufjörður (p276)
2. Ísafjörður (p236)
3. Hlíðarfjall (p271)
4. Grenivík (p278)
5. Stafdalur and Oddsskarð (p317)

Glaciers/Ice Caves

1. Katla Ice Cave (p151)
2. Langjökull (p204)
3. Sólheimajökull (p150)
4. Mýrdalsjökull (p150)
5. Vatnajökull (p166)
6. Snæfellsjökull (p217)
7. Kverkfjöll ice caves (p346)

National Parks

1. Þingvellir National Park (p51)
2. Vatnajökull National Park (p168)
3. Snæfellsjökull National Park (p216)

ICELAND

THE GUIDE

The Westfjords
p220

North Iceland
p249

West Iceland
p191

The Highlands
p327

East Iceland
p302

REYKJAVÍK ✪
p42

Southwest Iceland & the Golden Circle
p99

Southeast Iceland
p162

Chapters in this section are organised by hubs and their surrounding areas. We see the hub as your base in the destination, where you'll find unique experiences, local insights, insider tips and expert recommendations. It's also your gateway to the surrounding area, where you'll see what and how much you can do from there.

Vatnajökull (p166)
ANDREW MAYOVSKYY/SHUTTERSTOCK

Researched by
Alexis Averbuck

Reykjavík

DYNAMIC CAPITAL FULL OF SURPRISES

Discover and shop creative art and design, sip coffee or craft beer streetside, soak in geothermal pools, spot whales and dance under the midnight sun.

The world's most northerly capital combines creative people, colourful buildings, eye-popping design, wild nightlife and a capricious soul. Reykjavík is strikingly cosmopolitan for its size. It's merely a large town by international standards, compared with London or Paris, yet it's loaded with captivating art, rich culinary choices, fantastic live music, and cool cafes and bars. When you slip behind the shiny tourist-centric veneer (it is a great base for tours to the countryside, so during summer it's often busy in the centre) ,you'll find a populace and a place that mix aesthetically minded ingenuity with an almost quaint, know-your-neighbours sense of community.

Reykjavík is Iceland's human heart, the commercial, industrial and cultural centre of the country. Nearly two-thirds of all Icelanders live in the capital region: 250,000 inhabitants of colourful corrugated houses, grey suburbs and an ever-growing number of apartment complexes. The most common bird, the joke goes, is the building crane. It's a far cry from its settlement in the late 800s CE when Reykjavík was just a simple collection of farm buildings (which persisted for centuries).

Most international travellers arrive at Keflavík International Airport, making Reykjavík a natural starting point for any Iceland trip. You can unwind from a long flight with a soak at the Blue Lagoon (pictured), Sky Lagoon or the public Sundhöllin, then dive into local life.

To first-time visitors, the capital tends to be warmer than expected and spread over a wider area, though the city centre – from the Old Harbour to the Hlemmur food hall – is less than 3km long, making it easy to explore on foot. For a bird's-eye view of the city, head to Hallgrímskirkja, whose soaring church tower is among the tallest structures in the country. It anchors a charming city centre with the largely pedestrianised shopping street Laugavegur. Old Reykjavík in historic Miðborg encircles serene pond Tjörnin. The Old Harbour area of Vesturbær invites whale-watching expeditions and seafront strolls with concert hall Harpa shimmering in the distance.

Add a backdrop of snow-topped mountains, churning seas and crystal-clear air, and the chances are you'll fall helplessly in love, heading home already saving to return.

ALEKSANDRA TOKARZ/SHUTTERSTOCK

THE MAIN AREAS

HISTORIC MIÐBORG
Classic, fascinating Old Reykjavík. **p48**

LAUGAVEGUR
Buzzing shopping and residential district. **p62**

VESTURBÆR & THE OLD HARBOUR
Charming harbour with whale watching, shops and sights. **p74**

LAUGARDALUR & HLÍÐAR
Parks, pools and play. **p84**

KÓPAVOGUR & HAFNARFJÖRÐUR
Surprising southern suburbs. **p91**

> **For places to stay in Reykjavík, see p96**

THE GUIDE

REYKJAVÍK

Left: Skólavörðustígur (p62); Above: Hallgrímskirkja (p62)

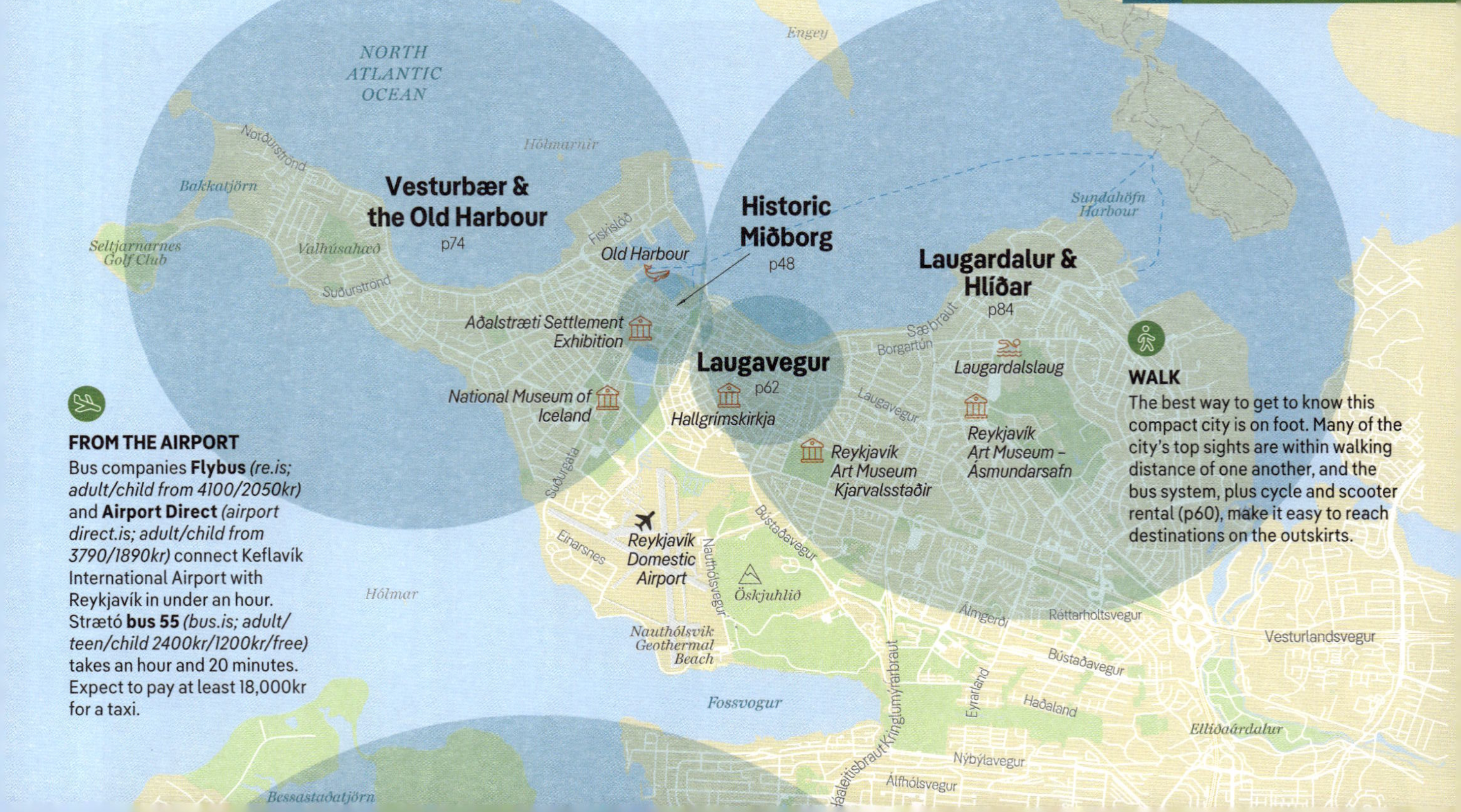

NORTH ATLANTIC OCEAN
Engey
Hólmarnir
Norðurströnd
Bakkatjörn
Seltjarnarnes Golf Club
Valhúsahæð
Suðurströnd
Vesturbær & the Old Harbour
p74
Fiskislóð
Old Harbour
Historic Miðborg
p48
Sundahöfn Harbour
Laugardalur & Hlíðar
p84
Sæbraut
Borgartún
Laugardalslaug
Aðalstræti Settlement Exhibition
Laugavegur
p62
National Museum of Iceland
Hallgrímskirkja
Laugavegur
Reykjavík Art Museum Kjarvalsstaðir
Reykjavík Art Museum – Ásmundarsafn
Suðurgata
Einarsnes
Reykjavík Domestic Airport
Nauthólsvegur
Bústaðavegur
Öskjuhlíð
Hólmar
Nauthólsvík Geothermal Beach
Fossvogur
Almgerði
Réttarholtsvegur
Vesturlandsvegur
Bústaðavegur
Kringlumýrarbraut
Eyrarland
Hađaland
Elliðaárdalur
Nýbýlavegur
Álfhólsvegur
Háaleitisbraut
Bessastaðatjörn

FROM THE AIRPORT
Bus companies **Flybus** *(re.is; adult/child from 4100/2050kr)* and **Airport Direct** *(airport direct.is; adult/child from 3790/1890kr)* connect Keflavík International Airport with Reykjavík in under an hour. Strætó **bus 55** *(bus.is; adult/teen/child 2400kr/1200kr/free)* takes an hour and 20 minutes. Expect to pay at least 18,000kr for a taxi.

WALK
The best way to get to know this compact city is on foot. Many of the city's top sights are within walking distance of one another, and the bus system, plus cycle and scooter rental (p60), make it easy to reach destinations on the outskirts.

Find Your Way

Reykjavík is a small, walkable city. It's easy to get around without a car, but you may want to take the bus or rent a bicycle or e-scooter if you're heading across town or to a further-flung neighbourhood. Taxis work for short hops, too. Cars and tours are best for getting into the countryside.

TAXI & CARS

Book taxis online, by phone or via the Hreyfill app. They are most economical for short hops within town. Uber and Lyft don't operate here. Parking in central Reykjavík is limited and governed by meters/payment apps (eg Parka). It's easiest to park on the edge and walk in.

BUS

Reykjavík has an extensive network of buses (p56) operated by Strætó (bus. is, connecting the suburbs, and extending to Akranes, Borgarnes, Hveragerði, Selfoss and along the Ring Road. Bus stops are marked with a yellow letter 'S'. Download the Klappið app.

Plan Your Days

Whether you've got 24 hours or several days, prepare to make unforgettable memories in Iceland's charming, beautiful capital before you've even hit the magnificent countryside.

Reykjavík Art Museum (p51)

Day 1

Morning
Start with a walk around Old Reykjavík near **Tjörnin pond** (p48) then peruse the city's best museums, such as the impressive **National Museum** (p52), **Reykjavík Art Museum** (p51) and **Settlement Exhibition** (p54).

Afternoon
Wander up arty **Skólavörðustígur** (p62), browsing crafts, design and jewellery boutiques, to enthralling **Hallgrímskirkja** (p62). For a perfect view, take an elevator up the tower, then circle down to stroll and shop Icelandic fashion around **Laugavegur** (p62).

Evening
Sit for people-watching and drinks at **GILLIGOGG** (p61), **22 Bar** (p73) or **Bingo** (p73) then head to dinner. For casual eats, hit **Posthús Mathöll** (p58), or try Icelandic fusion at **Mat Bar** (p69). Many cafes – like **Kaffibarinn** (p73) – turn into party hangouts at night.

You'll Also Want to...
You could spend weeks roaming Reykjavík and still not discover everything this tiny capital has to offer. Culture, life, weather...it's always changing and inventive.

HAVE ICE CREAM, NO MATTER THE WEATHER
Join the national ice-cream mania and seek out the homemade treat, topped with oodles of candies. You'll find families, couples and solo flyers thronging **ice-cream shops** (p77) all over the city.

EXPLORE COASTAL TRAILS & BEACHES
Stroll the cityfront promenade with photogenic sculpture **Sun Voyager** (p70), **Höfði Lighthouse** (p84) and **Recycled House** (p86). Cruise the **Old Harbour** (p74) and climb **Púfa** (p78), or brave a dip at **Nauthólsvík Geothermal Beach** (p89).

LISTEN TO LIVE LOCAL MUSIC
Music festivals (p56) and **live music** (p73) are an Icelandic staple. Musicians gig in spaces from theatres to art galleries, and of course **Harpa** (p56) regularly hosts festivals, performances and comedy. Check what's on around town and go.

Day 2

Morning
Enjoy brunch at **Grái Kötturinn** (p68) or get a blast of sea air and stroll to the **Old Harbour** (p74) and the food stalls at **Grandi Mathöll** (p77). Sail out on a **whale- or puffin-spotting tour** (p80).

Afternoon
Check out the art at **Þula** (p78), **Nýló** (p77) and the other free galleries in the **Marshall House** (p77). Get ice cream at **Omnom chocolate factory** (p77) or taste gin at **Þoran Distillery** (p79).

Evening
Circle back to the centre for a soak at **Sundhöllin** (p71), then try Reykjavík's famed hot dogs at **Bæjarins Beztu** (p59). On weekends, join Reykjavík's notorious pub crawl. Start at beer-lovers' **Kaldi** (p72) or **Skúli Craft Bar** (p72), then dance at **Kiki** (p73), **Prikið** (p73) or **Lemmy** (p73).

Day 3

Morning
Get fresh-baked rolls at one of the city's excellent **bakeries** (p114). If you haven't already, soak at the **Sky Lagoon** (p91) in Kópavogur, or, for a relaxed combo of geothermal pools, botanical gardens, charming Café Flóra and cool art, drop into **Laugardalur** (p84).

Afternoon
Go record shopping at the city's excellent **music stores** (p72) and find out what's on for **live music** (p73) that night.

Evening
Book ahead if you'd like to wrap up at one of Iceland's top restaurants, such as **Dill** (p59), **Óx** (p59) or **OTO** (p59). Or if you're travelling during the winter and the forecast is good, spend an evening looking for the Northern Lights on **Seltjarnarnes** (p83).

GO FOR A SWIM, SOAK & CHAT
Local pools are as much social scenes as they are places to swim. Hop between giant kids' splash-pools and hot-pots, cold plunges and saunas at popular **Sundhöllin** (p71), **Laugardalslaug** (p86) and sleeper hit **Vesturbæjarlaug** (p92).

FIND THE NORTHERN LIGHTS
Are you feeling lucky? From September to April you'll have a shot at **spotting the Aurora Borealis** (p77). Check the forecast, then book a **boat ride or tour** (p75) or head out on your own to top viewing spots.

IMMERSE IN ICELAND'S WILDLIFE & TRADITIONS
Choose between the thrilling fun of the **Lava Show** (p79) and **FlyOver Iceland** (p79) or the enriching open-air farm museum **Árbær** (p89), **Reykjavík Maritime Museum** (p77), hilltop **Perlan** (p89) and **Natural History Museum of Kópavogur** (p95).

RIDE HORSES ACROSS RED LAVA
Icelandic horses are unlike any others in the world. They're more petite, and have five gaits, instead of the usual three. Go out for a trot in **Heiðmörk Nature Reserve** (p77) and its vivid red pseudocraters, **Rauðhólar** (p92).

Historic Miðborg

CLASSIC, FASCINATING OLD REYKJAVÍK

GETTING AROUND

Old Reykjavík is super compact and easily walkable. It's well served by Strætó buses (p56). One of the main bus stops in the city centre is Lækjartorg, at the junction with Austurstræti. Parking in central Reykjavík is limited. There are three paid **parking zones** *(reykjavik.is/en/parking/obligation-to-pay)* with different rates and rules on length of stay. Pay at street meters or on payment apps Parka, EasyPark, SíminnPay or Verna. With those, you activate when you start parking, then close out when you leave and they charge you accordingly. It's easiest to find parking on the edge and walk in.

Historic Miðborg, or the area dubbed Old Reykjavík, is the jaunty heart of the capital and its cultural centre. Anchored by placid Tjörnin lake, the neighbourhood is tops for a wander. Sights radiate out from the oldest settlements in the city's history. You can learn about them at the Settlement Exhibition, or the more expansive National Museum. It's also the area with the seats of government: city hall and Alþingi (Parliament). Art highlights include the Reykjavík Art Museum's superb Hafnarhús. Stroll from glistening seafront concert hall Harpa to Ingólfstorg square with its cafes and historic houses, then onward to Austurvöllur park. When the weather's fine, scenic Tjörnin is a magnet for Reykjavikers and visitors alike. If you're looking to spend a day museum-hopping, shopping and snacking, this is the place to do it. Independent cafes and souvenir shops line the streets. Bars and dance clubs dot the neighbourhood, too, making it a key part of the city's famed bar crawl under the midnight sun.

Stroll Lake Tjörnin

MAPS P49 & P50

Swans, scenery and sculptures

When the weather is fine, take a stroll around idyllic city-centre lake Tjörnin and you'll find lots of surprises. It echoes with the honks and squawks of more than 40 species of visiting birds, including swans, geese and Arctic terns.

Pretty, sculpture-dotted parks like **Hljómskálagarður** line the southern shores, and their paths are much used by cyclists and joggers. Take a minute to check out *The Unknown Bureaucrat*, a sculpture of a man being crushed by a rock, and *The Black Cone*, a cracked rock-based sculpture designed as an ode to peaceful civil disobedience. The lake is adjacent to the postmodern **Ráðhús** (Reykjavík City Hall), which has a topographical map of Iceland – a good way to get acquainted with this unique terrain.

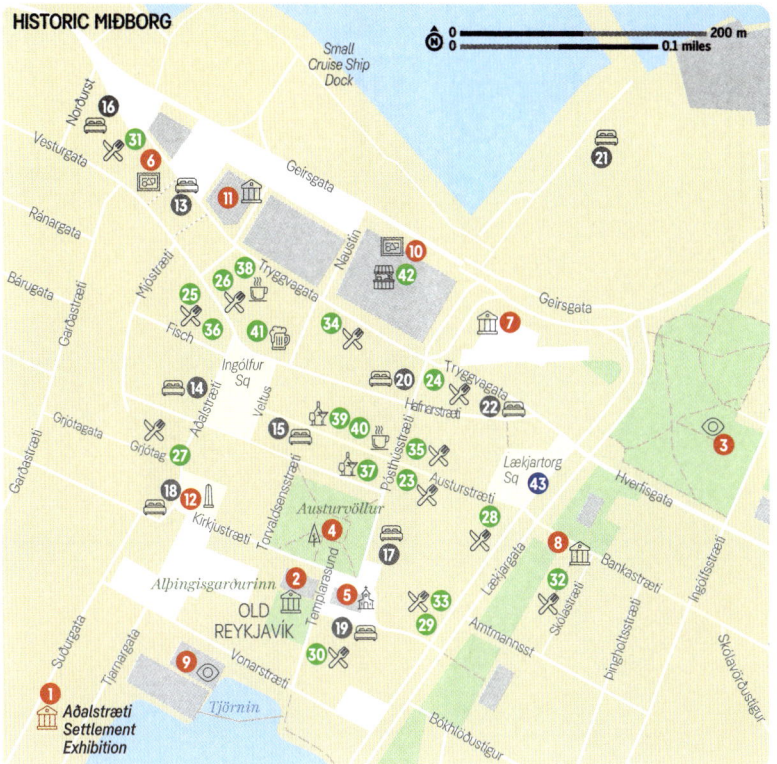

HIGHLIGHTS
1 Aðalstræti Settlement Exhibition

SIGHTS
2 Alþingi
3 Árnarhóll
4 Austurvöllur
5 Dómkirkja
6 i8
7 Icelandic Phallological Museum
8 Icelandic Punk Museum
see 4 Jón Sigurðsson Statue
9 Ráðhús
10 Reykjavík Art Museum – Hafnarhús
11 Reykjavík Museum of Photography
12 Skúli Magnússon Statue

SLEEPING
see 23 Apotek
13 Black Pearl
14 CenterHótel Plaza
15 City Center Hotel
16 Exeter Hotel
17 Hótel Borg
18 Hótel Reykjavík Centrum
19 Kvosin Downtown
20 Radisson Blu 1919
21 Reykjavík EDITION
22 Reykjavík Konsulat Hotel

EATING
23 Apotek Kitchen + Bar
24 Bæjarins Beztu
25 Café Rosenberg
26 Fiskfélagið
27 Fiskmarkaðurinn
28 Grillmarkaðurinn
29 Icelandic Street Food
30 La Barceloneta
31 Le Kock
32 Mama Reykjavík
33 Messinn
34 Napoli
35 Pósthús Mathöll
36 Vegan World Peace

DRINKING & NIGHTLIFE
37 GILLIGOGG
see 29 Icelandic Craft Bar
38 Iða
39 Jungle Cocktail Bar
40 Laundromat Cafe
41 Sæta Svínið Gastropub

SHOPPING
42 Kolaportið

TRANSPORT
43 Lækjartorg Bus Stop

☑ TOP TIP

Nightclubs in the Old Reykjavík quarter offer some of the city's best late-night DJ sets and intense dance scenes (p73), but they start late – after midnight. To get deals on drinks, though, pop in early for happy hour, circling back to dance in the wee hours.

HISTORIC MIÐBORG REYKJAVÍK

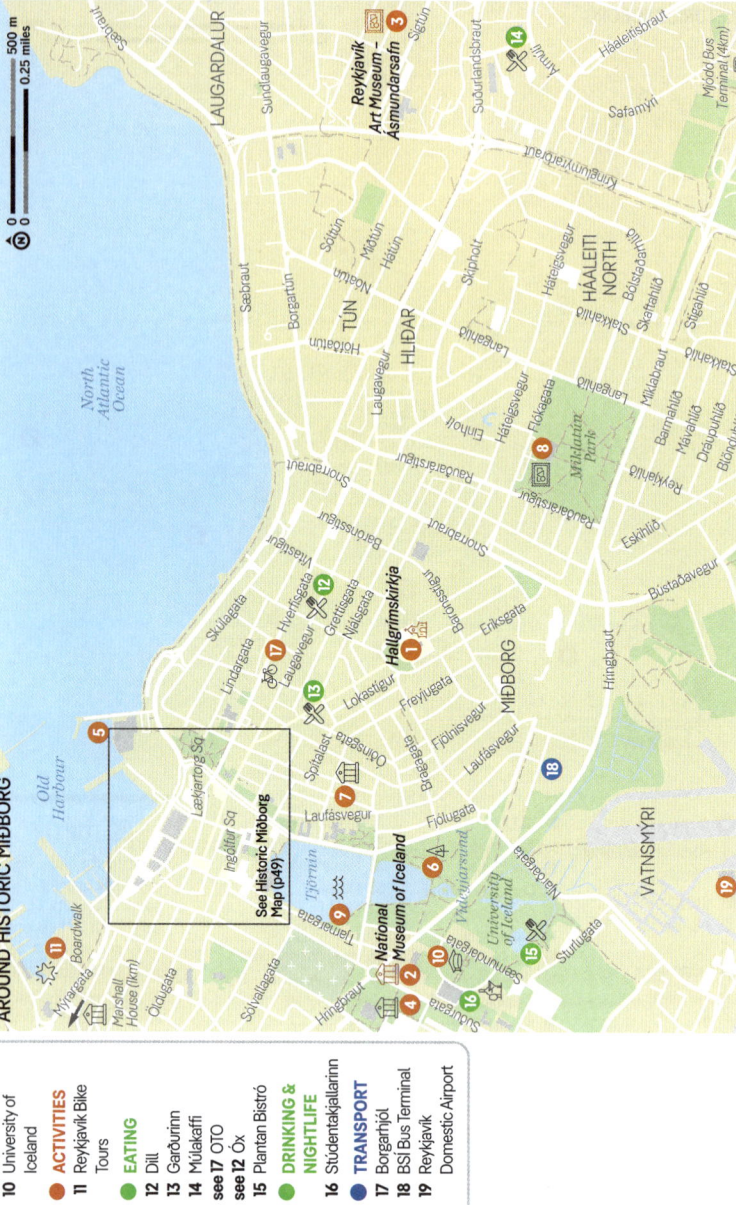

AROUND HISTORIC MIÐBORG

★ HIGHLIGHTS
1. Hallgrímskirkja
2. National Museum of Iceland
3. Reykjavík Art Museum – Ásmundarsafn

● SIGHTS
4. Árni Magnússon Institute for Icelandic Studies
5. Harpa
6. Hljómskálagarður Park
7. National Gallery of Iceland
8. Reykjavík Art Museum – Kjarvalsstaðir
9. Tjörnin
10. University of Iceland

● ACTIVITIES
11. Reykjavík Bike Tours

● EATING
12. Dill
13. Garðurinn
14. Múlakaffi
   see 17 OTO
   see 12 Ox
15. Plantan Bistró

● DRINKING & NIGHTLIFE
16. Stúdentakjallarinn

● TRANSPORT
17. Borgarhjól
18. BSÍ Bus Terminal
19. Reykjavík Domestic Airport

The National Gallery of Iceland (p69), the National Museum of Iceland (p52) and the **University of Iceland** are also nearby.

Visit Parliament
MAP P49

Appreciate Icelandic independence at the Alþingi

The imposing grey **Alþingi** (Parliament House; *althingi.is*) is the centre of modern Icelandic government, and it's home to the oldest public garden in Iceland, **Austurvöllur**, a favourite spot for cafe lounging or lunchtime picnics. The statue in the centre is of **Jón Sigurðsson**, who led the campaign for Icelandic independence.

The parliament building was constructed of Icelandic basalt to replace parliament's original meeting place in Þingvellir National Park (p120), and it opened its doors in 1881. It was designed by Danish architect Ferdinand Meldahl (1827–1908) when Iceland was still under Danish rule. Check the website to attend sessions (four times weekly mid-September to early June) when parliament is sitting.

To the left you'll see Iceland's main cathedral, the small but perfectly proportioned 18th-century **Dómkirkja** *(domkirkjan. is)*, with a plain wooden interior animated by glints of gold.

Peruse Icelandic Art
MAPS P49 & P50

Immerse at Reykjavík Art Museum

The **Reykjavík Art Museum** *(artmuseum.is; adult/child 2430kr/free)* is Iceland's largest institution dedicated to the visual arts. It's split across three locations. The **Hafnarhús**, near the waterfront in Old Reykjavík, is a marvellously restored warehouse converted into a soaring steel-and-concrete exhibition space. Browse well-curated exhibitions of cutting-edge contemporary Icelandic art, which change frequently – expect installations, videos, paintings and sculpture. And you can always count on the comic-book-style paintings of political artist Erró (Guðmundur Guðmundsson). Nearby **i8 gallery** *(i8.is; free)* exhibits some of the country's top working artists, many of whom show overseas as well. They also have a location at Marshall House (p77) in Grandi, along with other galleries.

A ticket to the museum is valid for two other locations: Kjarvalsstaðir (p87) in Klambratún Park, an urban green space not far from the city's core; and **Ásmundarsafn** in Laugardalur. They showcase painter Jóhannes Kjarval and sculptor Ásmundur Sveinsson respectively. Each building has its own

(continues on p56)

ICELAND'S EARLIEST SETTLERS

Rumour, myth and tales of fierce storms and barbaric dog-headed people kept most explorers away from the great northern ocean, *oceanus innavigabilis*. Irish monks who regularly sailed to the Faroe Islands looking for seclusion were probably the first to stumble upon Iceland. It's thought that they settled around the year 700 but fled when Norsemen began to arrive in the early 9th century. Viking Ingólfur Arnarson is credited with being the country's first permanent inhabitant. The Norwegian fugitive landed in Southeast Iceland, before continuing around the coast. He made his home in this promising-looking bay that he named Reykjavík (Smoky Bay), after the steam from its thermal springs.

 EATING IN HISTORIC MIÐBORG: FISH FORWARD
MAP P49

Fiskfélagið: The 'Fish Company' takes Icelandic seafood through far-flung inspirations, Fiji coconut to Spanish chorizo. *11.30am 2.30pm Mon Fri, 5-10.30pm daily* €€€

Fiskmarkaðurinn: Chefs infuse local seafood with Asian flavours at this intimate restaurant and sushi bar. *5.30-10pm* €€€

Messinn: Amazing pan-fried dishes: fish in a sizzling cast-iron skillet with buttery potatoes. *11.30am-9pm Sun-Thu, to 10pm Fri & Sat* €€€

La Barceloneta: If you have a hankering for seafood paella and tapas, this is your place, right near Tjörnin. *11.30am-3pm Wed-Fri, 4.30-9.30pm Wed-Sun* €€

TOP EXPERIENCE

Explore the National Museum

The superb National Museum of Iceland provides a meaningful overview of Iceland's history and culture. You'll see how this wild volcanic island over 600km from its closest neighbour became a country. Brilliantly curated exhibits lead you through the struggle to settle the forbidding island, the radical changes wrought by the introduction of Christianity, the lean times of domination by foreign powers and Iceland's eventual independence.

DON'T MISS

- Medieval ship
- Bronze Thor
- Drinking horns
- *Hnefatafl* game set
- Viking graves
- Valþjófsstaðir church door
- Guðbrandur's Bible
- Jón Sigurðsson papers & possessions

Settlement-Era Finds

The premier section of the museum describes the Settlement Era – including the rule of the chieftans and the introduction of Christianity.

The Age of Settlement is traditionally defined as between 870 and 930, when political strife on the Scandinavian mainland caused many to flee. Most North Atlantic Norse settlers were ordinary citizens: farmers and merchants who settled across Western Europe, marrying Britons, Westmen (Irish) and Scots.

PRACTICALITIES
- thjodminjasafn.is
- adult/child 3000kr/free
- 10am-5pm

Start with a look at the kind of ship medieval explorers would have used on their journey to Iceland. Displays in this part of the museum feature swords, drinking horns, silver hoards and the most prized item: a tiny Eyrarland bronze statue from around 1000 CE, widely understood to represent the Norse god Thor with his hammer.

Exhibits explain how the chieftains ruled and how people survived on little, lighting their dark homes and fashioning bog iron. There's everything from the remains of early *skyr* (an Icelandic cheese that's like yoghurt) production to intricate pendants and brooches. Look for the Viking-era *hnefatafl* game set (a bit like chess). This artefact's discovery in a grave in Baldursheimar led to the founding of the museum.

Viking Graves

Look down! Encased in the floor are Viking-era graves with precious burial goods: horse bones, a sword, pins, a ladle, a comb. One of the tombs containing an eight-month-old infant is the only one of its kind ever found.

Among Iceland's first Norse visitors was Norwegian Flóki Vilgerðarson, who uprooted his farm and headed for Snæland around 860. He navigated with ravens, which, after some trial and error, led him to his destination and provided his nickname, Hrafna-Flóki (Raven-Flóki). Hrafna-Flóki sailed to Vatnsfjörður on the west coast but became disenchanted with the conditions. On seeing the icebergs in the fjord he dubbed the country Ísland (Iceland) and returned to Norway. He did eventually settle in Iceland's Skagafjörður district.

Christian Artefacts

Reykjavík remained just a simple collection of farm buildings for centuries. In 1225 an important Augustinian monastery was founded on the offshore island of Viðey (p88), although this was destroyed during the 16th-century Reformation.

The section of the museum that details this introduction of Christianity is chock-a-block with rare art and artefacts. Make sure to seek out the priceless 13th-century Valþjófsstaðir church door carved with the story of a knight, his faithful lion and a passel of dragons. There's also Guðbrandur's Bible. The Bible was the first book printed and widely distributed in Iceland. About 500 copies were printed, and this one still has its original binding intact.

The Modern Era

Upstairs, collections span from 1600 to today and give a clear sense of how Iceland struggled under Danish rule, developed a constitution then home rule, and finally gained independence on 17 June 1944, before going on to modernise.

Simple objects use every scrap of materials – check out the gaming pieces made from cod ear bones, and the wooden doll that doubled as a kitchen utensil. Also look for the perfectly preserved papers and belongings of Jón Sigurðsson (1811–1979), the architect of Iceland's independence.

THE SAGA AGE

The late 12th century kicked off the Saga Age, when the epic tales of the earlier 9th- to 10th-century settlement were recorded by historians and writers. These sweeping prose epics, or 'sagas', detail the family struggles, romance, vendettas and colourful characters of Settlement, and are the backbone of medieval Icelandic literature, and a rich source for historical understanding.

TOP TIPS

● The ground-floor cafe (open 11am to 4pm) offers wi-fi and a welcome respite, with wraparound windows looking out on a flowing fountain.

● Bring headphones for the free audio-guide app which has loads of useful detail in nine languages. The one for kids is in Icelandic or English only.

● Leave extra time for the museum's rotating photographic exhibitions.

● Across the street, the **Árni Magnússon Institute for Icelandic Studies** houses a collection of medieval vellum manuscripts and related artefacts.

● Strætó bus 11 serves the museum from downtown.

TOP EXPERIENCE

Time Travel at the Aðalstræti Settlement Exhibition

This is one of those museums kids visit on school field trips and for good reason. The Aðalstræti Settlement Exhibition, a fascinating archaeological ruin-museum spanning Aðalstræti 10 and 16, is based around a 10th-century Viking longhouse and other Settlement Era finds from central Reykjavík, and reconstructs how the city came to be with fascinating multimedia displays.

DON'T MISS

Viking longhouse ruins

Ancient boundary wall

Great auk bones

Interactive displays

Aðalstræti 10 general store

Viking Longhouse

The Aðalstræti complex is constructed around a 10th-century Viking longhouse unearthed here in 2001–02. Mainly a series of foundation walls now, it was thought to be inhabited for only 60 years. Look for areas of the longhouse with animal bones deliberately built into the structure (for good fortune, perhaps) and for the old spring.

PRACTICALITIES
- borgarsogusafn.is
- adult/child 3000kr/free
- 10am–5pm

Tephra Layers & the Significance of 871 CE

Tephra layers are the layer of fragments from a volcanic eruption, and they are used to date sites around Iceland.

According to the 12th-century *Íslendingabók* (a historical narrative of the Settlement Era), Ingólfur Arnarson fled Norway with his blood brother Hjörleifur, landing at Ingólfshöfði (southeast Iceland) in 871 CE. They continued around the coast, and Ingólfur was then led to Reykjavík by a pagan ritual: he tossed his high-seat pillars (a symbol of authority) into the sea as they approached land. Wherever the gods brought the pillars ashore would be the new home of the settlers. Ingólfur named Reykjavík (Smoky Bay) after the steam from its thermal springs. Hjörleifur settled near the present town of Vík, but was murdered by his slaves shortly thereafter.

The Aðalstræti longhouse was built on top of the 871 tephra layer, but don't miss the fragment of boundary wall at the back of the museum, which was below the tephra layer, and is thus older still. It's the oldest human-made structure in Reykjavík, predating even Ingólfur Arnarson.

Ancient Artefacts

Fine exhibitions imaginatively combine technological wizardry and archaeology for a glimpse into early Icelandic life. Through a series of interactive exhibits, the museum tells the story of how Reykjavík evolved from rugged farmstead to modern capital.

Arcing around the side of the exhibit, softly lit niches contain artefacts found in the area, from great auk bones (the bird is now extinct) to fish-oil lamps and an iron axe. More recent finds from ancient workshops near the current Alþingi include a silver bracelet and a spindle whorl (for making thread) inscribed with runes (reading 'Vilborg owns me').

High-Tech Displays

Among the captivating displays are interactive multimedia tables explaining the area's excavations, which span several city blocks. Don't miss the wrap-around panorama showing how things would have looked at the time of the longhouse and a space-age-feeling panel that allows you to steer through different layers of the longhouse's construction.

Aðalstræti 10 Shop

This quaint, dark-brown wooden building is the area's oldest and has been incorporated into the museum. Take your time to follow exhibits and photographs illustrating Reykjavík through time, and wander through a replica of an old general store.

RISE OF REYKJAVÍK

After being settled in the late 800s CE, Reykjavík was just a simple collection of farm buildings for centuries. It expanded in the 1700s when local sheriff Skúli Magnússon, the 'Father of Reykjavík', created factories to bypass a Danish monopoly. WWII was another boom period, and the city's architecture and cultural offerings have exploded once again with the recent rise in tourism to Iceland.

TOP TIPS

● Excellent English-language tours run at 11am from May to August.

● Multilingual audio guides are free.

● The kids' corner has traditional Icelandic toys, rune spelling exercises and computer games.

● Reykjavík Culture Card gets a 10% discount in their shop.

● If you need a refreshment, pop across historic Fógetagarðurinn square, in which you'll see a Skúli Magnússon Statue, to Skúli Craft Bar (p72) or down the street to Gaeta Gelato (p77) or the **Uppsalir Bar & Café** in Hótel Reykjavík Centrum.

(continued from p51)

architectural style, and they're all just as interesting from the outside as they are from the inside.

You can also create an art walk using the museum's Reykjavík Art Walk Mobile app.

Fascinating Photographs
MAP P49

Pause at the Reykjavík Museum of Photography

Dive deep into Icelandic photography at the unassuming **Reykjavík Museum of Photography** *(borgarsogusafn.is; adult/child 1350kr/free)*, which shares a building with the city library and the city archives. The museum's collection, on the 6th floor, includes more than six million photographs dating as far back as 1860, with work from professional photographers as well as amateurs. It features industrial and commercial photography in addition to press photographs and portraits. There are also some personal photo collections here.

And if seeing these collections inspires you to think about your own photo archive, you're in luck. The museum has a photo studio and hosts events aimed at helping visitors preserve their photos.

If you take the lift up, descend by the stairs, which are lined with vintage B&W photos.

Sparkle Inside Harpa
MAP P50

Extraordinary concert hall with top performances

With its ever-changing facets glistening on the water's edge, Reykjavík's sparkling **Harpa** *(harpa.is)* concert hall and cultural centre is a beauty. The award-winning glass-and-steel facade was designed by Icelandic-Danish artist Olafur Eliasson. His mission was to prism the city, its light and Iceland's changing weather in kaleidoscopic reflections inside the building.

Don't just marvel at Harpa's beauty from the outside without going in. If you're in town during a performance, try to catch one. Harpa is home to the Iceland Symphony Orchestra, Icelandic Opera, Reykjavik Big Band, a classical music series and a local jazz club. It also hosts regular top-tier concerts and music festivals…but even a wander inside when nothing is happening is an experience. The lobby houses design boutiques and a cafe, and restaurant La Primavera perches on the upper level.

BUS TIPS

Download the Klappið app if you have a smartphone with signal, for buying Strætó public **bus tickets** *(bus.is; adult/teen/child 670/335kr/free, valid for 75 minutes)* and track buses in real time. You can also use a card for contactless payment, but no cash is accepted. Buses run from 7am to 11pm or midnight (from 11am on Sunday) every 15 to 30 minutes. Weekend night services cover some routes, from around 1am to 4.30am.

Many buses loop around Tjörnin and the city centre before heading onwards. Bus 55 links **BSÍ bus terminal** (the base for Reykjavík Excursions and its Flybus) and Keflavík International Airport (adult/teen/child 2400kr/1200kr/free). **Mjódd Bus Terminal**, 8km southeast of the centre, is the hub for long-distance Strætó buses.

EATING IN REYKJAVÍK: BEST VEGETARIAN & VEGAN — MAPS P49 & P50

Vegan World Peace: Tried and true for salads and vegan fare with Asian flourishes. *11am-9pm Mon-Sat, from 4pm Sun* €

Plantan Bistró: In the Nordic House cultural centre, this endlessly creative spot champions plant-based food. *10am-5pm Tue-Sun* €€

Mama Reykjavík: Globally inspired vegan stews, juices, salads and sandwiches in a space for wellness, art and spirituality. *11am-9pm* €€

Garðurinn: Asian, Middle Eastern and Mediterranean flavours in veg and vegan soups and dishes. *11am-6.30pm Mon-Thu, to 7pm Fri, noon-5pm Sat* €€

EXPLORE OLD REYKJAVÍK

Take in the highlights of Reykjavík's earliest settlement area, dating to just before 871 and centred in the Old Reykjavík quarter.

START	END	LENGTH
Settlement Exhibition	Harpa	1.7km; 1½ hours

The history of Reykjavík – and this walk – begins at the 1 **Settlement Exhibition** (p54) on Aðalstræti ('Main Street'). This fascinating archaeological ruin-museum is based around a 10th-century Viking longhouse and combines technological wizardry and archaeology to give a glimpse into early Icelandic life. Across the street is a 2 **bronze statue of sheriff Skúli Magnússon**, the 'father of modern Reykjavík'. In the 1750s, when the town was a simple collection of farm buildings and the country belonged to Denmark, Magnússon set industrialisation in motion by establishing weaving, tanning and wool-dyeing factories. A few more steps down Krikjustræti is the city's most fateful development: 3 **Alþingi** (p51; Parliament). When Iceland gradually won back its autonomy from Denmark, Reykjavík was chosen as the location for a restored Alþingi. The current basalt building from 1881 houses 63 lawmakers. Turn right at Templarasund to stroll city pond 4 **Tjörnin** (p48) and visit the waterside 5 **Ráðhús** (p48; City Hall). Find an interesting 3D topographical map of Iceland inside. Head down Lækjargata to landmark hot-dog stand 6 **Bæjarins Beztu** (p59). On the other side of the street is 7 **Kolaportið flea market** (p59), open weekends. Complete the walk at 8 **Harpa**, the shimmering concert hall perched on the water's edge. Zip inside to admire vaulted glass panels and wonderful harbour sight lines, or browse its shops.

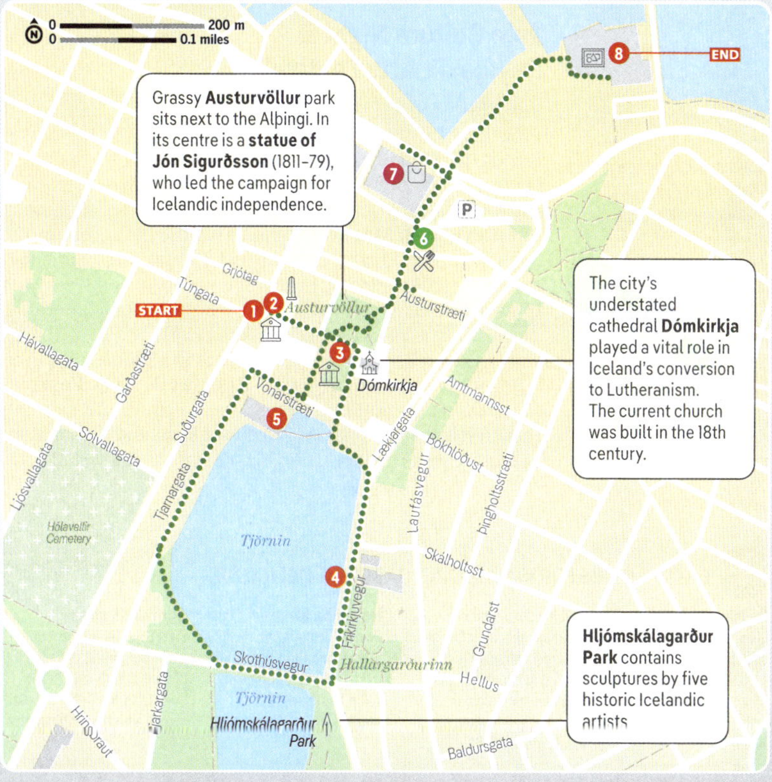
0 200 m
0 0.1 miles
Grassy **Austurvöllur** park sits next to the Alþingi. In its centre is a **statue of Jón Sigurðsson** (1811–79), who led the campaign for Icelandic independence.
The city's understated cathedral **Dómkirkja** played a vital role in Iceland's conversion to Lutheranism. The current church was built in the 18th century.
Hljómskálagarður Park contains sculptures by five historic Icelandic artists
START
END
Grjótag
Túngata
Austurvöllur
Austurstræti
Hávallagata
Garðastræti
Suðurgata
Vonarstræti
Dómkirkja
Amtmannsst
Sólvallagata
Lækjargata
Bókhlöðust
Ljósvallagata
Tjarnargata
Laufásvegur
Þingholtsstræti
Hólavallir Cemetery
Tjörnin
Skálholtsst
Fríkirkjuvegur
Grundarst
Skothúsvegur
Hallargarðurinn
Hellus
Tjörnin
Hljómskálagarður Park
Bjarkargata
Hringbraut
Baldursgata

HISTORIC MIÐBORG REYKJAVÍK

BEST CULTURAL FESTIVALS

Þorrablót: Nationwide midwinter feast with traditional treats. *Jan/Feb*

Winter Lights Festival: Dark days get lit up with Museum Night, Pool Night and light installations. *(vetrarhatid.is) Feb*

DesignMarch: Hundreds of design and art exhibitions and workshops. *(honnun armidstod.is) Mar*

Food & Fun: International chefs join local restaurants to compete for awards. *(foodandfun.is) Mar*

Reykjavík International Literary Festival: Gathers international writers for four days of readings and panels. *(bokmenn tahatid.is) Apr*

Reykjavík Pride: Celebrate LGBTIQ+ culture and traditions with 100,000 people. *(hinsegindagar.is) Aug*

Reykjavík International Film Festival: Homegrown and international independent filmmaking, with screenings and talks. *(riff.is) late Sep-early Oct*

Bæjarins Beztu hot dog

You can learn more on a 45- to 60-minute guided tour *(adult/child 4900kr/free)*, in English, bookable online.

Join Culture Night & Reykjavík Arts Festival

MAP P49

Celebration of capital life

First held in 1996 as a birthday celebration for the city of Reykjavík, **Culture Night** *(menningarnott.is)* is easily the biggest single event in Iceland. The downtown-wide event generally takes place on the first Saturday after 18 August. The **Reykjavík Marathon** *(rmi.is)* is the first event of the day, with around 10,000 participants. Casual, family-oriented events include enjoying the 'waffle grants' where residents invite hundreds into their homes or gardens, for a hot waffle. The final big event is a concert at **Árnarhóll**, ending with fireworks around 11pm. From there, Reykjavík nightlife takes over.

If you're in town in June, **Reykjavík Arts Festival** *(listahatid.is)* should be your go-to. Iceland's premier cultural festival showcases two weeks of local and international theatre performances, film, dance, music and visual art.

EATING IN HISTORIC MIÐBORG: CASUAL & DELICIOUS

MAP P49

Pósthús Mathöll: Lively, central food hall with loads of options including popular Funky Bhangra: think burger meets Indian. *11.30am-10pm* €€

Le Kock: Some of Reykjavík's best burgers paired with drinks at Tail and doughnuts at its bakery Deig (which has earlier hours). *11.30am-11pm* €€

Icelandic Street Food: Showcases home-cooked food: from fish stew and lamb soup to sugar-dusted waffles. *11am-10pm* €€

Apotek Kitchen + Bar: Equally known for delicious menu of small plates and its top-flight cocktails, stylishly located inside a historic pharmacy. €€€

Rummage through Cool Wares at the Kolaportið Flea Market
MAP P49

Find vintage bric-a-brac, clothes and more

Dive into the huge industrial building near the harbour to find **Kolaportið flea market** *(kolaportid.is)*, a Reykjavík institution on weekends from 11am to 5pm. Wend through a vast tumble of secondhand clothes, old toys, antiques and cheap imports. A food section sells traditional eats like *rúgbrauð* (geothermally baked rye bread) and *brauðterta* ('sandwich cake'; a layering of bread with mayonnaise-based fillings). If you're looking for a wool sweater that won't break your budget, this is the place to try. Bring cash in case that must-have-item's seller doesn't take cards or digital payments.

Munch Favourite Hot Dogs
MAP P49

Visit Bæjarins Beztu truck

It's a rite of passage to seek out the city's famous hot dogs at the **Bæjarins Beztu truck** *(bbp.is; 9am-1am Sunday-Thursday, to 6am Fri & Sat)* near the harbour (patronised by Bill Clinton, Anthony Bourdain, Kim Kardashian and late-night bar-hoppers). Its hot dogs are made of lamb, pork and beef. Use the vital phrase '*eina með öllu*' (one with everything) to get the quintessential favourite with sweet mustard, ketchup, remoulade and crunchy onions. It's since expanded into a chain with locations throughout the region.

Do Your Laundry while Browsing Books at a Cafe
MAP P49

Cafe-diner with a twist

No one wants to spend their holidays doing laundry, but sometimes you just need clean clothes. The book-lined **Laundromat Cafe** *(thelaundromatcafe.is)* doubles as a laundrette, making it easy to wash and dry your clothes while you read books, sip coffee or enjoy a meal in the vibrant diner.

Rock Out at the Phallological Museum & Punk Museum
MAP P49

Get edgy in small museums

Oh, the jokes are endless here… Enjoy the unique **Icelandic Phallological Museum** *(phallus.is; adult/child 3500kr/free)*

BEST REYKJAVÍK MUSIC FESTIVALS

Iceland Airwaves: Overflows with music in intimate bars, cool clubs and prestigious theatres. Around 200 acts from 30 countries at one of the world's premier new music showcases. *(icelandairwaves.is)* Nov

Dark Music Days: A winter music festival at Harpa concert hall featuring Icelandic composers. *(darkmusicdays.is)* Jan

Lóa Festival: Music, street food and skateboarding come to Laugardalur Park. *(loafestival.is)* Jun

Innipúkinn Festival: Indie music fest held in clubs in central Reykjavík for a weekend. *(innipukinn.is)* late Jul or early Aug

Reykjavík Jazz Festival: Reykjavík toe-taps through a week dedicated to jazz across the city. *(reykjavikjazz.is)* Aug

---

EATING IN REYKJAVÍK: THE FINER THINGS
MAPS P49 & P50

Óx: Watch chef Vigfusson prepare 16 courses in his grandfather's kitchenette; wine pairings, too. *6.30-10pm Wed-Sat, plus 1-3pm Sat* €€€

Dill: New Nordic cuisine at this Michelin-starred bistro journeys guests across the Icelandic countryside. *6-10pm Tue-Fri or Wed-Sat alternate weeks* €€€

Grillmarkaðurinn: Farm-to-table dining: Icelandic lamb, beef, Arctic char and *skyr* (like a yoghurt). *5.30-10.30pm Mon-Fri, to 11.30pm Sat & Sun* €€€

OTO: Italian-Japanese fusion may not seem like a natural pairing, but dishes sing with creativity and nuance. Delish cocktails, too. *5.30-11pm Tue-Thu, to 11.45pm Fri & Sat* €€€

CYCLING & SCOOTING IN REYKJAVÍK

By Nordic standards, Reykjavík is hardly a city of cyclists. Blame the wind – statistics cannot explain how often it blows in the opposite direction to the way you are riding. But major improvements to bike paths, led by former mayor Dagur Eggertsson (known for attending meetings with famous leaders with a bike helmet), have made cycling a serious alternative to cars. Shared-use paths – designed for cyclists and pedestrians – connect the inlets of the capital region by threading along the coastline, running all the way from the tip of the Seltjarnarnes peninsula to downtown Hafnarfjörður. Rent bikes (or take tours) with **Reykjavik Bike Tours** (icelandbike.com), **Bike Company** (bikecompany.is) or **Borgarhjól** (borgarhjol.is). Or you can zip around on e-scooters using the **Hopp** (hopp.bike) or **Zolo** (en.zoloiceland.is) apps.

with its huge collection of phalluses – actually very well done. From pickled pickles to petrified wood, browse 286 different members representing all Icelandic mammals and beyond. Featured items include contributions from sperm whales and a polar bear, minuscule mouse bits and silver castings of each member of the Icelandic handball team.

If you're into punk music or Björk, Iceland's best-known musician, you can't miss the small **Icelandic Punk Museum** (facebook.com/Bankastraeti0; adult/child 1500/750kr), a few blocks away. This may be the only museum in the world that occupies a city's former public toilets. Follow the music and head downstairs to enter this ode to punk culture. Walk through exhibits, news clippings, quotes and the stories of punk legends glued to the white tiles of the bathroom stalls. There's also a listening station featuring music from artists including the multifaceted Björk, who was in an all-girl punk band as a teenager.

Explore Your Creativity
Try your hand at art, knitting, cooking and more

Love arts, crafts and culture? Satisfy your curiosity by learning from the locals with **Creative Iceland** (creativeiceland.is).

EATING & DRINKING IN HISTORIC MIÐBORG

MAPS P49 & P50

Café Rosenberg: You'll find welcoming Café Rosenberg in a historic brick building with worn wooden floors, plump couches and a spacious main room. *11am-8pm* €

Iða: Both bookstore and cafe, perfect for whiling away a day. Settle in for coffee, cake or soup. *8am-6pm Mon-Fri, from 10am Sat & Sun* €

Stúdentakjallarinn: University of Iceland's cafe serves everything from coffee to burgers and turns into a bar at night. *11am-11pm Mon-Wed, to 1am Thu-Sat* €€

Napoli: Technically a bakery of pizza...fresh made and baked to perfection, for takeaway. *11.30am-10pm Sun-Thu, to 11pm Fri & Sat* €€

Icelandic Punk Museum

Get involved with knitting *(22,500kr)*, cooking *(adult/child 29,900/14,950kr)*, graphic design, arts, crafts, music…you name it. This service hooks you up with local creative people offering workshops in their specialities.

Special Christmas Buffets
Lavish feasts at historic venues

If you're in town in December, book ahead for a lavish Christmas buffet, or *Jólahlaðborð*. These traditional arrays of local and international cuisine are a perfect way to sample Icelandic dishes like smoked lamb, pickled herring and smoked salmon. The buffets happen all around town throughout the month (but usually not on Christmas itself). **Múlakaffi** *(mulakaffi.is)* is a popular choice, and also has Þorrablót (p58) buffets. Or, if you want to go glam, the art-deco luxury **Hótel Borg** *(hotelborg.is)* has an off-the-charts *Jólahlaðborð*.

The founder of this historic hotel made a fortune as a circus performer in the US, and dreamed of investing in a magnificent luxury hotel back home. Since opening in 1930, it's become a magnet for heads of state and visiting celebrities, and it ran Iceland's only legal pub in the 1940s.

GUIDED TOURS

Walking tours – like **CityWalk** *(citywalk.is)*, **City Library literature tours** *(borgarbokasafn.is)* and **Haunted Walk** *(hauntedwalk.is)* – or bike (p60), **Tuk Tuk Tours** *(tuktuktours.is)* and bus tours show you the capital. **Your Friend in Reykjavík** *(yourfriendinreykjavik.com)* offers folklore- and foodie-themed tours of the centre. Another option for creative foodies is the **Reykjavik Food Tour** *(thereykjavikfoodwalk.com)* where you'll stroll the centre sampling at restaurants.

Whale-watching, puffin-spotting and sea-angling trips (p80) allow jaunts offshore. Smartphone apps feature everything from art and design to film locations.

The city is also the main hub for tours (p108) to amazing landscapes and activities around Iceland, some of which can pick up in Reykjavík.

 DRINKING IN HISTORIC MIÐBORG: PUBS & COCKTAIL BARS — MAP P49

Jungle Cocktail Bar:	GILLIGOGG:	Sæta Svínið Gastropub:	Icelandic Craft Bar:
Upbeat and friendly with some of the best cocktails in town, plus who doesn't love a jungle theme? *4pm-1am Sun-Thu, to 2am Fri & Sat*	Classy, burnished feel with delish mixed drinks and outdoor seating alongside Austurvöllur square, perfect on fair-weather days. *hours vary*	Tuck into meaty and creative pub food while quaffing a litre of the local ale at this three-storey feature of Reykjavík's pub scene. *11.30am-11.30pm*	A mellow hangout with good views onto bustling Lækjargata and local brews including Einstök Arctic Ale on tap. *11.30am-1am*

Laugavegur

BUZZING SHOPPING AND RESIDENTIAL DISTRICT

GETTING AROUND

Within the neighbourhood it's easiest to walk as many of the roads are one way or pedestrianised. Several buses (p56) run between the key Laugavegur bus stop at the eastern end of the street, through to central Lækjartorg Sq, before continuing onward. Others run along the seafront road, Sæbraut. E-scooters (p60) are also a fun way to get around.

Public parking (p48) is tough to find and zoned with different rules and prices. Pay with a meter or app.

Reykjavík's main street for shopping and people-watching is bustling, often-pedestrianised Laugavegur. The narrow, one-way lane and its side streets blossom with the capital's most interesting shops, cafes and bars. At its western end, its name changes to Bankastræti, then Austurstræti. Running uphill off Bankastræti, artists' street Skólavörðustígur ends at spectacular modernist church, Hallgrímskirkja. The waterfront offers excellent views of Faxaflói bay and majestic Mt Esja, from the iconic *Sun Voyager* sculpture.

This is prime Reykjavík, where colourful houses hide the central city's best swimming pool, and boutiques, galleries and cafes vie for your attention. Plan on browsing and meandering, though the streets can get thick with folks midday in high summer. On weekend nights, it becomes the centre of the city's *djammið* (party scene).

The further you stray from the two main drags, the quieter and more residential the streets become. So make sure to walk for pleasure's sake, taking in a more typical Reykjavík 101 way of life.

Ascend Reykjavík's Iconic Church MAP P66
Sweeping views from Hallgrímskirkja

Reykjavík's soaring church defines the city skyline and is one of the tallest structures in Iceland, visible from 20km away. Named after poet Reverend Hallgrímur Pétursson (1614–74), who wrote Iceland's most popular hymn book, *Passion Hymns*, **Hallgrímskirkja** *(hallgrimskirkja.is; church free, tower adult/child 1400/200kr)* is also one of the best places to get a bird's-eye view of the city. Head to the top of the 74.5m-high tower to look out on Reykjavík's colourful houses, the Atlantic Ocean and Mt Esja. On a clear day, it's possible to see as far as the Snæfellsjökull glacier. A lift carries visitors part of the way up the tower (no prebooking of tower tickets), but you have to climb

Hallgrímskirkja

a few flights of stairs to reach the very top. Try for a local's pronunciation: Hallgrímskirkja is pronounced hatl-krims-kirk-ya.

The church's best-kept secret may be its organ recitals and 50-person **choir** *(listvinafelag.is)* that regularly performs concerts. You can see concerts and prices, plus mass schedules (usually 11am Sunday and 10am Wednesday) online. The tower is closed during some of these.

On the church's front plaza, gazing proudly into the distance, is a statue of the Viking **Leifur Eiríksson**, the first European to discover America. A present from the USA on the 1000th anniversary of the Alþingi (Parliament) in 1930, it was designed by Alexander Stirling Calder (1870–1945), the father of modern mobile-creator and sculptor Alexander Calder (1898–1976).

Studio Museum & Free Sculpture Garden

MAP P66

Take in art and city views at the Einar Jónsson Museum

Einar Jónsson (1874–1954) was one of Iceland's foremost sculptors, with his dramatic allegorical style. Chiselled representations of Hope, Earth and Death burst from basalt cliffs, weep over naked women, and slay dragons. Pop across the street from Hallgrímskirkja to the **Einar Jónsson Museum** *(lej.is;*

(continues on p68)

HALLGRÍMSKIRKJA'S ARCHITECTURE

The columns on either side of the white-concrete church's signature tower represent volcanic basalt, part of architect Guðjón Samúelsson's desire to create a national architectural style. The church's size and radical design caused controversy, however, and Samúelsson (1887–1950) never saw its completion – it took 41 years (1945–86) to build.

In contrast to the high drama outside, the Lutheran church's interior is plain. The most eye-catching feature is the vast, gleaming 5275-pipe organ, installed in 1992. It was made in Germany by Johannes Klais Orgelbau and individuals sponsored each pipe – their names are inscribed on them. Towards the altar is the quaint older organ, still in use. The foyer hosts occasional art exhibitions.

EATING IN LAUGAVEGUR: BAKED GOODS & PASTRIES

MAPS P64 & P66

Sandholt: Usually crammed with folks hoovering up baguettes, croissants, pastries and sandwiches. *7am-7pm Sun-Thu, 6.30am-9pm Fri & Sat* €

Brauð & Co: Watch hipsters make some of the city's best home-baked breads and pastries. *6am-6pm Mon-Fri, to 5pm Sat & Sun* €

Kattakaffihúsið: Vegan pastries at the Cat Cafe – felines greet customers and nap in the window. *10am-5.30pm* €€

Wake & Bake: No better place for absurdly delicious freshly baked cookies, stacked bagels or muffins paired with strong coffees. *8am-5pm Mon-Sat, from 9am Sun* €

LAUGAVEGUR REYKJAVÍK

LAUGAVEGUR WEST

SIGHTS
1. Einar Jónsson Sculpture Garden
2. House of Collections
3. National Gallery of Iceland
4. Tjörnin

SLEEPING
5. Canopy by Hilton
6. CenterHotel Arnarhvoll
7. Galtafell Guesthouse
8. Hótel Holt
9. Loft Hostel
10. REY Apartments
11. Sunna Guesthouse

EATING
12. 101 Reykjavík Street Food
13. Bæjarins Beztu
14. Baka Baka
15. Chickpea
16. Grái Kötturinn
17. Hafnartorg Gallery
18. Kattakaffihúsið
19. Mat Bar
20. Pósthús Mathöll
21. Skál
22. Snaps
23. Sushi Social

DRINKING & NIGHTLIFE
24. Bastard Brew & Food
25. Bingo Drinkery
26. Bodega
27. Daisy
28. Einstök Bar
see 29 ELLÝ
29. Kaffibarinn
30. Kaldi
31. Kramber
32. Lebowski Bar
33. Lemmy
34. Mokka Kaffi
35. Prikið
36. Röntgen
37. Skúli Craft Bar

ENTERTAINMENT
38. Bird
39. Gamla Bíó
40. Gaukurinn
41. Hannesarholt
42. Iðnó
43. Mengi
44. National Theatre
45. Pablo Discobar

SHOPPING
46. 12 Tónar
47. 66° North

- 18 Andrá
- 19 Arason
- 60 Aurum
- 51 Buy My Chic
- 52 Epal
- 53 Fischersund
- 54 Fríða
- 55 Handknitting Association of Iceland
- 56 Hildur Hafstein see 52 Hildur Yeoman
- 57 Hürra
- 58 Kaolin
- 59 Kirsuberjatréð
- 60 Kogga
- 61 Kolaportið
- 62 Mamma Mia Vintage
- 63 Orr
- 64 Rammagerðin
- 65 Skúmaskot
- 66 Smekkleysa
- see 52 Stefánsbúð
- 67 Thorvaldsens Bazar
- 68 Vínbúðin – Austurstræti
- 69 Wasteland

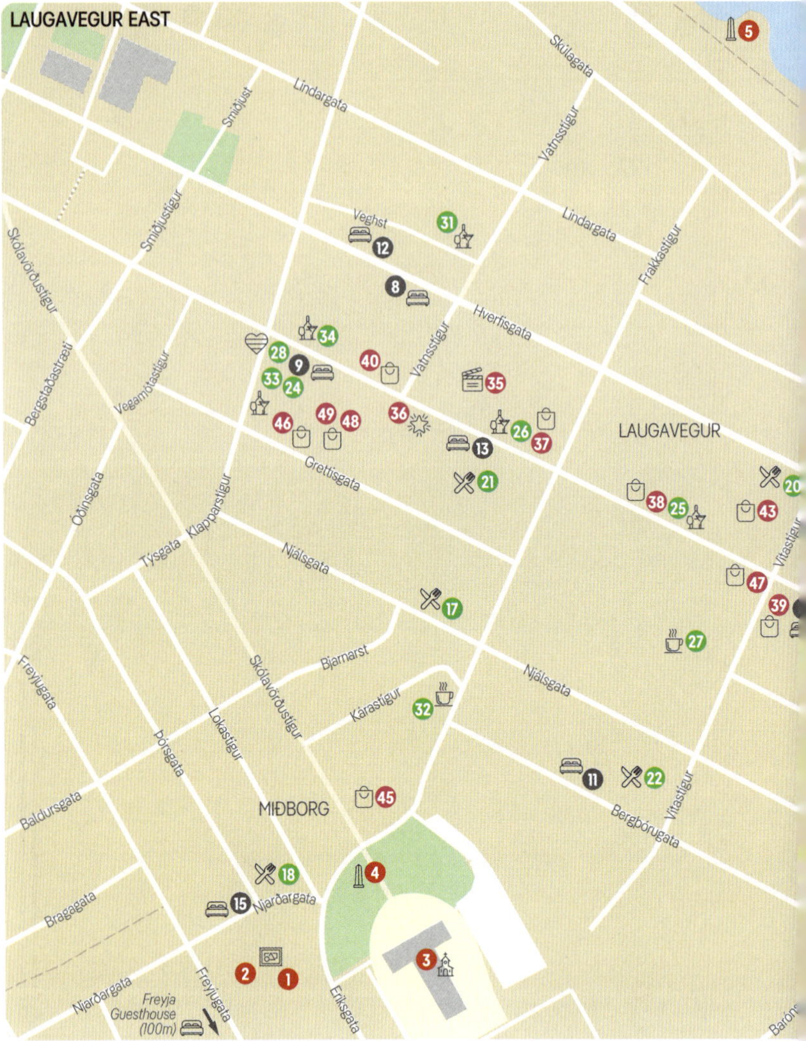

LAUGAVEGUR EAST

● SIGHTS
1. Einar Jónsson Museum
2. Einar Jónsson Sculpture Garden
3. Hallgrímskirkja
4. Leifur Eiriksson Statue
5. Sun Voyager

● ACTIVITIES
6. Sundhöllin

● SLEEPING
7. Alda Hotel
8. CityHub
9. Hótel Frón
10. KEX Hostel
11. Nest Apartments
12. Reykjavik Residence
13. Sand Hotel
14. Skuggi Hotel
15. Sunna Guesthouse

● EATING
16. Arabian Taste
17. Brauð & Co
18. Café Loki
19. Hlemmur Mathöll
20. Kemuri
21. Sandholt
22. Vitabar
23. Wake & Bake

● DRINKING & NIGHTLIFE
24. 22 Bar
25. Amma Don
26. Cernin Vínbar
27. Kaktus Espressobar
28. Kiki
29. Microbar
30. Plantan Kaffihús
31. Port 9
32. Reykjavík Roasters
33. Veður
34. Vínstúkan Tíu Sopar

● ENTERTAINMENT
35. Bíó Paradís
36. Dillon

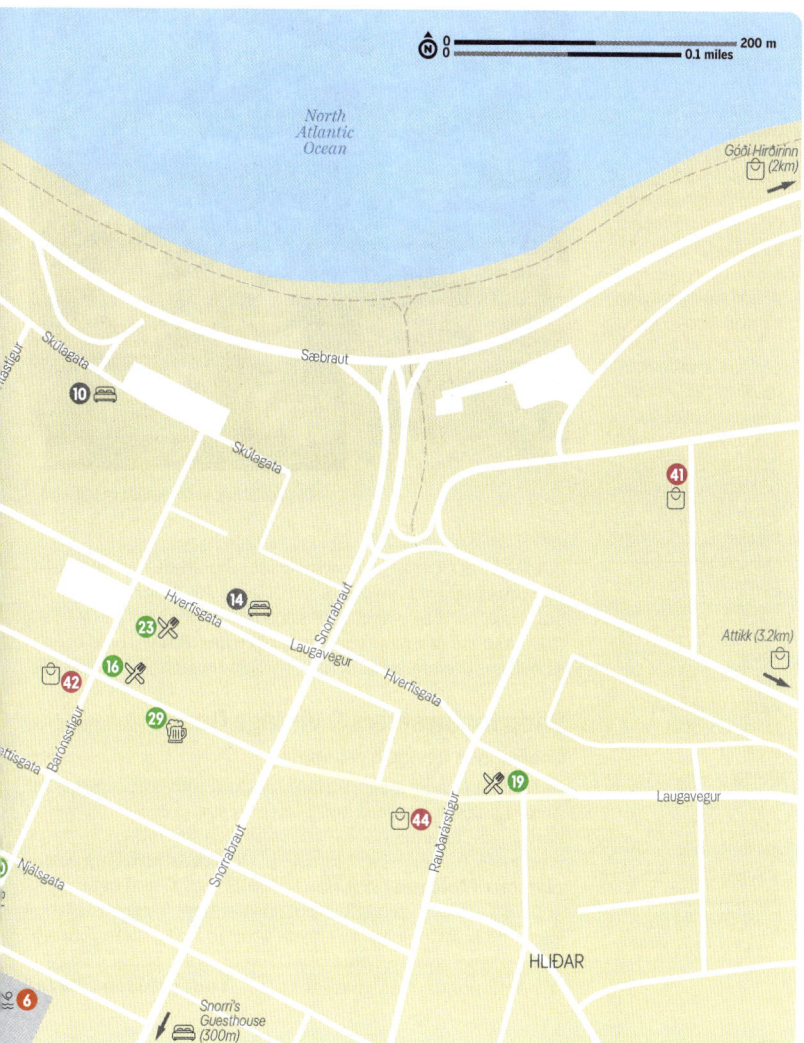

- **SHOPPING**
- **37** Aftur
- **38** Emil & Lina
- **39** Geisladiskabúð Valda
- **40** Herrafataverslun Kormáks & Skjaldar
- **41** Hringekjan
- **42** Kron
- **43** KronKron
- **44** Lucky Records
- **45** Orrifinn
- **46** Reykjavík Record Shop
- **47** Rokk & Rómantík
- **48** Spúútnik
- **49** Verzlanahöllin

☑ TOP TIP

Learn the Icelandic word for 'food hall' (*mathöll*) and you'll never go hungry in Reykjavík. Since Hlemmur Mathöll (p84) opened in a former bus terminal, these indoor courtyards with six to eight food vendors have multiplied. For lunch try Hlemmur or the Grandi Mathöll (p77). At night, dine at **Hafnartorg Gallery** and Pósthús Mathöll (p58).

BEST DESIGN SHOPPING

Skúmaskot: Handmade porcelain, women's and kids' clothing, paintings and cards. *(facebook.com/skumaskot.art.design)*

Kirsuberjatréð: Women's art-and-design collective with handmade clothes, fishskin-leather purses and bowls made from radish slices. *(kirs.is)*

Rammagerðin: Souvenir shop loaded with woollens, crafts and collectables. *(icelandgiftstore.com)*

Fischersund: Concept store by Sigur Rós frontman Jónsi and his sisters: perfumes, herbs, ethereal music and art. *(fischersund.com)*

Epal: Large Icelandic home-goods store. *(epal.is)*

Kaolin: Interesting array of ceramic arts and crafts. *(kaolinkeramikgalleri.com)*

Kogga: Tiny ceramic studio in the lower level of an old Reykjavík house. *(kogga.is)*

Handknitting Association of Iceland

(continued from p63)

adult/child 1500kr/free), which fills the studio he designed. The upper storeys have good city views. Jónsson designed the building, built between 1916 and 1923, when this hill was on the outskirts of town. The **sculpture garden** with 26 bronzes behind the museum is free, so wander in and have a look.

Shop for Sweaters & Vintage Goods MAPS P64 & P66
Cool unique Reykjavík shopping

Independent boutiques, restaurants and souvenir shops dominate Laugavegur, making it easy to spend hours browsing handmade jewellery, local crafts, bags and clothes. If you're hankering for some local knitwear, the **Handknitting Association of Iceland** *(handknit.is)* sells traditional hats, socks and *lopapeysur* (Icelandic woollen sweaters). You can also buy yarn and knitting patterns if you want to make them yourself.

For a wool sweater that won't break your budget, browse the Kolaportið flea market (p59), **Thorvaldsens Bazar**

EATING IN LAUGAVEGUR: QUICK BITES & BRUNCHES — MAPS P64 & P66

Baka Baka: Baked goods and small plates play second fiddle at night when the wood-fired pizza dominates. *7.30am-9pm Sun-Thu, to 10pm Fri & Sat* €

Arabian Taste: Perennial favourite for delicious wraps, shawarma, falafel and grills into the wee hours. *10am-11pm Sun-Thu, to 2am Fri & Sat* €

Vitabar: Sidle up to the bar to order your short-order burger with crispy hand-cut fries. *11.30am-11pm, bar to 1am or 2am Fri & Sat* €

Grái Kötturinn: Tiny six-table cafe that feels like an eccentric bookshop/art gallery that serves hearty brunches. *8am-2.30pm* €€

Snaps: Megahit for classic bistro mains – think steak or *moules frites* (mussels and fries) and tempting brunches. *7-10am & 11.30am-11pm* €€

Sushi Social: Grab a happy-hour cocktail from 5pm to 6pm nightly and dig into delish sushi. *5-10.30pm* €€€

Chickpea: Casual counter of Mediterranean fusion sandwiches, wraps and salads, all vegetarian. *10am-8pm Mon-Sat* €

Kemuri: A short menu of delectable, vegetarian Polish dumplings are all the rage, with daily specials. *noon-8pm Mon-Thu, to 9pm Fri-Sun* €€

(thorvaldsens.is) or **Verzlanahöllin** *(verzlanahollin.is)* secondhand stores. Everything is more expensive in Reykjavík, and that's made vintage shopping an art. The city centre has a batch of well-curated secondhand shops like **Spúútnik** *(spuutnikreykjavik.com)*, tiny **Buy My Chic** *(buymychic.is)* and street-trendy **Mamma Mia Vintage** *(mammamiavintage.shop)*. Other names include **Wasteland** *(instagram.com/wastelandreykjavik)* – a smorgasbord of bargain hunting. Just into the Hliðar neighborhood, try **Hringekjan** *(hringekjan.is)* or **Góði Hirðirinn** *(godihirdirinn.is)*, and **Attikk** *(attikk.is)* is a bit further out but features high-end and couture brands.

Make like a Scandi Fashionplate   MAPS P64 & P66
Shop iconic Icelandic clothes and shoe designers

Reykjavík's vibrant design culture makes for great clothes shopping: from cool Scandi fashions to sleek fish-skin purses. **Stefánsbúð** *(stefansbud.com)* rounds up a batch of hard-to-find designers all under one roof, as does **Andrá** *(andra reykjavik.com)* with an emphasis on the high-end specialists. **Hildur Yeoman** *(hilduryeoman.com)* makes frothy, slinky dresses and swimsuits. **Rokk & Rómantík** *(rokkogromantik.is)*, **Aftur** *(aftur.is)* and **Húrra** *(hurrareykjavik.is)* are leaders in edgy, original streetwear, jewellery and fragrance. **Kron Kron** *(kronkron.com)* carries high fashion with Scandinavian designers' silk dresses and knit capes, while **Kron** *(kron.is)* offers its outlandishly wonderful handmade shoes. **66° North** *(66north.is)* is the go-to for swanky outdoor gear.

While perhaps technically menswear, **Arason**'s *(arasonofficial.com)* classic cashmere hoodies, denim jackets and more are really unisex. **Herrafataverslun Kormáks & Skjaldar** *(herrafataverslun.is)* evokes a bygone era with old-school men's suits, hunt clothing and accessories. For the fancy kids, hit **Emil & Lina** *(emiloglina.is)*.

And don't forget the other innovative designers in the Old Harbour.

See What's on at the National Gallery   MAP P64
The bountiful art and creativity of the National Gallery of Iceland

Stop in at the **National Gallery of Iceland** *(listasafn.is; adult/child 2400kr/free)*, a pretty stack of marble atriums and spacious galleries overlooking Tjörnin (p48). Its ever-changing

BEST JEWELLERY STORES

If you spring for high-end jewellery, don't forget visitors are eligible for a 15% tax refund (p352), under certain conditions.

Aurum: Guðbjörg's whisper-thin silver jewellery is sophisticated stuff, often inspired by leaves and flowers. *(aurum.is)*

Orrifinn: Subtle jewellery that captures the natural wonder of Iceland and its history: delicate anchors, axes and pen nibs. *(orrifinn.com)*

Orr: A creative couple craft delicate, nature-inspired jewellery using pearls, semiprecious stones and lustrous metals. *(orr.is)*

Fríða: Intricate gold handcrafted on-site, run by a wife and husband team. *(fridaskart.is)*

Hildur Hafstein: Wander through the incense haze to browse funky Asian-inspired jewellery made right here with local stones and gems. *(hildurhafstein.is)*

EATING IN LAUGAVEGUR: ICELANDIC PICKS   MAPS P64 & P66

Skál!: Combines unusual flavours (fermented garlic, birch sugar, Arctic thyme salt) with Icelandic ingredients to impressive effect. *noon-3pm Wed-Sun, 5-11pm or midnight daily* €€€

Mat Bar: Intimate, atmospheric place, fusing Mediterranean and Nordic cuisine in tapas-sized shared plates, and cocktails too. *5-10pm Mon-Thu, to 11pm Fri & Sat* €€€

Cafe Loki: Convenient cafe for classic home-style Icelandic dishes and delicious *skyr* desserts across from Hallgrímskirkja. *8am-10pm* €€

101 Reykjavik Street Food: Casual spot perfect for a quick bowl of soup, *plokkfiskur* (fish stew) or fish and chips. *11am-10pm* €€

ICELANDIC BEAUTY PRODUCTS

Iceland's pure water, wild herbs and traditional salves have led to a thriving beauty/wellness industry. Stock up on masks, creams and balms at pharmacies like ÍslandsApótek, Lyfjabúrið or Lyfja. Look for excellent **Sóley Organics** (soleyorganics.com), which emphasises handpicked, organic herbs. There's a store in Grandi, but it's cheaper at airport duty free. Other indie brands with a sustainability focus include **Villimey** (villimey.is), made in the Westfjords, and **Angan** (anganskincare.com). **Blue Lagoon** (skincare.bluelagoon.com) sells its signature brand – not necessarily sustainable, but with name recognition. **Herbal Apothecary** (jurtaapotek.is) makes ointments, teas and oils. Fischersund (p68) crafts scents and soaps.

exhibits draw from a fascinating 15,000-piece collection and it hosts the occasional international show. The museum can only display a small sample at any one time and exhibitions range from 19th- and 20th-century paintings by Iceland's favourite artists (including Jóhannes Kjarval and Nína Sæmundsson) to sculptures by Sigurjón Ólafsson and others. Admission also includes rotating exhibits and the interdisciplinary *Resistance* show at the museum's House of Collections.

In their stewardship of the **Ásgrímur Jónsson Collection** and home, the museum sometimes offer shows and events at Jónsson's former atelier. Iceland's first professional painter, Jónsson (1876–1958) was the son of a farmer and his work incorporates folk tales and Icelandic nature.

Pose Alongside an Iconic Sculpture MAP P66
Seek out the waterfront Sun Voyager

Beyond museums, you'll find unique murals and sculpture all over town, but it's Jón Gunnar Árnason's shiplike **Sun Voyager** (*Sólfar*) sculpture that seems to catch visitors' imaginations. Scooping in a skeletal arc along the seaside, it offers a photo shoot with snowcapped mountains in the distance.

Catch an Icelandic Flick with Subtitles MAP P66
Indie movies at Bíó Paradís

Looking for something to do tonight? The totally cool cinema **Bíó Paradís** (bioparadis.is), decked out in movie posters and vintage officeware, screens specially curated Icelandic films with English subtitles and international flicks. It's a chance to see movies that you may not find elsewhere.

Go Flightseeing by Plane or Helicopter
Soar above volcanoes, glaciers and springs

A helicopter or flightseeing tour may be one of the most expensive ways to explore Iceland *(69,000kr to 200,000kr)*, but seeing this incredible landscape from above can be worth the price. Flights from Reykjavík Domestic Airport soar over volcanic eruptions, geothermal springs and colourful mineral-streaked landscapes. Land on a glacier, a volcano, or both. Companies include **Atlantsflug** *(flightseeing.is)*, **Norðurflug** *(helicopter.is)* and **Glacierheli** *(glacierheli.is)*. If you can't

---

DRINKING IN LAUGAVEGUR: CAFES MAPS P64 & P66

Reykjavík Roasters: High-end coffee institution with hardwood tables and a relaxed air, plus a branch in Hlíðar. *7am-6pm Mon-Fri, 8am-5pm Sat & Sun*

Kaktus Espressobar: Mismatching furniture and houseplants in the window. Popular with the cool crowd. *7.30am-5pm Mon-Fri, 9am-5pm Sat & Sun*

Mokka Kaffi: Soak up the vibe at Reykjavík's oldest coffee shop from the 1950s; waffles, sandwiches and coffees. *9am-6pm*

Plantan Kaffihús: Scrumptious pastries and vegan breakfast bowls with top-tier coffee and hot chocolate. *8am-6pm Mon-Fri, from 10am Sat & Sun*

House of Collections, National Gallery of Iceland

spring for the flight, visit the show FlyOver Iceland (p79) for simulated thrills.

Unwind & Soak with Locals
MAP P66

Revel in neighbourhood pool culture at Sundhöllin

Iceland's public pools are some of the best in the world, and thanks to the abundant geothermal supply, there are 17 public **pools** in and around Reykjavík. Pools are also one centre of the city's social life (as in many Icelandic towns); children play, teenagers flirt, business deals are made and everyone catches up on the latest gossip at the baths. Volcanic heat keeps the temperature at a mellow 29°C, and most baths have *heitir pottar* (hot-pots) – Jacuzzi-like pools kept a toasty 37°C to 42°C – and saunas and cold plunges.

Every neighbourhood has its own *sundlaug*, but **Sundhöllin** *(reykjavik.is)*, near Hallgrímskirkja, is special. Built in 1937 and designed by the legendary architect Guðjón Samúelsson, it's kitted out with a sauna, steam rooms, cold plunge pools and several heated pools. Relax in its rooftop hot tub, gazing at the open sky.

Admission to public City of Reykjavík *(reykjavik.is)* pools is 1380kr and free for children aged 15 and under (a bargain

POOL & LAGOON ETIQUETTE

In pool and lagoon locker rooms, take your shoes off at the racks by the door and leave them there.

Then, do not enter a public pool with dry hair. It means you are an amateur, guilty of breaking the rule that you must shower naked (no bathing suit) with soap before getting in the pool. Thanks to the abundance of hot water, pools are low on chlorine and Icelanders like to keep it that way. Shampoo or liquid soap is usually provided in the shower.

Another rookie mistake is leaving your towel in the locker room then wetting the entire room on the way out. So, use towel racks by showers.

Women no longer have a different dress code to men: going topless is allowed for everyone.

 DRINKING IN LAUGAVEGUR: WINE BARS — MAPS P64 & P66

| Vínstúkan Tíu Sopar: Chat with the friendly owner to find the vintage that's right for you, paired with small plates. *5pm-midnight Sun-Thu, 5pm-1am Fri & Sat* | Port 9: Rub shoulders with actors and the media elite under low lighting, with a secret hangout vibe (it's tucked down a tiny street). *4-11pm Tue-Sun* | Kramber: Relaxed, eclectic atmosphere with wines, but also on-point cocktails, to keep the whole group happy. *3-11pm Tue-Sat, to 9pm Sun* | Cernin Vínbar: Fancy wine and cheese pairings at a premium, in a sleek, modern room. *4-11pm Thu-Sun* |

LOCAL LIQUORS

Icelanders have a lot of time in winter to perfect their crafts. It's no wonder then that a slew of good local distilleries and breweries have sprung up. Here's a quick cheat sheet for your next bar-room order.

Microdistillery **64° Reykjavík** (reykjavik distillery.is) produces Katla vodka, aquavit, herbal liqueurs and schnapps from foraged fruits and botanicals.

Brennivín is caraway-flavoured 'black death' schnapps, nicely neon green and a whopping 80 proof.

Myriad gins include Ólafsson Gin, Reykjavík Gin and Wild Icelandic Pink Gin.

Opal is a flavoured vodka in menthol and licorice varieties (52 proof).

Reyka (reyka.com), Iceland's first distillery, in Borgarnes, is not open to the public. To have a tasting or tour, visit Þoran Distillery (p79), and south of town Eimverk Distillery (p93) and Hovdenak Distillery (p93).

Smekkleysa

after the Blue Lagoon). Save even more with a 10-ticket card for 6300kr. They are open from early morning to evening. Bring towels and bathing suits, or at some places you can rent them on-site.

Reykjavík's Record Stores   MAPS P64 & P66
Browse Icelandic music

Love Icelandic music? Hit the record stores to browse, listen and purchase good old-fashioned vinyl or CDs. The two-floor shop at indie **12 Tónar** (12tonar.is) is a cool place to hang out: listen to tunes, drink coffee, grab a beer and catch a gig (summer concerts and DJs). Or try **Lucky Records** (luckyrecords.is), **Reykjavík Record Shop** (facebook.com/reykjavikrecordshop) and tiny **Geisladiskabúð Valda** record store.

Don't miss **Smekkleysa** (smekkleysa.net), the home of historic Bad Taste Records where Björk and The Sugarcubes got their start. It's now got both a shop and coffee bar.

In the Old Harbour, you can visit **Alda Music** (aldamusic.is) for vinyl and CDs, too.

DRINKING IN REYKJAVÍK: CRAFT BEER   MAPS P64 & P66

Skúli Craft Bar: At the forefront of the craft-beer wave; 14 craft beers on tap, non-alcoholic ales, beer flights. *noon-11pm Sun-Thu, to 1am Fri & Sat*

Kaldi: Effortlessly cool with a smoking courtyard and piano, Kaldi serves its own microbrews. *noon-1am Sun-Thu, to 3am Fri & Sat*

Einstök Bar: Friendly bartenders serve 10 of the famed brewery's beers on tap. *noon-1am Sun-Thu, to 3am Fri & Sat*

Microbar: Low-key spot with 14 microbrews on tap, beer flights and happy hour. *3pm-midnight Sun-Thu, to 1am Fri & Sat*

Party under the Midnight Sun MAPS P64 & P66
Cruise the capital's bar and music scene

Reykjavík is renowned for its weekend party scene that goes strong into the wee hours, and spills over onto some of the weekdays (especially in summer). *Djammið* in the capital means 'going out on the town', or you could say *pöbbarölt* for a 'pub stroll'.

Most action is near Laugavegur and Austurstræti, with another cluster of pubs and dance clubs near Ingólfstorg in the heart of Old Reykjavík.

Things get going late, usually midnight and later on weekends. During the week, places stay open to around 1am and on Friday and Saturday to 4am or 5am. Some clubs have cover charges after midnight.

Cheap beer, of course, is nonexistent here, but check smartphone app **Barhopp** for happy hours. Warm and welcoming craft beer bars (p72) and wine bars (p71) are an inviting bunch, to warm up before a night out at the clubs. Or pregame with your own booze from the national store **Vínbúðin** *(vinbudin.is)*. Pro tip: buy alcohol at the duty free when you arrive at Keflavík Airport.

Bodega *(bodega.is)* is aces for outdoor seating, with a happy hour from 4pm to 6pm. A new breed of cocktail bars and pubs run the gamut from **Daisy** *(instagram.com/daisy.rvk)* to **Bingo Drinkery** *(instagram.com/bingo.rvk)*. **ELLÝ** *(ellybar.is)* and **22 Bar** *(22bar.is)* are handily central on Laugavegur.

For a more sedate hang, kick back at the handsome library bar at **Hótel Holt**. **Amma Don** *(ox.restaurant)* is worth seeking out. It's a speakeasy serving top-notch cocktails.

After 10pm, mingle with the Reykjavík in-crowd at **Röntgen** (over the age of 30) and **Prikið** (under 30), which really get going the later it gets. **Lemmy** *(lemmy.is)* is a rock music bar staple.

Midnight. The dance floor at gay bar **Kiki** *(kiki.is)* is pumping, and classic **Kaffibarinn** *(kaffibarinn.is)* is packed. Dance to DJs...like at the trio of **Pablo Discobar** *(pablodiscobar.is)* and **Bird** *(instagram.com/bird_rvk)*, where fun karaoke meets live shows, or **Gaukurinn** *(gaukurinn.is)*. Rock bands hit the tiny corner stage at **Dillon** *(dillon.is)*, and there's a great garden out back for sipping from more than 170 whiskies.

Stop for a late-night hot dog at Bæjarins Beztu (p59) or a wrap at Arabian Taste (p68) if you need sustenance along the way.

BEST LIVE LOCAL MUSIC

The ever-changing Reykjavík performing-arts scene features shows at bars and cafes, theatres and Harpa. To see who's playing, consult free English-language newspaper *Grapevine* (grapevine.is), websites Visit Reykjavík (visitreykjavik.is) and What's On in Reykjavík (whatson.is/magazine), Setlist (setlist.is) or city music shops.

Gamla Bíó: Premier 1926 art-deco cinema turned small concert venue. *(gamlabio.is)*

Iðnó: Lakeside for special shows. *(idno.is)*

Mengi: Small, edgy program of music and visual and performing arts. *(mengi.net)*

Hannesarholt: Gallery and intimate music venue in the house of a former prime minister. *(hannesarholt.is)*

Tjarnarbíó: Theatre with occasional music. *(tjarnarbio.is)*

National Theatre: From Icelandic plays to musicals and opera. Kids' shows, too. *(leikhusid.is)*

DRINKING IN LAUGAVEGUR: BARS MAPS P64 & P66

Prikið: A coffee shop and diner from 1951 by day, pub and live-music/DJ venue by night. *8am-1am Mon-Thu, to 4.30am Fri, 11am-4.30am Sat, to 1am Sun*

Veður: Cosily cool, with a beautifully lit bar, welcoming vibe, acclaimed cocktails and long happy hour (noon to 7.30pm). *2pm-1am Sun-Thu, to 3am Fri & Sat*

Lebowski Bar: With *The Big Lebowski* playing on multiple screens, this is the fan bar you didn't know you needed. *11am-1am Sun-Thu, to 4.30am Fri & Sat*

Bastard Brew & Food: Pub pairing drinks and craft beers with a creative menu and bottomless weekend brunch. *noon-1am*

Vesturbær & the Old Harbour

CHARMING HARBOUR WITH WHALE WATCHING, SHOPS AND SIGHTS

GETTING AROUND

A very short walk from central Reykjavík, this compact, characterful neighbourhood is ripe for exploring on foot. Strætó bus 14 runs to the Old Harbour from Laugardalur, via the BSÍ terminal and Lækjartorg Sq in Old Reykjavík. Choose the Mýrargata stop for whale-watching and Grandagarðu for the Reykjavik Maritime Museum.

In summer, the **ferry to Viðey** *(elding. is)* leaves from here a few times per day. There are also bike and segway outfitters here: **Reykjavik Bike Tours** (p60) and **Reykjavik Segway Tours** *(reykjaviksegwaytours.com)*.

☑ TOP TIP

Find visitor resources at **Visit Reykjavík** *(visitreykjavik.is)*, **Grapevine** *(grapevine.is)* and **Iceland Review** *(icelandreview.com)*.

The Vesturbær area of Reykjavík includes several distinct neighbourhoods as well as the city's charming historic harbour. The Grandi area on the west side of the harbour is named after a fish factory, but it's now dotted with interesting tourist attractions, galleries and eateries. The inland Vesturbær district is quietly residential, and the Seltjarnarnes Peninsula juts into the sea in the far northwest, a local favourite for walks and Northern Lights viewing.

One of the best things about the area around the Old Harbour is the casual, eclectic vibe. Try for a fine-weather day, when you can comfortably walk along the sparkling water, taking in the moored boats and sweeping views back to Harpa and Hallgrímskirkja. Then stroll between art galleries, shops and museums. It's also the place where you'll catch whale-watching, puffin-spotting or harbour cruises, and in summer boats run out to Viðey island. Then dine well at diverse restaurants on the harbourfront or along Grandagarður.

Get Your Photo Op at the Old Harbour   MAP P76
Stroll the seafront

Reykjavík's natural harbour was a key force in helping transform the area from remote farmland into a national capital and fishing powerhouse. Largely service harbours until recently, the **Old Harbour** and, on its western edge, the **Grandi** (Örfirisey) area, have blossomed into tourist hot spots, with key art galleries, museums, restaurants and shops. Whale- and puffin-viewing trips depart from the Old Harbour, and as boat bells ding, photo ops abound with views of snowcapped Mt Esja and Harpa concert hall. Nearby, Seltjarnarnes peninsula (p83) is one of the city's premier walking areas, with a well-maintained trail along the wave-crushed coastline. It's also a top spot for winter Northern Lights viewing.

- **SIGHTS**
1 Church of Seltjarnarnes
2 Grótta Lighthouse
3 Whales of Iceland
- **ACTIVITIES**
4 Kvika Footbath
5 Nesvöllur
6 Sundlaug Seltjarnarness
7 Vesturbæjarlaug
- **EATING**
8 Brauð & Co
9 Gaeta Gelato
10 Grandi Mathöll
see 7 Hagavagninn
11 Ísbúð Huppu
12 Ísbúð Vesturbæjar
see 8 Kaffihús Vesturbæjar
13 Litla Valdís
14 Raðagerði Veitingahús
- **SHOPPING**
15 Farmers & Friends

Go Aurora Borealis Hunting
MAP P76

In search of the Northern Lights

Witnessing the aurora borealis anywhere can be magical, but there's nothing quite like watching the Northern Lights dance above you at sea. From September to April, Northern Lights cruises depart from Reykjavík's Old Harbour in the evening. Cruises are typically between two and three hours long and offer another cruise should your search not pan out the first time. Try Elding (p81) or Special Tours (p81).

On land, going with a tour operator has the benefit of an experienced guide and a driver skilled in winter conditions. Many companies also provide heavy-duty winter wear. Check cancellation policies. Some companies go ahead, even when the sky is cloudy and the forecast bleak.

Aurora Basecamp (*aurorabasecamp.is*) offers indoor, widescreen simulation of Northern Lights before searching for the real thing with your guide.

You don't have to book a tour or rent a car to see auroras. When the conditions are right, you can spot them from the edge of Seltjarnarnes peninsula (p83) or from Öskjuhlíð (p89)

SEEING THE NORTHERN LIGHTS

The Northern Lights, visible in the dark between September and April, are caused by solar activity. A flow of charged particles from the sun, called the solar wind, slams into the Earth's magnetic field and causes atoms in the upper atmosphere to glow. The lights appear quite suddenly, their intensity varying – scientists publish a daily forecast *(aurora forecast.is)*.

The best time to see the Northern Lights is around the equinoxes (September/October and March/April). Searching for the auroras is a waiting game – and success can come down to dressing warmly. Dress warmly andead for dark, cloudless skies beyond the city lights.

VESTURBÆR & THE OLD HARBOUR REYKJAVÍK

OLD HARBOUR

★ HIGHLIGHTS
1. Old Harbour

● SIGHTS
2. Aurora Reykjavík
3. Grandi
- see 5 i8 Grandi
- see 5 Kling & Bang
4. Lava Show
5. Marshall House
- see 5 Nýló
6. Omnom Chocolate
7. Reykjavík Maritime Museum
8. Saga Museum
- see 5 Stúdió Ólafur Elíasson
9. Þoran Distillery
10. Þúfa
- see 5 Þula Gallery

● ACTIVITIES
11. Elding Adventures at Sea
12. Katla Whale Watching
- see 11 Mr Puffin
13. Reykjavik Bike Tours
14. Reykjavík By Boat
15. Reykjavik Segway Tours
16. Special Tours
17. Viggson Sailing
- see 11 Whale Safari

● SLEEPING
18. Grandi
- see 27 Local 101
19. Reykjavik Marina

● EATING
20. Fish & Chips Vagninn
21. Forréttabarinn
22. Hamborgara Búllan
23. Himalayan Spice
- see 8 Matur og Drykkur
- see 23 Sægreifinn (Sea Baron)
- see 20 Valdís
24. Viet Noodles

● DRINKING & NIGHTLIFE
25. Hygge Coffee & Micro Bakery
- see 5 La Primavera
26. Lady Brewery
27. Litli Barinn
28. Reykjavík Röst
29. Slippbarinn

● ENTERTAINMENT
30. FlyOver Iceland

● SHOPPING
31. Farmers & Friends
32. Jens
33. Kiosk
- see 33 Krínolín
- see 23 Smiðsbúðin
34. Steinunn

If weather doesn't cooperate, head to **Aurora Reykjavík** (*aurorareykjavik.is; adult/child 3900/1900kr*) to learn about the classical tales explaining auroras and the scientific explanation, then watch a surround-sound, panoramic, high-definition re-creation of Icelandic auroras. It also offers tours.

Get Ice Cream (Yes, Really)   MAPS P75, P76 & P85
Icelandic ice-cream culture

Icelanders do not let the sunshine dictate the correct time frame for ice-cream consumption. If the weather is good enough to leave the house, locals go for it. **Ísbúð Vesturbæjar** (p82; *isbudvesturbaejar.is*) and **Ísbúð Huppu** *(isbud huppu.is)* lead the way in soft-serve ice cream mixed with sweets and flavours; kids especially love the *bragðarefur* made with three selections from the candy bar.

For quality over quantity, Old Harbour establishments **Valdís** *(valdis.is)* – which now has a branch called **Litla Valdís** near Laugavegur – and **Omnom** *(omnomchocolate.com)*, a chocolate factory, have a highly colourful selection of flavours. Top ice-cream aficionados praise **Skúbb** (p89; *skubb.is*) for its creamy goodness; the shop is near the Laugardalslaug pool, a 30-minute walk from downtown. **Gaeta Gelato** *(gelato.is)* has three branches bringing gelato into the game.

Dive Deep at the Reykjavík Maritime Museum   MAP P76
Learn about the city and the sea

If you want to understand Iceland, you have to understand how the country has been defined by its relationship with the sea. There's no better place to do that than the **Reykjavík Maritime Museum** *(borgarsogusafn.is; adult/child 2450kr/ free)*. This museum chronicles 150 years of fishing. Learn how traditional and modern fishing methods differ and what it took to survive the rough seas without the technology of today. The museum is housed in a building that used to be a fish-freezing plant. Make time for one of the daily guided tours (March to October) of the 816-tonne former coastguard ship *Óðinn (1870kr)*.

Embrace Art & Culture at Marshall House   MAP P76
Support local art

The restoration of Marshall House is a key factor in Grandi's rise as an arty enclave. Once a massive fishmeal factory, it's now home to several innovative arts spaces. The artist-run exhibition space **Nýló** (Living Art Museum; *nylo.is; free*) was founded by a group of local artists in 1978 and houses a collection of more than 2000 items dating as far back as

BEST LOCAL SPOTS FOR THE AURORA BOREALIS

To vastly increase your chances of spotting this Arctic phenomenon, seek deeper darkness.

Grótta Lighthouse: The coastal walk to the tip of the Seltjarnarnes peninsula takes only an hour from the city centre.

Öskjuhlíð: To capture a photograph of the Northern Lights over the Reykjavík skyline, this hill is an excellent vantage point.

Heiðmörk Nature Reserve: Best for solitude. It's possible to reach the area by public transport to Norðlingaholt, but a private car makes the trip smoother.

Lake Kleifarvatn: Remote Reykjanes Peninsula locale with big views.

Road to Bláfjöll Mountain: Good option when driving on your own and there's no (or only light) snow.

 EATING & DRINKING IN THE OLD HARBOUR: OUR PICKS — MAPS P75 & P76

| Sægreifinn: Sidle into harbour shack 'Sea Baron' for the capital's most famous lobster soup plus fish skewers grilled on the spot. *11.30am-10pm €€* | Forréttabarinn: Creative plates loaded with seafood; duck, beef and lamb dishes too. Kick back in its airy and relaxed bar area. *4-10pm, bar to 11pm €€€* | Grandi Mathöll: Food hall with long trestle tables harbourside and diverse stalls ranging from lamb, Korean food and fish and chips to veggie delights. *11am-9pm €€* | Matur Og Drykkur: Inventive versions of traditional Icelandic fare as mini-portion tasting menus with attentive service. *6-11pm Wed-Sun €€€* |

ETHICS & EATING

Some Icelandic restaurants tout dishes like whale (*hvál/hvalur*), shark (fermented and called *hákarl*) and puffin (*lundi*). Before ordering, consider that what may have been sustainable with 350,000 Icelanders becomes taxing on species and ecosystems when 2.3 million tourists annually get involved. Find whale-free restaurants at *icewhale.is/whale-friendly-restaurants*.

Fin whales: Classified as endangered globally; their status in the North Atlantic region is hotly debated.

Greenland shark: Used for *hákarl*, it has a conservation status of 'vulnerable' globally.

Atlantic puffin: Iceland's iconic puffin is classified as a vulnerable species globally because of rapid European population decline.

Þúfa

the 1960s. The space was designed to serve as a canvas for artistic experimentation; a place for up-and-coming artists to display even their most avant-garde projects.

Then swing in to **Kling & Bang** (*kob.this.is/klingogbang; free*) and **i8 Grandi** (*i8.is; free*), two perennially cutting-edge art galleries that are favourites with locals. The spaces close between exhibitions, so check online before you go. **Þula** (*thula.gallery; free*) is interesting, too, for its abstract and conceptual artists.

Alas, closed to the public, **Stúdíó Ólafur Elíasson** (*olafur eliasson.net*) is where internationally acclaimed Icelandic-Danish artist Ólafur Elíasson (responsible for the iconic honeycomb glass-and-steel facade of the Harpa concert hall) works his magic.

Finish with a fine meal at excellent Northern Italian restaurant **La Primavera** (*laprimavera.is*).

Climb Þúfa Hill   MAP P76

Harbour views and fresh air

Þúfa (th-oo-fha, meaning tussock) is an 8m, perfectly round, grassy mound made from about 4080 tonnes of gravel and covered in grass. This subtle but grand piece of public art – it's one of the largest pieces of public art in Iceland – comes

---

 EATING IN THE OLD HARBOUR: RELAXED INTERNATIONAL — MAP P76

Hamborgara Búllan: Savoury patties at the Old Harbour's outpost of burgerdom and Americana are perennial local favourites. Other branches around town. *11am-9pm* €

Himalayan Spice: Scrumptiously rich Himalayan dishes featuring curries, dumplings and grilled meats and veg. *noon-8pm* €€

Viet Noodles: Extensive menu of reasonably priced and tasty Vietnamese rice, pho and noodles in a simple setting. *11.30am-10pm Mon-Fri, from noon Sat & Sun* €€

Fish & Chips Vagninn: Fish and chips near the Maritime Museum and from food trucks around town; check hours at *fishandchipsvagninn.is*. *noon-8pm* €€

from Ólöf Nordal, the same artist who created the Kvika Footbath (p83) on the Seltjarnarnes peninsula. Climb the hill for sweeping views of Reykjavík's harbour and the bay, **Faxaflói**. And ponder the reminder of the country's rich fishing history – it's topped with a style of hut that would have historically been used to dry fish.

Tour an Old Harbour Gin Distillery   MAP P76
Sip bevvies at Þoran Distillery and Lady Brewery

It's worth booking ahead for a visit to the **Þoran Distillery** *(thoran.is; tour and tasting from 4400kr)*. There, the friendly distiller, Biggi, will walk you through how Icelandic gin is made and you'll sample his award-winning Marberg gin *(marberg.is)*. He also makes Limoncello Atlantico *(limoncello.is)* and Bróðinn Brennivin *(brodinn.is)*.

Nearby, the woman-owned microbrewery **Lady Brewery** *(ladybrewery.com)* currently only allows prebooked tours with large groups. But you can stop in to see if their store is open and you can buy some of their impressive craft beer.

Strap in to FlyOver Iceland   MAP P76
Simulate Iceland by air

Surveys suggest 75% of tourists visit for Iceland's nature, but sometimes rain and weather conspire against you. Many of the best indoor options are in the Old Harbour/Grandi area. **FlyOver Iceland** *(flyovericeland.com; adult/child 5690/3690kr)* is a sensational cinematic experience where viewers hang suspended, feet dangling, before a 20m spherical screen, as if steering a plane over the ice-capped Hvannadalshnúkur and the isolated lighthouse of Þrídrangar. Showtime is 30 minutes and kids must be at least 1m tall.

Sizzle at a Lava Show   MAP P76
Feel the heat of flowing molten rock

It isn't always possible to time your Icelandic holiday with a volcanic eruption. Even if you could, you might not want to. That doesn't mean you can't see real flowing lava. Started by an Icelandic couple who visited the site of the Fimmvörðuháls volcanic eruption in 2010 and haven't been able to stop thinking about it, **Lava Show** *(lavashow.com; adult/child 6590/3590kr)* re-creates a volcanic eruption by superheating real molten lava

(continues on p82)

BEST BOUTIQUES & DESIGNERS

Hidden among the docks and warehouses of the Grandi area is excellent shopping.

Steinunn: Collection of celebrated Icelandic designer Steinunn Sigurðardóttir, featuring her innovative knitwear. *(steinunn.com)*

Krínolín: Head here for creative Icelandic outerwear.

Kiosk: You never know what you'll find at this designers' cooperative lined with creative women's fashion. Designers take turns staffing the store. *(kioskgrandi.com)*

Farmers & Friends: More commercial, with gorgeous boots, clothes and accessories in earthy tones at this design company's flagship store. Also a branch on Laugavegur. *(farmersmarket.is)*

Jens: Fine jewellery featuring runes and stones from a well-established family of designers. *(jens.is)*

Smiðsbúðin: Creations of a pair of skilled goldsmiths. *(smidsbudin.is)*

 DRINKING IN THE OLD HARBOUR: CAFES & BARS   MAP P76

Hygge Coffee & Micro Bakery: Linger over excellent coffee, fresh bread, creative pastries and blue birch rolls with outdoor seating streetside. *8am-5pm* €

Reykjavík Röst: Local harbourfront fave for richly brewed coffee and decadent baked goodies. Brews on tap too. *8am-6pm* €

Litli Barinn: Wine, craft beer and cocktails pair with a short but inventive and well-prepared food menu in the Local 101 Hotel. *3pm-10.30pm* €€

Slippbarinn: An inviting place, bedecked with vintage record players, to sip cocktails looking out onto the Old Harbour. *noon-11pm Sun-Thu, to midnight Fri & Sat*

Watching a humpback whale

TOP EXPERIENCE

Go Whale & Puffin Spotting

Iceland is one of the best places in the world for whale watching, and you can join the boats departing year-round from Reykjavík's Old Harbour to catch glimpses of these magnificent beasts as they wave their fins, spout and dive. Trips are also tops for puffin spotting, birdwatching, fishing and winter Northern Lights viewing.

DID YOU KNOW?

Cute, clumsy and endearingly comic, the puffin is one of Iceland's best-loved birds. Although known for its frantic fluttering, the bird is surprisingly graceful underwater and was once thought to be a bird-fish hybrid.

Go Whale Watching

You don't have to travel far from Reykjavík to spot these magnificent creatures. Several whale-watching cruises depart from Reykjavík's Old Harbour, and it's not uncommon to spot whales within 16km of the coastline.

Iceland is home to more than 20 species of whale, and on boats from Reykjavík you're most likely to see humpback and minke whales. The humpback is known for its curious nature and spectacular surface displays. The minke has a streamlined, slender, black body, a white striped pectoral fin and a tendency to leap entirely out of the water. If you're lucky you might also spot a sleek black-and-white orca, either solo or in a pod.

Sperm, fin, sei, pilot and blue whales also swim in Icelandic waters and have been seen by visitors.

It's possible to see whales off the coast of Reykjavík all year long, but reasonable temperatures and ample daylight hours make April to September the best months for whale-watching trips.

Porpoises & Dolphins

Tiny, shy harbour porpoises *(Phocoena phocoena)* are easiest to spot in placid conditions. More gregarious white-beaked dolphins *(Lagenorhynchus albirostris)* often travel in larger pods and approach the boats year-round.

Puffins & Seabirds

Birdlife is abundant, especially during the warmest months when migrating species arrive to nest. You may see Arctic terns, gannets, guillemots and kittiwakes, but the zippy, cute puffins *(Fratercula arctica*, or *lundi* as they're called in Icelandic) are the real stars. They're best known for their bright orange beaks and huge personalities. They spend most of the year at sea but seek out land each spring for four to five months to breed and birth pufflings, and they generally keep the same mate and burrow (a multiroom apartment!) from year to year.

They arrive in April in huge numbers (an estimated 10 million birds), departing for warmer climes by mid-August. Three uninhabited islands off the coast (Akurey, Engey and Lundey, referred to as the Puffin Islands) are hot spots.

Puffins tend to spend their days fishing at sea, so try to plan your puffin-spotting excursions for the evening when they're returning to their burrows.

Over the last decade, the puffin stock has gone into a sharp decline in the south of Iceland. They still visit – Vestmannaeyjar (p147) islands' puffins are the largest colony in the world – but in smaller numbers and with less breeding success. The reason is uncertain, but it's thought that warming ocean temperatures have caused their main food source – sand eels – to decline. It's also possible that hunting and egg collection have had an effect.

Tour Operators

Elding Adventures at Sea *(https://elding.is)* Whale exhibition, angling and puffin-watching trips and Northern Lights tours. Also runs the ferry to Viðey island (p88).

Whale Safari *(whalesafari.is)* Whale-watching and puffin tours in a Zodiac.

Mr Puffin *(puffintours.is)* Birdwatching.

Reykjavík By Boat *(reykjavikbyboat.is)* Small-boat bird and whale watching and fishing.

Special Tours *(specialtours.is)* Sea angling and whale watching in a small, fast boat; puffin, combo and Northern Lights tours too.

Viggson Sailing *(viggsonsailing.com)* Small, family-run operator with puffin and sea angling trips.

Katla Whale Watching *(katlawhalewatching.is)* Whale watching, puffin tours and sea angling.

Fish Partner *(fishpartner.com)* Fishing day tours with custom and multiday possibilities.

COMMERCIAL WHALING

In the late 19th century, Norwegian hunters built 13 whaling stations in Iceland, and hunted until stocks practically disappeared in 1913. Icelanders established their own whaling industry in 1935, until whale numbers again became low and commercial hunting was banned by the International Whaling Commission (IWC) in 1986. Iceland resumed commercial whaling of minke and fin whales in 2006, which still causes controversy today. Whale-watching companies launched a Meet Us Don't Eat Us campaign *(icewhale.is)*.

REYKJAVÍK IN WINTER

It's bitterly cold and the sun barely rises, but there are advantages to wintery Iceland. Many bus tours continue to operate in winter, taking you to frozen white Gullfoss, caves full of icicles and snow-covered mountains. There are also snowmobiling, back-country skiing and heliskiing tours.

Northern Lights (p272): A major joy is watching the glory of auroras in the dark sky.

Reykjavík Skating Hall: Opens its doors September to mid-May. Some also skate on central Tjörnin lake when it freezes. *(skautaholl.is)*

Bláfjöll: Downhill skiing, cross-country and snowboarding. *(skidasvaedi.is)*

Winter Food Experiences: Christmas buffets (p61) and Þorrablót (p58) midwinter feasts.

Music Festivals (p59): Like Iceland Airwaves and Dark Music Days.

(continued from p79)

and letting it flow like glowing honey at 1100°C into a darkly lit room of 88 seats. Lava Show has a second location in Vík.

Gaze at the Whales of Iceland   MAP P75

Full-sized models of Icelandic whales

You don't have to go out on a boat to get up close to whales in Iceland. Head inside **Whales of Iceland** *(whalesoficeland.is; adult/child 4300/2150kr)* to see a collection of nearly two dozen life-sized replicas of the whales found off the coast. See a huge blue whale like those that surface near Húsavík. Check out a sperm whale and snuggle up to an adorable beluga whale. These models are soft, squishy and made to be touched.

The museum worked with marine biologists to create a collection of audio guides in more than a dozen languages. One of its missions is to promote marine preservation through education.

Go Viking at the Saga Museum   MAP P76

Journey into Iceland's Viking past

The endearingly bloodthirsty **Saga Museum** *(sagamuseum.is; adult/child 4000/1200kr)* is where Icelandic history is brought to life by eerie silicon models and a multi-language soundtrack featuring the thud of axes and hair-raising screams. Don't be surprised if you see some of the characters wandering around town, as moulds were taken from Reykjavík residents (the owner's daughters are the Irish princess and the little girl gnawing a fish). There's also a station where visitors can try on Viking gear for photos.

Laid-Back Hangout at Pools & Hot-Pots   MAP P75

Soak and chat at Vesturbæjarlaug

Vesturbæjarlaug *(reykjavik.is; adult/child 1380kr/free)* is the public pool in Reykjavík with the strongest neighbourhood spirit. It was, in fact, built in 1961 with local donations and volunteer work. The original 25m swimming pool is crowded for swimming, but fortunately, most folks are fine just hanging out in hot water doing nothing after work. There's also a steam room, sauna, three hot-pots and one cold plunge.

 EATING IN VESTURBÆR: OUR PICKS   MAP P75

Hagavagninn: Favourite for fair-priced burgers (vegan patties, too) with pickled onions and a few tables out front for alfresco eating. *11.30am-9pm* €

Brauð & Co: Branch of beloved bakery with fantastic pastries, cinnamon rolls, cookies and whole-grain breads, plus coffee. *7am-5pm Mon-Fri, 8am-4pm Sat & Sun* €

Kaffihús Vesturbæjar: Hipster stronghold, with delightful dishes from soups and top-notch sandwiches to vegan burgers. *8am-11pm Mon-Fri, from 9am Sat & Sun* €€

Ísbúð Vesturbæjar: Reykjavík staple for soft-serve ice cream and a staggering supply of toppings, or get a shake with your candy mixed in. *noon-11.30pm* €

OCEANFRONT WALK IN SELTJARNARNES

Surrounded by wild ocean, Seltjarnarnes peninsula at Reykjavík's western edge is a place to escape for inspiring walks and abundant birdlife.

START	END	LENGTH
Church of Seltjarnarnes	Sundlaug Seltjarnarness	7km; 2 hours

Begin near the peaked 1 **Church of Seltjarnarnes** and follow the coastal trail. As you go you'll see waves rushing in to lava-strewn beaches, fish-drying racks sitting by the shore, Mt Esja rising across the bay and Arctic terns screaming overhead.

If you're feeling peckish, pop into one of Reykjavík's best Italian restaurants, cosy 2 **Raðagerði Veitingahús**, with a menu of pizzas, bruschetta and great brunches.

Stop at the tiny 3 **Kvika Footbath**. Icelandic artist Ólöf Nordal carved the tiny pool out of a coastal rock, and it's fed by a warm geothermal spring. Soak your feet while taking in mountain and water views.

4 **Grótta Lighthouse** anchors a nature reserve surrounded by rugged coastline and black sand. On a clear day you can see as far as Snæfellsnes Peninsula. Arctic terns form a colony on the rocks (stick to marked paths) while tufted ducks hang out in an adjacent pond. You can only safely walk to the lighthouse's islet when tides are low.

The trail curves around the flat expanse of the 5 **Nesvöllur** golf course. At the golf club, the excellent restaurant Ness creates seasonally rotating menus featuring fresh fish, local produce and expansive views.

Finish with a hot soak at the local pool, 6 **Sundlaug Seltjarnarness**, with its mineral-water swimming pool, waterslide and steam bath.

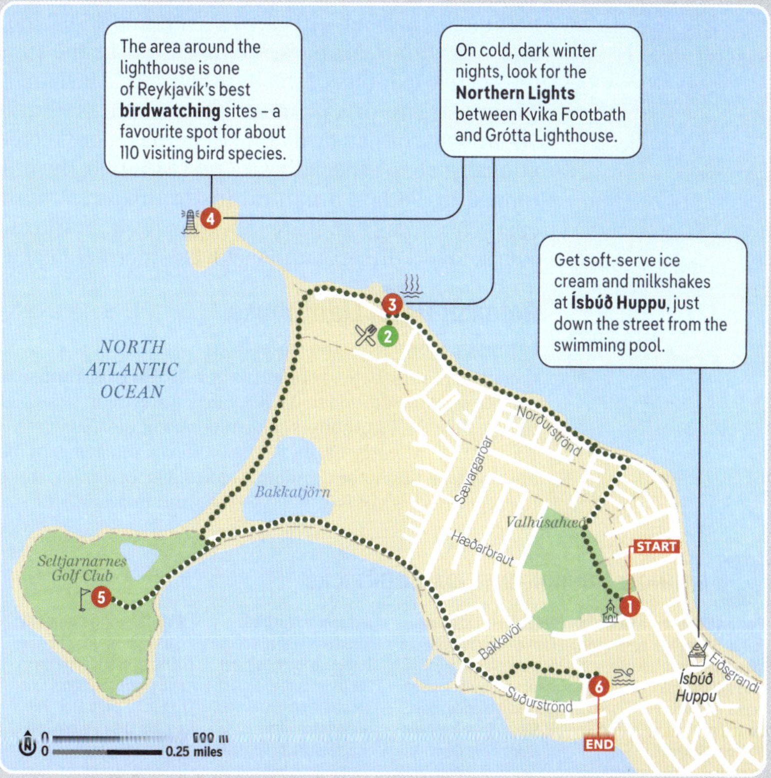
The area around the lighthouse is one of Reykjavík's best **birdwatching** sites – a favourite spot for about 110 visiting bird species.
On cold, dark winter nights, look for the **Northern Lights** between Kvika Footbath and Grótta Lighthouse.
Get soft-serve ice cream and milkshakes at **Ísbúð Huppu**, just down the street from the swimming pool.
NORTH ATLANTIC OCEAN
Bakkatjörn
Seltjarnarnes Golf Club
Norðurströnd
Sævargarðar
Valhúsahæð
Hæðarbraut
Bakkavör
Suðurströnd
Eiðsgrandi
Ísbúð Huppu
START
END
1
2
3
4
5
6
0
500 m
0
0.25 miles

Laugardalur & Hlíðar

PARKS, POOLS AND PLAY

GETTING AROUND

These areas are sprawling, so easiest to reach by bus. Strætó bus 14 runs all the way across town: from Laugardalur park to Old Reykjavík and finally the Old Harbour. Buses 12 and 16 also serve the Laugardalur area, and the Skarfabakki Harbour for Viðey.

For Perlan and Öskjuhlíð, bus 18 stops nearest, and bus 13 is the next best. It takes about half an hour to walk to it from the city centre, and a taxi takes five minutes.

The neighbourhoods to the east of the city centre are Tún, Hlíðar and Laugardalur. Walk along the coast from cheery yellow Höfði Lighthouse and you'll find waterfront museums before you head inland to the park at Laugardalur. It was once the main source of Reykjavík's hot water; now it's a local favourite for its huge geothermal swimming complex – with indoor and outdoor pools, alfresco hot-pots and a swirling waterslide. It's also got a spa, arenas, a skating rink, botanical gardens with a cool cafe and kids' zoo, and entertainment park. Round it out at the fun, interactive exhibits of the Reykjavík Art Museum – Ásmundarsafn or a jaunt to Viðey island.

Southwest of Laugardalur, Hlíðar has more recreational spaces, especially around Öskjuhlíð, the hill topped by Perlan, a natural history museum with epic city views from its observation deck. In the far south, take a dip at Nauthólsvík Geothermal Beach.

Relax at Höfði Lighthouse

Fantastic views from the waterfront

Completed in 2019, cheery bright-yellow **Höfði Lighthouse** is a relatively new addition to the Reykjavík waterfront. Designed to resemble the lighthouses that stood along Reykjavík's Old Harbour in the early 1900s, it was built as a replacement for another that had to be decommissioned. On a clear day, take in excellent views of Faxaflói (p79) bay and majestic Mt Esja.

 EATING & DRINKING IN HLÍÐAR: OUR PICKS

| **Perlan Restaurant & Cafe** (p89): Sip a drink or dine on salads and pizza under a glass dome with 360-degree views of Reykjavík (Perlan ticket required for entry). 11.30am-6pm €€ | **Reykjavík Kitchen:** A family-owned restaurant specialising in fresh fish, beef and lamb. It only serves Icelandic beer. 11.30am-3pm Tue-Sun, 5-10pm daily €€ | **Hlemmur Mathöll:** Food hall where vendors rustle up multicultural foods including Danish smørrebrød (rye bread) and Vietnamese noodles. 11am-11pm €€ | **RVK Brewing Company:** Fabulous flights of some of its 22 craft beers on tap, plus occasional live music. 3-10pm Sun-Tue, 1-10pm Wed, 1-11pm Thu, 1pm-midnight Fri & Sat |

LAUGARDALUR & HLÍÐAR

⭐ HIGHLIGHTS
1. Höfði House
2. Laugardalslaug
3. Reykjavík Art Museum – Kjarvalsstaðir

● SIGHTS
4. Áfangar
5. Berlin Wall
6. Höfði Lighthouse
7. Imagine Peace Tower
8. Klambratún
9. Monastery Ruins
10. Öskjuhlíð
11. Perlan
12. Recycled House
13. Reykjavík Botanic Gardens
14. Reykjavík Zoo & Family Park
15. Schoolhouse
16. Sigurjón Ólafsson Museum
17. Sundbakki

see 9 Viðey Church
see 9 Viðeyarstofa

● ACTIVITIES
18. Laugar Spa

● SLEEPING
19. Dalur – HI Hostel
20. Eyja Guldsmeden
21. Fosshotel Reykjavík
22. Hilton Reykjavík Nordica
see 31 Lækur Hostel
23. Reykjavík Campsite
24. Tower Suites

● EATING
25. Café Flóra
26. Hlemmur Mathöll
27. Perlan Restaurant & Cafe
28. Reykjavík Kitchen
29. Skúbb
30. Viðeyjarnaust Day Hut

● DRINKING & NIGHTLIFE
31. Kaffi Lækur
32. Malbygg Taproom
33. RVK Brewing Company

Visit a Windswept Sculptor's Paradise

Explore the Sigurjón Ólafsson Museum

It's worth the effort to reach the peaceful seafront studio of sculptor Sigurjón Ólafsson (1908–82), which is now **Sigurjón Ólafsson Museum** (lso.is; adult/child 1000kr/free). Started by his widow at the waterfront home the couple shared, it showcases his powerful busts and driftwood totem poles. Even after the museum closes, you can see some of the sculptures outside.

HÖFÐI HOUSE & THE COLD WAR

Gleaming white-washed wooden **Höfði House** overlooking the water is where the Cold War began winding down. US President Ronald Reagan and Soviet President Mikhail Gorbachev met here in 1986. Reagan had come to discuss human rights and the Soviet occupation of Afghanistan while Gorbachev was squarely focused on limiting arms control. No agreements were announced here, but the meeting is seen as a major breakthrough. The discussions marked the first time human rights entered the conversation between the US and the Soviet Union.

The house is not open to the public, but you can look at a few sculptures outside, and find another remnant of the Cold War, a 3.8-tonne chunk of the Berlin Wall (*Berlínarmúrinn*). It was a gift commemorating the 25th anniversary of German reunification.

Check Out the Art at the Recycled House
When your home is public art

Just adjacent to Sigurjón Ólafsson Museum, a Viking warrior greets visitors to Icelandic filmmaker Harfn Gunnlaugsson's unusual property along the coast that's come to be known as the **Recycled House** but has nothing at all to do with recycling. You'll find small temples paying homage to Norse gods, Christian deities and Buddhist icons.

Reykjavík's Largest & Liveliest Pool Complex
Play at Laugardalslaug

Local favourite **Laugardalslaug** (*reykjavik.is; adult/child 1380kr/free*) is not as fancy as the Blue Lagoon or Sky Lagoon, but you're likely to hear far more Icelandic than foreign accents. The property includes a 50m pool primarily used for training as well as a separate play pool and indoor pool, children's pool, hot tubs and an 86m waterslide. You can also hit the fitness trail, steam bath, saltwater tub and play beach volleyball. A visit here really is a uniquely Icelandic experience. Pop next door to the **Laugar Spa** (*worldclass.is; spa access 7520kr*) for more saunas, steam room and gym, plus massages and other treatments. The spa is 18+.

Free Outing to the Reykjavík Botanic Garden
Lush flowers and foliage with summer cafe

Stroll the **Reykjavík Botanic Garden** (*grasagardur.is; free*) through over 5000 varieties of subarctic plant species, colourful seasonal flowers and birdlife. The garden aims to help

Reykjavík Botanic Garden

visitors understand the variety of flora that can flourish even in northern climates where harsh conditions are common. An alpine garden shows off perennials and bushes from the world's mountain ranges. Don't miss the rose garden or wonderful summer cafe, Café Flóra (p89).

Play at the Reykjavík Zoo & Family Park
Happy place for your children

Delve into the sprawl of Laugardalur park to bring the kids to the **Reykjavík Zoo & Family Park** *(mu.is; adult/child 1700/1170kr, 1-/10-ride ticket from 565/9300kr)*, which gets packed with happy local families. Don't expect lions – think seals, foxes and farm animals. The family park section has a mini-racetrack, child-size bulldozers, a giant trampoline, boats and rides.

Large Park with Famous Art
Branch of Reykjavík Art Museum at Klambratún park

The angular glass-and-wood **Kjarvalsstaðir** *(artmuseum.is; adult/child 2430kr/free)*, which looks out onto **Klambratún** park, is named for Jóhannes Kjarval (1885–1972), one of Iceland's most popular classical artists. He was a fisherman until his crew paid for him to study at the Academy of Fine Arts in Copenhagen, and his wonderfully evocative landscapes share space alongside changing installations of mostly Icelandic 20th-century paintings. The expansive park outside is a grand place to play basketball, beach volleyball or at the playground.

> ☑ **TOP TIP**
> **Reykjavík City Card** *(visitreykjavik.is; 24/48/72hr 5500/7700/9500kr)* offers admission to eight of Reykjavík's municipal pools and to most of the main galleries and museums, plus discounts on some tours, shops and entertainment. It also gives free travel on the city's Strætó buses and on the ferry to Viðey. Kids don't need one, since they already get discounted or free admission.

EXPLORE VIÐEY ISLAND

Tiny uninhabited Viðey makes a wonderful day trip. Surprising modern art, an abandoned hamlet and great birdwatching add to its spell.

START	END	LENGTH
Viðeyarstofa	Ferry dock	6km; 2–3 hours

Step off the ferry and the only sounds you'll hear are wind, waves and bumblebees buzzing among tufted vetch and hawkweed. Viðey was settled around 900 and farmed until the 1950s. Powerful sheriff Skúli Magnússon (1711–94) built 1 **Viðeyarstofa** as his home in the 1750s. Now it houses a cafe serving basic fare. The adjacent 18th-century wooden 2 **church** has Skúli's tomb. The 3 **ruins of a powerful monastery** built in 1225 are behind the Viðeyarstofa.

Visit Yoko Ono's 4 **Imagine Peace Tower** (2007), a 'wishing well' for world peace that blasts a dazzling column of light into the sky every night between 9 October (John Lennon's birthday) and 8 December (the anniversary of his death).

Locals in the know come prepared with cook-out supplies and head to glass-fronted 5 **Viðeyjarnaust Day Hut** on a beautiful headland. It has a public BBQ. Trails leading northwest take you around ponds – there's great birdwatching (30 species breed here) and botany (over one-third of all Icelandic plants grow on the island) – shipwreck monuments, the low cliffs of Eiðisbjarg, and Vesturey, the island's northern tip. Influential American sculptor Richard Serra installed huge basalt sculptures, 6 **Áfangar** (Milestones; 1990), across this part of the island.

In the southeast, stop at the 1928 7 **School-house** for a photo exhibition, then find the abandoned fishing village at 8 **Sundbakki**. Making your way back towards the ferry dock, trails pass tiny Paradíshellir (Paradise Cave).

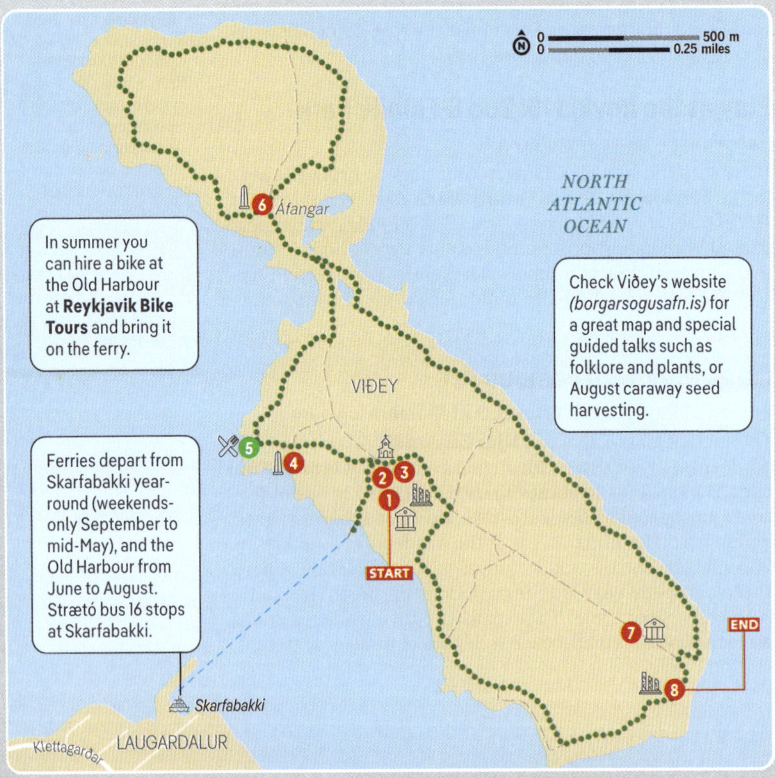
0 500 m
0 0.25 miles
NORTH ATLANTIC OCEAN
6 Áfangar
VIÐEY
5
4
2 3
1
START
7
8
END
Skarfabakki
LAUGARDALUR
Klettagarðar
In summer you can hire a bike at the Old Harbour at **Reykjavik Bike Tours** and bring it on the ferry.
Ferries depart from Skarfabakki year-round (weekends-only September to mid-May), and the Old Harbour from June to August. Strætó bus 16 stops at Skarfabakki.
Check Viðey's website *(borgarsogusafn.is)* for a great map and special guided talks such as folklore and plants, or August caraway seed harvesting.

Experience Old Iceland at Árbær Open Air Museum

Visit a historic building and see craft demonstrations

Don't be surprised to see history walking past you in the form of costumed staff at this history/folk museum at the edge of Reykjavík. **Árbær Open Air Museum** (*borgarsogusafn.is; adult/child 2450kr/free*) is built on former farmland and is made up of historic buildings transported here from other parts of Iceland. They are arranged to form an old town square, a village and a farm. During summer, staff demonstrate spinning wool, milking cows and smoking meat. Year-round tours in English lasting about an hour run at 1pm with no extra charge.

Natural Wonders with Views at Perlan

Reykjavík landmark perched atop the city's geothermal water tanks

Silver, dome-shaped natural history museum **Perlan** (*perlan.is; adult/child 6290/4090kr*) shines on top of Reykjavík's highest hill, **Öskjuhlíð**, which is crisscrossed with walking and hiking paths. Inside, the Wonders of Iceland exhibits begin with a vast ice cave, 100m (328ft) long and built with 350 tonnes of snow and layers of ash from the 2010 Eyjafjallajökull eruption, and continues to the bird-nesting cliffs at Látrabjarg, and interactive rooms on volcanoes, earthquakes and glaciers.

On a clear day, the top-floor restaurant, bar and ice-cream shop slowly turns, with unobstructed 360-degree city and bay views through the glass dome and from an observation deck. You have to buy a Perlan ticket to get in.

Head to the Beach

Sea swimming at Nauthólsvík

Welcome to the beach of Reykjavík. **Nauthólsvík** (*nautholsvik.is; adult/child 920kr/free*) is where locals bring foreign friends to test their strength – swimming in an Icelandic ocean requires a bit of mettle. Over summer the ocean's temperature can reach double digits (like, say, 10°C!), but during winter a very, very cold plunge is part of the program. Afterwards, people linger in the hot tub (38°C year-round) overlooking the beach.

WHAT TO EXPECT IN ÁRBÆR

Around 20 quaint old buildings have been transported from their original sites to Árbær Open Air Museum (Árbæjarsafn). Alongside 19th-century homes are a turf-roofed church, domestic animals, barns and boathouses – all very picturesque.

The property includes an old shop from Reykjavík's most famous shopping street, a 19th-century labourer's cottage, the first Boy Scout cabin built in Iceland, and homes of local blacksmith and fishing families. Walk through an old city-centre stable, and learn about historic building techniques and how turf houses were able to withstand harsh Icelandic winters and unpredictable rainy summers.

The exhibits inside are as interesting as the buildings themselves: toys Icelandic kids played with in the last century and American classic cars.

 EATING & DRINKING IN LAUGARDALUR: OUR PICKS

Cafe Flóra: Sun-dappled tables fill a greenhouse in the Botanic Gardens next to a flower-lined terrace. Dishes feature wholesome local ingredients. *10am-6pm May-Sep* €€

Skúbb: Kids and grownups alike head to Skúbb for some of the city's best ice cream. *2-11pm Mon-Fri, from noon Sat & Sun* €

Malbygg Taproom: Stout lovers take notice! This brewery bar is tops, and has lagers, sours and IPAs, too. You can take a brewery tour. *4-11pm Thu-Sat*

Kaffi Lækur: Food is simple but the happy hour (4-7pm and 10-11pm Tue-Sat) is good at this cafe in Laugalækur Hostel. *10am-10pm or 11pm*

ATV RULES & SAFETY

To drive an ATV in Iceland, you must hold a driving licence in your home country and be at least 17.

Safety equipment, helmets, thermal overalls and gloves are provided by tour operators. You can also expect a short orientation and a little bit of time to practise before you set off on your adventure.

Dress in warm layers and plan for unpredictable weather. Always keep your helmet and goggles on when riding or driving, and never exceed the speed limits set by your guide.

Children as young as six can join ATV tours as passengers.

Nauthólsvík (p89)

The Nauthólsvík cove is artificially constructed, and the yellow sand – brought from elsewhere – is a hot commodity for sunbathing, volleyball and other beach activities on warm summer days. There are changing rooms.

Hop on an ATV
Rugged adventure awaits

You don't need to go far from Reykjavík to have an off-road adventure. All-terrain quad bikes and buggies are an excellent way to explore the rugged landscape inaccessible by car. Ride solo or partner up with a friend on a dual-passenger bike. Regardless of what you choose, expect excellent views of the city, Faxaflói bay and geothermal areas, on a truly off-the-beaten-path adventure you'll never forget. Loads of companies offer tours. We like **Safari Quads** (*safari.is; tours from 17,000kr*) and **ATV Reykjavík** (*atvreykjavik.is; tours from 15,000kr*).

Kópavogur & Hafnarfjörður

SURPRISING SOUTHERN SUBURBS

Reykjavík's bustling suburbs are Mosfellsbær to the north, and Kópavogur, Garðabær and Hafnarfjörður to the south. Plan to base yourself in Reykjavík proper, but then make a foray to Kópavogur, the first suburb south of Reykjavík, for Sky Lagoon. Relax in its geothermal waters and enjoy the peaceful views that feel like the edge of the Earth. You might also come for its museum and concert hall or Smáralind shopping mall.

Looking to escape into the raw outdoors? Head to Heiðmörk Nature Reserve where you can explore natural lava caves, jog scenic running trails, hike towering red rocks or have a gorgeous picnic.

On the surface, Hafnarfjörður, 12km south of Reykjavík, is a simple harbour town (best known for its annual Viking Festival). But it also has a strong mystical bent. It rests on a 7300-year-old flow that, according to locals, hides a parallel elfin universe. Also, the home of Iceland's president perches on its idyllic Álftanes peninsula.

Oceanfront Sky Lagoon Bliss
Peaceful sweeping views while you soak

There's nothing like soaking in warm water with an ocean view. Wildly popular **Sky Lagoon** (skylagoon.com; from 15,990kr) beckons with a human-made seaside geothermal lagoon, swim-up bar and cascading waterfall. Its seven-step bath ritual includes a cold plunge, sauna and homemade salt scrub and is part of all packages, but you can skip any steps you don't want.

You'll find this idyllic oasis just beyond the warehouses and industrial buildings that dominate the Kópavogur area. Reykjavík, although just a 7km drive north, is out of sight. The farm-like houses you see on the other side of the inlet? The Bessastaðir residence of Iceland's president.

Kids under 12 are not allowed in, which gives the lagoon a more serene feel.

GETTING AROUND

Strætó buses to Kópavogur call at the Hamraborg stop (look for the church). Buses run every 15 minutes and the journey takes around 20 minutes. Bus 1 leaves from Harpa via the Lækjartorg stop in central Reykjavík and continues on to Hafnarfjörður.

The **Flybus** (re.is) between Reykjavík and Keflavík International Airport will stop at Hafnarfjörður's Hotel Viking, and **Airport Direct** (airportdirect.is) stops in Kópavogur.

☑ TOP TIP

The Sky Lagoon may get all the attention, but don't leave this area without venturing into the magnificent Rauðhólar pseudocraters at the Heiðmörk Nature Reserve. These pseudocraters are bright red because of iron in the lava.

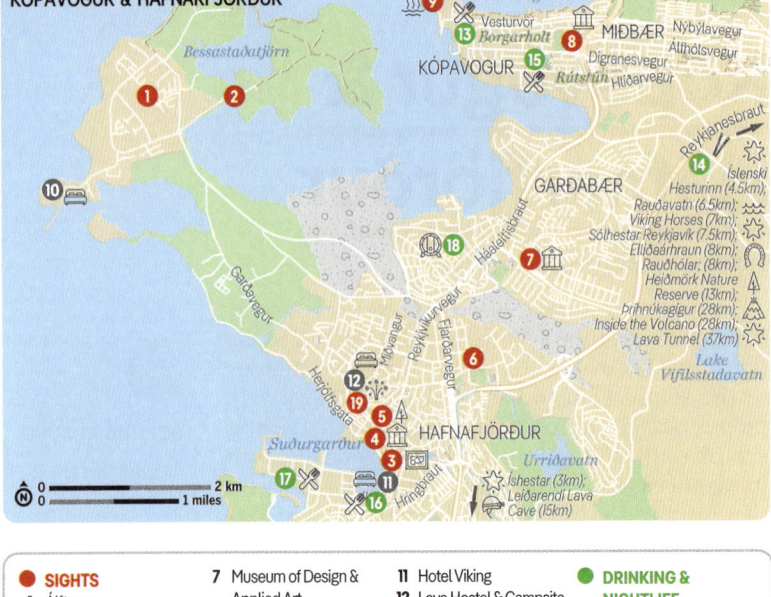

SIGHTS
1 Álftanes
2 Bessastaðir
see 8 Gerðarsafn Art Museum
3 Hafnarborg Centre of Culture & Fine Art
4 Hafnarfjörður Museum – Pakkhúsið
5 Hellisgerði
6 Hovdenak Distillery
7 Museum of Design & Applied Art
8 Natural History Museum of Kópavogur
see 8 Salurinn

ACTIVITIES
see 4 Hidden Worlds
9 Sky Lagoon

SLEEPING
10 Hlid Fisherman Village
11 Hotel Viking
12 Lava Hostel & Campsite

EATING
13 Brasserie Kársnes
see 13 Brikk
14 Krua Thai
15 Mossley
16 Pallett
17 Sól
see 4 Tilveran
see 16 Von Mathus & Bar

DRINKING & NIGHTLIFE
18 Eimverk Distillery

ENTERTAINMENT
see 4 Bæjarbíó
19 Hafnarfjörður Viking Festival

Hike Around Heiðmörk Nature Reserve

Towering trees, craters and caves

Heiðmörk Nature Reserve is only about 18km southeast of Reykjavík's centre, but it feels like an entirely different planet. Walk among towering Sitka spruce trees and little lakes. Wander across **Rauðhólar** (Red Hills), a collection of vibrant red craters that are part of larger **Elliðaárhraun** lava field (not to be confused with Reykjavík's large Elliðaárdalur park). Explore natural caves. Go for a hike, check out the wildflowers or simply take in the silence and solitude at this nearly 32 sq km oasis.

Ride Horses Across Lava Fields

An unforgettable ride for all levels

There are lots of places in Iceland to go horse riding, but there's no place like the wild Rauðhólar (Red Hills) that form part of the 3.6-sq-km Heiðmörk Nature Reserve at the eastern edge of Kópavogur. Many tour operators offer beginner-friendly rides across this unusual landscape of red craters and rocks, actually part of a larger lava field. A route for more advanced riders leads around the **Rauðavatn**, a lake within the reserve.

Book with **Viking Horses** *(vikinghorses.is)*, a family-run company offering small-group rides. **Íslenski Hesturinn** *(reidskolinn.is)* offers private and group riding tours across these volcanic landscapes, as does **Sólhestar Reykjavík** *(solhestar.is)* and **Íshestar** *(ishestar.is)*.

Descend into a Volcano
Hike to and be awed inside Þríhnúkagígur

If you loved Jules Verne's *Journey to the Centre of the Earth*, this is a one-of-a-kind experience you can't miss. Head inside the dormant **Þríhnúkagígur** volcano, making the 120m descent to the bottom of the crater in an open cable lift with **Inside the Volcano** *(insidethevolcano.com; tours adult/child 49,000/25,000kr)*.

The volcano last erupted around 4000 years ago, and the marvellous descent to the chamber floor that once gurgled with hot lava takes just seven minutes. Visitors can either hike 3km (about 50 minutes) across gorgeous lava fields to the volcano or book a private helicopter ride. The trail can be uneven and the last 10 minutes are a climb up the side of the volcano.

This experience operates from early May through October, and children eight and above are welcome if they can do the hike.

Visit Local Distilleries
Cheers to local liquors

This area of the capital region is a hub for Icelandic distilleries. Take the chance to sample Icelandic liquors on-site. **Hovdenak Distillery** *(hovdenakdistillery.is; by appointment only)* makes gin, vodka, rum and aquavit. Head to **Eimverk Distillery** *(flokiwhisky.is; tour and tasting 5200kr)*, a family-run distillery that opened in 2009, to learn how it makes Iceland's only single-malt whisky, Floki. Vor is its pot-distilled gin, and Viti, a signature Icelandic Brennivín. Þoran Distillery (p79) is now in the Old Harbour.

BEST LAVA TUBES & CAVES

Lava tubes are formed when lava hardens over a flowing magma channel. These huge tubes are accessible with a guide.

Lava Tunnel (Raufarhólshellir): A 1360m-long tunnel from the 11th century.

Vatnshellir: Snæfellsjökull National Park's 8000-year-old lava tube.

Viðgelmir – The Cave: At 1.5km-long, Viðgelmir is the largest in Iceland.

Caves of Hella: Ancient human-made caves of mysterious origin.

Leiðarendi Lava Cave: Untouched Reykjanes Peninsula 915m lava tunnel without tourist infrastructure. You'll have to crawl to access certain areas. If you're an inexperienced hiker or claustrophobic, choose another lava tunnel first.

EATING IN KÓPAVOGUR: OUR PICKS

Brikk: A bright bakery with lots of pastries and light lunch items like soups and sandwiches. *8am-4pm Mon-Fri, from 9am Sat & Sun* €

Brasserie Kársnes: This local favourite offers a creative à la carte menu and a four-course chef's tasting menu. *3-10pm Mon-Wed, from 11.30am Thu-Sun* €€€

Krua Thai: Authentic Thai food with rich flavours, generous portions and reasonable prices. *11.30am-9pm Mon-Fri, from noon Sat, from 5pm Sun* €

Mossley: A comfortable neighbourhood restaurant serving up burgers, tacos, sandwiches and more. *11.30am-10pm Sun-Thu, to 11pm Fri & Sat* €€

VOLCANO TOURISM

Volcanic eruptions are a big draw for tourists, but viewing them takes special preparation. You'll need to be flexible with your travel arrangements. New eruptions can happen at any time and viewing points close if they're deemed unsafe. The active and recent fissures (p110) near Grindavík on the Reykjanes Peninsula are the most easily visible eruption sites.

Pack your sturdiest hiking boots and prepare for potentially a multi-hour hike across rough, rocky ground. Visibility can be low, and there may be gas in the air. Follow all safety rules on-site. Helicopter tours (p70) give a bird's-eye view, and hiking tours lead to viewing points.

If that's all a bit much for you, you can also go deep into dormant Þríhnjúkagígur crater (p93).

Catch a Concert or Show
Classic former cinema to mod concert hall

Looking for a night out? Hafnarfjörður's **Bæjarbíó** (baejarbio.is) hosts concerts and theatre, and there's no better place to get a reminder of what Icelandic life was like as Europe emerged from WWII. This venue opened in 1945 and is the only Icelandic cinema that's been preserved in its original form.

Fast-forward to Iceland's first specially designed concert hall, **Salurinn** (salurinn.is) in Kópavogur. It's built entirely from local materials (driftwood, spruce and crushed stone) and has fantastic acoustics.

Enchanted Lava Grottoes of Hellisgerði
Visit a hidden world

If this magical garden feels like a fairy wonderland, there might be a very good reason for that. According to folklore, Hafnarfjörður is home to one of Iceland's largest colonies of *huldufólk* (hidden people). Peaceful **Hellisgerði** is filled with lava grottoes where moss blankets lava formations and is apparently one of the favourite places of the *huldufólk* – the *álfar* (elves), *ljósálfar* (fairies) and *dvergar* (dwarves) purported to live in parallel worlds to ours.

EATING IN HAFNARFJÖRÐUR: OUR PICKS

Pallett: Welcoming, quirky cafe that feels more like an indie bookshop. Everything's homemade. *8am-5pm Tue-Fri, from 10am Sat, from 11am Sun* €

Von Mathus & Bar: Exquisite, creative small plates, hearty mains and three-course set menus. Top cocktails. *11.30am-2.30pm Tue-Fri, 5-9pm Wed-Sun* €€€

Tilveran: Delicious Icelandic home-cooking with a neighbourhood feel featuring generous portions of fresh seafood. *11.30am-1pm & 6-9pm Mon-Fri, 6-10pm Sat* €€

Sól: High-concept restaurant in a greenhouse, floating above growing veg, with views towards the sea from which much of the food comes. *5.30-9.30pm Wed-Sun* €€€

Bessastaðir

A 1½-hour **Hidden Worlds** *(alfar.is; 6000kr)* tour leaves from the tourist office, which also sells elf maps.

Visit the Home of Iceland's President
Peaceful peninsula site of Bessastaðir

The official residence of Iceland's president, **Bessastaðir** *(forseti.is)*, on the serene peninsula **Álftanes**, is a site that's played a key role in Icelandic history. This spot was settled around 1000 and claimed by the king of Norway after the murder of beloved historian and writer of Icelandic sagas Snorri Sturluson (p204), who had operated it as a farm. The understated white building here has been a school and a residence. It was donated to the state in 1941 and eventually turned into the presidential residence. Visitors are welcome inside the church and on the grounds, a very different experience to visiting other high-profile presidential palaces, where fences and security may make it hard to get a close-up view.

Make Like a Viking
Travel back in time at the Hafnarfjörður Viking Festival

Once a year, the tiny town of Hafnarfjörður turns into a vibrant village of Vikings. Arrive here in mid-June, during **Hafnarfjörður Viking Festival** *(visithafnarfjordur.is; free)*, and you may feel you've travelled back in time 1000 years. Dozens of members of a local Viking club reenact battles during the five- to six-day festival. Sample freshly roasted lamb, swap stories with new friends and experience a festival unlike any other.

BEST SUBURBAN MUSEUMS

Gerðarsafn Art Museum: Beautifully designed and named for sculptor/stained-glass artist Gerður Helgadóttir. Excellent modern-art exhibitions. *(gerdarsafn.is)*

Natural History Museum of Kópavogur: Iceland's unique geology and wildlife are showcased. Highlights include an orca skeleton and Mývatn's unusual *marimo* balls (algae clusters). *(natkop.is)*

Hafnarfjörður Museum – Pakkhúsið: Divided over several buildings. Start at Pakkhúsið, for displays on Hafnarfjörður's history. *(museum.hafnarfjordur.is)*

Hafnarborg Centre of Culture & Fine Art: Bright contemporary gallery with rotating exhibitions of well-chosen art. *(hafnarborg.is)*

Museum of Design & Applied Art: Icelandic design, from unique furniture to knitwear, shoes and album art. *(honnunarsafn.is)*

Places We Love to Stay

€ Budget €€ Midrange €€€ Top End

Historic Miðborg   MAP p49

Exeter Hotel €€ Don't let its simple exterior fool you. This is a stylish, industrial-chic property with a bakery, restaurant and sauna.

CenterHótel Plaza €€ Business-oriented rooms with great views from the higher levels. It's in an enviably central spot.

Hótel Reykjavík Centrum €€€ Two historic central buildings, with a spry, light feel across neatly proportioned rooms, suites and apartments.

City Center Hotel €€€ Straightforward central option: it's modern, easy on the eyes, and 5th-floor rooms have balconies.

Hótel Borg (p61) €€€ Art-deco luxury hotel on Reykjavík's main square with a glamorous restaurant and a fab spa.

Black Pearl €€€ Fully kitted-out apartments just back from the waterfront. King-sized beds, designer furniture and balconies, some with water views.

Apotek €€€ Iconic 1917 building designed by Guðjón Samúelsson, with contemporary rooms in muted tones and a popular restaurant-bar.

Reykjavík Konsulat Hotel €€€ Hilton's plush hotel where service is impeccable and welcoming bedrooms are rich in antique flourishes and modern comforts.

Kvosin Downtown €€€ Suites at this superbly located historic hotel range from 'Junior' and 'Executive' to 'Valkyrie'.

Reykjavik EDITION €€€ Steps from Harpa, the city's first five-star hotel is an oasis of luxury with rooms that feature panoramic harbour views.

Radisson Blu 1919 €€€ Central hotel that's a favourite among business travellers. Though part of a large chain, a strong sense of style lingers.

Laugavegur & Skólavörðustígur   MAPS p64 & p66

Loft Hostel € Clean sociable hostel with dorms with linen included and ensuite bathrooms, private ensuite rooms, a kitchen and a cafe.

Sunna Guesthouse € Room and apartment configurations are simple and sunny with honey-coloured parquet floors. Several have Hallgrímskirkja views. Limited free parking.

KEX Hostel € Megahostel with heaps of style (think vaudeville meets rodeo). Unofficial headquarters of backpackerdom and popular local gathering place.

Freyja Guesthouse €€ Beautiful, welcoming rooms with shared bathrooms in the residential streets near Hallgrímskirkja. Also has a family suite with private bathroom.

REY Apartments €€ Modern, two- to eight-person apartments scattered across several Escher-like stairwells. Branch of Hótel Óðinsvé.

Reykjavík Residence €€ Lodging comes in a variety of configurations, from suites and studios with kitchenettes to two- and three-bedroom apartments.

CityHub €€ If you don't mind a tight squeeze, try this Japanese-style capsule hotel with a rooftop hot tub.

Galtafell Guesthouse €€ Four one-bedroom apartments in a converted historic mansion, plus three double rooms that share a kitchen.

CenterHótel Arnarhvoll €€ Glossy waterfront hotel with unimpeded views of the bay and Mt Esja. Small, Scandi-design rooms with large windows.

Snorri's Guesthouse €€ No-frills guesthouse with clean rooms and a shared kitchen on the edge of the action.

Hótel Frón €€ Hodgepodge of buildings with doubles and apartments of varying quality overlooking Laugavegur (streetside rooms get noisy at weekends).

Alda Hotel €€€ Boutique touches lift Alda above the crowd: good buffet breakfast, a small sauna and hot tub, and free cell phone use. Front rooms noisy at weekends.

Nest Apartments €€€ Four thoroughly modern apartments with neat antique touches make a superb home away from home on this central, peaceful street.

Sand Hotel €€€ Art-deco echoes meet Nordic design and 21st-century luxury: in-room espresso machines, bluetooth speakers, fine linens and soft towels.

Canopy by Hilton €€€ Comfortable rooms styled in tones echoing ocean, volcanic rock and ice, some with sea or mountain views. Loaner bikes, wholesome breakfasts and a gym.

Hótel Borg (p61)

Skuggi Hotel €€€ King-sized beds, charcoal-toned decor and an excellent location just off Laugavegur. Plus there's free parking.

Hótel Holt €€€ Cool blast to the luxurious past. Built in the 1960s as one of Reykjavík's first hotels, Holt is decked out with original art.

Vesturbær & the Old Harbour MAP p76

Local 101 €€ Modern, tidy and well-decorated, blocks from the harbour with an excellent restaurant-wine bar called Litli Barinn.

Grandi €€€ Simple, spacious rooms steps from the harbour and the centre of Reykjavík. Some rooms have balconies and expansive city views.

Reykjavik Marina €€€ Comfortable hotel with a hint of rustic charm and a variety of room types, including singles and family rooms.

Laugardalur & Hlíðar MAP p85

Reykjavík Campsite € Sprawling campground for tents, RVs and vans with showers, kitchens, luggage storage and laundry.

Dalur – HI Hostel € The bus stops just outside this clean hostel with family rooms, bike rental, guest kitchen, barbecue and spacious deck.

Lækur Hostel € Clean dorm rooms with shared bathrooms and kitchen facilities at this airy hostel where linens are included.

Eyja Guldsmeden €€ Attentive service, excellent breakfasts and four-poster beds. An edge-of-downtown location and free parking might seal the deal.

Tower Suites €€€ It doesn't get much more exclusive than this – the 20th floor of a waterfront skyscraper accessed by private lift and frequented by Hollywood A-listers.

Fosshotel Reykjavík €€€ Giant high-rise hotel with modern rooms and all the normal mod cons (flat-screen TV, hairdryer). Smaller, older Fosshotels dot the capital.

Hilton Reykjavik Nordica €€€ Spacious Scandinavian chic makes this Hilton an effortless stay: amenities include 24-hour room service, gym, spa and gourmet restaurant Vox. Upper floors have sea views.

Hafnarfjörður MAP p92

Lava Hostel & Campsite € Overlooking the otherworldly sculptures of the Víðistaðatún park, this basic hostel has stylish decking and good facilities, including kitchen and washing machine.

Hlid Fisherman Village €€ This charming collection of cabins on an ocean-swept point offers privacy, family-friendly rooms and a restaurant.

Hotel Viking €€ Can't make the Viking Festival? Stay at this unique hotel for family-friendly rooms and decor that's sure to make you feel like a Viking.

Above: Katla Ice Cave (p151); Right: Seljalandsfoss (p139)

Researched by
Alexis Averbuck

Southwest Iceland & the Golden Circle

VOLCANO, GLACIER AND BLACK-SAND ADVENTURES

Lava fields, glacier-topped volcanoes, waterfalls and charming coastal towns and islands create outdoor adventures galore: come here to sample the best of Iceland.

Black beaches stretch along the Atlantic, geysers spout from geothermal fields and waterfalls glide across escarpments while brooding volcanoes and glittering ice caps score the inland horizon. The beautiful Southwest has many of Iceland's legendary natural wonders, so it's become a relatively crowded and more developed area. The Golden Circle – a tourist route comprising three famous sights: Þingvellir, Geysir and Gullfoss – draws the largest crowds, but visit during off-hours or venture into the wilderness and you'll find quiet hiking routes and otherworldly scenes.

The further you go, the better it gets. Tourist faves such as the silica-filled Blue Lagoon on the actively volcanic Reykjanes Peninsula and the rift valley and ancient parliament at Þingvellir are just beyond the capital. As you work your way east, Rte 1 (the Ring Road) emerges into austere volcanic foothills punctuated by surreal steam vents around Hveragerði, then swoops through a coastal plain full of verdant horse farms and greenhouses, before the landscape suddenly begins to grow wonderfully jagged after Hella and Hvolsvöllur. Churning seas lead to the Vestmannaeyjar archipelago.

At the region's far reaches lie powerful Hekla, Eyjafjallajökull and Katla volcanoes, topped by giant glaciers, busy Skógar and Vík, and hidden highland valleys Þórsmörk and Landmannalaugar. Enormous rivers such as Þjórsá cut to black-sand beaches. The South Coast's family farms, some rich with Saga heritage, offer lovely rural guesthouses and true Icelandic hospitality.

THE MAIN AREAS

REYKJANES PENINSULA
Volcanic region rimmed by fishing villages. **p104**

THE GOLDEN CIRCLE
Famous rift valley, geysers, waterfalls and more. **p116**

HVOLSVÖLLER
Horse farms and river-valley gateway to the highlands. **p136**

VÍK
Black-sand beaches, glaciers and volcanoes. **p153**

Reykjanes Peninsula, p104

Dramatic promontory with active volcanoes, crater lakes, charming hamlets and Iceland's famous Blue Lagoon, plus the busy Keflavík International Airport.

Find Your Way

Road trips are huge in Iceland: imagine being on the open road with volcanoes, glaciers and waterfalls on one side, farms and beaches on the other. Tours are popular, too. Limited public buses travel this area.

The Golden Circle, p129
Rift valley and ancient parliament Þingvellir, the OG (original geyser) and giant glacial waterfall Gullfoss, bordered by agricultural valleys and rivers.

CAR
It's easy to drive since road quality is good in the Southwest. Rent a car at Keflavík Airport to start your road trip immediately or take the bus into Reykjavík (you won't need a car while you're in the capital) and pick up a rental (4WD is best) when you leave. Countless tours run here, too.

BUS
Strætó public buses (straeto.is) trace the Ring Road, run inland near (but not to) the Golden Circle and out to the coast at Þorlákshöfn, Eyrarbakki and Landeyjahöfn. Highland Buses (p136) serve Þórsmörk and Landmannalaugar.

HIKE
Hiking is a major feature of the Southwest, especially around inland valleys and glaciers. Hitchhiking is never entirely safe, and it's not recommended, but it does remain fairly common; you can consult carpooling site samferda.net/en.

Hvollsvöllur, p136
Small-town gateway to the South's marquee waterfalls and glaciers, highland treks and the offshore puffin-friendly Vestmannaeyjar islands.

Vík, p153
Busy little town anchoring the Katla Geopark with black basalt beaches and rock formations in the shadows of glaciers and volcanoes.

THE GUIDE

SOUTHWEST ICELAND & THE GOLDEN CIRCLE

Plan Your Time

Get a taste of Southwest Iceland on a long layover or spend a week exploring its lesser-known fringes. The South Iceland (south.is) and Reykjanes Peninsula (visitreykjanes.is) sites are packed with maps and ideas.

Brúarfoss (123)

A Long Layover

● Take advantage of plenty of daylight and hit the road – rent wheels or join a tour. Walk between the continental plates and through Iceland's historic former parliament at **Þingvellir National Park** (p116), then marvel at spouting **Geysir** (p124) and misty, roaring **Gullfoss** (p126).

● Relax at **Laugarás Lagoon** (p127), **Secret Lagoon** (p127) or **Hrunalaug** (p127) and have drinks at **Vínstofa Friðheima** (p125) and farm-to-table dinner at **Friðheimar** (p127), inside a greenhouse where tomatoes grow year-round, or at **Flúðasveppir Farmers Bistro** (p127).

● Climb the magma chamber turned crater at **Kerið** (p128). Stop at the **Blue Lagoon** (p104) for a blissful spa break and a meal on the way to the airport, or take a late-night hike to see Iceland's latest volcanic zone around **Fagradalsfjall** (p110).

Seasonal Highlights

In summer, there are days when the sun barely sets and Iceland enters the season of the 'midnight sun'. Winter brings long stretches of darkness, ideal for aurora viewing.

APRIL TO AUGUST
Peak puffin season. Puffins arrive in late April or early May and stick around until August. March and April equinox also bring top Northern Lights viewing (p272).

MAY
Fishing season gets underway. Catch brown trout and Atlantic salmon, but wait until June to fish for Arctic char. Breezier weather brings occasional snow. It's a good time for those who prefer smaller crowds.

JUNE
Celebrate Icelandic National Day (17 June) when even the smallest towns mark the occasion. Endless daylight is upon you, and visitors kick off the summer season en masse. Mountain F roads begin to open.

Three Perfect Days Filled with Nature

● In addition to the time in the Golden Circle and Reykjanes Peninsula, have a full day revelling in waterfalls. Seek out brilliant inland cascades from **Brúarfoss** (p123), **Hjálparfoss** (p135), **Háifoss** (p135) and **Gluggafoss** (p138) to the Ring Road stars **Seljalandsfoss** (p139), **Nauthusagil** (p139), **Skógafoss** and **Kvernufoss** (p149).

● Spend half a day on a guided glacier walk on the ice tongue at **Sólheimajökull** (p150) or embark on a snowmobile adventure in **Katla Geopark** (p150).

● Then wrap up in the evening, avoiding the crowds, at the black basalt columns, sea stacks and rocky buttes of **Reynisfjara** (p155) near buzzy **Vík** (p153), and the windswept **Dyrhólaey** (p153) rock arch and headland. Finish with a beer and a bite at **Smiðjan Brugghús** (p156).

Taking Your Time

● With more time, you can add to your escapades, from walking through an **ice cave** (p151) at the Katla volcano, to **riding horses** (p116) from meadows to beaches (p155). Or be awed on **ziplines** (p131, p156) and with a tandem **paraglide** (p156) above fantastical land- and seascapes.

● Set sail for the fascinating **Vestmannaeyjar islands** to see **puffin colonies** (p147) and a small town tucked between lava flows where you can see its **volcanic history in action** (p147). Birdwatch (p134) around the fishing villages **Eyrarbakki** (p133) and Stokkseyri.

● When the roads are open in summer, camp and hike in **Þórsmörk** (p143), a lush kingdom surrounded by brooding glaciers. At **Landmannalaugar** (p146), traverse multicoloured peaks past pristine lakes, then set off on Iceland's most famous hike, the **Laugavegurinn** (p144).

JULY
Check out the Icelandic Horse Competition (Landsmót) or run an ultra marathon *(marathon.is)* in the highlands. Prices peak and accommodation bookings are essential for June, July and August. Most F roads are open.

AUGUST
Enjoy concerts, bonfires and fireworks displays at the Vestmannaeyjar National Festival **Þjóðhátíð** (p149). Don't skip the Sunday singalong. Say goodbye to the puffins.

SEPTEMBER
The autumn equinox creates prime Northern Lights season in September and October. Look for a viewing spot with clear skies and minimal light pollution. The highland F roads close and tourism ebbs.

DECEMBER
This is one of Iceland's coldest and darkest months. Expect excellent aurora viewing conditions and unique Christmas traditions from *Jólahlaðborð* (Christmas buffet; p61) to mid-winter festivals. It's also ice cave (p108) season.

Reykjanes Peninsula

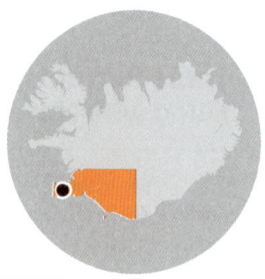

SEISMIC THRILLS | BLUE LAGOON | CHARMING VILLAGES

The Reykjanes Peninsula expands in drama as you leave the highway between Reykjavík and Keflavík International Airport. You'll find a gorgeous (and active!) volcanic zone at the meeting of the tectonic plates where vivid eruptions draw tourists from around the world. Vast lava fields are punctuated by bubbling mudpots and crater lakes, while lighthouses, lava-formed cliffs and birdwatching opportunities dot the coast.

You'll also find the Blue Lagoon, Iceland's most famous attraction, a silica-laden complex of geothermal baths. The busiest towns are amenity-rich Keflavík and Njarðvík, but the delightful, windswept fishing hamlets of Garður and Sandgerði are just minutes to the west of the airport on a small northwestern spur. Grindavík, on the south coast, has been impacted by recent eruptions. The rest of the Reykjanes Peninsula, from dramatic Reykjanestá cape in the southwest to the Reykjanesfólkvangur Wilderness Reserve in the east, is an untamed landscape of multihued craters, mineral lakes, springs and coastal lava fields.

GETTING AROUND

You'll need private transport to reach the southern and more remote parts of the peninsula, or go on a tour. The Blue Lagoon offers buses between Keflavík Airport or downtown Reykjavík via online booking *(destination bluelagoon.is)* or you can go with Flybus *(re.is)*. Public Strætó *(bus.is)* bus 55 serves Keflavík and the airport from Reykjavík. Bus 89 gives limited service from Keflavík to Garður and Sandgerði villages.

☑ TOP TIP

The Reykjanes Peninsula is a UNESCO Global Geopark *(reykjanesgeopark.is)*, formed to research and protect the region's local culture and unusual geology (pillow lava, oceanic ridge, meeting of tectonic plates, and a whopping four volcanic systems). Also, check *safetravel.is* before exploring eruption zones (p110) on your own.

Bathe in the Blue Lagoon

Relax in geothermal waters

When you think of Iceland, no doubt one of the first things that comes to mind is the **Blue Lagoon** *(bluelagoon.com; adult/child under 13 from 13,700kr/free)*. Walking out in a fluffy white bathrobe to the milky blue water, surrounded by lava, is the epitome of relaxation and luxury.

The Blue Lagoon was initially a delightful curiosity, a pleasant byproduct of geothermal energy production. It has since become one of the most recognisable spas in the world – and for good reason. In a magnificent black-lava field, 47km southwest of Reykjavík, this luxe spa is a place where steam rises from teal blue water and people float by daubed in white

Blue Lagoon

mud...like you're on another planet. If you're on a long layover and have time for just one thing, this is an excellent option (prebook a bus from the airport or Reykjavík on the lagoon's site *destinationbluelagoon.is*).

Take in the unreal scenery while soaking in warm geothermal water that's bright blue because of its nourishing silica, algae and minerals. Flowing from the futuristic Svartsengi geothermal plant, the super-heated spa water (at a perfect 38°C) is 70% seawater, 30% freshwater.

Spend a day here or settle in at one of two on-site hotels. Sample Michelin-starred Icelandic cuisine, or take a piece of this magical place home, with products from its skincare line.

The Blue Lagoon's world-famous silica may work wonders for your skin, but it isn't as good to your hair. Wear a swimming cap or use a leave-in conditioner to keep your hair from getting stiff. Always practise Iceland pool etiquette (p32): have a thorough naked pre-pool shower using soap and shampoo.

Top tips: pre-book or be turned away. Get e-tickets online or vouchers from tour firms. Avoid summer between 10am and 2pm. Go early or after 7pm (prices then are less, too). Luggage checks enable stops to/from the airport.

BEST DAY HIKES NORTH & EAST OF REYKJAVÍK

Mt Esja: Well-worn trails up Reykjavík's 914m-high mountain; most end at Steinn (the rock) at 600m (three hours). To reach the trailhead by bus, take bus 15 from Reykjavík towards Mosfellsbær, get off in Háholt and change to bus 57 to the Esjustofa Hiking Centre.

Glymur (p202): Iceland's second-highest waterfall; 7km loop trail, view over Hvalfjörður. Hiking experience required. At least three hours. Take a dip in spectacular Hvammsvík Hot Springs (p199) after.

Akrafjall: A steep, challenging trail with panoramic views that even the rain will struggle to diminish.

Reykjadalur: Popular valley of hot springs, accessible on foot only from car park outside Hveragerði. Four hours.

EATING AROUND THE BLUE LAGOON: LUXURY IN THE LAVA

Blue Café: The Blue Lagoon's most casual eating establishment: sandwiches and light meals. *same hours as lagoon* €€

Max's Restaurant: Dine casual in lava fields at the Northern Light Inn. Don't skip the cocktails; do try the fish of the day. *noon-3pm & 5.30-9.30pm* €€

Moss Restaurant: This Michelin-starred restaurant in the Blue Lagoon's Retreat Hotel offers seasonal tasting menus merging Asian flavours and local ingredients. *6-11pm Wed-Sun* €€€

Lava Restaurant: Blue Lagoon restaurant with an à la carte menu: fish, lamb and beef, plus an evening multi-course menu. *11.30am-9pm* €€€

REYKJANES PENINSULA

★ HIGHLIGHTS
1 Blue Lagoon

● SIGHTS
2 Básendar
3 Bridge Between Continents
4 Brimketill
5 Fagradalsfjall
see 6 Garðskagi Museum
6 Garður Lighthouse
7 Grænavatn
8 Gunnuhver
9 Hópsnes
10 Hópsnes Lighthouse
11 Hrafn Sveinbjarnarson III
12 Hvalsneskirkja
13 Icelandic Museum of Rock 'n' Roll
14 Indjánahöfði Nature Preserve
15 Kleifarvatn
16 Krýsuvíkurberg Bird Cliffs
17 Litli-Hrútur
18 Reykjanesfólkvangur Wilderness Reserve
19 Reykjanestá
20 Reykjanesviti Lighthouse
21 Stekkjarkot
22 Stóra-Sandvík Inlet
23 Sudurnes Science & Learning Center
24 Sundhnúksgígar
25 Valahnúkur
see 21 Viking World

● ACTIVITIES
26 4x4 Adventures Iceland
27 Seltún

● SLEEPING
see 42 Courtyard Reykjavik Keflavik Airport
28 Guesthouse 1x6
29 Hótel Berg
30 Stapakot B&B

- **EATING**
- **see 1** Blue Café
- **31** Bryggjan
- **32** Cafe Petite
- **33** Fish House
- **34** Issi
- **35** Kaffi Duus
- **see 12** Kaffi Gola
- **36** Kef Restaurant
- **37** Kökulist
- **see 1** Lava Restaurant
- **38** Max's Restaurant
- **see 1** Moss Restaurant
- **39** Olsen Olsen
- **40** Oriento
- **41** Papa's
- **see 6** Röstin
- **42** Sigurjónsbakarí
- **see 23** Sjávarsetrið
- **43** Skeifan Söluturn

- **DRINKING & NIGHTLIFE**
- **44** Litla Brugghúsið

- **TRANSPORT**
- **45** Fagradalsfjall Parking 1

HELP ME PICK:

Guided Tours

Joining an organised tour may not be your idea of an independent holiday, but Iceland's rugged terrain and high costs can make it appealing. Tours can save you time and money, and can get you into stunning, isolated spots where your hire car will never go. Many tours are by bus, others are by 4WD or super-Jeep. Many give you adventure activity options such as whitewater rafting, horse riding, glacier hiking, snowmobiling or quad biking.

If you like...

Adventure & Glacier Exploration

Icelandic Mountain Guides *(mountainguides.is)* Offers an incredibly diverse range of activities, plus multiday hiking, mountain climbing, biking and skiing tours. Hard-core expeditions too.

Midgard Adventure *(midgardadventure.is)* One of the best local adventure operators in South Iceland with immense expertise and a great vibe to boot.

SOUTHCOAST ADVENTURE

Southcoast Adventure *(southadventure.is)* Small operator with regional knowledge for highland tours, snowmobiling, volcano tours and glacier hikes.

Troll Expeditions *(troll.is)* Growing South Coast glacier, ice cave and volcano operator.

Arctic Adventures *(adventures.is)* Specialises in action-filled tours – from straight-up sightseeing to mountain biking, sea kayaking and even surfing.

Katlatrack *(katlatrack.is)* Ice-cave and glacier tours from Vík.

Arctic Surfers *(arcticsurfers.com)* The OGs of Icelandic surfing.

Asgard Beyond *(asgard beyond.is)* Creates bespoke tours.

Saga Travel *(sagatravel.is)* A company with strong ties to North Iceland, and a diverse year-round program of tours from Reykjavík, Akureyri and Mývatn.

From Coast to Mountains *(fromcoasttomountains.is)*, **Local Guide** *(localguide.is)* & **Secret Iceland** *(secreticeland.com)* Excellent operators in the southeast.

Katla Geopark operators (p150) explore from glacier tongues and ice caps topping volcanoes to unusual ice caves.

Bicycles

Reykjavík Bike Tours *(icelandbike.com)* Bike hire and tours of Reykjavík and surrounds.

Bike Company *(bikecompany.is)* Mountain-bike tours throughout the region.

Icebike Adventures *(icebikeadventures.com)* Mountain-bike specialist in Hveragerði.

Horse Riding

Horse farms abound in the southwest, so you'll be spoiled for choice, from lava fields around Reykjavík (p92) to the Golden Circle (p116) and the plains around Selfoss (p132) or even a black-sand beach at Vík (p155).

Bus Tours

Reykjavík Excursions *(re.is)* Popular large company; extensive summer and winter programmes.

Grayline Iceland *(grayline.is)* Comprehensive day trips and plenty of activities.

Gateway to Iceland *(gtice.is)* Small groups and good guides.

Hidden Iceland *(hidden iceland.is)* Luxe off-the-beaten-path tours with sustainability emphasis.

Flightseeing

Atlantsflug *(flightseeing.is)* Flightseeing tours from Reykjavík and Skaftafell.

Iceland Air *(icelandair.com)* Combination air, bus, hiking, rafting, horse riding, whale-watching and glacier tours.

Norðurflug *(helicopter.is)* Helicopter flights over Reykjavík, the volcanoes and beyond.

Ice cave at Mýrdalsjökull (p150)

HOW TO

Book ahead So you get your top choice activity at the date and time you can actually make it.

Be flexible Weather and mountain F-road openings (p134) don't always cooperate with your plan. Operators can re-book, so leave some flex in your schedule.

Call or email Reach out if in doubt. Operators are responsive. Solo travellers, ask about joining others' tours where you don't meet the minimum booking number.

Book local Support local operators like Midgard Adventure, Southcoast Adventure, Arcanum, etc, ideally avoiding less-informed mass-providers or intermediaries scooping up profits.

Where to base yourself

Many operators offer Reykjavík pick-ups, and a day tour from Reykjavík is one of the most efficient ways to see spectacular natural wonders if you're on a short holiday. But if you're in Iceland on a longer stay and planning to base yourself in Reykjavík and use day-long tours to explore the countryside, you'll spend (some may say waste) a significant amount of time being transported in and out of the capital.

If a series of short tours is what you're after, choose a base in the countryside closer to the attractions that pique your interest. This will also help spread your Icelandic krona beyond the capital. Another advantage of this approach: often the best and most personalised tours are with small-scale local operators who have grown up exploring the ice caves, glaciers, mountains and trails in their backyards, and can give you a real local insight (as opposed to large city-based companies that shuttle busloads to popular destinations).

There are hundreds of tour operators in Iceland. The list here represents some of the most reputable tour operators, with an emphasis on the Southwest region (look in our regional chapters to see other local guides). Check operators' websites to get a sense of what is on offer, and ask locally at your guesthouse if you haven't pre-booked. Tight-knit communities know the best operators in their area

Ogle the Cooling Craters of Fagradalsfjall

Hike around volcanic craters, fissures and lakes

Volcanic eruptions have become a big draw for tourists, but viewing them takes special preparation. New eruptions can happen at any time and viewing points will close if they're deemed unsafe - be flexible with your plans. Always check *safetravel.is* before exploring eruption zones on your own.

You'll want to bring your sturdiest hiking boots, water, proper clothing and prepare for a six- to eight-hour hike across several kilometres of rough, rocky ground. Visibility can be low, and there may be gas in the air. You won't able to get too close because new fissures and craters can emerge.

The **Fagradalsfjall** volcano erupted in 2021, the **Litli-Hrútur** volcano erupted in 2023, and in 2023-25 **Sundhnúksgígar** crater chain fissures began erupting around Grindavík. You can hike around Fagradalsfjall where paid parking lots *(1000kr)* have been established at trailheads. Check *visitreykjanes.is* for current safe routes; usually you would park at **Fagradalsfjall Parking 1**. **Reykjanes Geopark** *(reykjanesgeopark.is)* maintains hiking maps and the Wapp smartphone app has GPS waypoints. It's possible to access the starting point of these hikes by car, but a guided tour is your best bet for exploring safely if you are at all unsure. Helicopter tours (p108) give a bird's-eye view.

In response to the Grindavík area eruptions, dikes have been built around the Blue Lagoon, and parts of Grindavík which were inundated by lava have been fenced off. When in doubt, ask first before going.

To find simpler volcanic action on the peninsula, try Indjánahöfði Nature Preserve at Kleifarvatn and 300-sq-km Reykjanesfólkvangur Wilderness Reserve at Seltún (p112) hot springs and crater lake Grænavatn (p112). Or head to the Gunnuhver (p113) geothermal area.

Search for Shipwrecks

Wreckage with stories to tell

The **Hópsnes** peninsula near Grindavík is home to the rusting skeletons of almost a dozen old shipwrecks scattered across the shoreline. These sites show just how dangerous the water - and the fishing business that keeps this town and much of Iceland going - can be. Most wrecks have signs that tell the ship's story, though salt has eroded the text on some markers. One of the best known shipwrecks in this area is the **Hrafn**

BEST NATURAL WONDERS ON REYKJANES PENINSULA

Reykjanesfólkvangur Wilderness Reserve: Showpieces are Lake Kleifarvatn, bubbling Seltún (p112; Krýsuvík) geothermal zone and Krýsuvíkurberg bird cliffs (p113).

Fagradalsfjall: Volcanic fissures and recent eruptions have hiking areas when not active.

Valahnúkur: Bird's-eye view of magical coastline. Reykjanesviti lighthouse (p113)sits near geothermal Gunnuhver (p113).

Bridge Between Continents: Epic geological journey in just a few metres - traverse North American and Eurasian tectonic-plate rift.

Stampar: Caldera row a short walk from the marked car park, just off Rte 425.

Brimketill: Seaside pool (p113) carved by the ocean. Legend says trolls once bathed here.

 EATING IN GRINDAVÍK: CASUAL SPOTS

Bryggjan: Spacious harbourside restaurant on the top floor with views. Best known for its lobster, lamb and vegetable soups. *11am-4pm* €€

Fish House: Tops for fresh fish, langoustine and crab dishes accompanied by a beer and a friendly, chilled-out atmosphere. *11am-8pm* €€

Papa's: Fish and chips are a treat, although you'll also find locals crowding in for pizza, salad, burgers and pulled-pork sandwiches. *11.30am-8pm Tue-Thu* €€

Skeifan Söluturn: Since some restaurants close due to volcanic activity, this is a reliable simple grill with hot dogs and pizza. *11am-5pm* €€

Fagradalsfjall volcano

Sveinbjarnarson III. The fishing boat ran ashore on a cold February morning in 1988 but all on board survived.

While you're here, check out the bright orange **Hópsnes Lighthouse**. You'll also find hiking and biking trails in this area.

Behold Black-Sand Lakes, Hot Springs & Bird Cliffs

Get wild at Reykjanesfólkvangur Reserve

For a taste of Iceland's raw countryside, visit the 300-sq-km **Reykjanesfólkvangur Wilderness Reserve**, a mere 40km from Reykjavík. Established in 1975, the reserve protects the elaborate lava formations created by the dramatic Reykjanes ridge volcanoes. Its three showpieces are **Kleifarvatn**, a deep mineral lake with submerged hot springs and black-sand beaches; the spitting, bubbling Krýsuvík geothermal zone at Seltún (p112); and the Southwest's largest bird cliffs, the epic Krýsuvíkurberg (p113). The whole area is criss-crossed by walking trails. Get good maps at Keflavík, Grindavík or Hafnarfjörður tourist offices. You'll see parking turnouts at the head of the most popular walks, including the loop around Kleifarvatn, and on the tracks along the craggy Sveifluháls and Núpshlíðarháls ridges.

SALTFISH, SAY WHAT?

Saltfiskur (saltfish) is an Icelandic culinary tradition. This method of preserving cod in salt built the Icelandic economy in the late 19th and 20th centuries and continues to support the local fishing industry. Freshly caught cod is split, washed, beheaded. The fish are then stacked with salt between each layer and left to dry.

Saltfish preservation was central to Icelandic diets and remains a staple in parts of the Mediterranean and Africa. It's often cooked in tomato broth or soup to soften it back up. Grindavík's saltfish museum Kvikan (*visitgrindavik.is*) was closed at the time of writing due to volcanic activity. The town also has restaurants serving saltfish (like Salthúsið), but they were damaged by lava in 2024–25.

EATING & DRINKING AROUND THE REYKJANES PENINSULA

Sjávarsetrið: Heaps of seafood in marine-fancy surrounds in Sandgerði. One of the peninsula's best. *11.30am-10.30pm Tue-Fri, from noon Sun* €€

Röstin Restaurant: Above the Garðskagi Museum in Garður. Large glass windows and awesome sea views and summer deck. *5-8.30pm Mon-Wed, from noon Thu-Sun* €€

Kaffi Gola: Go for cakes, waffles, sandwiches and coffee at this beloved small cafe alongside Hvalsneskirkja, with views of meadows and ocean. *11am-5pm* €

Litla Brugghúsið: Remote Garður brewpub tucked into fishing warehouses with porters, IPAs and more. If you can't visit Thursday, try these beers at Röstin. *4.30-6pm Thu*

DARK TALES OF KLEIFARVATN

This deep, brooding lake, Kleifarvatn, sits in a volcanic fissure, surrounded by wind-warped lava cliffs and black-sand shores. A walking trail runs around the edge, offering dramatic views and the crunch of volcanic cinders underfoot. While you're walking, think about this: legend has it that a wormlike monster the size of a whale lurks below the surface – but the poor creature is running out of room, as the lake has been shrinking ever since two major earthquakes shook the area in 2000.

For a macabre fictional book on this event, seek out Arnaldur Indriðason's thriller *The Draining Lake* (2004).

Seltún

Explore Hot Springs & Mud Pools
Colourful bubbling springs at Seltún

Colourful geothermal area Austurengjar, about 2km south of Kleifarvatn, in **Seltún** (often called Krýsuvík after the nearby abandoned farm) is among the easiest to visit on the Reykjanes Peninsula. Wooden walkways cross the uneven earth and signs explain what you're seeing. Hot steam rises from blue pools in shades of orange and yellow earth. Listen for the bubbling of mud pools and steaming sulphuric solfataras (volcanic vents) which shimmer with rainbow colours from the minerals in the earth. Smell the sulphur in the air, and hear the hissing of vents in the mud. (There are bathrooms, too.)

Just to the north, don't miss **Grænavatn**, an explosion crater filled with gorgeous teal water, caused by a combination of minerals and warmth-loving algae.

Whip Across Lava Fields on a Quad Bike
ATV and buggy adventures around the peninsula

Zip through the open air along black-sand beaches with **4x4 Adventures Iceland** *(4x4adventuresiceland.is; per person 15,900isk for 2 people on an ATV),* the major provider for quad-bike and buggy rides around the peninsula: explore lava fields and see shipwrecks. A driver's licence is required (p90).

Cross Rare Bird Species off Your List
Birdwatching around the edges of the peninsula

There's no shortage of birdwatching in Iceland, a country with few bird predators. Several excellent spots are in this area, as Reykjanes Peninsula is one of the first destinations for birds coming from the west. Head to the shore to look for gulls – you may spot a rare one, such as Ross's gull, Franklin's gull or Bonaparte's gull.

About 3km south of Seltún across the Krýsuvíkurhraun lava fields, a dirt track leads down to the coast at **Krýsuvíkurberg Bird Cliffs** (marked on the main road as Krýsuvíkurbjarg). These sweeping black cliffs stretch for 4km and are packed with some 57,000 seabird breeding pairs in summer, from guillemots to occasional puffins. A walking path runs the length of the cliffs.

Look for whooper swans, geese, ducks and red-necked phalaropes at the **Stóra-Sandvík Inlet** in the far west. Or head to the **Reykjanestá** cape around **Reykjanesviti Lighthouse** to see the arctic terns, fulmars, kittiwakes, razorbills and gannets. Garður (p114) is great for birdwatching, too.

If you're looking for breeding species, plan your trip between late May and June when migrant birds have arrived. To add rare species to your list, pack a raincoat and visit between September and November.

Discover a Dramatic Lava Rock Pool
Nature's coastal creation

Behold the drama of **Brimketill**, the pool eroded into the lava rocks at the edge of the Atlantic, purported to be the hangout of giantess Oddný. Go on a sunny day to see the rock formations beneath the crashing ocean, and the full range of blues. A walkway and viewing platform (don't venture off) make it easy to spot about 11km west of Grindavík. In the winter, this is an excellent spot for aurora-borealis viewing.

Seek Out Seething Mudpots
The bubbling geothermal area of Gunnuhver

The **Gunnuhver** geothermal area is in the heart of the Reykjanes Geopark where the North Atlantic ridge rises from the ocean, creating craters, lava fields, bird cliffs and geothermal hot spots like this one. Boardwalks allow you to get close to the eerie site, which is filled with bubbling pools and billowing steam. Iceland's largest mudpot (at 20m or 65ft) boils vigorously and is impossible to miss. Some observation areas get frighteningly close to the smoking geothermal activity – be careful in strong winds. The area was named after a female ghost named Guðrún Önundardóttir (or Gunna) who was, the story goes, lured and trapped here by a priest.

Take in Epic Scenery from a Lighthouse
Cliffs, rock formations and distant islands

Make your way to the remote 26m **Reykjanesviti Lighthouse** *(parking 1000kr)*, built in 1908 and perched on Bæjarfell Hill. Walk the coastal edge and see the strangely shaped **Valahnúkur** cliffs formed from hardened volcanic layers (tuff, breccia and pillow lava) in an eruption in the early 1900s. Tuff consists of volcanic glass, which is the result of 1200°C magma cooling rapidly. You can park close to the cliff and climb up for spectacular views of the coast and Eldey, 15km offshore and a popular habitat for cliff-dwelling birds like guillemots,

SUSTAINABLE TRAVEL

The Icelandic tourism boom has placed enormous pressure on the local population, fragile environment and growing infrastructure.

Heed local warnings and advice: When an Icelander tells you that your car isn't suitable for a particular road, or an area is off limits, listen. Change your plans.

Recognise your impact: You may think that staying overnight in your campervan by a roadside isn't a problem. But it is when thousands of people do it – that's why there are laws banning it. Try to travel outside of the busy season, slow down and stay longer, and buy local.

Plan properly: Check weather-forecast and road-condition websites (p351). Pack a good map, appropriate gear and flexibility.

Respect nature: Stick to marked roads, don't litter. Learn more on p359.

HIKING SAFELY

The specifics of gear required in Iceland will vary, depending on your activity, time of year, remoteness of the trail and how long you'll be exploring (day hike versus multiday trek; staying in a hut versus camping). Always have good maps and GPS gear, and there's one constant: the changeability of the weather, and the risk it poses.

Check roads *(road.is)*, weather *(vedur.is)* and alerts *(safetravel.is)* before setting out (and log your plan with Safe Travel). Also download the 112 app and check in en route; it has a one-touch emergency button, in case you need it. Always check local conditions and change your plan if it's not safe. When you stop into huts, write your plan in the guestbook.

gannets and kittiwakes. Also check out the bronze sculpture of a great auk, an ode to a now-extinct flightless bird that once nested here. The last two auks in the world are believed to have been killed in the mid-1800s on Eldey. The visitor centre at Reykjanesviti has a small cafe.

Walk from Europe to North America
A bridge between continents

It's not often that you can walk from Europe to North America, but in this corner of Iceland it's easy to do – and in just a few minutes. The **Bridge Between Continents** is a 15m footbridge across the sandy rift between the Eurasian and North American tectonic plates. The bridge, named Leif the Lucky Bridge after Icelandic explorer Leif Erikson, is surrounded by lava fields and small craters.

Moody Black-Stone Church
Contemplate Hvalsneskirkja

For an evocative moment, find the lonely black-stone church, **Hvalsneskirkja**, at Hvalsnes 6.3km south of Sandgerði. It's featured in a famous Icelandic hymn by Hallgrímur Pétursson (1616–74), written at the death of his young daughter, who was buried here.

Get Nautical in Garður & Sandgerði
Serene seaside villages

The tiny fishing villages of Garður and Sandgerði harbour a couple of fun spots to learn more about local maritime life.

Positioned on the tip of the peninsula by the **Garður Lighthouse**, **Garðskagi Museum** *(facebook.com/byggda safngardskaga; free)* is open May to September with a pleasing mishmash of boating memorabilia, farming equipment and vintage Icelandic goods. There's a good restaurant, Röstin (p111). All-in, it's a lovely spot for watching the sunset. You may spot birdlife, seals and dolphins offshore here, too.

EATING IN KEFLAVÍK: BAKERIES, DINERS & CAFES

Sigurjónsbakarí: Welcoming spot for coffee and pastries near Keflavík International Airport. *7am-5.30pm Mon-Thu, to 4pm Fri & Sat* €

Kökulist: Bakery items from donuts to cinnamon rolls and pies, plus lots of options for light breakfasts and lunches. *7am-6pm* €

Olsen Olsen: This US-style diner transports you to peachy Route 66, with red plastic seats and Elvis pictures. *11am-11pm* €

Cafe Petite: Adorable place with pool tables and deck for a beer, coffee or slice of cake hidden behind other buildings. *4pm-midnight* €

Issi: The area's go-to for fast, cheapish fish and chips between a gas station and the seafront in a small kiosk. *11am-8pm* €€

Kef Restaurant: Inside Keflavík's eponymous hotel. Indulgent weekend brunch and fine tasting dinner menus. *11.30am-11pm* €€

Oriento: Delicious Mediterranean fare from souvlaki and gyros to burgers in a cheap-and-cheerful diner. *11am-11pm* €€

Kaffi Duus: Friendly, nautical-themed cafe-restaurant-bar, decorated with walrus tusks. Overlooks the small-boat harbour and Giantess sculpture. Some Indian dishes. *10am-5pm* €€

Viking World

In Sandgerði, visit **Sudurnes Science & Learning Center** *(thekkingarsetur.is; adult/child 6-15/child under 6 600/300kr/free)* for its fascinating exhibit on Polar explorer Jean-Baptiste Charcot, whose ship *Pourquoi Pas?* wrecked near here in 1936 (all but one sailor perished). There are original artefacts from the wreck. Other displays include stuffed and jarred Icelandic creatures (look out for the walrus) and a small aquarium.

Jam Out at the Rock 'n' Roll Museum
Keflavík's free music museum

Delve into the history of the awesome Icelandic music scene, from Björk to Sigur Rós and Of Monsters and Men, at **Icelandic Museum of Rock 'n' Roll** *(rokksafn.is; free)*. You can listen to music along the way and there's also the Music Hall of Fame, instruments for you to jam on, a cafe and a shop where you can stock up on local tunes.

Climb Aboard a Replica Viking Ship
Taste Viking life

At the eastern end of Njarðvík's waterfront, the spectacular **Viking World** *(vikingworld.is; adult/child 3420kr/free)* is a Norse exhibition centre built in one beautiful, sweeping architectural gesture. The centrepiece is the 23m-long *Íslendingur*, an exact reconstruction of the Viking Age *Gokstad* longship. It was built almost single-handedly by Gunnar Marel Eggertsson, who then sailed it from Iceland to New York in 2000 to commemorate the 1000th anniversary of Leif the Lucky's journey to America.

On the point near Viking World, keep an eye out for **Stekkjarkot**, a restored turf house, abandoned in 1924, with parts dating to the 19th century.

FISHING VILLAGES GARÐUR & SANDGERÐI

From Keflavík, if you follow Rte 41 for 9km, through the village of **Garður**, you'll reach beautiful wind-battered **Garðskagi** headland and its two lighthouses, one of the best places in Iceland for birdwatchers. It's a big breeding ground for seabirds, and it's often the place where migratory species first touch down. You might also see seals (and maybe whales), and superb views over the ocean to Snæfellsjökull.

Sandgerði sits 5km south of Garður and has pleasant beaches along its southern coastline. The surrounding marshes are frequented by more than 190 bird species. Continue 8.5km south and you can walk to the ruins of Saga Age fishing village **Básendar**, which was destroyed by a tidal wave in 1799.

The Golden Circle

RIFT PARLIAMENT | EPIC GEYSIR | GRAND WATERFALLS

GETTING AROUND

The Golden Circle is easy to drive on your own, and it allows you to visit at your leisure (and out of peak hours), overnight in the area, and explore attractions further afield. There's paid parking at many of the major sights. Download the Parka app to avoid queuing at machines.

You can also choose from myriad bus/van/Jeep tours which can be done in about eight hours. Many operators offer additional activities like ATV rides, horse riding and glacial adventures or Blue Lagoon or Sky Lagoon visits. No public buses serve the main sights of the Golden Circle, but Strætó bus 72 loops south of it from Selfoss to Flúðir and Reykholt, and bus 73 has a spur to Laugarvatn.

The 300km Golden Circle route features three knockout sights: Þingvellir National Park, where Iceland's parliament was founded in 930 CE and where the tectonic plate boundary pulls apart the landscape with canyons and cracks; Geysir, where water erupts more than 100 times a day; and finally the roaring and voluminous waterfall Gullfoss. Plus, it covers two continents!

If you're completing the Golden Circle in the traditional direction, starting at Þingvellir, then the route from Gullfoss back to the Ring Road (Rte 1, towards Selfoss) will be the final stage of your trip. Along the way you'll find plenty to lure you to stop. Most people follow Rte 35, which passes through Reykholt, known for its river rafting. You can also detour slightly to Flúðir, with its geothermal greenhouses where everything from tomatoes to red roses flourish, or stop at hot springs like the new Laugarás Lagoon, and Skálholt, once Iceland's religious powerhouse.

Horse Riding through Remote Valleys
Day rides and multiday treks

Icelanders have been crisscrossing this area on horseback for generations, and you can too. A few designated horse trails run through Þingvellir National Park. **Parliament Horses** *(facebook.com/parliamenthorses)* is just north of the park. In the Mosfellsdalur valley on the Rte 36 approach from Reykjavík, you can go horse riding with **Laxnes** *(laxnes.is; 2hr ride 18,400kr)*. **Eldhestar** *(eldhestar.is)* in Hveragerði takes guests on a 125km six-day ride through Maradalur, a valley of unusual volcanic formations, before cutting across the lava fields and forests.

Learn about Green Energy
See water in action at Ljósafoss Power Station

Take the kids to the 1937 **Ljósafoss Power Station**, which catches the outflow of Úlfljótsvatn, the lake just south of

Horse riding, Mosfellsdalur valley

Þingvallavatn, and turns it into electricity. The elaborate state-of-the-art multimedia exhibition will show them the principles of electricity, hydropower, and geothermal and renewable energy.

Eat Ice Cream at a Working Dairy Farm
Watch the cows and jump on the trampoline

The kids will also love the working dairy farm **Efstidalur II** *(efstidalur.is)* with brilliant views of hulking Hekla, serving tasty, farm-fresh meals and amazing ice cream made from its milk. The fun ice-cream bar has windows looking into the dairy barn. Outside the trampoline is a smash-hit and you can stay over in its good guesthouse.

Linger at a Lovely Hot Spring Lake
Kick back and soak at Laugarvatn

Laugarvatn (population 350) sits on the western shore of the lake of the same name, fed not only by streams running from the misty fells behind it, but by the hot spring **Vígðalaug**, famous since medieval times. At **Fontana** *(fontana.is; adult/child 5890/3750kr),* a swanky lakeside soaking spot, it

(continues on p123)

ACCOMMODATION IN THE SOUTHWEST

The south is the most developed region outside of Reykjavík, with lodging in all of the towns along the Ring Road, plus many farms with guesthouses. Increasingly, hotels are staying open year-round.

Book well ahead during summer and holidays, especially in the far south and southeast, as visitor numbers often exceed beds.

If you have your own gear, camping is by far the cheapest option and readily available in the summer. There are municipal campgrounds in each town (some you can pay on the Parka app), but be prepared for weather to change frequently. You may find one campground is windy and another not too far away is calm and sheltered. Wild camping is not allowed.

EATING AROUND ÞINGVELLIR & LAUGARVATN: OUR PICKS

Silfra Restaurant: Beautifully presented, well-proportioned meals featuring locally sourced, seasonal ingredients at Ion Adventure Hotel south of Þingvellir. *noon-2pm & 6-10pm* €€€

Lindin: In a charming little silver house facing Lake Laugarvatn, with high-concept Icelandic fare featuring local ingredients (including reindeer burgers). *hours vary* €€€

Vinastræti Veitingahús: Cheerful bistro with Italian grilled sandwiches, pizzas and an airy rustic dining room in Laugarvatn. *11.30am-4pm & 5-8.30pm* €€

Babylon Bistro: Spacious and welcoming in Laugarvatn's Héraðsskólinn hotel serving burgers, fish and chips and pizzas. *noon-9pm* €€

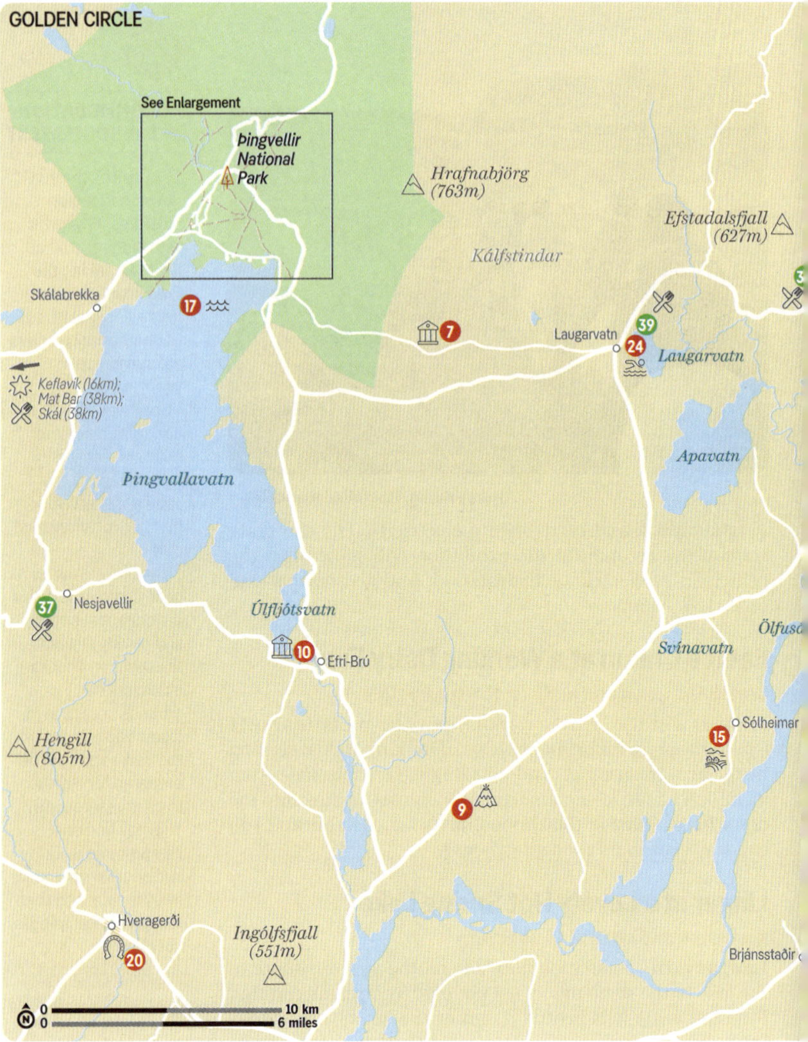

GOLDEN CIRCLE

★ HIGHLIGHTS
1. Geysir
2. Gullfoss
3. Þingvellir National Park

● SIGHTS
4. Almannagjá
5. Alþingi Site
6. Brúarfoss
7. Caves of Laugarvatn
- see 5 Drekkingarhylur
8. Faxafoss
- see 6 Hlauptungufoss
9. Kerið
10. Ljósafoss Power Station
- see 5 Lögberg
- see 6 Miðfoss
11. Öxarárfoss
12. Silfra
- see 13 Skálholt
13. Skálholtsdómkirkja
14. Slakki Petting Zoo
15. Sólheimar Eco-Village
- see 1 Strokkur
- see 16 Þingvallabær
16. Þingvallakirkja
17. Þingvallavatn

● ACTIVITIES
18. Arctic Rafting
- see 1 Blesi
19. Brúarhlöð
20. Eldhestar
21. Geysir Golf Course
- see 28 Geysir Hestar
22. Hrunalaug
23. Laugarás Lagoon
24. Laugarvatn Fontana
- see 24 Laugarvatn Swimming Pool
25. Parliament Horses
26. Reykholtslaug
27. Secret Lagoon
28. Skjol

● SLEEPING
- see 1 Geysir Campground
- see 28 Geysir Hestar
29. Hótel Geysir
30. Hótel Gullfoss
31. Náttúra Yurtel

- 32 Nyrðri-Leirar Campsite
- see 15 Sólheimar Eco-Village
- 33 Syðri-Leirar Campsite
- 34 Vatnskot Campsite

● **EATING**
- see 24 Babylon Bistro
- 35 Efstidalur II
- see 26 Fish & Chips
- 36 Flúðasveppir Farmers Distro
- see 26 Friðheimar
- see 15 Græna Kannan Cafe
- see 13 Hvönn
- see 24 Lindin
- see 27 Minilik Restaurant
- see 26 Restaurant Mika
- 37 Silfra Restaurant
- see 28 Skjól Cafe
- 38 Sólskinsbúðin
- see 2 Tourist Centre Cafe
- 39 Vinastræti Veitingahús
- see 23 Ylja

● **DRINKING & NIGHTLIFE**
- see 26 Vínstofa Friðheima

● **INFORMATION**
- 40 Hakið Visitor Centre
- see 32 Leirar Service Centre

☑ TOP TIP

The Golden Circle is the most popular tourist route in Iceland. If you have your own wheels, in peak summer with all that daylight, plan your visits for early morning or late evening to avoid the bulk of the tours plying this route. You can check the live traffic monitor *(visiticeland.com/visitor-numbers)* to further avoid peak times.

Tectonic plates

TOP EXPERIENCE

Walk Through History at Þingvellir National Park

UNESCO World Heritage Site Þingvellir National Park is Iceland's most important historical spot. Viking settlers established the world's first democratic parliament, the Alþingi, here in 930 CE. Come and see where meetings were conducted outdoors in an immense, fissured rift valley, with rivers and waterfalls all around. This is the kind of place that will make even hardcore urbanites grab a pair of hiking boots.

DON'T MISS
Almannagjá
Lögberg
Öxarárfoss
Þingvallabær & Þingvallakirkja
Silfra
Þingvallavatn

Behold Tectonic Plates

Þingvellir (*thing*-vet-lir) sits on the tectonic-plate boundary where North America and Europe are tearing away from each other at 1–18mm per year. The world's oldest parliament, Alþingi (*al*-thingk-ee), was here. From 930 to 1798, meetings were held among this awe-inspiring geology, which created a natural amphitheatre. The plain is scarred by dramatic fissures, ponds and rivers, including the great rift **Almannagjá**. A path descends into the fault between the clifftop **Hakið Visitor**

PRACTICALITIES
- thingvellir.is
- parking fee from 1000kr, site entry free
- site 24hr, visitor & information centre hours vary

Centre and the **Alþingi Site**. There's also a viewing platform, and trails are 1.5km to 10.5km long, so it's easy to find a hike to suit. South is **Þingvallavatn**, where you can descend into Silfra (p122) gorge between the tectonic plates.

The river Öxará cuts the western plate, tumbling off its edge in a series of pretty cascades. The most impressive is **Öxarárfoss**, north of the Alþingi site. In the Middle Ages, people were put to death by drowning in **Drekkingarhylur** pool between the 20m cascade and **Lögberg**.

Compare Ancient Ruins to Historic Buildings

Near the dramatic Almannagjá fault and fronted by a boardwalk is the **Lögberg** (Law Rock), where the Alþingi convened annually and the *lögsögumaður* (law speaker) recited existing laws. After Iceland's conversion to Christianity the site shifted to the foot of the Almannagjá cliffs, marked by the Icelandic flag.

Straddling the Öxará river are ruins of temporary camps called **búðir** (booths). These stone foundations were covered during sessions and acted like stalls, selling food and beer. The largest, and one of the oldest, is **Biskupabúð**, north of the church. **Þingvallabær**, the rift farmhouse, was built for the 1000th anniversary of the Alþingi in 1930 by state architect Guðjón Samúelsson. It's now the park warden's office and prime minister's summer house. **Þingvallakirkja** was one of Iceland's first churches. Originally consecrated in the 11th century, the current building dates from 1859. There's a small cemetery outside the church. You can also get to it by using Car Park 2 at the end of Rte 362, and follow the footpath from there.

Understand Þingvellir's History

Many of Iceland's first settlers had run-ins with royalty back in mainland Scandinavia. These chancers and outlaws decided that they could live happily without kings in the new country, and instead created district *þings* (assemblies) where justice could be served by and among local *goðar* (chieftains).

Eventually, a nationwide *þing* became necessary. Bláskógur – now Þingvellir (Parliament Fields) – lay at a crossroads by a huge fish-filled lake. It had plenty of firewood and a setting that would make even the most tedious orator dramatic, so it fitted the bill perfectly. Every important decision affecting Iceland was argued out on this plain – new laws were passed, marriage contracts were made, and even the country's religion was decided here. The annual parliament was also a great social occasion, thronging with traders and entertainers.

Over the following centuries, escalating violence between Iceland's most powerful groups led to the breakdown of law and order. Governance was surrendered to the Norwegian crown and the Alþingi was stripped of its legislative powers in 1271. It functioned solely as a courtroom until 1798, before being dissolved entirely. When it regained its powers in 1843, members voted to move the meeting place to Reykjavík.

TOURS & EXHIBITIONS

Free one-hour guided tours in English run most days from June to August. These were at 10am and 2pm at the time of research, but check ahead online for the schedule and start point. No booking is necessary.

Year-round, the Hakið Visitor Centre also has an informative multimedia exhibition *(adult/child 1200kr/free)* on the site's geology and history.

EATING, LODGING & CAMPING

A year-round campsite at **Nyrðri-Leirar** is adjacent to the park's service centre north of the lake, which has a small cafe. Restrooms and laundry are available year-round. Showers close December to March. Campsites at **Syðri-Leirar** and **Vatnskot** are open from June to August. There's a snack bar at Hakið Visitor Centre in the south. **Silfra Restaurant** (p117) has slow-food ingredients and a bar.

TOP TIPS

- Þingvellir's **Hakið Visitor Centre** (p120) is in the south and has an exhibition on the site's history and a snack bar and shop.

- Þingvellir's **Leirar Service Centre** is on Rte 36 on the north side of the lake and handles camping and fishing licenses, plus has a small cafe.

- There are a few different car parks around the sights; you can pay parking fees with the Parka app or at a machine in the Hakið Visitor Centre.

- Dark skies here make for ideal aurora-borealis viewing from September to May...a chance to see bright greens, reds and pinks dance through the sky.

Find Fissures with Fables

There are other smaller fissures on the eastern edge of the site. During the 17th century, nine men accused of witchcraft were burned at the stake in **Brennugjá** (Burning Chasm). Nearby are the fissures of **Flosagjá** (named after an enslaved person who jumped his way to freedom) and **Nikulásargjá** (after a drunken sheriff discovered dead in the water). The southern end of Nikulásargjá is known as **Peningagjá** (Chasm of Coins) for the thousands of coins tossed into it by visitors (an act forbidden these days).

Enjoy Iceland's Largest Lake

Fish for brown trout and Arctic char on **Þingvallavatn** (p121), Iceland's largest lake, from late April to mid-September. Get a permit *(2500kr)* at the **Leirar Service Centre** and learn local regulations. The fishing card (p127) offers some access.

Snorkel or Dive Between Continents at Silfra

Diving at **Silfra** tops many bucket lists. This water-filled crack between the tectonic plates is the only place in the world to swim between continents. The crystal-clear water flows 60km from the Langjökull Glacier, winding through porous lava rock for decades before emerging here. Marine life is limited to bright green algae. This glacial water maintains a consistent temperature of 2°C to 3°C. You can only dive or snorkel on a guided tour. Reserve ahead with **Dive.is** *(dive.is)*, **Arctic Adventures** *(adventure.is)* or **Troll** *(troll.is)*.

You can park in lot No 5 for walking trails offering glimpses of the fissure and marvel at the rocks you see through the pure glacial water.

Silfra

(continued from p117)

is possible to relax inside a cedar-lined steam room that's fed by a naturally occurring vent below then take a cold swim in the lake. Time your visit around daily **geothermal bakery tours** *(adult/child 3350/1650kr)* to watch fresh pots of bread emerge from hot black sand. Sample this one-of-a-kind fresh bread with local smoked trout and Icelandic butter. Tours go year-round at 11.45am and 2.30pm; from June through September there's also one at 10.15am.

There's also a public pool, **Laugarvatn Swimming Pool** *(facebook.com/ithrottahusLaugarvatn; adult/child 1200/590kr)*.

Journey into Cave-Dwelling History
Traditional cave homes

The **Caves of Laugarvatn** *(cavesoflaugarvatn.is; adult/child 2000/1000kr)* invite you to get to know characters in period costumes, revealing what rural Icelandic life was like 100 years ago on half-hour guided tours of two human-made caves. It's 10km west of Laugarvatn.

See Bright Blue Cascades at Brúarfoss
Waterfall hike

The brilliant blue waterfall called **Brúarfoss** originates at the Langjökull glacier, and it's that glacial meltwater flowing in the rivers Brúará and Hvítá that gives this waterfall its bright blue colour. The falls plunge 3m into an azure pool punctuated by white rapids. Pay to park in the main car park *(750kr)*, from where the falls are a few minutes' walk – or take the scenic route by parking for free in the southern Brúará Trail car park and enjoying a 7km round-trip hike to the waterfall, which will pass **Hlauptungufoss** and **Miðfoss** along the way. There's usually a snack truck in the main car park from June to August.

Hike Breccia Rock Formations
Picnic at Brúarhlöð canyon

Seek out **Brúarhlöð** canyon *(parking 1000kr)*, an overlooked spot where the voluminous Hvítá river cuts through extraordinary breccia rock formations. Sharp cliffs rise from glacial water running through this narrow gorge, showing off hints of blue and green as it flows. The best views of this unique canyon are from above and don't require an arduous hike to access. The trail is under 1.5km (about 15 to 20 minutes) each way with an elevation gain of just 29ft. Expect to be tempted by the peaceful picnic spots you pass on the way.

Go White-Water Rafting
Fun on the Hvítá river

Ride the Hvítá river through a majestic river-sculpted canyon just below thundering Gullfoss. Giant rock walls seem

RESPECTING THE POWER OF NATURE

Tantalising as the sights of Iceland may be, with its black-sand beaches and glaciers glinting along the roadside, it is paramount to realise that there are real dangers involved. For example, the famous Reynisfjara beach near Vík is known for rogue waves, and tourists are regularly rescued or drown there, and people have died falling into Brúarfoss.

As for glaciers, no one should go onto them without experienced, local guidance. Crevasses form suddenly and are often invisible (beneath snow), gasses can be emitted by volcanic activity, and flooding (sometimes invisible from above) can destabilise the ice even further. Also, it is illegal to drive off-road. Always check local conditions and change your plan if it's not safe. Download the 112 Iceland app and log your treks with *safetravel.is*.

TOP EXPERIENCE

Visit Iceland's Iconic Geyser

Geysir (*gay*-zeer; literally 'gusher') is the original hot-water spout after which all other geysers are named. Set in the beautiful Haukadalur geothermal region, about a 90-minute drive from Reykjavík, the Great Geysir has been active for around 800 years. Now relatively dormant, its neighbour Strokkur steals the show with steady eruptions. The geysers here have drawn visitors for more than 100 years.

Strokkur geyser

TOP TIPS

- Giant Geysir Center across the street has a mall-like shop and N1 petrol station.
- You can eat at its restaurant, cafe (Glima), soup outlet (Supa) or fast-food joint (Kantina).
- **Hótel Geysir** (p160) bustles with tour groups tucking into a buffet. Nearby **Skjól Cafe** has pizzas, salads and snacks.

PRACTICALITIES

- The Strokkur and Geysir area was free to enter at time of writing. Parking costs 1000kr
- Open 24hr

Bubbling Haukadalur Valley

You'll see smoke rising on the horizon as you approach colourful geothermal valley Haukadalur. Vibrant shades of yellow (sulphur), green (copper) and red (iron) colour the ground. You'll also find mud pools, hot springs and fumaroles – vents in the earth that emit volcanic gas.

Look for Spouts at Geysir & Strokkur

The best-known geyser, Geysir, used to gush water up to 80m. Earthquakes can stimulate activity, though nowadays eruptions are rare. Luckily for visitors, trusty Strokkur, the valley's most active geyser, sits alongside, shooting an impressive 15m to 30m plume before the water vanishes down its enormous hole. Strokkur may not shoot water as high as Geysir, but it's far more reliable, going off about every 15 minutes.

Stand downwind only if you want a shower. You can grab super photos from up the valley, looking back at the volcanic hills and erupting geyser.

Choose Among Outdoor Activities

The walking path connects Geysir to **Blesi**, a beautiful hot spring with steam rising off blue and turquoise water. Hike in nearby Haukadalur forest or hit the nine-hole **Geysir Golf Course**. **Geysir Hestar** (*geysirhestar.com*) offers horse riding and **Skjol** (*skjolcenter.is*) has ATVs and e-bikes.

to softly rise out of the water and it may be one of the most picturesque rafting locations in the world. The glacial river's name means 'white river' – a reflection of its white caps – and the rapids (class II) are suitable for first-time rafters. Expect waves, splashes and at least a little thrill.

The water is only 'warm' enough between May and September. Tour companies provide life jackets, wetsuits and helmets. Rafters must be aged at least 11 and know how to swim. A base camp offers showers, saunas, changing rooms, a restaurant and bar. Book ahead with **Arctic Adventures** *(adventures.is; from 19,900kr)* or **Arctic Rafting** *(arcticrafting.com; from 19,900kr),* a local company that's been leading river-rafting tours here since 1985, and kayaking, too *(28.990kr).*

Fish for Salmon at Faxafoss
Waterfall with abundant fish

Faxafoss is an underrated waterfall just a 20-minute drive from its famous neighbor Gullfoss. What this waterfall lacks in height (7m), it makes up for in width (80m) and with fish. It's located on the **Tunguﬂjót**, one of Iceland's best-known rivers for catching brown sea trout. The trout can weigh up to 13.5kg, but these huge fish aren't the only draw in this stretch of river. During the season (late June through September), you'll also find a wide pool filled with salmon at the base of Faxafoss. Fishing permits are required, with only fly-fishing allowed. Salmon measuring over 68.5cm must be released back into the water.

There's a fish ladder next to the waterfall and a boardwalk that provides easy access to its base.

Visit a Bishop's Church & Farm
Historic Skálholt

A village with about 100 residents holds the weight of Iceland's history: **Skálholt** *(skalholt.is)* was a bishopric that ruled Iceland's souls from the 11th to the 18th centuries. In the wealthy settlement was a school, farms, a monastery and living quarters. The great cathedral that once stood here was destroyed by a major earthquake in the 18th century, but visitors can step inside the huge Evangelical Lutheran church, **Skálholtsdómkirkja**, built between 1956 and 1963. It has a **museum** *(admission 500kr),* runs **Hvönn** restaurant and hosts summertime concerts.

TOWNS IN THE SOUTHERN GOLDEN CIRCLE

Near Geysir and Gullfoss, the Haukadalur and Hvítá valleys are dotted with farms and geothermal greenhouses – a sustainable-produce paradise.

Reykholt: This rural township (population 300) – one of several Reykholts around the country – is centred on the Reykjahver hot spring and is traditionally a greenhouse village. The main attraction is the spectacular, deep Hvítá river: South Iceland's centre for white-water rafting.

Flúðir: This little agrarian community is connected to Reykholt via a bridge on Rte 359.

Laugarás: Hamlet with new lagoon and kid-favourite Slakki Petting Zoo.

Selfoss: The largest gateway town, on the river Ölfusá. It has an impressive array of grocery stores and eating and accommodation options.

EATING & DRINKING IN FLUÐIR: RICH VARIETY

Minilik Restaurant: This colourful Ethiopian restaurant offers authentic food, including vegetarian options, and a welcoming vibe. *6-9pm Tue-Sun* €€

Fish & Chips: Stop at this food kiosk for a quick road-trip meal or pick up picnic provisions: of course fish and chips, but also burgers. *noon-9pm* €

Restaurant Mika: Everything from bread to sauces and chocolate is made from scratch at this family-run restaurant. *noon-4pm & 5-9pm* €€

Vínstofa Friðheima: The wine bar at Friðheimar (p127), with an extensive selection, located inside a greenhouse. *noon-10pm* €€

TOP EXPERIENCE

Feel the Roar at Gullfoss

Iceland's most famous waterfall, Gullfoss (Golden Falls) is a spectacular double cascade dropping a dramatic 32m. As it descends, it kicks up magnificent walls of spray before thundering down a rocky ravine. On sunny days the mist creates shimmering rainbows, while in winter the falls glitter with ice. Although it's popular, its remote location on the edge of the Highlands still makes you feel the ineffable forces of nature.

TOP TIPS

- The tourist centre has a shop and **cafe** (lamb soup, salads, sandwiches, cakes and coffee).
- Nearby **Hótel Gullfoss** (p160) has a restaurant, too.
- Gullfoss has 3.2km of walking paths, but don't step over the barriers – they're there to protect both you and the fragile environment.

PRACTICALITIES

- gullfoss.is
- free
- falls open 24hr, cafe/shop hours vary

Feel the Power of the Waterfall

Dropping into the rugged canyon of the Hvítá river, Gullfoss has two cascades: the first drop is 11m and the second is 21m. In summer, Gullfoss is at its fullest, and around 38 million tonnes of water charge through daily. Light prisms through the mist into rainbows rising over carpets of bright green moss. In winter, the falls are spectacular when they freeze in places, enormous icicles shimmering.

Maximise Views & Photo Ops

A tarmac path leads from the main car park and visitor centre to a grand lookout over the falls. Stairs continue down to the level of the falls. For wheelchair-accessible parking, drive in on the spur below the tourist centre at falls-level. A path (don't stray off) continues down the valley towards the falls for the most captivating video shots. There's also a lesser-known viewing spot on the eastern riverbank.

Saving the Falls

In 1907, Gullfoss almost became a hydroelectric dam. Sigríður Tómasdóttir (1871–1957) walked barefoot to Reykjavík to protest. Gullfoss was donated to the nation, and since 1979 it's been a nature reserve. Look for the memorial to Sigríður near the foot of the stairs from the visitors centre.

Luxe Soak & Top Meal at Laugarás Lagoon
The Golden Circle's new lagoon and restaurant

The hottest entry in the Golden Circle soaking game is the beautifully designed **Laugarás Lagoon** (*laugaraslagoon.is; admission from adult/child 6,900/3500kr*), which opened in 2025. The soft arches of its building are planted with native grasses to blend with the exquisite location on the banks of the Hvítá. You can immerse yourself in a vast complex of pools, taking in the river views and changing temperatures and relaxing at its waterfall feature. Modern dressing rooms and a bespoke skincare line developed with a preeminent herbalist add to the charms, though a top highlight of the lagoon is its **Ylja** restaurant, run by Gísli Matt, a leading chef who creates inventive, hyper-local Icelandic cuisine – eg at Vestmannaeyjar's Slippurinn and Næs (p146) and Reykjavík's Skál! (p69) and Mat Bar (p69). The menu uses locally sourced produce and evolves with the seasons. They harness the geothermal heat for some of the cooking techniques.

Note: children under eight are not allowed at the spa.

Lounge in a Spacious Historic Hot Spring
The wild charms of the Secret Lagoon

Unwind in a broad, calm geothermal pool, mist rising and ringed by natural rocks. It's Iceland's oldest swimming pool, **Gamla Laugin** (*secretlagoon.is; adult/child 4200/200kr*), an oasis in Flúðir that traces its history to 1891. Many Icelanders learned to swim here in the early 1900s, and it is now known as **Secret Lagoon**. The water is consistently around 38°C and the walking trail along the edge of this lovely hot spring passes the local river and a series of sizzling vents and geysers. Surrounding meadows fill with wildflowers in summer. The lagoon gets packed with tour-bus crowds at midafternoon, so come earlier or later.

You'll find changing rooms, lockers and a cafe, plus swimsuits and towels available for rent.

Discover a Secluded Hot Spring
Natural feel with valley views

The hot spring **Hrunalaug** (*hrunalaug.is; adult/child 3000/free*), just outside Flúðir, is so far off the beaten path you might get it all to yourself. This tiny hot spring has three small pools, each at a different temperature. It's privately owned by a local

RULES OF THE ROD

Southern Iceland's rivers are known for their ample stocks of salmon and Arctic char. There are several places to rent fishing gear in the area. If you bring your own equipment, you have to disinfect it before you can use it in Iceland.

You do need a permit for fishing here. For lake fishing, opt for an annual fishing pass. This **Fishing Card** (*Veiðikortið; veidikortid.is*) provides a permit for 37 lakes across the country for a year for 9900kr. You can load the e-permit on your smartphone.

Rivers issue a limited number of permits each day. You'll need to purchase in advance for a specific date and location. Check *island.is/en/angling* for more info.

Prime fishing season in this area is from July through September.

 EATING IN THE HVÍTÁ RIVER VALLEY: FARM-TO-TABLE FARE

Friðheimar, Reykholt: Book well ahead to dine in a charming greenhouse where tomatoes grow year-round. Taste tomato beer and tomato ice cream. *11.30-4pm* €€

Flúðasveppir Farmers Bistro, Flúðir: Delish mushroom soup, burgers and more, with locally grown toppings at Iceland's only mushroom farm. *noon-5pm* €€

Græna Kannan Cafe, Sólheimar: Their own organic food in a buffet; daily soup comes with a cup of their roasted coffee. *cafe 11am-5pm, cafeteria 11.30am-1pm* €€

Sólskinsbúðin, Flúðir: This adorable farmers market is the spot to stock up on local strawberries and bell peppers. *9am-5pm* €

Kerið

SUSTAINABLE, LOCAL FOOD

Chef and food activist **Gísli Matt Auðunsson** gives us his insights on healthy eating in the Golden Circle. *gislimatt.is*

The region around Laugarás is rich with amazing farmers and producers growing some of the best food in the country. At our new restaurant at the Laugarás Lagoon we focus on working with local growers to create food with a story, with a connection to the land, the place and the people. We also focus on zero waste, hopefully making our restaurant a place that is a value to the community, the farmers and the environment.

Be sure to visit **Sólheimar**. It's a special eco-village and a wonderful community growing their own vegetables, roasting coffee for their cafe and making arts and crafts.

farmer and in 2025 they were building bathrooms and a new changing room (the old one was a sheep barn).

If all these pricier hot springs are a bit much for you, make a beeline to **Reykholtslaug** *(blaskogabyggd.is; adult/child 1200/590kr),* Reykholt's small, friendly hot-pots, swimming pool and water slide.

Go Art Shopping at Sólheimar Eco-Village
Fresh lunch and fresh art

It's worth finding your way to the special Sólheimar Eco-Village, a collection of homes and greenhouses using ecologically sound practices to create a sustainable community. Day visitors should go to the Græna Kannan Cafe (p127), where soups and a small lunch buffet are made from ingredients grown on the farm. Don't miss the art gallery there, which has summer exhibitions of the residents' fantastic artwork. If you can't buy a piece and wait for the exhibition to close to collect it, don't worry, many immediate gratification pieces stock the eclectic shop.

If you feel like staying longer, they operate two guesthouses.

Hike the Colourful Kerið Magma Chamber
Stroll the shores of a crater lake

One of Iceland's best-known volcanic craters, **Kerið** *(kerid.is; 600kr)* is a 6500-year-old magma chamber that collapsed, leaving vivid red and sienna earth surrounding an ethereal green lake. It's 16km northeast of Selfoss and is the most striking of several crater lakes in Iceland's western volcanic zone. Much of Kerið is made of rich, red volcanic rock, but its least steep slope is a bed of mossy green during summer. Hints of yellow are a reflection of the land's sulphur content.

You can walk around the lake – Björk once performed a concert from a raft in the middle of it – in about 30 minutes or walk from the viewing platform down to the lake in about 15 minutes.

Beyond The Golden Circle

Roam the dales and river valleys around the Golden Circle to find geothermal rivers, horse riding and the edges of the Highlands.

To the south of the Golden Circle at the Ring Rd, Hveragerði emerges from otherworldly lava fields and hills pierced, surreally, by natural steaming vents. Selfoss is the largest town in southern Iceland, a bustling centre of commerce with a newly built town centre. It's surrounded by the rain-kissed flat fields of Flóahreppur, the heartland of dairy farming and horse breeding (and riding). On the coast, slip away to the quiet fishing villages Eyrarbakki and Stokkseyri, alongside the bird-lovers' Flói Nature Reserve. To the east, the powerful Þjórsá is Iceland's longest river, a fast-flowing, churning mass of milky glacial water that courses 230km from Vatnajökull down to the Atlantic. Rte 32 follows the western side of the river and leads to volcanic fields and the Highlands.

Places
Mosfellsbær p129
Langjökull p129
Hveragerði p130
Selfoss p132
Raufarhólshellir p133
Eyrarbakki p133
Þjórsárdalur Valley p135

GETTING AROUND

For rural Iceland, this part of the country has the best road infrastructure. The Hellisheiði mountain ridge between Reykjavík and Selfoss can be windy and snowy in winter; during bad weather, consider the alternate Rte 39 via the southern coast. Strætó bus 51 between Reykjavík and Vík and Höfn stops at the N1 station in Selfoss. Bus 52 loops south to Landeyjahöfn, and several local buses serve the villages around Hveragerði and Selfoss.

Mosfellsbær
TIME FROM ÞINGVELLIR NATIONAL PARK: **20MIN**

Tour the home of a Nobel Prize writer

Nobel Prize–winning author Halldór Laxness (1902–98) lived in Mosfellsbær all his life and his classy riverside home is now the **Gljúfrasteinn Laxness Museum** (*gljufrasteinn.is; adult/child 1500kr/free*). The 1950s-styled house still retains its original furniture, writing room and Laxness' fine-art collection (the needlework is by his wife Auður). An audio tour leads you around. Look for Laxness' beloved Jaguar parked out the front. Mosfellsbær is easy to access via the Reykjavík to Þingvellir road (Rte 36).

Langjökull
TIME FROM GULLFOSS: **2HR**

Snowmobile on a glacier

There's no feeling quite like whizzing across a glacier on a snowmobile. Langjökull, in West Iceland, is usually accessed from around Húsafell, but tour companies **Mountaineers of Iceland** (*mountaineers.is; adult/teen/child 6-11 years 31,900/23,925kr/free*) will pick up from Gullfoss and take you in a 4WD vehicle on an F road to the base camp. You'll

NATURE'S OVEN

Icelanders have used the hot springs here to bake rye bread for generations. *Hverabrauð* (hot-spring bread) is steam-cooked underground for 24 hours in the heat of the geothermal springs. Bakers bury stainless steel pots of flour, sugar, baking powder, salt and milk, digging up the pots of the bread the next day.

The Icelandic rye that emerges is cakey with just a hint of sweetness, and goes perfectly with smooth, creamy Icelandic butter. **Ylja** (p127) uses geothermal heat in its cooking. You can take a bread-making tour at **Laugarvatn Fontana** (p117), or buy some in Hveragerði and try it for yourself.

need a driver's license to operate a snowmobile, and operators provide thermal suits and helmets. Children over six can join as passengers.

Sleipnir Glacier Tours *(sleipnirtours.is; adult/teen/child 4-11 years 22,900/11,450kr/free)* runs monster-truck tours to the glacier.

Hveragerði   TIME FROM ÞINGVELLIR NATIONAL PARK: 40MIN

Hike to a geothermal river

The small town of Hveragerði emerges from otherworldly lava fields and hills pierced, surreally, by natural steaming vents. It's the hot-springs capital of the world, with a highly active geothermal field, which heats hundreds of greenhouses. Nationally, the town is famous for its horticultural college and naturopathic clinic, **NLFÍ Health Clinic & Spa** *(heilsustofnun.is)*. There are also some fantastic hikes in the area, though routes are sometimes packed in summer.

One of the most popular hikes in the country is up **Reykjadalur** *(parking per hr 250kr)*, a geothermal valley where you can bathe in a small river warmed to bathing temperatures by geothermal activity (bring your swimsuit). From the trailhead car park, it's a 3km hike through fields of sulphur-belching plains (it takes roughly one hour, one way). Stick to marked paths, lest you melt your shoes, and leave no rubbish.

Sizzling sights around Hveragerði

In town, the geothermal park **Hveragarðurinn** *(visithveragerdi.is; adult/child 400kr/free)* has mudpots and steaming pools where visitors can dip their feet (but no more). There's also a small cafe serving tea, coffee and geothermally baked bread.

Head to the Sunnumörk shopping centre for a look between tectonic plates. The crack was discovered during construction. And the **Tourist Information Centre** *(southiceland.is)* has a 6.6 richter seismic simulator *(300kr)*.

EATING IN HVERAGERÐI: OUR PICKS

Gróðurhúsið: (Greenhouse, in English) Food hall with many vendors – tacos, noodles and ice cream to fried chicken – and excellent vibes. *hours vary* €€

Varmá: Scenic restaurant overlooking the gorge. Icelandic dishes use local ingredients and geothermal cooking techniques. *5.30-10pm* €€€

Hofland Eatery: Grill specialising in beef, pizzas galore and beer with a casual feel on the backside of the shopping centre. *11.30am-9pm* €€

Rósakaffi: Rose garden, coffeeshop serving cakes and lunch, and gift shop rolled into one. *11.30am-1.30pm Mon-Thu, to 8pm Fri & Sat, to 5pm Sun* €€

Skyrgerðin: Lamb, fish, veg and Italian pastas...something for everyone, in a homey, historic building. *11.30am-1.30pm Mon-Fri, 6-9pm Wed-Sat* €€

Ölverk: Family-owned microbrewery powered by geothermal energy offers craft beer and delish wood-fired pizza. *11.30am-10pm Wed-Sun* €€

Almar: Large, bustling bakery (pastries, doughnuts, cookies) that also serves sandwiches, salads and soup with fresh bread. *7am-6pm Mon-Fri, from 9am Sat & Sun* €

Reykjadalur Café: This little cafe near the start of the Reykjadalur trail serves homemade soups, flatbread, cakes and coffee. *11am-6pm* €€

Reykjadalur

If you'd like a more casual soak, pop into beloved **Sundlaugin Laugaskarði** *(laugaskard.is; adult/child 1220/420kr)* for pools, hot-pots and a steam room, just across the river from the waterfall **Reykjafoss**.

Bike, horseback ride or fly through the lava fields

A favourite way to get up the valley is on mountain bike. Book ahead with **Icebike** *(icebikeadventures.com; from 9500kr per day),* who will also hook you up with route maps. Or take to horseback with excellent **Sólhestar** *(solhestar.is)* and **Eldhestar** (p116) *(eldhestar.is).*

Looking for more thrills? **Mega Zipline** *(megazipline.is; adult/child from 9490/6900kr)* will whip you through the air for 1km, the longest line in Iceland. You must be over eight years old and weigh between 30kg and 120kg (66lb to 264lb).

Take in inspiring Icelandic art

Art lovers should make sure to stop into the free modern-art gallery **Listasafn Árnesinga** *(listasafnarnesinga.is; free),* which puts on superb exhibitions. When it's quiet the staff are more than happy to walk guests around the gallery, offering an insight into the art. It also has a fine cafe serving hot drinks and cakes.

Follow the steam and learn about its power

The sleek shell of **Hellisheiði Geothermal Power Plant** *(on.is; adult/child 2500/free)* is one of the few plants that provides 30% of Iceland's electricity. A multimedia exhibition and tour lay out the details of harnessing the Earth's hot-water power and the origins of geothermal energy. Plus you can see the turbine room, and view Iceland's rocks and minerals. There's a cafe on-site. It's 17km west of Hveragerði off Rte 1.

En route you can stop off at the usually uncrowded bubbling springs and mudpots at **Hveradalir** *(parking 1000kr)* near the Skíðaskálinn í Hveradölum restaurant.

BEST WOOL & SOUVENIR SHOPPING

In addition to fascinating wool-dying studio Hespa (p132), the south has great spots to shop crafts.

Þingborg: Handmade wool products made by a local women's collective specialising in farm-to-sweater clothing and natural wool colours. Between Selfoss and Hella. *(thingborg.is)*

Uppspuni Mini Mill & Yarn Shop: Wool comes from the farm's own sheep, processed in a mill downstairs. West of Hella. *(uppspuni.is)*

Una Local Products: Hangar in Hvolsvöllur loaded with handmade crafts: fish-skin purses, woolly sweaters, jewellery, leather goods, you name it. *(facebook.com/unalocalproduct)*

Gallerý GIMLI Icelandic Handkraft: Stokkseyri's handmade wool items, from baby socks and mittens to cardigans.

Vinnustofan Rosin: Small family-run sheep farm and shop sells handmade wool sweaters, socks and mittens near Geysir. Cash only.

BEST HORSE RIDING

In addition to Hveragerði's Sólhestar and Eldhestar, the region is ripe with horse farms; many have lodging.

Núphestar: Family-run, with short rides around Þjórsá river area. *(nupshestar.is)*

Hekluhestar: French-Icelandic family specialising in six- to eight-day Highland rides. *(hekluhestar.is)*

Herríðarhóll: Multiday horse tours and short rides with a German-Icelandic family. *(herridarholl)*

Skeiðvellir: Horse-breeding farm with a visitor centre, horse petting and rides. *(iceworld.is; Icelandic Horse World)*

Sólvangur Icelandic Horse Centre: Eyrarbakki stable with rides suitable for beginners. *(hesturinn.is)*

Bakkahestar: Beach rides with friendly horses and patient instructors in Eyrarbakki. *(bakkahestar.is)*

Cora's House & Horses: Cosy farm with rides near Raufarhólshellir. *(coras.is)*

Raufarhólshellir

Selfoss
TIME FROM ÞINGVELLIR NATIONAL PARK: **30MIN**

Get to know the town where chess master Bobby Fishcher lived

Selfoss is the largest town in southern Iceland, an important centre for getting business done, and in the midst of a dramatic building project, creating a downtown of replicas of historic Icelandic buildings. It makes for a great lunch stop in the pedestrian-friendly town centre paired with a swim at **Sundhöll Selfoss** *(arborg.is; adult/child 1750/350kr)*.

Perhaps its most famous resident was chess champion Bobby Fischer. The little **Bobby Fischer Center** *(fischersetur.is; adult/child 1700kr/free)* houses his memorabilia and you can visit his grave 2km northeast in **Laugardælirkirkja's** cemetery.

See natural wool dying in action

Artists, knitters and the craft curious should make a beeline to **Hespa** *(hespa.is)* where the informative Guðrún Bjarnadóttir brews natural dyes for Icelandic wool and happily talks you through her methods and sources. Her studio is stocked with beautiful wools, knitting kits and patterns and fun learning games she created herself (she's a former professional teacher). You can reach out even when she's closed in winter, and she can sometimes open the studio. It's one of several musts for fibre lovers (p131).

Want to learn even more? Take a multiday knitting and wool-dying workshop with designer Hélène Magnússon *(icelandicknitter.com)*.

Eat Icelandic donuts at a turf house

Being so close to the most travelled portion of the Ring Road south of Selfoss, it's a wonder you can fall into **Flóahreppur**, a rural region of rolling pastures leading to the ocean. This small agricultural area has laid-back horse farms and harbours the **Íslenski Bærinn Turf House** (*islenskibaerinn.is; adult/child 2000/1000kr*). Turf houses used soil as insulation, keeping early Icelanders sheltered from harsh weather. The exhibits here explain how turf houses were built and how they've evolved over time. Over summer, there's a coffee house serving traditional *kleinu* (twisted doughnuts).

Feast like a Viking

Ingólfsskáli Viking Restaurant (*ingolfsskali.is*), between Hveragerði and Selfoss on Rte 374, may appear touristy, but you can try your hand at archery and axe-throwing then feast on dried stockfish, fermented shark and pan-fried char. Vegan options, too. The architecture will make you feel like you're on a Viking ship.

Raufarhólshellir

TIME FROM ÞINGVELLIR NATIONAL PARK: **50MIN**

Hike through rock formations in a lava tunnel

Hankering to head into a lava tube? The **Lava Tunnel** (*thelavatunnel.is; adult/child 8400/free*) known as Raufarhólshellir was created by hot-flowing lava in the 11th century. Take a one-hour tour through the 1360m-long tube (Iceland's third largest) and see its wonderful lava columns. In winter cold air is funnelled down and trapped inside, producing amazing ice formations.

A longer three- to four-hour tour guides visitors deep into the cave, where you'll have to climb over boulders and squeeze though tight spaces. That tour requires good balance and reasonable physical fitness. Both tours are best done in sturdy hiking shoes and a light jacket, even during summer. Temperatures inside are typically around 2°C (35°F). Helmets and headlamps are included with your visit.

Eyrarbakki

TIME FROM ÞINGVELLIR NATIONAL PARK: **40MIN**

Embrace fishing village life

It's hard to believe, but tiny Eyrarbakki was Iceland's main port and a thriving trading town well into the 20th century. Farmers from all over the south once rode here to barter for

DON'T CALL THEM PONIES

Icelandic horses have five gaits or paces. Most horses have three: walk, trot and gallop. Icelandic horses add *tölt*, a relaxed pace that's perfect for taking in the scenery; and flying pace, a faster, more adventurous full gallop – more commonly used with show horses.

As you're mounting your horse, you'll notice it's smaller than what you may be used to riding. Icelandic horses are shorter than most, coming in at around 1.3m to 1.4m when they're full-grown. For comparison, full-grown quarter-horses are generally between 1.5m and 1.6m while Clydesdales are around 1.8m in height. Whatever you do, don't call these petite horses 'ponies'.

EATING IN SELFOSS: OUR PICKS

Old Dairy: Lively food hall with pizza, tacos, Thai food and *skyr*-smoothies. Outdoor seating for people-watching. *11.30a-9pm Sun-Thu, to 9.30pm Fri & Sat* €

GK Bakerí: Hip sourdough bakery on the main street, serving sticky cinnamon buns and fresh coffee. *7am-5pm Mon-Fri, 8am-4pm Sat, 8am-2pm Sun* €

Kaffi Krús: Popular main-street cafe and restaurant; excellent pizza (try the duck or langoustine), burgers and outdoor space. *11am-9pm* €

Tryggvaskáli: Antique-laden romance and riverfront views in Selfoss' first house. *4-9pm Mon-Thu, to 10pm Fri, 11.30am-3pm & 5-10pm Sat & Sun* €€€

Fröken: Swishy Icelandic food restaurant in the 'new' old town. A good bet for date night, with yummy cocktails, too. *noon-10pm* €€€

MAR Seafood: Delicious Icelandic seafood pairs well with the full bar and welcoming, wood dining room. *11.30am-9pm Mon-Sat, from 5.30pm Sun* €€

Bókakaffið: Cool independent bookshop (with both new and secondhand books) serving coffee, cake and nostalgia. *noon-6pm Tue-Fri, 11am-5pm Sat* €

Konungskaffi: Excellent coffees and fresh-baked goodies in a contemporary-mod coffeehouse with some outdoor seating. *8am-6pm* €

WHAT TO KNOW ABOUT F ROADS

Bumpy tracks called F roads are shown on maps and signs with an 'F' for *fjall* (mountain) before the road number (F26, F88 etc). Don't confuse F roads with regular gravel roads, which are normally fine for 2WDs with high enough clearance.

- F roads open only in summer and dates vary with weather; always check *road.is*.
- You must have a 4WD (or take a bus or super-Jeep tour) and check that your insurance covers you (it's usually invalidated by river crossings).
- Educate yourself about what lies ahead (eg river crossings).
- While some F roads may seem to blend into the surroundings, driving off marked tracks is strictly prohibited in Iceland; it damages fragile ecosystems.
- Fill up on petrol and pack extra food and water in case you get stuck.

supplies at the general store – crowds were so huge it could take three days to get served!

Now it's best known for its museum **Húsið á Eyrarbakka** (*byggdasafn.is*) in one of Iceland's oldest houses (1765), with displays explaining the town's history and its other annexes like a maritime museum. Nearby **Stokkseyri** is a quaint oceanfront hamlet with art-nouveau **Knarraros Lighthouse**, and the fishing town of **Þorlákshöfn**, to the west, is where the ferry to the Vestmannaeyjar leaves from when it's too stormy to leave from Landeyjahöfn. They're also home to **Black Beach Tours** (*blackbeachtours.is*), which can take you quad-biking on lesser-known beaches.

Look for wetland birds from land or kayak

The **Flói Nature Reserve** (*fuglavernd.is*) is the hidden wetland attraction of Eyrarbakki. More than 70 bird species have been spotted. In spring and summer, greylag and white-fronted geese pass through, as do wigeon, tufted duck and waders like snipe. You can take to these marshlands, pools and ponds by kayak, too, with **Kajakferðir Stokkseyri** (*kajak.is; rental/tours from 6500/8900kr*) and see what you can spot.

EATING NEAR EYRARBAKKI: SEAFOOD

Rauða Húsið: Find this charming restaurant in an old house in Eyrarbakki, dishing up lobster, cod, lamb and veg. *5-9pm Wed-Fri, from noon Sat & Sun* €€€

Fjöruborðið: Head to Stokkseyri to feast on lobster soup and this restaurant's signature lobster tails, right by the shore. *noon-9pm* €€

Hafið Bláa: An oceanfront restaurant for fresh lobster and water views, just west of Eyrarbakki near Flói Nature Reserve. *5-9pm Tue-Sat, from 3pm Sun* €€€

Heima Bistro: Þorlákshöfn's workaday favourite for fish and chips, burgers and cake, too *11.15am-9pm Tue-Fri, from 1pm Sat & Sun* €€

Þjóðveldisbærinn

Þjórsárdalur Valley

TIME FROM GEYSIR: **45MIN**

Explore the secret circle bordering the Highlands

Sometimes referred to as the 'Secret Circle', the **Þjórsárdalur Valley** is a magnificent detour through the lush landscape of the south to the interior's multihued lava. Due to the lack of transport to this region – and time, for many – this is southern Iceland minus the crowds. (For now...A major hotel and luxury lagoon called **Mountain Retreat & Baths**, developed by the Blue Lagoon, is set to open in 2027.)

Twenty-six kilometres northeast of **Árnes** – which has a cafe and visitor center **Þjórsárstofa** *(thjorsarstofa.is)* – along Rte 32, take a signposted turn to delightful waterfall **Hjálparfoss**. The azure falls tumble in two chutes over twisted basalt columns and into a deep pool: a good place for a picnic.

On Rte 327, off Rte 32, the notable ruins of medieval longhouse **Stöng** were buried by white volcanic ash in 1104 during one of the eruptions of nearby **Hekla volcano**. This ancient farm once belonged to Gaukur Trandilsson, a 10th-century Viking who lived a tempestuous life. Excavated in 1939 during Iceland's first proper archaeological dig, the discovery was used to help date Viking houses elsewhere. These include the foundations of a farm, a house, a barn, a smithy and a church. It's not to be confused with **Þjóðveldisbærinn** (Commonwealth Farm; *thjodveldisbaer.is; adult/child 1000kr/free*), a nearby reconstruction of Stöng, open to visitors June to September.

A walking path from Stöng (or a 4WD-only river-fording road) takes you a couple of kilometres to the small lush valley **Gjáin**, full of twisting lava, otherworldly caves and spectacular waterfalls. From Gjáin, 10km along the 4WD-only, pot-hole-laden Rte 332, get an astounding view of 122m **Háifoss** waterfall plunging off the edge of a majestic plateau. Thick lava formations, over two million years old, carpet the canyon below.

HOODED HEKLA

The name of Iceland's most famous and active volcano, Hekla, means 'Hooded One', as its 1491m-high summit is almost always shrouded in ominous-looking clouds. Hekla has vented its fury numerous times throughout history, and during the Middle Ages it was believed to be the gateway to hell.

Viking-era farms were wiped out by the eruption of 1104, which buried everything within a radius of 50km. Since then there have been 15 major eruptions; the 1300 eruption covered more than 83,000 sq km in ash. The most recent eruption (in 2000) produced a pyroclastic flow (high-speed, highly destructive torrent of rock particles and gas which can reach 800°C). Hiking on Hekla is discouraged because it's due to erupt any day.

Hvolsvöllur

ADVENTURE BASE | MAGNIFICENT CASCADES | CANYONS & VALLEYS

GETTING AROUND
Your own wheels make travel easier, but **Strætó buses 51** Reykjavík–Vík–Höfn and 52 Reykjavík–Landeyjahöfn stop in Hella and Hvolsvöllur.
 Late June to early September **Reykjavik Excursions** *(re.is/highland-bus)* Highland Buses to Landmannalaugar stop in Selfoss and Hella. Trex *(trex.is)* Highland Buses to Landmannalaugar stop in Hella. All Highland Buses to Þórsmörk stop in Hvolsvöllur, too.
 Reykjavik Excursions also has a Skógar bus which stops in Hvolsvöllur for six hours. Reserve ahead with Reykjavik Excursions to take a bike *(4500kr)* or arrange baggage transfer *(2000kr)* in the highlands, if you're hiking Laugavegurinn (p144).

As you work your way east from Selfoss, the Ring Road passes near Urriðafoss and on into the Rangárþing Ytra district and the small agricultural community of Hella on the banks of the pretty Ytri-Rangá river (which has its own falls, Ægissíðufoss). It's an important horse-breeding area all the way into the Rangárþing Eystra district's farms around Hvolsvöllur. This was the setting for the bloody events of *Njál's Saga*, one of Iceland's favourites; today, though, besides the turf house at Keldur, the Saga sites exist mainly as place names. Hvolsvöllur itself had not been much more than a pit stop, with a couple of petrol stations and a cluster of houses, but its enormous volcano education centre and access to top activities and sights, makes it a popular base for South Iceland adventures to the wonderfully jagged terrain of Landmannalaugar, Þórsmörk and volcanoes like Eyjafjallajökull with their waterfalls...and the awesome glaciers of Katla Geopark beyond.

Tremble Through an Earthquake
Experience volcanic action at the Lava Centre
There may be no better place for a museum dedicated to the study of lava, earthquakes and volcanic activity. The **Lava Centre** sits in the shadows of several volcanoes, including the notorious **Eyjafjallajökull**, whose 2010 eruption caused the closure of large swaths of European airspace; Hekla, one of Iceland's most active volcanoes; and Katla, one of Iceland's largest volcanoes.

Interactive displays bring the wild south Icelandic terrain to life, explaining how volcanoes work and why there are so many of them here. You'll experience a few seconds of shaking and get an idea of what an earthquake would feel like at three different strengths. A cinema screens soaring drone footage and there's also a good cafe-restaurant. Don't leave before heading to the building's roof to check out the volcano views.

HVOLSVÖLLUR

✪ HIGHLIGHTS
1 Seljalandsfoss

● SIGHTS
2 Ægissíðufoss
see 8 Drífandi
3 Eyvindarholt Farm
see 3 Gljúfrabúi
see 8 Gluggafoss
4 Keldur
5 Lava Centre
see 3 Nauthúsagil
6 Sólheimajökull
7 Sólheimasandur
8 Þórðarfoss
see 3 Þorsteinslundur

▲ ACTIVITIES
9 Caves of Hella
10 Midgard Adventure
11 Óbyggðaferðir
12 Seljavallalaug

● SLEEPING
see F Aurora Lodge
13 Erú Guesthouse
14 Fljótsdalur HI Hostel
15 Hótel Rangá
see 10 Midgard Base Camp

● EATING
16 Bongó
see 10 Eldstó Art Café
see 5 Gallerí Pizza
17 Groovís
18 Hekla Street Food
19 Hygge Restaurant & Bar
20 Ísbúð Huppu
see 10 Midgard Restaurant
see 18 Stracta Rótin
see 10 Valdís

● DRINKING & NIGHTLIFE
see 9 American School Bus Cafe

☑ TOP TIP

The Hvolsvöllur area *(visithvolsvollur. is)* has great access to all manner of adventures around the south. If you're here in winter, inquire with local adventure tour operators like Midgard Adventure (p159) to see where they can access with their vehicles.

THE STORY OF NJÁL'S SAGA

One of Iceland's best-loved (and longest) sagas is also one of the most complicated (better read it!). But the upshot is that a petty squabble between the wives of friends and neighbours Gunnar Hámundarson and Njál Þorgeirsson leads to feuds and battles that ultimately leave almost every character dead.

Doomed hero Gunnar of Hlíðarendi (in Fljótshlíð) falls for and marries beautiful, hot-tempered Hallgerður, who has long legs but – ominously – a 'thief's eyes'. Hallgerður has a falling-out with Bergþóra, wife of Njál. Hallgerður and Bergþóra begin murdering each other's servants and it all goes south from there. At one important point Gunnar slaps Hallgerður – which later comes back to haunt him. (Spoiler alert: Hallgerður's two previous husbands were killed as a result of slapping her.)

Gluggafoss

Picnic in Fljótshlíð by Waterfalls
The charms of the window falls Gluggafoss

Venture away from the Ring Road at Hvolsvöllur onto Rte 261 and you'll follow the mossy green edge of the lush Fljótshlíð hills, offering great views of waterfalls on one side, and the Markarfljót river delta and Eyjafjallajökull on the other. Tourism immediately drops off, and it's primo territory for a picnic (get groceries in Hvolsvöllur) at small grove **Þorsteinslundur** at the base of **Drifandi** waterfalls. Or continue on past **Þordarfoss** to special **Gluggafoss** *(parking 1000kr)* dropping some 45m from the cliff above, fed from the Merkja River. It tumbles through crevices in between rocks or 'gluggars' (windows). The lower falls cascades around 10m and you can walk behind it.

The surfaced section of the road ends soon after the farm and church at **Hlíðarendi**, once the home of Gunnar Hámundarson from *Njál's Saga*. With a large 4WD you can continue along road F261 towards Landmannalaugar (p144) and Tindfjöll – a hiker's paradise. Though it seems tantalisingly close, Þórsmörk can only be reached via Rte F249. **Óbyggðaferðir** *(atvtravel.is)* runs quad-bike tours if you want to venture further.

EATING IN HVOLSVÖLLUR & HELLA: OUR PICKS

Midgard Restaurant: Excellent locally sourced, creative Icelandic dishes with a bit of international fusion. Vegan options and a bar, too. *7.30-10am, 12.30-9.30pm* €€

Eldstó Art Café: Homemade specials (such as traditional Icelandic flatbread with smoked lamb), burgers, fish stew, coffee and cakes, amid ceramics. *10am-10pm* €€

Stracta Rótin: Local Hella favourite for freshmade pizza and pasta in a cheery room. Reserve ahead at peak times. *noon-9pm Sun-Wed, to 10pm Thu-Sat* €€

Hygge Restaurant & Bar: Up the Fljótshlíð valley from Hvolsvöllur you'll find this popular eatery serving generous portions of chickpea curry and Arctic char. *noon-10pm* €€€

Walk Behind Famous Seljalandsfoss
Chasing waterfalls

Iceland has thousands of waterfalls, but some of the most popular and impressive are located on the Ring Road drive from Hvolsvöllur to Vík. You'll see one of Iceland's most famous waterfalls, the glistening 60m-high **Seljalandsfoss** *(parking 1000kr)*, thundering off the lower escarpments of Eyjafjallajökull *(ay-ya-fiat-la-yo-gootl)* volcano from miles away. A misty, slippery path runs around the back of the waterfall; wear sturdy boots and waterproof clothing. There's also a cafe and small shop selling souvenirs.

Just 650m further inland, the humble **Gljúfrabúi** gushes into a hidden canyon. Access it either by driving down on Rte 249 (road to Þórsmörk) or follow the walking path from Seljalandsfoss car park.

Plane Wreck Photo Ops
The story of two DC-3s

A US Navy militarised Douglas DC-3 airplane crashed in 1973 at barren black-sand beach **Sólheimasandur**. All seven crew members walked away. The wreckage became a popular photo spot (see Justin Bieber's 'I'll Show You' video), drawing visitors from around the world to walk the hour from the car park *(850kr)*. Now there's also a shuttle bus *(one way/return 2000/3200kr)*.

In 2023, another wrecked DC-3 was moved from Sauðanes in north Iceland to **Eyvindarholt Farm** *(eyvindarholt.is; parking 1000kr)* up Rte 249 because tourism was disrupting farm operations where it had crashed – so you can get your plane pic there, too.

Scramble to Hidden Cascades in a Mossy Ravine
Adventure to Nauthusagil

Not far from Seljalandsfoss, the road to Þórsmörk (4WD required) hides one of the most thrilling and adventurous scrambles to a waterfall, along a river and through an ancient moss-covered canyon called **Nauthusagil**. Although the walk through the ravine is short (roughly 1.5km, one hour out and back), you have to be reasonably steady on your feet (unless you don't mind getting wet). It requires walking planks, navigating and hopping dozens of pebbles and boulders, using

(continues on p142)

READY FOR YOUR CLOSEUP?

Iceland has become a Hollywood darling for location shooting due to its immense, alien beauty and the 20% production rebate. Try to spot Iceland in *Tomb Raider* (2001), *Die Another Day* (2002), *Batman Begins* (2005), *Flags of Our Fathers* (2006), *Prometheus* (2012), *Oblivion* (2013), *Thor: The Dark World* (2013), *Star Trek: Into Darkness* (2013), *The Secret Life of Walter Mitty* (2013), *Captain America* (2016), *Justice League* (2017) and HBO's *Game of Thrones*. Christopher Nolan's *Interstellar* (2014) and *The Odyssey* (2026) and Star Wars installments *The Force Awakens* (2015) and *Rogue One* (2016) were also shot here.

Musicians shoot videos here, too. Don't miss Sigur Rós' concert film *Heima* (2007), starring the Icelandic people and their roaring falls. Bon Iver's 2011 'Holocene' is six minutes of bliss.

 EATING IN HVOLSVÖLLUR & HELLA: FOOD TRUCKS & PIZZA

Food Truck Company: Mexican food? In a food truck next to the supermarket in Hvolsvöllur? Yep! Smoothies and juices, too. *hours vary* €€

Gallerí Pizza: The Hvolsvöllur pizzeria is a busy, no-frills place with vinyl booths and 20 different pies. Burgers, too. *11.30am-9pm* €€

Hekla Street Food: Hella's cheap-and-cheerful food truck for fish and chips and burgers. *5.30-8pm Wed-Mon* €€

American School Bus Cafe: Full menu of coffees and teas, with baked treats and a few sandwiches. Yes, in a school bus in Hella. *8am-7pm* €€

DRIVING TOUR

South Coast Highlights

Driving the Ring Road, many of Iceland's most famous sites are right there beside you, as if the route was designed to blow your mind. Waterfalls Seljalandsfoss and Skógarfoss, and glacial lagoon Jökulsárlón – you can spot them all from the road. So instead of pointing out the obvious, this road trip offers some short and worthwhile detours on the drive from Hella to Höfn, passing Vík midway.

❶ Caves of Hella
This 50m-long human-made cave (p142) is up to 11m below the soil at its deepest point. Dating back 700 to 1100 years, five ancient chimneys and various carvings remain intact, supposedly made by monks.

The Drive Off the Ring Road, follow Rte 242 and signs to a car park with a 1.8km walking trail to Seljavallalaug pool.

❷ Seljavallalaug
Seljavallalaug, the country's oldest swimming pool, owes its stunning location between a steep mountain and a river to practical reasons: here it can be warmed with runoff from a small hot spring.

The Drive From the Ring Road, follow Rte 221 to the car park and tour base camp. Guides will walk 800m with you to reach the foot of the Sólheimajökull glacier.

❸ Sólheimajökull
One of the easiest glaciers to reach is Sólheimajökull (p150). This icy outlet glacier unfurls from the main Mýrdalsjökull ice cap and is a favourite spot for glacial walks and ice climbing.

To walk on the glacier you should go with any of the area's tour operators; tours depart from the car park.

Fjaðrárgljúfur

The Drive The Fjaðrárgljúfur canyon is not far west of Klaustur (Kirkjubæjarklaustur), 3km north of the Ring Road via Rte 206.

④ Fjaðrárgljúfur

The darkly picturesque canyon of Fjaðrárgljúfur (p151), carved out by the river Fjaðrá, has been well and truly discovered, thanks to Instagrammers and one Justin Bieber (who filmed a music video here). A thrilling walking trail follows its southern edge for a couple of kilometres.

The Drive Fuel up in Kirkjubæjarklaustur, the only settlement for the next 200km. Tours to Ingólfshöfði depart from Fagurhólsmýri by the Ring Road.

⑤ Cape Ingólfshöfði

Cape Ingólfshöfði has a spectacular sandy beach and a rich history chronicling the arrival of Iceland's first settlers. Go on a From Coast to Mountains (p169, p173) tour in the back of a large wagon with fascinating Einar. In summer you might even see puffins.

The Drive On the Ring Road, 12km west of Jökulsárlón, turn at the signpost 'Fjallsárlón' and drive about 2km until reaching the car park.

⑥ Fjallsárlón

The massive Fjállsárlón (p178) lagoon is less crowded than its famous neighbour Jökulsárlón (p180). It has only one cafe and one boating operator, which offers 45-minute excursions.

The drive Continue on the Ring Road, past the one-lane bridge over Jökulsárlón's outlet, to the only sizable town in southeast Iceland.

⑦ Höfn

Browse restaurant menus in Höfn (p185), arguably Iceland's seafood capital. Reserve a table at Otto Matur & Drykkur for a memorable meal or drop by Hafnarbúðin, best known for its langoustine baguette.

THE EDDAS

The medieval monastery at **Oddi**, in Rangárvellir, 8km south of Hella on Rte 266, was the source of the Norse Eddas, the most important surviving books of Viking poetry. The *Prose Edda* was written by poet and historian Snorri Sturluson (p204) around 1222. It was intended to be a textbook for poets, with detailed descriptions of the language and meters used by *skalds* (court poets). Its epic poem 'Gylfaginning' reveals Norse creation myths and stories about the gods and Ragnarök.

The *Poetic Edda* was written later in the 13th century by Sæmundur Sigfússon. It's a compilation of works by unknown poets, some predating Iceland's settlement. A favourite is the one about giant Thrym stealing Þór's hammer and demanding goddess Freyja in marriage for its return.

Today Oddi is a church and farmsteads.

Caves of Hella

(continued from p139)

precarious ropes (optional) and traversing walls with chains. Those with less balance and fitness may find it easier to wear rubber boots and just walk through the river at times. It's about 10km north of Gljúfrabúi with a parking area.

Iceland's Oldest Turf House
Travel back in time at Keldur

About 5km west of Hvolsvöllur, unsurfaced Rte 264 winds about 8km north along the Rangárvellir valley to the medieval turf-roofed farm at **Keldur** *(thjodminjasafn.is; adult/child 2500kr/free)*, which dates to the late 12th century. This historic settlement once belonged to Ingjaldur Höskuldsson, a character in *Njál's Saga*. The structure is managed by the National Museum and has interesting historical exhibits and a pastoral setting. It's only open to visitors during the summer, but you can see their exteriors all year.

Tour the Caves of Hella
Four caves, many mysteries

As the Ring Road approaches Hella from the west, you'll see the turnoff to **Caves of Hella** where you can go on a guided tour of four of 12 human-made caves, including one believed to have been a chapel. The caves are sparsely decorated with crosses and ancient wall carvings, so the real highlight is the stories the guide tells. Add some extra thrills afterwards by driving five minutes south on Rte 25 to the cascades at **Ægissíðufoss**.

 EATING ON THE RING ROAD: BEST ICE CREAM

Bongó, Hveragerði: A cute, small shop with delicious ice cream inside the Greenhouse Hotel and food hall. *3-9.30pm Wed-Sun* €

Ísbúð Huppu, Selfoss: Tasty ice cream and even better milkshakes. Take a number and wait to be called. *2-11pm Mon-Fri, from noon Sat & Sun* €

Groovís, Selfoss: If there's one thing that makes ice cream better, it's doughnuts. Go here for both, in the centre of the new old Selfoss. *1-10pm* €

Valdís, Hvolsvöllur: Branch of the beloved ice cream shop from Reykjavík, choc full of exotic flavours. *noon-10pm Mon-Fri, from 10am Sat & Sun* €

Beyond
Hvolsvöllur

Roam deep into the awe-inspiring Highlands, out to the puffin-rich Vestmannaeyjar islands or simply marvel at waterfalls and history in Skógar.

This area is about making a little extra effort. Adventure inland to the magnificent Highlands' Fjallabak Nature Reserve, home to ancient rhyolite hills and a hot springs valley at Landmannalaugar. Ford rivers to reach Þórsmörk, a green valley surrounded by volcanoes. Connect the two on one of Iceland's most well-known multiday hikes: Laugavegurinn. Escape offshore by ferry to a puffin-filled island in Vestmannaeyjar, whose fate was forever changed when a volcano erupted in 1973.

On the other hand, you can easily remain on the Ring Road, skirting the base of hulking Eyjafjallajökull, to reach Skógar. You'll see enormous Skógafoss from the road, can hike to hidden Kvernufoss or climb to see two dozen waterfalls along the ambitious Fimmvörðuháls trail into Þórsmörk.

Places
Southern Highlands p143
Vestmannaeyjar p147
Skógar p149

GETTING AROUND

Strætó bus 51 from Reykjavík stops in Skógar. The ferry to Heimaey *(herjolfur.is)* in Vestmannaeyjar departs from Landeyjahöfn (35 minutes), which is served by bus 52, or, in rough weather, Þorlákshöfn (three hours). Flights to the island sometimes function in winter from Reykjavík. Check Iceland Air or Norlandair.

Trex *(trex.is)* and Reykjavík Excursions *(re.is)* have Highland Buses (p136) from Reykjavík, Hella and Hvolsvöllur (where it is best to get on if travelling from Vík).

Southern Highlands
DISTANCE FROM HVOLLSVÖLLUR: VARIES

Hiking in verdant Þórsmörk

Named after the Norse god Thor (Þór), the nature reserve **Þórsmörk** is a hiker's paradise, a verdant realm clasped by snowcapped mountain ridges, wildflower-filled valleys, curling gorges, icy rivers and three looming glaciers (Tindfjallajökull, Eyjafjallajökull and Mýrdalsjökull). It's easier to get to than Landmannalaugar – but you'll still need a ride.

You'll find hiking ideas online *(fi.is)* and get trail maps at base camps. Take the **Valahnúkur Circle** for a quick aerial view; it's about a 2½-hour round-trip from base camp **Húsadalur – Volcano Huts** *(volcanotrails.com)*. You'll see two glaciers, braided glacial rivers and endless moss-covered mountains.

Tindfjöll Circle is a longer loop, and the most popular of the 'short hikes' in the area. The trek takes three to six hours depending on your base camp – it's quickest from **Básar** *(utivist.is)* and **Langidalur** (Skagfjörðsskáli; *fi.is*). It will take you along the **Tindfjöll** gorge and ridge, with sweeping valley views. Parts of the trail are narrow with steep drop-offs.

Stakkholtsgjá Canyon is a short but astounding trek along the riverbed of a narrow canyon with moss-covered walls and a dramatic twisting gorge with a hidden waterfall. It's about a 1½-hour round-trip, but it's hard to get there without a private

(continues on p146)

HIKING TOUR

Landmannalaugar to Þórsmörk

The two- to five-day hike from Landmannalaugar to Þórsmörk – commonly known as Laugavegurinn – is where backpackers earn their stripes in Iceland. The word Laugavegurinn means 'Hot Spring Road', and it is easy to understand why. Expect wildly coloured mountains, glacier rivers and the glaciers themselves. It is the most popular hike in Iceland and the infrastructure is sound, with carefully positioned huts along the zigzagging 55km route. Book huts months in advance *(fi.is)*, or camp.

❶ Landmannalaugar

From Landmannalaugar (p146) it's a relatively easy start to your adventure, 12km (four to five hours) to the first hut, or you could combine stops 1 and 2 in one day, arriving in Álftavatn after a full eight to 10 hours of hiking. You'll need to fill up on fresh water in Landmannalaugar, as there's no source until you reach the first hut.

The Walk The route passes the boiling earth at Stórihver and sweeping fields of glittering obsidian. To extend the walk, take the quieter route via Skalli; the information hut in Landmannalaugar has a handout.

❷ Hrafntinnusker

At Hrafntinnusker, try a couple of short local hikes without your pack before setting off. There are views at Söðull (20 minutes return) and Reykjafjöll (one hour return), and a hidden geothermal area behind the ice caves (three hours return); ask the warden for walking tips.

The Walk Walking the 12km (four to five hours) to Álftavatn you'll see the looming ice caps of

Hiking Laugavegurinn

Tindafjallajökull, Mýrdalsjökull and the infamous Eyjafjallajökull.

❸ Álftavatn

Two huts here, both with drinking water and mattresses, hold 72 people in total. Opening coincides with the opening of local F roads (from early to late June, depending on the weather), making the hut accessible with a 4WD. It closes in mid-September.

The Walk To reach Emstrur (15km, six to seven hours), you'll need to ford at least one large stream.

❹ Emstrur-Botnar

Emstrur has 60 beds divided across three huts on barren ground. Don't miss the detour to spectacular Markarfljótsgljúfur – a gigantic multihued canyon. It's well marked from Emstrur, and takes about an hour to reach (you can come back the same way).

The Walk It's a 15km (six- to seven-hour) relatively flat walk to Þórsmörk. If you're not planning on staying in Þórsmörk, you need to arrive before the last bus leaves in the afternoon/evening.

❺ Þórsmörk

Barrenness turns to brilliantly verdant lands dotted with lush Arctic flowers in Þórsmörk (p143): your reward for the final steps.

The Walk From Þórsmörk, this optional extension hike (24km, eight to 10 hours) starts with lush green mountains until, suddenly, you are walking on snow. The path goes between two glaciers, passing lava from a 2010 eruption.

❻ Extension to Skógar

You'll reach Skógar after the truly awesome Fimmvörðuháls (p149; *fimmvorduhals.is*) hike. The final part is known as the waterfall way, along the canyon of Skógá river. Complete it within a day or overnight at the huts of Baldvinsskáli and Fimmvörðuskáli halfway.

Eldfell

GETTING TO ÞÓRSMÖRK & LANDMANNALAUGAR

You can't drive all the way into Þórsmörk with a rental vehicle. A 4WD with excellent clearance can plough down Rte F249 to the crossroads for Húsadalur and Básar at gushing, dangerous Krossá river. Leave your vehicle and walk via a seasonal footbridge or go by bus. Volcano Huts *(volcanotrails. com)* has a bus. Trex and Reykjavík Excursions have Highland Buses (p136) to Þórsmörk and Landmannalaugar.

Landmannalaugar tracks open mid- to late June *(check road. is)*. Experienced drivers with an appropriate, insured 4WD (ask the rental company) can drive F208 from the north just beyond Highland Center Hrauneyjar (p337), or F225 or F208 from the south. Reserve parking well ahead *(parka.is; 1200kr)*. Pre-booking is required 20 June to 14 September from 9am to 4pm. Other times, a reservation is not needed, but the fee must be paid.

(continued from p143)

tour; try to negotiate a ride with the daily amphibious buses heading in the same direction.

Base camps and their lodging are generally open June to September, with huts and camping spots. It's crucial to book hut space in advance and, in most cases, bring your own sleeping bag. Wild camping is strictly forbidden.

Multicoloured hills and hot springs in Landmannalaugar

Mind-blowing multihued mountains, soothing hot springs, rambling lava flows and clear-blue lakes make **Landmannalaugar** one of Iceland's most unique destinations, and a must for explorers of the interior. Part of the magnificent **Fjallabak Nature Reserve**, Landmannalaugar (600m above sea level) includes the largest geothermal field in Iceland outside the Grímsvötn caldera in Vatnajökull National Park (p168). Its many-coloured peaks are made of rhyolite – a mineral-filled lava that cooled unusually slowly, causing those intense pigments.

The area is the official starting point for the famous Laugavegurinn hike (p144), and you can make some excellent day hikes, too (eg to **Stútur** crater, **Frostastaðavatn** and **Ljótipollur**, an incredible magenta crater filled with bright-blue water).

Follow the wooden boardwalk just 200m from the Landmannalaugar info hut, and you'll find a steaming river and

 EATING & DRINKING IN HEIMAEY: OUR PICKS

Næs: Delicious Icelandic fare in a bistro headed by chef Gísli Matt Auðunsson (p128); creativity meets comfort food. *11.30am-8.30pm* €€

Pítsugerðin: Top spot for a pizza. All pies are baked in a wood-burning oven. Classic styles, plus a vegan pizza. *noon-9pm* €€

Gott: Fresh fusion food, using organic, healthy ingredients in a wood-floored dining room with coloured chairs. *11.30am-9pm* €€

Brothers Brewery: Take a tour and have a beer flight (IPA, ale, stout) at this taproom at an ambitious brewery. *noon-7pm Sun-Tue, to midnight Wed-Sat*

natural pool filled with bathers. Both hot and cold water flow from beneath Laugahraun and combine to form an ideal warm bath. 'Landmannalaugar' could be interpreted as the 'People's Pools'...and here they are.

Landmannalaugar Hut & Camping Complex (*fi.is*) also has a bare-bones shop, **Mountain Mall** *(facebook.com/mountainmall)*. If you drive, you must reserve parking in advance in summer.

Vestmannaeyjar DISTANCE FROM HVOLLSVÖLLUR: 1HR

Find puffin paradise

A visit to Vestmannaeyjar is very much a wander, from one cliff to another, like a puffin. The archipelago is home to the world's largest Atlantic puffin colony. Every summer, puffins arrive at their seaside burrows at Heimaey's cape **Stórhöfði**, **Heimaklettur** and elsewhere to do a little dance, make a little love.

Puffin season runs April to August (prime for baby puffins). The best lookout is on Stórhöfði, the rocky peninsula at Heimaey's southern end topped by **Stórhöfðaviti** lighthouse. You can find a small birdwatching hut (especially helpful when weather is rough) about halfway up the hill; go from the first turnout on the right, marked with a hiking sign, to the end of a trail across sheep pasture. **Kervíkurfjall** and **Stakkabót** are also good places for puffin viewing.

Pick up a good island map at **Eymundsson** bookshop or the Beluga Whale Sanctuary (p148).

Volcanic adventure and the aftermath

The 221m-high volcanic red cone, **Eldfell**, appeared from nowhere in the early hours of 23 January 1973 (p148). Heat from the volcano provided Heimaey with geothermal energy from 1976 to 1985, and today the ground is still hot enough in places to bake bread or char wood. From town, it's a 1.5km hike to the top of Eldfell, up the collapsed northern wall of the crater. Stick to the path, to help prevent erosion.

Explore Mars-like landscape **Eldfellshraun** on the east of the Island. You can criss-cross it on a maze of otherworldly hiking tracks that run down to the **Skansinn** fort and all around the bulge of the raw, red eastern coast where a fish farm is being constructed. Here you'll find small black-stone beaches, the **Gaujulundur** lava garden and a lighthouse.

You'll see twisted lava formations close to some houses: don't miss the fantastic **Eldheimar** on the edge of the lava. It's a museum revolving around one house excavated from 50m of pumice. It was once home to Gerður Sigurðardóttir and Guðni Ólafsson, their two children and baby. During the eruption the family was forced to leave in the middle of the night with only time to grab one item, a baby bottle.

Helgafell (226m) erupted 5000 years ago. Its cinders are grassed over today, and you can scramble up here without much difficulty from the football pitch on the road to the airport.

BEST PUFFIN, WHALE & VOLCANO TOURS

Ribsafari: See the millions of puffins that nest here every year from a speed-boat. Sometimes you can spot orcas, too. *(ribsafari.is)*

Eyjatours: Combine puffin spotting with a trip to Eldfell volcano and the farmstead where the island's first Viking family settled. *(eyjatours.com)*

Kayak & Puffins: Kayak across the Klettsvík bay looking for puffins, eider ducks and more on rugged cliffs. *(instagram.com/kayakandpuffins/?hl=en)*

Volcano ATV: ATV trips tour the island. *(volcanoatv.is)*

Lyngfell: Horse rides along black-sand beaches and along the cliffs when the wind is low. *(facebook.com/lyngfell)*

Eyjascooter Tours: Rugged e-scooters zip you around the island. *(eyjascootertour.com)*

Viking Tours: Combos of boat, ATV and bus tours. *(vikingtours.is)*

HEIMAEY'S VOLCANIC HISTORY

At 1.45am on 23 January 1973 a mighty explosion blasted through the winter's night as a 1.5km-long volcanic fissure split the eastern side of the island. The eruption area gradually concentrated into a crater cone, **Eldfell** (p147), which fountained lava and ash into the sky.

Normally the fishing boats would have been at sea, but the previous afternoon a gale had prevented them from sailing. Now calm, the harbourful of boats evacuated most of the island's 5273 inhabitants to the mainland. Incredibly, there was just a single fatality (from toxic gases).

Over the next five months more than 30 million tonnes of lava poured over Heimaey, destroying 360 houses. One-third of the town was buried beneath the lava, and the island increased in size by 2.5 sq km.

Visit a beluga whale sanctuary

Meet Little Grey and Little White. In 2019, this pair of beluga whales that previously lived at an aquarium in China came, via plane, to Vestmannaeyjar for showbiz retirement. Their new home is a 32,000-sq-metre sea pen at the pristine creek called Klettsvík, but they are frequently brought inside the **Beluga Whale Sanctuary** *(belugasanctuary.sealifetrust.org; adult/child 3560/2610, under 6yr free)* near the harbour. The aquarium is also an informal bird hospital, where adorable baby puffins gather energy for life ahead.

Discover a 15th-century fort

Find your way to 15th-century fort Skansinn (p147), a lovely green area by the sea. The oldest structure on the island, Skansinn was built to defend the harbour (not too successfully – when Algerian pirates arrived in 1627 they simply landed on the other side of the island).

In the 1840s an island woman, Sólveig, went abroad to be trained as a midwife. Tiny wooden house **Landlyst** was Sólveig's maternity hospital (and is the second-oldest building on the island). Today it contains a small display of her equipment. **Stafkirkjan** is a reconstruction of a medieval wooden stave church.

EATING ON RTE 1 SOUTH OF EYJAFJALLAJÖKULL: OUR PICKS

Gamla Fjósið: In a former cowshed, this charming eatery's focus is on farm-fresh and grass-fed meaty mains, from burgers to spicy meat stew. *11.30am-9pm* €€

Faxi Bakery: Bodacious bagels and baked goods plus sandwiches and soups and top espresso coffees, next to Eyjafjallajökull info area. *8am-6pm* €

Umi Restaurant: In the hotel of the same name, put on the ritz with Icelandic-Japanese fusion on the edge of a river- and ocean-adjacent plateau. *6.30-10pm* €€€

Skálakot: Reserve ahead for a meal (even breakfast!) at the restaurant at this horse farm and high-end lodge. *8-10am, noon-2.30pm & 6-9.30pm* €€€

Skógafoss

WHAT'S THE NATIONAL FESTIVAL?

The blow-out three-day **Þjóðhátíð** is the country's biggest outdoor festival. Held at Herjólfsdalur festival ground in the Vestmannaeyjar islands over the first weekend in August, it involves music, dancing, fireworks, a big bonfire, gallons of alcohol and a light display with an eruption of red torches, a nod to Heimaey's volcanoes. Upwards of 17,000 attend.

Historically, the festival was first celebrated when bad weather prevented Vestmannaeyjar people from joining the mainland celebrations of Iceland's first constitution (1 August 1874). The islanders held their own festival a month later, and it's been an annual tradition ever since.

Extra flights run from Reykjavík, but you must book transport and accommodation months in advance.

Climb for puffins and views

Get some vigorous hikes in to check out puffins and get incredible views. You can hike up the mountain from grassy **Herjólfsdalur**. The top of the craggy precipice **Stóraklif** is an intense 30-minute climb from behind the N1 petrol station at the harbour. As it gets steeper you're 'assisted' by ropes and chains (but don't trust them completely). Further out on the pier, Heimaklettur (p147) is more perilous, with wild rickety ladders. Both are top puffin-breeding grounds. When rainy, slick or windy, neither is a good idea.

Skógar

DISTANCE FROM HVOLLSVÖLLUR: **40MIN**

Chase waterfalls at Skógafoss and Kvernufoss

Skógafoss *(parking 1000kr)* is another immediate sight on the Ring Road. The 62m-high waterfall topples over a rocky cliff at the western edge of little tourist town Skógar in dramatic style. Climb the steep staircase alongside for giddy views, or walk to the foot of the falls, shrouded in sheets of mist and rainbows. Legend has it that a settler named Þrasi hid a chest of gold behind Skógafoss. The top of the waterfall is the start of the dramatic Fimmvörðuháls trek. If you're not up for that much of a hike, chase the two dozen or so waterfalls you'll find along the 8km stretch of the Skógá River that leads to Skógafoss.

It's also worth the 15-minute walk to delightful **Kvernufoss** *(parking 750kr)*, a lesser-known, sequestered 20m waterfall that you can walk behind. The short trail to it starts at the far east of the Skógar Folk Museum car park.

Fimmvörðuháls hike into the Highlands

The epic **Fimmvörðuháls** *(fimmvorduhals.is)* trail – named for a pass between two brooding glaciers – dazzles the eye with a parade of wild inland vistas. Linking Skógar and Þórsmörk,

(continues on p152)

Sólheimajökull

TOP EXPERIENCE

Katla Geopark

Katla is one of Iceland's fiercest and most striking volcanoes. It's surrounded by a UNESCO World Heritage geopark that accounts for nearly 10% of the land in Iceland. Starting from Hvollsvollür in the west and spanning beyond Vík and Kirkjubæjarklaustur to Skeiðarársandur, it encompasses volcanoes, glaciers, ice caves and more...all excuses to get out of the car and play.

DON'T MISS

- Katla Geopark Visitor Center in Vík (p155)
- Sólheimajökull
- Katla Ice Cave
- Fjaðrárgljúfur
- Lakagígar
- Science expeditions

Go Glacier Hiking

Spend a half-day hiking on **Sólheimajökull**, a massive ice tongue coming off Iceland's fourth-largest glacier **Mýrdalsjökull** and emerging between the volcanoes Katla and Eyjafjallajökull. It's a rare spot for sweeping views from a glacier. At about 8km long and 1.6km wide, with its shades of white, blue and black, this is one of the most popular spots in Iceland for glacier hiking.

These hikes are suitable for beginners and available year-round, but you must go with a guide, as the crevasses and

PRACTICALITIES
- katlageopark.com
- free
- 24hr

dangers are real. Rte 221 leads 4.2km off the Ring Road to a small car park and the **Arcanum base camp** *(parking 1000kr)*. Tour leaders will walk you 800m across a field of ash and sand from the Eyjafjallajökull volcanic eruption to the ice. The glacier itself is retreating, and hiking it offers a fascinating geology lesson.

Journey into an Ice Cave

Head underground into the **Katla Ice Cave** to see black ash from centuries of eruptions encased in ice. Notice the older blue ice layers and trapped air bubbles as you move through this space beneath an offshoot of Mýrdalsjökull. The black-striped layers of ice you see are key for determining the age of glaciers like this one. A few steps have been carved into the ice to make it easier to navigate. Otherwise, this ice cave remains in its natural state. Tours depart from Vík or Reykjavík.

Snowmobile on a Glacier

Go snowmobiling on top of Mýrdalsjökull, the icecap that tops Katla, Iceland's largest volcano. It's Iceland's southernmost glacier and an estimated 250m deep. Full-day tours start with a briefing and include a monster truck ride to the snowmobile site. This experience has to be booked with a tour company and cannot be done independently. You will need a driver's license to drive a snowmobile. Tour operators provide thermal suits and helmets.

Hike a Magical Canyon

There's nothing like walking through a lush green fairy tale, and there may be no more fairy-tale place for a hike than **Fjaðrárgljúfur** canyon, made early-Insta-famous by Justin Bieber's video. The canyon's name translates to 'feather', and as the crystal-clear Fjaðrá river twists through what looks like a hand-carved piece of Earth, you can see why.

Marvel at a Crater Row

It's almost impossible to comprehend the immensity of the Laki eruptions, one of the most catastrophic volcanic events in human history. Nowadays the lava fields around **Lakagígar** belie the apocalypse that spawned it some 235 years ago. Its black, twisted lava formations are overgrown with soft green moss. It's a fascinating place to visit, and one that sees relatively few visitors.

Help Do Science in the Park

A new initiative makes it possible to join expeditions in the Geopark furthering scientific research. Year-round, you can help map glaciers and the coastline of black-sand beaches. And for part of the year you can head to lesser-visited and retreating **Tindfjallajökull**. Trips are for two to six people – check the Geopark's website for what trips are available: some are day trips, others last 12 days, and prices vary accordingly.

TOP TIPS

- Glacier hikes operate year-round, but you should never do this on your own.
- Professional guides know the terrain and provide necessary safety equipment, such as crampons and helmets.
- Opt for a warm inner layer and a waterproof outer layer of clothing.
- Choose sturdy shoes to which you can easily attach crampons.
- Specially modified trucks are the main way to access these areas.
- Batteries drain faster in cold temperatures. Bring a power bank for phones and cameras.
- Neighbouring parks are the Skaftafell portion of Vatnajökull National Park *(vjp.is)* to the east and Fjallabak Nature Reserve to the northwest.

Skógar Museum

> ### WINTER'S BRIGHT SIDE
>
> There's a silver lining to visiting Iceland during winter when the darkness can stretch for as long as 19 hours a day. Long nights like these are when the aurora borealis emerges, dancing across the sky in shades of green, red and pink. Look for viewing spots with minimal light pollution, like Þingvellir National Park or Dyrhólaey. Some tours drive the countryside looking for the Northern Lights and some hotels offer a wake-up service when they're spotted.
>
> Also, ice caves (p157) become solid and safe for visiting in the coldest months, and you can still do glacier walks – and the glaciers take on that blue hue so beloved by photographers. Even some of the Highlands can be visited with snowmobiles or super-Jeeps.

(continued from p149)

the truly awesome 23.4km hike showcases all of Iceland's varied terrain in one fell swoop. Plan for at least eight to 10 hours, including stops to rest. It's best to tackle the hike from late June to early September, but get local advice on conditions, and check *safetravel.is*. Download the 112 Iceland app and check in your location. There should be intermittent mobile-phone signal so take GPS coordinates before you set off; pack wisely; and expect all four seasons along the way (snow and whiteouts are common). If in doubt, go with a guide, who will help negotiate two treacherous passes.

You have to book well in advance to get space in the huts **Baldvinsskáli** *(fi.is)* or **Fimmvörðuskáli** *(utivist.is)*. The latter is managed by Útivist, who offers hiking tours.

Go back in time at Skógar Museum

Make the time to visit wonderful **Skógar Museum** *(skogasafn .is; adult/child 2750/free)*, which covers all aspects of Icelandic life from turf houses to tech. The vast collection was put together by Þórður Tómasson over roughly 75 years. He retired as the museum's curator at the age of 92, but published his last book on local folklore in 2021, a year before passing away at the age of 101. You can book a guided tour in advance.

EATING & DRINKING IN SKÓGAR: OUR PICKS

Mia's Country Van: Cheerful food truck specialising in fish and chips, perfect for a road-trip lunch with remoulade, lemon or sweet chili sauce. *hours vary* €€

Freya Café: Pretty cafe inside Skógar Museum serving up tasty salads, Icelandic soups and pricier mains, plus coffees and desserts. *9am-6pm* €€

Skógafoss Bistro-Bar: The best thing about this hotel restaurant with a varied menu and beer selection is its views of Skógafoss. *noon-9pm* €€

Heimamenn Cafe & Minimart: This small cafe serves fish and chips, veggie lasagna, soup and cakes, 2km west of Skógar. Has a teeny mini-mart. *11.30am-4pm* €€

Vík

BLACK-SAND BEACHES | TEETERING PUFFINS | ADVENTURE TOURS

Walk the streets of the welcoming little community of Vík (aka Vík í Mýrdal) and try to guess how many people live here by the volume of traffic. Three thousand? On paper, the population is just shy of 640. Counting the commercial activity from tourism, it is the de facto booming capital for a very beautiful portion of the South Coast. Iceland's southernmost town, it's also the rainiest, but that doesn't stop the madhouse atmosphere in summer, when every room within 100km seems to be booked solid.

The beautiful basalt beach Reynisfjara and its puffin cliffs lie just to the west. There's also the rocky plateau Dyrhólaey and the volcanoes running from Skógar to Jökulsárlón glacier lagoon and beyond. Along the coast, white-capped waves wash up on black sands and the cliffs glow green from all that rain. Put simply, it's pretty special.

Get Magnificent Views from a Headland

Thrilling Dyrhólaey rock formations

Viewers of the 2021 dystopian Netflix series *Katla* can probably guess the colour of the beach on Iceland's southern tip: black as magmatic rock from the chambers of the Earth.

The sandy shore is dramatic from above and below, not the least for the crashing waves. For the bird's-eye view – and maybe a look at puffins – **Dyrhólaey** *(parking 750kr),* pronounced *deer-*lay, rises dramatically from the surrounding plain 10km west of Vík, with crashing black-sand beaches and amazing views. It's best known for its soaring cliffs, coated in bright green in certain seasons, snowy white in others, and a rock arch that's large enough for a boat to pass through in calm seas. The best view of the archway is from Reynisfjara along the coast. There are two parking areas, one on the top of the cliff near the Dyrhólaey Lighthouse and one at the base.

According to *Njál's Saga* (p138), the most dramatic in medieval literary genres, the sole survivor of the fire that wiped out Njál's clan – a man named Kári – had his farm here. Another

GETTING AROUND

Vík is a major stop for the Reykjavík–Höfn Strætó bus 51. Buses stop at the N1 petrol station in the centre of town on Austurvegur/Rte 1.

Vík is an easy self-drive destination. The Ring Road (Rte 1) runs right through the centre; it's 2¼ hours from Reykjavík by car. Just beware high winds and make sure you open your car door so it won't be torn off.

☑ TOP TIP

Reynisfjara is a striking but dangerous beach where deadly sneaker waves can come in at any time. They're called sneaker waves because they sneak up on people (!) and sweep them away (this happens pretty regularly). This is no place for swimming, long walks or selfies with your back to the water.

Vík SOUTHWEST ICELAND & THE GOLDEN CIRCLE

THE GUIDE

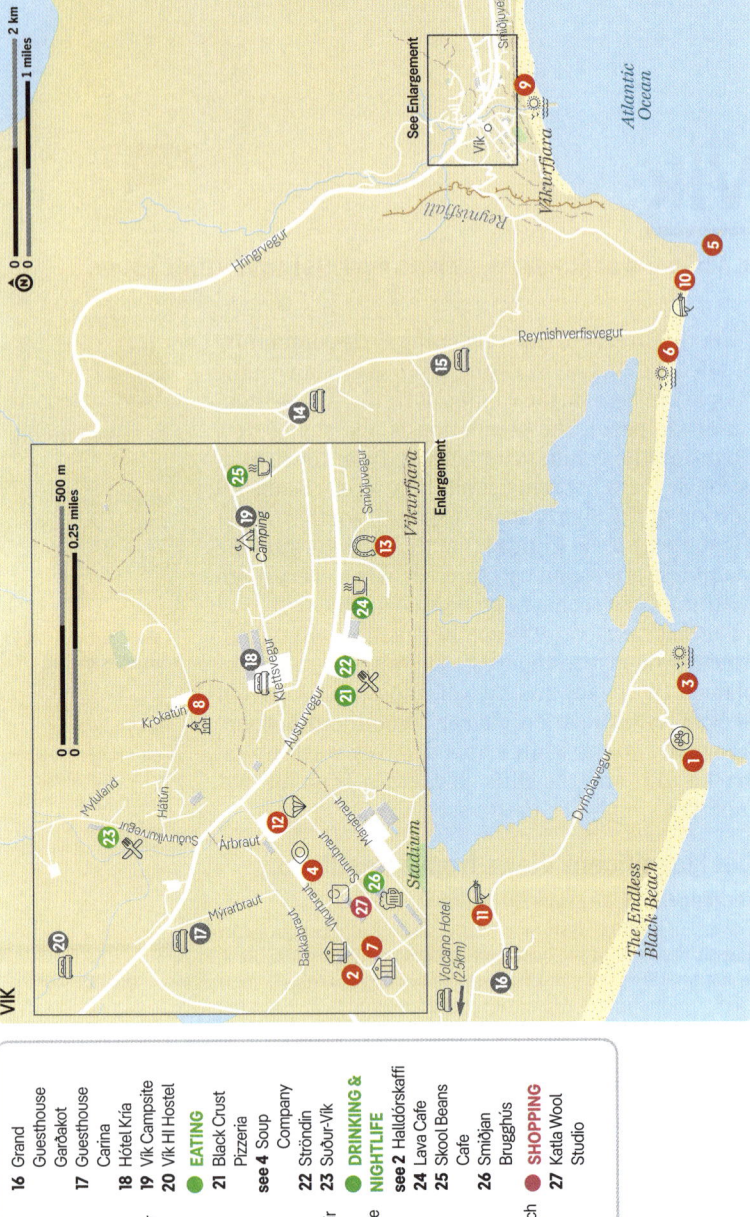

Vík

SIGHTS
1. Dyrhólaey
2. Katla Visitor Center
3. Kirkjufjara
4. Lava Show
5. Reynisdrangar
6. Reynisfjara
7. Skaftfellingur Museum
8. Vík í Mýrdal Church
9. Víkurfjara

ACTIVITIES
10. Hálsanefshellir
11. Loftsalahellir
12. True Adventure
13. Vík Horse Adventure
see 12 Zipline Iceland

SLEEPING
14. Barn
see 14 Black Beach Suites
15. Gistiheimilið Reynir
16. Grand Guesthouse Garðakot
17. Guesthouse Carina
18. Hótel Kría
19. Vík Campsite
20. Vík HI Hostel

EATING
21. Black Crust Pizzeria
see 4 Soup Company
22. Ströndin
23. Suður-Vík

DRINKING & NIGHTLIFE
see 2 Halldórskaffi
24. Lava Cafe
25. Skool Beans Cafe
26. Smiðjan Brugghús

SHOPPING
27. Katla Wool Studio

Viking Age connection is the cave **Loftsalahellir**, reached by a track just before the causeway to Dyrhólaey, which was used for council meetings in Saga times.

A hiking trail connects the top of Dyrhólaey with the black sands of **Kirkjufjara**.

The islet is a nature reserve that's rich in birdlife; over the nesting season (from 1 May to 25 June) the road is closed overnight, from 7pm to 9am.

Which Way to the Beach?
Famed Reynisfjara black-sand beach

On the western side of Reynisfjall, the high ridge above Vík, Rte 215 leads 5km down to the famed black-sand beach **Reynisfjara** *(parking 1000kr).* Braving weather and crowds you'll be rewarded with a broad sweep of beach backed by an incredible stack of basalt columns that look like a magical church organ, and outstanding views west to Dyrhólaey. The cliffs are pocked with caves like **Hálsanefshellir** formed from twisted basalt, and puffins belly-flop into the crashing sea during summer.

Immediately offshore you'll see the towering **Reynisdrangar** sea stacks. Tradition says they are the mast of a ship that trolls were stealing when they got caught in the sun. A bracing walk up from Vík's western end takes you to the top of Reynisfjall (340m), which offers superb views.

At all times watch for rogue waves: people are regularly swept away.

Ride Horses on a Black-Sand Beach
Calm beach for fantastic rides

To ride horses along a black-sand beach without the threat of being washed away by a terrifying sneaker wave, head to the beach nearest to Vík, called **Víkurfjara**. This beach is calmer than Reynisfjara, making it possible to ride horses here while taking in sweeping views of the Reynisdrangar rock formation. **Vík Horse Adventure** *(facebook.com/vikhorseadventure; rides from 15,200kr)* makes it easy for just about anyone to tour this area with a four-legged guide.

BEST OUTINGS IN VÍK

While Reynisfjara and Dyrhólaey may get all the press, there's more to do in little Vík.

Víkurkirkja: Walk to the idyllic white church above town for sweeping ocean views.

Katla Geopark Visitor Center: In a tin-clad house built in Vestmannaeyjar in 1831 and moved to Vík in 1895. With displays on Katwla Geopark, the tourist office with good maps, Halldórskaffi (p156) and a shop. *(kotlusetur.is; katlageopark.com)*

Skaftfellingur Museum: Contains a 100-year-old ship and information about the Icelanders who relied on it.

Lava Show: Book ahead to see the hot, melted rocks show, also located in the Old Harbour of Reykjavík. *(lavashow.com/vik)*

EATING IN VÍK: OUR PICKS

Suður-Vík: The friendly ambience, in a warmly lit building, helps elevate this restaurant beyond its competition. Food is Icelandic hearty. *noon-9pm* €€€

Soup Company: It's all in the name. Slurp up creamy cauliflower soup, beef goulash and lamb stew. *11.30am-10pm* €€

Ströndin: Behind the N1 petrol station is this semi-smart wood-panelled option enjoying sea-stack vistas. Go local with lamb soup or global with burgers. *noon-11.45pm* €€

Black Crust Pizzeria: Pricey black dough or sourdough pizzas with generous and creative topping combos. *noon-9pm* €€

BEST TOUR OPERATORS

Many Reykjavík tour companies also make the drive out here.

Katlatrack: Runs tours of the area taking in local landmarks and activities on the Mýrdalsjökull glacier.

Zipline Iceland: Zip along over a brilliant green canyon.

True Adventure: Paraglide in tandem with a guide over this spectacular section of the South Iceland coast.

Vík Horse Adventure: Offers half-hour and full-hour horse rides that are suitable for beginners.

Troll Expeditions: No longer strictly local, this growing firm has all manner of tours on the South Coast.

Midgard Adventure: Loads of day tours, including super-Jeep trips, canyoning and ice climbing.

See Sweaters Being Knit
The knitwear of Katla Wool Studio

A better alternative to the massive Icewear chain store, **Katla Wool Studio** *(woolkatla.com)* is tucked into the back streets of town. In addition to mountains of Icelandic knitwear, there's a workshop where you can see the knits being made. Browse sweaters, mittens, blankets and small knit toys. Or pick out a kit for knitting or crocheting up the wool yourself.

Take to the Air
Zipline over a canyon, paraglide through the skies

Need more thrills? You can zipline over Grafargil (Grave Canyon) and epic South Icelandic valleys with **Zipline Iceland** *(zipline.is; adult/child 11,900/7900kr)*, from April to October. Getting to the zipline platform requires a short car ride as well as a hike of about 3km through beautiful scenery to the platforms for the four ziplines between 30m and 240m long. You have to weigh 30kg to 120kg and be at least eight years old.

Vík's black-sand beaches and rock structures are mesmerising just as they are. But from May to September you can take to the skies for a unique perspective on these natural wonders. Paraglide in tandem with a guide from **True Adventure**

 DRINKING IN VÍK: BREWS & COFFEES

Smiðjan Brugghús: Vík's hippest (and only) microbrewery, with craft beers on tap and windows onto the brew room. Bar food. *11.30pm-midnight*

Skool Beans Cafe: A micro roaster located inside an old yellow school bus. A great spot for creative coffees and pastries. *hours vary*

Halldórskaffi: Lively, timber-lined all-rounder popular for coffee and cake, or its crowd-pleasing menu of burgers, pizza and lamb fillet. *noon-9pm*

Lava Cafe: This bare-bones cafe behind the Krónan supermarket is most useful for a quick coffee or breakfast near the Ring Road. *8am-6pm*

Ziplining, Grafargil

(*trueadventure.is; 35,000kr*) for a panoramic view of Reynisdrangar rock stacks as you soar over crashing waves and puffin-dotted cliffs. There's no need to jump off a cliff or out of an airplane: simply hang on as the instructor begins down a slope and you'll be lifted into the air by the canopy. No experience is required. You'll spend 10 to 15 minutes in the air on a one-hour ride and use the rest of the time preparing. You'll need to be at least 12 years old and weigh 30kg to 120kg.

For both outings, you'll want to dress in layers and with a waterproof outer layer. Wear a thin hat that'll slip under your helmet as well as gloves and hiking boots.

ICE CAVES & SAFETY

The South and Southeast of Iceland, especially around Vatnajökull National Park (p168), is where professional guides, every winter, drive super-Jeeps to the foot of the glacier searching for a natural entrance. The landscape changes every summer and it is unsafe to visit these ice caves outside the frozen months from October to March when any caves become unstable. In recent years there have been deadly accidents when tours have gone outside of the safe season.

Tours depend on weather conditions and available sunlight. Tour operators include **Local Guide** (*localguide.is*) and **Arctic Adventures** (*adventures.is*).

FARMSTAY BOOKINGS

Hey Iceland (*heyiceland.is*) is a booking engine for guesthouses and cottages on farms or rural properties, and the local alternative to Booking.com and Airbnb. For more on accommodation, see p160.

Beyond Vík

Depart from Vík in either direction for iconic South Coast terrain: mountain, glacier, waterfall, ocean. To the east, you enter the austere sandar.

Places
Mælifell p158
Mýrdalssandur p158
Fjallabaksleið Nyrðri p159

GETTING AROUND

The Ring Road from Hella to Vík gets busy over summer. Traffic eases up the closer you get to Höfn. If you're heading east, fuel up in Vík because there's nothing in the big sandur until you reach Kirkjubæjarklaustur.

Vík is the last stop on the Strætó bus 51 Reykjavík–Höfn route before Kirkjubæjarklaustur.

As the Ring Road arcs east from Skógar to Vík, the haunches of the foothills rise to the glaciers, mountains and volcanoes inland, while rivers descend from mysterious gorges and course across the broad sweep of pastures to black-sand beaches and the crashing ocean.

This rural area may be dotted with farmhouses (many of which have guesthouses), but considering the volume of summertime visitors, it still feels alternately dramatic and pastoral. Then you enter the sandar (broad, flat glacial outwash plains) to the east, and all signs of life diminish.

The whole area is encompassed in Katla Geopark, which finally gives way in the east, just after Kirkjubæjarklaustur, to the even larger Vatnajökull National Park (p168).

Mælifell
DISTANCE FROM VÍK: **40MIN**

Dramatic green valley and mountain hikes

On the edge of the Mýrdalsjökull glacier, the 642m-high Mælifell ridge and the countryside around it are spectacular, if you are properly equipped and experienced. The simple, idyllic campsite and huts at **Þakgil** *(thakgil.is)*, in a green bowl among stark mountains and dramatic rock formations, makes a convenient base for exploring.

Buy groceries and food in Vík – there are no facilities in the isolated Mælifell ridge area.

You can drive with 4WD to Þakgil, 15km along an extremely rough dirt road (Rte 214) that branches off Rte 1 about 5km east of Vík; there is also a hiking trail from Vík.

Mýrdalssandur
DISTANCE FROM VÍK: **15MIN**

Austere, amazing sand flats

The vast black-lava sand flats of **Mýrdalssandur**, east of Vík, are formed from material washed out from underneath Mýrdalsjökull during Katla eruptions. This phenomenon is called a *jökulhlaup* (glacial flood; p174).

This 700-sq-km desert is bleak and desolate (some say haunted), but quite awe-inspiring. It looks lifeless, but keep your eyes open for Arctic foxes and seabirds, and it kicks off a parade of drama to the east across the world's greatest sandur, Skeiðarársandur (p173).

A mountain with a Yoda-shaped cave

Venture about 13km east of Vík and just south of Rte 1, and you'll find the small peak of **Hjörleifshöfði** (221m) rising above the black sands of Mýrdalssandur, and you can get great views towards Vestmannaeyjar. This area is now marketed as **Viking Park** *(vikingpark.is; parking from 1000kr)*.

It is believed that the hill was once surrounded by sea and was thus an island. You can still find the remains of the grave of Viking settler Hjörleifur Hróðmarsson, after whom the mountain is named. He was the brother-in-law of Iceland's first Norse settler, Ingólfur Arnarson, and was killed by his Irish slaves.

If you're a *Star Wars* fan, **Gígjagjá** is the Icelandic cave you can't miss. It's Yoda shaped! Follow the gravel road around Hjörleifshöfði, and you'll find it on the southern side.

On the other side of Rte 1, the green hill of **Hafursey** (582m) is another option for walks from Vík.

Fjallabaksleið Nyrðri

DISTANCE FROM VÍK: **2 DAYS**

Adventure behind the glacier

In high summer the Fjallabak (pronounced *fiat*-la-back; Fjallabaksleið Nyrðri) Route (F208) makes a spectacular alternative to the coast road between Hella, in southwest Iceland, and the Ring Road east of Vík, if you have a large 4WD. Its name translates as 'Behind the Mountains', and that's exactly where it goes.

Note that a 2WD vehicle wouldn't have a hope of completing even a small portion of the route, and car-hire companies prohibit taking even some 4WD vehicles on F roads (p351). Since most of the Fjallabak Rte is along rivers (or rather, in rivers!), it's not ideally suited to mountain bikes either. People attempt it, but it's not casual cycling by any stretch.

Well-established trekking company **Fjallabak** *(fjallabak.is)* leads multiday guided treks and assisted backpacking tours throughout the southern back country, with a speciality in the Fjallabak Nature Reserve (p146) area, which the Fjallabak Rte passes through. **Midgard Adventure** *(midgardadventure.is)* is another top option.

HOW TO AVOID BEING SKUA-ED

The great sandar on Iceland's southern coast is the world's largest breeding ground for great skuas (*Stercorarius skua; skúmur* in Icelandic). These large, meaty, dirty-brown birds tend to build their nests among grassy tufts in the ashy sand. You'll often see them harassing gulls into disgorging their dinner, killing and eating puffins and other little birds, or swooping down on *you* if you get too close to their nests.

Thankfully (unlike feather-brained Arctic terns), skuas will stop plaguing you if you run away from the area they're trying to defend. You can also avoid aerial strikes by wearing a hat or carrying a stick above your head.

Places We Love to Stay

€ Budget   €€ Midrange   €€€ Top End

Blue Lagoon

Silica Hotel €€€ Spa hotel with a geothermal lagoon a 10-minute walk from the Blue Lagoon.

Northern Light Inn €€€ Stylish rooms line the lava field 1km from Blue Lagoon.

Retreat Hotel €€€ Luxury resort with a private lagoon, spacious suites, yoga and Michelin-starred meals.

Keflavík   MAP p106

Guesthouse 1x6 €€ Created using driftwood and volcanic stones, where every room is unique.

Stapakot B&B €€ Well-decorated red guesthouse with shared bathrooms on a waterfront levee.

Hótel Berg €€ Boutique hotel overlooking the small harbour, with a dreamy rooftop pool.

Courtyard Reykjavik Keflavik Airport €€€ Best of the on-airport chain hotels for an easy walk to your flight.

Around Þingvellir

Skógarhólar Lodge €€ Five-bedroom lodge with access to horse-riding, with a barbecue grill and a full kitchen.

Lake Thingvellir Cottages €€ Four pine cottages with kitchenettes and views of the lake sit near the national-park entrance along Rte 36.

Ion Adventure Hotel €€€ Chic, with sustainable practices, it has a geothermal pool, spa and restaurant.

Laugarvatn

Héraðsskólinn € Unique lakeside boutique hostel (built in 1928 by Guðjón Samúelsson). Some private rooms with shared bathrooms.

Hótel Laugarvatn € Small hotel with single, double and family rooms. Offers breakfast buffet.

Björk Guesthouse €€ Central with spacious, clean rooms and helpful owners.

Geysir   MAP p118

Geysir Campground € Simple campground, a short walk from the geysers, has mountain views, laundry and a playground.

Geysir Hestar €€ Rustic guesthouse and private cottages on a working horse farm.

Hótel Geysir €€ Stylish hotel with 77 rooms a five-minute walk from its namesake geyser.

Náttúra Yurtel €€€ Mongolian yurts with electricity, private toilets, underfloor heating.

Gullfoss   MAP p118

Hótel Gullfoss €€€ Clean rooms and comfortable beds, and a restaurant, as close to the waterfall as you can get. Ask for a room facing the valley hot-pots.

Flúðir, Reykholt & Laugarás

Brekkugerdi Guesthouse, Laugarás € Welcoming, comfortable guesthouse with ensuite bathrooms in some rooms. Tucked into the trees.

Skyggnir B&B, Flúðir € Breakfast is included in the homey guesthouse with views of pastures near Hrunalaug.

Blue Hotel Fagrilundur, Reykholt €€ Log cabin exterior encloses a modern hotel with generous breakfast.

Torfhús Retreat, Reykholt €€€ Luxury cabins made of reclaimed oak, complete with every creature comfort. Geothermic basalt pool.

Fellskot Guesthouse, Reykholt €€€ Charming horse-farm house makes a cosy base, featuring comfortable rooms with country views and shared kitchen.

Hveragerði

Hótel Kvika €€ Modern rooms in a brilliant backdrop, with rocky foothills behind and the sweep of a lush valley reaching towards the coast.

Hótel Örk €€ Hotel favoured by tour groups, with tidy rooms, hot tub, sauna and swimming pool with a little slide.

Inni Boutique Apartments €€€ Swanky apartments handy for families in a quiet residential area.

Greenhouse Hotel €€€ A comfortable hotel that looks and feels like a greenhouse. Best thing is lobby and food hall downstairs.

Selfoss

Gesthús Selfoss € Choose between camping and doubles in two-room cabins with shared kitchen and bathroom, by the park.

Hotel South Coast €€ Comfortable rooms in Nordic style. Rich breakfast buffet, and eight wheelchair-accessible rooms.

Icelandic Cottages €€€ Ubercool cottages in the lava fields 18km east of Selfoss have terraces and BBQs, and sleep up to six.

Eyrarbakki & Stokkseyri

Bakki Hostel & Apartments € Six-bed dorms share a living area and kitchen, plus studios and one-bedroom apartments, some with sea views.

Sea Side Cottages €€ Living up to their name, these two quaint cottages are just metres away from the pounding Atlantic, behind a protective berm.

Black Sand Hotel €€€ New hotel with ocean views just across from Flói Nature Reserve.

Camp Boutique €€€ Glamp out on the water's edge for a unique holiday experience.

Þjórsárdalur

Steinsholt € Relax at this homey guesthouse with horse-riding tours in raw nature.

Skaftholt Guesthouse € This small guesthouse with great views and kitchen opened in 2025 on a nonprofit eco-farm.

Sandartunga Camping € Super bare-bones with just water and toilets. The blessing is its grand setting in lava fields and valley.

Hella

Loa's Nest € Pure countryside bliss at this guesthouse with shared kitchen and morning waffles.

Stracta Hótel €€ Straightforward hotel at a good-value price in central Hella.

Glass Cottages Iceland €€€ Glass cottages at sprawling lava fields north of Hella are every bit as magical as they look.

Hvolsvöllur   MAP p137

Midgard Base Camp € Smart bunk beds in dorms, private rooms with fab views. Rooftop hot tub and sauna.

Fljótsdalur HI Hostel € Peaceful, remote base for highland walks, with a beautiful garden and mountain views that make your knees tremble.

Aurora Lodge €€ Riverside rural joy with friendly staff, spacious rooms and relaxing lounge.

Brú Guesthouse €€ Called a guesthouse but actually modern cottages with kitchens and killer views.

Hótel Rangá €€€ Icelandic luxury with fine dining and a backdrop of Northern Lights.

South of Eyjafjallajökull

Hamragarðar € Campground next to waterfall Gljúfrabúi, with good but busy facilities.

Paradise Cave Hostel € Busy dorms, private rooms, small kitchen and a cafe near Seljalandsfoss. Breakfast included.

Skálakot €€€ Fresh-faced horse farm with luxury art-deco hotel rooms and refined restaurant.

UMI Hotel €€€ Every room at this boutique hotel has a mountain or ocean view and a private bathroom.

The Garage €€€ Beloved guesthouse with studios and a friendly owner who sometimes bakes for guests.

Vestmannaeyjar

Hrafnabjörg Guesthouse € Picturesque B&B that'll quickly make you feel at home.

Glamping & Camping € In the bowl of an extinct volcano, Herjólfsdalur campsite has hot showers, laundry room and cooking facilities.

Hótel Vestmannaeyjar €€ Clean, comfortable hotel perfectly located in the centre of town.

Skógar

Guesthouse Skógafoss €€ Austere but reasonably priced (for busy Skógar) small guesthouse with kitchen.

Hótel Skógafoss €€ Busy hotel where half of the rooms have views of Skógafoss. Bistro on-site.

Sólheimahjáleiga Guesthouse €€ Cosy renovated farm buildings, 11km east of Skógar. Both private and shared bathrooms, plus a kitchen.

Vík   MAP p154

Barn € Sprawling, modern hostel on a farm with great views outside of Vík, with options ranging from dorms to pricier private rooms.

Vík HI Hostel € A small but dated hostel with decent dorms and a lived-in vibe.

Vík Campsite € Under a grassy but windy ridge at the eastern end of town.

Grand Guesthouse Garðakot €€ Generous guesthouse with shared kitchen on a pastoral sheep farm.

Guesthouse Carina €€ Neat, spacious rooms with clean shared bathrooms in a large converted house near Vík's centre.

Black Beach Suites €€€ Modern, well-equipped studio apartments. Wake up to water views through floor-to-ceiling windows.

Volcano Hotel €€€ Small hotel, 11.5km west of Vík, with a good restaurant. Books up early.

Gistiheimlilið Reynir €€€ Family-owned silver strip of rooms looks out over the ocean at Dyrhólaey.

Hótel Kría €€€ Sleep in the shadows of mountains at this luxurious hotel near the beach in Vík.

Researched by
Anthony Ham

Southeast Iceland

RAW GLACIAL BEAUTY, CHARMING HAMLETS

The mighty Vatnajökull ice cap dominates the Southeast, with its huge rivers of frozen ice cracking steep-sided valleys. Verdant farmsteads offer welcome sanctuary.

Blow your mind as you traverse the 200km stretch of Ring Road from Kirkjubæjarklaustur to Höfn, transporting yourself across vast deltas of grey glacial sand, past marooned-looking farms, around the toes of craggy mountains, through surreal lava fields and by groaning glacier tongues and ice-filled lagoons. The only thing you won't pass is a town – this is small farm country.

The giant Vatnajökull – Europe's most massive ice cap – dominates the region, its twisting tongues of frozen ice carving valleys opening at the sea. One of several glacial lagoons, Jökulsárlón is a photographer's paradise where wind and water sculpt calving icebergs into fantastical shapes and sweep them out to Fellsfjara where they sparkle in the sun like diamonds.

The unfathomable coastal deserts of glacial sand are remnants of calamitous collisions between fire and ice. With so much natural upheaval on display, it's not surprising that Skaftafell (the southern branch of the enormous Vatnajökull National Park) is such a popular oasis for sightseers and hikers. This sheltered enclave between the glaciers and the sand deltas throbs with life and colour.

North, as you edge towards the Eastfjords, the small seaside town, Höfn (pictured), is a warming sight, offering the chance to dine well and stroll its peaceful surrounds. In short, this section of the Ring Road is a trip that must be taken.

THE MAIN AREAS

SKAFTAFELL
Premier glacier and waterfall hikes. **p166**

JÖKULSÁRLÓN & AROUND
Glittering icebergs float to black-sand beaches. **p178**

HÖFN & AROUND
Fabulous food and views. **p185**

For places to stay in Southeast Iceland, see p189

THE GUIDE

SOUTHEAST ICELAND

Left: Höfn (p185); Above: Jökulsárlón (p180)

SOUTHEAST ICELAND | THE GUIDE

Find Your Way

You'll need to have your own wheels or join a tour to explore the 200km of untouched volcanic wonderland from Kirkjubæjarklaustur to Höfn. Book well ahead to stay overnight, as the few beds are in hot demand. Höfn's small airport serves Reykjavík domestic airport.

Skaftafell, p166
Iceland's favourite national-park pocket is a resplendent area of green amid icy masses and vast sand deltas.

Jökulsárlón & Around, p178
Admire the ever-changing ice sculptures at this bewitching lagoon that empties out onto black-sand beaches.

Höfn & Around, p185
Dine in the town's restaurants, sampling delicious seafood treats, then walk out along the wild coastline for stellar views.

CAR
By far the most convenient way to stop for photo ops and hikes, a car gives freedom. Fuel up frequently as petrol pumps are few and far between. Never drive on glaciers. Get groceries in Kirkjubæjarklaustur and/or Höfn. Routes heading inland require a 4WD.

TOURS
Occasional buses and a multitude of tours drive the Ring Road, connecting Reykjavík and popular towns in Iceland's Southwest with eastern destinations such as Jökulsárlón.

Skaftafell (p166)

Plan Your Time

How deep you dive in the timeless Southeast with its eons-old glaciers is up to you: from a quick awe-inspiring zip to plentiful activities including kayaking, ice caving, glacier walking and puffin viewing.

Pressed for Time

If you really have to zoom through, then stop off at **Fjaðrárgljúfur** (p175) for a magnificent view of canyon and waterfalls. Get groceries in Kirkjubæjarklaustur or eat at excellent restaurant **Kjarr** (p176), then enjoy the otherworldly photo ops in the **sandar** (sand deltas; p173). Hike in **Skaftafell** (p169) on its vista-blessed heath before capping off the mammoth day at **Jökulsárlón** (p180) glacier lagoon.

Three Days to Explore

With extra time, get off the Ring Road into more remote regions like spectacular **Laki** (p176) reserve. The family-friendly **puffin tour** (p172) to Ingólfshöfði is a gas. Or tour one of the glacier lagoons (Jökulsárlón, Fjallsárlón or Heinabergslón) by kayak, amphibious boat or Zodiac. Join a **glacier walk** (p170) or **snowmobile tour** (p171), or ride in style up on the glacier in a **super-Jeep** (p171).

Seasonal Highlights

SPRING
Glacier walks and snowmobiling are generally available year-round (weather permitting), but sudden, extreme changes of weather are always possible; go with a tour.

SUMMER
Puffins visit Ingólfshöfði from May to early August. Everywhere along this stretch of Ring Road is crowded; book ahead for accommodation. Bring warm clothes just in case.

AUTUMN
Boat trips on Jökulsárlón generally run from May to October. Interior F roads close in September or October and don't open again until June.

WINTER
Winter sparkles with the Northern Lights and the chance to visit ice caves that form under the glacier edges.

THE GUIDE

SOUTHEAST ICELAND

Skaftafell

HIKING | GLACIERS | ICE CAVES

GETTING AROUND

All visiting vehicles must pay for parking at Skaftafell (if you go to Jökulsárlón in the same day, then you'll pay 50% of the rate there – and vice versa). Signs indicate rates (1040kr for a normal-sized car) and how to pay (input your licence plate number via a website, the Parka app, kiosks at the lot, or screens inside the visitor centre). The fee is for one day, and is valid until midnight each day.

Skaftafell is a stop (in front of the visitor centre) on the Reykjavík–Höfn Strætó bus route 51.

☑ TOP TIP

Skaftafellsstofa Visitor Centre has helpful staff, maps, a summertime cafe and internet access. Follow the rules: all flora, fauna and natural features are protected, open fires are prohibited and rubbish must be carried out. Stick to marked paths.

For many, the jewel in the crown of Vatnajökull National Park, Skaftafell encompasses a breathtaking sweep of peaks and glaciers. It's the country's favourite wilderness: join the more than 500,000 visitors per year who come to marvel at thundering waterfalls, twisted birch woods, the tangled web of rivers threading across the sandar, and brilliant blue-white Vatnajökull with its tongues of ice, framing rugged mountainsides.

Skaftafell deserves its reputation, and few visitors – even those who usually shun the great outdoors – can resist it. In the height of summer it may feel like every traveller in the country is here. However, if you're prepared to get out on the more remote trails and take advantage of the fabulous hiking on the heath and beyond, you'll leave the hubbub behind. For example, you can find serenity by visiting the famous waterfall, Svartifoss, under the midnight sun, when everyone else is asleep.

Wonder at Vatnajökull & its Outlet Glaciers

Walk to the ice face

Vatnajökull is the world's largest ice cap outside the poles. At 7800 sq km, it's more than three times the size of Luxembourg, with an average thickness of 400m to 600m (and a maximum of 950m). Beneath this enormous blanket of ice lie countless peaks and valleys, including a number of live volcanoes and subglacial lakes, plus Iceland's highest point – the 2110m mountain Hvannadalshnúkur (p173).

Huge outlet glaciers, pleated with crevasses, flow down from the centre of Vatnajökull to the lowlands along Iceland's South Coast. There are around 30 of them, with many visible (and accessible, to varying degrees) from the Ring Road (Rte 1) in the southeast.

A very popular trail offers an easy one-hour walk (path S1; 3.7km return) to **Skaftafellsjökull**, a relatively small glacier tongue that ends within 1.5km of **Skaftafellsstofa Visitor**

SKAFTAFELL

SOUTHEAST ICELAND SKAFTAFELL

SIGHTS
1. Falljökull
2. Hrannadalshnúkur
3. Kristínartindar
4. Morsárlón
5. Sel
6. Skarnipa
7. Skaftafellsjökull
8. Skálafellsjökull
9. Svartifoss
10. Svínafellsjökull
11. Vatnajökull National Park

ACTIVITIES
12. Arctic Adventures
13. Atlantsflug
14. From Coast to Mountains
15. Glacier Adventure
16. Glacier Horses
17. Glacier Jeeps
18. Glacier Journey
19. Glacier Trips

see 12 Icelandic Mountain Guides
20. Local Guide
21. Tröll Expeditions

SLEEPING
22. Ferðaþjónustan Svínafelli
23. Fosshotel Glacier Lagoon
24. Hótel Skaftafell
see 21 Nónhamar
see 22 Potato Storage
25. Skaftafell Campsite

EATING
see 14 Cafe Vatnajökull
see 25 Glacier Goodies
26. Söluskálinn Freysnesi
see 25 Visitor Centre Cafe

INFORMATION
27. Skaftafellsstofa Visitor Centre

VATNAJÖKULL NATIONAL PARK

Vast, varied and spectacular, Vatnajökull National Park was founded in 2008, when authorities created a megapark by joining the Vatnajökull ice cap with two previously established national parks: Skaftafell in Southeast Iceland and Jökulsárgljúfur in the northeast. With recent additions, the park now measures over 14,967 sq km – approximately 15% of the entire country (it's one of Europe's largest national parks) – and it's on the UNESCO World Heritage list. The park contains a staggering richness and some of Iceland's greatest natural treasures: Vatnajökull ice cap and countless glistening outlet glaciers and glacial rivers; incredible waterfalls like Svartifoss; the storied Lakagígar crater row (p151); Askja (p339) and other volcanoes. The park's website *(vatnajokul sthjodgardur.is)* is crammed with information on trails, campsites, access roads and maps.

Svartifoss

Centre *(vatnajokulsthjodgardur.is)*. The marked trail begins at the visitor centre and leads to the glacier face, where you can witness the bumps and groans of the ice (although the glacier is pretty grey and gritty here). It has receded greatly in recent decades so land along this trail has been gradually reappearing. Pick up the brochure describing the trail's geology.

Close to Skaftafell, companies guide glacier walks on tongues such as **Falljökull**, where Icelandic Mountain Guides has a hut.

As you head east on the Ring Road from Skaftafell, a sign points the way to **Svínafellsjökull**. A gravel road near Hótel Skaftafell (p189) leads to a car park, from where it's a 500m walk to the northern edge of the glacier and fine photos. A picturesque bike trail (15km return) between Skaftafell and Svínafell opened here in 2023.

Walking to the Waterfall Svartifoss
Basalt cascades and glacier views

Seek out your perfect view of famous Svartifoss (Black Falls), a stunning, moody-looking waterfall flanked by geometric black basalt columns. The relatively easy 1.8km trail leads up from the visitor centre via the campsite. To take pressure off the busy trail, park staff recommend an alternate path back. From the waterfall, continue west up the track to Sjónarsker, where a view disc names surrounding landmarks, plus an unforgettable vista stretches across Skeiðarársandur (p173). From here you can visit the traditional turf-roofed farmhouse **Sel**. This two-hour, 5.3km return walk (path S2), including Svartifoss, is classified as easy.

Or, for a challenging hike (path S5/S6), from Svartifoss head east over the heath to the viewpoint at **Sjónarnípa**, looking across Skaftafellsjökull. Allow three hours return (7.4km).

Hiking the Skaftafellsheiði Loop
Take hiking trails across the heaths

On a fine day, tackle the five- to six-hour walk (path S3; 16.7km) around Skaftafellsheiði (Skaftafell Heath), a hiker's dream (except when it's closed during the spring thaw because you'd be knee-deep in mud). It begins by climbing from the campsite to Sjónarsker, continuing across the moor to 610m-high Fremrihnaukur. From there it follows the edge of the plateau to the next rise, Nyrðrihnaukur (706m), which affords a superb view of **Morsárdalur**, and **Morsárjökull** and the iceberg-choked lagoon at its base. At this point the track turns southeast to an outlook point, **Gláma**, on the cliff above Skaftafellsjökull. The route continues down to Sjónarnípa and then back to the campsite.

For the best view of Skaftafellsjökull, Morsárdalur and the Skeiðarársandur, it's worth scaling the summit of **Kristínartindar** (1126m). The best way follows a well-marked 2km route (classified as difficult) up the prominent valley southeast of the Nyrðrihnaukur lookout, and back down near Gláma.

Getting out into the Back Country
Going beyond the crowds

Skaftafell is ideal for both day hikes and its longer treks through wilderness regions. Although they take longer and require greater levels of planning and fitness, these trails are the best way to leave behind the hordes that descend on Skaftafell in summer.

Before setting out, stop in to talk to the rangers at the visitor centre who are keen to help you prepare and inform you of potential risks, and leave a travel plan at *safetravel.is*. Pick up a good map outlining shorter hiking trails, or one of the larger topographical maps.

Most visitors stick to popular routes on Skaftafellsheiði, and from mid-June to mid-August, rangers usually guide free daily interpretive walks from the visitor centre.

The seven-hour hike (20.9km return) from the campsite through the upper **Morsárdalur** and valleys to the glacial lake of **Morsárlón** is more serious, but enjoyable. Alternatively, cross the Morsá river at the foot of Skaftafellsheiði and make your way across the gravel riverbed to the birch woods at Bæjarstaðarskógur. The complete walk to/from Bæjarstaðarskógur takes about five hours (15.8km return).

A long day hike beyond Bæjarstaðarskógur leads into the rugged **Skaftafellsfjöll**. Or, summit the 862m-high **Jökulfell ridge**, which affords a commanding view of the vast expanses of **Skeiðarárjökull**. Even better is an excursion into the Kjós dell.

Glacier Hikes & Ice Climbing
Explore out on the ice

One highlight of any visit to the southern reaches of Vatnajökull is a glacier hike where you get to strap on crampons and

LOCAL TOUR OPERATORS

From Coast to Mountains (p171): Owner Einar, Iceland's first ice cave guide, offers climbs of Hvannadalshnúkur peak, and cave and puffin tours.

Local Guide: Family-owned and in the area for generations; first-rate local knowledge, year-round glacier hikes and ice climbs.

Glacier Horses: Short horse rides in view-blessed countryside, 9km east of the park. Bookings are essential.

Tröll Expeditions: Offering glacier hikes, ice climbing, and wintertime ice cave tours from their base 18km east near Hof. They have an office next to Skaftafell visitor centre.

Icelandic Mountain Guides: Family-friendly 'Blue Ice Experience' on the ice run from Skaftafell four to eight times daily year-round.

Glacier Adventure: Glacier walks plus winter ice-cave exploring from their base at Hali Country Hotel, 68km east.

SHIFTING SANDS OF HISTORY

The historical Skaftafell was a large farm at the foot of the hills west of the present campsite. Shifting glacial sands slowly buried the fields and the district came to be known as Hérað Milli Sanda (Land Between the Sands). After all the farms were annihilated by the 1362 eruptions, it became the 'land under the sands' and was renamed Öræfi (Wasteland). Cute Svínafell, just east, offers camping and lodging and was once home to Flosi Þórðarson, who burned Njáll and his family to death in *Njáll's Saga*. It was also the site where Flosi and Njáll's family were finally reconciled, thus ending one of the bloodiest feuds in Icelandic history. In the 17th century, Svínafellsjökull nearly engulfed the farm, but it has since retreated.

Ice cave tour, Vatnajökull

crunch your way around (atop) a glacier. You can see waterfalls, ice caves, glacial mice (moss balls, not actual mice!) and different-coloured ash from ancient explosions. As fascinating as the glaciers are, they are also riven with fissures and are always potentially dangerous – never venture out onto one without both a guide and the right equipment.

Icelandic Mountain Guides *(mountainguides.is)* and **Arctic Adventures** *(glacierguides.is)* have information and booking huts beside Skaftafellsstofa Visitor Centre, where you can talk to experts and get kitted out for glacier walks (warm clothes are essential; waterproof gear and hiking boots are available for hire).

Locally owned companies throughout the Southeast, like excellent Glacier Adventure over on Breiðamerkurjökull (p181), also offer more challenging ice treks and ice climbs, or combos, such as a glacier hike plus a lagoon boat trip.

Getting Up on the Vatnajökull Ice Cap
Snowmobiling, hiking and super-Jeep joyrides

Access to the bulk of Vatnajökull is only for experienced folks set up for a serious polar-style expedition: the ice cap is cracked with deep crevasses, made invisible by coverings of fresh snow, and there are often sudden, violent blizzards. You can travel way up into this ice wilderness on organised snowmobile or super-Jeep tours.

FOR LODGING IN THE SOUTHEAST

Inside the park, the only option is to camp. There's very little accommodation nearby, and hotels in the Southeast book up. Bring either a tent or a firm hotel booking.

Companies lead activities on the broad glacial spur Skálafellsjökull (p169), 840m above sea level and with spectacular 360-degree views. Most travellers choose to do an awesome snowmobile ride. You're kitted out with overalls, helmets, boots and gloves, then play follow-the-leader along a fixed trail – great fun.

Although tours often last around three hours, only one hour is actually spent on the glacier.

Glacier Jeeps *(glacierjeeps.is; snowmobile tour per person 27,600kr, super-Jeep glacier tour per person 27,500kr)* and **Glacier Journey** *(glacierjourney.is; snowmobile tour per person 29,500kr, super-Jeep glacier tour per person 29,000kr)* both offer snowmobiling and super-Jeep tours. Glacier Jeeps also offers a glacier hike. Snowmobile drivers need a driving licence (passengers don't).

Glacial Ice Caves in Winter
Discover a subterranean world

Wonder at glorious dimpled caverns of exquisite blue light accessible (usually at glacier edges) only from around November to March. This truly is a thing of wonder, seeing the ice cap or glacier from within.

The caves can be viewed only in cold conditions, not least because they become unstable and unsafe in warmer weather. Temporary ice caves are created anew each season by the forces of nature, and are scouted by local experts. They *must* be visited with guides, who will ensure safety and correct equipment. As with glacier hikes, tours generally involve getting kitted out (crampons, helmets etc), then driving to the glacier edge and taking a walk to the cave. Reasonable fitness and mobility are required.

With their rapid growth in popularity, the largest and most accessible ice caves become crowded when tour groups arrive (from as far afield as Reykjavík). Day tours from Reykjavík are not an especially good idea, due to travel time (four-hour drive, one way). Often, these guided groups visit the same cave – it's disappointing to find queues to enter.

We recommend you go with a local company. **From Coast to Mountains** *(fromcoasttomountains.com; 3hr ice-cave tour per person 27,500kr)* and sister company **Local Guide** *(localguide.is; 3hr ice-cave tour per person 23,900kr)* are the regional experts on ice caves in the Southeast, and can get you to more remote, private caves if you have time, stamina and cash.

Other good, locally owned companies include **Glacier Adventure** *(glacieradventures.is)*, **IceGuide** *(iceguide.is)*, **Glacier Journey** *(glacierjourney.is)*, **Ice Explorers** *(explorers.is)* and **Glacier Trips** *(glaciertrips.is)*. Some tours depart from Skaftafell, while most depart from Jökulsárlón car park (57km east of Skaftafell) – check when booking.

SOARING OVER THE GLACIERS

Sightseeing flights by **Atlantsflug** *(flightseeing.is)* offer a brilliant perspective on all this natural splendour. They leave from the tiny airfield on the Ring Road, just by the turnoff to the Skaftafellsstofa Visitor Centre. Choose between tour options, with views over Landmannalaugar, Lakagígar, Skaftafell peaks, Jökulsárlón and Grímsvötn.

If you love a thrilling scenic overflight, you can pair your glacier flight with a helicopter ride over scintillating Askja at highland farm Möðrudalur (p342).

For general sightseeing helicopter tours out of Reykjavík or Gullfoss, **Glacier Heli** *(glacierheli.is)* is another professional operator of long-standing.

EATING IN & NEAR SKAFTAFELL: OUR PICKS

Cafe Vatnajökull: Welcoming roadside eatery with fresh-made snacks and excellent coffee. A rare alternative to petrol-station dining in these parts. *10am-5.30pm* €

Visitor Centre Cafe: In summer, this busy cafe sells sandwiches, cake and hiking snacks (*skyr* etc), plus hot food (soup) with vegetarian options. *9am-9pm Jun-Sep, shorter hours rest of year* €

Glacier Goodies: The food truck near the visitor centre makes a small menu of well-executed dishes: lobster soup, fish and chips, baby back ribs. *11.30am-9pm mid-May-Sep* €

Söluskálinn Freysnesi: Get meals and a few supplies year-round here at the petrol station opposite Hótel Skaftafell, 5km east of the park. *9am-8pm Jul-Sep, shorter hours rest of year* €

Beyond Skaftafell

Glaciers lord over lava fields, waterfalls and the largest sandy glacial outwash plains in the world.

Places

Ingólfshöfði p172
Hvannadalshnúkur p173
Núpsstaður p173
Kirkjubæjarklaustur p174
Foss á Síðu p175
Landbrotshólar & Eldhraun p175
Fjaðrárgljúfur p176
Laki p176

Soulful glaciers and brooding mountains line the eye-popping stretch of the Ring Road between Skaftafell and little Kirkjubæjarklaustur hamlet in the east and the iceberg-filled lagoon Jökulsárlón in the west. The unfolding landscape, from lava fields to pseudocraters, glaciers to waterfall-laden escarpments, makes it difficult to keep your eyes on the road – come with an empty data card in your camera, and you'll use it all.

Towards the coastline, the Ingólfshöfði reserve is visited by guided tour only, but offers an expansive view on land and sea, with puffins to boot. And inland, the Lakagígar (Laki crater row) makes for secluded, magnificent hiking, while Hvannadalshnúkur, Iceland's tallest mountain, is the province of the pros.

GETTING AROUND

Kirkjubæjarklaustur is a stop on the Reykjavík–Vík–Höfn bus route. Buses stop at the N1. Buses travelling east call at Skaftafell and Jökulsárlón. Super-Jeep trips using the Fjallabak Route (F208) to Landmannalaugar or going to Laki leave from here. You'll obviously have more freedom if you have your own wheels, but parking fees at each site can quickly add up.

Ingólfshöfði

TIME FROM SKAFTAFELL: **30MIN**

Take a tractor to see puffins

While everyone's gaze naturally turns inland in this spectacular part of Iceland, there are reasons to look offshore too – in particular to the 76m-high Ingólfshöfði (pronounced *in-golvs-huv-thi*) promontory, rising from the flatlands like a strange and beautiful dream.

In spring and summer, this superb, isolated nature reserve is visited by nesting puffins, skuas and other seabirds, and you may see whales offshore. It's also of great historical importance – it was here that Ingólfur Arnarson, Iceland's first settler, stayed the winter on his original foray to the country in 874 CE.

The reserve is open to visitors on tours with **From Coast to Mountains** (*fromcoasttomountains.com; adult/child 11,500/5750kr*). Tours begin with a fun and spectacular 30-minute ride across 6km of shallow tidal lagoon in a tractor-drawn wagon. After a short but steep sandy climb, there's a 1½-hour guided walk round the headland. The emphasis is on birdwatching, with stunning mountain backdrops to marvel over on clear days. The puffins usually appear sometime in May and leave Iceland around mid-August.

Go for a post-tour (excellent) coffee or cake at welcoming Cafe Vatnajökull (p171), just up on the Ring Road.

Hvannadalshnúkur

Hvannadalshnúkur

TIME FROM SKAFTAFELL: **30MIN**

Climb Iceland's highest mountain

Iceland's highest mountain, Hvannadalshnúkur (2110m), pokes out from Öræfajökull, an offshoot of Vatnajökull. This lofty peak is actually the northwestern edge of an immense 5km-wide crater – the biggest active volcano in Europe after Sicily's Mt Etna. It erupted in 1362, firing out the largest amount of tephra in Iceland's recorded history.

Einar, the owner of **From Coast to Mountains** *(fromcoasttomountains.com; per person 55,000-100,000kr),* holds the record (over 300!) for ascents of Hvannadalshnúkur, and his grandfather was on the team that first ascended it.

Núpsstaður

TIME FROM SKAFTAFELL: **30MIN**

Explore the world's largest glacial sand plain

The **sandar** are fantastically flat sweeps of sand sprawling along Iceland's southeastern coast. High in the mountains, glaciers scrape up silt, sand and gravel that is then carried by fast-flowing grey-brown glacial rivers, or (more dramatically) by glacial bursts, down to the coast and strewn across huge, barren plains. The sandar here are so impressive that the Icelandic word (singular: sandur) is used internationally to describe these glacial outwash plains.

Immediately to the west of the world's largest sandur, **Skeiðarársandur**, a precipitous 767m-tall palisade of cliffs known as Lómagnúpur, towers over the landscapes. It's the inspiration for many legends, and looks particularly good as a backdrop to the turf-roofed farm at **Núpsstaður**, where buildings date back to the early 19th century, and the idyllic chapel is one of the last turf churches in Iceland.

WINTER AROUND SKAFTAFELL

Winter travel in the region is booming, with the strong draws of the Northern Lights and ice caves (p171). These caves form within the ice of a glacier and become solid and safe for visiting only in the coldest months. You can also still do glacier walks in winter – and the glaciers look more pristine, taking on the iridescent blue hue so beloved by photographers. In the right conditions, Svartifoss freezes in January to February (on the flip side, in winter the falls are not always accessible, due to slippery, unsafe tracks). Between December and March, access to trails is weather-dependent, and some may require crampons. There are also restricted daylight hours, so always talk to park staff about your best options.

EMBRACING ICELANDIC WINTER

Though daylight hours are short, Icelandic winter provides adventure in addition to the fun of chasing the shimmering Northern Lights. Learn more on p272.

Eldhraun

JÖKULHLAUP!

The section of Ring Road that passes across Skeiðarársandur was the last bit of the national highway to be constructed, in 1974 (until then, folks from Höfn had to drive to Reykjavík via Akureyri). Long gravel dykes have been strategically positioned to channel floodwaters away from this highly susceptible artery. They did little good, however, when within a few hours in late 1996 the Grímsvötn (or Gjálp) eruption created a massive *jökulhlaup* (glacial flood, releasing up to 3000 billion litres of water and dragging icebergs the size of three-storey buildings – three Ring Road bridges were washed away like matchsticks. There's a memorial of twisted bridge girders and an information board along the Ring Road just west of Skaftafell.

Inland **Núpsstaðarskógar**, a beautiful low-growing woodland area on the slopes of the mountain Eystrafjall, is best explored on a tour (due to the perils of crossing the Núpsá river). In July and August, **Icelandic Mountain Guides** (*mountainguides.is*) runs a guided five-day (65km) backpacking hike through Núpsstaðarskógar, over to Grænalón (an ice-dammed marginal lake), across the glacier Skeiðarárjökull and then into Morsárdalur in Skaftafell.

Do not drive off-road in these expanses. It is illegal, and hugely destructive to the fragile environment.

Kirkjubæjarklaustur   TIME FROM SKAFTAFELL: 1HR

Exploring the Twin Falls

Many a foreign tongue has been tied in knots trying to say Kirkjubæjarklaustur. It helps to break it into bits: *Kirkju* (church), *bæjar* (farm) and *klaustur* (convent). Otherwise, do as the locals do and call it 'Klaustur'.

Klaustur is tiny, even by Icelandic standards – a few houses and farms scattered across a brilliant-green backdrop. Still, it's the only real service town between Vík and Höfn, and it's a major crossroads to several dramatic spots in the interior, including Landmannalaugar and Laki.

 EATING IN KIRKJUBÆJARKLAUSTUR: OUR PICKS

Skaftárskáli: They don't come any simpler than this all-day grill-bar, with quick bites and fast food. *8am-10pm Jun-Aug, shorter hours rest of year* €

Kjarr: Mod new bistro at the foot of the Systrafoss with superb Arctic char (from pure water directly under the nearby lava field) and other fresh, seasonal fare. *noon-10pm* €€

Systrakaffi: This busy restaurant gets slammed in summer, but has a wide-ranging menu from burgers to carefully cooked lamb. *noon-9.30pm* €€

Klaustur Restaurant: Popular sunny, enclosed dining terrace and bar featuring local produce (Arctic char, slow-cooked lamb shank) in the hotel of the same name. *5-9.30pm* €€

At the western end of the village, the lovely double waterfall, **Systrafoss**, shimmers down the cliffs and a sign outlines three short walks in the pretty wooded area (Iceland's tallest trees grow here!). The lake, **Systravatn**, reached by a leisurely climb up steps cut into the hill beside the falls, was once a bathing place for nuns. A marked 2.5km walking path leads from the lake to descend near the basalt columns of **Kirkjugólf** *(Church Floor)*, and takes in glorious views.

Stop by the helpful tourist office inside the visitor centre for good local information, a short film on the Laki eruption plus coverage and exhibitions on Katla Geopark and Vatnajökull National Park. This is the base for the lesser-visited western pocket of the national park, best accessed from the **Fjallabak Route** (Rte F208), which connects to popular Landmannalaugar and arcs up from the western side of the river Skaftá, between Vík and Kirkjubæjarklaustur. It's only accessible by 4WD or super-bus.

Foss á Síðu

TIME FROM SKAFTAFELL: **50MIN**

Visit more nearby falls

Around 11km east of Kirkjubæjarklaustur and right on the Ring Road, Foss á Síðu is a real eye-catcher. It combines the big drop from the cliffs with a series of levels at lower levels – during especially strong winds, however, it actually goes straight up!

Landbrotshólar & Eldhraun

TIME FROM SKAFTAFELL: **1HR**

Witness Iceland's largest pseudocrater field and lava flows

West of the village of Kirkjubæjarklaustur and south of the Ring Road, the vast, dimpled, vivid-green pseudocrater field Landbrotshólar undulates into the distance, the largest in Iceland at about 50 sq km. Pseudocraters form when hot lava pours over wetlands. The subsurface water boils and steam explodes through to make these barrow-like mounds – not real craters. The origin of the lava of Landbrotshólar has been a matter for debate, but it's now believed to be the 10th-century Eldgjá eruption. To the west, the pseudocraters give way to eerie lava field Eldhraun, averaging 12m thick, that appears to alter as light conditions change. It contains more than 15 cu km of lava and covers an area of 565 sq km, making it the world's largest recorded lava flow from a single eruption (Laki).

You'll emerge in the west near **Hrífunes** (pronounced something like ri-voo-ness), a perfectly placed hamlet, in the peaceful and impossibly green surrounds of Skaftártunga, with many excellent guesthouses.

WHY I LOVE SKEIÐARÁRSANDUR

Alexis Averbuck, writer

Wild Skeiðarársandur is the largest sandur in the world, covering 1300 sq km. As you drive from the south, up the east coast, you pass lava fields and pseudo-craters, and emerge into this moody glacial outwash plain stretching 40km between ice cap and coast (from Núpsstaður to Öræfi). Mists swirl down off the glaciers, which are just becoming visible in the distance, and the vibe is absolutely one-of-a-kind. Since the Settlement Era, Skeiðarársandur continues to grow, swallowing farmland. The region used to be relatively well-populated (for Iceland), but in 1362 the volcano beneath Öræfajökull (known as Knappafellsjökull) erupted and the *jökulhlaup* (flooding caused by volcanic eruption beneath ice) laid waste. The area was renamed Öræfi (Wasteland).

THE LAKI ERUPTION

In the summer of 1783, a vast set of fissures erupted, forming around 135 craters. The Laki craters fountained molten rock 1km into the air for eight months, spewing out over 15 cu km of volcanic material, creating the lava field Eldhraun (p175), covering 565 sq km. Far more devastating were the hundreds of millions of tonnes of ash and sulphuric acid that poured from the fissures. The sun was blotted out, grass died off, and around two-thirds of Iceland's livestock perished from starvation and poisoning. Some 9000 people – a fifth of the country's population – were killed and the remainder faced the Móðuharðindin ('Hardship of the Mist'), a famine that followed. Across the northern hemisphere, clouds of ash blocked the sun. Temperatures dropped and acid rain fell, causing devastating crop failures.

Fjaðrárgljúfur

TIME FROM SKAFTAFELL: 1HR

Look down upon a storied canyon

The verdantly twisting picturesque Fjaðrárgljúfur canyon (p151), topped by waterfalls and carved out by the river Fjaðrá, has been well and truly discovered, thanks to Instagrammers and one Justin Bieber (who filmed a video clip here). The view from the viewing platform at the top is simply glorious – gaze into the gorge's gorgeous rocky, writhing depths and emerald-green surrounds, with a crashing waterfall to one side.

The main parking area (follow the signs for Fjaðrárgljúfur) leaves you with a 2km uphill hike: it's a decent climb, but takes you past three viewpoints. The much smaller top car park (good for people with limited mobility, follow the signs to Laki) is 500m from the top of the canyon. Both cost 1040kr per vehicle *(parka.is)*. We strongly recommend the longer walk from the lower car park.

The canyon is just west of Kirkjubæjarklaustur, 3km north of the Ring Road via Rte 206.

Laki

TIME FROM SKAFTAFELL: 1½HR

Hike a volcanic landscape

It's almost impossible to comprehend the immensity of the Laki eruptions, one of the most catastrophic volcanic events in human history. Nowadays the smoothly variegated scree hills and twisted lava fields covered with delicate green moss bely the apocalypse that spawned them some 235 years ago. It's a fascinating place to visit and hike, with relatively few visitors.

Although Laki (818m) peak did not erupt, it loaned its name to the 25km-long Lakagígar Crater Row (p151), which stretches northeastwards and southwestwards from its base. Scramble up a steep path for 40 minutes to one hour from the parking area. From the top, exhilarating 360-degree views encompass

Laki

the fissure, undulating lava fields, lakes and glinting glaciers in the distance.

The crater row itself is fascinating to explore, with multi-coloured dunes, lava tubes and unusual wildlife like the Arctic fox and snow bunting. At the foot of Laki, marked paths lead through the two closest craters.

An absolute highlight of the Laki experience, **Fagrifoss** (Beautiful Falls) exceeds its name. One of Iceland's most bewitching falls, rivulets of water shimmer over immense black rocks. To get here, it's a short walk from the parking; the turnoff is 24km along Rte F206 to Laki.

Another excellent walk is to **Tjarnargígar Crater Lake**; extend it to 1½ hours through lava channel Eldborgarfarvegur.

Visiting the area requires a large, robust Jeep and 4WDing experience (rivers must be forded). If you don't meet these requirements, join a tour. Family-owned **Secret Iceland** *(secret iceland.com)* in Kirkjubæjarklaustur offers excellent super-Jeep tours that get you to the crater field first-thing so you hike Laki mountain completely alone, then return, stopping for wonderful little-known hikes, with knowledgeable guides who provide informative geological and historical commentary along the way.

The nearest campsite, operated by the national park, with hut facilities, toilets and showers, is at Blágil, about 11km from Laki, off Rte F207.

Always stick to marked paths and roads in this ecologically sensitive region – part of Vatnajökull National Park. Rangers staff a hut with excellent information at the Laki car park when the road to Laki is open (usually mid-June until early September).

FOR HIGHLAND EXPEDITIONS
The Laki region begins the march into Icelands' wild highlands. To learn more about the main summertime routes across this stark interior and how to tackle them, see p327.

Jökulsárlón & Around

GLACIER SCENERY | 'DIAMOND' BEACH | WILDLIFE

Spectacular, luminous-blue icebergs drift through Jökulsárlón (pronounced yokul-sar-lon) glacier lagoon, right beside the Ring Road between Höfn and Skaftafell. About a million people per year make the pilgrimage here.

The icebergs calve from Breiðamerkurjökull, an offshoot of Vatnajökull, crashing down into the water and drifting towards the Atlantic Ocean. They can spend up to five years floating in the 25-sq-km-plus, 250m-deep lagoon, melting, refreezing and occasionally toppling over with a mighty splash, startling the birds and the seals that like to frolic in the shallows here. They then move on via Jökulsá, Iceland's shortest river, out to sea at Fellsfjara.

Just southwest of Jökulsárlón, another wonderful and less-visited glacier lagoon, Fjallsárlón, beckons, while Breiðamerkursandur is one of the main breeding grounds for Iceland's great skuas, with Arctic foxes (and echoes of the sagas) never far away. This is one of Iceland's most popular corners, and it truly is a place of wonder.

GETTING AROUND

You pay 1000kr to park at Jökulsárlón, if you can find a place. The main car park on the north side of the road fills up fast, with the overflow also close to full by a mid-summer's morning. Drivers beware: the bridge on the Ring Road that passes over the Jökulsá river is a single-lane bridge – and a tricky one to navigate. It's hard to see what is approaching from the other side, and there is a lot of traffic plus drivers distracted by the scenery.

Buses run between Reykjavík and Jökulsárlón daily in July and August, between Reykjavík and Höfn twice daily year-round, or between the visitor centre at Skaftafell and Jökulsárlón twice daily in July and August only.

Floating Fjallsárlón Glacier Lagoon
Sand plains and intimate lagoons

A sign off the Ring Road indicates Fjallsárlón, where icebergs calve from Fjallsjökull and Zodiac tours cruise among the bergs. While not as immediately spectacular or visually arresting at first sight as Jökulsárlón, 10km further east, **Fjallsárlón** is one beautiful lagoon that often ends up being just as special (and just as picturesque if you get away from the main viewing areas). As crowds grow with each passing year at Jökulsárlón, Fjallsárlón is increasing in popularity as a smaller (around 3 sq km) alternative to its busy, larger (25 sq km) neighbour.

The best way to explore is with **Fjallsárlón Glacial Lagoon Boat Tours** (*fjallsarlon.is; adult/child 10,500/5500kr*), which offers 45-minute Zodiac trips among lagoon icebergs

JÖKULSÁRLÓN AND AROUND

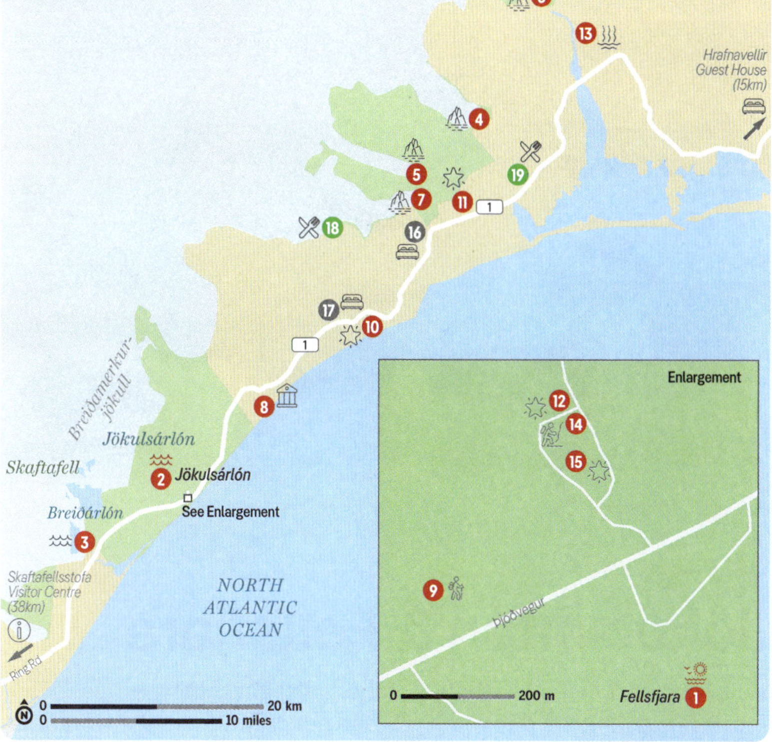

★ HIGHLIGHTS
1 Fellsfjara
2 Jökulsárlón

● SIGHTS
3 Fjallsárlón
4 Fláajökull
5 Heinabergsjökull
6 Hoffellsjökull
7 Skálafellsjökull
8 Þórbergssetur

● ACTIVITIES
9 Breiðármörk Trail

see 3 Fjallsárlón Glacial Lagoon Boat Tours
see 8 Glacier Adventure
10 Glacier Jeeps
11 Glacier Journey
12 Glacier Lagoon Amphibious Boat Tours
13 Hoffell
14 Ice Explorers
15 Ice Lagoon Adventure Tours
see 11 IceGuide

● SLEEPING
16 Guesthouse Skálafell
17 Kálfafellsstaður Guesthouse

● EATING
see 15 Fancy Sheep
see 3 Frost
see 12 Heimahumar
18 Jöklasel
see 12 Jökulsárlón Café
19 Jón Ríki
see 15 Northern Light Bite
see 8 Þórbergssetur Restaurant

☑ TOP TIP

Countless tours take in Jökulsárlón, a true Iceland highlight. With summer's plentiful light, visit in early morning or late evening to avoid crowds. Follow rules: flora, fauna and natural features are protected, drones and fires are prohibited and rubbish must be carried out. Stick to marked paths to preserve delicate terrain.

(April to October; minimum age five). The trail to the boat's departure point at the lagoon shore is gently intrepid, and there's also an intimacy to a tour on this lagoon – you don't have to travel far to reach the glacier snout and the lack of huge crowds is grand.

The same operators (with an office in the Fjallsárlón car park) also offer 3½-hour excursions to the stunning **Ice Cave**

(continued on p182)

Jökulsárlón

TOP EXPERIENCE

Jökulsárlón & Fellsfjara

Which is best? In the wee hours, alone, with light shifting on ice forms? Or during the day when you can not only admire the wondrous glinting ice sculptures in the lagoon and on the beach – some of them striped with vivid ash layers from volcanic eruptions – and scout for seals, but also take a thrilling lagoon boat trip?

DON'T MISS

Amphibious boat tour

Zodiac boat tour

Kayak alongside the glacier

Walk the lagoon shore

Breiðármörk Trail

Fellsfjara

Jökulsárlón on film

On the Water

In summer, the lagoon is a hub for boat tours and some kayaking – a chance to get out among the bergs. Check in 30 minutes before to avoid missing out.

Amphibious Boat Tours

Take a memorable 40-minute trip in the amphibious boat operated by **Glacier Lagoon** (*icelagoon.is; adult/child 6900/3500kr*). It trundles along the shore like a bus before

PRACTICALITIES
- vatnajokulsthjodgardur.is
- parking per 24hr 1000kr
- ranger station 842 4355, open 9am–5pm

driving into the water – high on novelty value. On-board guides regale you with factoids about the lagoon, and you can taste 1000-year-old ice. Trips run from from May to October (sometimes longer) out of the eastern car park – up to 40 a day in summer. Prebook online.

Zodiac Tours

Glacier Lagoon and **Ice Lagoon Adventure Tours** (*icelagoon.com; per person 15,900kr*) offer Zodiac tours of the lagoon. The 1¼-hour experience has a maximum of 10 passengers per boat and travels at speed up near the glacier edge (not done by the amphibious boats) before cruising back at a leisurely pace. Book ahead online. Glacier Lagoon's minimum age is 10 years and 1.3m height; Ice Lagoon Adventure Tours' is eight years.

Kayak

The chance to get out among the icebergs in a quiet kayak could be our favourite way to explore – no engine noise! **IceGuide** (*iceguide.is; per person 16,900kr*) leads hour-long paddles May to early October from its van on the eastern car park. Prebook online – minimum age 14, maximum weight 120kg (265lb).

Walking the Lagoon

Lagoon boat trips are excellent, but you can get almost as close to those cool-blue masterpieces by walking along the shore, and taste ancient ice by fishing it out of the shallows. On the Ring Road west of the car park, there are designated parking areas where you can visit the lake at less-touristed stretches of shoreline. And the national park has set up walking routes with information detailing geological features.

Rangers lead daily tours at 11am June to September from near the food trucks. Also, consult the maps on the park website for a series of trails from easy to challenging, such as route B1 from the car park to the glacier ridge, **Helguhóll**.

A favourite, longer route, the **Breiðármörk Trail** (p182), connects Jökulsárlón's western car park to the lagoons Breiðárlón (10km one way) and Fjallsárlón (15.3km; p182).

Ice Explorers (*explorers.is; per person 17,900kr*) and **Glacier Adventure** (p171; *glacieradventure.is; per person from 16,400kr*) guide half-day glacier hikes on **Breiðamerkurjökull**.

Fellsfjara

Cross from the lagoon car parks underneath the Ring Road bridge out to the mouth of the Jökulsá river. Tourists dubbed the site '**Diamond Beach**', and the name has stuck on marketing brochures. You'll see why: ice boulders and bergs glitter photogenically on the black-sand beach as part of their final journey into the ocean.

A GROWING LAGOON

Slow-moving rivers of ice (glaciers) flow down from Vatnajökull, Iceland's largest ice cap, advancing and retreating with the millennia. The lagoon may look like a relic of the last Ice Age, but it's only about 80 years old. Until the mid-1930s Breiðamerkurjökull reached the Ring Road. It's now retreating rapidly (up to a staggering 500m per year), and the lagoon is growing.

TOP TIPS

- Look for approaching traffic plus distracted drivers on the single-lane Ring Road bridge.

- Two large car parks on the ocean side of the Ring Road (signposted Eystri- and Vestri-Fellsfjara) are best for campers. Walk under the bridge to the lagoon.

- In June and July, avoid nesting and dive-bombing Arctic terns near the lagoon's eastern car park.

- Closest accommodation east: around Hali (13km; no camping; next campsite is in Höfn), or west: Fosshotel Glacier Lagoon (28km), camping at Svínafell (52km) or Skaftafell (60km).

THE F985

One notable road in the area northeast of Höfn is the 4WD-only track F985. It branches north from the Ring Road, about 35km east of Jökulsárlón and 45km west of Höfn, to the broad glacial spur Skálafellsjökull. This 16km-long track is practically vertical in places, with iced-over sections in winter, so best visited on tours with Glacier Jeeps (p171) and Glacier Journey (p171; snowmobile or super-Jeep up on the glacier).

Don't even think of attempting to drive Rte F985 in a 2WD car – you'll end up with a huge rescue bill – or in a small 4WD, or if you're inexperienced with such a vehicle on such routes.

(continues from p179)

(adult/child 24,500/18,375kr) at the Breiðamerkurjökull glacier tongue, a four-hour **glacier hike** *(per person 14yr & over 19,800kr)*, and longer overnight expeditions.

Hike Between the Lagoons
Jökulsárlón to Fjallsárlón

For the most part, hiking in this part of Iceland is a fairly short affair – usually from a visitor centre car park to the nearest glacier tongue or waterfall. That's why we love the **Breiðármörk Trail**, which represents a genuine opportunity to get some miles under your belt without launching a major expedition.

The walking trail begins in the western car park at Jökulsárlón and follows the plain between the Ring Road and the steep-walled mountains of the interior. The path leads west to Breiðárlón (10km one way), a rarely visited lagoon, and on to Fjallsárlón (15.3km). It's classified as challenging (at least five hours with no water along the route), though much of it is over level ground and there are no rivers to ford. The Skaftafellsstofa Visitor Centre on the outskirts of Kirkjubæjarklaustur sells a trail map (250kr).

There is a long-term plan to eventually build out this walking route from Skaftafell in the west to Lónsöræfi in the east.

The Wildlife & Sagas of Breiðamerkursandur
Great skuas and happy endings

The region of Breiðamerkursandur is backed by a sweeping panorama of glacier-capped mountains and sandy plains, often fronted by deep lagoons such as Fjallsárlón. It has two main calling cards, though they're not tied to any specific place.

The Breiðamerkursandur area is one of the main breeding grounds for Iceland's great skuas. Thanks to rising numbers of these ground-nesting birds, there's also a growing population of Arctic foxes, making this whole stretch of coastline west of Jökulsárlón filled with wildlife-watching potential.

And there's a whiff of typically Icelandic legend attached to the area. Historically, Breiðamerkursandur figures in *Njáll's Saga*, which ends with Kári Sölmundarson arriving in this idyllic spot to 'live happily ever after' – which has to be some kind of miracle in a saga!

EATING AT JÖKULSÁRLÓN: FOOD TRUCKS & QUICK SNACKS

Jökulsárlón Café: In the main lagoon car park; offers basic snacks but is usually overwhelmed. *9am-7pm Jun-Sep, to 6pm Mar-May & Oct, to 5pm Nov-Feb* €

Heimahumar: This excellent food truck at the southern end of the main car park does a warming lobster bisque, lobster roll, hot dogs and hot drinks. *11.30am-6pm mid-May–mid-Sep* €

Northern Light Bite: Another of the Jökulsárlón food trucks, this one keeps it simple with fish (local cod) and chips. *11.30am-6pm mid-May–mid-Sep* €

Fancy Sheep: Lined up with the other food trucks alongside the Jökulsárlón car park, Fancy Sheep holds its own with lamb or beef burgers, pumpkin soup or fries. *11.30am-6pm mid-May–mid-Sep* €

Hoffellsjökull

Get Your Glacier Boots On

Exploring Vatnajökull's eastern glacier tongues

Kvíárjökull glacier snakes down to the Kvíá river and is easily accessible from the Ring Road; look for the sign for **Kvíármýrarkambur** just west of the bridge over the river. Leave your car in the small car park and follow the path into the scenic valley.

Vatnajökull National Park authorities are working with lots of local landowners between Ingólfshöfði and Höfn to gain public access to areas of raw natural beauty (and take pressure off popular Skaftafell and Jökulsárlón in the face of rising tourist numbers). These areas are signed off the Ring Road – for now, they are not especially well known, so you stand a good chance of finding yourself a tranquil pocket of glaciated wonder.

Uniquely, three glacier tongues – Skálafellsjökull (p170), **Heinabergsjökull** and **Fláajökull** – converge on the Hjallanes and Heinaberg area. A fourth, **Hoffellsjökull**, lies further east, closer to Höfn. Remarkable walking trails and scenery include glacier lakes and moraines. And best of all, they're still something of an easy, DIY adventure with a palpable sense of discovery still possible.

Heinabergsjökull is 8km off the Ring Road on a gravel road, signposted east of Guesthouse Skálafell (p189), where they can provide information. Walking trails from Guesthouse Skálafell include the 8km Hjallanes loop or a 7.5km hike to Heinabergslón (the icy lagoon at the foot of Heinabergsjökull). From Heinabergslón an 8.3km trail leads to Fláajökull. Brilliant 3½-hour kayaking trips (including two hours on the water) on Heinabergslón are operated by **IceGuide** (*iceguide.is; per person 14yr & over 20,900kr*).

Hoffellsjökull is accessed from the road to **Hoffell** guesthouse. A signed, 4km gravel road (which washes out in heavy

VATNAJÖKULL NATIONAL PARK

Súsanna Ruth Magnúsdóttir (Iceland) and Josh Persello (Australia), park rangers for Vatnajökull National Park at Jökulsárlón.

Favourite time of year? Winter (Súsanna and Josh)

Why? The glaciers are more blue, and it's ice-cave season (Súsanna). The icebergs, too are really blue, and it all has a dusting of snow. (Josh).

Do you ever tire of this place? The weather is always changing, so there's always something new going on (Josh).

Favourite way to experience Jökulsárlón? Zodiac boats, because they take you all the way to the glacier on the lagoon (Súsanna). Glacier hiking for me (Josh).

How to escape the crowds? Go to Nýgræðuöldur and Fjallsárlón. (Súsanna). Everyone says their favourite glacier is Fjallsjökull (Josh).

BEER IN THE SOUTHEAST

Look out for Vatnajökull Beer: marketed as 'frozen in time' beer, it's brewed from 1000-year-old water (ie Jökulsárlón icebergs), flavoured with locally grown Arctic thyme. You'll find it in restaurants around the Southeast (it's brewed in Selfoss). More broadly in Iceland, the main brands of Icelandic beer – Egils, Gull, Thule and Viking – are all fairly standard lager or pils brews. Look out, too, for seasonal beers – the ones brewed for the Christmas period are especially popular. Down here in the Southeast, farmhouse restaurant **Jón Ríki** is an example of the growing number of smaller craft breweries scattered around Iceland – its house brews range from a mango IPA to a jalapeno-and-pumpkin ale.

Þórbergssetur

rain) leads to the glacier, which calves into a small lake. This is a good glacier to walk to from the guesthouse; upon your return, you can soak in the hot-pots there.

Stop by the visitor centres in Skaftafell (p166) or Kirkjubæjarklaustur, or the ranger hut at Jökulsárlón, to ask about road conditions, find out if any areas are newly accessible, and buy the *Heinaberg, Hjallanes, Hoffell* map. Or visit the Jökulsárlón & Heinaberg section of the national park website *(vatnajokulsthjodgardur.is)*.

Celebrating a Local Writer & Arctic Char
Feed body and soul

Cleverly crafted museum **Þórbergssetur** *(thorbergur.is; adult/child 1000kr/free)*, with its inspired exterior looking like a shelf of books, pays tribute to the most famous son of this sparsely populated region – writer Þórbergur Þórðarson (1888–1974). Þórbergur was a real maverick (with interests spanning yoga, Esperanto and astronomy), and his first book *Bréf til Láru* (Letter to Laura) caused huge controversy because of its radical socialist content.

It's in the Hali Country Hotel, 13km east of Jökulsárlón, and is also home to a quality restaurant specialising in Arctic char.

EATING AROUND JÖKULSÁRLÓN: OUR PICKS

Jöklasel: The base hut for Glacier Jeeps is situated at the top of Rte F985, 840m above sea level. The on-site cafe, Iceland's highest, has epic views with coffee and snacks on offer. *10.30am-1.30pm Jul & Aug* €

Frost: The visitor centre at Fjallsárlón is home to Frost, a cafe with hot dishes, soups, salad and snacks. *9.30am-4pm Jun-Sep, 11am-4pm Oct-May* €€

Jón Ríki: Stylish farmhouse restaurant at Hólmur with a small in-house brewery, grilled langoustine, panna cotta for dessert, sourdough pizza and the jalapeno-and-pumpkin ale. *6-8.30pm Mon-Fri* €€

Þórbergssetur Restaurant: In the Hali Country Hotel, 13km east of Jökulsárlón, this museum restaurant does excellent Arctic char. *9am-9pm* €€

Höfn & Around

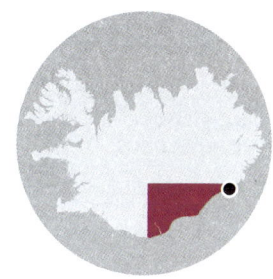

ICELANDIC FOOD | WILD COUNTRY | COASTAL SCENERY

Although it's no bigger than many European villages, the Southeast's main town feels like a sprawling metropolis after driving through the emptiness on either side. Its setting, strung out across a long, windswept peninsula with fabulous coastal and ocean views, is stunning; on a clear day, wander the waterside or climb to its picturesque headland, find a quiet bench and just gaze at Vatnajökull and its guild of glaciers. Suitably for a welcoming oasis on such a wild stretch of coastline, Höfn has a stirring cast of restaurants – it's the best place for a meal anywhere along Iceland's South Coast.

Northeast of Höfn, the pretty bay of Lón is a classic South Coast stretch of shore, with a black-sand beach and a lonely, end-of-the-world feel about it. The road heading northeast beyond Lón is another of those sweeping panoramas and long, lonely kilometres that Iceland does so well.

Höfn's Culinary Scene
Fine dining in 'The Harbour'

Höfn is a fantastic place to eat, with the widest selection of choices anywhere along Iceland's southern coast.

The town's name simply means 'harbour', and is pronounced like an unexpected hiccup (just say 'hup' while inhaling). It's an apt name – it has always relied heavily on fishing and fish processing, and is famous for its *humar* (often translated as lobster, but technically it's langoustine), although those on the menu these days are often imported.

There are a few excellent choices and the better ones are all within walking distance of each other around the southern end of town. It wouldn't be a trip to Höfn for us without dinner at Pakkhús (p186) – the lamb, octopus and langoustine are all superb; try the local sheep-dung-smoked whisky as an apéritif. Occupying the oldest house in town, Otto Matur & Drykkur (p186) is another excellent choice for tender Icelandic lamb, salmon and more. For something more casual and

GETTING AROUND

It's easiest to see the region with your own wheels, and if you're planning on diverting off the Ring Road, make sure you have a 4WD. But if you're bussing, timetables may refer to Höfn as Höfn í Hornafirði (meaning Höfn in Hornafjörður) to differentiate it from all the other *höfn* (harbours) around Iceland. Höfn has a small airport serving Reykjavík's domestic airport.

☑ TOP TIP

Unless you don't mind waiting, we recommend an early dinner in Höfn – many restaurants don't take reservations, and waiting lists in summer can be long. In contrast, most Ring Road travellers stop to use the town's services, so prebook accommodation, especially in summer.

HUMARHÁTÍÐ – FOR HOW LONG?

Every year in late June or early July, Höfn's **Humarhátíð festival** (facebook.com/Humarhatid) takes over the town, with competitions, live entertainment, themed menus in restaurants and much merriment. It's all designed to honour *humar* (langoustine). Fishing is a mainstay for Höfn, but overfishing has long threatened the local industry: in some recent years the catch has been so scarce that its commercial fishing has been halted for a time. As for Höfn, so, too, for Iceland, for which fishing makes up 40% of the country's exports, at a time when annual catches are falling (by 3% in 2023 alone) and the nation's commercial fishing fleet has fallen to around 1500 boats, with the number of fishing trawlers down by 50% since 2004. For now, the festival continues.

HÖFN AND AROUND

- **SIGHTS**
  1. Seamen's Monument
  2. Viewpoint
- **ACTIVITIES**
  3. Ósland
  4. Sundlaug Hafnar
- **SLEEPING**
  5. Guesthouse Dyngja
  6. Old Airline Guesthouse
- **EATING**
  7. Hafnarbúðin
  8. Íshúsið Pizzeria
  9. Kaffi Hornið
  10. Nettó
  11. Ósinn
  12. Otto Matur & Drykkur
  see 8 Pakkhús

EATING IN HÖFN: OUR PICKS

Hafnarbúðin: Tiny old-school diner with big breakfasts, fast-food favourites and fine langoustine baguettes. *9am-10pm Sat-Thu, from noon Fri Jun-Aug, shorter hours rest of year* €

Íshúsið Pizzeria: Family-friendly Ice House doles out thin-crust, stone-baked pizzas, everything from Hawaiian to 'lobster festival'. *noon-9pm* €€

Otto Matur & Drykkur: Occupying the oldest house in Höfn (1897), this elegant space is high on Nordic style and delicate dishes like lamb or salmon. *5.30-9pm* €€

Pakkhús: Boisterous harbourside warehouse with high-level kitchen creativity and great service. Wait for a table in its downstairs bar. *noon-9pm* €€

less pricey, Hafnarbúðin does a big, tasty langoustine baguette that's ideal for picnic lunch.

Walk out to Wild Views

Explore beyond the southern end of town

Höfn huddles around a harbour and it makes sense – the town and its sheltered bay has always offered refuge for boats returning from fishing out on the wild Arctic seas. Beyond the town's southern limits, the road leads out onto the **Ósland** promontory, about 1km beyond the harbour, with a walking path round its marshes and lagoons full of seabirds. In winter, with no buildings to block their path, the winds coming in off the ocean can be icy and ferocious. Crowning the promontory's high point, such as it is, is the **Seamen's Monument**. From the monument, you can follow a nature trail that has been set up to model the solar system to scale.

The views from the monument across the water towards Vatnajökull are superb. They're similarly good from the **viewpoint** atop the cute little rising headland at the southwestern end of Hofðavegur.

In such places, swimming may be the last thing on your mind, but in summer, swim you can, at **Sundlaug Hafnar**, the town's popular outdoor swimming pool with waterslides, hot-pots and a steam bath.

FOR ICELANDIC FOOD FUN

Icelandic cuisine ranges from the foraged to the foragers (sheep) plus bounteous seafood. Learn more about the Icelandic food scene on p34.

Strolling Sandy Spits

Lón's seabirds and soaring mountains

The name **Lón** (Lagoon; pronounced 'lone') describes this shallow bay enclosed by two long spits between the sheer mountains Eystrahorn and Vestrahorn. The best access for strolls on the sandy eastern spits is via Eystrahorn.

At the western end of Lón, commanding Vestrahorn and its companion Brunnhorn form a cape between Skarðsfjörður and Papafjörður. Travel down the signposted road to Stokksnes to explore this striking area, known as Horn. Here you'll find the excellent **Viking Cafe** (*vestrahorn.is*), a farm owner charging for car-park camping, and

FOR WILDERNESS LOVERS

Another outpost of the grand Vatnajökull National Park includes the East's Snæfell region (p310), which is much less visited than the spots easily accessible from the Ring Road.

 WHERE TO EAT IN & AROUND HÖFN

Viking Cafe: In a wild setting under moodily Gothic Vestrahorn mountain in Stokksnes, you'll find this cool little outpost, where soup, coffee, waffles and cake are served. *7.30am-8pm* €

Nettó: Supermarket (with bakery) in the central Miðbær shopping centre. Stock up – in either direction, it's miles to the next grocery selection. *9am-7pm* €

Kaffi Hornið: Casual log-cabin bar and restaurant with varied menu plus, of course, local seafood. *11.30am-9pm* €€

Ósinn: Outshining the hotel it inhabits, this place in Hótel Höfn is open year-round and offers a creative menu that includes pearl-barley salads, langoustine pizzas and salmon teriyaki. *5.30-10.30pm* €€€

Lón (p187)

ICELAND'S FIRST SETTLERS

Iceland's South Coast may now draw tourists in ever-growing numbers, but nearly 13 centuries ago, as the closest geographical point to mainland Scandinavia, it was also where the Vikings first came ashore. Credit for the first intentional permanent settlement on Iceland, according to the 12th-century *Íslendingabók*, or Book of Settlement, goes to Ingólfur Arnarson, who fled Norway with his blood brother Hjörleifur. He landed at Ingólfshöfði (115km southwest of Höfn) in 871, then continued around the coast and set up house in 874 at a place he called Reykjavík (Smoky Bay), named after the steam from thermal springs there. Hjörleifur settled near the present town of Vík, but was murdered by his slaves shortly after.

land access to a black-sand beach with an old Viking village film set, where seals laze and the backdrop of Vestrahorn creates superb photos.

To the northwest an enormous colony of swans nests in spring and autumn in the delta of Jökulsá í Lóni river.

Going further from Höfn, the 105km between Höfn and Djúpivogur is yet another impossibly scenic stretch, with farms, austere scree hills, black-sand beaches and bird-filled wetlands.

In the middle of nowhere, Stafafell farm is an excellent starting point for hikes. Get route descriptions online at *stafafell.is*.

Places We Love to Stay

€ Budget   €€ Midrange   €€€ Top End

Skaftafell   MAP p167

Skaftafell Campsite € Large, year-round site with laundry facilities, paid hot showers. No cooking at the campsite; the nearest wi-fi is in the visitor centre.

Ferðaþjónustan Svínafelli € Well-organised campsite with six basic cabins (sleeping four), spotless amenities block at Svínafell, 8km east.

Potato Storage €€ Brand-new apartments on a peaceful Svínafell farm offer welcome respite after a day's hiking.

Nónhamar €€€ Small, modern cottages 19km east of the park in Hof; sleep two or three.

Hótel Skaftafell €€€ One of very few hotels in the area, so in hot demand, despite being merely functional, 5km east, with a restaurant.

Fosshotel Glacier Lagoon €€€ Superb four-star hotel out on the plains with sleek Nordic design and all-encompassing views.

Kirkjubæjarklaustur

Kirkjubær II Campground € Good kitchen, paid showers and laundry in the main part of town.

Iceland Bike Farm €€ Stay in a countryside 'glamping hut' and take fat-tyre mountain bike rides (also available to nonguests).

Magma Hotel €€€ Winning hearts with beautiful design, peaceful surrounds and friendly staff, by a lake with lush views.

Hótel Klaustur €€€ Klaustur has friendly staff and attractive decor in its well-equipped rooms, plus a sunny enclosed dining terrace and bar-lounge.

Hrífunes

Glacier View Guesthouse €€ In clear weather, see Vatnajökull and Mýrdalsjökull from the lounge. It's a fine, simple place with a warm welcome.

Hrífunes Guesthouse €€ Stylish farmhouse, cosy lounge and stunning photos by a local photographer who runs tours (phototours.is).

Hrífunes Nature Park €€ Enjoy stellar views, Northern Lights in winter and an outdoor wood-fired hot tub with modern small houses.

Hótel Hrífunes by Ourhotels €€€ Cosy rooms with wood floors and walls, and views over the nearby grasslands and hills; serves a decent breakfast.

Jökulsárlón & Around   MAP p179

Hrafnavellir Guest House €€ Seven small cabins about 25km east of Höfn on a super-peaceful patch with views across the river delta.

Kálfafellsstaður Guesthouse €€ Embrace the farmstay experience within a 20-minute drive of the glacier lagoon.

Guesthouse Skálafell €€ Friendly working farm with a handful of agreeable rooms in the farmhouse, and in motel-style units and cottages.

Höfn & Around   MAP p186

Old Airline Guesthouse €€ Central and sparkling, with five rooms (shared bathrooms), plus a large lounge and guest kitchen.

Guesthouse Dyngja €€ Pristine, six-room guesthouse in a prime harbourfront locale, with self-service breakfast and an outdoor deck.

Milk Factory €€ Renovated dairy factory with 17 modern, hotel-standard rooms, including two with disabled access.

Lambhús €€ Ducks and horses, plus 11 cute, compact self-catering cottages (sleeping four to five), 31km from Höfn.

Seljavellir Guesthouse €€ Superb spot with 20 smart, minimalist rooms – all with splendid views – about 6km from Höfn.

Dynjandi €€ Cosy three-room guesthouse on a photogenic horse farm at the foot of mountains about 9km from Höfn.

REY Stays €€ Cute little cabin rooms that face out onto the mountains just off the Ring Road 5km from Höfn; one of the better price-quality ratios in the area. Also has a two-bedroom apartment nearby.

Árnanes Country Lodge €€ This polished, rural 18-room locale is 6km from Höfn and has motel units and guesthouse rooms.

Above: Kirkjufell (p211); Right: Road to Ingjaldshóll (p218)

For places to stay in West Iceland, see p219

Researched by
Jade Bremner

West Iceland

STUNNING VOLCANIC AND GLACIAL TERRAIN AND WILD COASTLINES

West Iceland offers everything from empty windswept beaches and historic villages to striking volcanic and glacial landscapes in one neat little package.

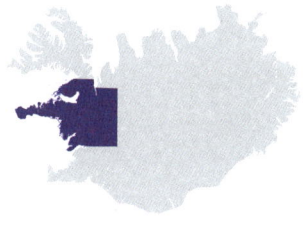

Largely overlooked by most visitors, West Iceland (known as Vesturland; *west.is*) is an impressive blend of Iceland's geological offerings. It's about as far from Reykjavík as the Golden Circle, with one big difference – no crowds. At times you're likely to have parts of this wonderful region all to yourself.

The diverse and fascinating landscape on the long arm of 100km Snæfellsnes Peninsula is known for its glacier, Snæfellsjökull, while the area around its national park has terrific bird and whale watching, lava-field hikes and horse-riding opportunities. The charming harbour village Stykkishólmur, with its scattering of brightly coloured buildings from the late 19th century, makes an ideal base with some surprisingly good restaurants and a ferry out to Flatey Island and the Westfjords beyond.

Inland, beyond Reykholt, you'll encounter lava tubes and remote highland glaciers, including enormous Langjökull with its unusual ice cave. The coast and rolling meadows of the Dalir region are even less visited, and have remote windswept promontories calling for exploration.

Two of the best-known Icelandic sagas, *Egil's Saga* and *Laxdæla Saga*, took place along the region's brooding waters, marked today by haunting cairns and a terrific museum in lively Borgarnes.

Good roads and regular buses mean that the features of the West are an easy trip from Reykjavík, offering a cross-section of the best Iceland has to offer in a very compact region, all without the hordes of tourists in other areas.

THE MAIN AREAS

BORGARNES
Saga-soaked watertront town. **p194**

STYKKISHÓLMUR
Quaint harbour, base for Snæfelsnes. **p205**

SNÆFELLSNES PENINSULA
Gorgeous glacier-topped reserve and wild coast. **p213**

Find Your Way

Buses serve the region's main villages, but to reach the furthest corners, your own car or a tour is necessary. The *Baldur* car ferry (p205) connects Stykkishólmur on Snæfellsnes Peninsula and Brjánslækur in the Westfjords, via Flatey Island.

CAR
Roads are largely excellent and easy to navigate in western Iceland. The rugged dirt roads are few, with only a handful of F roads off-limits to 2WD. Most villages have petrol stations.

BUS
Because of the good bus services passing through Borgarnes, you can reach many destinations in the West using local Strætó buses. Reykjavik to Akureyri routes run through Borgarnes, Bifröst and Staðarskáli, so it's easy to continue onwards towards the north.

Stykkishólmur, p205
Wander past chocolate-box houses in this buzzy harbour town with good eating options and ferries to Flatey.

Borgarnes, p194
Step back into Saga times at the impressive Settlement Centre in this little town.

Snæfellsnes Peninsula, p213
Wander crunchy lava fields, along windswept coastlines, and over Snæfellsjökull, the icy heart of this magical park.

Saxhóll Crater (p217)

Plan Your Time

The West makes for several easy loops: oft-forgotten Hvalfjörður, into the upper valley to the west of Borgarnes and out along the Snæfellsnes Peninsula.

Pressed for Time

Start at the **Hvammsvík Hot Springs** (p199) in Hvalfjörður to soak in the warm pools and cold-plunge in the ocean before driving on to the Snæfellsnes Peninsula. Circle the tip of the peninsula, through **Snæfellsjökull National Park** (p216), gawping at the cliffs and waterfalls, the ice cap and the craters, before dining in **Stykkishólmur** (p205).

Three Days to Explore

Hike into the canyon **Rauðfeldsgjá** or up the **Saxhóll Crater** (p217) and hop on a whale- and puffin-watching boat tour. Continue on to the Dalir, visiting **Eiríksstaðir** (p210) for saga stories and **Erpsstaðir** (p210) for ice-cream confections. Then go inland for activities such as waterfall hiking at **Glymur** (p202), crater climbing at **Grábrók** (p198) or caving at **Víðgelmir** (p204).

Seasonal Highlights

SPRING
Iceland awakes from winter. Mountain roads slowly become passable again and puffins arrive in May.

SUMMER
Lots of daylight, activities and mountain roads open. Hikers welcome; puffins leave by mid-August.

AUTUMN
Breezier weather, optimal visiting conditions for those who prefer solitude as the tourist season begins to wind down.

WINTER
Long nights with likely Northern Lights viewings and ice activities from snowmobiling to ice caving.

Borgarnes

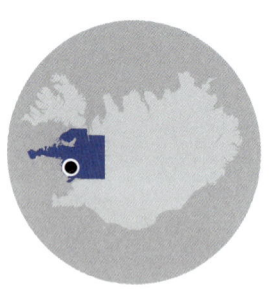

VIKING ROOTS | LOCAL LIFE | SAGA LAND

GETTING AROUND

Borgarnes is the major transfer point between Reykjavík and Akureyri, Snæfellsnes and the Westfjords. The bus stop is at the cluster of petrol stations (N1, Orkan). Bus 57 goes to both Akureyri and Reykjavík and runs seven days a week. Bus services are reduced in winter.

☑ TOP TIP

West Iceland's main tourist information centres are in Borgarnes at Ljómalind craft co-op and the national park offices in Malarrif and Hellissandur. Read up in advance to enjoy the saga-soaked region: *Egil's Saga, Laxdæla Saga, Heimskringla, Eyrbyggja Saga, Saga of Erik the Red* and *Saga of the Greenlanders*, to name a few.

Unassuming Borgarnes has got it going on. For such a tiny place, it bubbles with local life. One of the original settlement areas for the first Icelanders, it's loaded with history and sits on a scenic promontory along the broad waters of Borgarfjörður. Zip past the busy petrol stations and go into the old quarter to encounter the fun small-town vibe and one of Iceland's best museums, the Settlement Centre. There you can learn about the establishment of human civilisation in Iceland, plus the dramatic antics of poet-warrior Egill Skallagrímsson. His homestead and sites from the saga describing his life dot the town.

The laid-back vibe and cheerful restaurants and bars, welcoming guesthouses and top-notch geothermal pool make Borgarnes a good base before exploring further afield.

Go on a Saga Tour

Deep dive into Egil's Saga

To go deep into how the sagas of the local area tie to the landscape around Borgarnes, download the detailed Locatify SmartGuide smartphone or iPad app and load the 'Egil's Saga, Borg on the Moors' tour, which tells the stories of local landmarks from the tale. The Settlement Centre has marked eight of the sites with cairns, including **Brákin**, **Borg á Mýrum** and **Skallagrímsgarður**, the burial mound of Skallagrímsson's father and son.

The Borg á Mýrum farm is named for the large rock *(borg)* behind the farmstead (private property); you can walk up to the cairn for views all around, and visit the small cemetery, which includes an ancient gravestone marked by runes.

Þorgerður Brák was Egill's nursemaid, thought to be a Celtic slave. In one of the more dramatic moments in *Egil's Saga*, she heroically saves Egill's life, then dies in the strait, between Borgarnes and the islet offshore, named Brákarsund for her.

BORGARNES

★ HIGHLIGHTS
1. Ljómalind
2. Settlement Centre

● SIGHTS
3. Borg á Mýrum
4. Borgarfjördur Museum
5. Brákin
6. Skallagrímsgardur
7. Viewing Disc

● ACTIVITIES
8. Borgarnes Swimming Pool

● SLEEPING
9. B59 Hotel & Hostel
10. Bjarg
11. Helgugata Guesthouse
12. Kría Guesthouse

● EATING
13. Bara
14. Blómasetrið–Kaffi Kyrrð
15. Dirty Birger & Ribs
16. Englendingavík
see 2 Settlement Centre Restaurant

In June the town celebrates an annual festival, **Brákarhátíð**, in her honour.

Delve into the Story of Iceland's Discovery
Excellent museum and landmarks

Egil's Saga starts by recounting the tale of Kveldúlfur, grandfather of the warrior-poet Egill Skallagrímsson, who fled to Iceland during the 9th century after a falling out with the king of Norway. Kveldúlfur grew gravely ill on the journey, and instructed his son, Skallagrímur Kveldúlfsson, to throw his coffin overboard after he died and build the family farm wherever it washed ashore – this happened to be at Borg á Mýrum, a local farmstead. Egill Skallagrímsson grew up to be a fierce and creative individual who killed his first adversary at the age of seven, went on to carry out numerous raids on Ireland, England and Denmark, and saved his skin many a time by composing eloquent poetry.

Learn about him at Borgarnes' excellent **Settlement Centre** (krlandnum.is; adult/child 3700/1300kr), housed in an

REYKA VODKA

Throughout Iceland you'll likely see Reyka Vodka. It's produced in Borgarnes, at the country's first distillery – completely made in Iceland, partly of Iceland. It's filtered through a 4000-year-old Artic lava field and distilled using wheat and barley. It's also made using glacial water and renewable geothermal energy, powered by underground volcanoes. The sustainable process takes around five hours, producing small batches only. It's one of the purest, smoothest, crispest vodkas out there. It's available at local liquor stores, and served in bars in humorously-named cocktails such as Blue Lagoon, the Long Iceland Viking Woo Woo and other takes on classic drinks.

imaginatively restored warehouse by the harbour. The museum is divided into two fascinating dimly lit exhibitions with displays, artefacts and Viking models depicting the stories of the area; each takes about 30 minutes to visit while listening to an audio guide (available in several languages). The Settlement Exhibition covers the discovery and settlement of Iceland. **Egil's Saga Exhibition** recounts the amazing adventures of Egill and his family. It also has a top-notch gift shop and the adjacent **Settlement Centre Restaurant**, built into a rock face, serving local classics such as lamb and fish stew.

Hilltop Views
Climbing Hafnarfjall

The dramatically sheer mountain **Hafnarfjall** rises south across the fjord from Borgarnes. It's about 844m tall, and approximately – give or take a millennium or two – four million years old. You can climb it (7km, roughly 4½ hours round trip) from the trailhead on Rte 1, near the southern base of the causeway into Borgarnes. There's a small birch wood at the base. Be careful of slippery scree cliffs on ascent but you'll get sweeping views from the top.

If that's a bit much, head to the much lower **Viewing Disc**, a small disc on the hill town just northeast of the campsite, which labels the peaks all around.

Embrace Town Culture
Geothermal pool and local culture

The charm of Borgarnes lies in its zippy daily life. Start at beautiful **Borgarnes Swimming Pool** *(borgarbyggd.is; adult/child 1290/385kr),* with hot-pots and steam room, all part of

Hafnarfjall

a large fjordside sports complex. This is a wonderful place to relax with views of the sea.

Seek refreshment at **Blómasetrið–Kaffi Kyrrð**, the quaint flower and gift shop that is also a cosy cafe with hot drinks, beer and snacks. Or sleep over at the family's guesthouse. Browse **Ljómalind** *(ljomalind.is)* crafts co-op and farmers market, a long-standing collaboration between local producers. It stocks everything from fresh dairy products from Erpsstaðir (p210) and organic meat to locally made bath products, handmade wool sweaters, jewellery and all manner of imaginative collectables.

The small municipal **Borgarfjördur Museum** *(safnahus.is; prices vary)* has engaging rotating exhibits (usually in peak tourist season), from the story of children in Iceland over the last 100 years to contemporary art shows.

EATING IN BORGARNES: OUR PICKS

Bara: Welcoming bar serving Icelandic craft brews and top fish and chips. Fun, friendly vibe. *5pm-1am Fri-Sat, to 10pm Mon-Thu* €€

Englendingavík: Casual, wonderful waterfront deck, serving tasty homemade dishes, from roast lamb to fresh fish. *noon-9pm* €€

Settlement Centre Restaurant: Light-filled eatery built into the rock face serving traditional Icelandic and international eats. Popular lunch buffet. *10am-9pm* €€

Dirty Birger & Ribs: Junk food fix of loaded burgers from pulled pork to beef with bacon or blue cheese. Chug down with a beer. *11am-10pm* €€

Beyond Borgarnes

Fecund farms with deep history lead to powerful stone-strewn lava tubes and highlands; this is the gateway to the ice caps beyond.

Places

Hvanneyri p198
Bifröst p198
Hvalfjörður p199
Reykholt p200
Húsafell p201
Kaldidalur Valley p204

GETTING AROUND

Borgarnes is a major transit hub for **Strætó** *(straeto.is)* buses throughout the region and to the Westfjords and North. September to May, bus 81 runs inland to Reykholt. Having your own wheels is much easier and gives you the freedom to hit more obscure areas at your own pace, with the chance to stop for photo ops en route.

As you head inland from Borgarnes and its broad Borgarfjörður (fjord) up the river-twined valleys, you'll find more sites rich in early Settlement lore, such as Reykholt, home to historian and chieftain Snorri Sturluson. Húsafell is the jumping-off point for activities on – and in – Langjökull ice cap, and has hot springs and peaceful vibes. The nearby lava fields networked with underground tubes are there to be discovered by intrepid families, as are an Icelandic goat farm and a number of horse farms offering rides through the countryside. To the south, scenic Hvalfjörður fjord is home to a terrific hike to Glymur, Iceland's second-tallest waterfall, plus an inviting hot springs experience, making for a dreamy way to wrap it all up.

Hvanneyri

TIME FROM BORGARNES: **15MIN**

Learn about wool and women

Find your way to off-the-beaten-path village Hvanneyri, 12km east of Borgarnes, and in among fjordside homes you'll find the **Agricultural Museum of Iceland** *(landbunadarsafn. is; adult/child 1600kr/free)*, inside an old cowshed, with more than 1000 artefacts from old salmon fishing devices to large tractors. Exhibitions feature the lives of agricultural women and the history of salmon fishing. Nearby is **Ullarselið** *(ull. is)*, a fantastic wool shop filled with combed, spun, knitted, matted, woven and check-woven delights. Handmade sweaters, scarves, hats and blankets share space with skeins of beautiful hand-spun yarn, and interesting bone and shell buttons. It's open mid-May to September.

Bifröst

TIME FROM BORGARNES: **25MIN**

Roadside craters

Formed around 3000 years ago during an eruption, the striking and perfectly formed crater **Grábrók** rises 173m above sea level, just off Rte 1, in the Norðurárdalur valley, near the village of Bifröst. Part of Grábrókarhraun lava field, it sits in a 600m-long fissure near two other beautiful scoria cones (Grábrókarfell and Litla Grábrók or Smábrók, meaning 'small panties'). Both of their mossy craters are visible from atop Grábrók, which has soaring views over the lava field. It takes around 40 minutes to climb (free), then circle the rim of the

Grábrók

crater along a well-maintained 1.5km pathway; you can also climb into the crater. At the base of the hill, don't miss a visit to the **Old Brekky Corral**, built in 1872 and once used to herd sheep in autumn, a practice that dates back to Viking times in Iceland – an annual gathering of livestock that usually runs free. This corral remained in use until 1922.

Hvalfjörður

TIME FROM BORGARNES: **30MIN**

Hike and take hot dips

Hvalfjörður (pronounced *kval*-fyur-thur) and the surrounding area feels suddenly pastoral despite being a mere 30-minute drive from the capital. Although lacking the majesty of the Snæfellsnes Peninsula further on, the sparkling fjord with shimmering waterfall Glymur (p202) offers excellent day-trip fodder. Those in a hurry to get to Borgarnes and beyond should head straight through the 5.7km-long road tunnel beneath the fjord. Cyclists aren't permitted in the tunnel.

The highlight of the area is the **Hvammsvík Hot Springs** (*booking.hvammsvik.com; dips from 8200kr*). Take a cold plunge in the ocean then warm up in the eight natural hot springs of different temperatures and sizes.

As you round the north side of the fjord, keep your eyes peeled for the **Saurbæjarkirkja**, the turfed church at the Saurbær farmstead. It's worth a look for its beautiful stained-glass work by Gerður Helgadóttir. It is named for Reverend Hallgrímur

ICELANDIC WOOL

Wherever you are in Iceland, you'll see people wearing Icelandic wool, typically *lopapeysa*, classic Icelandic sweaters. Icelandic wool is a unique material perfect for Iceland's often wet and cold climate thanks to its two-layer structure, developed over more than 1000 years. The outer layer, called *tog*, is long, coarse and naturally water-resistant, while the inner layer, *þel*, is soft and super warm. Icelandic sheep have been isolated since Viking times, so their wool hasn't been mixed with other breeds and doesn't undergo lots of chemical processing like other wool. It's considered a sustainable material due to its natural properties and minimal environmental impact. Sheep roam freely, the wool breaks down naturally, and the process supports local craftspeople and rural life in Iceland.

EATING IN HVALFJÖRÐUR: OUR PICKS

Stormur Bistro: In a barn at the Hvammsvík Hot Springs; open sandwiches, cakes and their famous seafood soup. *9am-9pm* €€

White Falcon Cafe: Inside the War & Peace Museum try Kleina (Icelandic doughnuts) in this fun vintage setting. *1.5pm Wed-Fri, 11am-5pm Sat & Sun May-Aug* €€

Esjustofa Café: Situated at Esjustofa Hiking Center for coffee, soup and salmon bagels after a Mount Esja hike. *hours vary* €€

Hotel Laxarárbakki: With an emphasis on local produce and Icelandic classics including cod stew and fish of the day. *4-8pm* €€

MILITARY BASE

Hvalfjörður (meaning Whale Fjord) is a 30km long and 84m deep fjord that played a big role in WWII. Its sheltered harbour made it a tactical spot for Allied forces, and during WWII the fjord contained a submarine and warship station. More than 20,000 American and British soldiers passed through, especially for convoys heading to the Soviet ports at Murmansk. The British first occupied Iceland in May 1940 to block any German advances. In July 1941 the US took over and built a massive fuel station and an ammo depot at Hvammsvík. The fjord had repair shops, storage, living quarters and more. It became the last pit stop for US and British merchant ships before sailing towards the Soviet Union. Allied forces heavily guarded the fjord's narrow mouth to keep those convoys safe on their perilous journeys.

Snorrastofa

Pétursson, who served here from 1651 to 1669, and composed Iceland's most popular religious work, *Passion Hymns*.

On the southern side of Hvalfjörður you'll find dramatic **Mt Esja** (914m), a great spot for wilderness hiking. The most popular trail to the summit begins at **Esjustofa Hiking Center** (with a cafe), just north of Mosfellsbær. There are several routes up the mountain, but most people hike 2.8km to the viewpoint at Steinn. The trail gets much more technical after that.

Learn about Iceland's role in WWII

The **War & Peace Museum** *(warandpeace.is; adult/child 2800kr/free)* houses artefacts from uniforms and weapons to radio equipment from Iceland's occupation by Britain and the US from 1940 to 1945. It tells the fascinating story of the Arctic convoys that went on long and difficult voyages from the Hvalfjörður base to the Soviet Union. There's a small cafe here serving tea in vintage cups, plus soups, bread and cakes among retro memorabilia. There's also a campground at the Military Training Center (1500kr per person) with barbecues, a playground and a swimming pool.

Reykholt

TIME FROM BORGARNES: **30MIN**

Roam Reykholt's historic Snorri sites

Reykholt is a sleepy outpost (just a few farmsteads really) that on first glance offers few clues to its past as a major medieval settlement. It was home to one of the most important medieval chieftains and scholars, Snorri Sturluson, who was killed here, and today the main sights revolve around him. The interesting medieval study centre **Snorrastofa** *(snorrastofa.is; adult/child 1200kr/free)* is devoted to him and is built on his old farm, explaining Snorri's life and accomplishments, including a 1599 edition of his *Heimskringla* (sagas of the Norse kings).

At the age of 36, Snorri was appointed *lögsögumaður* (law speaker) of the Alþingi (Icelandic parliament). In the following decades he endured heavy pressure from the Norwegian king to promote the ruler's interests but, instead, Snorri busied himself with his writing until the unhappy Norwegian king Hákon finally snapped and issued a warrant for his capture – dead or alive. Snorri's political rival and former son-in-law Gissur Þorvaldsson saw his chance to impress the king and possibly snag the position of governor of Iceland in return. He arrived in Reykholt with 70 armed men on the night of 23 September 1241 and hacked the historian to death in the basement of his farmhouse.

The most important relic of Snorri's farm is **Snorralaug** (Snorri's Pool), a circular, stone-lined pool fed by a hot spring, which may be the oldest handmade structure in Iceland. The stones at the base of the pool are original 10th century, and it is believed that this is where Snorri bathed. A wood-panelled tunnel beside the spring (closed to the public) leads to the old farmhouse – the site of Snorri's gruesome murder.

The quaint old church dating from 1896 is open to the public; a 1040–1260 cistern for a smithy was found beneath it in 2001 – look for the viewing glass in the floor.

Meet Icelandic goats

It's little known that Iceland's population of goats, one of the smallest, most isolated goat populations in the world, has been in danger of extinction. Farm workers walk you through pretty fields with Icelandic goats at the **Icelandic Goat Centre** *(geitur.is; adult/child 7-17 years 1800/950kr)*. The farm's most famous resident, Casanova, a bright-eyed goat who had a starring turn in *Game of Thrones* (running from a dragon), passed away some years ago, but many charming ruminants remain and the gift shop is full of goodies, goat-related and otherwise. Find the farm, Háafell, on dirt road Rte 523, northeast of Reykholt. Coffee or tea included.

Húsafell

TIME FROM BORGARNES: **50MIN**

Playing in the high country

Tucked into an emerald, river-crossed valley, with the Kaldá river on one side and a dramatic lava field on the other, **Húsafell Recreation Base**, with its encampment of summer cottages, campsite, bistro and geothermal swimming pool, and hot-pots with mountain views, is a popular outdoor retreat for Reykjavík residents, and the main access point for nearby Langjökull glacier. The star of the show in the Húsafell holiday village is the chic **Hótel Húsafell** *(hotelhusafell.com)*, offering spacious, comfortable rooms. Art is the original work of local artist Páll Guðmundsson, and the restaurant is one of the best in the region, creating dishes from local sustainable and foraged ingredients. It's also the base for **Canyon Baths** hot springs and **Into the Glacier** *(intotheglacier.is; tours from 24,000kr)*, for LED-lit tunnel and cave tours.

Nearby **Gamli Bær** guesthouse, in a quaint, renovated 1908 farmhouse, is full of charm and with country views and a hot-pot, run by jovial Sæmi.

(continues on p204)

BEST HOT SPRINGS IN THE WEST

Deildartunguhver: Find Europe's biggest hot spring about 5km west of Reykholt, just off Rte 50, near the junction with Rte 518. Look for billowing clouds of steam rising from scalding water bubbling from the ground (180L per second and 100°C).

Krauma: Bathing complex at Deildartunguhver offering sleek hot pools, a cold pool and two steam rooms. There's also a restaurant and food truck.

Hvammsvík Hot Springs: Book ahead to soak in these fjord-front hot-pots and then cold plunge just offshore if you dare.

Canyon Baths: Húsafell's fabulous wilderness hot-pots newly opened only for prebooked visits.

Snorralaug: Thought to be the oldest hot spring in Iceland is this tiny circular spring flanked by a stone patio in the village of Reykholt.

HIKING TOUR

Glymur Waterfall Hike

A diverse, scenic, moderately challenging 7.5km (4.7 mile, three to four hours) trail, suitable for outdoorsy families, leads to Glymur, the second-highest waterfall in Iceland at 198m. The path leads through a cave, over a river via a tree trunk and a cable, and up a spectacular mossy deep palagonite canyon. There's also the option to make it a longer circular trail through the valley.

❶ Botnsdalur Fields

Follow the gravel road and park at the trailhead where there's a map of the trail (take a picture of it). The route starts beyond a gate on a fairly flat dirt trail through green pastures. Take the left fork with the Glymur sign and enjoy views of green mountains in the distance (snow tipped in winter). The route is officially open between June and October, when a log is positioned, making the Botnsa River crossing possible. There are, however, adapted versions of the trail, which can be walked all year.

The Hike: This easy section is less than 2km long through fairly flat, wide dirt paths, until you reach Þvottahellir Cave.

❷ Þvottahellir Cave

Meaning 'Wash Cave' or 'Cave of the Laundry', as it was used to dry clothes on rainy days, Þvottahellir Cave is an atmospheric natural lava tube with a series of steps leading down to Botnsa River. Stop for a photo op at the natural round window or arch as you descend the stairs into the rock.

The Hike: Several stairs lead through low ceilings and through a hole in the rock. Stones can be loose underfoot so use walking poles if unsteady on your feet.

❸ Botnsa River

Fed by glacial waters from the deep Hvalvatn Lake above, formed by molten lava and up to 180m deep in places, the Botnsa

Botnsa River

River rushes for 10km along a deep canyon. A short walk left of the Þvottahellir Cave will bring walkers to a tree trunk, placed across the river between June and October (to avoid it being swept away during floods in the rainier seasons). When the tree trunk is not there, it's possible to clamber up the steep and unmaintained left side of the hill (although the trail is unofficial and slippery on slate) to get a vantage point of the waterfall.

The Hike: Hold onto the cable to steady yourself when crossing the Botnsa along the thick tree trunk over the river.

❹ Canyon Views

Follow the path next to the river, up the hill for dramatic canyon and crevice views. This river is regulated by a dam at the lake, flowing roughly 4m every second, but its speed has reached 60m a second (don't attempt river crossings when the river is rushing). On the way up, don't forget to turn your head for soaring mountain views down the valley all the way to 30km-long Hvalfjörður (Whale Fjord).

The Hike: This bit works the calves as you ascend higher, climbing roughly 300m to the falls. The path can be slippery so wear good boots.

❺ Glymur Waterfall

Rising to 198m, Glymur was for years considered the highest waterfall in Iceland, tumbling from lofty heights down the gorge. However, after Morsárjökull glacier in Vatnajökull National Park retreated, Morsárfoss was recorded at 228m. From here it's possible to continue up the cliff and wade through the river (bring water shoes or waterproof boots) and take the well-marked trail back down Svartihryggur ridge for spectacular fjord views. Otherwise, retrace your steps back down the canyon or cross the river for a longer loop (roughly 6.5km total) down the ridge.

THE STORY OF SNORRI STURLUSON

The chieftain and historian Snorri Sturluson (1179–1241) is one of the most important figures in medieval Icelandic history, and he was one of the main chroniclers of Norse sagas and histories. He composed the *Prose Edda* (a textbook of medieval Norse poetry) and *Heimskringla* (a history of the kings of Norway), and is also widely believed to be the hand behind *Egil's Saga* (p194).

Snorri was born at Hvammur near Búðardalur, raised and educated at the theological centre of Oddi near Hella, and later married the heir to the historic farm Borg á Mýrum near Borgarnes. He eventually left Borg and retreated to the wealthy church estate at Reykholt, which was home to between 60,000 and 80,000 people and was an important trade centre.

(continued from p201)

Exploring lava features

The name of spectacular **Hraunfossar** waterfall, about 6km west of Húsafell, translates to 'Lava Field waterfall' because the crystalline water streams out from below the lava field all around. Walk a little further on the marked trail to reach **Barnafoss**, another churning chute. East of Húsafell, along Rte 518, the vast, barren lava flows of Hallmundarhraun make a wonderful eerie landscape dotted with gigantic lava tubes. These long, tunnel-like caves are formed by flows of molten lava beneath a solid lava crust; it's possible to visit the 1100-year-old, 1.5km-long **Viðgelmir – the Cave** *(thecave.is; adult/youth/child 8500/4000kr/free)* on a tour. If you have caving gear (helmet, torch etc), **Surtshellir**, along Rte F578 (rental cars not allowed), is a dramatic, 2km-long tube connected to Stefánshellir, half its size.

Hidden drives

If you've got a large 4WD that's insured for F roads, it's possible to continue from Húsafell into the interior along the epic, but challenging, back-country Rte F578 beyond Surtshellir. This dramatic and supposedly haunted 2km-long, 10m-high lava tube connected to Stefánshellir sits under sheets of lava around 20m thick. The bumpy and very rough route beyond is a further adventure that has views of Langjökull glacier, goes through the mossy remote Hallmundarhraun lava field and passes the lakes at Arnarvatnsheiði, before going on to Hvammstangi. You'll likely be driving it alone. Note that Rte F578 is usually only open seven weeks a year due to weather; check *road.is* to see if its passible during your trip.

Kaldidalur Valley

TIME FROM BORGARNES: **80MIN**

Getting out onto Langjökull and the Kaldidalur Corridor

Southeast of Húsafell, the extraordinary Kaldidalur valley skirts the edge of a series of glaciers, offering incredible views of the **Langjökull** ice cap (the second-largest glacier in Iceland) and, in clear weather, Eiríksjökull, Okjökull and Þórisjökull. Do not attempt to drive up onto the glacier yourself. Tours depart from Reykjavík or Húsafell for the Into the Glacier (p201) ice cave, a major tourist attraction (tours only available between November and April). The enormous (300m-long) human-made tunnel and series of caves head into the glacier at 1260m above sea level, and contain exhibitions, a cafe and even a small chapel. **Mountaineers of Iceland** *(mountaineers.is; tours from 35,000kr)* and **Tröll Expeditions** *(troll.is; tour prices vary)* offer snowmobiling on the ice cap, but check which side they are leaving from (sometimes it's over by Gullfoss in the Golden Circle, p126).

The Kaldidalur Corridor, also simply known as unsurfaced Rte 550, is slow but dramatic going (mountain ice, barren rock) and is often fogged in in summer. It links south to the Golden Circle, offering the option to create an extended loop from Reykjavík. Access to Rte 550 is limited to sanctioned vehicles – ask your rental outfit before setting off.

Stykkishólmur

FOOD AND DRINK | WEST ICELAND BASE | QUAINT ARCHITECTURE

The charming town of Stykkishólmur, the largest on the Snæfellsnes Peninsula, is built up around a natural harbour tipped by a basalt islet. It's a picturesque place with a laid-back attitude and a sprinkling of brightly coloured buildings from the late 19th century. With a comparatively good choice of accommodation and restaurants, and handy transport links, Stykkishólmur makes an excellent base for exploring the region and the national park.

Several artists have small galleries with ceramics, woollens and other crafts, so it's a good place to look for local handmade wares. There's also free wi-fi throughout the town. What's not to love?

> **TOP TIP**
>
> In addition to its more formal sit-down restaurants, **Stykkishólmur** *(visitstykkisholmur.is)* is great for casual eats. There's everything from food trucks on the harbour (fish and chips, ice cream) to a traditional bakery, pizzeria, burger joint and fancier restaurants.

Explore the Coastline from the Water
Puffins, angling and shipwrecks

To see this mesmerising landscape in all its glory, take a local boat tour, skirting the coastline and viewing fjord islands, bird colonies (puffins can be spotted spring until August) and basalt formations (natural columns formed by the cooling and contraction of lava). **Kontiki** *(kontiki.is)* runs easy kayaking tours *(11,900kr)* to search for puffins and seals. It also ventures to an abandoned shipwreck. The rusty Dutch ship *Porgeir GK* dates to 1925, and met its end during a storm before before being banked off a nearby island. **Ocean Adventures**

GETTING AROUND

You can get to Reykjavík (2½ hours) by changing in Borgarnes by bus. Buses run out of the peninsula to Hellissandur via Vatnaleið (crossroads of Rtes 54 and 56), Grundarfjörður, Ólafsvík and Rif. All services are greatly reduced in winter.

The **Baldur car ferry** *(ferja.is/on)* crosses Breiðafjörður between Stykkishólmur and Brjánslækur in the Westfjords (2½ hours) via Flatey (1½ hours), where it stops for five minutes. From early July to early August, when there are two boats per day, you can take the first ferry to Flatey, then the second ferry onward or back to Stykkishólmur. Book ahead to bring your car or camper.

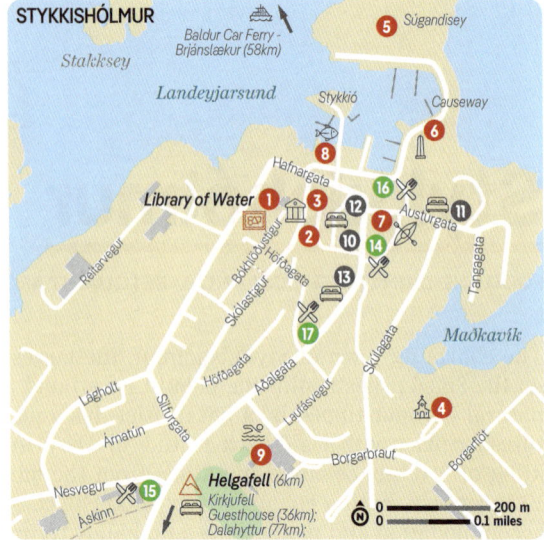

GETTING YOUR WISH AT HELGAFELL

To ascend Helgafell, pay the fee at the base, but to get your three wishes, you must ask with a pure heart and follow three important steps.

Step 1 Start at the grave of Guðrun Ósvífursdóttir.

Step 2 Walk up to the Tótt (the chapel ruins), not uttering a single word, and (like Orpheus leaving Hades), never looking back.

Step 3 Once at the ruins, face east while wishing. And never tell your wishes to anyone or they won't come true.

★ HIGHLIGHTS
1 Library of Water

● SIGHTS
2 Eider Center and Cafe
3 Norska Húsið
4 Stykkishólmskirkja
5 Súgandisey
6 Viking Longboat Sculpture

● ACTIVITIES
7 Kontiki
8 Ocean Adventures
9 Stykkishólmur Swimming Pool

● SLEEPING
10 Akkeri
11 Fransiskus Hotel
12 Hótel Egilsen
13 Stykkishólmur Inn

● EATING
14 Narfeyrarstofa
15 Nesbrauð
16 Sjávarpakkhúsið
17 Skipper Restaurant

(oceanadventures.is) lets you try your hand at angling *(from 25000kr)* for cod, halibut, wolffish, haddock and ocean perch, and also offers a puffin-viewing tour with boats going to puffin nesting site Elliðaey *(13,000kr)*.

Climbing Helgafell for Good Luck
Historic hill with lore

The holy mountain Helgafell (73m), about 5km south of Stykkishólmur proper, was once venerated by worshippers of the

EATING IN STYKKISHÓLMUR: OUR PICKS

Sjávarpakkhúsið: Old fish-packing house transformed into a wood-lined fine-dining eatery with harbourfront outdoor seating. *6-9pm €€*

Narfeyrarstofa: Book a table on the 2nd floor for romantic antique lamps and harbour views at this excellent restaurant. *6-9pm €€*

Nesbrauð: Stock up on sugary confections such as *kleinur* (traditional twisty doughnuts) or *ástar pungur* (literally 'love balls'; fried balls of dough and raisins). *7.30am-3pm Mon-Fri, 8am-3pm Sat €*

Skipper Restaurant: Family-owned no-frills restaurant-cum-pub with solid burgers and fish and chips. *noon-10pm €*

god Þór. Although quite small, the mountain was so sacred in Saga times that elderly Icelanders would seek it out near the time of their death. Today locals believe that wishes are granted to those who climb the mount.

In the late 10th century, Snorri Goði, a prominent Þor worshipper, converted to Christianity and built a church at the top of the hill; its ruins still remain. The nearby farm of the same name was where the conniving Guðrun Ósvífursdóttir of *Laxdæla Saga* lived out her later years in isolation. Her grave marks the base of the mount.

Stay at wonderful **Helgafell 2 Guesthouse**, with two bungalows and a studio, if you want to overnight on the lambent pond alongside the mountain.

Celebrate Icelandic Water
Installation and hot-pots

For relaxing views of town and bay, head up the hill to the **Library of Water** (*facebook.com/vatnasafn; adult/child 900kr/free*). This window-lined space showcases an installation by American artist Roni Horn (b 1955). Light reflects and refracts through 24 glass pillars filled with Icelandic glacier water. There's also a chess set if you feel like lingering. Visit the Norwegian House to get an access code to the Water Museum.

To actually get *in* the water, head inland to **Stykkishólmur Swimming Pool** (*adult/child 1500/500kr, under 6 years free*), where waterslides and hot-pots are the highlights at the town's geothermal swimming pool in the municipal sports complex alongside the campsite.

WATCH (DON'T EAT) WHALES & PUFFINS

Whale-watching boats also leave from Ólafsvík/Grundarfjörður (p213), Húsavík (p280) and Akureyri (p271). Puffins feature at Ingólfshöfði (p172) and, of course, the Vestmannaeyjar archipelago (p147).

FOR FANS OF ICELANDIC BAKED GOODS

Compare Stykkishólmur's *kleinur* and *ástar pungur* with those at Möðrudalur (p342) on the edge of the East and the highlands.

STROLLING THROUGH TOWN & HISTORY

Discover Stykkishólmur's museum, church and brilliant fjord views on this walk around town

START	END	LENGTH
Norska Húsið	Súgandisey	2km; 1 hour

Stykkishólmur's quaint maritime charm comes from the cluster of wooden warehouses, shops and homes around the town's harbour, most dating back about 150 years. One of the most interesting (and oldest) is the ❶ **Norska Húsið**, now the regional museum, built by trader and amateur astronomer Árni Thorlacius in 1832.

For duck aficionados, head just behind to the ❷ **Eider Center and Cafe** which explains everything you need to know about duck farming and duvet making in this, the centre of eider farming.

Walk along the town's main road (Rte 58) and turn onto Borgarbraut to Stykkishólmur's futuristic church, ❸ **Stykkishólmskirkja**, with its sweeping bell tower that looks like a whale vertebra. It was designed by Jón Haraldsson, and the interior features hundreds of suspended lights and a painting of the Madonna and Child floating in the night sky.

Follow Skúlagata back to the harbour, past the metal ❹ **Viking Longboat Sculpture**, and cross the causeway at the tip of Stykkishólmur Harbour. Cap off your stroll of town at the basalt island of ❺ **Súgandisey** with its scenic lighthouse and grand views across Breiðafjörður.

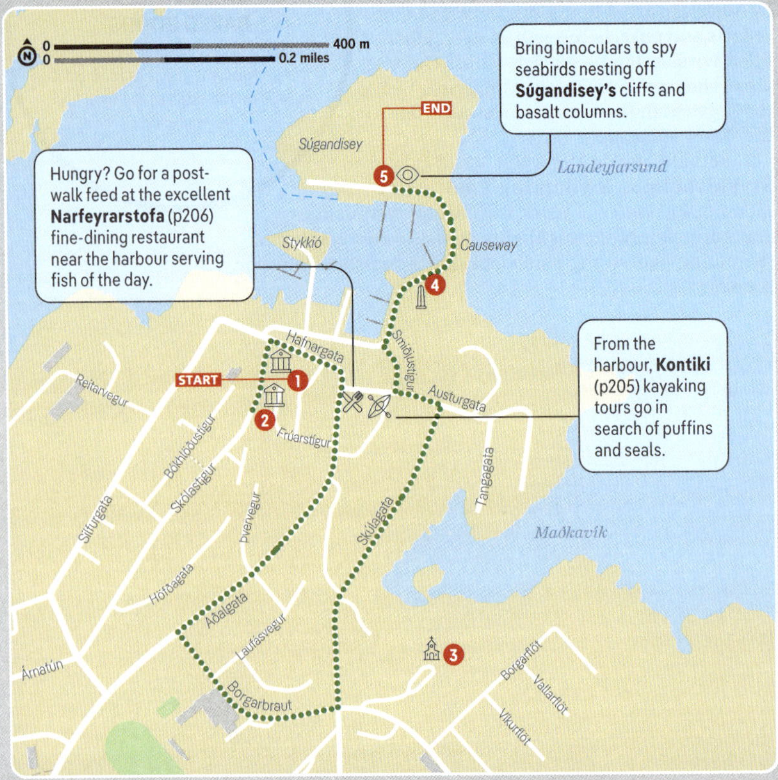

> Bring binoculars to spy seabirds nesting off **Súgandisey's** cliffs and basalt columns.

> Hungry? Go for a post-walk feed at the excellent **Narfeyrarstofa** (p206) fine-dining restaurant near the harbour serving fish of the day.

> From the harbour, **Kontiki** (p205) kayaking tours go in search of puffins and seals.

Beyond Stykkishólmur

Gentle Grundarfjörður and its iconic mountain Kirkjufell, windswept island Flatey, plus saga country make for super exploring.

From Stykkishólmur, on the Snæfellsnes Peninsula's populated northern coast, moving west you'll pass rugged lava fields to reach smaller townships, including charming Grundarfjörður with its famous mountain Kirkjufell and accompanying resplendent waterfalls. Between Stykkishólmur and the Westfjords, the rolling fields of the Dalir, one of Iceland's bread baskets, are also home to two fascinating saga sights focusing on Erik the Red (Eiríkur Rauðe) and Leifur Eiríksson. The Erpsstaðir dairy farm is also a perfect pit stop for refreshments.

Across the broad Breiðafjörður (that's what the name means: broad), tiny Flatey Island is an idyllic windswept isle calling out for a serene overnight.

Places
Flatey p209
Búðardalur p209
Grundarfjörður p211
Bjarnarhöfn p212
Dalabyggð p212

GETTING AROUND

Strætó bus 59 connects Borgarnes–Bifröst–Búðardalur–Skriðuland–Króksfjarðarnes–Hólmavík. It has connections to Reykjavík from Borgarnes. Bus 57 Reykjavík–Akureyri runs through Bifröst and Staðarskáli (to Reykjavík or to Akureyri).

Ferjuleiðir ehf *(ferja.is/en;* single journeys from Brjánslækur, from 4200kr) runs ferries to Flatey, which can be visited as a day trip in summer when there are two boats a day.

Flatey
TIME FROM STYKKISHÓLMUR: 1½HR

Wander Old Iceland

Of Breiðafjörður's innumerable islands, little Flatey (literally 'Flat Island') is the only one with year-round inhabitants. In the 11th century Flatey *(flatey.com)* was home to a monastery, and today the appealing island is a popular stopover for travellers heading to (or from) the Westfjords, as well as filmmakers: several movies and series have been shot here. Push the slow-mo button on life, and get a glimpse of old-fashioned windswept Iceland, amid bright candy-coloured houses and swooping Arctic terns.

Hótel Flatey, built in 1890, is open from the last week in May until the end of August, and has some of the most charming, nook-like vintage rooms in Iceland, and the on-site restaurant is fantastic as well, serving a small menu of fish and tenderloin mains. On some summer evenings, slip down into the basement bar for live music. One of the island's farms, about 300m from the pier, **Krákuvör** (438 1451) offers camping on a meadow sweeping to the shore.

Búðardalur
TIME FROM STYKKISHÓLMUR: 1¼HR

Stop in a dairy town

Founded as a cargo depot in Saga times, the pint-sized town of Búðardalur (pronounced boo-thar-dalur) occupies a pleasant position looking out over **Hvammsfjörður**, at the mouth of the

SAGA-FILLED DALIR DISTRICT

The scenic corridor of rolling fields and craggy river-carved buttes between West Iceland and the Westfjords is known as Dalir. It served as the setting for the *Laxdæla Saga*, written in the 13th century, and the most popular of the Icelandic sagas, believed to have been written by a woman. The story revolves around a love triangle between Guðrun Ósvífursdóttir, said to be the most beautiful woman in Iceland, and the foster brothers Kjartan Ólafsson and Bolli Þorleiksson. In typical saga fashion, Guðrun had both men wrapped around her little finger and schemed until both were dead. Most Icelanders know the stories by heart and hold this area in great esteem.

Laxá river. A current claim to fame is its dairy, which produces most of the cheese in Iceland. The local supermarket carries a good sample. If time permits, add in a stop at **Leifsbúð**, a little cafe near the water offering coffee, cakes and soup; upstairs a multimedia exhibition focuses on Leifur Eiríksson and the exceptional Guðriður Þorbjarnardóttir (p218).

Swing into **Bolli Craft** *(facebook.com/bollicraft)* for cool local arts and crafts including handmade sweaters, sheephorn buttons and charming elves.

Just north of the spot where Rte 590 heads west off Rte 60 you'll find the encampment at **Laugar**, the birthplace of *Laxdæla Saga* beauty Guðrun Ósvífursdóttir. Historians believe they've found Guðrun's bathing pool: **Guðrúnarlaug** (also known as the Saga hot-tub), the free circular hot pool, is well marked above the entrance to **Dalahótel**, a fine place to overnight, and has a small changing kiosk. Tungustapi, in the distance, is a large elf cathedral.

Eat farm treats

When the peanut gallery starts moaning, 'Are we there yet?', you know it's time to head to **Erpsstaðir** *(erpsstadir.is)*, the perfect place to stretch your legs. Like a mirage for sweettoothed wanderers, this dairy farm on the gorgeous Rte 60 (between Búðardalur and the Ring Road; with high mountain valleys, streams and waterfalls) specialises in delicious homemade ice cream. You can tour the farm, greet the buxom bovines, chickens, rabbits and even guinea pigs, then gorge on a scoop. The farm also sells *skyr* (yoghurt-like dessert) and cheese; try the rocket-shaped *skyr-konfekt* (meant to look like an udder), a delicious dessert made with a hard white chocolate shell encasing thick *skyr*. It'll blow you away. Want to stay? They have a rental house, too.

See inside a Viking longhouse

The farm **Eiríksstaðir** *(eiriksstadir.is; adult/child under 12 years 2800kr/free)* was home to Eiríkur Rauðe (Erik the Red), father of Leifur Eiríksson, the first European to visit America. Although only a ruin of the original farm remains, a fascinating reconstructed turf house built using only the tools and materials available at the time is an excellent blast into the past. Period-dressed guides show visitors around, and while seated around a traditional indoor fire explain interesting details of Settlement Era living: how Viking longhouses were cleverly built slotted together and could be moved to different locations; that people in a Viking longhouse would sleep sitting up to avoid fire smoke; or that Viking women (who could be warriors, but typically worked in the house) had an average life expectancy of under 30 years due to childbirth and the smoke inside the longhouse (which, of course, they didn't understand was poisonous at the time). Historians also tell the fascinating story of Erik the Red, who went on to found the first European settlement in Greenland – named as a clever marketing scheme by Erik, who was exiled from Iceland and wanted to convince people to move to this icy northern place. His exploits were captured in *Saga of Erik*

Kirkjufell

the Red and *Saga of the Greenlanders*. Eiríksstaðir's shop is the place to pick up Viking history books and memorabilia.

Grundarfjörður

TIME FROM STYKKISHÓLMUR: **30MIN**

Take an iconic waterfall snap

Spectacularly set on a dramatic bay, little Grundarfjörður is backed by waterfalls and surrounded by ice-capped peaks often shrouded in cottony fog. More prefab than wooden, the town feels like a typical Icelandic fishing community with a great vibe. The surrounding landscape can't be beaten, with its iconic **Kirkjufell** (463m), guardian of the town's northwestern vista. Translating to 'Church Mountain', it was also known as 'The Sugar Top' by Danish sailors. It's said to be one of the most photographed spots in Iceland, appearing in *Game of Thrones* season one in a scene with Jon Snow. Locals may help you find a guide to climb it, as it can be technical. Two spots involving a rope climb make it dangerous to scale when wet or without local knowledge. The bottom of the mountain dates back a million years and contains fossils of organisms that lived during the Ice Age.

Kirkjufell is backed by the roaring **Kirkjufellsfoss** (Church Mountain Falls), which runs from the Kirkjufellsá river down the Helgrindur volcano. It's made up of three waterfalls for

---

SECRET SPOTS

Marta Magnúsdóttir, former Iceland Chief Scout and Valeria Coffee owner, offers her favourite things to do in the area. *Instagram.com/marta-magnusdottir*

If I have friends visiting me it will include one or all of following.

A visit to the swimming pool, an Icelandic tradition. In Snæfellsnes there are four public pools; all are fantastic but **Grundarfjörður** pool offers the best view.

Showing our (lack of) skills at one of our superb golf courses such as **Vestarr Golf Course**; they are managed by volunteers and welcome visitors to play nine holes.

Last but not least, those rainbow air balloon trampolines you see everywhere, in **Stykkishólmur**, and the towns around. Well, they are so fun! Remove your shoes and go for some goofy jumping!

🍴 EATING IN GRUNDARFJÖRÐUR: OUR PICKS

Bjargarsteinn Mathús: Superb waterfront restaurant creating Icelandic dishes with an emphasis on fresh seafood. *6-9.30pm Tue-Thu, 6-10pm Fri-Sun* €€

Valeria Coffee: Who better than a friendly Colombian ex-pat and Icelandic partnership to import, roast and serve some of the best coffee in Iceland? *8.30am-4pm Tue-Fri, 9am-4pm Sat-Mon* €

Græna kompaníið: Vegetarian coffee house serving soup of the day with vegan bread, plus cakes and coffee. *noon-9pm* €

Kaffi 59: Cosy cafe serving burgers with patties made of local beef, plus pizzas, fish and chips, local lamb chops, and soup of the day. *noon-9pm* €

WEST ICELAND EXPLORATION

Noel Bas Barrera, the seasoned chef of Sjávarpakkhúsið (p206), shares his tips for how to get out into the raw open spaces of West Iceland.
@noel_brx
@sjavarpakkhusi

I feel like here in the west of Iceland it is one of the most beautiful and quiet places. Close to Reykjavík, small towns, cosy, no stress. Living in the middle of nature. If I am not working, then I go somewhere, always. Kayak in Stykkishólmur with Kontiki (p205). Climb to Glymur (p202) waterfall. I go in my camper car and trek, trying to discover new places.

The whole Snæfellsnes Peninsula is fantastic: Hellnar (p216) with its really nice cafe, tiny and in front of the ocean...one of my favourites. I love the lonely road through the Berserkjahraun (Berserkers' lava field). Go by bicycle or go with a car, about 15km west of the intersection of Rte 54 and Rte 56.

---

more camera fodder. Look out for birdlife in this area: of the 75 species breeding in Iceland, 55 of them nest on Snæfellsnes Peninsula. The seabed fauna and flora is some of the richest in the North Atlantic.

Bjarnarhöfn

TIME FROM STYKKISHÓLMUR: 25MIN

Try ethical shark meat

The farmstead at Bjarnarhöfn is the region's leading producer of *hákarl* (fermented shark meat), a traditional Icelandic dish. The **Bjarnarhöfn Shark Museum** *(bjarnarhofn.is; entry 2000kr)* has exhibits on the history of this culinary curiosity, along with the family's fishing boats and processing tools. A video explains how the Greenland shark, which is used to make *hákarl*, is poisonous if eaten fresh; fermentation neutralises the toxin. Note that Greenland shark is classified as near threatened, and is the longest-living vertebrate on the planet, with some living over 500 years. Staff at the museum explain that once locals worked out how to ferment the meat, they discovered numerous heath benefits including high protein and omega-3 fatty acids. The sharks were once fished as there was a limited source of food in Iceland. Now the farm only prepares accidental catches by fishers, that would otherwise be discarded.

Your visit to the museum comes with a bracing nibble of possibly the most ethically sourced *hákarl* you can try, accompanied by either *rúgbrauð* (Icelandic rye bread) or Brennivín (aka 'black death') schnapps. Ask about the drying house out the back – you might find hundreds of dangling shark slices drying, the last step in the process. It's off Rte 54 on a turnoff from Rte 577, on the fjordside, northeastern edge of Bjarnarhafnarfjall (575m).

Dalabyggð

TIME FROM STYKKISHÓLMUR: 2HR

Drive lonely Rte 590

The dramatic coastline of the oft-forgotten peninsula between the Snæfellsnes Peninsula and the Westfjords is traced by the 85km track Rte 590 (OK for 2WD; along Rte 60 look for the turnoff at Fellströnd). Windswept farmsteads lie frozen in time, and boulder-strewn hills, crowned with flattened granite, roll skyward. Keep an eye out for white-tailed eagles.

Near the beginning of the track, the farm at Hvammur produced a whole line of prominent Icelanders, including Snorri Sturluson of *Prose Edda* fame. You can spend the night at remote, lovely **Guesthouse Nýp** *(nyp.is)*. If you can't get in there, try **Vogur Country Lodge** *(vogur.org)*. Some of the local farms in these parts have remained in the same hands for more than 1000 years.

Snæfellsnes Peninsula

LAVA TUBES | HIKING | WHALE WATCHING

Snæfellsjökull National Park encompasses much of the western tip of Snæfellsnes Peninsula and wraps around the rugged slopes of the glacier Snæfellsjökull (pronounced sneye-fells-yo-kutl), the icy fist at the end of the long Snæfellsnes arm. Around its flanks lie lava tubes, protected lava fields home to native Icelandic fauna, and prime hiking and coastal bird- and whale-watching spots.

When the fog swirling around the glacier lifts you'll see the mammoth ice cap, which was made famous when Jules Verne used it as the setting for *Journey to the Centre of the Earth*. In his book, a German geologist and his nephew embark on an epic journey into the crater of Snæfells, guided by a 16th-century Icelandic text.

To the east of Snæfellsjökull National Park, coastal Rte 574 passes the hamlets of Hellnar and Arnarstapi, with their glacier tour companies and interesting sea-sculpted rock formations. It continues east along the broad southern coastal plain, hugging huge sandy bays such as Breiðavík on one side, and towering peaks with waterfalls on the other.

Go Whale Watching & Puffin-Spotting

Wildlife watching from the ocean

Láki Tours *(lakitours.com; from 14,000kr)* has excellent fishing, puffin-spotting and whale-watching trips from Grundarfjörður or Ólafsvík. Whale-watching tours from Ólafsvík (mid-February to September) cover the area's best cetacean habitat – orca, fin, sperm, blue, minke and humpback can all be seen.

Puffin tours (June to late August) from Grundarfjörður go to the wonderful basalt island Melrakkaey, with puffins, kittiwakes and other seabirds. Cute and endearingly comic, the puffin (*Fratercula arctica*, or *lundi* as they're called in Icelandic) is one of Iceland's best-loved birds. It's a member of

GETTING AROUND

The best way to get around Snæfellsnes Peninsula is in your own rented wheels – the views are glorious and you can stop off at sites impossible to reach by public transport. Strætó bus *(straeto.is)* runs to the area (2½ hours from Reykjavík with a change in Borgarnes). All services are greatly reduced in winter.

☑ TOP TIP

Malarrif and Hellissandur each have a National Park Visitor Centre. The park's online map is also excellent and rangers have an active summer program of free park guided tours – check online or on their facebook page.

the auk family and spends most of its year at sea. For four or five months it comes to land to breed, generally keeping the same mate and burrow from year to year.

Giant & Troll Stroll

Coastal walk between Hellnar and Arnarstapi

Hellnar is a tiny fishing village (once huge), overlooking a rocky bay where waves incessantly beat against the steep black cliffs, forming awe-inspiring formations and home to seabird rookeries. Whales are regularly sighted here too. In folklore this is home to the guardian spirit of Bárður, part giant, part troll and part human (from the *Snæfellsáss Saga*), who is said to live in a cave below. The nearby Bárðarlaug lake was supposedly Bárður's bathing pool, though the pond is no longer hot. The area can be explored via an easy 2.5km **coastal path** to/from Arnarstapi following the jagged coastline through a nature reserve, passing lava flows and eroded stone caves and past a statue of the deity. During tumultuous weather, waves spray through the rocky arches; when it's fine, look for nesting seabirds. Ancient, velvety moss-cloaked lava flows tumble east through the Hellnahraun. **Fjöruhúsið** *(facebook.com/FjoruhusidHellnum)* is tops for a seafront soup or cake.

Riding the Rolling Coastline

Southern Snæfellsnes by horseback

Local farm **Stóri Kambur** *(storikambur.is; tours from 14,500kr per person)* offers one- to two-hour rides on the beach, some with a historical saga theme. It's a family-run chance to embrace the open air and relaxation of the quiet southern coast of Snæfellsnes with glacier views (when it's clear), plus there are short kids' rides, and cottages to let. Equine enthusiasts can also try friendly horse farm **Lýsuhóll** *(lysuholl.is; beach tours from 34,000kr),* which also has a guesthouse and cottages.

The geothermal source for **Lýsulaugar** *(lysulaugar.is; adult/child/under 9 years 1500/500kr/free)* pumps carbonated, mineral-filled waters in at a perfect 37°C to 39°C. Don't be alarmed that the pool is a murky green – it's rich in green chlorella algae and is supposed to have a soothing and healing effect on the body. No chemicals (such as chlorine) are added to the water.

GOING BERSERK

The common term 'berserk' comes from the old Norse word *'berserkr'*, describing warriors in a trance-like fury, but there's also a West Iceland link. Berserkjahraun hails from the *Eyrbyggja Saga,* telling the tale of a farmer who grew weary of having to walk on jagged lava. He employed two berserkers to work on his farm. When one of them took a liking to his daughter, he asked local chieftain Snorri Goði for advice, but Snorri also had a crush on her. Snorri recommended setting the berserker an impossible task: promise the daughter's hand in marriage if he clears a passage through the lava field – surely impossible. To the horror of both, the berserkers ripped a passage straight through. The farmer trapped the berserkers in a sauna and murdered them, allowing Snorri to marry his daughter. A path through the 4000-year-old lava field of **Berserkjahraun** still remains, and a grave was discovered containing the remains of two large men.

 WHERE TO EAT NEAR SNÆFELLSJÖKULL NATIONAL PARK

Fjöruhúsið: Renowned fish soup by the bird cliffs at the trailhead of the scenic Hellnar–Arnarstapi path. *11am-5pm* €

Samkomuhúsið: Arnarstapi's tried-and-true old school eatery for Icelandic specialities like lamb soup and fish and chips. *noon-4pm Mon-Fri, to 3pm Sat & Sun* €€

Sker Restaurant: Reliable fish dishes, BBQ and pasta in a cosy atmosphere in Ólafsvík. *8am-9.30pm* €€

Stapinn: Laid-back Arnarstapi cafe serving burgers, fish and chips and soups, plus a selection of fried cheeses. *11am-8pm* €

Djúpalónssandur

TOP EXPERIENCE

Snæfellsjökull National Park

Snæfellsjökull National Park offers an abundance of natural features and a spectacular ice cap. Stay on the park's edges (it has no accommodation or camping) and make forays in – distances are short so it's easy to explore a smorgasbord of experiences quickly. Malarrif and Hellissandur are home to visitor centres that sell maps, give advice and offer free guided tours in summer.

DON'T MISS

- Öndverðarnes
- Saxhóll Crater
- Snæfellsjökull
- Djúpalón Beach & Dritvík
- Malarrif rock stacks

Djúpalón Beach & Dritvík

On the southwest coast, Rte 572 leads off Rte 574 to wild black-sand beach **Djúpalónssandur**. It's a dramatic place to walk, with rock formations (an elf church, and a *kerling* – a troll woman), two brackish pools (for which the beach was named) and the rock-arch Gatklettur. Some of the black sands are covered in pieces of rusted metal from the English trawler *Eding*, which was shipwrecked here in 1948. An asphalt car park and public toilets allow tour-bus access, and crowds.

Down on the beach you can still see four lifting stones where fishing-boat crews would test the strength of aspiring fishers. A series of rocky sea stacks, some of which are thought to be a troll church, emerge from the ocean up the coast as you tramp north over the craggy headland to reach the black-sand beach

PRACTICALITIES
Scan this QR code for hiking trail maps and wildlife guides

at Dritvík. From the 16th to the 19th century, Dritvík was the largest fishing station in Iceland, with up to 60 fishing boats, but now there are only ruins near the edge of the lava field.

Snæfellsjökull

It's easy to see why Jules Verne selected Snæfell for *Journey to the Centre of the Earth*: the peak was torn apart when the volcano beneath it exploded and then collapsed back into its own magma chamber, forming a huge caldera. Today the crater is filled with the Snæfellsjökull ice cap (highest point 1446m) and is a popular summer destination.

Saxhóll Crater & Sauðhóll

About 11.5km north of the Djúpalón exit, on Rte 574, follow the marked turnoff to the roadside scoria **Saxhóll Crater**, which was responsible for some of the lava in the area. There's a drivable track leading to the base, from where it's a 300m climb for magnificent views over the enormous Neshraun lava flows. Or trek south into the greener crater Sauðhóll.

Vatnshellir

The 8000-year-old Vatnshellir lava tube with multiple caverns lies 32m below the earth's surface, 1km north of Malarrif. The car park is visible from Rte 574, and the tube can only be visited by guided tour with **Summit Adventure Guides** *(summitguides.is; adult/child 5400/2400kr)*. A 10 minute drive east is **Rauðfeldsgjá Gorge**, a dramatic mossy crevice that you can walk inside by hopping on rocks.

Öndverðarnes

At the westernmost tip of Snæfellsnes, Rte 574 cuts south, while Rte 579, a tiny gravel and occasionally surfaced track, heads further west across an ancient lava flow to the tip of the **Öndverðarnes** (pronounced und-ver-thar-nes) peninsula, which is great for whale watching.

Exploring a Golden Beach

As the paved road winds through charcoal lava cliffs you'll pass **Skarðsvík**, a golden beach with basalt cubes. A Viking grave was discovered here in the 1960s; it's easy to see why this was a favoured final resting place.

The Point

After Skarðsvík the track is unpaved and bumpier (though still manageable for a 2WD). Park at the turnoff (left side) to walk through craggy lava flows to the imposing volcanic crater **Vatnsborg**, or continue driving straight on until you reach a T-intersection. It's 1km to the left to the dramatic Svörtuloft bird cliffs (Saxhólsbjarg), with excellent walkways, and the tall, orange **Svörtuloft Lighthouse**. To the right, a bumpy track runs parallel to the sea for 2km to a squat, orange lighthouse. From its parking area, you can walk to the very tip of the peninsula, for whale watching, or walk 200m northeast to **Fálki**, an ancient stone well that was thought to have three waters: fresh, holy and ale!

MALARRIF & LÓNDRANGAR

Malarrif Lighthouse and visitor centre are about 2km south of Djúpalónssandur. A trail leads 1km east along cliffs to rock pillars at Lóndrangar, which surge into the air in surprising pinnacles. **Þúfubjarg bird cliffs** lie further east. Lóndrangar and Þúfubjarg are also accessible from Rte 574.

TOP TIPS

● The best way to reach the glacial summit is to take a tour with **Summit Adventure Guides** or **Icelandic Mountain Guides** *(mountainguides.is; tours from 52,000kr)* These companies approach the peak from the south, on Rte F570.

● Rte F570's northern approach (near Ólafsvík) is frustratingly rutty (4WD required) and frequently closed due to weather-inflicted damage.

● Even the well-trained and outfitted are not allowed to ascend the glacier without a local guide; contact the National Park Visitor Centre in Hellissandur or Malarrif for more information.

EXPLORER GUÐRIÐUR ÞORBJARNARDÓTTIR

Among Iceland's most celebrated explorers, Guðriður Þorbjarnardóttir certainly earned her nickname the 'Far Traveller'. A small sculpture marks the site of her family's farm (now abandoned) at **Laugarbrekka**. Born in Hellnar before the year 1000, Guðriður had a serious case of wanderlust. Not only was she one of the first Europeans to reach Vinland (thought to be Canada's Newfoundland), she bore a child while she was there: the first European born in North America! Later, Guðriður converted to Christianity and embarked on an epic pilgrimage to Rome, where some say she met the pope and recounted her experiences.

Guðriður features in *Saga of Erik the Red*, *Saga of the Greenlanders*, *The Far Traveler* by Nancy Marie Brown and *The Sea Road* by Margaret Elphinstone.

Ingjaldshóll

Small Towns, Curious Churches
Charming fishing settlements

Quiet, workaday Ólafsvík won't win any hearts with its fish-processing plant. Although it's the oldest trading town in the country (it was granted a trading licence in 1687), few of the original buildings survive. But the waters offshore and west to the tip of the peninsula are the region's best for whale sightings. Blink-and-you'll-miss-it **Rif** is a harbour hamlet that makes Ólafsvík look like a teeming metropolis. Dramatic **Svöðufoss**, with its barrelling cascades and dramatic hexagonal basalt, rockets along in the distance.

Between Rif and Hellissandur, spot the lonely church (built 1903) at **Ingjaldshóll**, the setting of *Víglundar Saga*. If the church doors are open, you can see a painting depicting Christopher Columbus' possible visit to Iceland in 1477; it's thought he came with the merchant marine and enquired about Viking trips to Vinland. The **Freezer Hostel** (*thefreezerhostel.com*) has the best nightlife around: check online for its music and theatre gigs.

Places We Love to Stay

€ Budget   €€ Midrange   €€€ Top End

Borgarnes & Reykholt
MAP p195

B59 Hotel & Hostel € Nicely decorated rooms and apartments, plus a choice of cheaper accommodation in the hostel.

Bjarg €€ This attractive series of linked cottages 1.5km north of Borgarnes overlooks the fjord and mountains.

Helgugata Guesthouse €€ Friendly Ludmila keeps this tidy guesthouse, perched on the cliff overlooking the twinkling fjord beyond.

Kría Guesthouse €€ On the seafront in a private home on a quiet residential street, Kría's two rooms have great water views.

Steindórsstaðir €€ Set on a farm 2km from Reykholt; offers clean, cosy rooms with countryside views, and a hot tub.

Fossatún €€ Family-friendly spot with a guesthouse, restaurant, hotel, cottage and numerous curved shaped camping huts next to a roaring waterfall.

Stykkishólmur
MAP p206

Stykkishólmur Inn € Warm and cosy guesthouse, with simple reasonably priced rooms, including singles with their own bathrooms, parking and a great Icelandic breakfast.

Dalahyttur €€ Three tiny cottages (each sleeping four) with a kitchenette, dining area, bathroom with a shower and sweeping views of Hólsfjall mountain and beyond. Also nine double rooms.

Akkeri €€ Smack in the centre of town; minimalist, comfortable rooms with swanky bathrooms – one has a balcony.

Hótel Egilsen €€€ Pretty red Norwegian-style house with lots of cosy character and tiny rooms in a timber house that creaks when winds howl off the fjord.

Fransiskus Hotel €€€ Renovated wing of a monastery built in the 1930s by Catholic sisters, and hospital complex; modern rooms, some with private bathrooms.

Kirkjufell Guesthouse €€€ Modern, well-equipped farmhouse guesthouse with a top waterfall-filled fjord setting just outside Grundarfjörður. Five comfy bedrooms share three bathrooms.

Snæfellsnes Peninsula
MAP p214

Grundarfjörður HI Hostel € Oiled outfit offering accommodation for most tastes from smart shared dorms to larger shared apartments. Sleeping arrangements are spread across the town. Sign up to HI for a discounted price.

Hellissandur Campground € Camping in a spiky lava field, with clean showers and a play park for children.

Við Hafið Guesthouse € It's not the prettiest of buildings but it has clean, simple rooms inside, plus shared bathrooms and kitchen facilities.

Freezer Hostel € One of the coolest and most social places on the peninsula, this Rif hostel has live music most nights and individually designed shared or individual rooms, some more trippy than others. Icelandic scenes painted on the walls. Shared bathrooms.

Miðhraun – Lava Resort €€ Sprawling and family-friendly with cottages, restaurant, geothermal baths, playground and farm animals. Super quiet option. It has a gorgeous restaurant in a converted barn.

Guesthouse Snjófell €€ Basic clean rooms, some with wooden floors, plush a good buffet breakfast and a bar/lounge to relax in.

Fosshotel Hellnar €€€ Sun-filled comfortable rooms and a good restaurant serving Icelandic fare and organic wines and beers; run with sustainability in mind.

Hótel Buðir €€€ Windswept inn, once a 17th-century trading post, with historic photos on the wall, on a lava field next to a gorgeous, remote coastline – room 28 has the best views (and a teeny balcony).

Researched by
Jade Bremner

The Westfjords

OFF-BEAT ICELAND

Epic drives twist and turn along the dramatic and mystical roads, with fjord after fjord views. At Europe's westernmost tip stoic puffins congregate for sunset. This isolated area has a long and fascinating history of folklore tradition, including witches and sea monsters.

The people of northwest Iceland – known as Vestfirðingar – have over the years threatened to secede from the rest of the country by establishing the Democratic Republic of the Westfjords. It is a joke, but it's telling: the massive northernmost peninsula, home to only 7000 people, the majority in the capital of Ísafjörður (pictured), does feel like a land of its own. It's believed that its isolation is one of the reasons it was home to such a large concentration of sorcerers and witches. About two-thirds of all 17th-century Icelandic witchcraft trials came from the Westfjords, and the Museum of Icelandic Sorcery & Witchcraft in Hólmavík explores the history of their practices. It's here that you can attend an annual festival of witchcraft and try 'witchcraft beer' or visit the Icelandic Sea Monster Museum – many of which have been spotted in and around the town of Bíldudalur.

On a map of Iceland, the Westfjords region is already in juxtaposition – the coastline appears to be drawn with a shaky hand, shaped by fjord after fjord after fjord: the Nordic word for narrow inlets with deep sea and steep mountains. The difference has to do with geological age. The land is Iceland's oldest and resembles that of neighbouring Greenland in many ways.

The natural curves make driving full of twists and turns. Consider this for scale: the region itself is merely one-fifth of Iceland's size but its circular drive covers some 950km altogether, known as the Westfjords Way, a bucket-list four-wheel endeavour. More than any other region in Iceland, the Westfjords is a summer destination. The birds of Látrabjarg, nesting in millions on Europe's westernmost tip, at least, agree summer is the best time to enjoy the rugged wilderness of narrow fjords and steep cliffs.

MONSDIAS/SHUTTERSTOCK

THE MAIN AREAS

ARNARFJÖRÐUR
Dynjandi waterfall and quirky museums. **p226**

ÍSAFJÖRÐUR
The largest town in the region and adventure base. **p236**

HÓLMAVÍK
Folklore heritage and whale watching. **p244**

For places to stay in the Westfjords, see p247

THE GUIDE

THE WESTFJORDS

Left: Ísafjörður (p236); Above: Hornbjarg cliff (p241)

Find Your Way

A vast size and small population set the Westfjords up as the ultimate road-trip destination, more about the journey than the must-sees. We've picked the places that capture its natural landscape and culture.

Ísafjörður, p236
A colourful community in bright tin-clad buildings, hemmed in on all sides by towering peaks and the dark waters of the fjord.

Arnarfjörður, p226
Home to two museums – the Icelandic Sea Monster Museum and Samúel Jónsson's Art Farm – that subtly capture the isolation of the 'Westfjords Alps'.

Látrabjarg Peninsula, p234
Sharp cliffs the length of a town and the largest bird cliffs in Europe, occupied by hundreds of puffins in summer.

Hornstrandir Peninsula, p241

Be among the small but steady number of travellers trekking to Hornbjarg, the iconic cliff that most people will only see on postcards.

Hólmavík, p244

The second-largest industry in Hólmavík – after fishing – is studying and sharing stories from the past: residents thrive on folklore.

AIR

Icelandair flies between Ísafjörður Airport, 5km south on the fjord, and Reykjavík's domestic airport twice a day. Hire a car at the airport or take the shuttle into Ísafjörður. Norlandair flies from Reykjavik to Bíldudalur and Strandir a few times a week.

CAR

Hire a car, preferably a 4WD, to explore the wild landscape of Westfjords. Expect gravel off the main Westfjords Way – the loop connecting most towns and villages – and take care during winter.

FERRY

The only way to reach the Hornstrandir Peninsula, a remote nature reserve without a road. Scheduled departures leave from Ísafjörður from June to September. In Breiðafjörður, the car ferry *Baldur* sails year-round between the southern Westfjords and Snæfellsnes Peninsula.

223

Plan Your Time

Quick visits to the Westfjords hardly exist, unless you arrive by plane to Ísafjörður. Allow at least several days to complete the circular drive known as the Westfjords Way.

Dynjandi waterfall (p226)

Pressed for Time

● Take Iceland's westernmost detour with a long, winding drive to **Látrabjarg Peninsula** (p234), five hours from the Ring Road. From June to mid-August the peninsula tip is one of Europe's liveliest bird cliffs, with puffins hanging out by the car park, fish in their mouth. Spend the night in **Patreksfjörður** (p235), the only sizeable settlement beyond **Ísafjörður** (p236).

● The next day, take the mountain road to **Arnarfjörður** (p226) to learn about the mythical Icelandic creature known as Fjörulalli or 'Shore Laddie' at the **Icelandic Sea Monster Museum** (p230). Then go north to see the jewel of the Westfjords – **Dynjandi waterfall** (p226).

Seasonal Highlights

Summer is the time to visit Hornstrandir, Látrabjarg, Mt Bolafjall and Strandir. Darkness and snow bring the action to Ísafjörður – skiing, concerts and hot baths.

JANUARY
In Ísafjörður, the first rays of sun rise above the mountain ridge and touch parts of town after weeks of absence.

FEBRUARY
Off-piste skiing in the 'Westfjords Alps' (p228) near Flateyri and Þingeyri; cross-country tracks from Ísafjörður.

APRIL
Music festival **Aldrei fór ég suður** (p238; over Easter weekend) attracts many of Iceland's best musicians and a devoted crowd.

Five Days to Travel Around

- Bring swimsuits and dive about shoulder-deep into local leisure life at **Pollurinn** (p234), a geothermal hot-pot in **Tálknafjörður** (p234). Drive the cliff-edge foggy and mystical Arnarfjörður road to colourful sculptures made by naïvist **Samúel Jónsson** (p229), passing the gorgeous beaches of **Hringsdalur** (p229) and nearby ancient pagan graves dating to the Viking Age.

- Set up base at the cosmopolitan capital **Ísafjörður** (p236). Wander past timber houses and fishing heritage in time for the seafood buffet at **Tjöruhúsið** (p239).

- Travel exciting one-lane mountain tunnels for lunch at **Vagninn** (p239) in **Flateyri** (p241) and through another set of tunnels to the **Bolafjall platform** (p240), made from 60 tonnes of steel.

A Week or More

- Take a dramatic road trip to the westerly point of **Látrabjarg** (p234). In summer, puffins swoop around the soaring 14km stretch of sea cliffs; don't forget to stop at Iceland's oldest steel ship, the wreck of *Garðar BA*, which is beached nearby.

- Let the mists of the majestic **Dynjandi** (p226) waterfall hypnotise you with its dizzying cascades en route to a scheduled boat to **Hornstrandir** (p241), Iceland's majestic reserve on the Arctic edge. Return to the grid with tired legs and the memory of seeing **Hornbjarg** (p241), the iconic cliff.

- Linger in the up-and-coming **Hólmavík** (p244) to try witchcraft beer at **Galdur Brewery** (p246), visit a **museum** (p244) telling the history of local sorcery and go whale watching without the crowds.

- Rent a bicycle at the atmospheric cafe **Simbahöllin** (p228) and ride to the lighthouse at **Svalvogar**, a journey favoured by the growing number of cyclists pedalling the **Westfjords Way** (p227).

MAY
Icelandic **Sorcery Festival** (p245), with music, talks and workshops in Hólmavík. Scheduled boat tours to Hornstrandir begin at the end of the month.

JULY
Temperatures up to 20°C; excellent for hiking and cycling. The gruelling cycling tournament, **Westfjords Way Challenge** (p227) bike race, takes place.

AUGUST
Pufflings – the baby puffins – prepare to leave their burrows at **Látrabjarg Peninsula** (p234). This is the last chance to spot them for the season.

OCTOBER
The tourist season dies down, earlier than in other regions, with some cafes and museums shut as early as September.

Arnarfjörður

WATERFALLS | FOLK LAW | CYCLING

GETTING AROUND

With the 2020 opening of the Dýrafjarðar tunnels, starting some 9km from the waterfall, the falls are accessible year-round. The notorious mountain road to Bíldudalur, known as Dynjandisheiði, was still being paved during our visit in 2025. The passage will remain challenging over winter, if not closed completely.

☑ TOP TIP

Around 23km southeast of Bíldudalur, the run-off water of a hot spring warms the fjord-side concrete pool Reykjafjarðarlaug to about 34°C. Less visible is a riverbed further behind the locker rooms – follow the path for 30m. This natural, turf-fringed bath – always open but prettiest at sunset – is over 40°C.

There was a time when Arnarfjörður had its own currency, Péturs-króna, issued by the largest company in the fjord's settlement of Bíldudalur. Fish was caught in its calm waters, sheltered by many inlets and creeks, and exported directly to Spain. Trade within Iceland, however, had alpine barriers: the largest of the mountains in the mountainous Westfjords sealed off the area. That spell of isolation wasn't entirely broken until 2020 with the opening of the Dýrafjarðargöng, mountain tunnels connecting Arnarfjörður to the northern part of the Westfjords. Dynjandi waterfalls, the icon of the Westfjords, can now be visited and admired year-round.

Driving – or, as some prefer, cycling – along the foggy coast of Arnarfjörður may inspire the sight of something mysterious in the distance, as in the past when Iceland's greatest gallery of sea monsters inhabited the fjord.

Possibly Iceland's Greatest Waterfall
Soothing cascades

The Westfjords' best-known site, the **Dynjandi** *(ust.is/parking; parking fee 750kr)* waterfall is actually a cascade of six falls in the river Dynjandi. But the grand and picturesque Fjallfoss on top (climbing a 100m up the hill, around 1km) tends to steal the limelight from its smaller siblings below; they're worth checking out as you walk the path, about 20 minutes up to the main vista.

Fjallfoss is neither powerful nor tall by Icelandic waterfall standards – and that makes its popularity even more special. Many seasoned travellers regard it as a favourite, and one reason may be proximity. The water spreads wide over the rocks without a splash like a veil coming down the mountainside, allowing visitors to get close without soaking in spray. It is possible to climb right up next to it and not get wet, and watching the water crawl down the cliffs is also a soothing and calm experience.

HIGHLIGHTS
1. Dynjandi
2. Jón Sigurðsson Museum
3. Samúel Jónsson's Art Museum

SIGHTS
4. Hringsdalur
5. Icelandic Sea Monster Museum
6. Svalvogar Lighthouse

ACTIVITIES
7. Naustahvilft
8. Path Towards Óshlíð
9. Sandafell

SLEEPING
see 5 Bíldudalur Campground
see 5 Harbour Inn
10. Heydalur
11. Korpudalur HI Hostel
12. Tálknafjörður Campground

EATING
see 3 Hrafnseyri Cafe
13. Simbahöllin
see 5 Vegamót

Camping is no longer allowed at Dynjandi, despite good bathroom facilities. Drones are forbidden during the nesting season, from May to September.

Cycling Tours
Quiet roads and incredible paths

The Westfjords' entire coastal loop – 960km of winding roads and steep mountain passes – is (to some people) a splendid cycling path. Every year, some 100 cyclists complete the loop in just five days as part of the **Westfjords Way Challenge** (*cyclingwestfjords.com*), along with many more independent travellers touring the Westfjords on a bike for up to two weeks.

Part of the Westfjords' appeal as a cycling destination is what sets its roads apart from the rest of Iceland: less traffic, with long stretches of wild, unspoiled scenery.

The best of the Westfjords Way is arguably the route between Arnarfjörður and Dýrafjörður via Svalvogar. The 49km circuit starts in the village of Þingeyri. The trip is strenuous, but on reasonably even ground. Experienced cyclists can loop the peninsula in about six to eight hours. For a less-demanding ride, cycle the first half to the orange **Svalvogar lighthouse** and then backtrack to Þingeyri. Fat bikes are available at the old-style coffee house **Simbahöllin** (p228; *simbahollin.is*), housed in a 1915 grocery store; prices follow the route plan, starting at 10,900kr (lighthouse and back) or 13,900kr around the **Svalvogar circuit**.

ACCOMMODATION

For its vast size, the Westfjords has scarce hotel accommodation, with just a few hundred rooms to choose from (many are closed in winter). Try homes and farmstays for more options; due to low property prices, the region has some excellent Airbnbs. See p247 for recommended places to stay.

TRADING HUB FOR DANISH MERCHANTS

Bíldudalur, the only settlement in the vast Arnarfjörður, has one of the finest fjord-side settings in the country – arriving by road from either direction, you're treated to spectacular views. The settlement dates back to the 16th century, when it was a trading hub for Danish merchants. It peaked in size during the early industrialisation of Iceland's fishing fleet to a whopping population of 350 people, compared with 290 residents today.

The town's name is still associated in Icelandic culture with green peas: for much of the 20th century the village ran Iceland's largest cannery. The old cannery, opposite the church, is now occupied by monsters. Yes, monsters (see the Icelandic Sea Monster Museum; p230).

Sandafell

Westfjords Legend
Learn about the architect of Iceland's independence

Jón Sigurðsson was born on 17 June 1811, at Farmstead Hrafnseyri. The interesting, modern **Jón Sigurðsson Memorial Museum** *(hrafnseyri.is; free, June to 8 September)* outlines his life and has a reconstruction of the turf house he grew up in, plus a 19th-century church and a small cafe. Arrive on Iceland's National Day (17 June, on Jón's birthday!) for a free cake and serious speeches on sovereignty and strength.

Free cake or not, Jón himself preferred life on the banks of Copenhagen's canals. He left Iceland at the age of 22 and never returned, pushing against Iceland's loyalty to the Kingdom of Denmark with legal arguments, not the romantic nationalism of the freedom fighters before him.

Climbing Sandafell Mountain
For scenery just like the Alps!

The people of the Westfjords have a humble way of describing the region. Ísafjörður on a sunny day? Ibizafjörður. The sharp summits towering over Dýrafjörður on both sides? The Westfjords Alps.

EATING AROUND ARNARFJÖRÐUR: OUR PICKS

Hrafnseyri Cafe: Traditional Icelandic pastry served on the property of Iceland's independence hero. *11am-5pm Jun-Sep* €

Vegamót: Grill with a view over the harbour in Bíldudalur, and a good mini-market. *11am-8pm Mon-Fri, noon-8pm Sat & Sun* €

Simbahöllin: Inside a former general store dating to 1916, this landmark coffee house in Þingeyri, serves cakes, Belgian waffles and tasty soups. *10am-5pm* €€

Hótel Flókalundur Restaurant: The place to grab a burger, pizza or fish of the day in Flókalundur. Lovely fjord views. *noon-9pm* €

Dýrafjörður sure is stunning. Hike to **Sandafell** (367m) above Þingeyri for a fantastic view. The quickest route is around 4.5km and takes approximately one to two hours round trip, from the car park marked 'Sandafell bílastæði' on Google Maps.

The tallest mountain among the peaks (and in all of Westfjords) is **Mt Kaldbakur** (989m), the highest mountain on the north side of Eyjafjörður. With an SUV, drive to **Kvennaskarð**, between Arnarfjörður and Dýrafjörður, and allow four to six hours to complete the 12km round trip.

Valleys of Surprise
Samúel Jónsson's art farm

The drive out to the tip of Arnarfjörður, along Rte 619 beyond Bíldudalur, is absolutely magnificent. The tiny dirt track rims soaring mountains, lush pastured valleys collectively known as Ketildalir and untouched sandy beaches, such as **Hringsdalur**, and looks onto the churning fjord and the incredible landscape on its northern side. A high-clearance vehicle is more comfortable, as fallen rocks can scatter the road. Towards sunset and on partly cloudy days, the light shifts continually, and rainbows often form.

Where the road ends on Rte 619, the art show begins at **Samúel Jónsson's Art Museum** *(samueljonssonmuseum. jimdofree.com; adult/child 500kr, bring cash for the honesty box)*. Selárdalur valley is where the farmer from Brautarholt, named Samúel Jónsson, made his mark on Iceland's popular art history. Jónsson has been described as the 'artist with the infantile heart' but his life story certainty lacks the elements of innocence: his three children all died young and his sculptures and paintings received little attention. He went twice to Reykjavík over his lifetime, and was exposed primarily to art and architecture through books and postcards.

Age 72, he displayed his art to the world by spending his pension on the construction of a colourful church with an onion dome (which is open for visitors and has displays about the artist). The regional church, some 2km up the road, had refused to accept an altarpiece he made. Next to the church he constructed a flamboyant home to showcase his work. Outside are numerous naive sculptures, including the *Lions Court* created from a postcard Jónsson saw of the Alhambra in Spain.

HIKING IN THE WESTFJORDS

Halla Mía, a journalist in Ísafjörður, shares her recommendations for hikes in the Westfjords. @hallamia

Naustahvilft (p238): This steep but short hike is also known as the Troll Seat. Legend has it that it was formed by a female troll who sat down to wash her feet in the fjord. Offers great views over the town of Ísafjörður and the fjord. Allow 1½ hours.

Óshlíð (p239): Used to be the road to the remote fishing village of Bolungarvík. After it got replaced by a tunnel, the road is slowly being reclaimed by nature. A beautiful path for walking but also biking and running. Allow three hours.

Hornstrandir Nature Reserve (p241): Take a boat to Veiðileysufjörður, hike to Hornvík and spend a day in Hornbjarg. Then walk to Hlöðuvík and from there to Hesteyri, a challenging but unique experience. Allow four days.

TOP EXPERIENCE

The Icelandic Sea Monster Museum

Celebrating Bíldudalur's legacy of spotting freaky creatures from the sea, and occasionally crawling on land, the Icelandic Sea Monster Museum, or Skrímslasetrið, has exhibitions that go beyond folkloric anecdotes, with stories dating from hundreds of years ago to the modern day, and many living locals claiming to have seen sea monsters. The museum gives visitors a sense of what could possibly be lurking in the depths of the nearby fjords.

Sea monster

TOP TIPS

- The museum cafe is a good place to fuel up with pizza, coffee and even cocktails.
- Kids will love the museum's gift shop, which sells all manner of monster memorabilia.

PRACTICALITIES
- skrimsli.is
- adult/child under 10 1500kr/free
- 10am-6pm 15 May to 15 September

Monster Sightings

Museum owner Lilja Rut Rúnarsdóttir claims that there have been hundreds of sea monster sightings in this part of Iceland. The last reported sighting was in 2024 by a local farmer. Some monsters have been seen so frequently they have names. Nocturnal Skeljaskrímsli (or Shell Monster) is covered in a shell-like skin. Fjörulalli (Shore Laddie) has fangs and webbed feet, Hafmaður (Sea Man) is an ugly beast with a big belly and Faxi (Combed Monster/Sea Horse) has a bright red mane and flashing green eyes.

Model Monsters

Step into a low-lit tunnel with models of monsters based on people's accounts, including Arnarfjörður, which is believed to have attacked a local farm named Krosseyri twice and has reportedly dragged men into the sea. Stories date back to the 18th century. There's a model of Shore Laddie, a monster personally seen by the museum's owner, and cabinets are filled with smaller monsters, such as the Little Seahorse of Arnarfjörður, said to look like a seal with flippers at the front, but shaped like a horse at the rear.

Interactive Exhibits

A central bookshelf contains dozens of accounts of local sea monster encounters, with video interviews, images and audio bringing these legendary creatures to life. Delve into the Story Trunk, a large map with 20 stories from the Arnarfjörður area.

Beyond
Arnarfjörður

A truly wild-feeling area, where white, black, red and pink beaches meet shimmering blue water, and towering cliffs and stunning mountains cleave the fjords.

By some standards, the beach of Rauðisandur exists on the wrong latitude. If it was located, say, 20 degrees further south on the globe, colourful towels and sun umbrellas would line the 10km beach of reddish sand that is uniquely tropical-looking for Iceland. Sunbathing is possible on a bright summer day but most visitors come wearing walking shoes; the area is excellent for long and short hikes. Further on the peninsula is the region's most popular destination, Látrabjarg – a 14km stretch of bird cliffs, one of Europe's largest, home to millions of nesting seabirds in summer.

Accommodation options are rich thanks to big-town Patreksfjörður with a population of 800 people – and, like it or not, rising with every new fish farm.

Places
Rauðisandur p231
Látrabjarg p234
Tálknafjörður p234

Rauðisandur TIME FROM ARNARFJÖRÐUR: 2¼HR
Thrilling drive to a red beach

The steep and narrow drive (often single lane) to **Rauðisandur** is an experience in itself. The nerve-jangling, pot-holed and gravel descent has sharp switchbacks and sheer drops. Go slowly (don't attempt in the dark or bad weather) and enjoy the awesome views of lush mountains all around. Be aware

(continues on p234)

🧭 GETTING AROUND

Major roads are well paved, but many leading to sights are gravel and driving is slow. At the time of writing the mountain road to Arnarfjörður, known as Dynjandisheiði, was being paved. Expect challenging conditions in snow.

The **Baldur car ferry** *(ferja.is/en)* connects the southern Westfjords to Stykkishólmur on the Snæfellsnes Peninsula, departing from Brjánslækur terminal daily in summer, with a stop at Flatey Island *(7400kr, plus 7400kr for a car; 2½ hours)*. Driving the same distance takes about four hours.

Norlandair *(norlandair.is)* offers daily flights between Reykjavík and Bíldudalur (40 minutes). Bus 62 with **Strætó** *(straeto.is)* connects Patreksfjörður and Ísafjörður five times a week via the Brjánslækur ferry terminal. The bus stops at Dynjandi waterfall but there's no other service from there to nearby settlements.

DRIVING TOUR

Taste of the Westfjords Way

Entering the Westfjords is a 950km commitment; a loop zigzags the fjord landscape along the Westfjords Way. Sure, there are big-name attractions, but more than anything the journey is about exploring the wild subarctic landscape and small-town coastal life. This section of the drive offers some of the many highlights on the route in a digestible 150km section.

❶ Hellulaug

There are several pools in the Westfjords, and Hellulaug is distinctive for being right on the beach, offering a view of the freezing ocean while being shielded from the road. It's a breeze to access from the main road while still feeling private, so you can easily hop in for a dip while watching the fjord waters. At high tide, do as the locals do and jump in the frigid sea, then run back to the hot pool (38°C) to warm up.

The Drive: It's a remote (usually empty) 40-minute drive between grassy hillsides, over a river on a single-lane bridge along paved Rte 60, followed by a left turn onto gravel and super-scenic fjord-side Rte 63.

❷ The Abandoned Barn Fossfjörður

The old, A-shaped barn – with a rusting roof and a perfect silver grey frame - has become an Instagrammer's delight. The image captures the silence of the landscape and the loss of scale against the wide open fjord. Is the abandoned farm small, or surprisingly big? Maybe both. Nearby is a great, illustrated lesson in the Icelandic language: 'foss' means waterfall and 'á' means river and from the small bridge over Fossá is a waterfall named Fossfjörður – the Waterfall in Waterfall River.

The Drive: Take the Dýrafjarðargöng mountain tunnels to reach the tiny village of Þingeyri

Valagil Waterfall

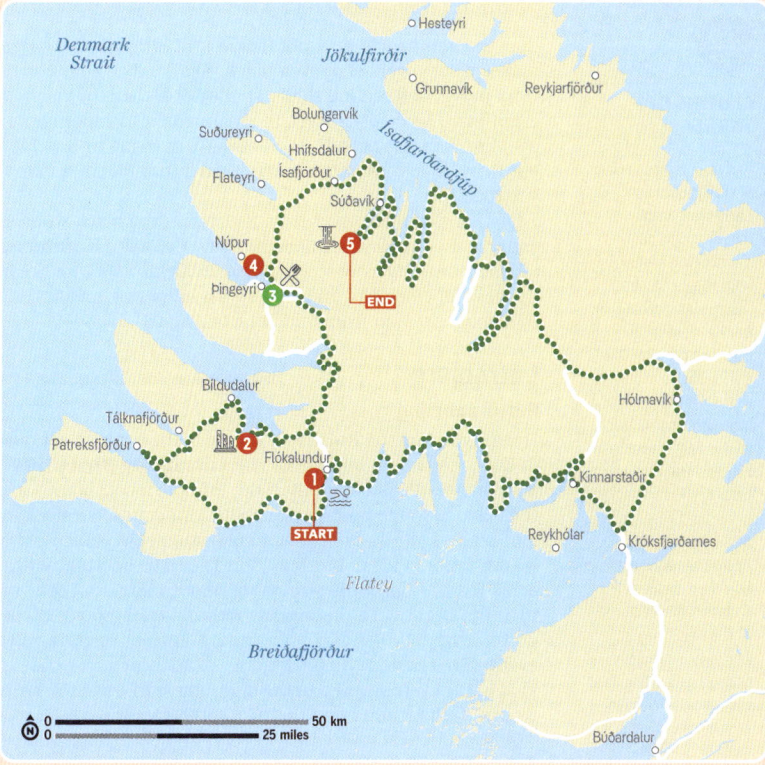

(1½ hours). The landmark green house on main street is hard to miss.

③ Simbahöllin

Simbahöllin (p228) is a cool cafe in Þingeyri, inside a restored 1915 general store with friendly staff serving tasty Belgian waffles during the day and hearty lamb tagines at night. Outdoor seating in an old bus, fjord views and a cosy vibe ensure this is one of the Westfjords' best boltholes. It's only open from June to September.

The Drive: Follow Rte 622 for 25km along the edge of Dýrafjörður, flanked by mountains that reflect in the twinkling waters on sunny days. Keep left to cross the fjord by bridge onto Rte 60, before turning left onto single lane Rte 624.

④ Skrúður

One of Iceland's oldest botanic gardens sits on the lower slopes of the fjordside valleys on Dýrafjörður's northern edge. Teeny **Skrúður** *(free, 5am-midnight)* was established as a teaching garden in 1909. You'll see arched whalebones at one entrance and spy colourful flowers in the summer months.

The Drive: Follow Rte 60 through scenic mountains and curving round the dramatic waters of Ísafjarðardjúp. Turn off into the valley car park on the right (marked only by a walking sign) then walk to Valagil Waterfall. The drive is 60km (roughly one hour).

⑤ Valagil Waterfall

A gigantic gorge with cascading waterfalls is revealed after a mellow walk along a lush valley. The trail is about 4km, round trip, at the landward end of Álftafjörður. The marked trail starts at a small car park about 9km south of Súðavík; the tallest waterfall is visible throughout the walk. From here it's 29km back to Ísafjörður.

CLOWNS OF THE SEA

Arriving in late spring and remaining at Látrabjarg until mid-August, puffins are striking seabirds with their colourful triangular-parrot-like beaks, nesting in burrows high on the cliffs. These monogamous creatures find a mate and come back to the same nest to breed annually; each pair lays just one egg per year. Baby puffins, named pufflings, fledge at night to avoid predators. Dubbed the 'clowns of the sea', they're actually incredibly competent in the sea, diving up to 60m to catch small fish, such as sand eels. But on land their appearance and whimsical clumsiness has earned them their comical moniker. Puffins can live more than 20 years in the wild – visitors who return year after year may see the same puffins coming to nest.

(continued from p231)

that the 'red beach' may not look red at all – the sun often makes it seem yellow or even black. The sandy colour comes from pulverised scallop shells, spoiled elsewhere by volcanic eruptions. Once at sea level, the road reaches a junction: for a 1.5km walking path to the beach, turn right to Saurbær. For drive-in access to the beach, turn left to Melanes campsite (p247).

Further down the road from Saurbær – the black wooden church – is a small white house hosting **Franska Kaffihúsið** (French Cafe; *facebook.com/FranskaKaffihusid*) for fresh waffles, delicious flan and coffee with killer beach views (it's open noon to 6pm from mid-June to August).

Látrabjarg
TIME FROM ARNARFJÖRÐUR: 2¾HR

Puffin spotting

Heading further on Rte 612, to the tip of the peninsula, is one of Europe's largest bird cliffs. The **Látrabjarg Bird Cliffs** – also the westernmost point of the European continent – are the place to watch puffins, razorbills, guillemots, cormorants and other seabirds from June to mid-August. A camera with a long zoom is ideal, but many birds can be spotted within arms length. The cliffs stretch for about 14km, and soar up to 440m high, with the longest walking trail (about 20km) dotted with wildflowers on the grassy clifftops in spring and eventually reaching Rauðisandur (p231) beach. It's best to visit in the evening (even in the midnight sun) when the birds return to their nests and there's a terrific view of the North Atlantic and dramatic cliffside. Seals and occasional whales can be spotted in the distance. On the road back, stop at the shipwreck **Garðar BA** for some Instagram fodder. Iceland's oldest steel ship, a rusty whaling and fishing vessel dating to 1912, was placed on the beach near Patreksfjörður when it was deemed no longer seaworthy. **Stúkuhúsið** *(stukuhusid.is)* a cool eatery nearby with friendly staff serving soup, sandwiches and succulent fresh fish as well as homemade chocolates.

Tálknafjörður
TIME FROM ARNARFJÖRÐUR: 2HR

Meet the locals

In a village of 250 people, it's all hands on deck; at lunchtime fish farmer workers head to the low-key joint **Hópið** *(11am-11pm Sunday to Friday, to 1am Saturday)*, a bar-cum-restaurant with a pool table and occasional pub quizzes and football on TV. There's an Icelandic lunch buffet with local cuisine prepared with considerably more attention to detail than other places, offering a true taste of the Westfjords. In the evening it's all about pizza.

You can meet with Tálkafjörður locals again in the evening sun at the free geothermal hot-pot **Pollurinn** *(24 hours)*. While the name means 'The Puddle', this hot-pot highlight of the Westfjords is a natural bath created with lots of cement and run-off water from a 1977 drilling project. Enter

Látrabjarg Bird Cliffs

day or night: the lockers are always open and feel free to use the donation box. Backed by mountains and sweeping fjord views, it's a place where locals often kick back with a beer in the evening (cans only, no glass). Take Rte 617 some 3.5km beyond Cafe Dunhagi – the hot-pot is signposted with a tiny white sign. To bathe in warm and clean water, however, visit the **Tálknafjörður Swimming Pool** (talknafjordur.is; adult/child 1300/570kr). It has a 25m outdoor pool, hot-pots, and a green waterslide with a shallow leisure pool that's a great choice for kids. The pool in neighbouring **Patreksfjörður** is a firm recommendation, too, with excellent views.

Tálknafjörður trail

Set amid rolling green hills and rocky peaks, Tálknafjörður is surrounded by magnificent scenery. Multiple **hiking routes** – many of which are old riding paths for horses – extend over to the neighbouring Arnarfjörður. A quick jaunt is Bæjarfell, rising a 100m above town (1.6km out and back) for gorgeous views and hills covered in bright purple Nootka lupines in June and July. For something much longer, follow the cairn-marked route to Bíldudalur along Tunguá river. The trail is 14km one way and the last stretch into Bíldudalur is on the highway (Rte 63). For a flatter short walk, the area around the Tálknafjörður Campground (p247) is green and delightful.

FOLLOW THE MONEY

It might be small but Tálknafjörður has a big connection to fish – and as the saying goes, odour from fish factories is the 'smell of money' in coastal communities. Tálknafjörður is different though: money doesn't exactly come from the bounty of the sea but trickles down from the fjord's horizon. Six fish pens, farming hundreds of thousands of salmon and trout, put the scale of Iceland's lucrative aquaculture boom on full display. Iceland farmed more than 54,700 tonnes of fish in 2024, and around 28,000 tonnes of this was salmon produced in sea pens in the Westfjords. Expect to see a fair amount of salmon on the menus in the local areas.

Ísafjörður

DINING OUT | SHOPPING | ADVENTURE BASE

☑ TOP TIP
From Ísafjörður, tour operators including **Sjóferðir** *(sjoferdir.is; 20,000kr)* sail to the island of Vigur, home to an incredible number of Arctic terns and coastal birds over the summer. The island, once farmed, has a cute cafe, and the tiniest post office in Europe (where you can send a postcard home). Tours run for three hours.

After a time spent travelling in the Westfjords, Ísafjörður feels like a bustling metropolis. With a population of around 2700, an airport, plus hip cafes, authentic gift shops, fine restaurant choices and even a cinema, it's by far the largest settlement in the region. Ísafjörður was first settled in the 16th century thanks to its abundance of fish, and has become a convenient base for Westfjords adventure tours. There is hiking in the hills around the town, skiing in winter, and regular summer boats ferry hikers across to the remote Hornstrandir Peninsula.

The centre of Ísafjörður is a charming and often colourful grid of old timber and tin-clad buildings, hemmed in on all sides by towering peaks and the dark waters of the fjord with a harbour at one end.

Ísafjörður History & Culture
Old houses and rock music

Ísafjörður gets its name from Danish merchants who were unable to pronounce 'Skutulsfjörður' – the name of the fjord it stands by, on an arcing spit that extends into the unpronounceable fjord.

The remote Westfjords' capital has long been shaped by incoming ships. Up until the early 20th century, Ísafjörður was Iceland's third-largest settlement, and timber houses

---

 GETTING AROUND

The 9km-long Ísafjörður–Suðureyri–Flateyri tunnel beneath the mountains is single-lane in parts of the 6km stretch from Ísafjörður to Flateyri – pull-overs allow oncoming traffic to alternate.

Most places of interest within Ísafjörður are accessible on foot. Tungudalur valley can be reached by local bus. Strætisvagnar Ísafjarðar buses run to Flateyri, Suðureyri and Þingeyri. It helps to have a car to explore neighbouring Bolungarvík, Flateyri and Þingeyri.

Strætó buses travel from Aðalstræti 7 in Ísafjörður, from June to August, to Hólmavík (Rte 61) and Patreksfjörður (Rte 62). From there it's possible to get on another bus to Reykjavík.

ÍSAFJÖRÐUR

HIGHLIGHTS
1 Borea Adventures
2 Naustahvilft
3 West Tours
4 Westfjords Heritage Museum

SIGHTS
5 Arctic Fox Centre
6 Bolafjall Platform
7 Minnibakki Beach
8 Ósvör Maritime Museum

ACTIVITIES
9 Golfklúbbur Ísafjarðar
10 Iceland ProFishing
11 Path Towards Óshlíð
12 Raggagarður
13 Sundlaug Bolungarvíkur

SLEEPING
14 Einarshúsið
15 Hótel Ísafjörður
16 Ísafjörður Hostel
see 21 Old Bookstore
see 21 Old Bookstore Guesthouse
17 Tungudalur Campground

EATING
18 Heimabyggð
19 Kaffihús Bakarans
20 Tjöruhúsið
21 Vagninn

ENTERTAINMENT
22 Aldrei fór ég suður

INFORMATION
23 Hornstrandir Visitor Center

Naustahvilft

WESTFJORDS FOR KIDS

Haukur Sigurðsson, a photographer in Ísafjörður and father of two, shares his recommendations for family fun in the Westfjords. @haukursigurdsson

Raggagarður: This huge playground in Súðavík, 20km from Ísafjörður, was created by Vilborg Arnardottir in memory of her son Raggi. Joyously attractive, even for adults, with picnic and barbecue facilities.

Samúel Jónsson's Art Museum (p229): The naïve animal sculptures of Samúel Jónsson (1884–1969) capture the imagination of children. The 40-minute drive from Bíldudalur is stunning on a clear day and most of the museum is outdoors by a stony beach.

Holtsfjara: I have been to some great sandcastle competitions on this quiet beach in Önundarfjörður, rival to the better-known Rauðisandur beach and closer to Ísafjörður. (Marked on Google Maps as 'Önundarfjörður Pier'.)

from the merchant era define the central part of town; unlike Akureyri and Reykjavík, the old town never suffered major fires so original houses can still be seen at places such as charming Tangagata.

Today, however, around 70% of harbour revenue in Ísafjörður comes from tourism, and it is Iceland's third-busiest port of call for cruise ships. Meanwhile, the University Centre of the Westfjords attracts many international students reading coastal and marine management.

To find out about the days when young people flocked to Ísafjörður to learn how to haul fish, head to the **Westfjords Heritage Museum** (nedsti.is; adult/child 1600kr/free) in the old wooden houses on the harbour tip. It's crammed with maritime history exhibits, fishing and nautical exhibits, tools from the whaling days and old photographs of sun-drying fish, tall ships and more fish. It's only open between 15 May and 15 September.

In April, Ísafjörður almost doubles in size when revellers descend on the town for the annual **Aldrei fór ég suður** (aldrei.is) rock music festival, held in a local shrimp factory warehouse every Easter. It runs hand in hand with Skíðavikan or **Ski Week** (skidavikan.is), a celebration of outdoor sports in the area.

Climb to the 'Troll Seat'

Hike to Naustahvilft

For a scenic hike, head to **Naustahvilft** above the road from the airport, a massive 'bowl' in the mountain ridge known as the 'troll seat'. It's a short but challenging 1km climb, taking about 30 minutes. Take your time at the top to appreciate the views over the fjord and for the chance to see a plane landing on the airstrip below – a spectacular sight.

Legend holds that the seat was formed by a troll who was hurrying home before sunrise – trolls turn to stone if they get caught in the daylight. After gathering speed, she actually made it back a bit early, so decided to take a break and sit down, dipping her sore feet into the fjord to cool off and creating a big depression in the landscape with her giant bum. The peninsula where Ísafjörður town sits? That's supposedly what ended up between her feet. The deep harbour? That's where her feet were soaking. Of course, geologists will tell you it's a hanging valley carved out by glaciers during the last ice age.

Get Outdoors
Biking, skiing and golf

Locals in Ísafjörður value their outdoor escapes; the town is well known for hosting tournaments in everything from cross-country skiing to cycling.

Within walking distance from the town's western edge, **Golfklúbbur Ísafjarðar** *(golfisa.is; adult/child 4000/2000kr, club rental 2000kr)* is a nine-hole golf course offering reasonably priced rounds and a skiing area, along with walking and bike paths.

Mountain biking has a strong following, with trails for all experience levels. Check out a trail map at *mtbisafjordur.is*. Bikes are available for rent at **Borea Adventures** *(boreaadventures.com; adult/child 15,700/11,775kr)*. They also offer guided cycling tours suitable for beginners. Those in shape for six hours of cycling tackle the 'fjord hopping' tour *(36,800kr per person)*, which crosses mountains over to Bolungarvík. Borea also runs challenging multi-country backcountry ski trips *(four days from 30,900kr)*.

The calm fjords make Ísafjörður and the wider Djúpið (shorthand for the fjord system known as Ísafjarðardjúp) especially popular for kayaking. Tours are available with Borea Adventures and **West Tours** *(westtours.is; adult/child from 16,000/12,000kr)* and range from two hours to several days, sleeping on a remote beach somewhere in the company of seals and seabirds, where the mind switches gear and time spools slowly, one paddle at a time. The Westfjords are not about speed.

THE PATH TO ÓSHLÍÐ

Ísafjörður and Bolungarvík are just a 10-minute drive apart via the 5.4km mountain tunnel, open since 2010. Cyclists, runners and hikers have since taken over the old road around **Mt Óshlíð**. The 8km track is wonderfully scenic with looming mountains, but outside of summer seek local advice before you set off as the hill is prone to rockfalls and avalanches. Arriving in Bolungarvík, sweat or not, the swimming pool **Sundlaug Bolungarvíkur** *(adult/child 7-16 years 1350/330kr)* is a wonderful place to take a post-ride dip, and has two hot tubs, one with a hydromassage. The small village between Ísafjörður and Bolungarvík, **Hnífsdalur** (Knife's Valley), is home to a large fish factory and 100-something people. There's no shop or service here, beyond several Airbnbs.

EATING IN & AROUND ÍSAFJÖRÐUR: OUR PICKS

Tjöruhúsið: Ambitious, rustic seafood place. Serve-yourself buffet of hot skillets, and lively hosts. noon-2pm & 6-10pm Tue-Sun €€

Heimabyggð: A local favourite with an excellent lunch menu, coffee and homemade sourdough pizzas slathered with toppings. 9am-6pm Mon-Fri, 10am-5pm Sat, to 4pm Sun €€

Vagninn: In Flateyri, *plokkfiskur* (fish stew) with rye bread or spicy fish soup brightens the day. 5-11pm Sun-Thur, to 1pm Fri & Sat €€

Kaffihús Bakarans: Popular bakery with a deli counter piled high with freshly made goods. Ideal for a sandwich before a hike. 7am-5pm Mon-Fri, 9am-4pm Sat & Sun €

Beyond Ísafjörður

Every direction is a journey here. The watery borders of Ísafjörður lead to a remote peninsula and road along the longest fjord to a witchcraft village.

Places
Bolungarvík p240
Hornstrandir Nature Reserve p241
Flateyri p241
Súðavík p242

GETTING AROUND

Hire a car – or hitch-hike – to explore Strandir. Over summer, Strætó bus 61 runs between Hólmavík and Ísafjörður twice a week, in sync with bus 59 connecting Hólmavík to western Iceland via Borgarnes.

Norlandair flies (a very small plane) between Reykjavík's domestic airport and the airstrip at Gjögur (50 minutes, twice a week), 16km southeast of Norðurfjörður.

The largest of the region's fjords, 75km-long Ísafjarðardjúp takes a massive swatch out of the Westfjords' landmass and the watery borders of inhabited and unpopulated land; across from Ísafjörður's side is the Hornstrandir Nature Reserve accessible only by ferry. With barely a phone signal and not a single road, the pristine peninsula is a hiking destination. The road down Djúpið, as Ísafjarðardjúp is casually called, winds in and out of a series of smaller fjords, making the drive from the bustling city of Ísafjörður to Hólmavík like sliding along each tooth of a fine comb. North of Hólmavík, continue up the magnificently peaceful Standir coast until the track suddenly ends in Norðurfjörður, the capital of Iceland's smallest municipality, with a population of 44 and one trillion Arctic terns.

Bolungarvík
TIME FROM ÍSAFJÖRÐUR: **15MIN**

The Westfjords view
It is now possible to walk – safely – beyond the edge of Bolafjall mountain by standing on a massive platform made from 60 tonnes of steel. Completed in 2022, the ambitious **Bolafjall platform** offers the ultimate Westfjords views at 638m and is likely to send butterflies straight to your stomach. The panorama extends over to the Hornstrandir Nature Reserve and the fjord system of **Ísafjarðardjúp**. Some people claim to see Greenland!

Look behind you, at the black basalt cliffs and a giant radome (radar dome) – Bolafjall is a defence site, too. Hence the barbed wires and metal gates. The radar station is one of four NATO monitors in Iceland scanning the Atlantic airspace.

From June to early September it is possible to drive all the way to the mountaintop, some 9km from Bolungarvík. In light snow, the road remains open most of the way, but may require walking the last few kilometres. The mountain is notoriously windy.

From summit to sea, further west on Rte 630, the road ends following a dramatic descent through mountains on a dirt path at **Minnibakki Beach** (4WD recommended). The stony creek, with pockets of soft sand, is favoured by locals for family fun and a cold swim.

On the way back to Ísafjörður, just before entering the tunnel separating the twin towns, is the atmospheric **Ósvör Maritime Museum** (adult/child under 16 years 1700kr/free), a replica of a fishing station from the 19th century, with turf houses full of maritime and fish-processing memorabilia.

Hornstrandir Nature Reserve

TIME FROM ÍSAFJÖRÐUR: 1¼HR

The wildest corner

The northernmost tip of the Westfjords, accounting for 0.6% of Iceland's land mass, is one of Europe's last wildernesses. **Hornstrandir Nature Reserve** (ust.is/hornstrandiris; free) is a breathtaking beauty of soaring mountains and precipitous cliffs. A small but steady number of travellers make the journey, moving from one fjord to the next, taking anywhere from two nights to a week. Travellers are guaranteed fickle weather and a sighting of the Arctic fox in its brown summer coat. The foxes living in remote Hornstrandir seem oblivious to the fact that almost everywhere else humans hunt them: some even approach people, eating from the palm of their hand. The last full-time human resident of the rugged area moved away in 1952 – it never was an easy place to farm – but many descendants have turned family farmsteads into summer getaways. And the former doctor's house at Hesteyri now serves coffee and cake.

To get to Hornstrandir, you must first head to a harbour; there are no roads. Ísafjörður has daily departures with **Borea Adventures** (boreaadventures.com; single fares from 13,900kr) and **West Tours** (westtours.is; single fares from 14,000kr) from June to mid-August. Hornvík and Hesteyri are the two base camps, staffed by a lone ranger, and most hikes are tailored around the landmark **Hornbjarg cliff**. The most popular hike is four to five days, known as the the Royal Horn (Hornleið; p243), from **Veiðileysufjörður** to **Hesteyri** via the northern strip. Day tours from Ísafjörður to Hesteyri are available in July and August, with West Tours (p239; *history day trips from 17,900kr*), around five hours. **Arctic Adventures** (adventures.is) runs 11-hour day hikes between June and September (from 58,900kr per person including ferry transfers). The **Hornstrandir Visitor Center** on the main square in Ísafjörður offers practical travel information and a small exhibit on the Arctic fox.

To see Hornbjarg without a multiday hike, book a boat with **Strandferðir** (strandferdir.is; fares from 15,000kr), departing from various points including Norðurfjörður near Gjögur and Strandir on the eastern end of the Westfjords, a four-hour drive from Ísafjörður.

Flateyri

TIME FROM ÍSAFJÖRÐUR: 20MIN

Fish and birds

Part of the Ísafjörður municipality, Flateyri is a village on a sandbar in the stunning **Önundarfjörður** that has successfully blended its seafaring heritage with tourism. As elsewhere

WESTFJORDS' FISH FARMING BOOM

In April 2023 Bolungarvík celebrated resident number 1000; a baby-girl named Rannveig. 'Project Bolungarvík 1000+ has been completed', the town council happily declared, in the high spirit of settlements across the Westfjords reversing decades of population decline by welcoming investment in aquaculture – fish farming. Narrow fjords, sheltered from the open ocean with mild waves and currents, provide excellent conditions for fish farming but not without environmental impact. The wild North Atlantic salmon population – already an endangered species – is highly vulnerable to genetic introgression from farmed salmon routinely escaping sea pens. Supporters argue for the big picture: farming fish helps to feed a growing world population with less greenhouse gas emission than most other farming, compared to protein units.

WAS THAT A POLAR BEAR?

Since 2008 five polar bears have travelled from northeastern Greenland to Iceland, all but one over summer, when the lack of sea ice pushes bears to leave their usual territory in search of food. Most have arrived at Hornstrandir. The government policy is to kill them, claiming they are weak and aggressive after swimming hundreds of kilometres. If you see a polar bear, remain calm, don't run or make sudden movements or make threatening loud noises. Back away slowly, keeping the bear in sight. If the bear charges – fight.

Walruses are more common, being spotted roughly every two years. In the last few years, however, they have frequented random harbours across Iceland in greater numbers – five times in 2023. In 2024 the walrus affectionately named 'Wally' was spotted in Iceland after visiting Ireland.

in the Westfjords, developments in Iceland's fishing industry have devastated small-scale operations. Local fishers have instead turned to sea angling and made Flateyri into a leading base for sea-angling tours. **Iceland ProFishing** *(iceland protravel.com)* occupies the harbour with a row of cottages where guests overnight between sea-angling tours, hauling big species like cod and haddock. Their eight-night tours go for around 162,000kr.

Walking around Flateyri, note the adorable street art all over town: the Flatbird Trail was created to reflect on place and ecology and includes 12 species of migratory birds, painted by resident artist Jean Larson *(jeanlarson.com)*. The pieces cover whole walls of buildings and homes, merging real life and art, and includes these species: white wagtail, glaucous gull, Arctic tern, black-tailed godwit, raven, great cormorant, eurasian whimbrel, eider duck, snow bunting, eurasian wren, oystercatcher, whooper swan and European golden plover – see if you can spot them all. For bonus points, search out a painted nest with eggs in it, painted on a small wall next to a grey house.

Oldest store in Iceland?

Founded in 1914, the **Old Bookstore** *(Gamla Bókabúðin; gamla.is; donations welcome)* claims to be 'the oldest store in Iceland still in traditional operation'. Today's merchandise is, appropriately, very nostalgic: classic children's books, vintage housewares and colourful analogue cameras. The English selection covers a wide range of translations by Icelandic authors – set in the Westfjords, a trilogy by Jón Kalman begins with the title *Heaven and Hell*. Above the bookstore has been the family home for more than 100 years and the owners now welcome travellers to stay in their double guest room (p247) with fabulous sea and mountain views.

Súðavík

TIME FROM ÍSAFJÖRÐUR: **20MIN**

Meeting Arctic foxes

Housed in a renovated farmstead, the **Arctic Fox Centre** *(mel rakki.is; adult/child 1500kr/free)* tells the story of Iceland's only endemic mammal. Arctic foxes are believed to have arrived during the last ice age, around 10,000 years ago, probably by walking across the frozen sea. They survived by eating birds, eggs and carrion, plus fish, and berries when they were available. The museum recounts how fox hunting became part of life in Iceland when humans settled and began farming. The foxes were hunted to protect sheep and other farm animals until the 1950s. In the early 20th century farmers could be paid three times the price of a cow for a fox's pelt. In the museum are stuffed foxes, equipment for finding and hunting foxes and many facts about foxes (they don't shiver until -70°C and have 20,000 hairs per sq cm). The Arctic fox population is now stable with roughly 10,000 living in the wild. Fox hunting is now banned in 26 protected areas in Iceland, including Hornstrandir and the highlands. The museum cares for orphaned foxes, which can be seen up close in an enclosure outside.

THE ROYAL HORN IN FOUR DAYS

This isolated, extreme point in the Hornstrandir Nature Reserve is a route filled with adventure as it crisscrosses the peninsula around precipitous cliffs and lofty mountains.

START	END	LENGTH
Veiðileysufjörður	Hesteyri	44km; 4 days

Sail from Ísafjörður to ① **Veiðileysufjörður** to start the hike. Follow a cairn-marked trail up the slope and through the mountain pass from where you can descend the mountain on either side until you reach ② **Hornvík**. The hike from Veiðileysufjörður to Hornvík can take anywhere between four and eight hours (roughly 11km). There's a ranger station at the campsite in Hornvík where you can get the latest weather forecast and information about trail conditions.

Use your second day to visit ③ **Hornbjarg** (p241), one of Iceland's most beautiful bird cliffs with diverse flora and fauna, around 12km there are back. Spend another night at the campsite.

Day three is from Hornvík to ④ **Hlöðuvík**, around six hours (9km). The partly marked trail goes through a mountain pass and is relatively easy to find. At Hlöðuvík, the campsite is situated next to Hlöðuvíkurós (the mouth of the Hlöðuvík river). Facing north, Hlöðuvík is the perfect place to watch the spectacular midnight sun.

On the final day, hike through Kjarnsvíkurskarð (a mountain pass) and Hesteyrarbrúnir pass to ⑤ **Hesteyri** (around eight hours and 12km). Hesteyri village was abandoned in the mid-20th century. There are still several well-kept houses amid the fields of angelica and ruins of a whaling station are nearby. The coffee shop in Hesteyri is a good place to stop and you can wait here for your prebooked ferry back to Ísafjörður, or enjoy an extra night to explore the area.

Hólmavík

WITCHCRAFT | CRAFT BEER | VILLAGE LIFE

GETTING AROUND

The easiest way to explore Hólmavík and surrounding areas is by car. Local Strætó bus 59 travels from Hólmavík to Borgarnes; change to bus 57 to Reykjavík there (four hours). The same combination goes to Bifröst or Borgarnes, then Akureyri (eight hours). Check timetables as transfers may require an overnight stay in Bifröst or Borgarnes. The Ísafjörður bus is operated by **Hópferðamiðstöð Vestfjarða** *(vestfirdir. is)*. It's a three-hour journey, with around three buses per week, from mid-August to mid-September.

☑ TOP TIP

If your hotel or guesthouse doesn't offer breakfast, don't forget to buy in for self-catering. No restaurants in town open for the first meal of the day.

Hólmavík, a laid-back fishing town with a population of 375 people, is the main settlement on the rugged northern Westfjords Strandir coastline, sitting on the eastern shore of the calm Steingrímsfjörður fjord. The drive to this magnificently peaceful gateway to the region is nothing short of spectacular with its high passes, mountain roads and soaring views. Strandir was thought to be the home of the island's great persecuted sorcerers and many travellers come to Hólmavík to visit its quirky witchcraft museum or attend the Sorcery Festival in May. There are a surprising number of good food and drink options here and you can take a dip in the nearby geothermal tubs.

Capital of Folklore

Witchcraft and sorcery

While Hólmavík is traditionally a fishing village and a service town for the Strandir region, in recent years it has reinvented itself by telling stories from the past.

The Folklore Institute at the University of Iceland, on main street Höfðagata, bestows a significant sense of authority upon the folklore of the village. Recent studies have explored the life of peasant farmers through 19th-century diaries and the outrageous, bizarre and brief Witchcraft Era. Over a 30-year period from 1654, 100 people were burned alive for supernatural practices. Unlike the witches of New England's Salem trials, most of Iceland's convicted 'witches' were men. Often 'occult practices' were simply old Viking traditions or superstitions, but hidden *grimoires* (magic books) full of puzzling runic design were proof enough for the local witch hunters (the area's elite) to burn around 20 souls (mostly from among the poor) at the stake.

The **Museum of Icelandic Sorcery & Witchcraft** *(galdrasyning.is; adult/child 1400kr/free)* serves as a form of restitution for the victims of that dark era. Through narratives and recreation of artefacts, the museum commemorates the art of witchcraft. Don't miss the detailed descriptions of the spells, and the starling 'necropants' (p246). Open year-round.

There's also a **Sorcery Cafe** on-site serving homemade seafood or meat soup and a gift shop for those wanting to dabble in the dark arts (pick up some tarot cards, spell books or items with witchcraft symbols on them here). Don't forget to visit the **Sorcerer's Cottage** *(open year-round, free)*; part of the museum, its 32km north of Hólmavík in Bjarnarfjörður. The three-room turf-roofed house shows how sorcerers lived and the magic staves they used to deter evil, cast spells and bring good luck.

Sorcery Festival
Immerse yourself in a community of witches

The annual **Sorcery Festival** *(sorceryfestival.is/en; full festival/day tickets 21,000/from 4000kr)* in May is a witchcraft extravaganza that sees hundreds of followers of the dark arts visit Hólmavík. The festival features experts in magic presenting lectures and classes on subjects ranging from old techniques for contemporary magic to reading runes, working with staves and Iceland's creatures and landspirits or 'Hidden People'. There's also a craft market selling all kinds of witchy fashion and equipment, plus evening entertainment in the form of music (think creepy experimental sounds, death metal and Icelandic folk music). The highlight is a big Saturday-night parade through town to the sound of drums, with attendees in Viking, witch and old Norse costumes holding fire torches, before a ceremony is held around a big bonfire.

NECROPANTS

Of all the mystical practices in the area, perhaps the most bizarre is the legendary 'necropants' – trousers made from the skin of a dead man's legs and groin. It was commonly believed that if a donor made a verbal agreement, his corpse could be skinned upon his death and the resulting necropants would produce money when worn (with the scrotum always full of coins). In order for this to work, the skinned portion of the corpse had to be without holes; the sorcerer had to put the necropants on immediately; then a coin stolen from a poor widow had to be placed in the necropants' scrotum. The Museum of Icelandic Sorcery & Witchcraft (p244) has an alarming plastic replica of the magic practice – for a very visual image of the necropants.

Sheep Farming Museum
A layered history of Icelandic ancient breed

The year 2022 marked a major event for Iceland's way of living: sheep no longer outnumbered the national population. For 1000 years, the stoic, resilient animal kept the nation alive with its meat, milk and wool. The **Sheep Farming Museum** *(saudfjarsetur.is; adult/child 1200kr/free)*, a 10-minute drive from Hólmavík, tells the surprisingly complex and layered history of Icelandic sheep. The area's farming history is told through photos and artefacts, and lambs gambol in the backyard. Visitors can sometimes feed them with milk from a bottle.

Drink a Pint of Wizardry
Iceland's first witch beer brewery

A warehouse at the edge of town offers the chance to drink witch beer. The **Galdur Brewery** *(facebook.com/witchcraftbeer)* serves up lagers and IPAs with ales coded with runic witchcraft. All are made with pure Icelandic water and local ingredients. Try the Vetur Lager, with hits of liquorice, a salty sweet snack that has been enjoyed in Iceland since the first settlers and known for its medicinal anti-inflammatory properties. Open most afternoons and evenings; take away available.

Whale Watching Without the Crowds
Humpback whales, blue whales and dolphin spotting

The calm waters of Steingrímsfjörður are ideal for wildlife spotters prone to seasickness. Humpback whales and white-beaked dolphins are the most common sight here, but blue whales can also be spotted. **Láki Tours** *(lakitours.is; adult/child under 15 years 12,000kr/free)* offers daily departures from June to October, lasting about two to three hours.

The whales often feed close to shore, offering some of the best land-based sightings in Iceland. Locals often know where the whales are residing on a given week, but a good place to start is Rte 68 by the Sheep Farming Museum. Keep an eye out for the spouts or the fin of a humpback. If nothing else, the walk along the beach is lovely.

WHERE TO EAT AROUND HÓLMAVÍK

Cafe Riis: Landmark cafe in Hólmavík with pizzas, burgers, colourful cocktails and late opening. *noon-11pm* €€

Kaffi Norðurfjörður: Fantastic establishment overlooking Norðurfjörður's tiny harbour; open from lunch to dinner in summer. *11.30am-8pm* €€

Steinshús: A perfect stop for a coffee and meat soup between Ísafjörður and Hólmavík, summer only, *10am-6pm* €

Sorcery Cafe (p245)**:** Laid-back cafe serving homemade seafood or meat soup, locally sourced Icelandic lamb, plus wine, coffees and cakes. *10.30am-5.30pm* €

Places We Love to Stay

€ Budget €€ Midrange €€€ Top End

Arnarfjörður
MAP p227

Bíldudalur Campground € Grassy, fjord-side quiet campsite next to the sports centre (no pool), with a playground and bouncing pillow.

Rauðsdalur € Great-value guesthouse located on a family farm with 12 clean rooms and shared bathroom facilities, plus a very tidy kitchen and lounge area. Located on the south coast nearby two great hot-pots, in Brjanslaekur.

Reykjanes tjaldsvæði € Grassy campsite between Ísafjörður and Hólmavík with good facilities and a pool on Hótel Reykjanes' property; close to the Reykjanes Geothermal Beach.

Harbour Inn €€ Smart and modern rooms in this Bíldudalur family-owned guesthouse, with kitchen for guest use and dining room where they serve a good breakfast.

Heydalur €€ Quirky farmstay with a picturesque pool inside a greenhouse, and Kobbi, a talking parrot. Rooms have floral bedsheets and wooden floors.

Korpudalur HI Hostel €€ Wonderfully located on a farm in Önundarfjörður, some 20 minutes from Ísafjörður. Suited to families with three to five beds in a room, plus sleeping bag options and camping.

Melanes €€ Adorable hobbit-sized, two-person wooden sleeping huts beside the sweeping Rauðisandur cove. Camping is also available.

Fosshótel Westfjords €€€ Historic Patreksfjörður building renovated into this super-sleek, stylish hotel with modern rooms. One of the more upmarket places to stay in the area.

Hótel Látrabjarg €€€ On the Látrabjarg Peninsula, one of the closest stays to the puffin cliffs, this small hotel has 13 rooms with private bathrooms.

Ísafjörður
MAP p237

Ísafjörður Hostel € Smart hostel with pristine four-bed dorms, on a residential street in the old part of town. Sleeping-bag accommodation with shared bathrooms and a kitchen.

Tungudalur Campground € Camping in a green valley just outside Ísafjörður, with good vibes at the kitchen-dining hut, plus a playground.

Einarshúsið Guesthouse €€ Eight lovely rooms in a wonderful 1902 heritage home near the harbour in Bolungarvik. Rooms have sea and mountain views and there's a garden, terrace, restaurant and bar.

Malarhorn €€ In Drangsnes, the guesthouse has 10 double rooms, plus a cottage and sleeping-bag accommodation, all with breakfast. There's also a seaside restaurant and a boat taking people to Grímsey island.

Urðartindur €€ One of two guesthouses in Norðurfjörður, this one is family run with modern rooms and private bathrooms.

Hótel Djúpavík €€ Landmark hotel originally built for seasonal workers during the herring boom in Djúpavík. Clean rooms with wooden floors and old photos. Good restaurant with charming, wooden beams.

Old Bookstore Guesthouse €€€ One double room above the atmospheric Flateyri bookshop, the oldest continually running business in Iceland, with antique furniture and wooden floors.

Hotel Ísafjörður (Torg) **€€€** Beats the other Hótel Ísafjörður building (Horn); business-style rooms with the best views from the top floors of the fjord. Restaurant next to the lobby.

Hólmavík
MAP p245

Holmavík Campsite € Basic grassy budget option with swimming pool and laundry facilities.

Finna Hótel €€ Mini hotel with 17 smart, modern rooms over three floors, many with sea views. Breakfast is included and served in a room with fjord views.

Kriukot €€ Don't let the well-weathered exterior put you off, inside are clean, stylish and warm rooms that blend heritage beds, slender modern chairs and eastern influences. There's also self-catering and a comfy lounge; some rooms share a bathroom.

Gistihús Hólmavíkur €€ Welcoming B&B with two doubles and a twin, one with ensuite. Nice terrace and breakfast room.

Steinhúsið €€ The first concrete house ever built in Hólmavík is now a friendly guesthouse with a handful of family rooms with private bathrooms, a kitchen, and a communal living/dining space with fjord views.

Hótel Laugarhóll €€ One of the Westfjords' most appealing retreats with a gorgeous geothermal hot-pot and swimming pool and the three-room turf-roofed Sorcerer's Cottage nearby.

Above: Whale watching, Húsavík (p280); Right: Karl og Kerling (p290)

For places to stay in North Iceland, see p300

Researched by
Mary Fitzpatrick

North Iceland

ICELAND'S ARCTIC STRONGHOLD

Hike on remote peninsulas, raft glacial rivers and relax in cozy Akureyri, all against the spectacular backdrop of the Arctic Coast Way.

Iceland's north is a world of its own. Winters last longer, the snow is deeper, history looms larger, legends seem real and locals – at least those from the regional hub of Akureyri – have their own slight twist on Icelandic pronunciation. Immersing yourself here means hiking next to towering cliffs alive with soaring gannets and nesting puffins, sailing past snow-covered mountains that plunge into whale-filled bays, spotting isolated seal colonies and fjordside pastures full of stout Icelandic horses and visiting tiny Grímsey, Iceland's Arctic Circle toehold.

Despite its many attractions, Iceland's north receives well under half the visitor numbers of the more popular south. But this is also one of the region's draws.

Apart from lively Akureyri, which has its own international airport, Lake Mývatn, with its famous hot springs, the thundering waterfalls of Dettifoss and Goðafoss and the picturesque whale-watching centre of Húsavík, you'll have much of the north to yourself. This is especially so if you choose to explore the seldom-travelled Arctic Coast Way, which winds along the coastline for 900km from Hvammstangi in the west to Bakkafjörður in the east. Throughout, the north offers the chance to see a different side of Iceland, at once accessible and remote, with countless opportunities to experience the warmth and welcome of locals who are at home in the country's most northerly towns.

THE MAIN AREAS

SKAGAFJÖRÐUR
Horse riding, sheep round-ups and rich history. **p254**

AKUREYRI
Iceland's cosmopolitan northern hub. **p266**

HÚSAVÍK
Quaint harbour town and whale watching. **p280**

JÖKULSÁRGLJÚFUR CANYON
Hiking and dramatic waterfalls. **p288**

MELRAKKASLÉTTA PENINSULA
Bird-filled promontories and the Arctic Henge. **p294**

Find Your Way

Akureyri, p266
Watch the Northern Lights dance over the snowcapped mountains of Iceland's northern capital, known for its cosy cafes, botanical garden and swimming pool.

Skagafjörður, p254
Jump on a horse to discover the countryside and then follow in the footsteps of Viking-era outlaw Grettir the Strong.

In this book, North Iceland encompasses the area from the Vatnsnes Peninsula in the west to Bakkafjörður in the east. Explore in any direction, using either the Ring Road, the Arctic Coast Way, or a combination of both as your orientation.

Húsavík, p280

Small-town Iceland-by-the-sea at its finest, with wooden sailboats and whale watching on Skjálfandi Bay.

Jökulsárgljúfur Canyon, p288

Bring a raincoat for a close – and wet – view of Dettifoss' cascading waters, and hiking shoes for the two-day Canyon Trail.

Melrakkaslétta Peninsula, p294

Visit the Arctic Henge, hike along remote stretches of coastline, learn about leader-sheep and experience the warm welcome of Iceland's northernmost communities.

CAR

Hire a car to really explore. A 2WD will get you to most places, but 4WD is preferable in winter. Gravel roads are common along the coast. Most are in good condition, but check *road.is* before setting off.

BUS

Strætó *(straeto.is)* is the public bus network across Iceland, and within Akureyri. There are daily connections between Reykjavík and Akureyri via Skagafjörður. Buses to Húsavík, Mývatn and Siglufjörður depart from Akureyri.

PLANE

There are nonstop connections between Akureyri (international) airport and London on EasyJet, seasonally from Zürich via Keflavík on Edelweiss and on Norlandair between Akureyri and Nerlerit Inaat (Greenland), with more international flights planned.

Plan Your Time

Raft glacial rivers or catch a ferry to an offshore island in the summer, round up horses in autumn, ski from mountain summits over winter and spot puffins in the spring.

Dimmuborgir (p285)

Pressed for Time

● Spend a day or two in and around **Akureyri** (p266) enjoying its many attractions. Then, rent a car or join an organised tour. Depending on your time, you could head to **Húsavík** (p280), which can also be reached via bus from Akureyri, and set sail on a wooden boat to look for whales, or drive the full **Diamond Circle** (p287), also taking in the **Dimmuborgir** (p285) lava formations and the Hverir hot springs around **Lake Mývatn** (p284).

● Stop for a meal at **Vogafjós Cowshed Cafe** (p286), stretch your legs with a walk to the mighty **Dettifoss** (p288) waterfall or take a short hike at **Ásbyrgi** (p290). Finish with a relaxing soak at the atmospheric **Mývatn Nature Baths** (p286) or back in Akureyri at **Forest Lagoon** (p268).

Seasonal Highlights

Northerly winds bring cold air from Greenland's ice cap, pushing against the balmy Gulf Stream from the south. So if you don't like the weather, just wait a minute.

JANUARY

January is the time for soaking in a hot tub and trying to catch the Northern Lights. After the New Year's holiday is a good time to watch for budget prices for flights and hotels.

MARCH

Early March brings the **Mývatn Winter Festival** (p257), with ice fishing, dog-sledding and sports and family events, plus peak off-piste skiing around Tröllaskagi. Late March brings the first whale-watching tours of the season.

MAY

Potato farmers take a risk planting in May as temperatures can still drop below zero at night, but this is generally a beautiful month to travel, with shoulder-season prices and few crowds.

Five Days to Travel Around

- From **Akureyri** (p266), rent a car and explore along both sides of **Eyjafjörður** (p271). **Grenivík** (p278) makes a perfect excursion, with a stop en route at **Laufás Turf House Museum** (p278) and maybe some horse riding or kayaking.

- On Eyjafjörður's western side (where you can also travel by bus), catch the ferry over to **Hrísey** (p275), where it's easy to spend half a day enjoying the tranquility and walking. Carry on to **Siglufjörður** (p276) for a visit to the **Herring Era Museum** (p277), a stroll around the harbour and a meal at **Restaurant Siglunes** (p277).

- Circle back via **Hofsós** (p259), with its **Icelandic Emigration Centre** (p259), and **Hólar** (p258). In good weather, the drive back to Akureyri on Rte 1 through Öxnadalsheiði is stunning.

More Than One Week

- With more than one week, travel all, or at least some, of the **Arctic Coast Way** (p262) – from Vatnsnes Peninsula, with its **seals** (p261) and the iconic sea stack of **Hvítserkur** (p263), to **Skagaströnd** (p256), on to **Sauðárkrókur** (p257), and then up and over each of the peninsulas until reaching **Bakkafjörður** (p299).

- En route, detour as much as you like: try **horse riding in Skagafjörður** (254); step into the Arctic Circle on **Grímsey** (p276); spend time in **Raufarhöfn** (p295) and watch the sun set at the **Arctic Henge** (p296); discover the area around **Þórshöfn** (p298); and hike the two-day **Canyon Trail** (p292) between Ásbyrgi and Dettifoss. When heading back to Akureyri, don't miss exploring around **Lake Mývatn** (p284) to round off your grand North Iceland loop.

JULY
Compared with the rest of Iceland, summers are dry in Akureyri, Mývatn and Jökulsárgljúfur. Expect record temperatures, Iceland-style. Camping is a pleasure and Raufarhöfn's **Arctic Henge** (p296) is wonderful in the midnight sun.

SEPTEMBER
September is beautiful in the north, with clear air and autumn-hued landscapes. As days begin to shorten, it gets easier to spot the Northern Lights – and to enjoy watching for them in relatively moderate temperatures.

OCTOBER
Although storms and bad weather can shake things up, heavy snowfall is still rare. You will catch the end of the season at many places in October, with bargain hotel prices.

DECEMBER
Iceland's Christmas spirit comes out full force in the snow-covered north, with twinkling lights, Christmas displays and the **Yule Lads' annual bath** (p257) at Lake Mývatn. Check road and weather forecasts before travelling, particularly on Holtavörðuheiði and Öxnadalsheiði.

Skagafjörður

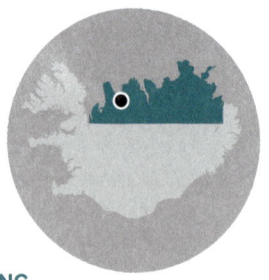

ICELANDIC HORSES | VIKING SAGAS | RIVER RAFTING

☑ TOP TIP

Reykjafoss waterfall and the nearby Fosslaug hot springs (38°C to 40°C year-round) are relatively seldom-visited gems about 7km southeast of Varmahlíð. Take Rte 752 south for 5km, go left on Rte 753 for 800m and then right onto a gravel track to the parking area, from where it's an easy walk.

Prosperous Skagafjörður is known for its horse breeding and sheep farming, for its glacial rivers and for its dramatic and often bellicose history. While travellers often pass through quickly, there are many attractions that make the region a fine place to linger. Explore open, river-laced landscapes on horseback and watch presentations at local farms showcasing the Icelandic horse's unique gaits. Call in at tiny Hólar, one of Iceland's first centres of Christianity. Learn about early-20th-century Icelandic emigration at the Icelandic Emigration Centre in Hofsós, followed by a swim in the town's beautifully situated pool. And discover the delightful regional hub of Sauðárkrókur, known for its good dining and well-presented virtual reality museum, where you can immerse yourself in Viking sagas that recall Iceland of a millennia ago. Afterwards, trace the footsteps of Grettir the Strong with a visit to Drangey, the tiny island where the famous outlaw was once exiled.

Riders' Stronghold
Where horses outnumber people

Skagafjörður is riding country, and the best way to discover its quiet corners is on the back of an Icelandic horse. This small

---

  GETTING AROUND

The regional centre of Sauðárkrókur is on the peninsula's western side. South is Varmahlíð, on the Ring Road, while diagonally across from Sauðárkrókur, on the fjord's eastern edge, is Hofsós. Skagaströnd sits by itself on the peninsula's western edge.

Bus 57 *(straeto.is)* stops at Sauðárkrókur and Varmahlíð on its route between Reykjavík and Akureyri, but for other destinations you will need a car. Rte 744, which crosses the peninsula between Blönduós and Sauðárkrókur, is wide and paved and makes a quieter alternative to the Ring Road.

Öxnadalsheiði, the mountain pass between Skagafjörður and Akureyri, frequently closes over winter and can be challenging driving during storms, even when open. Check road conditions first at *road.is*.

SKAGAFJÖRÐUR

🟊 HIGHLIGHTS
1. Drangey
2. Glaumbær
3. Hofsós Swimming Pool
4. Lýtingsstaðir

🔴 SIGHTS
5. 1238 The Battle of Iceland
6. Árnes Museum
7. Borgarsandur
8. Cathedral
see 3 Icelandic Emigration Centre
see 8 Icelandic Horse History Centre
see 6 NES Artist Residency
see 8 Nýibær Turf House
9. Spákonufell
10. Spákonufellshöfði
see 6 Spákonuhof – the Museum of Prophecies

🔴 ACTIVITIES
11. Bakkaflöt
12. Grettislaug
13. Langhús Horse Tours
14. Syðra-Skörðugil
15. Viking Rafting

⚫ SLEEPING
see 18 Brimslóð Atelier
16. Guesthouse Gimbur
17. Guesthouse Hofsstaðir
see 5 Hótel Tindastóll
see 12 Reykir Guesthouse
see 10 Salthús Guesthouse
see 3 Sunnuberg

🟢 EATING
18. Brimslóð Atelier
19. Dalakaffi
see 5 Grána Bistro
see 12 Grettis Cafe
20. Hótel Varmahlíð Restaurant
see 5 Jarlstofa
see 3 Retro Mathús
see 5 Sauðá
see 5 Sauðárkróksbakarí
see 18 Teni

🟢 DRINKING & NIGHTLIFE
see 8 Icelandic Beer Centre

⚫ INFORMATION
see 5 Sauðárkrókur Tourist Information Office

and stocky breed, which has been serving Icelanders since Viking days, is known for its hardiness, its lively personality and its unique gaits. Several farms in and near the region, including **Lýtingsstaðir** *(lythorse.com),* **Syðra-Skörðugil** *(sydraskordugil.is)* and **Langhús Horse Tours** *(icelandichorse.is)* offer activities for experienced and entry-level riders. These range from one-hour introductory tours to multiday tours for advanced riders. The shorter tours generally follow a beginner rhythm, sometimes incorporating variations of pace towards the second half. For multiday tours, you'll need to be skilled in riding and handling. Langhús offers a horse experience for children who are too young for regular riding tours, and Lýtingsstaðir and Syðra-Skörðugil offer farmstays. If you are interested in exploring the horse theme further, don't miss a visit to Hólar (p258), home to the Icelandic Horse History Centre. Also watch for the biennial **National Icelandic Horse Competition** (Landsmot Hestamanna), next scheduled for July 2026 in Hólar.

RÉTTIR

Autumn in Iceland brings round-up time, when sheep – after enjoying their summer pastures – are gathered up and sorted into their home folds in a paddock called a *rétt*. These round-ups take place all over the country, including many in Skagafjörður, where horses still do sheepherding work. Some farms, including **Syðra-Skörðugil** (p255) and the **Íslandshestar** *(islandshestar.is)* farms, offer visitors the chance to observe and sometimes participate. You may also see *stóðréttir*, or horse round-ups, when free-roaming horses are gathered from their summer grazing areas. One of the best-known is the **Laufskálarétt**, in Hjalta valley near Hólar. Round-ups are usually held from late September to early October, with dates and locations published in the Icelandic-only *Bændablaðið* (*bbl.is*; search under *fjar-og-stodrettir*).

Spákonufell

Land of Þórdís
Prophecies, art and hiking in Skagaströnd

If you are travelling the Arctic Coast Way (p262) and wondering how the rest of your journey might go, call in at **Skagaströnd**, 2km off Rte 745 on the Skagi peninsula's western edge. The town has been associated with divination since Viking days and is famed for its association with the late-10th-century soothsayer, Þórdís, one of the area's first residents. At **Spákonuhof** – the **Museum of Prophecies** *(tel 861 5089, 849 9351; adult/child 2000/1000kr, fortune-telling 6500kr)*, learn about Þórdís' story and have your fortune told. The museum is open from June through August (closed Monday), and otherwise by appointment. Just opposite is the late-19th-century **Árnes Museum** *(tel 455-2700; adult/child 2000/500kr)*, Skagaströnd's oldest house, where you can get insights into local life at that time and double-check on your fortune. Thanks to the **NES** *(neslist.is)* artist residency program, based by the harbour at the old fish factory, Skagaströnd is also gaining a reputation as one of north Iceland's artistic hubs.

Rising up behind town is **Spákonufell** (639m), the mountain below which Þórdís lived. According to legend, Þórdís buried a treasure chest near the top. It remains hidden, still waiting to be found by an unbaptised woman to whom ravens

 DINING IN & AROUND SKAGAFJÖRÐUR

Hótel Varmahlíð Restaurant: Try this place just above the junction, known especially for its well-prepared lamb dishes. *6.30-9pm May-Sep* €€

Grettis Cafe: Come for the warm welcome, wonderful cakes and rustic ambience at this small cafe at Grettislaug, plus the chance for a hot soak afterwards. *9am-11pm* €

Retro Mathús: Travellers in Hofsós praise this place for its lovely location overlooking the harbour, its wholesome food and competitive prices. *noon-9pm Tue-Sun, 6-9pm Mon Jun-Aug* €€

Dalakaffi: A lovely little seasonal cafe about 5km east of Hofsós with soups and homemade cakes and pastries. *noon-6pm Thu-Mon Jun-Aug* €€

will deliver the key. To everyone else it will just look like a rock. There are several paths up, with the more gradual one (although steep in parts) beginning at the golf course north of town and taking three to four hours return (7km). **Spákonufellshöfði**, just northwest of the harbour, offers a view-dial and walking trails.

Viking Saga
History and cuisine in Sauðárkrókur

Around the 13th century, when Iceland had neither a king nor a central government, *The Saga of Grettir the Strong* (p258), together with a medieval literature genre of family stories known as Sagas of the Icelanders, were penned to bolster the authority of the ruling chieftains. This was also the time that Iceland saw its first and only civil war. Viking enthusiasts of all ages can learn about these battles at **1238 The Battle of Iceland** *(1238.is; adult/child 3400/2400kr)* in **Sauðárkrókur**. The exhibit first covers history, weapons and more, finishing with an interactive virtual reality presentation where you can step into the midst of a battle. Afterwards, take time to stroll around Sauðárkrókur, which is a pleasant stop in its own right. Highlights include the black-sand beach of **Borgarsandur**, a helpful **tourist information office** at the Battle of Iceland exhibition, attractive old houses and a rewarding array of restaurants.

Ocean Swimming with Grettir the Strong
A chilly swim and warm soak

According to the medieval saga chronicling his life, Iceland's legendary outlaw Grettir the Strong was exiled on the small island of **Drangey**, 7km from the mainland northeast of Sauðárkrókur, following arson and retributions for the death of his brother. Thankfully, only one part of his biography still inspires people to action nowadays: the swim from Drangey to the mainland. About 20 people have completed this cold endeavour since Grettir's alleged escape, with one of the more recent swims in 2017, when friends Harpa Berndsen and Sigrún Geirsdóttir finished within four hours in water temperatures averaging about 10°C. Following his swim, Grettir apparently soothed his chilled bones with a soak in **Grettislaug** *(entry 2000kr)*, a small geothermal pool opposite the island, where modern-day soakers (swimmers or not) are welcome. It is run

BEST NORTH ICELAND FESTIVALS

Akureyri Art Summer: A long-standing festival held in July with events for all ages, mostly free.

Siglufjörður Folk Music Festival: Held in early July in Siglufjörður, focusing on Icelandic and Scandinavian folk music.

Fisherman's Day: Held on the first Sunday in June throughout North Iceland to honour local seafarers and seafaring culture.

Yule Lads' Bath: There is fun for all at the Yule Lads' annual bath, held in early December in Mývatn Nature Baths.

Mývatn Winter Festival: Ice fishing, cross-country skiing and more, plus food and family fun around Lake Mývatn in late February/early March.

Landsmót Hestamanna: Held every two years in rotating locations around Iceland to showcase Icelandic horses and equine traditions.

 DINING IN SAUÐÁRKRÓKUR: OUR PICKS

Grána Bistro: Known for its soup-and-salad lunch buffet plus sandwiches and delicious cakes. At the information centre in Sauðárkrókur. *10am-5pm €*

Jarlstofa: Fine dining at Hotel Tindastóll, featuring a mix of traditional Icelandic and new-Nordic cuisine with fresh, local ingredients, all excellently prepared. *5-10pm Apr-Sep €€€*

Sauðárkróksbakarí: This historic bakery is a local favourite, with delectable cinnamon rolls, great rye bread, sandwiches and warm drinks. *7am-5pm Mon-Fri, 9am-4pm Sat-Sun €*

Sauðá: This justifiably popular spot offers specialities such as pan-fried cod and lamb ribeye, with all ingredients locally sourced. *5-10pm Tue-Sun €€*

GRETTIR THE STRONG

Grettir Ásmundarson, better known as Grettir the Strong, lived in the early 11th century. Although good-hearted, he was strong-willed and impetuous and spent much of his time battling monsters, both mythical and human. This soon landed him in trouble and he was declared an outlaw – first, for three years for killing a suspected thief, and later for 20 years, due to being mistakenly accused of killing a dozen men in a fire.

Grettir ultimately made his way to Drangey, where he was killed by a combination of witchcraft and enemies shortly before his sentence was due to expire. You can read Grettir's story at the **Icelandic Saga Data Base** (*sagadb.org*) or in print (*The Saga of Grettir the Strong*, translated by Bernard Scudder).

by the indomitable Ingemar, who also serves soups, cakes and drinks at the adjacent cafe.

For the rest of us, **Drangey Tours** (*drangey.net*) offers daily four-hour boat tours (weather permitting) from Sauðárkrókur to the island from 1 June to 20 August. The company has been running for three generations, with skipper Helgi Hrafn at the helm of the small fishing boat bringing people to the island's tiny harbour. Passengers spend two to three hours on the island, walking and observing puffins and seabirds. Expect to hear many (often unbelievable) stories of Grettir. Back on the 'mainland' is the rustic **Reykir Guesthouse** (*jarlinn551@gmail.com*) and a beautifully situated campsite.

Horses & History in Hólar
Equine hub and ancient bishopric

History buffs and horse lovers heading up or down Rte 76 along the east side of Skagafjörð shouldn't miss the 11km detour through the wide and scenic Hjalta valley to tiny **Hólar**, one of Iceland's earliest centres of Christianity. At the village entrance is **Hólar cathedral** – one of Iceland's oldest churches. Dating to the mid-18th century, it is built on the site of earlier churches dating back to 1050, when the area was northern Iceland's main bishopric. Its interior is filled with

DINING BEYOND SKAGAFJÖRÐUR: OUR PICKS

Sjávarborg: The lunch buffet, seafood soup and views over the harbour are highlights of this stylish restaurant in Hvammstangi. *11.30-3pm & 5-10pm Mon-Fri, 5-10pm Sat & Sun* €€€

North West Restaurant: Speedy service and generous portions at this always-busy place on the Ring Road 13km east of the Hvammstangi turnoff. *11.30am-9pm* €€

Brimslóð Atelier: Enjoy a three-course dinner featuring New Nordic cuisine prepared by Icelandic chefs Inga and Gísli. On the waterfront in Blönduós. *advance booking only* €€€

Teni: This unassuming place at the Kjörbúðin supermarket shopping centre in Blönduós has favourably priced burgers, pizzas and fish. *noon-9pm* €

Hólar cathedral

historical treasures including a pre-Reformation altarpiece and a baptismal font dating to at least the late 17th century. In theory, the church is open from 10am to 6pm daily during the summer. Just up from the church is Hólar University, known for its equine sciences program. It is flanked by the **Nýibær turf house** *(free)* and the seasonal **Icelandic Horse History Centre** *(sogusetur.is; adult/child 1500kr/free)*. Opposite is the small **Icelandic Beer Centre** *(facebook.com/bjorsetur.islands)*, which hosts regular beer festivals. The area around Hólar is good for hiking; there is a route map with trail descriptions posted on the side of the university just below Nýibær turf house. While there is camping and self-catering accommodation *(visitholar.is)* in Hólar, note that there are currently no supermarkets, cafes or restaurants, so bring in whatever you will need for snacks and meals.

Emigrating Icelanders

Trace your Icelandic roots

About midway up Skagafjörður's eastern side is the old trading post of **Hofsós**. Its roots stretch back to at least the 16th century when it took over from the old settlement of Kolkuós, 10km to the south, as Skagafjörður's main port and provided sea access for the Hólar bishopric. Today, the tiny town, backed by a striking row of flat-topped mountains, is known for its lovely municipal **swimming pool** *(sundlaugar.is; adult/child 1300/415kr)* overlooking the fjord, and for the **Icelandic Emigration Centre** *(hofsos.is; 2000kr)* at the harbour. The centre is full of information about emigration from Iceland during the late 19th and early 20th centuries, when over 14,000 Icelanders – more than one-fifth of the country's population at the time – left the country. It is open from 11am to 6pm daily from June to September. Outside of these times, call *(tel 453-7935)* to arrange an appointment.

WHERE TO DO LAUNDRY?

After all that hiking and days on the road, it's time to do your laundry. Some hotels offer the service and most campsites have at least one washing machine where a load costs from around 800kr, plus drying facilities. However, you'll often have to wait in line at major campsites, especially during peak summer travel time. It is better to seek out small campgrounds with large facilities such as **CJA Camping** *(cja.is)* near Laugar or the scenic **66.12 North** *(facebook.com/camping66.12)* campground near the tip of the Tjörnes peninsula.

For those willing to pay, **Grand Laundry** *(tvottur.is)* in Akureyri offers 24-hour delivery, and sometimes can return clothes on the same day.

SLOWING DOWN BEYOND SKAGAFJÖRÐUR

When it is time to leave Skagafjörður, it's likely you'll pass through Blönduós (p261). But don't pass through too quickly: the Blönduós police district is famously diligent in traffic surveillance and driving the highway at 100km/h can set you back 20,000kr in fines. (At 110km/h, the fine is 50,000kr.)

It is also worth slowing down to take advantage of a local culinary treat. At the water's edge in the older part of town is the boutique guesthouse **Brimslóð Atelier** (p300; *brimslodguesthouse.is*), with fine meals (p258) and workshops (by appointment) in New Nordic cooking and Icelandic food heritage led by owners Inga and Gísli. They have authored several cookbooks, including *Into the North: Live well, Eat Well – The Icelandic Way*.

Rafting on the Austari-Jökulsá (East Glacial River)

Rafting Glacial Rivers
Easy paddling and challenging white water near Varmahlíð

The Ring Road junction settlement of Varmahlíð is known for its campsite, municipal swimming pool and busy service station. But Varmahlíð's main claim to fame from May/June to September is as a hub of north Iceland's best white-water rafting. The two main operators are **Bakkaflöt** *(bakkaflot.is)* and **Viking Rafting** *(vikingrafting.is)*. For adrenaline junkies, the action happens on four-to-six-hour extreme trips on the high-octane Austari-Jökulsá (East Glacial River), with Class 4+ rapids plus stretches of calm waters where you can catch your breath and appreciate the dramatic canyon scenery. If this isn't your idea of enjoyment, try a three-to-four-hour 'family rafting' trip on the more placid Vestari-Jökulsá (West Glacial River), with Class 2+ rapids. Both companies also offer kayaking, ranging from gentle paddles to customised, pro-level challenges. For all trips, the operators will give you overwear, but dress warmly and ideally bring a set of dry clothes for afterwards. Whatever you choose, make a complete experience of it with an overnight at the rafting company bases, both of which have lovely settings just south of the Ring Road. Both also offer restaurants and camping, and Bakkaflöt has cabins and a guesthouse.

Traditional Life in Old Iceland
Visiting Glaumbær turf farm

If you've ever wondered how it would be to live in a traditional Icelandic turf house, don't miss the 18th-century **Glaumbær Museum** *(glaumbaer.is; adult/child 2200kr/free)*. The traditional Icelandic turf farm was a complex of small separate buildings, connected by a central passageway, and you can see this style of construction here. The interior is full of period furniture, equipment and utensils and conveys a real feeling for the living conditions, especially how cramped things were. The beds, for example, are not long enough to lie flat while sleeping.

Beyond Skagafjörður

Small-town Iceland, knitted together by the Ring Road, has an appeal all of its own, plus seals and Arctic scenery around the Vatnsnes Peninsula.

West of Skagafjörður, just across the waters of Húnafjörð, is the Vatnsnes Peninsula. Driving around its approximately 75km-long periphery only takes about 90 minutes, excluding stops, but it is likely to be a highlight of your Iceland journey, with its coastal scenery, mythical, fog-draped rock formations and the chance to spot seals. The main town here, Hvammstangi, is notable as the westerly starting point of the Arctic Coast Way. Back on the Ring Road, finding attractions along the northwestern drive takes some work as neither villages nor nature will woo you off the road with splashy phenomena. For those willing to linger, the lively town of Blönduós makes a pleasant stop, with its seasonal textile museum.

Hvammstangi
Spotting seals

TIME FROM SKAGAFJÖRÐUR (SAUÐÁRKRÓKUR): **75MIN**

Hvammstangi is known as home to a small port, the large **Kidka** *(kidka.com)* knitwear shop and the start of the Arctic Coast Way. Before setting off, call in at the **Icelandic Seal Centre** *(selasetur.is; adult/child 1400/1100kr)* at the harbour, with its helpful proprietor and informative exhibits about the grey and – especially – harbour seals that frolic in the nearby waters. Spotting them is a highlight, and the best place to do this is at **Illugastadir** (p262), 25km to the north.

Blönduós
A Ring Road stop

TIME FROM SKAGAFJÖRÐUR (SAUÐÁRKRÓKUR): **40MIN**

Blöndós, a Ring Road default stop, is divided in half by the Blanda river. The traditional 'downtown' is to the west, with services along the highway at the settlement's edge. Linger to visit the seasonal **Textile Museum** *(textile.is; adult/child 2000kr/free)*, run by town expert Elín Sigurðardóttir, with its intricate embroideries and early Icelandic costumes. Next door is the **Icelandic Textile Centre** *(textilmidstod.is)*, home to the Iceland Knit Fest in June and the textile residency 'Ós'. At Blönduós' eastern edge is a footbridge to **Hrútey** island for picnics and walks.

Places
Hvammstangi p261
Blönduós p261

GETTING AROUND

Outside summer, check the weather forecasts and road conditions *(road.is)* before driving over Holtavörðuheiði, the mountain road marking North Iceland's western border. For more on travelling the Arctic Coast Way, see p262.

Bus 57 *(straeto.is)* between Reykjavík and Akureyri stops at the junction of the Ring Road with Rte 72 ('Hvammstangavegur'), 6km south of Hvammstangi, and at Blönduós.

Rte 35, known as the 'Kjölur Route' (p330), is an approximately 167km-long highland road leading from Rte 731 (off Rte 1, just south of Blönduós) to Gullfoss in the south. It is usually open from around mid-June for SUVs with proper insurance.

DRIVING TOUR

The Arctic Coast Way

There is no finer way to experience North Iceland than on a journey along the 900km Arctic Coast Way *(arcticcoastway.is)* between Hvammstangi and Bakkafjörður. While you could drive the route in several days, plan on at least a week to allow for exploration. The Arctic Coast Way can be driven from spring to autumn and in a 2WD, and easily combines with the Ring Road and Diamond Circle for a rewarding circuit taking in Lake Mývatn and the Ásbyrgi Canyon.

❶ Hvammstangi – The Journey Begins

The entire Arctic Coast Way is refreshingly unassuming and under-publicised and Hvammstangi (p261), its westerly starting point, is no different. Enjoy a meal at Sjávarborg (p258) and visit the Icelandic Seal Centre (p261) before following the mostly good, mostly gravel Rte 711 for 25km north to the old farm of **Illugastadir** (closed 1 May to 20 June), with camping *(tjalda.is/en/campsite/illugastadir-vatnsnesi)* and seal-spotting. From the parking area *(per day 1000kr)*, a path leads down and to the left for about 1.5km to a wooden viewing shed and a sheltered cove where it is common to see seals.

The Drive: Continue on Rte 711 around the Vatnsnes Peninsula's tip. The road is pot-holed just enough so that you'll need to slow down and enjoy the views. After 21km, watch for the signposted Hvítserkur turnoff on your left.

Hvítserkur

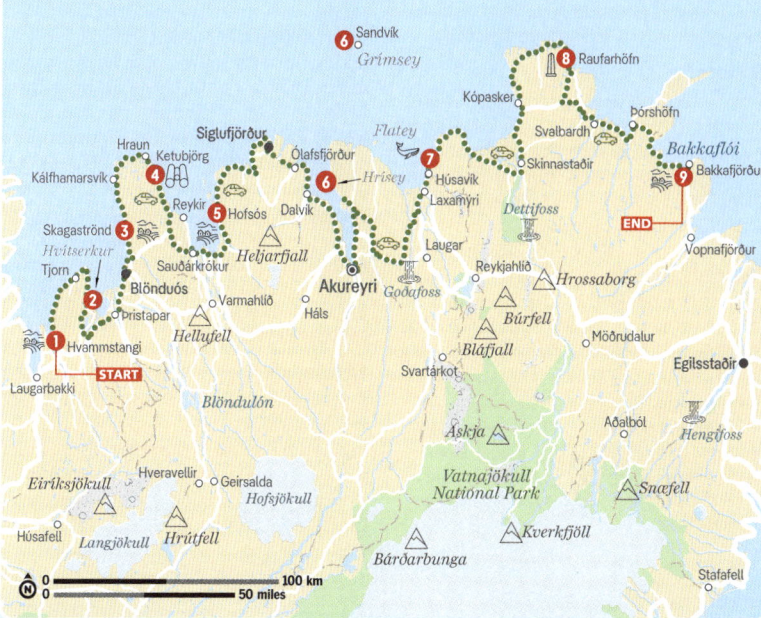

❷ Hvítserkur

According to legend, this imposing 15m-high rock formation is actually a troll who was so absorbed in his bad behaviour that he did not notice the approaching dawn and was petrified for eternity by the sun's first rays. From the parking area, follow the path 500m to the left for the best views. You can also walk about 700m down the right-hand path to a small, black-sand beach, where you may see some seals – or watch for them around Sigríðarstaðavatn lake, just south along the beach.

The Drive: About 9km south of Hvítserkur, the road forks. Turning left onto Rte 717 takes you 7.5km over a rough, narrow, rollercoaster-like track to the old rock fortress of Borgarvirki. But avoid this and continue south on the easy-to-negotiate Rte 711. The two rejoin at Rte 716, from where it is 3km further to the Ring Road and then 57km on good roads via Blönduós to Skagaströnd.

❸ Skagaströnd

Skagaströnd (p256) is the place to linger for fortune-telling and fine hiking. About 25km beyond town is **Kálfshamarsvík**. This once-thriving fishing village, 1.6km off the road, was abandoned in the 1940s and is now a ruin, although plaques (in Icelandic) near the lighthouse show where various buildings previously stood. Don't miss the fine basalt columns edging the lighthouse headland.

The Drive: The good, gravel Rte 745 takes you around the Skagi peninsula's tip through increasingly remote scenery. About 32km after Kálfshamarsvík, watch for the signposted parking area for Ketubjörg, with its cliffside cascades.

❹ Ketubjörg

There are two official lookout points here separated by about 2km of road. The westernmost one is wheelchair accessible. You can also hike between the two, watching here and at the lookout points for stunning waterfalls cascading from the cliffs into the sea.

The Drive: With the Skagi peninsula's most dramatic scenery now behind you, it's an easy 46km on to Sauðárkrókur, with camping and hot tubs at nearby Grettislaug. From there, continue along good roads to Hólar and on to Hofsós.

❺ Hofsós

Tiny Hofsós, on the western edge of Tröllaskagi ('Troll Peninsula'), makes a good overnight stop, if only for the chance to enjoy the views over the fjord from its municipal swimming pool (p259) and to call in at the Icelandic Emigration Centre (p259). From here, Rte 76 leading north is particularly beautiful as it takes you up and around the peninsula's tip and through a short tunnel to Siglufjörður (about one hour beyond Hofsós), where the Herring Era Museum (p277) is an essential stop.

The Drive: After Siglufjörður, the road almost immediately enters the long Héðinsfjarðargöng tunnels which bring you to Ólafsfjörður. From there, continue south via the 3.4km Múlagöng tunnel to Dalvík, Árskógssandur and the ferries to Grímsey and Hrísey.

❻ Grímsey & Hrísey – Island Detours

About 1.5km after exiting the eastern end of Múlagöng tunnel is a rest area facing north towards **Mígandifoss**, an unexpected ocean-plunging waterfall, with a view of Grímsey island on clear days. Grímsey (p276) itself makes a fine detour and lets you step into the Arctic Circle. If you'll be taking the ferry (p276), plan on overnighting in Dalvík – or at least call in at Gísli, Eiríkur, Helgi – Kaffihús Bakkabrædrai (p276) for fish soup before continuing to Árskógssandur for the ferry to Hrísey and some gentle island walks.

The Drive: From Árskógssandur, continue south on the tarmac Rte 82 towards Akureyri (p266), where you can relax and restock before resuming your Arctic Coast journey via end-of-the-road Grenivík, with its superb vistas over Eyjafjörður, and on to Húsavík on Rte 85.

❼ Húsavík

In Húsavík (p280), the highlights are whale watching, warm sea baths and hiking. From the town, the good Rte 85 takes you past tiny Lundey (Puffin Island; p81) in Skjálfandi Bay and on around the tip of the Tjörnes Peninsula. About 34km from

Icelandic Emigration Centre

Hringsbjarg

Húsavík, pause at the cliff-edge viewing platform of **Hringsbjarg** for an amazingly broad horizon and maybe a resting puffin. Hringsbjarg is not signposted, but the large car park makes it obvious.

The Drive: From Hringsbjarg, the good road winds steeply down towards the flat black beach of Öxarfjörður and the signposted turnoff to the beautifully situated 66.12 North campground before continuing via Ásbyrgi to the Melrakkaslétta Peninsula. Shortly before Kópasker, leave Rte 85 and turn north onto Rte 870, which takes you about 55km around the tip of the peninsula to Raufarhöfn.

8 Raufarhöfn & the Arctic Henge

In Raufarhöfn, treat yourself to a meal and an overnight at Hótel Norðurljós (p301), have a swim at the local pool and take in the 360-degree views from the Arctic Henge (p296). The town makes a perfect hub for enjoying nearby birding and hiking opportunities, including around Rauðinúpur and Hraunhafnartangi lighthouse (p295).

The Drive: From Raufarhöfn, it's an easy 20km south to rejoin the tarmac Rte 85 and then about 47km further southeast to Þórshöfn.

9 Þórshöfn & on to Bakkafjörður – The Journey's End

Pretty Þórshöfn (p298) is the gateway to Langanes, the Arctic Coast Way's final peninsula. With its cosy guesthouse and good infrastructure it also makes an ideal overnight base for hiking at Rauðanes Point and visiting the gannet colony at Skoruvík (p299). From Þórshöfn, it is just 44km further, following Rte 85 as it hugs the coast, to Bakkafjörður (p299), where the spectacular Arctic Coast Way ends as quietly and unassumingly as it began. Check out Bakkafjörður's harbour, hike to the lighthouse and relish the memories of the journey you have just completed. From Bakkafjörður you can return to the Ring Road via Vopnafjörður or turn around and do the Arctic Coast Way all over again.

Akureyri

COSY CAFES | OUTDOOR ADVENTURE | MUSEUMS & GARDENS

GETTING AROUND

Akureyri's city buses *(straeto.is)* are free for everyone. All routes start and end at Miðbær, just across Hringvegur from the Hof Cultural Centre. Line 6 services Akureyri Museum. Taxis between the airport and town cost about 3000kr, or you can walk the 3km along a fjord-side footpath.

Free parking is widely available. For pay parking, try **Parka** *(parka.is)*. To locate and rent a scooter, download the Hopp *(hopp.bike)* app; expect to pay around 1000kr for rides within the centre. Just outside Hof Cultural Centre on Strandgata are Strætó's long-distance bus stops for connections to Reykjavík, Siglufjörður, Húsavík and Egilsstaðir.

Akureyri (population 20,000) is Iceland's second city and a charming place, with excellent infrastructure, a welcoming vibe, cosy cafes and something of a late-night scene in the Hafnarstræti pedestrian area. In comparison with other towns in rural North Iceland, it feels downright cosmopolitan.

The city sits at the head of long, narrow Eyjafjörður, backed by stands of forest and snowcapped mountains. In the early days, Danish merchants influenced Akureyri's development, in part by promoting the planting of trees in well-tended gardens and thereby laying the foundation for today's Scandi-style parks at Kjarnaskógur and Lystigarður. In summertime, Akureyri's harbour – just a stone's throw from the Arctic Circle – is one of Iceland's busiest ports of call for cruise ships and also a jumping-off point for whale-watching tours. Lively winter festivals and some of Iceland's best skiing provide plenty of off-peak and off-piste appeal, making Akureyri a true year-round destination.

Sea Monsters & Storybooks
A visit to Akureyri Museum

For an overview of Akureyri's history, don't miss visiting the **Akureyri Museum** *(minjasafnid.is; adult/child 2600kr/ free),* about a 30-minute walk from the centre in Akureyri's old town. Its highlight is the **Schulte Collection** – the world's largest collection of historical maps of Iceland and elsewhere in Scandinavia. Some date back to the early 16th century and many are decorated with sketches of sea monsters and other denizens of the deep. Other museum exhibits showcase Akureyri as Iceland's bourgeoisie northern capital: the shiny gifts Frederik VIII of Denmark brought with him on a 1907 visit, old musical instruments and wooden sledges. The museum, overlooking a beautiful garden near the old Aðalstræti (Main Street), was also the first place in Iceland to cultivate trees when a nursery was established here in 1899.

AKUREYRI

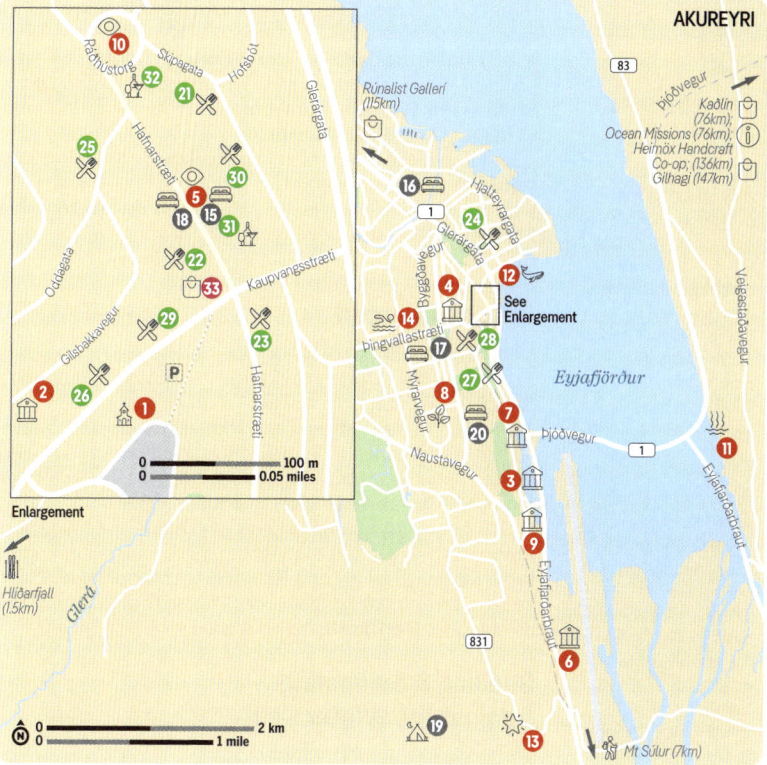

- **SIGHTS**
  1. Akureyrarkirkja
  2. Akureyri Art Museum
  3. Akureyri Museum
  4. Davíð Stefánsson Writers' Museum
  5. Hafnarstræti
  6. Icelandic Aviation Museum
  7. Laxdalshús
  8. Lystigarður
  9. Motorcycle Museum of Iceland
  see 3 Nonnahús
  10. Ráðhústorgið
  see 3 Toy Museum

- **ACTIVITIES**
  11. Forest Lagoon
  12. Keli Sea Tours
  13. Kjarnaskógur
  14. Sundlaug Akureyrar
  see 12 Whale Watching Akureyri

- **SLEEPING**
  15. Akureyri Backpackers
  16. Akureyri HI Hostel
  17. Berjaya Iceland Hotel Akureyri
  18. Hafnarstræti Hostel
  19. Hamrar Campsite
  see 28 Hótel Akureyri
  20. Sæluhús

- **EATING**
  21. Berlín
  22. Blaá Kannan
  see 7 Brynju Ís
  23. Eyja
  24. Greifinn
  25. Kaffi Ilmur
  26. Ketilkaffi
  27. Lyst
  28. North Restaurant
  29. Rub23
  30. Strikið

- **DRINKING & NIGHTLIFE**
  31. Græni Hatturinn
  32. R5

- **ENTERTAINMENT**
  see 12 Hof Cultural Centre

- **SHOPPING**
  33. Eymundsson Bookshop & Cafe
  see 5 Lopi Og List

Next door is a tiny, black-tarred timber church and **Nonnahús** (Nonni's House), the 19th-century home of children's writer Jón Sveinsson. His books – some of which have been translated into English – make cosy bedtime reading and the house gives a glimpse into the Akureyri of bygone days. Entry to Akureyri Museum is valid for one year and allows free admission to all seven of its affiliated museums. In addition to

☑ TOP TIP

Runners and cyclists will enjoy the smooth 14km path between Hof Cultural Centre and Hrafnagil village south of town.

STAINED-GLASS MYSTERY

Just as Reykjavík is defined by the Hallgrímskirkja, central Akureyri is defined by the iconic **Akureyrarkirkja**, which was also designed by Guðjón Samúelsson (p296). Inside the Akureyrarkirkja is a 3200-pipe organ, a series of reliefs of the life of Christ, and a ship suspended from the ceiling, reflecting an old Nordic tradition of votive offerings for the protection of loved ones at sea.

Perhaps the interior's most striking feature is the central stained-glass window above the altar. Although it was originally believed to have come from England's Coventry Cathedral, this story was later disproved – check out BBC's documentary *The Great Glass Mystery* (bbc.co.uk/mediacentre/latestnews/2014/great-glass-mystery). The church admits visitors some weekdays during the summer months, but it is generally locked.

Nonni's House these include the nearby **Toy Museum**, where kids can see what their counterparts of a century ago played with; Laufás turf-house farm near Grenivík (p278); and – just north of Akureyri's municipal swimming pool – the **Davíð Stefánsson Writers' Museum**, former home of Icelandic writer and poet Davíð Stefánsson.

For more niche interests, try the **Icelandic Aviation Museum** *(flugsafn.is; adult/child 1800kr/free)* at the airport, with its fine collection of old planes, and the **Motorcycle Museum of Iceland** *(motorhjolasafn.is; adult/child 2000kr/free)* – perfect for poking around on a rainy day.

Artistic Akureyri

Touring the Akureyri Art Museum

Just below the **Akureyrarkirkja** – Akureyri's landmark church – is the 'Gilið' or 'ravine' – Akureyri's art street, lined with several small galleries and craft shops, sporting a rainbow-hued sidewalk and crowned by the **Akureyri Art Museum** *(listak.is; adult/child 2200kr/free)*. This ambitious museum is by far the best art museum outside of Reykjavík, with a frequently changing array of exhibits and four floors showcasing classic and contemporary art, from photography to performance pieces and Icelandic to international. There are guided tours in English every Thursday at 12.30pm. The on-site cafe, **Ketilkaffi**, makes a good spot for a break.

Soaking & Swimming Against the Winter Chill

Warm soaks and waterslides

Akureyri is famously sunny, but this is still North Iceland. What better way to beat the chill than with a warm soak? Some years ago, during the building of the Vaðlaheiðar Tunnel on Akureyri's outskirts, the construction crew was struck by a stream of hot water midway into the 7km mountain dig. Fast forward several years and the result of that discovery is the **Forest Lagoon** *(forestlagoon.is; adult/child 6900/3450kr)*, open since 2022 and the winner of our vote for Iceland's best luxury hot springs. The resort is located on a green hillside, surrounded by the Vaðlaskógur Forest and distinguished from other spas in the region by its wooded ambience – a feeling that is maintained inside as well – and by its culture of upmarket relaxation. You can enjoy views over town from two overlapping baths of varying temperature. The Finnish

EATING IN AKUREYRI: CAFES

Blaá Kannan: The cakes and pastries are always fresh at this much-loved Hafnarstræti cafe; also has soup, panini and bagels. *9am-9pm Mon-Fri, from 10am Sat & Sun* €

Kaffi Ilmur: In a historical building (once a saddlery), this cafe offers tasty breakfast and lunch options, delicious freshly prepared lamb soup and homemade cakes. *9am-5pm* €

Lyst: A lovely setting in the Botanical Gardens. Wine, chocolates, cakes and next-level mains have made Lyst an Akureyri favourite. *10am-9pm Mon-Sat, until 7pm Sun* €€

Kettilkaffi: All-day brunch, homemade bread and cakes, and a focus on fresh and organic are the highlights at this Akureyri Art Museum cafe. *8am-5pm* €€

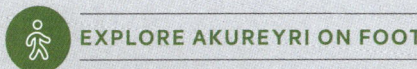

EXPLORE AKUREYRI ON FOOT

Discover Akureyri's attractions and off-beat charm on this walking tour of town.

START	END	LENGTH
Hof Cultural Centre	Akureyri Museum	2.5km; 3 hours with stops

The walk begins outside ❶ **Hof Cultural Centre**, home to the North Iceland Symphonic Orchestra and where cruise ships dock. Cross Hringvegur to the quiet town square, ❷ **Ráðhústorgið**, and then stroll down lively ❸ **Hafnarstræti**, the town's main shopping street and tourism hub, with hotels, cafes and eateries.

At ❹ **Eymundsson Bookshop & Cafe**, cross the road and climb (the upper parking lot is also accessible by car) the approximately 100 steps up to ❺ **Akureyrarkirkja** for views. The exterior towers were inspired by coastal Iceland's hexagonal basalt columns, such as those near Kálfshamarsvík (p263).

About 600m further on is the ❻ **Lystigarður** (Botanical Garden), a delightful spot for a stroll. The wealth of plant life on display here is impressive considering the garden's proximity to the Arctic Circle. You'll find examples of every species native to Iceland, as well as a host of high-latitude and high-altitude plants from around the world.

From here, follow Spítalavegur down to ❼ **Brynju Ís** ice-cream shop and the start of Akureyri's small old town. The wooden houses here – the oldest is the signposted 1795 ❽ **Laxdalshús** – used to stand by the shoreline. Continue along Aðalstræti, finishing up by ❾ **Nonnahús** (p267; Nonni's House) and the ❿ **Akureyri Museum** (p266). The Line 6 bus back to town stops in front of the museum, or walk along the waterside path.

> Just a five-minute walk further uphill from the church is **Akureyri's swimming pool**, an ideal spot for a break.

> The well-stocked **Eymundsson's** has Icelandic literature in English, plus an excellent selection of maps.

> Stop for a break at the Botanical Garden's delightful **Lyst cafe**.

WHERE TO BUY WOOL & HAND-KNITTED CLOTHING IN NORTH ICELAND

Heimöx Handcraft Co-op: Gorgeous wool sweaters made by the local hand-knitting society; it's in the house closest to Ásbyrgi's visitor centre.

Gilhagi: This sheep and goat farm is in a beautiful valley northwest of Ásbyrgi, and has an ambitious wool mill and shop.

Lopi Og List: A small, friendly shop on Akureyri's Hafnarstræti with an excellent selection of quality sweaters made by a group of local knitters.

Kaðlín: At the harbour in Húsavík, with sweaters crafted by a local hand-knitting co-op and 100% locally made handicrafts.

Rúnalist Galleri: Clothing and crafts made from natural yarns plus farm-fresh cheese, jams and more. It's at Stórhóll farm, 18km southeast of Varmahlíð on Rte 752.

dry sauna is also superb – you'll see guests moving ritually in and out of the cold plunge pool. Children are not allowed after 6pm, but they have their own stronghold at Akureyri's wonderful public pool, **Sundlaug Akureyrar** *(sundlaugar.is; adult/child 1350/300kr)*, with hot-pots, waterslides (the longer one is Iceland's longest) and a separate 25m lap-swimming pool. It is easy for water-lovers of all ages to spend several hours here, whether the weather is fine or not.

Outdoor Akureyri Unpacked
Ski slopes and cycling trails

Once the snow starts falling, winter turns Akureyri and its surroundings into one big winter playground. In a good year, ski season lasts from late November into April, with the focus on **Hlíðarfjall** *(hlidarfjall.is)*, the area's largest resort, rising up over Akureyri to the west. It has a range of slopes plus a small network of cross-country trails and offers rental of alpine skis and snowboards *(hlidarfjall.is/ski-rental)*. Day passes cost 7200/1950kr per adult/child, with occasional deals available to also use at the other major resorts in North Iceland: Sauðárkrókur, Siglufjörður, Ólafsfjörður and Dalvík. There's a small cafe on-site and Hótel Hálönd, just below. Lower down, you can cross-country ski in **Kjarnaskógur**

EATING & DRINKING IN AKUREYRI: OUR PICKS

Eyja: Wine bar and bistro with three-course options and a fish-of-the-day main. *4-10pm Sun-Thu, to midnight Fri & Sat* €€

Strikið: Large windows with fjord views lend glitz to this 5th-floor restaurant known for its Icelandic brunches and local focus (super-fresh sushi, lamb shoulder, shellfish soup). *11.30am-2pm & 5-9pm* €€€

Rub23: This sleek seafood-showcasing restaurant has a Japanese flavour, but also promotes its use of 'rubs' or marinades. Advance booking advised. *11.30-2pm & 5-10pm Mon-Fri, 5-10pm Sat & Sun* €€€

North Restaurant: Chef Gunnar Gíslason elevates Nordic cuisine to new levels, with fresh, locally sourced Icelandic ingredients and creative menus. At Hotel Akureyri. *6-9.30pm Wed-Sat* €€€

Forest Lagoon

forest, 5km south of Akureyri. Some trails are lit, but not all – better for spotting the Northern Lights.

While Akureyri's slopes are certainly fun, they don't merit comparison with famed European ski destinations. But off-piste mountain skiing, practised near Akureyri on both sides of Eyjafjörður, is unique. The towns of Siglufjörður and Grenivík are the primary base camps for summit-to-sea rides, either by snowcat or helicopter, usually sliding down Mt Múlakolla and Mt Kaldbakur, respectively. **Arctic Heli Skiing** (arctic heliskiing.com) offers multiday packages.

When there is no snow on the ground, enjoy Akureyri's growing network of hiking and cycling paths. Among the best are those at Kjarnaskógur and at Naustaborgir (on Akureyri's southwestern edge, adjacent to Kjarnaskógur). A more challenging option is the 11km hike up Mt Súlur (1213m), with views from the top. The trail begins on Súluvegur, just before the Glerá bridge (five to six hours return). Over summer, Hlíðarfjall ski resort keeps one of its chairlifts open to shuttle mountain bikers up to the **Hlíðarfjall Bike Park** (hlidarfjall. is) from late July to September. Bikes are available to rent at **Skíðaþjónustan** (skidathjonustan.com), which also rents cross-country and downhill ski equipment.

On the other side of the fjord, a forest hiking path leads to Vaðlaheiði mountain via the **Forest Lagoon**.

Whale Watching in Eyjafjörður

Narrow fjord with calmer waters

Húsavík (p280) is justifiably famed as one of Iceland's best whale-watching hubs, but several operators also run tours along Eyjafjörður, taking advantage of the increasing number of whales in the fjord's waters in recent years. Narrow, long and partially sheltered, the fjord's sailing conditions tend to

BEACH CLEAN-UP

Ocean Missions (oceanmissions.org) is an NGO focused on keeping Iceland's coastline and coastal waters clean and healthy. Between May and October, it hosts weekly beach cleaning events around Eyjafjörður and along the northeastern coast near its base in Húsavík. These clean-up events are popular in the summer, especially on World Ocean Day (8 June), which draws the largest crowd of helpers.

Ocean Missions also hosts trash-to-treasure workshops and occasional films and other activities aimed at drawing attention to the effect of marine litter on Iceland's fragile coastal ecosystems. With volunteer assistance, they have created a database monitoring microplastic pollution in northeast Iceland. Stop by their office for more background information and ideas on ways to help.

(continues on p274)

Northern Lights near Akureyri

TOP EXPERIENCE

The Northern Lights

There is a science to predicting the phenomena, but ultimately catching the Northern Lights comes down to a mix of luck and effort. North Iceland offers good chances – as does Iceland in general – with the added bonus of a snowy winter landscape.

PLAN AHEAD

- Choose when to go
- Find a base
- Follow the aurora forecast
- Escape city lights
- Avoid challenging road conditions
- Plan outdoor adventures or a hot-tub soak to fill the time

When to Go

There is a reason September is the third-most-visited month in Iceland: nights turn dark enough to see the Northern Lights while winter storms of road-shutting, plan-altering magnitude are rare. The forces creating the spectacular streaks of colours are active year-round; we just don't see them during bright summer nights. If catching them is a primary goal, visit during the darkest months, from November to February. By mid-April, the nights are too bright.

PRACTICALITIES
Check en.vedur.is/weather/forecasts/aurora for the Icelandic aurora forecast

Contrary to their name, the Northern Lights do not brighten with every northern latitude. They appear, instead, on top of the globe like a doughnut, known as the aurora oval. Middle-of-the-aurora-belt Iceland is a prime location throughout. While North Iceland has the benefit of shorter daylight hours – about one hour less in December, compared with Reykjavík – this is a minuscule benefit in scientific terms. The North, however, has the added advantage of being popular for outdoor adventures like hikes and skiing, so you will have plenty to fill your time when you're not chasing auroras.

In late 2024, the roughly 11-year solar cycle reached its 'maximum' – good news for readers of this book, since research shows that auroras tend to be more frequent during the years just after solar maximum. Thus, for Northern Lights seekers, 2026 through at least 2028 may well be ideal. To round out your astro-tourism, note that Iceland will also see a full solar eclipse in August 2026.

Find a Base

Many visitors lack the experience and expertise to handle Iceland's wintry road conditions. It doesn't help that in the north the sun can rise as late as 11.30am and set as early as 2.45pm, meaning drivers spend most of their day travelling in the dark. From November to February, a good base to spend several days will make travel safer and more relaxed, combined with searching on foot or with an organised tour. All you need is a dark spot. And this is easy in small-town North Iceland. In Akureyri, the higher hills of Hlíðarfjall and Kjarnaskógur forest are free of city lights.

Follow the Forecast

The Northern Lights are caused by solar activity. A flow of charged particles from the sun, called the solar wind, slams into the Earth's magnetic field and causes atoms in the upper atmosphere to glow. The lights appear quite suddenly, their intensity varying – scientists do a daily forecast based on solar winds in the previous three days to predict aurora strength. The **Icelandic Met Office** *(vedur.is/weather/forecasts/aurora)* publishes this forecast, with a nine-level activity range. (The scale deviates from a normal curve, usually hovering around level three, while any strength beyond level five indicates a rare solar storm.)

Make a Travel Plan

Going with a tour operator provides a good structure to the experience, and a chance to try something new like dog sledding *(snowdogs.is)* or snowmobiling *(myvatnsnowmobile.is)*. The best places for winter activity in the north are Akureyri, Mývatn and Siglufjörður. Guides will also have the resources and experience to help track the forecasts and seek out the lights. And they will often know the best viewing spots, and have back-up locations if the weather is not cooperating.

AURORA PHOTOGRAPHY

The Northern Lights are generally best photographed at shutter speeds of five to 15 seconds. A tripod is an absolute must for a strong picture; better yet, invest in a remote shutter release. While the newer smartphones are able to capture surprisingly good footage, most are hardly promising enough to make your work shine.

TOP TIPS

● Prepare like you are going to a mountain summit, with no trees or buildings sheltering you from the cool wind. Searching for the auroras is a waiting game and success can come down to that extra layer you thought was unnecessary. Invest in a thermal underlayer that will retain heat.

● Some people put too much emphasis on escaping city lights. It is enough to just leave immediate light pollution like street lights and houses to get a clear view of darkness; venturing 500km off the grid often won't make a difference.

WHALE WATCHING IN NORTH ICELAND

Madalena Gaspar is a marine biologist who works with Friends of Moby Dick *friendsofmobydick.is*

Skjálfandi Bay is an important feeding ground for several species, especially for humpbacks. We commonly observe feeding behaviour and often come across resting or sleeping whales. Sometimes, we are presented with spectacular acrobatics like breaching or tail slapping!

Even though the daily probability of spotting whales is high, they can choose to leave at any point. It's important to get out there with a sense of privilege and approach the experience with gratitude above all. Whale watching should be passive – observing whales behaving like they would if we were not around, never pushing for close encounters or interfering with their natural behaviour. And in my experience, that's when the most amazing interactions happen.

Humpback whale, Eyjafjörður

(continued from p271)

be smoother than at other destinations and tours are often shorter – averaging about two hours during summer. They can therefore be a good option for children and those prone to seasickness.

Expect to see humpbacks and minke whales, although the number of species swimming into Eyjafjörður are far fewer than in Húsavík's Skjálfandi Bay, where you have a real chance of seeing a blue whale. **Whale Watching Akureyri** *(whalewatchingakureyri.is)* dominates the Akureyri market, with a large steel ship offering indoor and outdoor viewing areas. It departs from behind Hof Cultural Centre. **Keli Sea Tours** *(keliseatours.is)* operates a single oak boat with morning and afternoon tours.

Before purchasing a ticket, it is worth asking where in Eyjafjörður the whales have been spotted in recent days. In winter especially, they tend to move towards the northern end of the fjord, creating time pressures for Akureyri tours. Depending on the whales' location, tour operators from Hauganes *(whales.is;* 35km north of Akureyri), Árskógssandur *(northsailing.is;* 2km beyond Hauganes) and Dalvík *(arcticseatours.is),* located towards the middle of Eyjafjörður, can sometimes be a better option.

EATING & DRINKING IN AKUREYRI: OUR PICKS

Græni Hatturinn: The bar is a side act at Akureyri's best live-music venue, but still has a range of good wines and local beers. *hours vary*

R5: Sample seasonal ales and the best of Iceland's craft-brew scene at Akureyri's most ambitious bar. *5pm-late*

Greifinn: Popular Greifinn is family-friendly and always full. Its no-frills menu features ribs and wings, burgers, pizzas and pastas and ice-cream desserts. *11.30am-9pm* €€

Berlín: All-day breakfasts and good coffee are the draws at this cosy timber-lined cafe. From 11.30am the menu adds lunch offerings as well. *8am-5pm* €

Beyond Akureyri

Explore Eyjafjörður's coastal towns, spot birds on Hrísey and step into the Arctic Circle on Grímsey.

At about 60km in length, Eyjafjörður is one of Iceland's longest fjords. As you venture along it, moving northwards from Akureyri, the scenery becomes increasingly dramatic, with steep mountain slopes cascading directly into the sea. To the west is Tröllaskagi ('Troll Peninsula'), where the towns of Siglufjörður and Ólafsfjörður, separated by two mountain ranges, were once a day-trip apart before the opening of the 14.2km-long Héðinsfjarðargöng tunnels in 2010. On the fjord's eastern side, the main town is Grenivík, with outdoor activities and stunning views. In the middle of the fjord is tranquil Hrísey island, while further north, surrounded by open ocean, is remote and lovely Grímsey, its northern tip just barely within the Arctic Circle.

Places
Hauganes to Dalvík p275
Grímsey p276
Siglufjörður p276
Grenivík p278
Strýtan p279

Hauganes to Dalvík TIME FROM AKUREYRI: 30-40MIN
Seafront settlements

Lining Rte 82 along Eyjafjörður's western edge are quiet coastal settlements that make for interesting stops. Hauganes, 35km from Akureyri, is known for its codfish-focused **Baccalà Bar**, with a patio shaped like a Viking longship. Work up an appetite with a swim in the sandy creek by **Hauganes Hot Tubs** *(adult/child 3000/1500kr)*, which is next to a campsite well suited to trailers and vans.

Just north is Árskógssandur, the departure point for the **ferry** *(ferjur.is/saevar; 2000kr return, 15min)* to **Hrísey**. The name Hrísey comes from the Icelandic word for dwarf birch (*hrís*), which once covered the island, and there are still some stands of forest. Officially, Hrísey is Iceland's second-largest offshore island after Heimaey, although many of its houses are only inhabited seasonally; check *visithrisey.is* for rentals. Whether you overnight or visit for the day, Hrísey is a tranquil place with several hiking trails, dozens of bird species and panoramas over the fjord. The seasonal restaurant **Verbúðin 66** (open Wednesday lunch and Saturday evening only) specialises in soup and fish and chips. There's also a small, well-stocked **convenience store** with a 24-hour self-help shed in front for off hours, and the **House of Shark Jörundur** at the **tourist information office**, detailing Hrísey's shark-fishing history,

GETTING AROUND

Beyond the Ring Road, the only gravel stretch is northwest of Siglufjörður via the short Strákagöng tunnel towards Hofsós.

Vaðlaheiðar Tunnel, Iceland's only toll road *(1700kr, payable online within 24 hours of tunnel passage)*, is the default route from Akureyri to Húsavík and Lake Mývatn. Over summer, it is possible to instead use Rte 84, adding about 15 minutes and some inspiring scenery to the trip.

Bus 78 *(straeto.is)* from Akureyri stops at Hjalteyri, Hauganes, Árskógssandur and Dalvík en route to Siglufjörður.

THE GRÍMSEY FERRY

This **ferry** *(vegagerdin.is)* is a comfortable workhorse of a boat with indoor seating, snack shop, beds *(1000kr)* and deck areas to watch the journey, which is spectacular heading up Eyjafjörður. About 40 minutes from Dalvík the boat passes Mígandi waterfall to the left and, nearby, the precarious old pre-tunnel Ólafsfjörður road.

Bus 78 links Akureyri with Dalvík, but the timing for catching the ferry is close. Contact the boat crew *(tel 853-2211)* when you are en route so they don't depart without you. Returning from Grímsey, the only options are a taxi to Akureyri *(tel 892 0808; 15,000kr)*, an overnight in Dalvík or your own vehicle (there is free overnight parking near the port). The open sea past Eyjafjörður can be choppy. If you are prone to seasickness, bring motion sickness tablets.

About 12km further north is Dalvík. It is nestled between Eyjafjörður and the rolling hills of Svarfaðardalur – the valley home of the folkloric Bakka brothers, who are known for their stupid solutions to simple problems. **Gísli, Eiríkur, Helgi – Kaffihûs Bakkabrædrai** honours the dubious trio with a friendly setting decked out in timber, vintage bric-a-brac and mismatched china. Tasty fish soup that comes with fresh bread and homemade cake rounds things out – this might just be the perfect small-town cafe. Dalvík's other claim to fame is as the ferry port for Grímsey.

Grímsey
TIME FROM AKUREYRI: **45MIN** + **3HR** OR **45MIN**

Step inside the Arctic Circle

Best known as Iceland's Arctic Circle toehold, remote Grímsey, about 40km from the mainland, is a serene little place where birds outnumber people by about 10,000 to one. The island is only about 5 sq km, but the welcome is big and the relaxation deep. Norlandair *(norlandair.is)* flies several times weekly to and from Akureyri, but it's more of an adventure to take the *Sæfari* ferry *(4000kr one way, 3hr)* from Dalvík. It is possible to catch the ferry back the same day, after two hours on the island, but spending the night is a better option, especially as hiking up and back to the Arctic Circle – currently beyond the Orbis et Globus artwork near the island's northern tip – will likely take at least this long. **Orbis et Globus** is a 7980kg concrete sphere by Kristinn Hrafnsson that was designed to be moved every year in accordance with the Arctic Circle's fluctuating position (due to the wobble of the Earth's tilt). In 2047, when the Arctic Circle will no longer intersect with the island, it is supposed to be pushed over the cliff into the sea. When hiking near the point, watch for the small '2047' stone marker.

From mid-April through July, puffins and other nesting seabirds are everywhere on Grímsey. On the island's southeastern corner is a **lighthouse** and around its southwestern corner are some impressive basalt columns. About midway between the ferry dock and the lighthouse is Grímsey's **church**. The original – built of driftwood in 1867 near the site of an 11th-century church – burned down in 2021. Grímsey's small community (year-round residents number less than 50) has rallied to raise funds to complete the new building, which also serves as the island's social centre. If you're interested in contributing, contact Gugga at Guesthouse Básar.

Siglufjörður
TIME FROM AKUREYRI: **75MIN**

The town at the end of the tunnel

Siglufjörður, with its colourful timber houses, owes its fortune to herring – small, silvery fish that move in massive schools. In its heyday, the town was home to thousands of workers, and fishing boats crammed into its small harbour unloading their catch for waiting women to gut and salt. For years, this herring export accounted for 20% of Iceland's entire foreign-trade revenue, fuelled by an influx of foreign ships

Orbis et Globus

and sailors as well as the town's many saloons and cinemas. On idle days, when ships had to stay in harbour to wait out a storm, the streets of Siglufjörður bustled.

But herring wander the northeast Atlantic without regard for human plans, and by 1969 they were gone completely. The award-winning **Herring Era Museum** (sild.is; adult/child 2400kr/free), set opposite the waterfront in three buildings that were part of an old Norwegian herring station, does a stunning job of recreating this era and the struggles that followed. It's open from June through September.

While today's population of 'Sigló', as it is known locally, is about 1200 people – a third of its herring-era size – local entrepreneurs have successfully reversed what was once a town in decline into a fun place to wander. Various ventures, such as the **Icelandic Folk Music Centre**, the **Herhúsið** artist residency and the **Siglufjörður Folk Music Festival** (facebook.com/FolkmusicFestival) have brought new life into old streets, and the microbrewery **Segull 67** (p278) and a collection of good restaurants make the town a fine spot for a stop.

Murder mysteries have helped, too! *Trapped*, the Icelandic TV series created by Baltasar Kormákur, was filmed largely in Siglufjörður, and the bestselling *Dark Iceland* crime series by Ragnar Jónasson is set in and around the town.

EXPLORE NATURE IN ACTION

Original North: E-bike tours from Akureyri's Forest Lagoon (p268) around Akureyri and the surrounding area. (originalnorth.is)

Mývatn Activity: Cycling and other activities in the area around Lake Mývatn. (myvatnactivity.com)

Saltvík Horse Farm: Two-hour coastal rides near Húsavík with glorious views over Skjálfandi bay. No special riding experience required. (saltvik.is)

Mývatn Tours: Local tourist agency, with day tours to Askja and other excursions. (myvatntours.is)

Húsavík Jet Ski: Cruise the coastline with local guides who love the sea and powerful engines. (husavikjetski.is)

 EATING IN SIGLUFJÖRÐUR: OUR PICKS

Restaurant Siglunes: Enjoy sizzling tajines and other Moroccan cuisine prepared with fresh Icelandic ingredients by chef Jaouad Hbib. Book ahead. *6-9pm daily, plus noon-2pm Sat & Sun* €€€

Fiskbúð Fjallabyggðar: The fishmonger in Siglufjörður serves fresh, well-prepared fish and chips inside the fish shop. *11am-4pm Mon-Thu, to 1.30pm Fri* €

Sunna Restaurant: The seafood-oriented menu at this upmarket restaurant at Hotel Sigló is tasty (if rather overpriced), but the pier-side setting is memorable. *6-9pm* €€€

Torgið: This informal harbourfront eatery has pizzas and hearty burgers behind a cheery yellow exterior. *noon-2pm Mon-Fri, 6-9pm Thu-Sun* €€

BEST THINGS TO DO AROUND GRENIVÍK

Polar Hestar: At Farm Grýtubakki, with one- to three-hour horse riding tours that cross small rivers and take in the surrounding fjord vistas. *(polar hestar.is)*

Cape Tours: Runs kayak tours of varying lengths and difficulty in Eyjafjörður. *(cape tours.is)*

Kaldbaksferðir: Reach the summit of Mt Kaldbakur in 45 minutes on a snow cat from January to spring with Kaldbaksferðir. Walk, slide or ski back to Grenivík. *(kaldbaksferdir.com)*

Viking Heliskiing: This Siglufjörður-based operator has tours based out of Grenivík's new Höfði Lodge from December 2025. *(vikingheliskiing.com)*

Watch the sunset: Grenivík offers some of the best views over Eyjafjörður. With luck, you may even see some whales.

At the southeastern end of the Héðinsfjarðargöng tunnels is Siglufjörður's sister city, **Ólafsfjörður** – beautifully locked between sheer mountain slopes. While it lacks Siglufjörður's energy and urban planning, it offers a good swimming pool and the cosy **Kaffi Klara**.

Grenivík

TIME FROM AKUREYRI: **40MIN**

The end of the road

You will need to make a special detour to reach Grenivík, the sole settlement on the eastern side of Eyjafjörður. But the stunning journey along Rte 83 is its own reward. And once here, you will be rewarded by magnificent vistas over the fjord, a small, seasonal **fishing museum**, kayaking and even free toilets – with a small plaque recognising those travellers who have truly reached the 'end of the road'. Shorter and multi-day hiking trails lead north along the coast (Látraströnd), to the top of the 1173m **Mt Kaldbakur** and northeast towards Fjörður. SUVs can drive the surrounding Flateyjarskagi peninsula all the way to Flateyjardalur, with several small rivers to ford. About 10km before Grenivík is the **Laufás Turf House Museum** *(minjasafnid.is; adult/child 2600kr/free)*,

EATING & DRIKING IN SIGLUFJÖRÐUR & ÓLAFSFJÖRÐUR

Aðalbakarí: On main street Aðalgata; serves pastries, sandwiches and a cold draft from the local Segull 67 microbrewery. *7am-4pm Mon-Fri, 9am-3pm Sat & Sun* €

Kaffi Rauðka: The outdoor tables at this harbourside cafe are a fine spot in summertime to take in the passing scene while enjoying pizza and a drink. *11.30am-9pm* €€

Segull 67 Brugghús: Sample tasty local brews at this microbrewery that also offers tours and tastings. Call first to arrange a time. *by appointment*

Kaffi Klara: On the main street in Ólafsfjörður, this cheery place has warm drinks, soups and light meals – it's an ideal spot to while away a rainy afternoon. *11am-5pm Mon-Fri, noon-5pm Sat & Sun* €

Grenivík

with its mid-19th-century church and comparatively spacious, well-preserved turf houses.

Strýtan

TIME FROM AKUREYRI: **25MIN** + **10MIN**

An underwater thermal chimney

Thoughts of scuba diving often involve sun-kissed beaches and tropical fish, so perhaps it's surprising that some of the northern hemisphere's most fascinating diving lies within Iceland's frigid waters. Most divers flock to crystalline Silfra (p122) near Þingvellir in the south, but the real diving dynamo, known as Strýtan, lurks beneath Eyjafjörður.

Strýtan, a giant 55m cone soaring up from the ocean floor, commands a striking presence as it spews out gushing hot water. This geothermal chimney – made from deposits of magnesium silicate – is truly an anomaly. The only other Strýtan-like structures ever discovered were found at depths of 2000m or more, while Strýtan's peak is just 15m below the surface.

In addition to Strýtan, there are smaller steam cones on the other side of Eyjafjörður. Known as Arnanesstrýtur, these formations aren't as spectacular, but the water bubbling out of the vents is estimated to be 11,000 years old. The water is completely devoid of salt, so you can put a thermos over the vent, bottle the boiling water and use it to make hot chocolate back at the surface!

Browse the range of tour options at **Strytan Divecentre** *(strytan.is),* based in Hjalteyri, about 20km north of Akureyri.

EYJAFJARÐARSVEIT

Eyjafjarðarsveit is the valley south of Akureyri rimmed by Rtes 821 and 829. With its fertile soil and amenable climate, it has long been one of Iceland's agricultural hubs. While local farmers produce beef, lamb, eggs and honey, and grow potatoes and greenhouse vegetables, it is dairy production for which the area is particularly known.

Its most famous resident is **Edda**, a giant, outdoor, metal cow sculpture made by local artist Beate Stormo, commissioned by the community and located about 27km south of Akureyri near the **Saurbæjarkirkja** turf church. Combine a look at Edda with a visit to the nearby ice-cream shop at **Holtsel** *(holtsel.is)* dairy farm and your explorations could turn into an *ísbíltúr* – the Icelandic word for 'driving around to get ice cream'.

Húsavík

WHALE WATCHING | MOUNTAIN SCENERY | UNIQUE MUSEUMS

GETTING AROUND

Bus 79 *(straeto.is)* plies several times daily except Saturday between Akureyri and Húsavík *(70 minutes, 3600kr)*. The bus stand in Húsavík is on Garðarsbraut, just south of Vallholtsvegur. Once here, Húsavík – barely 2km wide – is easily walkable.

☑ TOP TIPS

Eurovision fans should head to **Bar-Pizzeria Jaja Ding Dong** *(eurovisionhusavik. com; adult/child 2000/1000kr)*, just north of the harbour. Named after the film's silliest song, it honours Húsavík's role by blasting the Oscar-nominated song 'Húsavík (My Hometown)' by Molly Sandén and Will Ferrell.

Húsavík, Iceland's whale-watching capital and one of the country's earliest settlements, has become a firm favourite on travellers' itineraries. With its colourful houses, unique museums, small harbour full of oak whalers and sailing ships and snowcapped peaks across the bay, it is easily the northeast's prettiest fishing town. Beyond the busy harbour – which bustles with fishers at work, whale-watching passengers and waterside eateries – are the outdoor GeoSea baths, where you can while away an afternoon or summer's evening gazing out over the fjord. In the town centre, Húsavík's modest but attractive tree cover harmonises with its red-and-white wooden church, built in 1907 from Norwegian timber and still defining the town's image. Húsavík is also known for its starring role in the Netflix comedy *Eurovision Song Contest: The Story of Fire Saga*. Just north of town is a controversial silicon metal production plant, the area's largest employer.

Whale Watching on Skjálfandi Bay
Humpbacks, minke whales and dolphins

It is easy to guess the number-one activity in Húsavík: the town's harbour bustles with schooners and wooden boats boarding passengers for whale-watching tours, and wide, mountain-edged Skjálfandi Bay beckons.

Húsavík's whale-watching season runs from around April to October/November, with the range of species varying somewhat during these months. Peak sightings are generally around July and August, when humpbacks, blue whales, minke whales, white-beaked dolphins and harbour porpoises are all seen with some frequency. Blue whales also tend to be most common in summer.

'Classic' whale-watching tours last about three hours and take place on wooden ships. All operators are based at the harbour. **North Sailing** *(northsailing.is)* and **Gentle Giants** *(gentlegiants.is)* are the two largest, both with boats that can

SIGHTS
1 Bar-Pizzeria Jaja Ding Dong
2 Húsavík Museum
3 Húsavík Whale Museum

ACTIVITIES
4 Friends of Moby Dick
5 Gentle Giants
6 GeoSea Geothermal Sea Baths
7 Húsavík Adventures
8 Húsavík Swimming Pool
see 5 North Sailing

SLEEPING
9 Árból
10 Gamli Skólinn
see 1 Húsavík Cape Hotel
11 Húsavík Green Hostel

EATING
see 7 Gamli Baukur
12 Hérna
13 Naustið
14 Salka Restaurant

take between 70 and 90 passengers, and both offering a range of other excursions. **Friends of Moby Dick** *(friendsofmobydick.is)* is a smaller operator with personalised tours led by a marine biologist and a boat that takes about 40 passengers. On all tours, passengers stay out on deck the entire time, but warm overalls are provided (which you should pull on over your own warm clothing).

North Sailing, Gentle Giants and **Húsavík Adventures** *(husavikadventures.is)* also offer tours on Rigid Inflatable Boats (RIBs), which move twice as fast as the other vessels. RIBs can be a good choice when the whales are far out, but less so in high waves, as sighting whales requires a good view over the surface. Note that RIBs are not allowed to motor any closer to whales than other boats – all must keep at least a 50m distance.

A three-hour tour costs around 13,000/7000kr per adult/child, but many hotels in the region have their own promotion code for online bookings. Over summer, tours depart multiple times daily, usually with some same-day availability, although booking ahead is recommended. Boats also run frequently in April, September and October, but sailings drop off significantly in March and November. There are no tours from December to February.

Before booking, it's worth enquiring about how big the boat is and how many passengers may be on it and strolling down to the dock to have a look at the vessel. Bus groups tend to favour sailing slots around 10am and after lunch. The evening tours over the brightest months of summer are a delightful choice, sailing into the resting sun with few other boats around.

THE WHALES OF SKJÁLFANDI BAY

Captain Arnar Sigurðsson, founder and head captain of Friends of Moby Dick *(friendsofmobydick.is)*, offers some perspectives.

I have been at sea since I was a young boy hand- and net-fishing with my father, and have worked in tourism since 1994. Skjálfandi Bay has so much life, including puffins, seals and dolphins, but it's the big whales that visitors especially love to see. Beginning in the early 2000s, humpback whale numbers here increased, while minke whales decreased. This is still the situation today. But we also see many other species, including blue, fin, sperm, northern bottlenose and pilot whales. We are Húsavík's smallest whale-watching company and it is my family's business and legacy. We love showing visitors whales and follow the Whale Watching Code of Conduct.

Beyond the Whales – Húsavík's Museums
Whale skeletons and a polar bear

After going on a whale-watching tour, don't miss visiting the harbourside **Whale Museum** *(hvalasafn.is; adult/child 2500kr/free)*, which is packed with informative displays. These include several large whale skeletons, a narwhal tusk and a room dedicated to the effects of plastic pollution and to environmental challenges facing whales around the globe. There is also a film (included in the ticket price) highlighting ongoing controversies about whale hunting. Afterwards, for insights into local life and culture, head to the worthwhile **Húsavík Museum** *(husmus.is; adult/child 1700kr/free)*, about 300m east of the harbour. Its maritime section focuses on the local fishing and boatbuilding industries and also includes the stuffed remains of what was once Iceland's largest recorded polar bear, who floated to Grímsey on an iceberg in 1969.

Húsavík Outdoors
Hikes and hot tubs

While many visitors in Húsavík focus on the sea, there is also plenty to do on land. On the eastern edge of town, **Húsavík Mountain**, with its blue, lupine-covered slopes, offers good

 EATING IN HÚSAVÍK: OUR PICKS

Naustið: Wins wide praise for its super-fresh fish and simple skewers of seafood and vegetables, grilled to order. *noon-9pm* €€

Salka Restaurant: Sit indoors or out, enjoying harbourside vibes and a mix of traditional Icelandic and international cuisine. *11.30am-8.30pm* €€€

Gamli Baukur: Among shiny nautical relics, timber-framed Gamli serves spaghetti with shellfish and cod with green pesto. *11.30am-9pm* €€

Hérna: A small coffeeshop with homemade pastries, locally sourced tomato soup and Icelandic newspapers. *11am-5pm Mon-Fri* €

Húsavík Harbour on Skjálfandi Bay

hiking, with the route to the summit taking about two hours return. Start at Auðbrekka, by the municipal pool, for an easy to moderate path to the top. Or, explore the area on electric mountain bikes with **North E-Bike** *(northebike.is)*. You can also walk from Húsavík's public park, Skrúðgarður Húsavíkur, for about 2.5km to **Botnsvatn** lake or combine the lake with hiking on the mountain for a half-day's hike.

To warm up afterwards, head to **GeoSea** *(geosea.is; adult/child 6990/3590kr),* an outdoor, cliff-edge series of infinity pools that merge with Skjálfandi Bay and the mountain ridge of Víknarfjöll. GeoSea, which is about 1.5km north of the harbour, exists thanks to a geothermal drillhole that got mixed with seawater, pumping up salty water at just the right temperature for a relaxing soak. The baths are frequented by tourists and locals alike (annual membership is a bargain compared with the single admission price) and are busiest in the late afternoon and evening sun. If you are travelling with children or on a more limited budget, the municipal **Húsavík Swimming Pool** *(sundlaugar.is; adult/child 1250/500kr)* is just as fun, with its steam bath, hot tubs and waterslide.

WHALE-WATCHING CODE OF CONDUCT

Whales rely more on hearing than sight and researchers have little doubt that noise causes them stress – measured by their levels of the stress hormone cortisol in areas of increased maritime traffic and their behaviour towards aggressive whale-watching boats. These findings, however, are sometimes forgotten in the competitive business of whale spotting.

Passengers can hold companies to account by knowing the industry Code of Conduct agreed to by all major operators in Iceland. Its principles include only approaching whales at an angle (and not head-on), slowing to 5 knots (jogging speed) on approach, stopping entirely at a 50m distance and limiting boat numbers at sightings. For more, see the Code of Conduct published by **IceWhale** *(icewhale.is)*.

Beyond Húsavík

Stretching south and west from Húsavík is one of Iceland's most geothermally active regions, centred around bird-filled Lake Mývatn.

Places

Lake Mývatn p284

GETTING AROUND

Most of Mývatn's points of interest are linked by the lake's 36km loop road. A cycling and walking path runs along the eastern side from Reykjahlíð to Skútustaðir, with hiking paths branching off this.

Bus 56 (straeto.is) between Akureyri and Egilsstaðir stops at Goðafoss (50km northwest of Mývatn along the Diamond Circle route) and at Reykjahlíð, on the lake's northeastern corner. The only way to get to Mývatn by bus from Húsavík is via Akureyri. For the Diamond Circle route, you'll need your own vehicle.

Lake Mývatn, perched just off the edge of the highlands, is one of Iceland's coldest areas and one of its most visited, with bubbling mudpots, strange lava formations and steaming fumaroles, all set around a bird-filled lake. During the winter, Mývatn (pronounced mee-vaht) is picture-perfect, its edges often frozen and snow covering the surrounding mountains. Spring's thaw heralds the arrival of swarms of tiny midges ('Mývatn' means 'midge lake') and migratory birds. Western Mývatn offers some of Iceland's best birdwatching, including over two dozen duck species. With luck, you might even spot the country's legendary *hverafugl* ('hot spring bird'). Linking Húsavík and Mývatn via lovely waterfalls and dramatic canyons is the Diamond Circle driving route.

Lake Mývatn

TIME FROM HÚSAVÍK: **45 MIN**

Birders' Paradise

Lake Mývatn's western side offers excellent birding, with more than 115 recorded species. Fifteen species of ducks breed here regularly, including the tufted duck, greater scaup, Eurasian wigeon and common scoter, with 28 duck species recorded in total. The banks of Laxá river, which flows out of Lake Mývatn, are a prime habitat for harlequin ducks and Barrow's goldeneye. Also watch out for gyrfalcons (Iceland's national bird) on the hunt.

For more background, call in at **Sigurgeir's Bird Museum** (*fuglasafn.is; adult/child 2400/1400kr*), with its large collection of taxidermy birds encompassing more than 180 types from around the world, including most species resident in Iceland. Mývatn is also known for its *marimo* balls (*Cladophora aegagropila*) – spheres of green algae that are thought to grow naturally in colonies in only a handful of places in the world (including Mývatn and Japan's Lake Akan).

For a bird's-eye view of the lake, do the steep but straightforward climb up 529m **Vindbelgjarfjall** (also known as Vindbelgur), just southwest of the bird museum turnoff.

Hverfjall

Lakeside Lava

The attractions along Mývatn's eastern lakeshore are linked together with roads and hiking paths, making a good half-day excursion.

Reykjahlíð, to the lake's northeast, is the main village. There is little to it beyond a collection of hotels and basic services, with a well-marked track to Grjótagjá, a gaping fissure with a 45°C water-filled cave (no swimming). *Game of Thrones* fans may recognise this as the setting of a steamy scene with Jon Snow and Ygritte.

Dominating the lava fields on the eastern edge of Mývatn is the classic tephra ring **Hverfjall**. This nearly symmetrical crater appeared 2700 years ago in a cataclysmic eruption. Today, with its diameter of about 1km and its highest point rising 180m above the surrounding area, it is a Mývatn landmark.

Stretching southwest from Hverfjall is the giant jagged lava field of **Dimmuborgir** ('Dark Castles'). It is believed that Dimmuborgir's strange pillars and crags were created in an eruption 2000 years ago when the lava formed a lake over marshland. The marsh water started to boil and steam jets rose through the molten lava, cooling it and creating the pillars. As the lava continued flowing towards lower ground, hollow pillars of solidified lava remained. A series of easy, colour-coded walking trails runs from the signposted parking area through the landscape past some incredible lava formations. One of the most popular paths is the Church Circle trail (2.3km).

Mud cauldrons and piping fumaroles

Northern Mývatn's geological gems can be accessed from the Ring Road (Rte 1) as it winds its way through harsh, starkly beautiful terrain. There are plenty of paths for exploring the area on foot.

THE YULE LADS

When the Icelandic Postal Service receives letters addressed to Father Christmas, they are forwarded to the little post office in Reykjahlíð, Mývatn where Father Christmas' Icelandic colleagues have taken on the responsibility of replying to letters.

Thirteen days before Christmas, 13 mischievous troll brothers, called the Yule Lads, come down from their mountain cave to herald the holidays and frighten children to be good. Fortunately the letters are not delivered to the Yule Lads' home, where they might be stolen by their ill-tempered mother, 600-year old Gryla. The family even has a 'Christmas Cat', a giant feline with a habit of eating children.

The local theatre club performs as the Yule Lads in Dimmuborgir *(jolasveinarnir idimmuborgum. com)* every weekend in December (Icelandic only).

ÞEISTAREYKIR ROAD

If driving between Húsavík and Mývatn during summertime, consider taking the road less travelled via Þeistareykir. This mountain area, with a recently built paved access road from Húsavík, is home to the Þeistareykir Power Plant, one of Iceland's largest geothermal energy sources.

Next to the A-frame building visible from the road are the relatively unvisited Þeistareykir hot springs. There are no paths and fences, so it is essential to watch your step if you pass this way to appreciate the otherworldly beauty of the bubbling, steaming white, orange and pale blue panoramas.

In winter, it is best to avoid the Þeistareykir Road and drive instead on Rte 845 via Laugar, as the slightly shorter Rte 87 can be difficult with snow.

The magical, ochre-toned world of **Hverir** (also called **Hverarönd**; *parking from 1200kr*) is a lunar-like landscape of mud cauldrons, steaming vents, radiant mineral deposits and piping fumaroles. Belching mudpots and the powerful stench of sulphur may not sound enticing, but Hverir's display of Iceland's geothermal power grips most visitors. A walking trail loops from Hverir to **Námafjall** ridge. This 30-minute climb provides a grand vista over the steamy surroundings. Avoid in wet conditions.

About 10km north at **Krafla** is an active volcanic region with steaming vents and craters. Its most impressive – and, potentially, most dangerous – attraction is the **Leirhnjúkur** crater and its solfataras. In 1975, fires at Krafla began with a small lava eruption at Leirhnjúkur and after nine years of on-and-off action, Leirhnjúkur became the ominous-looking, sulphur-encrusted mud hole that visitors can see today. On the other side of Krafla Power Station is the volcanic explosion crater Víti from 1724. There is a circular path from the car park around the 300m-wide rim.

To relax after all this sightseeing, head to the powder-blue **Mývatn Nature Baths** (*myvatnnaturebaths.is; adult/child 7400kr/free*), which is North Iceland's smaller and more low-key answer to the Blue Lagoon, although at the time of writing major renovations were taking place. Arrive early or late to avoid tour groups.

 EATING AROUND LAKE MÝVATN: OUR PICKS

Vogafjós Cowshed Cafe: A window separates the dining area (with creatively prepared all-local produce) from the farm's dairy where cows are milked. Advance bookings essential. *noon-9pm* €€€

Fish & Chips Lake Mývatn: Lakeside Reykjahlíð is perhaps an odd place for seafood but this takeaway is good value; opposite Kjörbúðin. *11.30am-9pm* €

Eldey Restaurant: Well-regarded fine dining Icelandic style inside the high-end Hótel Laxá. *6-9pm* €€€

Daddi's Pizza: Top-notch, creatively topped pizzas near the edge of Lake Mývatn, with apple-cinnamon breadsticks for dessert. *noon-9pm* €

DISCOVERING THE DIAMOND CIRCLE

Discover the sights beyond Húsavík on this straightforward driving tour, taking in waterfalls, canyons and Lake Mývatn.

START	END	LENGTH
Húsavík	Húsavík	250km; 2 days

From 1 **Húsavík** (p280), follow Rte 85 south to 2 **Goðafoss**, where lawspeaker Þorgeir Ljósvetningagoði supposedly threw statues of the old Norse gods into the waterfall after converting to Christianity around 1000 CE (hence the name 'waterfall of the gods'). Parking areas on both sides of the falls are connected by a bridge.

Continue eastwards to Mývatn, stopping at the helpful 3 **Mývatn Visitor Centre** at Skútustaðir to check out its relief map and get hiking information. Nearby attractions include 4 **Dimmuborgir** (p285; walk amid amazing lava formations), 5 **Hverfjall** (p285) crater (396m, hike to the top from Dimmuborgir or from the northwestern crater parking area) and 6 **Grjótagjá** (a hot-water-filled cave). Further east are bubbling 7 **Hverir** hot springs and (10km north) 8 **Krafla power station** and the turquoise Víti Crater.

Finish Day 1 with a soak at 9 **Mývatn Nature Baths** – North Iceland's 'Blue Lagoon'.

The next morning, take Rte 862 along the Jökulsárgljúfur canyon to thundering 10 **Dettifoss** (p288). The falls are about 1km from the parking area, with a trail branching off to nearby 11 **Selfoss** (p288).

Continue north to 12 **Ásbyrgi** (p290) and then around the tip of the Tjörnes peninsula – an area known for its fossil-rich coastal cliffs, with some layers about two million years old – before finishing in Húsavík.

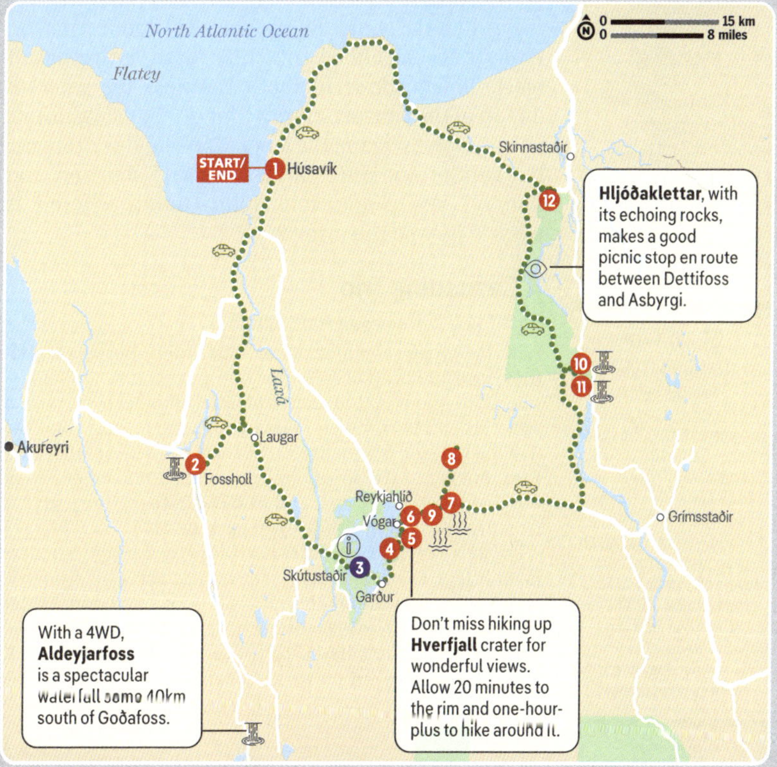
North Atlantic Ocean
Flatey
0 15 km
0 8 miles
START/ END
1 Húsavík
Skinnastaðir
12
Hljóðaklettar, with its echoing rocks, makes a good picnic stop en route between Dettifoss and Asbyrgi.
Laxá
10
11
Akureyri
Laugar
2
Fossholl
8
Reykjahlíð
Vógar
6 9 7
5
4
3
Skútustaðir
Garður
Grímsstaðir
With a 4WD, Aldeyjarfoss is a spectacular waterfall some 40km south of Goðafoss.
Don't miss hiking up Hverfjall crater for wonderful views. Allow 20 minutes to the rim and one-hour-plus to hike around it.

Jökulsárgljúfur Canyon

OVERNIGHT HIKING | CANYON PANORAMAS | POWERFUL WATERFALLS

GETTING AROUND

The tarmac Rte 862 from the Ring Road to the Ásbyrgi turnoff connects the Jökulsárgljúfur area with Mývatn and Húsavík, making Dettifoss' western side an easy Ring Road detour.

Jökulsárgljúfur lies within Vatnajökull National Park (p168) and has well-maintained hiking trails and designated cycling paths.

☑ TOP TIP

Hiking maps are available online (*vatnajokulsthjodgardur.is*) and at the Gljúfrastofa Visitor Centre in Ásbyrgi. The best way to experience Jökulsárgljúfur is on foot, ideally along the 32km Canyon Trail (p292), which is accessible for most levels of fitness and also offers shorter variations. The Jökulsárhlaup (*jokulsarhlaup.is*) trail run in early August completes the route in several hours.

In geological terms, Jökulsárgljúfur, which means 'Glacial River Canyon', is young at only about 4000 years old. The canyon stretches from south of Dettifoss up to Ásbyrgi and is characterised by soaring cathedral cliffs. It was formed by the melting of the mighty Vatnajökull, the largest glacier in Europe with many of Iceland's most active volcanoes beneath its ice cap. The river flowing through Jökulsárgljúfur is said to have an average discharge of one Olympic-sized swimming pool every 13 seconds, and over the millennia, 'super floods' the size of four Amazon rivers have scrubbed the cliffs, with entire basalt blocks flowing down like cork. Dettifoss, the waterfall on top of the canyon, gives a hint of Jökulsárgljúfur's power. Downstream, the landscape remains dramatic but gentler and offers hikes long and short around Ásbyrgi, Vesturdalur and Hólmatungur, where it is easy to escape the crowds.

A Cascading Trio

Dettifoss, Selfoss and Hafragilsfoss

With the greatest volume of any waterfall in Europe, **Dettifoss**, near the head of Jökulsárgljúfur canyon, is an impressive sight. About 400 cu metres of water thunder over its edge every second in summer, creating a plume of spray. But the flowing cascade is actually a trio, together with smaller **Selfoss**, further upstream and reached via a 700m detour from the main Dettifoss trail, and **Hafragilsfoss**, downstream from Dettifoss and with its own parking area.

The falls can be seen from either side of the canyon, but there is no bridge at the site itself. The easiest access is from the west via Rte 862, although check conditions first over winter on *road.is*, as snow often obstructs the route. In summer, you can also reach the falls' eastern side via the gravel Rte 864, but you will miss out on western-bank-only attractions like

JÖKULSÁRGLJÚFUR CANYON

● **SIGHTS**	5 Karl og Kerling	● **SLEEPING**	● **INFORMATION**
1 Ásbyrgi Canyon	6 Rauðhólar	9 Ásbyrgi Campsite	13 Gljúfrastofa Visitor
2 Dettifoss	7 Selfoss	10 Dettifoss Guesthouse	Centre – Ásbyrgi
3 Hafragilsfoss	● **ACTIVITIES**	11 Hótel Skúlagarður	
4 Hljóðaklettar	8 Hólmatungur	12 Nordic Natura	

PURPLE LANDSCAPES

Across the road from the Verslun supermarket in Ásbyrgi is an alien plant which is prevented from entering the national park by rangers armed with lawnmowers. The blue Nootka lupine, native to North America and a familiar sight in flower gardens there, has spread wildly in Iceland since its introduction in the late 1970s to halt soil erosion. (Among other places, you'll also see it on Húsavík Mountain; p282.)

Today, however, the lupine is considered an invasive plant, as it threatens not only the existing flora but also the barren volcanic interior. Encouraged by the warming atmosphere, lupine is spreading beyond Iceland's relatively temperate coastal areas and into the interior, previously thought too dry and cold to support its growth.

Vesturdalur and Hljóðaklettar. Both sides require a walk from the respective car parks of about 15 to 20 minutes.

Sunseekers & Petrified Trolls

Hiking around Ásbyrgi Canyon

With its 50m cliffs blocking the wind, **Ásbyrgi** – a horseshoe-shaped canyon at the top of Jökulsárgljúfur – can sometimes feel like a giant sun patio filled with vegetation and relative warmth. Hikes here – long and short – are popular. One of the easiest is the 1km-walk to **Botnstjörn**, a bird-friendly pond at the canyon's head where the Icelandic Forest Service has made a mark on the landscape with birch and pine trees lining the footpath. Its walls echo and the area was once used as a concert venue by avant garde band Sigur Rós. For a bird's-eye view, take the trail to **Eyjan** (3km) or **Klappir** (6km). All hikes begin from Ásbyrgi's **Gljúfrastofa Visitor Centre**, which also has maps and bathrooms. The nearby **Ásbyrgi campsite** is popular among sun-seeking Icelanders with trailers and camper vans.

South of the Visitor Centre along the Jökulsá river, and reached via foot (12km) or by road, is **Vesturdalur** – a pristine valley that marks the overnight stopping point along the Canyon Trail (p292). According to local folklore, trolls travelling at night become petrified at daybreak by the sun's rays. There are several examples at **Karl og Kerling** – rock pillars along the river's western banks within an easy walk from the Vesturdalur parking area.

Ásbyrgi

Also starting from the Vesturdalur car park is a 3km circular walking trail around **Hljóðaklettar** (Echo Rocks), where bizarre basalt swirls create acoustic effects that make it challenging to determine the direction of the roaring Jökulsá River. The formations are volcanic vents – the centre of a washed-away volcanic eruption – sturdy enough to withstand the river. If you have enough time, continue on to the **Rauðhólar** crater row (5km return).

South of Vesturdalur is **Hólmatungur**, which is an accessible detour along the Dettifoss drive. The most popular walk here is a 4.5km loop to Hólmá falls via Katlar – an area where the river channel narrows, creating roiling water and whirlpools.

VATNAJÖKULL NATIONAL PARK

Jökulsárgljúfur canyon is at the northern end of **Vatnajökull National Park** *(vjp.is)* and patrolled by rangers who also service **Askja** (p339) in the highland region. Gljúfrastofa, the visitor centre in Ásbyrgi, has the latest information on highland road conditions.

HIKING TRAIL

The Canyon Trail

The two-day, 32km Canyon Trail between Dettifoss and Ásbyrgi is a wonderful hike, suitable for anyone of at least moderate fitness. En route, it takes in dramatic gorge scenery, stands of forest, barren open areas, ponds and waterfalls. The trail can be hiked in either direction, with overnight camping in Vesturdalur. Starting at Dettifoss means you can look forward to good camping at Ásbyrgi at the end. To avoid backtracking, arrange a shuttle through Hótel Skúlagarður (p301) *(skulagardur.com)* or Nordic Natura *(nordicnatura.is)*.

❶ Dettifoss

Although the trailhead is at Dettifoss, it bypasses the waterfall, so before heading north, take the 1km loop towards the viewing platform. Once on the trail (just over the parking hill), there is a choice between the challenging, 10km black-marked Hafragil lowland route to the right (best avoided by those afraid of heights or carrying large packs) and the gentler (red-marked), 11.5km ravine route to the left. Whether you go left or right, the next stop is Hólmatungur.

The Hike: Arrive at Hólmatungur after 10km to 12km (three to four hours), marking the first half of day one. The terrain is rocky but with fine views and springs for refilling your water bottles.

❷ Hólmatungur

With its lush vegetation, tumbling waterfalls and air of tranquility, the

Vesturdalur

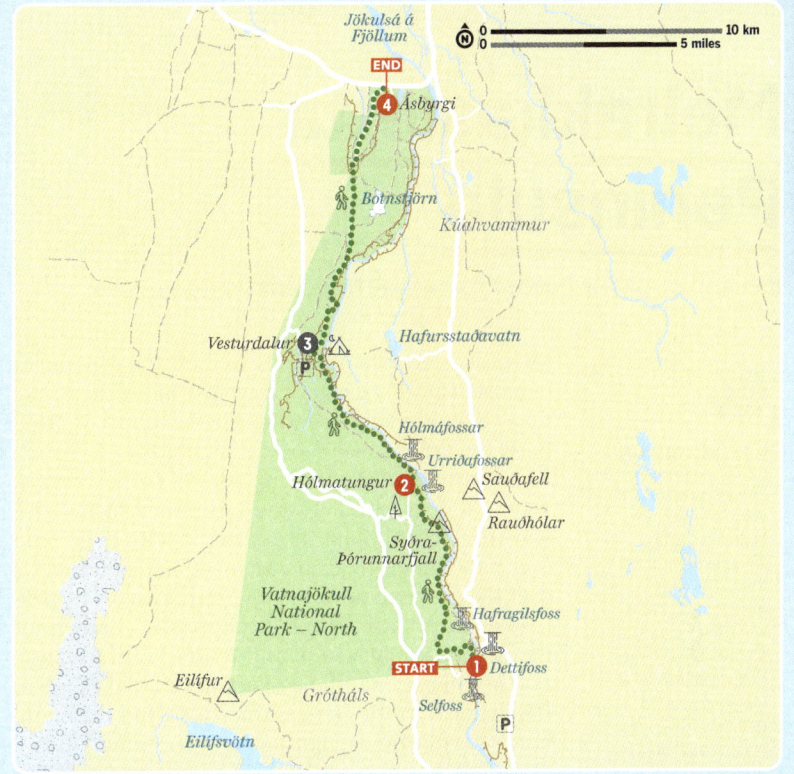

Hólmatungur area is one of the most beautiful in the park. From just after the parking area, you can go left, following the spring river Hólmá, or right along Jökulsá, with the chance for a short (1km) detour to the **Katlar** area, with its roiling water and whirlpools. The two paths rejoin at the cascading Hólmárfossar. Look out for **Karl og Kerling**, the troll-like stacks, about 1km before Vesturdalur.

The Hike: From Hólmatungur to Vesturdalur (8km, two hours), the path has an uphill section midway and at the spring river Stallá it is time to go barefoot and wade. The river is shallow but cold – a memorable part of the hike.

❸ Vesturdalur

The pristine Vesturdalur valley is a perfect overnight stop, with a basic campsite (toilets and running water only) next to a spring river. Bring a portable stove and refill your water bottles here to last until Ásbyrgi.

The Hike: Start the next day via **Hljóðaklettar** (p291), the main sight at Vesturdalur, on the pleasant 12km path to Ásbyrgi. Travellers without the time for a two-day hike often opt for this section as the terrain is soft and flat and the scenery diverse.

❹ Ásbyrgi

When you arrive at Ásbyrgi via the path to Klappir, you will be met with views over the entire horseshoe-shaped Ásbyrgi canyon (which is separated from the Jökulsárgljúfur canyon). Walk along the cliffs to Tófugjá, using rope and stairs, to the canyon floor. The finish line is at Ásbyrgi's Gljúfrastofa Visitor Centre. For hikers starting at Ásbyrgi, the trail is more uphill as it rises gradually towards Dettifoss.

Melrakkaslétta Peninsula

ICELAND'S NORTHERNMOST TOWN | ARCTIC HENGE | REMOTE HIKES

GETTING AROUND

You will need a vehicle to explore Melrakkaslétta. Outside of winter, Rte 870 is easily passable for 2WDs, while the tarmac Rte 85 offers the chance to do a Melrakkaslétta loop based out of Raufarhöfn. The closest bus routes to the area are between Akureyri and Húsavík and Akureyri and Egilsstaðir.

☑ TOP TIP

Midsummer is special at Raufarhöfn. Time your visit to catch the midnight sun framed by the stone arches of the Arctic Henge and take in the 360-degree views.

Melrakkaslétta Peninsula is well off the itineraries of most visitors, except for travellers along the Arctic Coast Way. But for those who take the time to venture here, the area is likely to be a highlight.

As you make your way up Rte 85 from Ásbyrgi, watch how green fields and red-roofed farms give way to a rugged coastline scattered with driftwood and punctuated by dramatic headlands and views over the open sea towards the Arctic Circle. The peninsula's two main towns are Kópasker, known for its earthquake museum, and Raufarhöfn, Iceland's northernmost 'mainland' community and home to the magical Arctic Henge. You'll also find the mainland's northernmost lighthouse at Hraunhafnartangi, its northernmost point (Rifstangi), and rock formations with colonies of gannets and other seabirds around Rauðinúpur. Despite its remoteness, Melrakkaslétta – with its roots in fishing and sheep farming – gives off a feeling of energy and self-sufficiency and offers travellers a warm welcome.

Exploring the Plain of the Arctic Fox
Windswept headlands and soaring gannets

Rte 870 is a 55km-long coastal road between Kópasker and Raufarhöfn that takes you past the driftwood-scattered beaches, fields, ponds and marshes of Melrakkaslétta, the 'Plain of the Arctic Fox'. Coming from Ásbyrgi, the first stop is **Kópasker**, an old fishing village known for its peaceful setting, large lamb-meat processing factory, good supermarket and its **Earthquake Centre**. Located in the school building, this informative exhibit commemorates a series of earthquakes that began in late 1975 and culminated in January 1976 in a 6.3-magnitude event that shook Kópasker, damaged many houses and broke the harbour wall. About 1km southeast of town, just off Rte 870 near the Snartarstaða church, is the seasonal **Snartarstaðir Folk Museum**, where you can get an idea of traditional local life and customs.

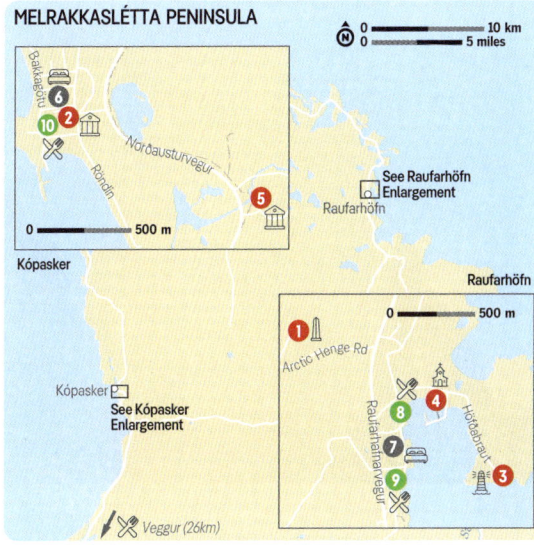

- **SIGHTS**
  1. Arctic Henge
  2. Earthquake Centre
  3. Lighthouse
  4. Raufarhafnarkirkja
  5. Snartarstaðir Folk Museum
- **SLEEPING**
  - see 8 Hótel Norðurljós
  6. Kópasker HI Hostel
  7. Nest
- **EATING**
  8. Hótel Norðurljós Restaurant
  9. Kaupfélagið Raufarhöfn
  10. Skerjakolla

From Kópasker, Rte 870 continues north and east, entering its most beautiful stretch near **Rauðinúpur** – a headland known for its sea stacks favoured by nesting gannets and for its puffins stoically watching the open sea. To reach the tip, turn left onto the Núpskatla road about 18km after Kópasker and continue about 7km further to an old farm where you can park and hike the approximately 2km remaining to the sea stacks. Stunning. Back on Rte 870, another 17km or so brings you to a rough 4km track branching northwards towards **Rifstangi**, mainland Iceland's northernmost point – edging out nearby **Hraunhafnartangi** for this honour by just 68m. Continue about 5km further along Rte 870 to the Hraunhafnartangi signpost, from where it is a 1.5km walk over a rocky path strewn with old fishing nets to the burial mound of the 11th-century Viking warrior Þorgeir and the Hraunhafnartangi lighthouse, which was moved here from Rifstangi in the 1940s. Note that much of this part of the peninsula is a protected eider duck nesting area and hiking is off-limits during nesting season from mid-April to July. From the Hrauhafnartangi turnoff, it's about 10km further to Raufarhöfn.

Living at the Edge

Raufarhöfn, Iceland's northernmost town

In Raufarhöfn, Iceland's northernmost mainland town, the midnight sun lasts longer, winter days are shorter, the northern lights seem to shimmer more vividly and the air has a unique clarity. Once one of Iceland's main herring centres, this sturdily built settlement is now reinventing itself as a tourism destination and makes a perfect base for exploring

GUÐJÓN SAMÚELSSON

If Iceland's churches seem to have something in common, it is because many of them were designed by the same architect. Guðjón Samúelsson (1887–1950) was the first Icelander to be educated in architecture. In the early years of Iceland's independent statehood he was known as the 'State Architect of Iceland' and worked to develop an Icelandic architectural style as he responded to calls when a town needed a new church or the country a national theatre.

Reykjavík's Hallgrímskirkja and the Akureyrarkirkja, designed around the mid-1930s to 1940s, are among his later works. Both are inspired by Iceland's geology, especially the coast's basalt columns. Raufarhöfn's church, completed in the late 1920s, is an earlier design – much simpler and more traditional in style.

Melrakkaslétta. The buildings in the central area were constructed to withstand the weather's challenges rather than for charm, but this is redeemed by a picturesque, fishing-boat-filled harbour, which is watched over by an orange **lighthouse**. Nearby is the small, beautiful **Raufarhafnarkirkja**, which was designed in the late 1920s by Guðjón Samúelsson, who also designed Reykjavík's Hallgrimmskirkja. For views and fine panoramas, follow the path from the church up to the lighthouse and then left around the headland back to the church (2km). Apart from its welcoming, small-town vibes, Raufarhöfn's main claim to fame is the Arctic Henge, watching over town to the northwest.

Myth & Magic at the Arctic Henge
Domain of the midnight sun

There is nothing anywhere else quite like it. Raufarhöfn's Arctic Henge (or Heimskautsgerðið, as it is locally known) is full of magic, myth and mystery. Despite the obvious parallels with England's Stonhenge, it is fully Icelandic. The idea was born in the late 1990s, led by Raufarhöfn businessman and visionary Erlingur Thoroddsen. Over the coming decade,

EATING AROUND THE MELRAKKASLÉTTA PENINSULA

Hótel Norðurljós Restaurant: Freshly prepared seafood dishes and soups served in cosy surroundings with views over the sea. *11.30am-1.30pm & 6-8.30pm* €€

Kaupfélagið Raufarhöfn: A charming cafe with driftwood, artwork, tasty breakfast buffet, afternoon cake and coffee and simple meals. *11am-7pm Mon-Sat, to 5pm Sun* €€

Skerjakolla: Kópasker's well-stocked supermarket is something of a local hub, and also serves pizzas, sandwiches, coffee and cake. *10am-6pm Mon-Fri, to 3pm Sat* €

Veggur: It's all Icelandic at this place on Rte 862, about a 30-minute drive south of Kópasker, with soups, grilled lamb and fish and chips, all locally sourced. *noon-8pm* €€

Arctic Henge

in collaboration with Icelandic artist Haukur Halldórsson, it gradually took shape as a structure that would bring together Raufarhöfn's 360-degree unobstructed horizons with the town's long hours of midnight sun while capturing the changing positions and moods of the sun's rays. Icelandic folklore and Norse mythology are woven in to the design with a (planned) circle of 72 stones. These represent a calendar year of trolls inspired by the dwarves' list of the Nordic creation myths of the *Völuspá*. Although the Arctic Henge is not yet complete, the essentials are in place – a 10m-high central structure ringed by four 6m-high arches corresponding to the four compass directions. The Arctic Henge is impressive at any time, but to really get a feel for its magic, try to coordinate your visit with the days around the summer solstice, or visit during dark, clear winter nights when you will have wide views of the movements of the stars and a real chance for seeing the Arctic Henge silhouetted against the Northern Lights.

LIFE IN THE FAR NORTH

Hólmsteinn Björnsson, manager at Raufarhöfn's Hótel Norðurljós (p301) *(hotelnordurljos.is)*, shares some insights:

There is much to experience in and around Raufarhöfn, an ideal hub between Dettifoss and Langanes. With its mix of coastline, lakes and heaths, Melrakkaslétta is home to Iceland's widest range of bird species and has several birdwatching cottages.

Between 1940 and 1968, Raufarhöfn, with Siglufjordur, was Iceland's main herring processing centre. There are remains of that era in town, plus many photos – some on display at Hótel Norðurljós.

The town's main attraction, the Arctic Henge, is still under construction but was visited by 25,000 guests last year. Based on old Norse mythology, it offers a unique experience around the summer and winter solstices, when the sun shines through three of the main gates.

Beyond Melrakkaslétta

Hike sandy tracks, linger in the lively settlement of Þórshöfn and reach the end of the Arctic Coast Way in Bakkafjörður.

Places
Þórshöfn p298
Bakkafjörður p299

GETTING AROUND

From Raufarhöfn, it is an easy drive on the tarmac Rte 874 south to the junction with Rte 85, which leads to Þórshöfn and on to Bakkafjörður. To join up with the Ring Road, follow Rte 85 further to Vopnafjörður, from where it is about 48km southwest through fine open landscapes to the Ring Road junction. The closest Strætó bus service is between Akureyri and Egilsstaðir.

Norlandair *(norlandair.is)* links Akureyri with Þórshöfn via Vopnafjörður several times weekly.

For exploring the Langanes Peninsula beyond Þórshöfn, you will need 4WD.

From Rauðanes point, with its rock formations and birding, to the lively harbour town of Þórshöfn to Fontur lighthouse at the tip of the Langanes Peninsula, the area beyond Melrakkaslétta offers hiking and exploring well off the beaten track. Visitors are few and far between in this remote corner of Iceland, but the welcome is warm and the infrastructure is just right for independent travellers looking to experience Northeast Iceland's nature and solitude. Þórshöfn is the best base outside of Raufarhöfn. From here, with views over the sea as your constant companion, you can easily reach Rauðanes for day hikes, explore the Langanes Peninsula or launch an excursion to Bakkafjörður and beyond.

Þórshöfn

TIME FROM MELRAKKASLÉTTA PENINSULA (RAUFARHÖFN): **55MIN**

Iceland's northeastern corner

With its good infrastructure, modern sports centre, cosy guesthouse and well-stocked shops, the friendly fishing settlement of Þórshöfn comes as a delightful surprise in this remote corner of the country. The town makes a comfortable base for hiking and enjoying the all-encompassing proximity of the sea. About 7km north of town, where the sealed Rte 869 past the airstrip meets the rough coastal track along the **Langanes Peninsula**, is an old 1879 vicarage. It has been converted to the seasonal **Sauðaneshús museum** *(husmus.is; adult/student 1500/1100kr)*, which documents local life. Back in town, finish the day with a swim or a soak at Þórshöfn's pretty **swimming poo**l, where there is also a gym.

A Rauðanes day hike

Jutting into the waters of Þistilfjörður northwest of Þórshöfn is the Rauðanes headland, with fine hiking along the coast to the point. The marked 7km trail takes you past secluded beaches, caves, striking rock formations and natural arches, with wonderful birdlife along the way. The turnoff is signposted about 28km west of Þórshöfn. From here, an unpaved track leads 1.5km to a car park and an information board with trail details. The loop's highlights are at the tip of the headland, where you have direct views onto bird-covered sea stacks. Allow about two hours return and bring water, as there is nowhere to fill your bottle.

The gannets at Skoruvík

From Sauðaneshús museum on Þórshöfn's northern edge, a rutted track (4WD) winds its way along the Langanes Peninsula coastline past driftwood and the bones of pilot whales that became stranded here in 2019. After about 30km you will reach Skoruvík, with its cliff-edge **viewing platform** overlooking the large rock pillar known as Stóri Karl – home to one of North Iceland's biggest colonies of northern gannets. Gannets are the North Atlantic's largest seabird and are known for their dramatic diving. Four-wheel drives with clearance can continue about 15km further to **Langanesviti lighthouse** at the peninsula's tip, stopping en route at the remains of the old fishing and trading station at **Skálar**, on the peninsula's eastern edge and reached via a track branching off the Fontur track about 5km east of the Skoruvík viewing platform.

Bakkafjörður

TIME FROM MELRAKKASLÉTTA PENINSULA (RAUFARHÖFN): **75MIN**

The end of the road

For those travelling the Arctic Coast Way from west to east, the small harbour settlement of Bakkafjörður is the end of the road. As with much of the rest of the Arctic Coast Way, it comes understated and without any fanfare other than its beautiful natural backdrop. Take time to walk from town out to the **Digranes Lighthouse** (about 8km return), and stroll over to the harbour, overlooking Bakka bay. About 7km southwest of town along Rte 85 is the pretty **Skeggjastaðakirkja**, built of driftwood and dating to 1845, making it the oldest church in these parts. Inside is an early-18th century pulpit.

LEADER SHEEP

Iceland is known for its unique leader sheep, considered as a subpopulation within the Icelandic sheep group. Leader sheep are a sort of superhero sheep. They are intelligent, usually larger than average, with a highly developed instinct for sensing danger and with the navigational and control skills to lead 'ordinary sheep' in bad weather and through challenging conditions. Worldwide there are estimated to be fewer than 1500 leader sheep, all of whom trace their lineage to Norður-Þingeyjarsýsla – the area around Melrakkaslétta and the Langanes Peninsula. The **Study Centre on Leader Sheep** *(fory stusetur.is, Jul-Aug)*, about 24km west of Þórshöfn, is dedicated to the study of these impressive animals. Also on-site is Cafe Silla and the small **Thistle Guesthouse** *(per person 8000kr)*.

 EATING IN & AROUND ÞÓRSHÖFN

Enn 1 Skálinn: At the petrol station in Þórshöfn, and pleasant for a hot drink or snack. *10am-9pm Mon-Fri, from 11am Sat & Sun* €

Holtið Kitchen Bar: Well-prepared seafood and lamb dishes, occasional lunch and dinner buffets and a billiards table. *noon-2pm & 6-9pm Jun-Aug* €€

North East Restaurant: At the harbour in Bakkafjörður, with burgers, thick-crust pizza and fresh fish. *11.30am-2pm & 5.30-9pm Jun-Aug* €€

Cafe Silla: At the leader sheep centre outside Þórshöfn, where the good coffee and cake seem to taste better when you're wearing an Icelandic wool sweater. *11am-6pm Jul-Aug* €

Places We Love to Stay

€ Budget   €€ Midrange   €€€ Top End

Skagafjörður MAP p255

Guesthouse Gimbur € North of Hofsós, this small family-run guesthouse offers a warm welcome and spacious rooms with seafront views.

Sunnuberg € On the main street in Hofsós near the municipal pool, this cosy guesthouse has rooms with private bathroom, plus a kitchen.

Guesthouse Hofsstaðir €€ Modern country hotel with 30 rooms, all with terrace, on a farm property some 20km from the Ring Road.

Salthús Guesthouse €€ Directly overlooking the water in Skagaströnd. Rooms have private bathrooms and there is hiking from the doorstep.

Hotel Tindastóll €€€ Iceland's oldest hotel dates to 1884. Rooms are period-style and full of character, with more modern ones available in the adjoining annex.

Beyond Skagafjörður

Hvammstangi Cottages & Hostel € A sleek hostel on the northern edge of town. The bunk-bedded rooms share bathrooms and a well-equipped kitchen and there are cottages nearby.

Albert Guesthouse €€ On rise above Hvammstangi's harbour with fresh, neat rooms (some with wheelchair access) and a breakfast buffet. No children.

Brimslóð Atelier (p260) **€€** Stylish, Scandi-style rooms directly overlooking the sea at the mouth of the Blanda River in Blönduós, and an excellent restaurant.

Akureyri MAP p267

Hafnarstræti Hostel € Tidy, stacked capsule beds in mixed dorms and pleasant, spotless common areas. Towels cost extra.

Hamrar Campsite € Family favourite just south of town on the edge of Kjarnaskógur forest, with a playground operated by the local scout group.

Akureyri HI Hostel € This cosy, excellent-value place is hostel-plus, with spacious common areas, comfortable, attractive rooms, a well-equipped kitchen and a Bónus supermarket nearby.

Akureyri Backpackers € A chilled travellers' vibe, popular bar, central location and rooms of varying size sharing bathrooms. Note that showers are in the basement and there's no kitchen.

Hótel Akureyri €€ Boutique-style hotel on the edge of town with well-equipped rooms (the front ones have fjord views).

Berjaya Iceland Hotel Akureyri €€ Rooms are compact but well-designed, showcasing Icelandic art. It's in the upper part of town near the swimming pool, and there's a restaurant.

Sæluhús €€€ This mini-village of modern studios south of the Botanical Garden is perfect for a few days' rest and relaxation.

Beyond Akureyri

Herring House € This stylish guesthouse in Siglufjörður, overlooking town near the church, has guesthouse rooms, cottages and personalised service.

Kaffi Klara Guesthouse € Small, tidy rooms above Kaffi Klara in Ólafsfjörður. A good spot to appreciate small-town vibes away from nearby Siglufjörður's more intense tourism scene.

Gullsól € Follow the stairs up through the trapdoor at cosy Gullsól to find tiny rooms perched above Grímsey's gift shop-cafe. It's a two-minute walk to the harbour.

Dalvík Hostel Gimli € Vintage-inspired decor, spacious rooms sharing bathroom and a kitchen. It's near the ferry dock and perfect for an overnight before/after Grímsey.

Hótel Siglunes €€ This Siglufjörður classic feels like a step back in time, with its patterned wallpaper, wood-panelled reading areas and fireplace. There's also an excellent restaurant.

Hótel Básar €€ A wonderful Grímsey getaway near the original Arctic Circle marker and a puffin-filled cliff. Rooms are cosy, there's a large kitchen and a helpful owner.

Sigló Hótel €€€ Smart rooms, plus an elegant restaurant and bar, suspended directly over the water at the Siglufjörður harbour, plus a stylish lounge and waterside hot-pot.

Húsavík MAP p281

Húsavík Green Hostel € Six tidy rooms with shared bathroom and well-equipped kitchen in a converted and conveniently located private house. Two-night minimum stay.

Gamli Skólinn €€ A perfect Húsavík base, with three beautifully decorated four- and six-person apartments on a quiet side street near the Húsavík Museum.

Árból €€ This 1903 heritage house has a leafy setting and spacious rooms spread over three levels. There's no kitchen.

Húsavík Cape Hotel €€€ A boutique option overlooking the harbour with fresh, modern rooms – ask for a corner room with views – and a breakfast buffet.

Beyond Húsavík

Vógar € Well placed for hiking around Dummuborgir and Hverfjall. Tidy rooms share bathrooms and a well-equipped kitchen.

Skútustaðir Farm Guesthouse €€ Various room types, some with private bathroom, plus a cottage, a guest kitchen and excellent ice cream. It's across from the Mývatn Visitor Centre.

Dimmuborgir Guesthouse €€ A block of simple ensuite rooms overlooking Lake Mývatn, plus a row of timber cottages.

Vogafjós Guesthouse €€€ Scents of pine and cedar fill the air in these log-cabin rooms set in a lava field just south of Reykjahlíð.

Jökulsárgljúfur Canyon   MAP p289

Dettifoss Guesthouse € This comfy spot is about 9km north of Ásbyrgi, with 11 rooms of varying sizes, shared bathrooms and a guest kitchen.

Hótel Skúlagarður €€ Near the Ásbyrgi tourist information centre, with a warm welcome, comfortable rooms (one with wheelchair access), a breakfast buffet and a restaurant.

Melrakkaslétta Peninsula   MAP p295

Kópasker HI Hostel € This homely hostel has rooms spread across several houses. Everything is well maintained, and there's birdwatching nearby.

Nest €€ Don't let the drab exterior put you off. Rooms – all sharing bathroom – are simple but tidy and there's a small shared kitchen. In Raufarhöfn.

Hótel Norðurljós €€€ Raufarhöfn's best, with spacious comfortable rooms, most with private bathroom, plus an excellent restaurant and a sea-facing terrace.

Beyond Melrakkaslétta Peninsula

North East Guesthouse & Camping € Your Bakkafjörður home at the end of the Arctic Coast Way, with simple rooms, camping and a restaurant overlooking the harbour.

Lyngholt Guesthouse €€ This impeccably maintained Þórshöfn guesthouse makes an excellent base, with its warm welcome, lovely kitchen and lounge area, cosy rooms and seasonal restaurant next door.

Grásteinn Guesthouse €€ Get away from it all at these boutique cottages on a remote and welcoming sheep farm 14km southwest of Þórshöfn.

Sigló Hótel, Siglufjörður (p276)

THE GUIDE

Researched by
Eygló Svala Arnarsdóttir

East Iceland

AS FAR FROM REYKJAVÍK AS POSSIBLE

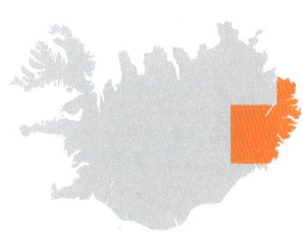

Characterised not only by deep fjords, towering mountains and wild nature, this remote region may surprise you with its unique history, culture and wildlife.

Heading east on Ring Road 1 along the southern coastline, after leaving the glacial wonders of the Southeast behind, you're soon greeted by awesome, rugged, multi-layered mountains. Here you'll find some of the oldest – and most colourful – rock in Iceland; about 13 million years old (ancient, yet infant on a global scale). These mountains have magnified storms, isolated communities, blocked out the sun, and caused mudslides and avalanches, but also provided shelter, food and joy. Another telltale sign that you've entered the East: reindeer. In winter and spring, they come to the lowlands for grazing and can sometimes be sighted amid sheep and horses. Off the shore is the formerly inhabited island Papey, known for its rich birdlife, its name a reference to Irish monks believed to have preceded the Norse settlers. Centuries later, in 1802, Iceland's first documented black settler found freedom and respect in Djúpivogur. One hundred years on, as activities of foreign fishers in Icelandic waters were peaking, French sailors had a hospital built in Fáskrúðsfjörður – today a hotel and museum. During WWII, allied troops set up camp in the Eastfjords, and their presence is still palpable. The East remains a melting pot of cultures, most prominently the artsy community of Seyðisfjörður. You're as far from Reykjavík as you can get. Expect colour, creativity and tranquillity alongside resourceful and welcoming people.

THE MAIN AREAS

FLJÓTSDALUR
Waterfalls, history and wilderness. **p306**

SEYÐISFJÖRÐUR
Art, design and adventurous hiking. **p316**

For places to stay in East Iceland, see p325

THE GUIDE

EAST ICELAND

Left: Laugavallalaug (p311); Above: Mjóifjörður (p???)

Find Your Way

East Iceland has very diverse nature and experiences that are all located at a relatively short distance from each other. We've picked some of the highlights that make a good base for further exploration.

Fljótsdalur, p306
Sheep-farming hub along lake Lagarfljót, marking the eastern border of Vatnajökull National Park. Hengifoss waterfall among many attractions.

Seyðisfjörður, p316
The region's culture capital is a 30-minute drive from Egilsstaðir. Superb shopping, tasty local food and pristine nature.

CAR
Car hire provides you with freedom and flexibility when exploring Iceland. Hire a 4WD for winter conditions and gravel roads. Find car rentals in larger towns, or arrive by ferry and bring your own.

BUS
There are sporadic public bus services in East Iceland. For fans of slow travel, this is an opportunity for a greener commute and in-depth discovery of each place. See *straeto.is* for more information.

Seyðisfjörður (p316)

Plan Your Time

To discover every nook and cranny of the eastern region, you'll need plenty of time – especially when planning long hikes – while the highlights can be covered in a few days.

If You Only Do One Thing

Seyðisfjörður (p316) is the vibrant beating heart of East Iceland, engaging through art and surrounded by stunning scenery. Listen to music and taste the most authentic sushi in Iceland. Walk the rainbow street to the blue church, browse around in **Blóðberg** (p317), invest in a hand-knitted *lopapeysa* (Icelandic woollen sweater), then walk up to sound sculpture **Tvísöngur** (p316) and take in the wondrous view.

If You Have More Time

Make room for all kinds of experiences. Go on a reindeer-sighting tour with Tinna Adventure in **Breiðdalsvík** (p314), marvel at Petra's stone collection in **Stöðvarfjörður** (p315), learn about the French history of **Fáskrúðsfjörður** (p320), camp out in **Hallormsstaðaskógur forest** (p309), watch the puffins in **Borgarfjörður Eystri** (p319), and hike up to **Hengifoss** (p307) in Fljótsdalur. Visit **Laugarfell** (p310) and adventure into the wild.

Seasonal Highlights

SPRING
Cool and unreliable weather, migrant birds arrive. Fewer tourists but some services are closed.

SUMMER
Height of the tourist season and the hottest weather. Dust conditions for hiking, biking and horse riding.

AUTUMN
Stunning foliage in Hallormsstaðaskógur. Dark nights and Northern Lights come out.

WINTER
List í Ljósi (p317) art festival is held in Seyðisfjörður. Ski areas open, snowfall permitting; frozen landscapes glitter.

Fljótsdalur

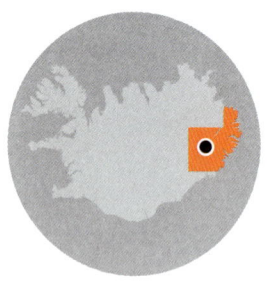

MEDIEVAL HISTORY | WONDROUS WATERFALLS | VAST WILDERNESS

GETTING AROUND

It's best to hire a car for travelling in and around Fljótsdalur. Hengifoss is only 30 minutes from Egilsstaðir and many of the main attractions are close by. A paved road (Rte 910) leads to Laugarfell on the edge of Vatnajökull National Park. Rte 931 leads you around lake Lagarfljót to Hallormsstaðaskógur forest. Rte 95 is a short cut to Breiðdalsvík and Stöðvarfjörður. Rte 939 – a scenic mountain road that is often closed in winter – goes to Djúpivogur.

☑ TOP TIP

Entrance to Snæfellsstofa Visitor Centre is free. More than an information centre about Vatnajökull National Park, it's also a museum about its flora and fauna where you're invited to touch and feel the objects on display. Ask about road conditions, hiking routes and guided tours, and a fun family orienteering game around Fljótsdalur.

Through green and peaceful valley Fljótsdalur flows Lagarfljót, a glacial river forming a 35km-long lake. Murky and mysterious, it covers an area of 53 sq km and is said to be the hideout of a vicious worm, which on occasion shoots up a hump, overturning boats. In the valley you'll find typical Icelandic sheep farms and also...a German-style manor! Built in the 1930s, Skriðuklaustur is the former home of author Gunnar Gunnarsson. This is also the site of a monastery and hospital, closed down in 1550, and the fascinating finds of an archaeological dig are displayed inside. Next door, Snæfellsstofa serves as the eastern gatekeeper to Vatnajökull National Park. The innermost farm in Fljótsdalur, on the highland's doorstep, is called Egilsstaðir, just like the region's largest town at the valley's other end. There, the Wilderness Center provides unique insight into the harsh life of farmers of centuries past.

Unearthing Skriðuklaustur's Secrets

Monastery and culture centre

Secrets lay buried here for centuries. The exact location of the **Skriðuklaustur** *(skriduklaustur.is; 1200kr)* monastery, which was in operation 1493–1550, had been forgotten, too. In 2000, after some digging around, archaeologist Steinunn Kristjánsdóttir and her team struck gold and their excavation project began. In the following 12 years they found evidence of buildings – a church, monastery and hospital – measuring 700 sq metres. In a forgotten graveyard, they uncovered the remains of almost 300 individuals. Thousands of artefacts were discovered, including a gold ring and statuette of St Barbara, indicating how grand the monastery had been and how well connected Iceland was with the outside world at that time. Although the names of the people buried at Skriðuklaustur are unknown, their bones have revealed some things about their identities and sufferings.

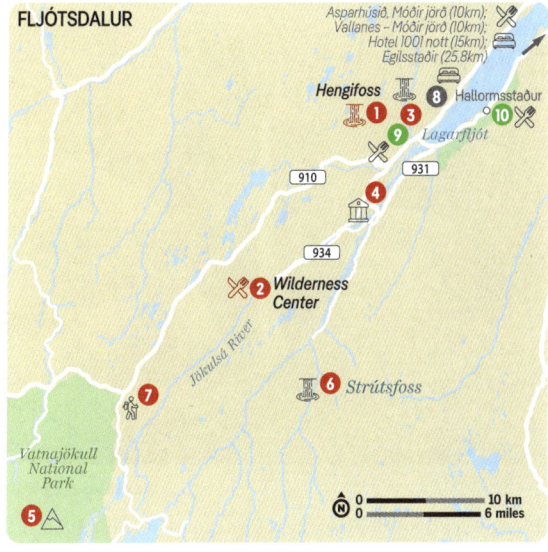

- **HIGHLIGHTS**
  1. Hengifoss
  2. Wilderness Center
- **SIGHTS**
  3. Litlanesfoss
  4. Skriðuklaustur
  5. Snæfell
  6. Strútsfoss
- **ACTIVITIES**
  7. Waterfall Circle
- **SLEEPING**
  8. Hengifosslodge
  see 7 Laugarfell
  see 2 Wilderness Center
- **EATING**
  9. Hengifoss Food Truck
  10. Lauf Restaurant
- **INFORMATION**
  see 4 Snæfellsstofa – National Park Visitor Centre

Included in the entrance fee is a guided tour of the museum at Skriðuklaustur. Learn about the excavation and its findings, then you can walk around the excavation site and afterwards journey into the past through a virtual reality tour of the church and monastery.

The museum at Skriðuklaustur is not only dedicated to the monastery but also to the life and work of author Gunnar Gunnarsson (1889–1975). The **Gunnar Gunnarsson Institute** was established here in 1997 to support literary projects and serve as a residence for artists, writers and scholars. Diverse cultural events are held here, including concerts and readings.

Hiking Hengifoss
Iceland's third-highest waterfall

Lace up your boots for the 40- to 60-minute hike to Hengifoss, which at 128m is Iceland's third-highest waterfall. The path is partly steep but well maintained. Just take it easy and enjoy the view of Fljótsdalur, which becomes more spectacular the higher up you go: the green valley, the massive lake and the sprawling forest on the other side.

As a special reward – and somewhat of a surprise – is another waterfall, **Litlanesfoss** (or Stuðlabergsfoss), midway.

THE GOOD SHEPHERD

'There they lay, the three of them, under the earth, humble, insignificant, scarcely recognizable as living beings. Yet they would awaken to deeds of which no other would be capable, which they alone could do, and for which only they were prepared. ... And over their heads the night wheeled on.'

Gunnar Gunnarsson's novella *The Good Shepherd* (1938) features fearless shepherd Fjalla-Bensi and his two trusted four-legged companions who battle a snowstorm while searching for lost sheep in the wilderness during Advent. Legend has it that Walt Disney was interested in making a cartoon based on Gunnar's story but that the author turned him down.

See *facebook.com/Skriduklaustur* for more information about readings and other events.

BEST HIKES IN FLJÓTSDALUR & BEYOND

Cableway – Wilderness Center: From the Wilderness Center, walk for 30 minutes to an old-fashioned cableway and pull yourself across a river.

Hengifoss: The 2.5km trail to the region's most famous waterfall is steep but fairly easy. Descend the canyon from the other side.

Strútsfoss: The 120m-high waterfall cascades over layered cliffs. The moderate trail is about 4km one way.

Waterfall Circle: From Laugarfell, the 8km loop leads past five waterfalls and one ravine. Afterwards, hop in the hot spring.

Snæfell: Reaching Iceland's highest non-glacial peak (1833m high) requires 4WD access along Rte F909 (open in summer). The 13km trail is for experienced hikers.

Litlanesfoss (p307)

It's smaller than Hengifoss but also quite magnificent, as it's framed with columnar basalt. Continue your walk into the Hengifossárgil gully and, soon, Hengifoss comes into view in all its glory. It tumbles down a spectacular layered cliff; these layers tell the story of different volcanic eruptions from the Tertiary period when Iceland was created.

On the Highlands' Doorstep
Travel back to the 1940s

As soon as you enter the gravel road that leads to the innermost farm in Fljótsdalur, you get the feeling that time has slowed down. Welcome to the **Wilderness Center** *(wilderness.is; 2800kr)*, on the doorstep of Europe's most expansive highlands.

The stately farmhouse that greets you was built in 1940 and has been meticulously renovated in its original style. Fourteen siblings grew up here – and nine of them lived here their entire adult lives. They were known for their handicraft, resourcefulness and their close relationship with nature and the wilderness.

The Wilderness Center is an example for slow tourism. Here, you can wind down and listen to stories over a cup of coffee and a slice of homemade *hjónabandssæla* (rhubarb oat cake),

 EATING IN & AROUND FLJÓTSDALUR: OUR PICKS

Hengifoss Food Truck: Homemade soup, waffles and ewe's-milk ice cream. Irresistible after a hike to Hengifoss. *11am-6pm May-Sep* €

Asparhúsið, Móðir jörð: Filling soup and freshly baked bread, vegetarian lunch buffet with local and organic barley and greens. *11am-5pm Tue-Sat, May & Sep, 10am-5pm Jun-Aug* €€

Lauf Restaurant: Tucked away in Iceland's largest forest lies luxury Hótel Hallormsstaður with an exquisite evening buffet. *6-9pm late May–mid-Sep* €€€

Wilderness Center: Try typical Icelandic farm fare for dinner, fish, meat or vegetarian, at an old-fashioned farm. Reservations required. *6-9pm 15 May-30 Sep* €€

sleep in a crowded but cosy *baðstofa* (old-fashioned Icelandic living room), soak in a hot spring with stacked stone walls, listen to birdsong and gaze up into the sky. In winter you might event catch the Northern Lights.

In an unassuming building you'll find a fascinating exhibition about the wilderness, humankind's relationship with the wild and the hardship of farmers past. Highlands' travel stories come to life through photos, videos and audio, along with an inventive set design, including an old-fashioned tent.

There are literary references to books by Gunnar Gunnarsson and Halldór Laxness. In Laxness' *Independent People*, the main protagonist Bjartur rode on a reindeer bull. The scene was actually inspired by a true story of a farmer from Fljótsdalur who tried to kill a sleeping bull but ended up trapped on its back.

To completely immerse yourself in nature, take long or short walks, with or without a guide, or better yet – discover nature from horseback. Longer tours go up to highlands' retreat Laugarfell (p310) – or even deeper into the wilderness.

The Thrill of Tölt
Becoming one with nature

The most natural way of experiencing Icelandic nature is from the back of an Icelandic horse. This unique breed has evolved in isolation since horses were first brought to the island around 1200 years ago, adapting to the harsh environment, and developing a special soft gait, called *tölt*. In Fljótsdalur and the surrounding area there are several horse-riding opportunities, offering everything from short rides for beginners to full-day or even multiday tours for experienced riders. While trotting on narrow dirt trails, descending rocky slopes and fording rivers, place your trust in your sure-footed steed, take in the view of the mountains, river canyons, massive Lagarfljót lake or sprawling **Hallormsstaðaskógur forest**, and feel how you become one with nature. Nothing beats the thrill of *tölting* through spectacular landscapes. Learn more at **Snæfellsstofa Visitor Centre** *(vjp.is)*.

HIGHLAND GEMS OFF FLJÓTSDALUR

Þórhallur Jóhannsson, ranger at Vatnajökull National Park, names his favourite spots in the eastern highlands, accessible from Fljótsdalur.
vjp.is

Sótavistir: A short and easy trail in the eastern Snæfell mountain with a view of Eyjabakkar. Legend has it that the troll Sóti rests there and that you can find his headstone in Sótavistir.

Snæfellsskáli Lodge: A tranquil and unique place at an altitude of 800m. The area is characterised by spring apple moss *(Philonotis fontana)*. The lodge was built by locals in 1970 and stands proud at the foot of Snæfell.

Grjótárhnjúkur: One of the peaks by Snæfell. It is possible to drive up it (Rte F909) and look across Vesturöræfi wastelands, all the way to Kverkfjöll and Herðubreið mountain in good weather.

Beyond Fljótsdalur

What's your fancy? Hunting for waterfalls, getting lost in a forest, soaking in hot and cold water or dining out?

Places
Laugarfell p310
Hallormsstaðaskógur p311
Egilsstaðir p312
Vallanes Organic Farm p313
Djúpivogur & Breiðdalsvík p314
Stöðvarfjörður p315

East Iceland is an incredibly diverse region where you can have varied experiences in a relatively compact area. The vast expanses of the highlands are a short drive from Fljótsdalur. On the other side of Lagarfljót lake lies Iceland's largest forest. Drop by organic barley and vegetable farm Vallanes to have a taste of the produce in its cafe, made with wood from its own forest. Thirty kilometres away, Egilsstaðir, the region's service centre, welcomes you with a selection of restaurants, cafes, bars – and Vök Baths. Drive southwards on Rte 95 and Rte 939 (often closed in winter) for about an hour and you'll end up in scenic seaside villages. You can have a different kind of adventure every day.

GETTING AROUND

In summer, it's tempting to take short cuts between Rte 931 and coastal towns Djúpivogur (via Rte 95 and Rte 939) and Breiðdalsvík (via Rte 95). If you do, it's better to have a 4WD. Check the weather and road conditions on *safetravel.is* before heading off and drive carefully. The longer, winding coastal road (Rte 1) – which is paved all the way – is enjoyable too.

Laugarfell

TIME FROM SNÆFELLSSTOFA: **35MIN**

Highway to the highlands

The controversial Kárahnjúkar hydropower plant opened in 2007, resulting in a paved road, Rte 910, and easy access to the eastern realms of Vatnajökull National Park. On the park's borders is **Laugarfell** *(laugarfell.is),* a highland retreat. In summer, the mountain lodge offers rustic accommodation, hearty breakfasts, lunches and dinners, and special lunch packs for hikers.

The 8km waterfall trail at Laugarfell is a fairly easy and extremely rewarding walk as it takes you to five different waterfalls on a round trip from Laugarfell, including the roaring 40m double waterfall **Kirkjufoss** in river Jökulsá í Fljótsdal. After your hike, relaxing in one of Laugarfell's two hot springs is more rewarding still. According to legend, the water has healing powers.

Higher into the highlands

Rte 910 leads onwards to **Kárahnjúkar**. There, you'll find Iceland's largest dam, Hálslón. When it fills up and overflows in late summer, massive waterfall Hverfandi appears on its western end and cascades 100m down into Hafrahvammagljúfur canyon.

From Laugarfell, Rte F909 leads to **Snæfell** (1833m), Iceland's highest mountain outside glacial regions. Summiting it requires experience and preparation. Snæfellsskáli lodge

Hafrahvammagljúfur

operates a campground and sleeping-bag accommodation. The road is only accessible in summer for 4WD vehicles. Rangers are happy to assist (call +354 842 4367 or email *snaefellsstofa@vjp.is*). After a successful mission, add your name to the list of conquerors at the lodge.

Tours on horseback, wheels or foot

Laugarfell has partnered up with the Wilderness Center (p308), offering a range of tours in different seasons. If you haven't seen enough waterfalls already, walk the waterfall trail along **Jökulsá í Fljótsdal**, where you'll see a total of 15 waterfalls! Experience nature from the back of an Icelandic horse, or rent a mountain bike.

There's also the 10- to 12-hour **Wonders of the Wilderness super-Jeep tour**, which is available in summer and winter. Highlights include **Hafrahvammagljúfur** canyon with spectacular vertical cliffs, Stuðlagil canyon (p324) with its distinct columnar basalt, and the geothermal waterfall in **Laugavallalaug**, a natural hot spring shower.

Hallormsstaðaskógur

TIME FROM SNÆFELLSSTOFA: 15MIN

Lose yourself

Have you heard the joke that goes: 'What do you do if you get lost in an Icelandic forest? Stand up!' The myth that Iceland is basically treeless is shattered as you enter Hallormsstaðaskógur, Iceland's largest forest, covering 740 sq km on the banks of Lagarfljót. From Snæfellsstofa Visitor Centre in Fljótsdalur it takes about 15 minutes to drive to the forest on Rte 931. Hallormsstaðaskógur has been a reserve since 1905 and includes 85 tree species from around the world. Most of them you can admire in the **arboretum**, including Swiss pine, mountain hemlock, subalpine fir, western red cedar and European aspen.

FIVE FUN FESTIVALS

Skógardagurinn mikli: The Great Forest Day is held around 24 June with games, music and a lumberjack competition. Local farmers serve roasted meat and other treats.

Á fætur í Fjarðabyggð: An entire week of hiking and family fun in late June. Diverse trails and easy walks, bonfires, concerts and a scavenger hunt. Organised by Mjóeyri Travel.

Ormsteiti: Harvest and culture festival in mid-September with concerts, markets, dances and other events in Egilsstaðir and surrounding regions.

Dagar myrkurs: The 'Days of Darkness' festival is celebrated throughout the East around Halloween with a focus on art, music, cosiness – and spooky events.

Jólakötturinn: Christmas market in mid-December, usually at Valgerðarstaðir in Fellabær, with Christmas trees, local delicacies and handicrafts.

FAVOURITE PLACES IN THE FOREST

Bergrún Arna Þorsteinsdóttir, assistant forest ranger in Hallormsstaðaskógur (p309) and co-owner of Holt og heiðar (forest products), shares some her favourite spots in the forest.

The birch forest in spring: It doesn't matter where exactly. Just stand among the birch trees in spring when everything is coming back to life, the leaves are opening up, the birds are nesting and the insects are crawling out of their burrows.

Atlavík: Whenever I go to the cove, I feel amazed by its magnetism. The tranquillity, the cliffs, the lake and the birch forest.

Fálkaklettur: It's thrilling to walk out onto the cliff in the middle of the blue hiking trail and take in the view of the forest.

Recreation in the woods

Through the forest lies 40km of paths for walking or biking. The longest leads up a mountain with a splendid view all the way to the highlands. Seven types of berries grow in the forest, and so it's a popular activity among locals to go berry-picking in late summer. When the foliage takes on its fiery autumnal costume, walking through the forest becomes an entirely different experience. In winter, when the frost glitters and a blanket of snow covers the ground and branches, it turns into a winter wonderland. In summer, native tourists 'chasing after the sun' (a special kind of Icelandic hobby) flock to Hallormsstaðaskógur to camp in the woods.

Egilsstaðir

TIME FROM SNÆFELLSSTOFA: **35MIN**

Exquisite taste of the East

In Egilsstaðir, the region's largest town, varied eateries and restaurants serve local delicacies, food sourced from surrounding farms and aquafarms, wild geese and reindeer caught in the highlands, berries and mushrooms gathered in the forests, and fish caught in the lakes, rivers and fjords.

Start your culinary discovery at an unassuming little fish and meat mongers, tucked away in an industrial neighbourhood. At **Kjöt & Fiskur** *(facebook.com/kjotogfisk)*, buy *gellur* (cod cheeks), leg of lamb for roasting, game, like black guillemot, or a typical old-fashioned lunch of the day *(around 2000kr)*.

At the other end of the scale, visit **Nielsen Restaurant** *(nielsenrestaurant.is)*, in the town's oldest house. The master chef, who used to work at Michelin-starred Dill, whirls up creative dishes with seasonal ingredients and a flurry of flavours (main courses 2600kr to 4900kr). Meanwhile, in an old mansion-turned-hotel by the lake, **Eldhúsið** *(english.lakehotel.is/restaurant)* offers a special farm-to-table three-course menu *(13,900kr)*. Cheese and other agricultural treats are sold at adjacent cafe **Fjóshornið** *(facebook.com/fjoshorn)*. Don't miss the cakes in **Tehúsið** *(tehusid.is)*, especially their take on rhubarb-oat cake, *hjónabandssæla (1200kr)*.

Iceland's only floating pools

Pay close attention or you might miss it. The grass-roofed building on the bank of Urriðavatn lake blends elegantly in with the surrounding landscape. A special take on Icelandic bathing culture, **Vök Baths** *(vokbaths.is; 7490kr)* offer relief from life on the road. The name *vök* references the holes that

---

 EATING IN EGILSSTAÐIR: OUR PICKS

Tehúsið: This hostel, bar, music venue, cafe and restaurant serves homemade soups, delicious cakes, hearty breakfasts. *10am-8.30pm* €

Askur Pizzeria: Stone-baked pizza with varied and sometimes unusual toppings. Local beer served in the taproom. *10.30am-9.30pm* €€

Eldhúsið: The restaurant at Lake Hotel Egilsstaðir has a selection of tempting courses, highlighting farm-fresh produce. *11.30am-10pm* €€

Nielsen Restaurant: In Egilsstaðir's oldest house, a Michelin-starred chef gets creative with local ingredients in seasonal dishes. *11.30am-2pm & 5-9pm Tue-Sat* €€€

Vallanes

formed in the frozen Urriðavatn in winter, hinting at the geothermal activity. The hot water is used for heating houses in Egilsstaðir – and now also for bathing in the lake.

There are four pools with different temperatures, two of which float in Urriðavatn lake – Iceland's only floating infinity pools. There's also a sauna and a cold mist tunnel. Order a smoothie, a beer or glass of wine at the swim-in bar and enjoy the view.

Vallanes Organic Farm

TIME FROM SNÆFELLSSTOFA: 30MIN

The warm embrace of Mother Earth

Between Hallormsstaðaskógur and Egilsstaðir, off Rte 931 by the southern bank of lake Lagarfljót, organic barley and vegetable farm **Vallanes** *(modirjord.is; buffet 4500kr)* is tucked away in a forest. Its produce, under the label Móðir jörð ('Mother Earth'), is carried at supermarkets and served by a range of restaurants. At cafe Asparhúsið (p308), built from the farm's own trees, enjoy a seasonal vegetable soup or salad, homemade bread or rhubarb cake.

Next, explore the greenhouses and take a walk in the woods – kids love easy adventurous trail **Ormurinn** ('The Worm'). If you'd like to stay, Vallanes offers lodges and cosy rooms in a renovated barn (p325). Emphasis has been placed on using natural materials, in addition to local timber, hemp furniture and wool duvets.

On the second Sunday in August a free forest festival is held at Vallanes, and in September or October a harvest festival.

Djúpivogur & Breiðdalsvík

TIME FROM SNÆFELLSSTOFA: 1½HR

Taking it slow

In summer (and in good weather in other seasons), you can cut the driving distance to Djúpivogur and Breiðdalsvík by at least an hour. From Fljótsdalur, take Rte 95 and then Rte 939 across scenic gravel road Öxi mountain pass to Djúpivogur; or Rte 95, a partly paved road, through Breiðdalur to Breiðdalsvík (check *road.is* for conditions).

Djúpivogur became the first town in Iceland to become a member of the Cittaslow movement in 2013. In short, it focuses on environmental protection and protecting cultural heritage, local food culture and production, friendliness and hospitality. As you enter the town, you're greeted by beautifully renovated old houses. In **Langabúð**, the village's oldest house, which dates back to 1790, you can fill up on hearty homemade soup and take a look at the heritage and sculpture museum.

At the harbour you'll find **Eggin í Gleðivík**, egg sculptures by Sigurður Guðmundsson, one for each of the 34 birds that nest in the area. Afterwards, stroll along the shore or around ponds on the outskirts of the town, and scout the different species from birdwatching huts. **Voxey Trips** offers wildlife and nature exploration by boat.

Retro vibe in tiny town

As you enter Breiðdalsvík, you're greeted by **Kaupfjelagið** (*facebook.com/kaupfjelagid*), a charming store and cafe. It's maintained as a museum but operated as a store, still carrying products that were sold when it opened over 60 years ago. It also facilitates the **Breiðdalssetur** (*breiddalssetur.is; free*) geology centre and Drill Core Library (DCL) of the Icelandic Institute of Natural History, with an impressive collection of kilometres of drill cores.

At **Hótel Breiðdalsvík** (p325; *breiddalsvik.is*), you can taste local food and Beljandi, the beer brewed across the street. The brewery's bar is open in summer. Family-run travel company **Tinna Adventure** (*tinna-adventure.is; tours 16,500-58,000kr*) offers nature exploration and reindeer-sighting tours, always with a focus on slow travel, mindfulness and local hospitality.

UNIQUE GEOLOGY

East Iceland's mountains are formed predominantly from lava flows that piled up in volcanic eruptions over millions of years. The gradual burial of older flows under newer ones caused the buried rock to heat up. Heated groundwater, which filled cracks and holes in the lava, dissolved the rock, transported the solutes, and precipitated them to form new minerals. When the Ice Age glacier tore through layers of rock, creating fjords and valleys, the minerals became visible. The glaciers dug deeper in East Iceland than most other parts of Iceland, so the quantity and diversity of minerals is greater, too, as explained by María Helga Guðmundsdóttir, geologist at Breiðdalssetur, the University of Iceland's research centre in Breiðdalsvík.

EATING IN DJÚPIVOGUR & BREIÐDALSVÍK: OUR PICKS

Langabúð Kaffihús: Enjoy the lunch of the day, a filling soup, or a traditional meat or fish dish in a charming old timber house. *9am-4pm Mon-Fri, from 10am Sat & Sun* €€

Hafið bistro: The varied menu ranges from pizzas to Polish dumplings. Good coffee and great selection of tempting cakes. *9am-8pm Mon-Fri, from 10am Sat & Sun* €€

Bláfell Restaurant: A feast of fresh local ingredients, the catch of the day, or lamb from a nearby farm. Try local beer Beljandi. *6-9pm* €€

Kaupfjelagið: Enjoy fish and chips, hamburgers, or a slice of cake and cup of coffee. *10am-8pm Mon-Sat, to 4pm Sun (in summer)* €€

Petra's Stone & Mineral Collection

Stöðvarfjörður

TIME FROM SNÆFELLSSTOFA: 1½HR

Amazing stone collection

Stöðvarfjörður is another unassuming seaside village worthy of exploring. The driving distance from Snæfellsstofa is the same whether you take Rte 95 through Breiðdalur (can be closed in winter) or Rte 1 along the coast.

The village's greatest attraction is **Petra's Stone & Mineral Collection**, an eccentric local woman's house turned museum dedicated to her and her husband's passion for collecting rocks. It's the largest of its kind in Europe. Petra's favourite pastime was walking out her front door, up the hills and to the mountains above, keeping an eye out for something unusual and sparkly. The house and garden are absolutely packed with colourful stones of various shapes and sizes, and it's amazing to think that almost all of them were collected by one woman. Petra passed away in 2012 but her children manage the museum.

Fascinating finds

If you drive westwards on Rte 1 towards Breiðdalsvík for 10 to 15 minutes, you can spy on shorebirds unobserved from the little turf-roofed **Óseyri birdwatching house**. A gravel road leads to **Stöð**, where in 2023 archaeologists discovered a longhouse predating the official settlement of Iceland (874 CE). It may have been the seasonal residence of a foreign chieftain operating a whaling station. A sandstone with a carving of a ship was also found; possibly Iceland's oldest image. Look out for a hiking sign to Stöðvarskarð. An approximately two-hour uphill walk leads to giant boulder **Einbúi** in Jafnadalur valley. A few minutes outside Stöðvarfjörður, along Rte 1 towards Fáskrúðsfjörður, stop by a sign indicating sea geyser **Saxa**. When it's windy you can watch the waves 'erupt'.

WHY I LOVE THE SOUTHERN EASTFJORDS

Eygló Svala Arnarsdóttir, Lonely Planet writer

Driving between Djúpivogur and Stöðvarfjörður on Rte 1 takes less than two hours, but there are countless roadside discoveries to be made. Behind every bend, there's something new to feast your eyes on. The ever-changing view of the rocky shoreline and rugged multicoloured mountains is a source of constant awe. Suddenly, a flock of swans appears, swimming in a placid fjord, or a herd of reindeer, grazing among the sheep and horses. Take it slow, make stops by parking or picnic signs, and take in your surroundings. Easily missed gems include **Teigarhorn**, a stately old house with a collection of zeolites and pyramid-shaped mountain Búlandstindur as a backdrop; **Nykurhylsfoss**, a thundering waterfall; **Blábjörg**, turquoise rocks; and **Streitishvarf**, ancient lava tubes.

Seyðisfjörður

HIKING HOT SPOT | WINING & DINING | CULTURE FESTIVALS

GETTING AROUND

It usually only takes 30 minutes to drive from Egilsstaðir to Seyðisfjörður on Rte 93. It's best to take your time, though, because the road lies across a mountain pass with many twists and turns. In winter, it can get slippery and visibility is sometimes poor due to drifting snow. Conditions are often foggy. Check *umferdin.is/en* for the latest road updates.

☑ TOP TIP

Seyðisfjörður is Iceland's only international ferry port. The MS *Norröna* ferry, operated by **Smyril Line** *(smyrilline.com)*, sails between Hirtshals in Denmark to Tórshavn in the Faroe Islands and onwards to Seyðisfjörður once a week from mid-March to late November. Bring your own vehicle or book travel packages.

Getting here is a bit of a fairy tale on its own. Up in the Fjarðarheiði pass, take in the incredible view of the fjord and surrounding mountains. As you snake your way down, you drive past the spectacular Gufufoss waterfall, and then the town of Seyðisfjörður – with its colourful houses, rainbow street and blue church – gradually appears, huddling between the shore of the narrow fjord and steep mountains. At certain times, the MS *Norröna* ferry also docks in Seyðisfjörður, dwarfing the charming wooden houses around the harbour. Stroll the rainbow street and browse a selection of Icelandic design in Blóðberg, the black-and-white store. Then drop by Handverksmarkaður by the harbour, which carries hand-knitted *lopapeysa* (sweaters) and souvenirs crafted by locals. Check out the latest exhibition in Skaftfell, listen to a summer concert, taste fresh sushi and enjoy fine wine. Soak up the creativity of this special place.

Tune into Seyðisfjörður's Artistic Vibe

Creative community

That stately white timber building from 1907 is **Skaftfell Art Center** *(skaftfell.is; free)*. This is the regional visual art centre for East Iceland, focusing on contemporary art. In addition to rotating exhibitions and regular cultural events, Skaftfell has an artist residency and a bistro, serving filling food, sweet treats, proper coffee and fine wine. The bistro was designed in honour of Swiss artist and Seyðisfjörður regular Dieter Roth by his son, Björn Roth, and Skaftfell's art library includes many of his books.

Take the 15- to 20-minute walk up to **Tvísöngur**. On a hill overlooking the town you'll find a sound sculpture by German artist Lukas Kühne, consisting of five concrete domes. Each has a frequency that represents one tone in the traditional Icelandic singing style *fimmundarsöngur* and is meant to amplify that particular tone. The **Blue Church Summer Concert** *(blaakirkjan.is; 1800kr)* series is held annually with

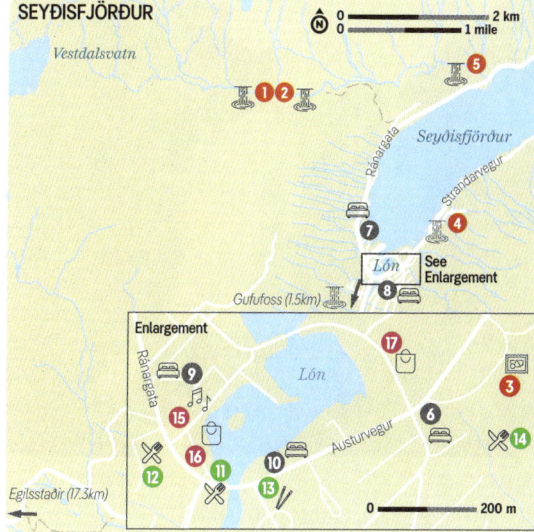

SEYÐISFJÖRÐUR

● SIGHTS
1. Selbrekkufoss
2. Selfossar
3. Skaftfell Art Center
4. Tvísöngur
5. Vestdalsfossar

● SLEEPING
6. Curry House Rooms
7. Hafaldan Harbour Hostel
8. Hafaldan Old Hospital Hostel
9. Hótel Aldan (Old Bank)
10. Hótel Aldan (Snæfell)

● EATING
11. Aldan Restaurant
12. Kaffi Lára – El Grilló Bar
13. Norð Austur Sushi & Bar
14. Skaftfell Bistro

● ENTERTAINMENT
15. Blue Church Summer Concerts

● SHOPPING
16. Blóðberg
17. Handverksmarkaður

Icelandic and foreign musicians of different genres performing every week throughout summer.

For shopping enthusiasts, **Blóðberg** (facebook.com/blodberg) carries everything from handmade chocolates to Icelandic design clothing, chic and practical in whimsical Icelandic weather. In **Handverksmarkaður** you can buy hand-knitted *lopapeysa* sweaters in all shapes, colours and sizes made by enthusiastic locals, or unique locally made jewellery.

In winter, Seyðisfjörður gets dark and quiet, some restaurants and tourism services close, and the sun disappears for four months. When it returns, on 18 February, residents celebrate with **sólarkaffi** ('sun coffee') and have pancakes. Around that date, the **List í ljósi festival** (listiljosi.com; free) is held to illuminate Seyðisfjörður with glowing artwork and genuine joy.

The Call of the Mountains

Hiking to heaven

If you'd like to discover the natural side of Seyðisfjörður, there are many different ways to do so. The walk up along the Fjarðaá river is among the easier options. It leads through a small forest, to an area where blueberries, bilberries and crowberries grow (they're usually ripe from mid-August) and to **Gufufoss** waterfall. It's possible to continue along a marked path on the river's southern bank to further waterfalls and a memorial at a height of 300m. You'll be rewarded with an incredible mountain view.

Experienced mountaineers may be up for the **Seven Peak Challenge**. Ask for a card with the names of the peaks at the information centre (by the ferry dock). At the summit of each mountain is a different hole puncher. When you've summited

---

SKIING IN THE EAST

A 10-minute drive from Seyðisfjörður on Rte 93 towards Egilsstaðir is **Stafdalur**, a skiing and snowboarding area with two disk lifts, one children's lift and slopes for snow-sport enthusiasts of all levels. A 5km cross-country skiing track is open whenever possible.

Oddsskarð, a larger ski area, lies 45 minutes from Seyðisfjörður. From Egilsstaðir, take Rte 1 to Reyðarfjörður, Rte 92 to Eskifjörður and then Rte 9549. There are two disk lifts, reaching 840m, and a children's lift. There are platforms for snowboarders, too.

Open daily December to May, weather permitting.

VESTDALUR NATURE RESERVE

Vestdalur is a valley and nature reserve on the western side of Seyðisfjörður along Rte 951, known for unique vegetation and cultural relics. It used to be one of the main mail and trade routes in East Iceland and remnants from the route can still be seen. The hike over to the next fjord, Loðmundarfjörður, takes a full day.

There are other routes in Vestdalur; for example, up to Vestdalsvatn lake and to the hollow where the 'Lady of the Mountain' was discovered in 2004. The mysterious human remains are believed to be of a young woman, who existed between 900 and 950 CE. In the hollow were also hundreds of glass pearls and gold, silver and bronze brooches, which may indicate that she was a sorceress.

Vestdalsfossar

all seven peaks, hand in your fully punched card and receive a certificate stating that you've completed the challenge. Henceforth you can call yourself: 'Fjallagarpur Seyðisfjarðar'. Every Fjallagarpur's name is documented in a registry and there's a special registry for those who complete the challenge in 24 hours. Always submit your travel plan and pay attention to the weather *(safetravel.is)*.

Vestdalsá Waterfalls

Wonders within reach

Opt for a short hike along Vestdalsá river and you'll be rewarded with a series of stunning waterfalls along Rte 951. There are two places where you can park your car: at Háubakkar (look out for a sign that says Vestdalur), and a bit further up the road where a sign says Vestdalsfossar at Vestdalseyri. You can walk up from Háubakkar to the smaller **Selfossar** and onwards to the viewing platform for the larger **Selbrekkufoss**. Walk back down, drive to the parking spot for **Vestdalsfossar** and follow the river to the platform where the tallest falls in the series, Arnarfossar, falls over reddish cliffs. Alternatively, leave the car at Háubakkar, walk between all of the falls and follow the road back to your car; about 6km in total. The hike is fairly easy and marked with sticks and signposts.

 EATING IN SEYÐISFJÖRÐUR: OUR PICKS

Norð Austur Sushi & Bar: Japanese cuisine meets Icelandic fishing culture. Fresh fish and fine sushi. *6-10pm Jun-Aug* €€

Aldan Restaurant: New Nordic-style cuisine with a French twist and fresh Icelandic flavours. *8am-10pm* €€

Kaffi Lára – El Grilló Bar: Juicy burgers, flavourful salads and fresh fish, but the lamb is the star of the menu. *11.30am-10pm* €€

Skaftfell Bistro: Warm and welcoming bistro, serving seasonal dishes with a French and Mediterranean twist. *4-10pm Tue-Thu, to 11pm Fri & Sat* €€

Beyond Seyðisfjörður

Deep fjords, tall mountains, peaceful seaside villages, each with their own attractions. Discover their history and natural wonders.

The Eastfjords await. By definition, they include every fjord along the rugged eastern coastline, from Djúpivogur to Borgarfjörður Eystri. Pre-tunnels, you had to drive in and out of every fjord to travel between villages. Pre-roads, people used to travel by sea or hike across mountain passes. While scenic drives and treks are enjoyable when you have time and the weather plays along, the tunnels are a welcome improvement – and more are in the pipeline. The larger towns are connected by paved roads but there are still places that are quite isolated – including Mjóifjörður with fewer than 15 inhabitants – and fjords like Loðmundarfjörður, which was abandoned in the 1970s. Many treasures can be discovered while journeying between the fjords.

Places
Borgarfjörður Eystri p319
Stapavík p320
Fáskrúðsfjörður p320
Reyðarfjörður, Eskifjörður & Neskaupstaður p321
Mjóifjörður p322
Vopnafjörður p323
Stuðlagil p324

Borgarfjörður Eystri TIME FROM SEYÐISFJÖRÐUR: 1½HR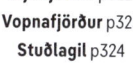
Colourful experiences

Drive from Seyðisfjörður towards Egilsstaðir on Rte 93, then take Rte 94 across a mountain pass to Borgarfjörður Eystri. The village, which lies in the placid fjord, framed by spectacular mountains, is called Bakkagerði. It's known for its lovely little **church** with altarpiece by famed painter Jóhannes S Kjarval (1885–1972), many of whose works were inspired by the area, as well as a tiny turf house, rich birdlife and **Álfaborg** – an elf-inhabited mound.

For hikers and bikers, there are plenty of trails for exploring nature at your own pace, from brief outings to multiday tours. The hike to **Stórurð** below Dyrfjöll peaks, where turquoise ponds have formed between massive boulders, is among the more popular. A marked trail leads from the parking area in Vatnsskarð Eystra. **Fjord Bikes** *(fjordbikes.com)* offers varied tours around Borgarfjörður Eystri, as well as snowshoeing and cross-country skiing in winter.

GETTING AROUND

Once you've driven the 30 minutes from Seyðisfjörður to Egilsstaðir, most other destinations in the vicinity can be reached in about 1½ hours. To the north lie Borgarfjörður Eystri and Vopnafjörður, via Stuðlagil, and to the south, Reyðarfjörður, Fáskrúðsfjörður, Eskifjörður and Neskaupstaður.

Puffins and other adventures

For more action still, try rib-safari tours by **Puffin Adventures** *(puffin.is; 18,500-23,900kr),* which include birdwatching – puffins and other seabirds – and sometimes seals and whales can be sighted, too.

TRAILBLAZING IN BORGARFJÖRÐUR EYSTRI

Árni M Magnússon, owner of Fjord Bikes, is making new biking trails and introducing new destinations to visitors. Here are three of his favourites.

Breiðavík: Black-sand beach covered with polished gemstone-like rhyolite rocks in green, red, blue and yellow. The trail to Breiðavík from Borgarfjörður Eystri is 12km with an incline of 500m.

Kækjudalur: Entering the valley is a grand experience as you have to move past huge boulders and the view is spectacular. Kækjudalur is a narrow mountain valley near Borgarfjörður Eystri, 7km long.

Hvítserkur: White and pink mountain made out of the oldest rock in Iceland, zircon, 130–240 million years old. The 15km trail is great for e-bikes. It can also be included in a 34km round trip to Breiðavík.

Approximately 5km out of town, down at the marina, is islet **Hafnarhólmi**, where puffins and other seabirds nest in summer. It has a birdwatching house where you can sit comfortably and watch puffins peek out from their burrows, fly out to sea to catch fish for their chicks and return with full beaks. The harbour also has a cafe, which doubles as storage and shower facilities for fishers, with a wonderful view out to sea.

Perfect your day with dinner and local beer at **Frystiklefinn** (*blabjorg.is*) restaurant, followed by a soak in the hot tub at **Musterið Spa** (*blabjorg.is; 5400-14,900kr*), or even a beer or seaweed bath.

Stapavík
TIME FROM SEYÐISFJÖRÐUR: **1HR**

Hike to rocky creek

Just before Rte 94 slings up across the mountain pass and over to Borgarfjörður Eystri, you'll notice a parking spot and information sign to the left of the road. It's the starting point of the easy 4.6km walk to Stapavík creek, along Selfljót river. Enjoy the view of the ocean and mountains on the other side of Héraðsflói bay, pay attention to the birds and flowers, and see if a seal swims by. The trail is mostly flat, but ascends a few small slopes before reaching the creek, a black-sand beach encircled by rocky cliffs.

You can walk down to the beach and admire the waterfall that tumbles down to the sea, and the vertical rock rising out of the sea after which the creek is named. Interestingly, in the early 20th century, cargo ships landed in Stapavík, and the winch used for securing the vessels can still be seen. For those keen on a more challenging hike, the popular Göngus-karð trail with an elevation of 415m goes from Stapavík over to Njarðvík by Borgarfjörður Eystri.

Fáskrúðsfjörður
TIME FROM SEYÐISFJÖRÐUR: **1HR**

French connection

Fáskrúðsfjörður is known for its French history, a history the residents treasure, judging by the bilingual street signs and **French Museum** (*facebook.com/frakkar2017; 2650kr*). Housed in the former French hospital, built in 1903 and now operated as a hotel, it includes a detailed encounter of the massive operations of French fishers off Iceland in the late 1800s and early 1900s. Fáskrúðsfjörður was one of the main fishing stations. At the museum, visitors are also invited to step on board a schooner.

 EATING IN BORGARFJÖRÐUR EYSTRI: OUR PICKS

Hafnarhús Cafe: Cosy cafe by the Hafnarhólmi birdwatching house. Soup, cakes and coffee. *10am-4pm Apr-Aug* €

Já Sæll Fjarðarborg: Local hangout serving burgers, lamb chops and everything barbecued. *11.30am-midnight Jun-Aug* €€

Álfheimar: Enjoy the scrumptious seafood buffet, including freshly caught fish. Great after a day of hiking. *6.30-9pm 15 Apr-15 Oct, reservations only +354 861 3677* €€

Frystiklefinn: A mix of Icelandic and international dishes with a focus on local ingredients. *5-9pm* €€

Stapavík

Ocean of memories

Thousands of names, appearing briefly, then disappearing into the waves. *Ocean of Memories* is a video artwork dedicated to the estimated 5000 French schooner sailors whose lives were lost in Icelandic waters. Hypnotisingly powerful, it turns Fáskrúðsfjörður's French history into a palpable experience mixed with a tinge of seasickness.

Locals look after the graveyard where the sailors who didn't end up in a watery grave were buried. They also celebrate an annual **French Days** festival – nurturing their relationship with Gravelines, the town from which most of the sailors came – at the end of July.

Reyðarfjörður, Eskifjörður & Neskaupstaður

TIME FROM SEYÐISFJÖRÐUR: 1HR–1HR 20MIN

Base for Allied operations

Reyðarfjörður nestles at the foot of majestic mountains in East Iceland's longest fjord. It takes one hour to drive there from Seyðisfjörður on Rte 1. In WWII it became the centre for Allied operations from Iceland. On 1 July 1940, British troops set up camp here, outnumbering the local residents 10 times over. Visit the **Icelandic Wartime Museum** *(museumguide.is/wartime-museum; 2100kr)* to learn more about the military occupation. From there, take a short walk along the river to marvel at **Búðarárfoss** waterfall. Afterwards, reward yourself with a pastry in **Sesam bakery** *(sesam.is)*.

Hiking centre

A 15km drive from Reyðarfjörður will take you to Eskifjörður, another picturesque fjord and seaside town. It's a great base for hiking; **Mjóeyri** *(mjoeyri.is)*, a local guesthouse and travel service, is one of the organisers of Gönguvikan, a week-long

HIDDEN MOUNTAIN VALLEY

Marzibil Erlendsdóttir, lighthouse keeper, weather observer, farmer and sheep dog trainer at Dalatangi in Mjóifjörður.

My favourite place here is **Afréttin**. You walk up Garðahjalli, a small mountain above the farm, and follow a narrow path northwards along the larger Flatafjall mountain. After about an hour, Afréttin – a mountain valley where we go to round up the sheep in autumn – appears. It gets so warm there, waterfalls tumble down the cliffs and the colours in mountain Grænafell are strikingly beautiful. The trail is steep, and it's only for experienced hikers who aren't afraid of heights. From Afréttin, it's possible to continue through Ytra-Afréttaskarð pass, across Skálanesbjarg mountain and over to Skálanes in Seyðisfjörður. Hiking tours in the area are organised by Mjóeyri Travel.

SUDDEN SNOWSTORM & ACT OF BRAVERY

During the allied occupation of Iceland in WWII, troops set up camp around the country, including in Reyðarfjörður, or Búðareyri, as the town was known. On 20 January 1942, a large group of British soldiers hiked up Eskifjarðarheiði mountain pass with full equipment for training purposes. They were planning to cross over to Eskifjörður but took a longer route due to slippery conditions. Suddenly a snowstorm hit and the situation looked dire. One of the men noticed a light – it was a candle in the window of farm Veturhús. He collapsed outside the door but was luckily found by Páll, the farmer's son, who'd gone to fasten the sheep house door. Páll and his brother Magnús braved the storm and carried 48 men into their house, saving many lives. Sadly, eight men perished.

hiking festival held annually in Fjarðabyggð municipality. Outside Eskifjörður is **Helgustaðanáma** *(free)*, a former Iceland Spar mine now under protection. The clear, transparent calcite mineral was used to create navigational instruments and for various inventions.

Sightseeing by boat

A tunnel takes you onwards to Neskaupstaður in Norðfjörður, the easternmost town in Iceland, enclosed by tall mountains. **Fjarðaferðir** *(fjardaferdir.com; 17,900kr)* offers sightseeing tours by rib boat to Páskahellir cave, Rauðubjörg cliffs and other natural treasures.

Neskaupstaður is also the ferry port for Mjóifjörður, the next fjord to the north. The ferry, a small boat called *Björgvin*, sails twice a week in winter. To book a trip, it's best to call +354 849-4797 or 849-4700.

Mjóifjörður

TIME FROM SEYÐISFJÖRÐUR: 1½HR

A secluded fjord

Mjóifjörður ('narrow fjord') is accessible by Rte 953 in good weather – it is not cleared regularly in winter. From Egilsstaðir, take Rte 1 towards Reyðarfjörður, and after 10km, turn left by the sign to Mjóifjörður, from where a gravel road winds its way down to the fjord. Take it slow and enjoy the view

EATING IN FJARÐABYGGÐ: OUR PICKS

Sesam Brauðhús (p321): Excellent bakery with sourdough breads, selection of pastries and soup of the day. *7.30am-4.30pm Mon-Fri, 9am-3pm Sat* €

Beituskúrinn: Simple, tasty, traditional food with international flair in a renovated bait shack. *2-9.30pm Mon-Fri, from noon Sat & Sun May-Sep* €€

Randulffssjóhús: Inside an old Norwegian herring processing station, sublime seafood is served with other regional treats. *11.30am-9pm Jun–mid-Sep* €€€

L'Abri: French cuisine meets Icelandic ingredients. Delicious food, stunning ocean view from the old French hospital. *6-10pm* €€€

Mjóifjörður

from the top. Once down, admire seven-tier waterfall **Klifbrekkufossar**. Continue along the road into quiet hamlet Brekkuþorp (home to fewer than 15 people) and stop by a curious shipwreck, once used for transporting herring offal to Neskaupstaður. In summer, cafe **Sólbrekka** *(mjoifjordur.is)* is open, and if you'd like to spend the night, there's a campground, guesthouse and cosy cottages with hot tubs at farm **Brekka**. Bring supplies and wind down in spectacular untouched nature, try angling from the pier, sea swimming, cycling or hiking.

Where adventures happen

Among trails is one leading from the cottages at Brekka up to **Brekkudalur** mountain valley. After a short but steep walk, take in the breathtaking view of the fjord. The trail continues across the mountains and over to Austdalur valley in Seyðisfjörður – but proper preparation is required for longer hikes. If you continue along Rte 953 along the fjord's northern side, you'll quickly reach majestic waterfall **Heljarfoss**, and a little further is **Smjörvogur**, a former natural prison. In winter, it's possible to take the ferry from Neskaupstaður, which goes there twice a week from Mjóifjörður. Buy a winter adventure package, enjoy the solitude of the isolated fjord and take snowshoe hikes. For bookings and activities, visit *mjoifjordur.is*.

Vopnafjörður

TIME FROM SEYÐISFJÖRÐUR: 1½–2HR

Take the high road

The northernmost town in East Iceland is Vopnafjörður, connected to Egilsstaðir by one of the most scenic mountain roads in Iceland. When travelling from Seyðisfjörður, take Rte 93 to Egilsstaðir, then Rte 1 northwards, and turn off the main road onto Rte 917. Open in summer only, this gravel road snakes 655m up Hellisheiði Eystri (not for inexperienced drivers),

---

SALMON & SWIMMING

Two of Iceland's best salmon fishing rivers, **Hofsá** and **Selá**, are located in Vopnafjörður. Hofsá, via Rte 920, has been popular among the English aristocracy and members of the royal family, including King Charles himself. Exclusive accommodation is available in lodges near the rivers. In addition to Atlantic salmon, Arctic char and sea trout can be caught there (see *thesixrivers foundation.com* for more information).

Swimming on the banks of a salmon river is a less expensive sport. The public swimming pool in Vopnafjörður, the small country pool **Selárdalslaug**, was built on the banks of Selá in 1950 and is still in operation. The location was chosen due to a natural hot water source nearby, but given its special surroundings, it is considered to be one of the most uniquely and beautifully placed public pools in Iceland.

The view from the top over the sandy beach of Héraðsflói is magnificent. Rte 85 via Rte 1 is the main route.

Treasures of nature and culture

Whichever route you take from Seyðisfjörður to Vopnafjörður, don't miss **Gljúfursárfoss**, a powerful waterfall on the southern side of Vopnafjörður fjord on Rte 917, and a little further on, **Ljósastapi**, a worthy rival to Vestmannaeyjar's elephant rock.

Vopnafjörður is known for its rich birdlife, especially around **Nýpslón**. The colourful common shelduck is among species sighted there. Local eider farm **Ytri-Nýpur** (*eiderdown comforters.com*) offers tours.

Bustarfell (*facebook.com/bustarfell; 1000kr*), on Rte 920, is one of the oldest and best-preserved traditional turf farms. It dates back to 1532 and is still owned by the same family. It is now preserved as a museum, taking visitors through the developments of Icelandic farm life of the past centuries. The museum and cafe are open in summer.

Stuðlagil

TIME FROM SEYÐISFJÖRÐUR: 1½HR

Klaustursel route

One of East Iceland's most popular attractions, river canyon Stuðlagil, lies just off the Ring Road. Take Rte 93 to Egilsstaðir, then Rte 1 northwards until you take a turn on Rte 923.

For a closer look but longer walk, drive to Klaustursel, cross a bridge and park 5km from the canyon. Take in the beauty of **Stuðlafoss** waterfall before continuing to Stuðlagil, watch grazing sheep and goats and listen to clucking geese.

As you reach the river canyon, marvel at the spectacular columnar basalt formations, up to 30m high, some including a layer of red rock, and exotic turquoise water. In some places, you can climb down into the ravine. Hold on to the ropes provided, and be careful because the rocks are often slippery.

Grund route

The drive to Grund is a little longer but it's easier to view Stuðlagil from there – albeit from a different angle. It also has a campsite, food truck, little handcraft store and bathrooms. Descend multiple stairs to reach the canyon; think of it as climbing the stairs to a church tower, just in reverse.

When you get down to the viewing platform at the edge of the canyon, it feels like standing in a cathedral, only this is nature's artwork, formed in an ancient eruption. Straight, slanting and irregular – some rusty red – the columns form a magnificent frame to the blue-green river.

At Grund, new paths are being made so that visitors can walk along the canyon and eventually down into it. Access, service and safety are continually being improved at both sites.

SCENIC PIT STOP

Shortly after Stuðlagil, on Rte 1, you'll notice a change in scenery. No trees, no grass, no sign of life, just barren landscapes and a black-sand desert. This is **Möðrudalsöræfi**, a highland plateau. It can get very windy here, and snowstorms are not uncommon.

At the intersection of Rte 1 and Rte 901, approximately two hours from Seyðisfjörður, is **Beitarhúsið**, perhaps the most curious pit stop on the Ring Road. The restaurant and cafe are an outpost from Möðrudalur á Fjöllum (p342) – Iceland's highest-located farm – built in the style of a stately turf house. Warm up on lamb soup or have *ástarpungar* doughnuts with your coffee while enjoying the view of Herðubreið mountain. You can fuel up your car, too!

Places We Love to Stay

€ Budget €€ Midrange €€€ Top End

Fljótsdalur & Around
MAP p307

Laugarfell (p310) **€€** Simple rustic accommodation in mountain lodge with shared bathrooms. Access to hot springs. Open in summer.

Wilderness Center €€ Unique accommodation in renovated farmhouse. Restaurant offers old-fashioned food. Activities, museum and spa. Also has dormitories.

Hengifosslodge €€€ Beautiful cottages with huge glass windows and view of lake Lagarfljót, with kitchenette and fireplace.

Hotel 1001 nott €€€ Family-run luxury hotel on the banks of lake Lagarfljót. Stylish rooms with large windows, access to hot tub, superb restaurant.

Vallanes – Móðir jörð €€€ Rooms and suites with kitchenette in renovated barn on organic farm Vallanes by lake Lagarfljót. Wood from the farm's forest. Also has cottages.

Egilsstaðir

Tehúsið Hostel €€ Simple, comfortable rooms and shared bathroom facilities. Great cafe and bar. Also has dormitories.

Hótel Edda €€ Simple, comfortable and centrally located near the local swimming pool. Restaurant's menu includes Icelandic specialities.

Ormurinn Cottages €€€ Studio cottages by Lagarfljót lake with a kitchenette and a terrace with a BBQ. Sleeps four.

Gistihúsið – Lake Hotel Egilsstaðir €€€ Family-run example of farming culture and hospitality, on the banks of Lagarfljót. Beautiful rooms, excellent restaurant and spa.

Hérað – Berjaya Iceland Hotels €€€ Charming and quirky, Hérað highlights chic design and comfort with Eastern flair. Restaurant has reindeer and other local specialities on the menu.

Seyðisfjörður
MAP p317

Hafaldan Hostel €€ Two locations: the hospital building (with access to sauna) plus the harbour building. With or without private bathroom; shared kitchen facilities. Also has dormitories.

Curry House Rooms €€ Cosy and stylish rooms in beautifully renovated house. Chic design, thoughtful details. Also has apartments for rent.

Hótel Aldan (Snæfell) €€ Comfortable rooms of classy design and varied sizes in historical building by the Fjarðaá lake. Shared kitchen.

Hótel Aldan (Old Bank) €€€ Luxury and comfort of historical grandeur. Built as a hotel in 1898 but later served as a bank. Aldan also offers apartments for rent.

Borgarfjörður Eystri & Around

Húsey HI Hostel € Secluded farmstay between two glacial rivers with comfortable rooms in old farmhouse. Shared bathroom and kitchen facilities. Horse riding and seal watching.

Álfheimar €€ Family-run hotel by the seaside. Simple, cosy and comfortable rooms. Guided hikes available. Restaurant serves fresh local food. Breakfast included.

Blábjörg Resort €€€ Modern comfort in renovated freezing plant. Varied rooms and prices. Hot tub and spa on-site. Excellent restaurant and local beer. Breakfast included.

Fjarðabyggð & Djúpivogur

Sólbrekka €€ Cosy cottages with kitchenette, hot tub and BBQ on the terrace. Fantastic view of secluded Mjóifjörður fjord. Sleeps four.

Hótel Breiðdalsvík €€ Comfortable rooms with access to sauna and hot tub. Good restaurant serving local fish and lamb – and local beer.

Mjóeyri (p321) **€€€** Charming huts by the quiet Eskifjörður seaside. Also has bedrooms with a shared bathroom.

Hildibrand Hotel €€€ Stylish family-run hotel offering self-catering apartments in Neskaupstaður inside the town's old co-op.

Fosshotel Eastfjords €€€ Design hotel inside the beautifully renovated 1903 French hospital by the Fáskrúðsfjörður harbour.

Hótel Framtíð €€€ Historical building by the Djúpivogur harbour. Comfortable and charming with in-house restaurant and bar.

Above: Kerlingarfjöll (p332); Right: Öskjuvatn (p343)

Researched by
Anthony Ham

The Highlands

RUGGED, RAW, WILD ICELANDIC INTERIOR

Challenging routes for the adventurous cross Iceland's hinterlands, accessible only in the height of summer, when roads open and soaring volcanic landscapes beckon.

The interior highlands' undulating multicoloured lava flows, creeping glaciers, roiling volcanoes and vast, unbroken horizons of sand, rock and mountain feel like another world. Gazing (or hiking) across the unspoilt, remote expanses, you could imagine yourself, as many have noted, on the moon or Mars. Those aren't overactive imaginations – Apollo astronauts trained here before their lunar landing and NASA trains here for Mars missions.

The highlands are home to Iceland's King and Queen of the Mountains, and the only sign of life you'll see (besides other homo sapiens) is an occasional delicate moss or flower, or the vibrant ripple of bright green where vegetation grows along a hot river. The isolation and the humbling scale of the natural world in its rawest form are the reason people visit. The solitude is exhilarating, the views unending. But there are practically no services, accommodation, bridges over rivers – or guarantees if something goes wrong, so travel to the highlands is not something to be undertaken lightly. It's vital to research road access, weather conditions and refuelling spots, and to choose the right vehicle and travel supplies for your trip (a 4WD is a necessity; you will need to self-cater).

You can simplify things by opting for a bus or super-Jeep tour. Be prepared with logistics. And for the kind of adventure you can only find in Iceland.

THE MAIN AREAS

KJÖLUR ROUTE
North–south with all rivers bridged. **p330**

SPRENGISANDUR ROUTE
North–south with large rivers to ford. **p335**

ASKJA ROUTE
Access from Iceland's north to Askja caldera, Herðubreið and Holuhraun. **p339**

THE HIGHLANDS

Find Your Way

Access to the highlands is not year-round, and depends on opening dates for mountain roads (and weather conditions). Check *umferdin.is/en* for practical information, plus road opening and closing dates for recent years, as well as *safetravel.is*, or phone 1777 for updates.

Kjölur Route, p330
Rte 35. Spice up endless vistas of rock and ice with stops at hot springs and climbable crags.

Askja Route, p339
Rte F88 or F905/910. Hike across the lava field, drinking in the caldera views, then gazing at the waters of Víti crater.

Sprengisandur Route, p335
Rte F26. Pity the melancholy ghosts and outlaws on Iceland's longest, loneliest north–south track.

THE GUIDE

TOURS
Consider travelling these routes on a tour: licenced tour operators sometimes gain access to roads before and after regular people are allowed in, and have knowledgeable guides.

4WD VEHICLES
Highlands routes are strictly for robust, high-clearance 4WD vehicles (not 4WD passenger cars or little Dacia Dusters), as jagged terrain and treacherous river crossings are common. Always ask rangers/visitor centres/experienced locals about current river conditions before going. The easiest route to drive is the Kjölur Route. Always make sure your rental vehicle is insured for F-road travel.

Note: Roads in this area are subject to flooding.

Herðubreið (p341)

Plan Your Time

The interior highlands have few sleeping options: basic campsites, a few huts (reserve ahead) and a couple of mountain lodges. If you're not going the whole way, stay on the edge of the highlands and make forays to the area.

Pressed for Time

Leave the Ring Road between Reykjahlíð and Egilsstaðir, and go either via Iceland's highest farm at **Möðrudalur** (p342) or the unique landform at **Hrossaborg** (p344). Cross the plains to oasis-like **Herðubreiðarlindir** (p339), from where you can admire the view of much-loved **Herðubreið** (p341). With a little more time, hike **Dragon Gorge** (p341), marvel at **Öskjuvatn** (p343) and swim in superb **Víti** (p343).

With a Few More Days

You could retrace your steps to the Ring Road and complete a north–south crossing along the **Kjölur Route** (p330) or the **Sprengisandur Route** (p335). Alternatively, continue beyond **Öskjuvatn** (p343) and go deeper into the remote highlands. This means more oasis vibes in **Hvannalindir** (p345), then on to the end of the road at **Kverkfjöll** and **Kverkjökull** (a northern tongue of Vatnajökull; p345).

Seasonal Highlights

SPRING
It's unusual to find any of the routes open this early (rarely before mid-June). Sudden and extreme changes in weather are always possible. If you go, go on a tour.

SUMMER
Most routes open around the middle of June, but it can be as late July. July and August are the only reliable months for taking these routes.

AUTUMN
You might be able to travel one or more of the routes in September, but there are no guarantees. Roads are usually closed by October.

WINTER
Possible to get to some areas, but only on guided tours by snowmobile, ski or super-Jeep, driven by local professionals.

Kjölur Route

HIGH-COUNTRY HIKING | SCENIC DRIVE | ADVENTURE ACTIVITIES

GETTING AROUND

While it is technically possible to drive a 2WD along the route, it is absolutely not sanctioned (posted signs are clear on this!). Car-hire companies expressly forbid the use of 2WD rentals on the route and your insurance won't cover you for any damage caused by, for example, the potholes and puddles that could almost swallow a small car. Road conditions in the north are better than those in the south. If you're in a 2WD and curious for a taste of the highlands, the first 14km of the route (north of Gullfoss) are sealed.

In summer, high-suspension Highland Buses follow this route at least once daily, travelling between Reykjavík and Akureyri.

What a drive! If you want to sample Iceland's high central deserts but don't like the idea of ford crossings, the 200km Kjölur (pronounced *kyu*-loor) route has had all of its rivers bridged. Although you'll need a 4WD vehicle, it's an accessible and achingly scenic adventure that gets you away from the Ring Road procession and out into the Icelandic wilds. The route gained a little stardust in 2023 with its first luxe highlands establishment: Highland Base Kerlingarfjöll.

From the south, Rte 35 starts just past Gullfoss, passing between two large glaciers before emerging between Varmahlíð and Blönduós on the northwest coast. It reaches its highest point (around 700m) between the Langjökull and Hofsjökull ice caps, near the mountain Kjalfell (1000m). Its northern section cruises scenically past Blöndulón, a large reservoir used by the Blanda hydroelectric power station.

The Kjölur route usually opens around mid-June, and closes sometime in September, depending on weather conditions.

Hit the Road on Horseback

Riding the open range

There are many ways to explore the Kjölur Route, but one of our favourites is on horseback. Apart from returning to the Icelandic past – this is how Icelanders once crossed the highlands – you'll slow down to a wonderfully relaxed pace, feel the wind in your hair and leave behind all engine noise. Bliss.

While day rides may be possible from some huts managed by adventure companies, the real adventure is to go on a multi-day trail ride that shadows the Kjölur Route along ancient trading, horse and pilgrimage trails. And remember: these are not generally trails for beginners and you'll need a reasonable level of experience to join such a trip.

Íslandshestar *(islandshestar.is; per person day tours from €95, 8-day Kjölur €2866)* is all about the multiday trail on its eight-day tour (which includes six days of riding) that

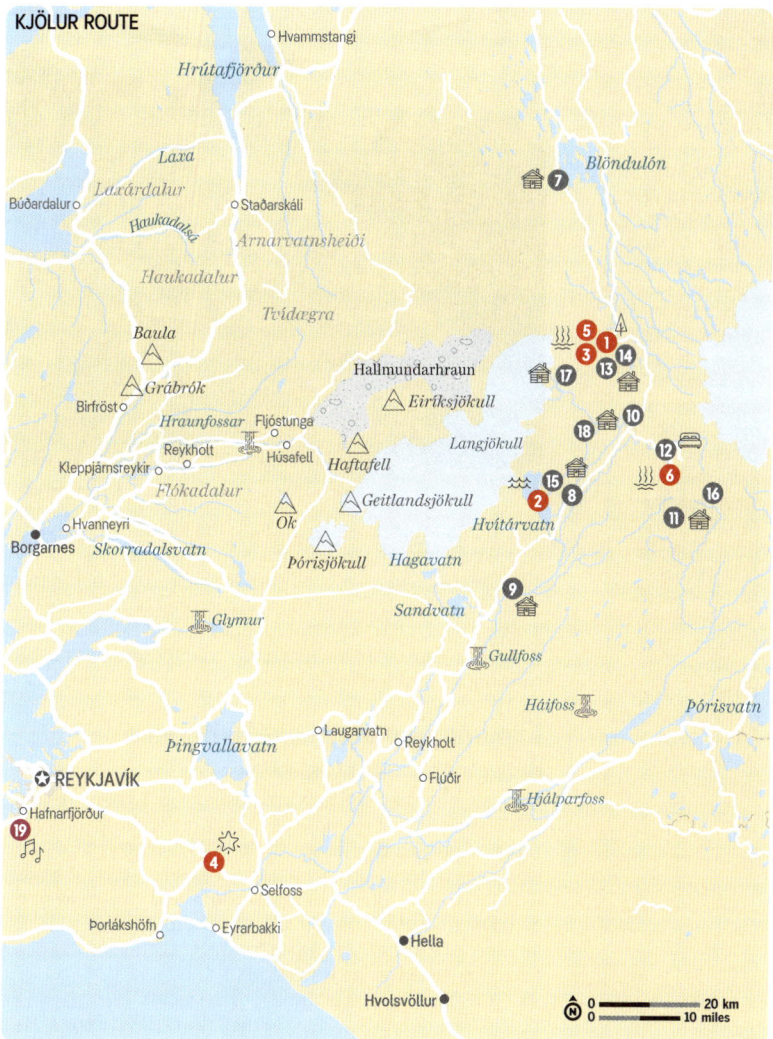

KJÖLUR ROUTE

● SIGHTS
1 Hveravellir Nature Reserve
2 Hvítárvatn

● ACTIVITIES
3 Bláhver
4 Eldhestar
5 Eyvindurhver
6 Hveradalir

● SLEEPING
7 Áfangi Hut
8 Árbúðir
9 Fremstaver
10 Gíslaskáli
11 Grákollur
12 Highland Base Kerlingarfjöll
13 Hveravellir New Hut
14 Hveravellir Old Hut
15 Hvítárnes Hut
16 Kisubotnar
17 Þjófadalir
18 Þverbrekknamúli Hut

● ENTERTAINMENT
19 Íslandshestar

☑ TOP TIP

Kerlingarfjöll, Árbúðir (Kaffi Kjölur) and Hveravellir offer food, but you need to bring self-catering supplies for all other overnighting options. Huts generally have kitchen access, but utensils are not guaranteed and campers are not allowed in some huts. Campers need to bring stoves (campfires are not permitted).

HIGHLAND DRIVING TIPS

Fill up before setting out: There are no petrol stations in the highlands, except at Hrauneyjar, south of the Sprengisandur route, and at Möðrudalur, north of the Askja route. Despite some websites' advice, there is *no* petrol available at Hveravellir on the Kjölur route.

Travel together: Try to travel in pairs, so if one vehicle bogs or breaks down, the other can drag it out, fetch help or transport passengers to shelter.

No off-road driving: In the highlands, as with everywhere in Iceland, stick to numbered roads and marked trails. Off-road driving is hugely destructive to the country's fragile environment, and illegal. There are now police in the highlands enforcing the law.

Kerlingarfjöll

overnights at its three huts along the route. It's a popular tour – book months in advance.

Eldhestar *(eldhestar.is; 7-day tour €2810)*, a horse farm based in Hveragerði near the southern end of the route, has a 180km, seven-day, six-night tour (six days of riding, at 20km to 45km a day). As in ancient times, you'll travel with a free-running herd of Icelandic horses.

Exploring Isolated Lake Hvítárvatn

Hiking and camping at a glacial lake

The pale-blue lake **Hvítárvatn** (pronounced *kvi*-towr-vatn), 35km northeast of Gullfoss, is the source of the glacial river Hvítá – a popular destination for Reykjavík-based white-water rafting operators. A glacier tongue of Iceland's second-largest ice cap, Langjökull, calves into the lake and creates icebergs occasionally, adding to the beauty of this rarified spot. It's an excellent way to get a taste for the highlands if you don't have time to cover the whole Kjölur Route.

In the marshy grasslands northeast of Hvítárvatn is Ferðafélag Íslands' *(fi.is)* oldest hut, **Hvítárnes Hut** *(N 64°37.007', W 19°45.394')*, built in 1930. It has a volunteer warden for most of July and some of August and sleeps 30. The kitchen has a gas stove, but no utensils (campers cannot use it). Beds must be reserved.

To get here from the Kjölur Route, drive the 4WD track to the hut from the Hvítárnes crossroads; if you're travelling by bus, it's an 8km walk from the crossroads.

Exploring the Coloured Hills of Kerlingarfjöll

Hot-spring valleys and striped hills

Until the 1850s, local Icelandic legends held that the Kerlingarfjöll mountain range (10km off Rte 35 on Rte F347) harboured the worst outlaws. It was thought that they lived deep in the heart of the 150-sq-km series of peaks in an isolated Shangri-la-type valley. So strong was this belief that it was only in the mid-19th century that anyone ventured into Kerlingarfjöll, and it was only in 1941 that the range was properly explored by Ferðafélag Íslands (Iceland Touring Association).

These days, it's a hauntingly beautiful detour off the main Rte 35. The colourfully dramatic landscape is broken up into jagged peaks and ridges, the highest of which is **Snækollur** (1477m), and it's scattered with hot springs. The striated steaming geothermal valley **Hveradalir** is a highlight. A stunningly colourful but difficult 5km hike ascends from Highland Base Kerlingarfjöll to this roiling pot of geothermal mist and colourful scree hills. Check on conditions before undertaking it, though – it's usually too muddy to be safe until well into July. Most people opt to drive the 15 minutes to a parking area at Mt Keis, from where Hveradalir is a short, steep walk downhill.

Prebook to join one of the several different guided hikes offered by Highland Base Kerlingarfjöll twice daily July to mid-September (one on Monday).

Living It Up at Highland Base Kerlingarfjöll
Summer and winter activities

Just because you're exploring one of Iceland's wildest and most remote areas, doesn't mean you need to rough it. For many years, Kerlingarfjöll was the site of a highland centre which Icelanders used for hiking and skiing in the region. In 2023 the Blue Lagoon company completed a massive renovation to transform it into a swankier new proposition, **Highland Base Kerlingarfjöll** *(highlandbase.is)*. Designed as a year-round venue, it has a rich offering in hikes as well as the chance to rent electric mountain bikes in summer.

Launched in October 2023, the **Highland Base Baths** have a trio of hot-pots, cold plunge and sauna, and there's also a natural hot springs a half-hour walk from the base.

In winter, Highland Base's partner **Amazing Tours** *(amazingtours.is)* leads adventures from a Hveradalir guided snowshoe trek to snowmobiling on Hofsjökull glacier and private back-country skiing. It also offers super-Jeep transfers to Highland Base in winter as the roads are closed *(22,000kr one way)*.

The complex offers a broad range of accommodation, from a hotel to shared and private huts, and camping. Plus there's a restaurant, with sweeping views, which serves lunch à la carte and a dinner buffet. It operates two mountain huts, allowing a three-day loop walk in the area.

Unwinding at the Hveravellir Oasis
Hot springs and hot drinks

The popular geothermal area of fumaroles and hot springs called **Hveravellir Nature Reserve** *(hveravellir.is; tel 452 4200)* is located about halfway between Gullfoss in the south and the Ring Road in the north. Among its warm pools

THE BADLANDS

Historically in Iceland, once a person had been convicted of outlawry they were beyond society's protection and aggrieved enemies could kill them at will. Many outlaws *(útilegumenn)*, such as the renowned Eiríkur Rauðe (Erik the Red), voluntarily took exile abroad. Others escaped revenge-killing by fleeing into the mountains, valleys and broad expanses of the harsh Icelandic highlands, where few dared pursue them.

Surviving in the harshest of conditions, Icelandic outlaws were naturally credited with all sorts of fearsome feats, and the general populace came to fear the vast badlands, which they considered to be the haunt of superhuman evil. The *útilegumenn* thereby joined the ranks of giants and trolls, and provided the themes for popular tales such as the fantastic *Grettir's Saga*.

HARSH COUNTRY

If you ever need a cautionary tale about the dangers of travelling in the Icelandic highlands, consider Beinahóll (Bone Hill), near Kjalfell.

In 1780, two brothers from Iceland's north set out late in the season with three others on a mission to buy sheep and horses in the south. They never returned. A search party sent out the following spring found a single emaciated animal. The remains of the five travellers were found in 1845, alongside the bones of sheep and horses. It appears that everyone had died in a blizzard. The area was thereafter called Bone Hill.

Local legends still hold that those camping near Beinahóll are likely to see mysterious shadows moving around, as well as unexplained animal bones...

Hveravellir

are the brilliant-blue **Bláhver**; Öskurhólshver (pronounced *usk*-ur-howls-kver), which emits a constant stream of hissing steam; and a luscious human-made bathing pool.

Another hot spring, **Eyvindurhver**, is named after the outlaw Fjalla-Eyvindur. Hveravellir is reputedly one of the many highland hideouts of this renegade. Lovely trails crisscross the area and you can pick up information from helpful staff at the **New Hut**, which has private rooms with shared bathrooms (no cooking facilities). The **Old Hut** sleeps about 30 in dorm beds (linen available for 2200kr) with cooking facilities. There's also a campsite, simple cafe and teeny store, as well as device charging and wi-fi hotspot for a fee. They also operate the **Áfangi Hut**, about 38km north, near Blöndulón reservoir.

A service fee *(1000kr)* applies for all day guests using parking, the hot-pot, toilets or showers.

DIY Hikes

Three-day scenic hikes

If hiking for three days across old-fashioned high-country trails sounds like your thing, two three-day hikes make for a fine highlands traverse. If you choose to go without a guide, make sure you tell someone where you're going before setting out – every year, local emergency teams have to go looking for lost hikers unprepared for weather that can close in rapidly, even in summer.

The **Old Kjalvegur Route** is an easy and scenic three-day hike (39km) from **Hvítárvatn** to **Hveravellir** (or vice versa) following the original horseback Kjölur route (west of the present road), via the Hvítárnes (p332), **Þverbrekknamúli** and **Þjófadalir** mountain huts *(fi.is)*.

For something a little more challenging, **Hringbrautin** is a challenging 47km circuit around Kerlingarfjöll. It starts and ends at Highland Base Kerlingarfjöll with huts at **Kisubotnar** and **Grákollur**.

Sprengisandur Route

HIGH-COUNTRY HIKING | FISHING | HOT SPRINGS

To Icelanders, the name Sprengisandur conjures up images of outlaws, ghosts and long sheep drives across the barren wastes, of sagas and the old ways. The Sprengisandur route (F26) is the longest north–south trail, and crosses bleak desert moors that can induce a shudder even today in a 4WD. An older route, now abandoned, lies a few kilometres west of the current one.

This route requires large river fords so is best kept to a tour or those with highland river-crossing experience and a hardy high-suspension 4WD vehicle. In addition to the in-demand accommodation at the Highland Center Hrauneyjar, there are huts along the route (BYO sleeping bag), and camping areas. It's necessary to prebook hut beds and pack all of your food (and remove all your rubbish). This route usually opens late, beginning some time between late June and mid-July, and closes sometime in September, depending on weather conditions.

Driving the Sprengisandur
Go on a 4WD highlands adventure

When speaking about the Sprengisandur, it's as easy to get bogged down in practicalities as it is to get stuck along some of the muddier sections of the route. And yes, nowhere are such practicalities more important – crossing between south and north is a serious undertaking and should only be done by those with a high-clearance 4WD and some experience of driving one.

But once you have taken care – and remain vigilant – of such matters, never lose sight of the fact that this is one magnificent drive. For those who undertake it this is an utterly unforgettable experience, a haunting highland traverse through landscapes that very few visitors to Iceland ever see.

Most people drive the route from north to south, and there are a number of ways to make that approach. The route proper begins at Rte 842 near Goðafoss in northwest Iceland. Some

GETTING AROUND

If you're one of those travellers who likes to push the regulations to the limit, this is not the place to do it. It would be sheer folly to try and take a 2WD along this route. Doing so is expressly forbidden under rental contracts and if you ignore this and have a problem, you won't be covered by insurance. Not to mention the fact that a 2WD simply won't make it. There is no public transport along this route, although a number of tour operators do offer this route as part of their tour portfolio.

☑ TOP TIP

There's no fuel along the route. Goðafoss to Hrauneyjar is 240km. The nearest petrol stations are: Akureyri (from the Eyjafjörður approach); Varmahlíð (from the Skagafjörður approach) or Fosshóll, near Goðafoss (if you're coming from the north along the main route through Bárðardalur).

In the south there is petrol at Hrauneyjar.

● **HIGHLIGHTS**
1 Aldeyjarfoss

● **SIGHTS**
2 Hrafnabjargafoss

● **ACTIVITIES**
3 Eldhestar
4 Ferðafélag Akureyrar
5 Fjalladýrð
6 Icelandic Mountain Guides
7 Mývatn Tours

● **SLEEPING**
8 Highland Center Hrauneyjar
9 Laugafell Hut
10 Nýidalur Hut

41km later, you'll pass through a metal gate as the road turns into F26. There's a billboard explaining the sights and finer points of the route, and 1km later you'll come upon one of Iceland's most photogenic waterfalls, **Aldeyjarfoss**. Churning water bursts over the cliff's edge as it splashes through a narrow canyon lined with the signature honeycomb columns of basalt. And just a bit further lie the multiple chutes of **Hrafnabjargafoss**, 1km down a signposted turnoff.

LANDMANNALAUGAR LOVERS

The famous Landmannalaugar highland locale (p144) is best reached from Southwest Iceland, though there is an alternate, lesser-travelled route, Fjallabak, which approaches from the southeast between Vík and Kirkjubæjarklaustur.

After the waterfalls, the Sprengisandur route continues southwest through 240km of territory that will appeal to those who dream of the bare, windswept moors of Yorkshire or the Scottish Highlands. They may not be for everyone, but these are brooding landscapes filled with mystery and character that just can't help but get under your skin. The route continues all the way to Þjórsárdalur. There are two other ways to approach Sprengisandur – the Eyjafjörður approach or the Skagafjörður approach – both of which link up to the main road about halfway through. We prefer the main route, but these two alternatives are equally wild and see even fewer vehicles.

From the north, the F821 from southern Eyjafjörður (south of Akureyri) connects to the Skagafjörður approach at Laugafell.

From the northwest, the 81km-long F752 connects southern Skagafjörður (the nearest town is Varmahlíð on the Ring Road) to the Sprengisandur route. The roads join near the lake Fjórðungsvatn (pronounced fyorth-ungs-vatn), 20km east of Hofsjökull.

Angling at the Volcano Lakes of Veiðivötn
Fish for trout under the midnight sun

The beautiful area of Veiðivötn (pronounced *veeth*-i-vutn), just northeast of Landmannalaugar, is a shimmering entanglement of small desert lakes in a volcanic basin. It's a continuation of the same fissure that produced Laugahraun in the Fjallabak Nature Reserve and besides gazing in wonder, it's a popular place for trout fishing.

It's about 30km from **Highland Center Hrauneyjar**, or there are basic huts and camping available in summer, plus fishing licences. Check the informative *veidivotn.is* site or email *ampi@simnet.is*. Licences for lakes further south are sold at **Landmannahellir**.

Access to this area is via Rte F228, east of Hrauneyjar, and you'll need to be self-sufficient in supplies, camping equipment and transport. Ask for directions (and let someone know you're going) at Hrauneyjar.

Hiking Around the Nýidalur Range
Trekking through the heart of Iceland

Nýidalur (also known as Jökuldalur), the range just south of the **Tungnafellsjökull** ice cap, was discovered by a lost traveller in 1845. With facilities including a campsite and huts, plus appealing hiking trails, it's the most popular rest spot for travellers along the Sprengisandur route. It's about 100km from Hrauneyjar.

The Vatnajökull National Park ranger *(vjp.is; tel 842 4377)* stationed here in summer *(July and August)* can advise on trail conditions and routes like the one up to Tungnafell or along Mjóháls ridge into Vonarskarð. Let them know where you are going before you head out.

There are two rivers en route to Nýidalur – the one 500m from the hut is usually difficult to cross (even for a 4WD). Ask locally for advice on conditions and always check weather forecasts as it can snow up there (830m) year-round.

The **Nýidalur Hut** *(fi.is; N 64°44.130', W 18°04.350'; July and August; 860 3334)* is actually two huts (sleeping up to 79 people) with kitchen facilities, showers *(1000kr)* and a summer warden *(July and August)*. Book your bed in advance. Campers cannot use hut facilities.

HIKING RESOURCES FOR THE HIGHLANDS

For independent hikers, the website of **Ferðafélag Akureyrar** *(ffa.is)*, the Touring Club of Akureyri, outlines details of the routes, including Askja Trail, known in Icelandic as Öskjuvegurinn. Along that route, the organisation's walking trail has huts across the Ódáðahraun, starting from Herðubreiðarlindir and ending at Svartárkot farm in upper Bárðardalur (pronounced bowr-thar-dalur) valley (Rte 843). Book hut beds well in advance or go on one of its guided treks.

The national-park website *(vatna jokulsthjodgardur.is)* is also loaded with hiking information. Independent hikers should inform a park ranger of their plans; leave a travel plan at *safetravel.is*; and whenever stopping at a hut, write your plan in the guestbook.

For hiker transport, your best bet is **Mývatn Tours** (p277) *(myvatntours.is)* or **Fjalladýrð** *(fjalladyrd. is)*. They can drop you at a hut and pick you up a few days later.

MULTIDAY HIGHLAND TOURS

Fjalladýrð: At Möðrudalur. Better known for its tours to Askja, but some of these also stray into Sprengisandur. *(fjalladyrd.is)*

Geo Travel: Based at Mývatn and Akureyri, this experienced operator runs day trips and overnight excursions. *(geotravel.is)*

Ferðafélag Akureyrar: Another excellent company, Ferðafélag Akureyrar organises five-day hut-to-hut hiking tours along the Askja Trail. *(ffa.is)*

Eldhestar: Leads six-day wilderness horse-riding treks along the Kjölur and Sprengisandur routes, for very experienced riders. *(eldhestar.is)*

Icelandic Mountain Guides: Offers tours all over Iceland, including 10-day winter ski trips on the Sprengisandur route. *(mountainguides.is)*

Laugafell

Hot Springs & Sunshine at Laugafell
Geothermal soaking and highland huts

Wonderful Laugafell is an 879m-high mountain with hot springs bubbling on its northwestern slopes. You can stay nearby at the hiker **huts** *(ffa.is; N 65°01.630', W 18°19.950' 462 2720; July and August; 833 5697)* operated by **Ferðafélag Akureyrar**, whose best feature is the geothermally heated, natural swimming pool. The two huts have 32 beds and a kitchen, plus they're heated using the local geothermal water. Cushy! There's a warden on-site in July and August.

Laugafell is on both the Skagafjörður approach (93km via Rte 752 and F752; p337) and the Eyjafjörður approach (87km south of Akureyri via Rte 821 and F821; p337) to the Sprengisandur route. A few tour companies out of Akureryi/Mývatn offer 4WD day tours to this area, including **Geo Travel** *(geotravel.is; 3hr tour from 35,000kr)*.

Askja Route

MOUNTAIN SCENERY | VOLCANIC LANDSCAPES | HIKING

The brilliant Askja route (Öskjuleið) runs across the multihued highlands to Herðubreið (1682m), the Icelanders' beloved 'Queen of the Mountains', the idyllic, green oasis Herðubreiðarlindir, and onward to the region's most popular marvel, the immense Askja (Öskju) caldera with its lake. Not to be forgotten is the little crater lake, Viti, alongside with its cerulean waters shining brighter than Askja's grander one.

Rock formations are another star of the show, with everything from one of Iceland's newest lava fields, Holuhraun, to dragon-shaped pinnacles at Drekagil, plus volcanic soils, lakes and rocks in myriad and glorious hues.

Part adventurous shortcut for those with a 4WD, part destination in its own right, Askja is arguably the most rewarding, the most spectacular of all of the extended detours off the Ring Road and into the highlands. Hiking – both long and short – is at the heart of exploring here.

☑ TOP TIP

Askja is part of the vast Vatnajökull National Park – see *vatnajokulsthjodgardur.is* for excellent information and hiking maps. The **Mývatn Visitor Centre** (p287) at Skútustaðir also has maps and information. National park rangers are stationed at **Drekagil** *(842 4357)*, **Herðubreiðarlindir** and **Askja** in summer, and give daily walking tours mid-July to mid-August at Askja, Herðubreiðarlindir and Holuhraun.

Hiking in Verdant Herðubreiðarlindir

Outlaw hideout in lush lands

The oasis Herðubreiðarlindir, a nature reserve thick with green moss, angelica and the pinky-purple flower of the Arctic river beauty *Epilobium latifolium,* was created by springs flowing from beneath the Ódáðahraun lava. You get a superb close-up

GETTING AROUND

Several operators run super-Jeep tours to Askja, from mid-/late June (when the route opens) until as late into September/October as weather permits. From Akureyri, it's a long day (up to 15 hours); a better base is Reykjahlíð at Mývatn (even then, the tour time is around 11 to 12 hours), or better yet Möðrudalur (nine or 10 hours). Two-day tours are better. If self-driving, there are no fuel stops anywhere on the route. The nearest ones are at Möðrudalur (90km from Askja) and Mývatn (120km from Askja). Plan accordingly.

There is no public transport along the route.

ASKJA'S VICTIMS

The eruption of the Askja volcano in 1875 may have laid waste to large swathes of northern Iceland, killing people and livestock. But it claimed still further victims 32 years later, in 1907, when German researchers Max Rudloff and Walther von Knebel went rowing on the lake. They completely vanished and their bodies were never found.

The deaths were never explained, with legends swirling around this haunting place suggesting that the lake may have hazardous quirks, possibly odd currents or whirlpools. More likely, the death was the result of taking to the deep, icy water in a rickety canvas boat, although rumours of supernatural explanations still persist. There's a stone cairn and memorial to the men on the rim of the caldera.

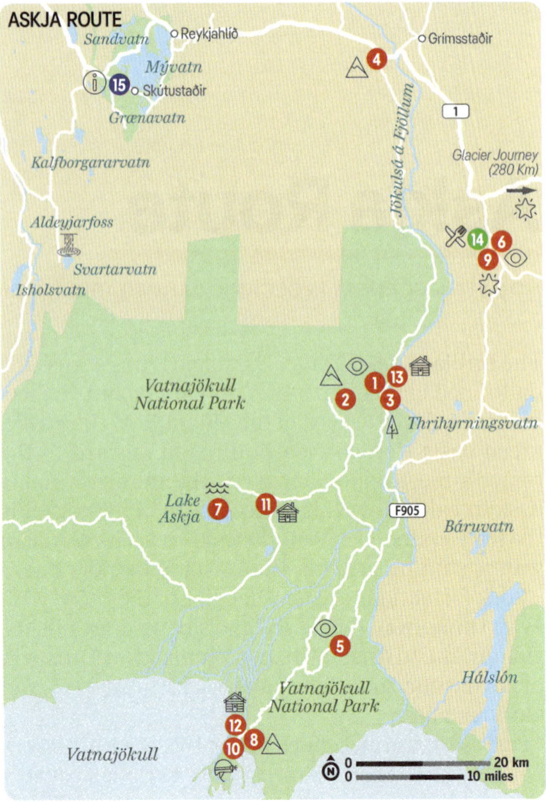

ASKJA ROUTE

SIGHTS
1 Fjalla-Eyvindur
2 Herðubreið
3 Herðubreiðarlindir
4 Hrossaborg
5 Hvannalindir
6 Möðrudalur
7 Öskjuvatn
8 Virkisfell

ACTIVITIES
9 Fjalladýrð
10 Kverkfjöll Ice Caves

SLEEPING
11 Drekagil Huts
12 Sigurðarskáli Hut
13 Þorsteinsskáli Hut

EATING
14 Fjallakaffi

INFORMATION
15 Mývatn Visitor Centre

view of Herðubreið from here (unless, of course, you're greeted by dense fog and/or a wall of blowing sand). Sometimes, the clouds cluster around the summit like a halo, which is a remarkable sight.

Stay at the appealing hut and campsite here, with a summertime ranger station. The popular 25-bed **Þorsteinsskáli Hut** *(ffa.is; N 65°11.544', W 16°13.360'; 822 5191)* offers a wonderfully green and welcoming landscape (much more so than at Drekagil). The cosy lodge at Herðubreiðarlindir has showers (1000kr) and a kitchen. Book hut beds in advance. It's also operated by the Touring Club of Akureyri and is the start of the **Askja Trail**, an ambitious five-day trek best tackled on one of its guided hikes.

And just in case the superb scenery and surrounds weren't sufficient, there's a touch of grim legend about this place. Behind the hut is a **Fjalla-Eyvindur** 'convict hole'. Outlaw Eyvindur (p343) is believed to have occupied it during the winter of 1774–75, when he subsisted on angelica root, raw horsemeat stored on top of the hideout to retain heat inside, and water from the stream running through the hole.

Herðubreiðarlindir is about 60km from Hrossaborg, at the northern point of Rte F88, and another 35km on to Drekagil.

Herðubreið, the Queen of the Mountains
Climb Iceland's favourite peak

Icelanders call Herðubreið (pronounced *hair*-the-breth), the country's most distinctive mountain (1682m), the 'Queen of the Mountains'. Majestic Herðubreið (meaning 'Broad Shoulders') is visible for miles around, and it crops up time and again in the work of local poets and painters, entranced by its beauty.

It's a *móberg* mountain, formed by subglacial volcanic eruptions. In fact, if Vatnajökull was to suddenly be stripped of ice, Grímsvötn and Kverkfjöll would probably emerge looking more or less like Herðubreið. From the **Þorsteinsskáli hut** in Herðubreiðarlindir, a marked trail runs to Herðubreið.

If you wish to climb the mountain, beware: as serenely beautiful as the queen may be, the hike is unrelenting and dangerous if you're not properly prepared. In the spring, falling rocks alter paths and topography. Clouds often shroud the mountain. A GPS is a must, as is a helmet, crampons and ice axe (and experience using them). Don't go alone, prepare for foul weather, and it is required that you discuss your intentions with the wardens at Herðubreiðarlindir.

Consider joining a tour – **Fjalladýrð** (p346) at Möðrudalur can arrange this, with a two-hour hike to the base of the mountain, a four-hour climb, a two-and-a-half-hour descent, then a further hike east to the oasis, before you drive back. It's a long, exhilarating 12-hour day. Prices vary depending on the number of participants.

Do Go Chasing Waterfalls in Drekagil
Walk up 'Dragon Gorge'

This really is the sort of landscape that lends itself to myths and legends, and there are times when the entire landscape seems alive. The name of the gorge, Drekagil, 35km southwest of Herðubreið, means 'Dragon Gorge', after the shapes of dragons in the craggy rock formations that tower over it. A hike up the twisting gorge (behind the Dreki huts) leads to an impressive waterfall, which is only accessible when the river is low enough to pass.

The **Drekagil Huts** *(ffa.is/en/huts/dreki)* are an ideal base for exploring the area. Day-use of the facilities (bathroom etc) costs 1000kr per person. You can also walk (or drive) 8km up the marked trail to Askja, and take a 20km trail

BIRTH OF A LAVA FIELD

On 16 August 2014, sensors picked up increased seismic activity around **Bárðarbunga**, one of many volcanoes underneath Vatnajökull. The magma in Bárðarbunga formed an 'intrusive dike' (tunnel of magma) through the ground under an outlet glacier named Dyngjujökull. On 29 August, the magma surfaced – a fissure eruption, complete with spectacular lava fountains, began in Holuhraun, a 200-year-old lava field about 5km away from the Dyngjujökull glacial edge.

The eruption continued for almost six months; then Iceland's largest for 230 years. Impressive stats: 85 sq km in area (larger than the island of Manhattan), averaging about 10m to 14m thick, and weighing about the same as a herd of 600 million elephants.

ICELAND'S HIGHEST FARM

Möðrudalur (p347) is the closest farm to the northern highlands, and Iceland's highest farm altogether (469m). You'll see its petrol pump and yummy cafe Beitarhúsið on the Ring Road between Egilsstaðir and Mývatn, and if you continue south 8km on Rte 901, you'll be welcomed at the main farm with a full range of accommodation from stylish private rooms to rustic guesthouse and view-blessed camping.

Its restaurant **Fjallakaffi** serves delicious local fare and it is the leading regional tour operator (called Fjalladýrð) for Askja and Kverkfjöll. To make the most of your time while you're here, we strongly recommend that you contact it in advance of your visit to see what's possible and to make the necessary bookings.

Holuhraun

to the Bræðrafell (pronounced *bri-thra-fetl*) hut. Book with Dreki summertime rangers *(842 4357; 8am-7pm)* first, as the hut is locked.

Walking Fresh Lava in Holuhraun

See some of Iceland's newest lava

There is a tendency to think of grand geological phenomena as ancient, as belonging to the distant past. Not in Iceland, not here. The huge lava field **Holuhraun** is as young as can be, created from 2014–15 during the Bárðarbunga eruption.

One spectacular way to see the lava field is from above – if they can tear themselves away from active volcanoes elsewhere, sightseeing flights from Reykjavík with **Glacier Heli** *(glacierheli.is)* grant you a sense of its vastness. For the rest of us, you can reach the edge of the field by road (F910), following signs from Drekagil for 24km to reach a car park. The marked trail clearly reveals the difference between the old lava field and the new, and the interplay of lava and river.

Stick to the trails marked with the yellow stakes, as some areas of the lava field are still unstable; other areas are off-limits due to the heat still being generated, and toxic fumes. Where you can walk, it's a surreal experience, your boots crunching on the gravel-like lava, with little puffs of ash rising from your footfalls in places, a reminder that this all happened very recently.

Park rangers at Drekagil provide information and safety precautions about Holuhraun and offer free one-hour walking tours starting at the car park (once daily mid-July to mid-August). Some Askja day tours also visit Holuhraun.

Investigating Askja & Its Two Crater Lakes
Cerluean waters, sensory delights in hell

The utterly remote and inspiring **Askja caldera** is the main destination for all tours in this northeastern part of the highlands. This immense 50-sq-km caldera shouldn't be missed – as you walk into the multicoloured snow-rimmed site you'll find it difficult to imagine the forces that created it.

The cataclysm that made it possible happened relatively recently (by geological standards at least – in 1875) when 2 cu km of tephra was propelled from the volcano. The force was so strong that debris landed in Continental Europe. Ash poisoned cattle in northern Iceland, sparking a wave of emigration to America.

After the initial eruption, a magma chamber collapsed and created a humongous, craterous 11-sq-km hole, 300m below the rim of the original crater. Part of this new depression filled with water and became the lake **Öskjuvatn**, the second-deepest in Iceland at 220m.

In the eruption a vent near the northeastern corner of the lake exploded and formed the tephra crater **Víti**, which contains geothermal water. This is one of two well-known craters called Víti, the other being at Krafla near Mývatn. (FYI: Víti means 'hell' in Icelandic.)

Wait for your first glimpse of the sapphire-blue lake Öskjuvatn, at the heart of the crater, as you crunch through sienna and magenta stones. The lake stands in contrast to the milky cerulean waters inside the small, steep crater Víti, adjacent to the caldera.

Although a bit on the chilly side (temperatures are around 25°C), a dip in Víti's milky blue pool is a sometimes-highlight of an Askja adventure (sometimes done sans swimsuit). Park officials carefully monitor the lake and sometimes close it to swimmers due to low PH levels and ongoing uncertainty regarding volcanic activity.

From Drekagil an 8km road leads to the Askja car park (which has toilets), and then it's a gorgeous 2.5km walk into and through the caldera (easy to moderate, depending on snow melt and weather conditions) across lava fields to reach Víti and the lake. Free, ranger-led, one-hour hikes leave from the Askja car park daily mid-July to mid-August.

For longer hikes, the closest huts and camping are at Drekagil (p341) and the more inviting, fertile area at Herðubreiðarlindir (p339). Bring your own food (none for sale here) and picnic by the Drekagil huts or on Öskjuvatn's shores on a fine-weather day.

Expanding into the Kverkfjöll Route
Get even more remote

Not literally far from Askja, but a veritable world away, the Kverkfjöll (pronounced *kverk*-fyutl) route creeps across the highlands to the Kverkfjöll area at the northern margins of the Vatnajökull ice cap.

(continues on p346)

FROM HIGHLAND LORE TO LUNAR LANDERS

The highlands are the setting of countless tales about Fjalla-Eyvindur ('Eyvindur of the Mountains'), a charming but incurable 18th-century kleptomaniac. He fled into the highlands with his wife and today you'll see hideouts attributed to him and hear lore of his ability to survive in impossible conditions while always staying one jump ahead of his pursuers.

If sci-fi is more your scene, visit the otherworldly grey-sand desert and jagged lava formations of **Ódáðahraun**, where 1960s NASA astronauts of the *Apollo* mission twice made astro-geologic field-training trips in the area south of the F910 east of Askja and near Drekagil. Nowadays NASA uses the area to test Mars Exploration Rovers.

DRIVING TOUR

Best of the Highlands

This route runs south off the Ring Road in Iceland's northeast, and plunges you into a highland world of high plateaus, ice-blue rivers and oasis-like springs, all the way to the northern rim of the Vatnajökull ice cap at Kverkfjöll. It's an incredible drive, but not for the faint-hearted – you'll need a high-clearance 4WD and 4WD experience. Or join a tour and let someone else do the hard driving for you!

❶ Hrossaborg

Setting south off the Ring Road down Rte F88 at Hrossaborg, around 35km east of Reykjahlíð, can feel like casting off into an ocean from a deserted shore. Hrossaborg itself is a 10,000-year-old crater shaped like an amphitheatre, used as a film set for the Tom Cruise sci-fi flick *Oblivion* (2013). It's a glorious spot, especially the views from the crater rim.

The Drive: The 57km route to Herðubreið is flat, following the Jökulsá á Fjöllum river. There are two river crossings. After hypnotic lava- and flood-washed plains, you reach Herðubreiðarlindir.

❷ Herðubreið & Herðubreiðarlindir

Your reward for a route that meanders across tephra expanses and winds circuitously through rough, tyre-abusing sections of the 4400-sq-km Ódáðahraun (pronounced o-dow-tha-roin; Evil Deeds Lava Field), is Herðubreið (p341), one of Iceland's most loved mountains. The view from the summit is extraordinary, but we don't recommend you go it alone. Park your car at the stunning

Kverkfjöll

Herðubreiðarlindir (p339) oasis area and admire the view, then join a tour or take a guide.

The Drive: It's only 33km from the Herðubreið turnoff to Drekagil; the route changes name from the F88 to the F910 after 20km.

❸ Drekagil

Drekagil (or Dreki to its friends) is the gateway to some of the most celebrated attractions in the Icelandic highlands. Hike up **Dragon Gorge** (p341), stand in awe at nature's awesome power and the sapphire-blue lake from the snowy rim of **Öskjuvatn** (p343), go for a swim (if allowed) in **Víti**.

The Drive: Return 13km back towards Herðubreið, then take the F910 south, then branch off onto the equally southbound F903.

❹ Hvannalindir

Hvannalindir (p346) makes up for Iceland's dearth of trees with lush vegetation of the deepest greens in the spare landscapes of the highlands. Hvannalindir is a magical place, and – not for the first time in Iceland – you'll find yourself shaking your head in disbelief. Enjoy distant views of Vatnajökull with its high mountains and snaking tongues of ice.

The Drive: Meander south and southwest until you reach the F902. As you go, watch for the paired and pyramid-like Upptyppingar hills.

❺ Kverkfjöll

Kverkfjöll is a cluster of peaks, the third highest in Iceland, formed by a large central volcano and it's partially capped by the ice of Kverkjökull (a northern tongue of Vatnajökull). There are few finer views in Iceland than the approach to Kverkjökull from the north. Kverkfjöll also refers to the hot-spring-filled **ice caves** (p346) that often form beneath the eastern margin of the Dyngjujökull ice due to the heavy geothermal activity in this area.

View from Virkisfell

KVERKFJÖLL PRACTICALITIES

Without a robust 4WD vehicle, the only way to visit is on a tour. If you do have your own vehicle, you can park and walk up to the viewing area for the mouths of the ice caves (entrance strictly prohibited) – anywhere further is highly ill-advised without a guide.

Some summers, the park rangers stationed at Sigurðarskáli hut offer guided hikes onto the Kverkjökull outlet glacier or to the geothermal area at 1700m, known as Hveradalur. Email *ferdaf@ferdaf.is* or call 863 9236 (in summer) to see what tours are being offered.

Fjalladýrð (from Möðrudalur) and **Geo Travel** (from Askja) offer two-day tours to Kverkfjöllkja. **Glacier Journey** (p171) guides snowmobile rides for experienced snowmobilers.

(continued from p343)

Along the rugged access road F902 (off Rte F910), thrilling sites include the twin pyramid-shaped **Upptyppingar hills** near the Jökulsá á Fjöllum bridge, and the **Hvannalindir** oasis, about 20km north of **Sigurðarskáli Hut** (Kverkfjöll's accommodation, campsite and information base). Check *vatnajokulsthjodgardur.is* for information and hiking ideas.

Down in Kverkfjöll, a 2km-return marked hike from behind Sigurðarskáli Hut takes you up **Virkisfell** (1108m) for a spectacular view over Kverkfjöll and the headwaters of the Jökulsá á Fjöllum (pronounced yuk-ul-sow ow fyu-tloom).

Besides being the source of the roiling Jökulsá á Fjöllum, central Iceland's greatest river, Kverkfjöll is also one of Iceland's largest geothermal areas. The lower **Kverkfjöll Ice Caves** lie 3km from the Sigurðarskáli hut; they're about a 15-minute walk from the 4WD track's end. Here the hot river flows beneath the cold glacier ice, and clouds of steam swirl over the river. It is not possible to enter the caves (they have claimed the life of one person), but depending on the year you can see different openings in the glacier ice.

Ranger-led tours continue up onto the glacier itself. The longer guided tours head over the glacier to the remarkable **Hveradalur** geothermal area. Always log any independent hike plans with the rangers.

In addition to Rte F88, the road to Kverkfjöll (F902; in Icelandic known as Kverkfjalaleið) usually opens mid- to late June. The Kverkfjöll route connects Möðrudalur (70km east of Mývatn, off the Ring Road) with the Sigurðarskáli hut via the F905, F910 and F902. Or, after visiting Askja, follow up with a 70km trip to Kverkfjöll by driving south along the F902. Drivers note: the petrol stop at Möðrudalur is the last place to fill up.

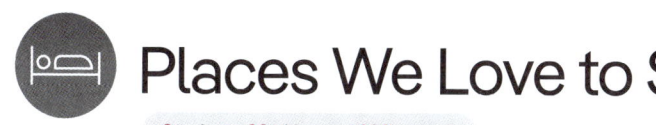

Places We Love to Stay

€ Budget €€ Midrange €€€ Top End

Kjölur Route MAP p331

Islandshestar Huts € There are three well-appointed but simple mountain huts on or just off Kjölur route: **Fremstaver** (N 64°27'02.6', W 19°56'25.9'; on the south slopes of the mountain Bláfell); **Árbúðir** (N 64°609.036', W 19°702.947'; on the banks of the Svartá river, about 42km north of Gullfoss) and **Gíslaskáli** (N 64°44'36.2', W 19°25'58.5; 4km north of the turnoff to Kerlingarfjöll).

Ferðafélag Ísland Huts € In the marshy grasslands northeast of Hvítárvatn is Ferðafélag Íslands' **Hvítárnes Hut** (p332; N 64°37.007', W 19°45.394'), which has a volunteer warden for most of July and August and sleeps 30. Others include **Þverbrekknamúli Hut** (p334; 64°43.100', W 19°36.860'), about 4km southeast of the mini ice cap Hrútfell; and **Þjófadalir** (p334; N 64°48.900', W 19°42.510'), at the foot of the mountain Rauðkollur, about 12km southwest of Hveravellir; neither is accessible by car.

Highland Base Kerlingarfjöll (p333) **€€€** There is a broad range of hotel, huts, houses and camping at this great, remote centre. It operates two mountain huts in the area and offers lots of activities.

Sprengisandur Route MAP p336

Laugafell Hut (p338) **€** Stay near Laugafell at the Ferðafélag Akureyrar hut, with 35 beds, a kitchen and a magnificent, geothermally heated, natural swimming pool. There's a warden on-site in July and August.

Nýidalur Hut € With a campsite, two huts (sleeping up to 79 people) and lots of hiking, Nýidalur makes for a great break in a Sprengisandur journey. The huts have kitchen facilities, showers and a summer warden (July and August). Book your bed in advance. Campers cannot use hut facilities.

Highland Center Hrauneyjar €€€ Somewhat unexpectedly, in the middle of lava and scree fields west of Þórisvatn in the Hrauneyjar region, you'll find Highland Center Hrauneyjar's year-round guesthouse and hotel (thus it's busy and charges high rates). The guesthouse has simple, smallish rooms and sleeping-bag accommodation, and a restaurant. The hotel complex has larger, more luxurious rooms; a bar and smart gourmet restaurant; and a hot-pot and sauna about 1.4km away. The latter is only open for groups of eight or more from October to May.

Askja Route MAP p340

Þorsteinsskáli Hut € Verdant Herðubreiðarlindir has an information office staffed by summer wardens, a campsite and the 30-bed, cosy lodge with showers and kitchen. Book your hut beds in advance.

Drekagil Huts € The Dreki huts, operated by Ferðafélag Akureyrar (Touring Club of Akureyri), sleep a total of 60, and there are showers, a kitchen, a ranger information centre (8am to 7pm) and a warden here. Camping is also permitted, but the wind (bringing dust) and cold may be oppressive for tent campers (consider the lusher site at Herðubreiðarlindir, 35km away).

Sigurðarskáli Hut € At Kverkfjöll, the large Sigurðarskáli hut has comfortable accommodation (sleeps 75) in a new hut, plus a well-maintained campsite. There are cooking facilities, toilets and showers. Campers pay extra if they want access to the kitchen and other facilities.

Möðrudalur €€€ With a cafe and petrol pump on the Ring Road, and a range of accommodation (stylish hotel-standard rooms, a simpler guesthouse and camping), it's one of the best such places in Iceland. It has an excellent restaurant, as well as being a travel hub for organising trips down the Askja Route and beyond.

TOOLKIT

Landmannalaugar (p146)

TOOLKIT

The chapters in this section cover the most important topics you'll need to know about in Iceland. They're full of nuts-and-bolts information and valuable insights to help you understand and navigate Iceland and get the most out of your trip.

Arriving
p350

Getting Around
p351

Money
p352

Accommodation
p353

Family Travel
p354

Health & Safe Travel
p355

Food, Drink & Nightlife
p356

Responsible Travel
p358

LGBTIQ+ Travellers
p360

Accessible Travel
p361

Take Care of Iceland
p362

Nuts & Bolts
p363

Language
p364

349

Arriving

Most international travellers flying to Iceland arrive at Keflavík International Airport, about 49km southwest of Reykjavík. Akureyri International Airport also has a couple of direct flights a week to London and Manchester in the UK. A weekly ferry service runs from northern Denmark to Seyðisfjörður and back, stopping at the Faroe Islands each way. Several cruise lines sail to Iceland from Canada, Europe and the UK.

Visas
Citizens or residents of the US, Australia, Canada, the UK, Japan, New Zealand, and EU and Schengen countries do not need a visa for visits under 90 days, in any period of 180 days.

Wi-Fi
Fast, free wi-fi is available at Keflavík International Airport and on local and airport buses. Most accommodation and many bars, restaurants and tourist sites also provide free wi-fi.

Border Crossing
You will need to go through passport control if you're coming from outside the Schengen Area. This includes visitors from North America, the UK and Australia.

Airport Buses
Airport buses are coordinated with flight schedules and are the most economical option – less than a third of the cost of a taxi from Keflavík International Airport to Reykjavík.

	Keflavík to Reykjavík	Akureyri Airport to city centre	Ísafjörður Airport to city centre
BUS	45–65min from 2280kr	7min free	7min 1000kr
TAXI	40min from 17,000kr	5min from 2000kr	6min from 3700kr
RENTAL CAR	40min from 20,000kr /day	5min from 16,370kr /day	6min from 15,000kr /day

AIRPORT SERVICES

Keflavík is the best-equipped of Iceland's airports. Several companies offer pick-up services that can include everything from assistance with baggage to personal escorts through security. Travellers can request VAT refunds at the airport by submitting original purchase receipts and Tax Free forms signed by retailers. You'll quickly notice that everything is expensive in Iceland, including alcohol and cigarettes. To save money, stock up at the duty-free shop before leaving Keflavík International Airport. Services are limited at Iceland's smaller airports. Airports in Akureyri and Ísafjörður have cafes. There's also a postbox for VAT forms in Akureyri.

Getting Around

Nothing beats the freedom of renting a car in Iceland, especially if you plan to explore small towns and off-the-beaten-path natural wonders.

TRAVEL COSTS

Bus
670kr per ride in Reykjavík

Car rental
Around 15,000kr per day

Petrol
Approx 315kr per litre

EV charging
Around 420kr per 100km

Road Conditions

Major roads in Iceland, like the Ring Road (Rte 1), are paved and well maintained throughout. Secondary roads may be gravel roads but are accessible to all types of vehicles. F roads are challenging roads, sometimes over mountains or through rivers, that should only be attempted by experienced 4WD drivers.

Trains & Buses

Unlike most of Europe, there's no public train system in Iceland. Reykjavík has an extensive bus system, but it's harder to get around by bus beyond Selfoss on the southern coast and Borgarnes to the north. Akureyri, Ísafjörður, Reykjanesbær and the Eastfjords also have local bus systems.

TIP

Download the Strætó app to purchase individual bus tickets. Activate your ticket before you ride.

RIDESHARING & HITCHHIKING

Iceland has about as many cars as it has people. And while it doesn't allow ridesharing services like Lyft and Uber, it does have a vibrant carpool scene. People submit routes they're driving on *samferda.net*, and passengers can request rides and offer to split costs. Because public transport is limited outside of Reykjavík, carpooling is a popular option for getting between cities. It's also not uncommon to see hitchhikers, particularly along Rte 1.

Ships & Ferries

Iceland is becoming an increasingly popular cruise destination with several lines sailing to Iceland from North America and Europe. It's also getting easier to circumnavigate the island on a cruise ship. There's a weekly ferry service from Denmark via the Faroe Islands (p316).

Planes

A domestic airport in Reykjavík connects the capital to three Icelandic cities: Akureyri in the north, Egilsstaðir in the east and Ísafjörður in the Westfjords.

Cycling

Iceland's Ring Road is a major draw for cyclists, but there are no bike lanes. Cold, rain and wind can make for uncomfortable conditions and contingency planning is key. Bike rentals are available in Reykjavík and a handful of other towns. Off-road biking is also popular and many trails allow bikes.

DRIVING ESSENTIALS

Drive on the right

Seat belts are required for all occupants

.05
Blood alcohol limit is 0.05%

Money

CURRENCY: ICELANDIC KRÓNA (KR OR ISK)

Cash or Card?

Don't feel pressured to visit an ATM. Most places in Iceland accept credit cards and digital payments, even in remote towns and for small purchases. Some public restrooms require payment; coins can be useful here, but many also have card payment options.

Chips & Pins

If you don't have a chip-based credit card, you'll need a pin to use your plastic in Iceland. Pins aren't required with chip-based cards, which are predominantly used for contactless payments.

Taxes & Refunds

Iceland's standard VAT is 24%. Books, food and accommodation are taxed at a lower 11%. Visitors who live outside of Iceland can claim a tax refund on transactions of 6000kr or more – ask for a form to fill in and a receipt from the shop, and drop these off at the airport.

Tipping

Taxes and service charges are always included in Iceland. Tipping is not expected, but rounding up restaurant bills or leaving an additional tip for exceptional service is always appreciated. Service charges may also be included in bills.

HOW MUCH FOR A...

Espresso **500kr**

Museum ticket **2500kr**

Golden Circle tour **10,000kr**

Northern Lights tour **9000kr**

HOW TO... Save Some Króna

The best way to save money is to limit restaurant and pub visits. Book campsites or self-catering accommodation and cook for yourself as much as possible. When you do go out to eat, opt for lunches at casual cafes, hot-dog stands or food halls. Alcohol is heavily taxed in Iceland – it is one of the most expensive places to drink in Europe, and US20 glasses of wine aren't unusual. Stock up at airport duty free before you hit the road.

LOCAL TIP

Skip the tours and self-drive with a group to save money – big attractions are easily accessible and mostly free (although watch out for parking fees). Smaller remote attractions don't charge for parking.

ICELAND FOR FREE

If you're looking for a cheap holiday, Iceland isn't it. After flights, a large portion of budgets go on accommodation and eating out. Then fill your itinerary with free activities. Visit waterfalls, national parks and geothermal areas across the country. Go hiking. Take in epic views. Walk across the red lava fields, black beaches, visit glacial lakes and nature reserves.

Check out Heiðmörk Nature Reserve, Harpa concert hall and the Reykjavík Botanic Garden. Set out in search of the Northern Lights. Believe it or not, the best things in Iceland are free.

Accommodation

Hotels

Iceland is expensive for accommodation. Many of Iceland's most luxurious hotels are located in and around Reykjavík, but you'll find a few scattered across the countryside. Don't be surprised if the nicest properties set you back 100,000kr a night during the busiest seasons. Bubbles and cabins with expansive glass walls are a way to experience the Northern Lights without the cold. Pay around 30,000kr to stay in one.

Hostels & Guesthouses

Hostels and guesthouses tend to be more affordable than hotels, but you may need to share bathrooms and other facilities. Expect to pay at least 5000kr for a hostel dorm. Some places offer private rooms, sometimes with ensuite bathrooms, or family rooms with plenty of space for everyone.

Sleeping-Bag Accommodation

Bring your own sleeping bag or sheets and you'll save money at some guesthouses, rural hotels, hostels and farmstays. Sleeping-bag accommodation is often dorms with bunk beds but no sheets, but that isn't always the case – you could find yourself sleeping in an attic or with a room to yourself. Expect to pay up to 50% less by choosing sleeping-bag accommodation.

Camping

Camping is an affordable way to see Iceland but is only allowed at designated campsites or private property with the owner's permission. Expect to pay between 1500kr and 2500kr per night per person. Iceland's network of campsites have toilets; some offer cooking facilities, heated lounge areas for communal eating and playgrounds for children.

HOW MUCH FOR A NIGHT IN A…

Hostel dorm
5000kr

3-star hotel
25,000kr

4-star hotel
40,000kr

Van Life

Campervans or 'Van Life' has become one of the most popular ways to experience Iceland, allowing travellers to go off-grid, live in the elements (while being protected from the elements) and self-cater. Van rental starts at around 16,000kr per night. You cannot park your van just anywhere – you will still be required to use campsites, which often have electricity hook ups.

HIGH SEASON & TOURIST TAXES

Summer is peak tourist season in Iceland. Prices tend to spike for accommodation and car hire, and you'll want to book tours and activities in advance as many are liable to sell out completely. Accommodation taxes were suspended from April 2020 to December 2023, but since January 2024 taxes have been reinstated. Hotels and guesthouses charge 600kr and campsites 300kr per room per overnight stay. For cruise passengers it's 1000kr per passenger, per night. Taxes are usually included in quoted prices.

Family Travel

Iceland doesn't need amusement parks or exciting rides to entertain children. The entire country is a natural wonderland that feels like exploring another realm. Go horse riding across red lava fields or whale watching off the coast. Explore ice caves and check out geysers. Learn about volcanoes. Chase Northern Lights or go in search of elves, trolls and fairies. Your kids won't get bored here.

Sights

With its ample natural wonders and wide variety of outdoor activities, Iceland may be the world's best playground. You'll find lots of kid-friendly hikes. Activities including snowmobiling, ATVs and ice-cave experiences welcome children with some age restrictions. The Blue Lagoon allows children two and older. The Sky Lagoon doesn't admit children under 12.

Facilities

Some hostels and guesthouses offer family rooms, which may help you save some krónur. Some hotels offer connecting rooms. Campsites offer discounted rates for children, and some campsites include playgrounds. You'll find lots of kid-friendly fare like hot dogs, hamburgers and chicken nuggets across the country, and many restaurants have children's menus. Most restaurants have at least one bathroom with a changing table.

KID-FRIENDLY PICKS

Perlan (p89)
Wander through a human-made glacier indoors.

Lava Centre (p136)
Learn about volcanoes and experience an earthquake for a few seconds.

Raufarhólshellir Lava Tunnel (p133)
Walk across a lava field and into one of Iceland's longest lava tunnels.

Húsavík Whale Watching (p280)
Take a boat tour from Húsavík harbour to look for blue whales.

Reykjavík Puffin Tour (p81)
Take a boat tour from Reykjavík's Old Harbour to look for puffins.

Laugardalslaug (p86)
This Reykjavík swimming pool is practically a waterpark.

Car Seats

Car-hire companies also rent car seats. Blue Car Rental, for example, offers booster seats for a one-time charge of 1000kr. Baby seats for children up to three incur a one-time fee of 4000kr. Child seats for children between four and eight are around 5000kr.

Breastfeeding

Breastfeeding is such a non-issue here that an Icelandic government official once addressed parliament during a live television broadcast while breastfeeding her six-week-old, and it was no big deal.

GLACIERS & ICE CAVES

Take kids six and older on a journey through a natural ice cave. Strap on crampons and head into the **Katla Ice Cave** (p151) to traverse icy paths and check out the various shades of blue and black. These markers tell stories of volcanic eruptions, glaciers and the formation of Iceland. Or head to Jökulsárlón glacier lagoon, which might feel a bit like seeing the home of *Frozen*'s Elsa of Arendelle. Most glacier snowmobiling tours are open to children eight and older, though drivers must be 18 and hold a valid driving licence.

Health & Safe Travel

INSURANCE

Iceland is generally considered a safe place to travel, with low levels of petty crime. One main risk is changeable weather, which can alter trail and road conditions. Eruptions and earthquakes can also happen here. Travel insurance policies offer coverage for these situations, but check the fine print to see if potentially dangerous activities like paragliding, ATVs or ice climbing are covered.

Personal Safety

Iceland is one of the safest countries in the world for visitors. It reports few violent crimes and murders compared with other countries. Mass shootings and sectarian violence are non-existent, and burglary rates are low. Theft, sexual assaults and car accidents do occur but are unlikely. Use common sense and never leave your drink unattended.

Nature

There are no mosquitoes or snakes, and only one kind of wasp in Iceland; the most dangerous creature is the timid Arctic fox. Animals won't try to kill you in Iceland, but nature might. Never walk on glacial ice without a guide or swim in a glacial lagoon – hypothermia can set in within minutes. Always be prepared for the weather to change, sometimes drastically, in minutes.

WEATHER RESOURCES

Check road conditions and weather with handy websites *safetravel.is*, *weather.is* and *vedur.is* for detailed localised forecasts.

ROAD SIGNS

Speed limit
Speed limits in kilometres

Gravel road
Bumpy gravel road ahead

4x4 only
Off-limits to anyone without a 4WD

Extremely difficult
Challenging terrain, even for experienced drivers

Road Safety

Iceland's roads present unique hazards that include wildlife, rivers and unpredictable weather. Follow speed limits, check weather conditions frequently, and don't attempt an F road without a 4WD. If you're skidding on a gravel road, turn into the skid as you would on ice to regain control of your vehicle. Take it slow on high mountain roads with sheer drops.

VOLCANIC ERUPTIONS

Historically volcanoes in Iceland have erupted every four to five years, but their frequency is increasing. They're now expected every year, particularly on the Reykjanes Peninsula. Eruptions are typically localised, but can pose health hazards from volcanic gases and ash. There are numerous warning systems in place for eruptions. Keep an eye on the Icelandic Meteorological Office website *(vedur.is)* for updates if travelling near an active volcano. Stay on designated trails and roads, and out of hazard zones.

Food, Drink & Nightlife

When to Eat

Breakfast (9–11am) Most coffee shops don't open until 8am. Many cafes open at 10am or later.

Lunch (11am–2pm) Many restaurants close in the late afternoon. Expect limited dining options between 3pm and 5pm.

Dinner (7–9pm) Restaurant kitchens start closing before 10pm, and it's hard to find anything to eat after then.

MENU DECODER

Matseðill Menu
Barnamatseðill Children's menu
Morgunmatur Breakfast
Smjör Butter
Drykki Drinks
Vatn Water
Bjór Beer
Eftirréttur Dessert
Bragðarefur Ice cream swirled with three toppings
Reikningur Bill
Servíetta Napkin
Fiskur dagsins Fish of the day
Flatkaka Med Hangikjot Flatbread with smoked lamb
Grænmetisæta Vegetarian
Sólagrænmetisætur Vegan
Kjöt Meat
Hangikjöt Smoked lamb
Kjúklingur Chicken
Hákarl Fermented shark, usually Greenland or sleeper sharks (check this is ethically sourced before ordering)
Harðfiskur Stockfish or dried fish
Plokkfiskur Fish stew (typically boiled cod or haddock, and often served with potatoes)
Pýlsur Hot dog
Humar A small Icelandic lobster, also known as langoustine
Rúgbrauð Icelandic rye bread, traditionally baked in the ground at a geothermal hot spring
Skyr A thick creamy yogurt that's technically a cheese
Ávextir Fruits
Kleinur Doughnut twist

Pick the Right Milk

HOW TO... Iceland has a vibrant dairy industry and one of the highest milk-consumption rates in the world. And while it's a small country, there's a surprising amount of variety in the Icelandic milk scene. This can be incredibly confusing, especially if your Icelandic is nonexistent. Most coffee shops offer dairy milk and non-dairy alternatives like almond milk, soy milk, coconut milk and oat milk.

Nýmjólk Full-fat milk
Léttmjólk Low-fat milk
Undanrenna Skimmed milk
Fjörmjólk Fortified and enriched skimmed milk
AB Mjolk Basically runny *skyr*. This will feel like adding a dollop of yoghurt to your coffee.
G-Mjolk Milk processed at ultra-high temperatures that's typically added to coffee.
Kókómjólk Chocolate milk; popular among adults as well as kids.

Land of Greenhouses

It won't take long for you to notice that the Icelandic countryside is dotted with greenhouses. These allow Icelandic farmers to grow cucumbers, strawberries, lettuces, peppers, mushrooms, herbs and flowers year-round. At **Friðheimar** (p127) in South Iceland, guests can dine inside a greenhouse on farm-fresh tomatoes grown on-site at the family-owned farm. Or head to **Farmers Bistro** (p127) where you can sample the bounty from Flúðasveppir, Iceland's only mushroom farm. It doesn't get any more farm-to-table than this.

FROM LEFT: NEW AFRICA/SHUTTERSTOCK, ALESIA.BIERLIEZOVA/SHUTTERSTOCK

HOW MUCH FOR A...

Coffee
400–600kr

Beer
1050–1800kr

Glass of wine
1500–1800kr

Pýlsur (hot dog)
400–700kr

Burger
2700–3300kr

Main course (dinner)
3000–9000kr

Soft drink
500–700kr

Dozen eggs
600–900kr

HOW TO... Eat Skyr

Skyr is a rich, creamy dairy product that's packaged like a yoghurt but technically defined as a cheese, like ricotta or mascarpone. Icelanders have been eating *skyr*, which is made from cow's milk, for centuries. It's high in protein but low in fat and packed with calcium and B vitamins.

Skyr can be eaten for breakfast or as a snack, or is used to make desserts like cheesecake, crème brûlée or an Icelandic twist on tiramisu. It can also form the base for drinks and smoothies, and there's a type of runny *skyr* that's essentially a milk.

Skyr is often eaten on the go, with individual servings packaged with disposable spoons. Pick up a carton at a shop or visit a *skyr* bar for a bowl topped with fruit, nuts, peanut butter and more. You may opt for a *skyr* and oatmeal breakfast like many Icelanders do.

You'll encounter *skyr* on lots of restaurant menus and a *skyr* bowl for breakfast is popular at many cafes in Reykjavík. At **Cafe Loki** (p69), you can try a *skyr* cake or *skyr* as a pastry topping. **Tapas barinn** on Vesturgata in Reykjavík is known for using *skyr* as a base for sauces and in its mousses.

To try *skyr* from the source, head to **Efstidalur II** (p117), a farm that makes *skyr*, feta and ice cream on-site. In Höfn, don't miss the *skyr* volcano at **Pakkhús** (p186).

Did You Know?

It takes four cups of milk to make a single cup of *skyr*, and it's that milk that makes *skyr* so much thicker and creamier than traditional yoghurts.

ICELAND & BEER: IT'S COMPLICATED

Icelanders were beer drinkers from the time this island was settled until prohibition came into effect in 1915. Wine was legalised in 1922 and spirits followed in 1935, but beer remained illegal until 1989. Icelandic lawmakers took the stance that beer would lead to more depravity because of its cheaper price. They declared that beer could contain a maximum of 2.25% alcohol by volume, half that of the average beer.

As Iceland fought for its independence, beer became closely associated with its Danish rulers. Drinking beer was considered unpatriotic. For years, home brewing and smuggling were the only ways to get full-strength beer in Iceland. Some people took to spiking their 2.25% beer with Brennivín, a cumin-and-caraway-flavoured local spirit that tastes a bit like liquorice. In 1979 an Icelandic businessman argued he should have the same right to buy beer at Iceland's duty-free shop as foreign visitors and flight crews. Davið Scheving Thorsteinsson lost his case, but his action helped to change attitudes in the country.

Beer became legal again in Iceland on 1 March 1989. Nowadays you can find quality craft breweries across the country. Beer is also sold at government liquor stores. Icelandic beer is made with Icelandic water, giving these lagers, pilsners, pale ales and stouts an exceptional taste that can't be matched. The two largest brewers in Iceland are Egill Skallagrímsson Brewery and Víking, but there are more than two dozen smaller beer brands. Look out for the words *brugghús* and *ölgerð* – both are markers of a brewery.

Responsible Travel

Climate Change & Travel

It's impossible to ignore the impact we have when travelling; Lonely Planet urges all travellers to engage with their travel carbon footprint, which will mainly come from air travel. While there often isn't an alternative, travellers can look to minimise the number of flights they take, opt for newer aircrafts and use cleaner ground transport, such as trains. One proposed solution – purchasing carbon offsets – unfortunately does not cancel out the impact of individual flights. While most destinations will depend on air travel for the foreseeable future, for now, pursuing ground-based travel where possible is the best course of action.

The **UN Carbon Offset Calculator** shows how flying impacts a household's emissions

The **ICAO's carbon emissions calculator** allows visitors to analyse the CO_2 generated by point-to-point journeys

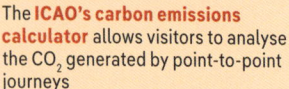

Order Fish Not Beef

Beef production is one of the largest drivers of climate change. Minimise the environmental impact of your holiday by opting for the fish of the day in this seafood capital of the world.

Bring a Water Bottle

Iceland is known for its pure, clean water. Bring a reusable water bottle, or pick up a new one in Iceland, and refill it at the tap.

Iceland is a geothermal energy pioneer that uses renewable sources to generate all of its electricity.

The orange Vakinn label shows that a tourism business meets the Icelandic Tourist Board's standards for ethical, professional and environmentally sustainable operations. There's a list of certified companies at *vakinn.is/en/certified-companies*.

EMBRACE SLOW TRAVEL

Make the most of your journey by settling into places and embracing slow travel. Use local transport and become part of a community. Share meals and transport, to minimise the carbon footprint of your trip.

STAY OFF THE MOSS

There's nothing Icelanders hate more than tourists damaging precious moss that can take hundreds of years to grow back. As tempting as it may be, stay off the moss, especially if there are signs telling visitors to keep off.

Rent Electric or Hybrid

You'll find lots of electric and hybrid car-hire options, and charging stations across the country. Some rental companies include free charging.

Shop Local

One of the things that makes Iceland so charming is its independent restaurants, bars and shops. Help keep these open by eating, drinking and shopping at locally owned businesses. Opt for locally grown produce labelled *íslenskt*.

Time Your Visit Just Right

The peak summer months can put a lot of pressure on Icelandic businesses and the environment. Visit at other times of the year to remove some of that pressure and save some money.

Stay on the Road

Icelandic roads can be narrow and rarely have hard shoulders. Avoid pulling over on natural features and in places without a hard shoulder unless it's an emergency – no matter how good the photo opportunity is.

Don't Eat Whale

About 2% of Icelanders report regularly eating whale meat; tourists are its most frequent consumer. Conservation groups are urging visitors to meet the whales not eat them, and more than 60 restaurants have pledged to stop serving whale.

Purchase carbon offsets to fund wetland restoration through the Icelandic Wetland Fund at *votlendi.is/carbon-offset*.

Iceland is home to the world's largest carbon-capture facility. The Mammoth plant in Hellisheiði can remove up to 36,000 metric tonnes of carbon each year, roughly like removing 8600 cars from the road, and runs all on renewable geothermal power.

2030 Car Pledge

Around half of the new cars registered in Iceland each year are electric or hybrid, totalling 11% of all cars. Iceland plans to ban the import of petrol and diesel cars by 2030.

RESOURCES

visiticeland.com/carbon-offset
Calculate the carbon footprint of your trip.

globalclimatepledge.com/global/iceland
Promise to be a responsible tourist in Iceland by signing the Icelandic Pledge.

CLOCKWISE FROM TOP LEFT: ALEXWALTNER/SHUTTERSTOCK, HAPPY WHALE/SHUTTERSTOCK, EUROBANKS/SHUTTERSTOCK

LGBTIQ+ Travellers

Icelanders are open and accepting of LGBTIQ+ travellers, and Iceland is considered one of the world's most friendly countries for people who identify as gay, lesbian, bisexual or transgender. Iceland was among the first to give same-sex couples equal access to adoption and IVF. Both Icelandic Parliament and the Church of Iceland support same-sex marriage, defined as a union between individuals.

Reykjavík Pride

This epic **Pride event** (hinsegindagar.is) takes over Reykjavík for a week each August. Thousands of people flood the Icelandic capital for what's become one of the country's largest annual events. The parade is the biggest part of Reykjavík Pride, but the event also includes lectures, concerts, a family festival and a post-parade dance party. Reykjavík held its first Pride parade in 2000 after several years of local protests. Some 100,000 people celebrate Pride in Reykjavík every year, a number equal to 70% of the city's population.

REYKJAVIK BEAR

If you're a bear (gay man who is larger, hairy and ruggedly masculine etc) or bear admirer, Iceland's premier bear party is an Icelandic event not to miss. This festival was started by a group of volunteers more than 15 years ago and has since grown into an international event attracting visitors from around the world. **Reykjavík Bear** (reykjavikbear.is) includes a Golden Circle Tour, a shirtless party, a visit to the Blue Lagoon and a night of clubbing.

Gay Reykjavík

Reykjavík is where you'll find the beating heart of the Icelandic gay scene. The city is so small there's no clearly defined gay neighbourhood. There's a gay bar in Reykjavík called **Kiki Queer Bar**, and you'll see rainbow flags and stickers in the windows of lots of other businesses.

DATING APPS

Tinder and Grindr are both popular in Iceland, but remember this is a country so small that there's an app to help people avoid dating potential relatives (islendingaapp.is). Whichever app you choose, expect to see the same small pool of people, especially outside of Reykjavík.

The National Queer Organisation

Samtökin '78 (samtokin78.is) was founded in 1978 and has been a driving force in promoting acceptance across Iceland. As well as counselling and support groups, it has an extensive offering of youth programs and is developing a queer certification program for workplaces in Iceland.

TOUR COMPANIES

Pink Iceland (pinkiceland.is) is a gay-owned tour operator founded by a local lesbian couple in 2011. This company won't just arrange your tours, they also arrange weddings and are happy to answer any questions about local LGBTQIA+ culture.

Out Adventures (outadventures.com) is a Canadian company that specialises in small-group tours for LGBTQIA+ travellers. They host a few trips to Iceland each year, including a countryside and Pride trip.

Accessible Travel

Accessibility is still a work in progress in Iceland, but the country has made major strides in recent years. Lifts and accessible bathrooms are the norm in modern buildings, and wheelchair ramps are increasingly common.

Ramping Up

Many businesses along Laugavegur, Reykjavík's main shopping street, now have wheelchair ramps, thanks to Ramp Up Reykjavík. The grassroots effort has driven the construction of some 450 ramps with plans for 1500 ramps by March 2026.

Airport

Keflavík International Airport offers travellers with reduced mobility assistance with checking-in, security screening, boarding and stowing hand luggage on board. Assistance must be requested through a passenger's airline at least 48 hours ahead of their departure.

Accommodation

Look for newer hotels and holiday rentals. Buildings constructed after 2012 are required to have lifts and accessible bathrooms. Many campsites and some hostels are accessible.

RESOURCES

Wheel Map *(wheelmap.org)* An online map for searching and marking wheelchair-accessible places.

Sjálfsbjörg *(sjalfsbjorg.is/english)* The National Confederation of Physically Disabled People provides short-term mobility equipment rental and curated lists of accessible hotels, restaurants and transportation services.

Wheelchairtraveling.com Destination-specific travel content for travellers in wheelchairs.

ATTRACTIONS

Key tourist sites including Gullfoss, the Geysir geothermal area and Þingvellir National Park are wheelchair-accessible. In Reykjavík, the Harpa concert hall, Hallgrimskirkja, National Museum, Perlan and some shops along Laugavegur Street are accessible.

LAGOONS

Several of Iceland's top lagoons including the Blue Lagoon, Sky Lagoon and Laugarvatn Fontana geothermal pools are wheelchair-accessible, as are many of the country's swimming pools.

Public Transport

Public buses are wheelchair-accessible, but users must enter and exit the bus on their own. Wheelchair accessibility is limited on buses outside of Reykjavík.

Taxis

Companies provide accessible taxi services in Reykjavík, including Hreyfill and City Taxi. City Taxi offers fixed-rate rides between Reykjavík and Keflavík International Airport. Call ahead to arrange.

Iceland Unlimited *(icelandunlimited.is)* offers accessible day tours of the Golden Circle, Reykjanes Peninsula and the southern coast. **GJ Travel** *(gjtravel.is)* and **BusTravel Iceland** *(bustravel.is)* can accommodate travellers with foldable wheelchairs; however, travellers must be able to enter and exit tour buses on their own.

Take Care of Iceland

Iceland is a small country that sometimes struggles under the weight of its popularity. Nature is its biggest resource, and visitors haven't always respected the land. The country launched the Icelandic Pledge *(pledge.visiticeland.com)* in 2017 to encourage respectful tourism. Sign it online and join the effort by following these guidelines.

Leave Places as You Found Them

There's no need to carve anything anywhere to let the world know you've been to Iceland. Leave places as you've found them, and take everything you bring with you when you leave.

Don't Venture off the Road

Tyres can do a lot of damage to delicate ecosystems, so stay on roads and off the moss. Off-road driving is illegal in Iceland, and pulling over just anywhere can be dangerous for you, other drivers sharing these roads, and the nature you came to see.

Camp in Designated Areas

Just because you have a tent doesn't mean you can set it up anywhere. Wild camping isn't allowed in Iceland. Only camp at designated areas.

Park in Designated Areas

Get the owner's permission before parking on private property or set up camp at one of the country's many campsites. Parking self-sufficient campervans or motorhomes just anywhere isn't allowed; park in designated spaces at campsites.

Use Designated Toilets

Icelanders are so annoyed with tourists using nature as their toilet that they've taken to shooting videos to shame them. Try not to end up as a viral video. Public toilets are available at campsites and other locations across the country.

DON'T BE LIKE JUSTIN BIEBER

Justin Bieber's 'I'll Show You' music video, filmed in Iceland in 2015, is a good lesson on what not to do in Iceland. In the music video, Bieber goes swimming in a glacier and frolicking through a pristine canyon with jagged rocky edges and postcard-perfect views.

In reality, swimming in a glacial lagoon is incredibly dangerous. The water is also icy cold, so it would be far less pleasant than soaking in one of the many geothermal lagoons that are scattered across the country.

And that canyon Bieber frolicked through? Officials had to close it in 2019 because so many fans were damaging the moss by rolling around on it. Look closely at the Bieber video, and you'll notice the moss starting to tear in places. While it looks like a lush carpet, Icelandic moss is delicate and can take years to regrow after being trampled.

There are few things Icelanders hate more than tourists that go destroying their delicate moss for silly reasons. Don't be that tourist.

Nuts & Bolts

OPENING HOURS

Supermarkets 7am–midnight. Some open as late as 10am and close as early as 8pm.

Government-owned liquor stores (Vínbúðin) Typically 11am–6pm Monday to Saturday. Some remote stores only open between 4pm and 6pm.

Shops 9am–6pm. Weekend hours may vary.

Bars To 1am Sunday to Thursday, and as late as 5.30am on Friday and Saturday.

Internet

Free wi-fi is widely available at hotels, restaurants, attractions and public libraries, but network availability can be limited in remote areas. Portable wi-fi devices are available to rent.

Weights & Measures

Iceland uses the metric system. Distances and speeds are measured in kilometres.

Smoking

It's illegal to smoke inside restaurants, bars and clubs, but smoking is allowed outdoors.

GOOD TO KNOW

Time zone
Western European Time (equal to GMT)

Country code
354

Emergency number
112

Population
394,000

Electricity
Type C and F, 230V/50Hz

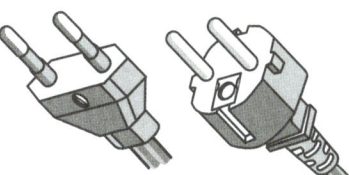

PUBLIC HOLIDAYS

There are more than a dozen public holidays in Iceland, when banks and government offices are closed. Businesses and non-essential services may be closed, and demand can be high for accommodation and restaurant tables.

The following dates are national public holidays in Iceland.

New Year's Day
1 January

Easter March or April; Maundy Thursday and Good Friday to Easter Monday (changes annually)

Labour Day 1 May

Ascension Day 18 May

Whit Sunday and **Whit Monday** May or June (changes annually)

Independence Day
17 June

Commerce Day
First Monday in August

Christmas Eve
24 December

Christmas Day
25 December

Boxing Day
26 December

Language

Most Icelanders speak English, so you'll have no problems if you don't know any Icelandic. However, any attempts to speak the local language will be much appreciated.

Basics

Hello. Halló. *ha·loh*
Goodbye. Bless. *bles*
Yes. Já. *yow*
No. Nei. *nay*
How are you? Hvað segir þú gott? *kvadh say·yir thoo got*
Fine. And you? Allt fínt. En þú? *alt feent en thoo*
Thank you. Takk/Takk fyrir. *tak/tak fi·rir*
Excuse me. Afsakið. *af·sa·kidh*
Sorry. Fyrirgefðu. *fi·rir·gev·dhu*
My name is ... Ég heiti ... *yekh hay·ti ...*
Do you speak English? Talarðu ensku?. *a·lar dhoo ens·ku*
I don't understand. Ég skil ekki. *yekh skil e·ki*

Directions

Where's the (hotel)? Hvar er (hótelið)? *kvar er (hoh·te·lidh)*
What's your address? Hvert er heimilisfangið þitt? *kvert er hay·mi·lis·fown·gidh thit*
Can you show me (on the map)? Geturðu sýnt mér (á kortinu)? *ge·tur·dhu seent myer (ow kor·ti·nu)*

Signs

Inngangur Entrance
Útgangur Exit
Opið Open
Lokað Closed
Bannað Prohibited
Snyrting/Salerni Toilets

Emergencies

Help! Hjálp! *hyowlp*
Go away! Farðu! *far·dhu*
I'm lost. Ég er villtur/villt. (m/f) *yekh er vil·tur/vilt*
Call ...! Hringdu á ...! *hring·du ow ...*
   a doctor lækni *laik·ni*
   the police lögregluna *leukh·rekh·lu·na*
Where are the toilets? Hvar er snyrtingin? *kvar er snir·tin·gin*

Eating & Drinking

What would you recommend? Hverju mælir þú með? *kver·yu mai·lir thoo medh*
Cheers! Skál! *skowl*
Do you have vegetarian food? Eruð þið með grænmetisrétti? *er·udh thidh medh grain·me·tis·rye·ti*
breakfast morgunmat *mor·gun·mat*
lunch hádegismat *how·day·yis·mat*
dinner kvöldmat *kveuld·mat*

Shopping & Services

I'm looking for ... Ég er að leita að ... *yekh er adh lay·ta adh ...*
How much is it? Hvað kostar þetta? *kvadh kos·tar the·ta*
It's faulty. Það er gallað. *thadh er gat·ladh*
Where's the ...? Hvar er ...? *kvar er ...*
   bank bankinn *bown·kin*
   market markaðurinn *mar·ka·dhu·rin*

NUMBERS

1 einn *aydn*
2 tveir *tvayr*
3 þrír *threer*
4 fjórir *fyoh·rir*
5 fimm *fim*
6 sex *seks*
7 sjö *syeu*
8 átta *ow·ta*
9 níu *nee·u*
10 tíu *tee·u*

DONATIONS TO ENGLISH

These words have their origin in Icelandic: berserk, blunder, cake, die, egg, fellow, geyser, happy, husband, ransack, saga, sky, window, yule.

Phrases to Sound Like a Local

Cool! Kúl! *kool*
No worries. Engar áhyggjur. *ayng-ahrr ow-higyrrö*
Sure. Vissulega. *viss-ö-lehkh-ah*
No way! Ekki séns! *ehky-i syens*
Just joking! Bara grín! *ba-rrah grreen*
Too bad. En leitt. *ehn layt*
What a shame. En leiðinlegt. *ehn layth-in-lehcht*
What's up? Hvað segirðu (gott)? *kvahth sagy-irr-th (gott)*
Well done! Vel gert! *vehl gyehrt*
Not bad. Ekki slæmt. *ehky-i slaimt*

GIMLI, MANITOBA, CANADA

The town of Gimli has a large Icelandic community, having been established for Icelandic immigrants fleeing poverty.

Icelandic Names

Icelanders use the ancient patronymic system, where *son* (son) or *dóttir* (daughter) is added to the father's or, less commonly, mother's first name. For example, Jónsdóttir or Gunnarsson.

Telephone book entries are listed by first names.

Icelandic Origins

Icelandic is a North Germanic language. Iceland was settled primarily by Norwegians in the 9th and 10th centuries. By the 14th century, Icelandic (Old Norse) and Norwegian had grown apart considerably, due to changes in Norwegian.

Reading the Sagas

Icelandic has changed so little through the centuries that the sagas and the *Poetic Edda*, written about 700 years ago, can be enjoyed by modern-day speakers of Icelandic.

Unique Alphabet

The Icelandic alphabet has 32 letters and includes some unique characters not found in the English alphabet, such as **þ** (thorn) and **ð** (eth). Both of these represent a 'th' sound, with 'þ' being unvoiced (as in 'think') and 'ð' being voiced (as in 'the').

Complex Grammar

Icelandic retains a complex grammar with four grammatical cases (nominative, accusative, dative and genitive) for nouns, adjectives and pronouns. This makes it a challenging language for many learners, but it also allows for great flexibility in word order, as the case endings indicate a word's function in a sentence.

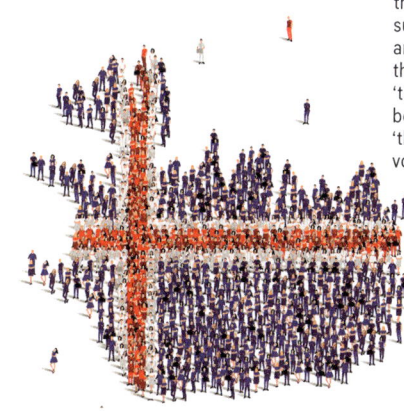

WHO SPEAKS ICELANDIC?

Icelandic *(Íslenska)* is spoken by about 390,000 people, mainly in Iceland.

THE ICELAND
STORYBOOK

Our writers delve deep into different aspects of Icelandic life

A History of Iceland in 15 Places

Viking exploration, Danish colonisation, religious conflict and modern development

Meena Thiruvengadam

p368

Meet the Icelanders

Sword-swinging, hard-headed Vikings or peace-loving, elf-whispering farmers?

Eygló Svala Arnarsdóttir

p372

Iceland Minus the Ice

In the future, Iceland will have less ice and more trees.

Egill Bjarnason

p374

Life Under Fire

Volcanoes shape the land, fertilise the soil, heat the water but also threaten life.

Eygló Svala Arnarsdóttir

p377

Iceland's Pop-Rock Juggernaut

Icelandic musicians draw on deep roots for rich modern-day creativity

Alexis Averbuck

p380

A HISTORY OF ICELAND IN
15 PLACES

Iceland packs 1200 years of history into a small island in the North Atlantic Ocean. Iceland itself is a result of shifting tectonic plates; a remote island created by the volcanic activity that mesmerises so many visitors. Its story is one of Viking exploration, Danish colonisation, religious conflict and modern development. By Meena Thiruvengadam

ONE OF THE northernmost inhabited places on the planet, Iceland is like a geology book come to life. Several chapters of Icelandic history are missing, but it's believed Norse and Celtic settlers came to this rugged island about the size of Switzerland over 1200 years ago.

In 930 CE, Iceland became the first country to establish a democratic parliament. In 1980, Iceland was the first in the world to democratically elect a female president. It had the world's first openly gay head of government in 2009, was the first country in the world to legalise abortion in 1935, and the first in the world to jail bankers after the 2008 financial crisis.

Icelanders have a history of resilience, a requirement for living in this environment. Plagues gutted the Icelandic population in the 15th century, and a volcanic eruption almost forced out the population in the 18th century. Denmark colonised Iceland in 1602, maintaining a grip on the country until 1944.

WWII ushered a fishing-based agricultural economy into the industrial age. An airport left behind by allied forces gave way to the rise of tourism, and the rest of the story is best told through these 15 places.

1. Húsavík
VIKINGS AND EUROVISION

This tiny North Icelandic town was home to one of Iceland's earliest Viking settlements. Archaeologists have found 9th-century Viking ruins nearby, suggesting this area predates Reykjavík by several decades and could be the earliest settlement in Iceland. Today, Húsavík is a hub for whale watchers and Eurovision fans. Nearly two dozen species of whale – including the gigantic blue whale – make appearances here. A Eurovision Museum opened in 2021. The 2020 Netflix film *Eurovision Song Contest: The Story of Fire Saga* was set and filmed in Húsavík, which is also the title of a song performed by Will Ferrell and Molly Sandén in the film.

For more, see page 280

2. Þingvellir National Park
WHERE DEMOCRACY BEGAN

Few places are more historically significant to Iceland than Þingvellir National Park. In 930 CE, this became the site of the Alþingi, the world's first democratic parliament. This is also where Iceland formally adopted Christianity in 1000 CE and where it declared independence from Denmark in 1944. Iceland's parliament met at a site along the Öxará river until the

18th century, and in 1930 this became the country's first national park. Follow the hiking path for a walk through early Icelandic history, and snorkel the Silfra fissure to see where the North American and Eurasian tectonic plates converge.

For more, see page 120

3. Árbær Open Air Museum
JOURNEY INTO THE PAST

Exploring its turf houses feels like walking into another time. Costumed guides usher guests through a collection of 20 historic buildings put together to form a town square, a village and a farm. While this was the site of a working farm in the 20th century, the structures here were relocated from Reykjavík.

For more, see page 89

4. Gásir
WHERE FORTUNES WERE MADE

This plot of land along the Eyjafjörður fjord, about 14km north of Akureyri, springs to life every summer during a medieval festival commemorating its history. Gásir was a key trading post in North Iceland and regularly made appearances in 13th- and 14th-century Icelandic sagas. This area is believed to have housed a trading post until the 16th century as Akureyri was developing into a commercial centre. The Gásir medieval festival takes travellers back in time every July with costumed actors and craftsmen who bring history to life.

For more on Akureyri, see page 266

5. Skálholtsdómkirkja
MORE THAN MEETS THE EYE

This cathedral may look relatively new, but it's a key piece of Iceland's Viking history. Built in 1963, the cathedral now standing at the site is the 10th to occupy the property. The history of this site can be traced to the 11th century, when sharp religious disputes defined the nation. Iceland's first church was built here around 1000 CE, when this was a large town and Christianity was rapidly spreading in Iceland. Iceland's last Catholic bishop was executed in Skálholt in 1550 alongside his two sons for opposing the Reformation imposed by the Danish king.

For more, see page 125

6. Reykholt
A READER'S DELIGHT

Head to this small town in West Iceland to walk in the footsteps of Snorri Sturluson, the country's best-known writer of sagas, the legendary family stories that defined the literary landscape of medieval Iceland. Sturluson lived here, writing his books on calfskin and taking breaks to soak in an idyllic pool that's one of Iceland's earliest archaeological remains. Sturluson was a legendary literary figure in Iceland – a feat in a country with some of the most voracious readers on the planet – and there's no better place to get acquainted with his work.

For more, see page 200

7. Eiríksstaðir
HOME OF LEGENDARY EXPLORERS

Take a detour to the 10th century at this West Iceland historic site that was the home of Eiríkur Rauðe (Erik the Red), father of legendary explorer Leifur Eiríksson. This is where the younger Eiríksson is believed to have been born. Archaeologists have found the remains of two buildings here, a Viking

Reykholt (p200)

longhouse and a separate pit house. The site is still visible to visitors, and a reconstructed longhouse shows what a typical Viking farmhouse would have looked like at the time. Each summer, costumed performers take visitors back in time to tell the story of this adventurous family.

For more, see page 210

8. Kirkjubæjarklaustur
A TINY VILLAGE WITH HUGE TALES

On the southern coast, Kirkjubæjarklaustur offers a peek into Iceland's Celtic history. Irish monks once lived in this little village, best known for a convent of Benedictine nuns that have inspired numerous folk tales. Kirkjubæjarklaustur was the site of a monastery in the 9th century, according to the *Book of Settlement*, Iceland's leading history text. A paved area of basalt stones resembles the Giant's Causeway in Northern Ireland, but its origin is just one of many Icelandic mysteries. The convent here closed in 1550 when Iceland moved away from Catholicism and toward Lutheranism.

For more, see page 174

9. Vestmannaeyjar
AFTER THE ERUPTION

These volcanic islands are largely uninhabited. Heimaey, the main island in this archipelago, offers a look at a key event in Icelandic history: the 1973 eruption of the Eldfell volcano, which decimated a thriving town, leaving it buried in a blanket of lava and ash. A swift evacuation left one casualty from the natural disaster. A museum on the island tells the stories of people forced to quickly leave home and shows how destructive volcanic activity can be to daily life. Another island that's visible from Heimaey, Surtsey, is the result of an underground volcanic eruption that lasted from 1963 until 1967.

For more, see page 147

10. Raufarhólshellir Lava Tunnel
A TUNNEL TO THE PAST

Journey thousands of years into the past just a half-hour's drive from Reykjavík. This is one of the largest lava tunnels in Iceland and one of the easiest to visit from Reykjavík. Walk through a tunnel carved by the boiling lava that ferociously flowed through here thousands of years ago. See the iron-oxide formations that have developed over the centuries, and learn what the interior of the tunnel can teach us about the history of this area. Two tour options are available, and safety gear is provided.

For more, see page 133

11. Keflavík International Airport
AN AIRSTRIP THAT CHANGED ICELAND

The airport that welcomes most visitors to Iceland is a remnant of WWII, a time when British and US forces occupied the country leaving behind a key piece of infrastructure. Keflavík International Airport opened in March 1943 and has been a key driver of commercial aviation growth in Iceland. This airport made it easier for Icelanders to travel the world and has helped Iceland become a layover tourism pioneer. Until 1987, civilian and military passengers shared a terminal. A separate civilian terminal, the Leifur Eiríksson Terminal, named after the first European to reach the Americas, has served all civilian travellers since.

For more, see page 350

Raufarhólshellir Lava Tunnel (p133)

Höfði House (p86)

12. Settlement Exhibition
HOW ICELAND CAME TO BE

Dive deep into Viking history with a short trip underground at this museum in downtown Reykjavík. The Settlement Exhibition surrounds a collection of excavated Viking ruins and tells the story of the settlement of Iceland. The remains of a Viking settlement here were unearthed in 2001 and are among the oldest human-made structures that have been discovered in Iceland. The Settlement Exhibition is connected to the Reykjavík City Museum – where you'll find the oldest house in central Reykjavík, dating to 1762 – by an underground tunnel.

For more, see page 54

13. Hallgrímskirkja
REYKJAVÍK'S DEFINING FEATURE

This Lutheran church is the tallest in Iceland and one of the tallest buildings in the country. A distinctive curved spire and side wings have helped it become an international symbol of Iceland since it was completed in 1986. Construction on the church began in 1945 and the tower, which has come to define the Reykjavík skyline, was among the first portions of the church to be completed. A statue of Leifur Eiríksson in front of the church predates its construction. The statue was a gift from the US to Iceland in honour of the 1000th anniversary of the convening of Iceland's parliament at Þingvellir.

For more, see page 62

14. Höfði House
A COLD WAR ICON

The gleaming white house overlooking the water became a Cold War icon in 1986 when US President Ronald Reagan and Soviet President Mikhail Gorbachev met here towards the end of the Cold War. The wooden house was built to serve as a French consulate in 1909 when French fishermen frequented the island. The structure was imported from Norway. It is the best-known of several 'catalog-style' homes in Iceland. Nowadays, this space is occasionally used for official events. Visitors can walk around the outside of the building and check out a chunk of the Berlin Wall.

For more, see page 86

15. Eyjafjallajökull
ICELAND'S BEST-KNOWN VOLCANO

In April 2010, this stratovolcano in South Iceland became a household name few people could pronounce when its eruption forced hundreds of people from their homes and wreaked havoc with European air traffic for six days. Several heads of state, including US President Barack Obama, German Chancellor Angela Merkel and French President Nicolas Sarkozy were among those affected. As a result of the eruption, Eyjafjallajökull became Iceland's most famous volcano. A glacier sits on top of the caldera, and Eyjafjallajökull is part of a volcano chain that stretches across Iceland. Before 2010, its last recorded eruptions were in 920 and 1612.

For more see page 136

MEET THE ICELANDERS

Sword-swinging, hard-headed Vikings or peace-loving, elf-whispering farmers? Who are the Icelanders really? EYGLÓ SVALA ARNARSDÓTTIR debunks some myths and reaffirms others while introducing her people.

ICELAND WAS SETTLED by independent Norse chieftains who would not bow to the rule of a dictator...or so the legend goes. Evidence suggests that the origin of the Icelanders is more complex than that. Archaeologist Þorvaldur Friðriksson argues in his book *Keltar* (2022) that Celtic influence on the Icelandic language and culture is more extensive than commonly perceived. He lists Icelandic words and place names that are Celtic, rather than Nordic, in origin, including *strákur* (*strácair* in Celtic) for boy. DNA research shows that more than 50% of female settlers were Celts. Today, some 18% of Iceland's approximately 390,000 residents are foreign citizens, along with immigrants who have taken up Icelandic citizenship, bringing with them colours and flavours from all over the world.

The Icelanders are fiercely protective of their legacy, independence and language: a nation of storytellers, yet the Icelandic language is under siege by English influences, as people are increasingly exposed to it. In the 19th century, during Danish colonisation, Danish influence on the Icelandic language was widespread, but Icelanders fought to save their native tongue. It seems another awakening is necessary. A language says a lot about its people. For example, *fé* means both 'sheep' and 'money', *vinna* means 'to work' and 'to win' and *yrkja* either grow crops or write poems. An industrious people, Icelanders tend to wear many hats. A sheep farmer might also work as a fireman, have an eiderdown business, run a farmstay and be a reindeer-hunting guide. One of the country's bestselling authors is an engineer and another one a lawyer.

The Icelandic humour is distinctively dark, from the ancient Eddic poem 'Þrymskviða', where Thor wears a wedding gown, pretending to be Freyja to reclaim his precious hammer and killing the groom, to Hugleikur Dagsson's death-themed cartoons. While Icelanders may seem cold – not wasting too many words, smiles, hugs or kisses – they usually warm up to you once the ice is broken, which might take a few drinks. At their core, Icelanders are hospitable and helpful. Through centuries, travellers lost in blizzards had to rely on the kindness of strangers.

Icelanders don't like to plan things a long time in advance, because the weather is so unreliable! If it happens to be sunny, you start haymaking. If it looks stormy, cancel the fishing trip. In summer, campers 'follow the weather', going wherever the forecast is best. Icelanders are rural by nature and love staying in countryside cabins. This connection with nature sometimes materialises as superstition. Foreigners often ask if Icelanders believe in elves. The short answer is no. Elves belong in folk stories; they were invented to explain irrational things. Yet, once in a while, for example during road construction, 'elf boulders' are moved out of respect for the hidden people. Even though most people don't believe in elves, they don't feel comfortable denying their existence. Why risk a curse?

> **The Book of Icelanders**
>
> *Íslendingabók* (islendingabok.is) is an online database containing genealogical information about the inhabitants of Iceland dating back more than 1200 years.

Pictured clockwise from top left: Boat captain, Jökulsárlón (p162); Storyteller surrounded by his antiques; Young man on Vatnajökull glacier (p166); Farmers near Selfloss (p288)

WHAT I LOVE ABOUT ICELAND

There was a time when I couldn't get away from here fast enough. My fellow Icelanders were narrow-minded, I thought, and nothing exciting ever happened. I lived abroad for many years – and, granted, I still miss the European summers. But once I returned, I experienced Iceland from an outside perspective and started appreciating the clean tap water, the abundant hot water, *skyr* (yoghurt-like dessert), and the close proximity to nature. And I appreciated my people more. With all their faults, they also have their charms, and there's a certain informality about them that often makes life easier. You don't lose hours every day commuting to work, and children grow up free and independent, playing outside on their own and cycling to soccer practice. Life, for the most part, is uncomplicated. And whenever the outlook is bleak, we take solace in our motto: *þetta reddast*, 'everything will work out in the end'.

Glacier in Vatnajökull National Park (p168)

ICELAND MINUS THE ICE

In the future, Iceland will have less ice and more trees. The real surprise is how fast predictions, along with the landscape itself, are changing. By Egill Bjarnason

A FEW YEARS ago, a completely new crop of news stories appeared in Icelandic media: celebrities, particularly musicians, who had fallen prey to biting midges on calm summer nights. 'Damn this newcomer', drummer Karl Tomasson – his arms swollen – said of the culicoides midges spreading across the southern lowlands at an alarming rate. Rappers posted pictures of their tattooed chests after being 'sniped at' during sleep.

The red bumps disappeared and the topic faded. The midges returned the next summer but, by then, as part of the landscape and everyday life.

Widespread Effects

When a glacier recedes it leaves behind piles of soil and rock, known as moraine. On every glacial floor, these hills of sediments show plainly and simply – stone-black versus snow-white – how far the glacier once reached. Look over the rest of Iceland, however, and the effects of climate change are less visible to an outsider.

Passengers on whale-watching boats today expect to see species of whales that were considered a novelty in Icelandic waters some 10 or 20 years ago, including the humpback whale, linked to changes in the ocean food web. Locals may not notice either, until a black-backed gull steals a steak from the barbecue. Aggressive seagulls are the side-effect of a collapse in the sand-eel stock – their preferred 'steak' – believed to be caused by warmer winter ocean temperatures. Nearly every seabird population is in decline. Puffins, a bird that symbolises Iceland in the age of tourism, is listed as 'vulnerable' by the International Union for Conservation of Nature, suffering a 70% fall in its population since 1975.

But who wants to read about starving puffins! As a reporter based in Iceland, the climate stories getting the widest reach have a positive spin – for example, a technical solution turning carbon dioxide into rocks or a public policy promoting electric cars, forestry and new agriculture. In reality, nature controls Iceland, not the other way around.

Shrinking Glaciers

In 2019, Vatnajökull National Park, the area surrounding Europe's largest glacier, became a UNESCO World Heritage Site precisely for its ephemeral landscape, a sort of lab, UNESCO notes, to 'explore the impacts of climate change on world glaciers and the landforms left behind when they retreat'. Under the Paris Climate Agreement,

STORYBOOK

a policy framework meant to keep temperatures from rising 2°C above pre-industrial levels, the mighty Vatnajökull, up to 1km in thickness, will still shrink to between 30% and 60% of its current size. The other 14 ice caps could go the same way, and the smaller will most definitely disappear. Breiðamerkurjökull, the glacial tongue calving icebergs into the famous Jökulsárlón glacier lagoon, is receding faster than any other glacial outpost due to rising ocean temperatures mixing with the lagoon. Ice caves, another popular sight at the base of Vatnajökull, are currently unsafe to visit outside the solidly frozen months from October to March; a time period that's bound to shrink if autumn and spring temperatures continue to rise.

Fighting Windmills

Drive the Ring Road in early summer and it's like barrelling down a road paved straight through purple-blue fields of lupine, as if the flowers came before the road. Far from it. The invasive Nootka lupine is an experiment that blew up in Iceland's face and left a permanent purple mark, brought to the country in an effort to fight soil erosion. Buoyed by climate change, it is spiralling towards places previously protected from the plant by cold temperatures and low rainfall.

If extreme rainfall continues, the effects will cause soil erosion by setting off landslides, previously a rare hazard. In 2020, parts of Seyðisfjörður were abandoned after a massive landslide, with plans to relocate the buildings.

Within a few years, drivers may also pass the first wind parks. Roughly 70% of electricity in Iceland is produced by hydroelectric power plants in rivers streaming from the glaciers. As the glacial melt increases – almost half of the total melt in the last 150 years has occurred within the last 30 years – the rivers grow more powerful, producing ever more electricity. But only for the time being. The state-run energy company Landsvirkjun is installing more wind turbines to prepare for a looming energy shift.

Changing Tides

Researching this book, I took the Arctic Coast Way from Hvammstangi to Langanes. The winding road passes pristine beaches with a wide ocean view: beyond the horizon are just a few tiny islands of dry land and definitely no trees. Yet the beaches are littered with driftwood – largely originating from trees felled by logging in the Yenisei catchment in central Siberia. The multiyear journey, thousands of kilometres long, is made possible by sea ice, according to a 2022 study Global and Planetary Change. With less ice, the driftwood is more likely to sink before it can make it to shore. By 2060, the study predicts that, based on sea-ice simulators, Iceland's driftwood supply will cease.

Midway along the 900km Arctic Coast Way, I stopped at the turf farm Glaumbær, constructed almost entirely from earthy material: turf, rocks, more turf. Windows were made with the afterbirth of a cow. The wealthy Glaumbær farm was inhabited until 1946 when the last two families moved out. Had it not been bought for protection, the structure would have rotted into the ground like any other turf farm. The first thing typically unearthed by archaeologists is driftwood – the lumber holding up roofs for most of Iceland's history – a pillar now sinking out of sight.

WHEN A GLACIER RECEDES IT LEAVES BEHIND PILES OF SOIL AND ROCK... LOOK OVER THE REST OF ICELAND, HOWEVER, AND THE EFFECTS OF CLIMATE CHANGE ARE LESS VISIBLE.

Breiðamerkurjökull (p181)
ERICA FRISK/SHUTTERSTOCK

LIFE
UNDER FIRE

Volcanoes shape the land, fertilise the soil, heat the water but also threaten to destroy life. By Eygló Svala Arnarsdóttir

THERE ARE 32 active volcanoes in Iceland and eruptions occur frequently. Volcanologists believe the recent series of eruptions on Reykjanes Peninsula may continue for several years, similar to Kröflueldar in North Iceland (1975–1984). The first three Reykjanes eruptions, from March 2021 to August 2023, were so-called 'tourist eruptions' – and didn't cause damage to infrastructure or pose severe risk to human lives.

Sudden Evacuation

Each eruption was preceded by powerful earthquakes, which affected the inhabitants of Grindavík, the town closest to the eruptions, the most. Objects fell from shelves and smashed against the floor, cracks formed in walls and people woke with a start in the night. On 10 November 2023, the intensity of the seismic activity prompted immediate evacuation. 'It was different from what we had experienced before; it seemed as if the quakes were directly below our feet,' recounted Mayor of Grindavík Fannar Jónasson in an interview on *visir.is*, one year on.

It turned out a magma channel was forming underneath the town. All residents of Grindavík, human and animal, were brought to safety before huge fissures opened up, tearing through roads and houses. Many moved to other towns on Reykjanes, in the capital area or further on, a close-knit community of almost 4000 people forced to split up.

Devastation, Destruction & Determination

On 18 December, an eruption began near Grindavík, lasting three days. Hope emerged that inhabitants could move back, and repairs had begun when on 10 January 2024 disaster struck. A man, who was working on filling a crack, fell into it when the ground beneath him caved. It was much deeper than originally believed and he was never found. The next eruption began four days later and many more were to follow.

Defense walls built to protect Grindavík, Svartsengi power plant and other infrastructure proved effective in redirecting lava flows. However, at one point, magma burst out from a fissure inside the town, destroying three houses. In another eruption, lava flooded part of the Blue Lagoon car park, burning down a small service building. The eruption on 16 July 2025 was the 12th in the series and more might be imminent. However, at the time of writing Grindavík is open and 1100 people have moved back, even though they may have to evacuate without notice and the threat of further eruptions is looming.

Historical Eruptions

Sub-glacial eruptions are usually the most dangerous. In 2010, a phreatic eruption in Eyjafjallajökull in South Iceland grounded aircraft around the world. Ashfall and massive flooding caused problems for farmers in the region, and part of the Ring Road was damaged. The most dan-

STORYBOOK

gerous eruptions in living memory include Vestmannaeyjar in 1973. Thousands of people had to be evacuated in the middle of the night. Houses were buried in lava and ash and a new mountain, Eldfell, was formed. One person died.

Through history, eruptions have caused devastation and destruction, including the eruption in Askja in 1875. Ashfall in East Iceland propelled mass emigration to North America. The poisonous gas from the Skaftáreldar (River Skaftá Fires) eruption in 1783–85 is believed to have caused the death of 75% of livestock and of every fifth inhabitant in Iceland. The eruption in Öræfajökull, Iceland's largest volcano, in 1362 caused severe ashfall and flooding, turning the lush region at its foot into wasteland. The Hekla eruption in 1104 had a devastating effect on life in the blooming Þjórsárdalur valley and marked the beginning of the end of farming in the area.

Not much is known about the effect of earlier eruptions, as they were rarely mentioned in sources. In the *Book of Settlement,* documenting the settlement of Iceland in the 9th century CE, eruptions are mentioned twice, briefly, in the context of people relocating as a consequence. Archaeologist Bjarni F Einarsson says that in spite of lack of written sources, it is clear that eruptions had immense consequences on habitation. He theorises that the 934 Eldgjá eruption, one of the largest to have occurred in the world in the past 2000 years, made a large region in South Iceland uninhabitable. Bjarni reasons that people fled to the mountains – closer to the eruption – because there, trees protruded from the ash and could be used for feeding livestock. The population eventually collapsed, and the remaining people moved back to the lowlands when the vegetation recovered. The Eldgjá eruption is believed to have slowed down the settlement of Iceland.

Ash Analysis

Now, thanks to volcanoes, the story of Iceland's settlements may have to be rewritten. Archaeologists use ash layers from eruptions to determine the age of relics found during excavations, among other methods. Bjarni is currently leading an excavation project in Stöðvarfjörður, East Iceland, where a layer from an eruption in Grímsvötn that occurred in 875 was found in a turf wall of a longhouse. Underneath is an older house, which dates back to 800–850, prior to the official settlement. Bjarni believes that these were seasonal dwellings that were used as a base for workers hunting and processing whales – oil made from whale blubber was a sought-after product at that time.

> ON 10 NOVEMBER 2023, THE INTENSITY OF THE SEISMIC ACTIVITY PROMPTED IMMEDIATE EVACUATION. A CLOSE-KNIT COMMUNITY OF ALMOST 4000 PEOPLE WAS FORCED TO SPLIT UP.

Geothermal Benefits

With volcanic activity comes geothermal activity, used for energy production, heating and bathing – naturally hot water is used for swimming pools and bathing lagoons around the country. Icelandic bathing culture has developed over centuries, at least going as far back as the Middle Ages when the sagas were written, describing people bathing in natural pools. Snorralaug, in which saga author Snorri Sturluson used to soak at his home in Reykholt, still exists. Bjarni says there is no evidence of Iceland's first settlers having used the natural hot water for bathing – they may have, even though the practice probably seemed alien to them at first. For hundreds of years, the hot ground and water have been used for baking and cooking, and the hot springs were convenient for doing laundry. In Laugardalur in Reykjavík there are pools that were used for doing laundry in the 19th and early 20th centuries, before houses had running water.

For better or for worse, volcanoes have shaped the country, culture and the Icelandic mentality. Icelanders take solace in the fact that a team of scientists monitors all of the country's volcanoes and that action plans are in place when eruptions near inhabited areas are foreseen. Life pretty much goes on as usual. Life under fire.

Fagradalsfjall (p110)
DANIELFREYR/SHUTTERSTOCK

Sigur Rós (p115)
MATTHEW EISMAN/GETTY IMAGES

ICELAND'S POP-ROCK JUGGERNAUT

Icelandic musicians draw on deep roots for rich modern-day creativity. By Alexis Averbuck

ICELAND BLOWS AWAY concerns such as isolation, continuous winter darkness and its small population with a glowing passion for music and all things cultural. From its earliest high-action medieval sagas, which were recited aloud, to the present day where many Icelanders play in a band, the country produces a disproportionate number of world-class musicians in all manner of styles. Their creativity and influences – like the grand landscape, Reykjavík life and capricious weather – blend with the literature and sounds of yore.

Roots

Until rock and roll arrived in the 20th century, Iceland was a land practically devoid of musical instruments and singing was the sole form of music.

The most famous song styles were *rímur* – poetry or stories from the sagas performed in a low, eerie chant (Sigur Rós have dabbled with the form) – and *fimmundasöngur*, which were sung by two people in harmony. Cut off from other influences, the Icelandic singing style barely changed from the 14th century to the 20th century. It also managed to retain harmonies that were banned by the church across the rest of Europe for being the work of the devil.

You'll find choirs around Iceland performing traditional music, and various compilation albums, such as *Inspired by Harpa – The Traditional Songs of Iceland* (2013), give a sample of Icelandic folk songs or *rímur*.

Eddic & Skaldic Poetry

Lyric writing goes back to the earliest days of Icelandic life. The first settlers brought their oral poetic tradition with them from other parts of Scandinavia, and the words of the poems were later committed to parchment in the 12th century.

Eddic poems were composed in free, variable meters with a structure very similar to that of early Germanic poetry. Probably the best known is the gnomic *Hávamál*, which extols the virtues of the common life – its wise proverbs on how to be a good guest are still quoted today.

Skaldic poems were composed by *skalds* (Norwegian court poets) and are mainly praise-poems of Scandinavian kings, with lots of description packed into tightly structured lines. As well as having fiercely rigid alliteration, syllable counts and stresses, Skaldic poetry is made more complex by *kennings*, a kind of compact word riddle. Blood, for instance, is 'wound dew', while an arm might be described as a 'hawk's perch'.

The most renowned skald was saga antihero Egill Skallagrímsson. In 948, after being captured and sentenced to death, Egill composed the ode *Höfuðlausn* (Head Ransom) for his captor Eirík Blood-Axe. Flattered, the monarch released Egill unharmed.

Early Instruments

The Vikings brought the *fiðla* and the *langspil* – both a kind of zither where a two-stringed box rests on the player's knee and is played with a bow. Never solo instruments, they served to accompany singers. In the 19th century, harmonicas and accordions arrived, but mostly, instruments were an unheard-of luxury until the 20th century. You can see some of the push-and-pull of international influence in the film *Djöflaeyjan* (Devil's Island; 1996), which depicts the lives of Icelandic families inhabiting the US military barracks left in Reykjavík after WWII.

Björk & the Sugarcubes

By most measures, the first modern-era internationally famous Icelandic musicians were The Sugarcubes. They received worldwide acclaim with their album *Life's Too Good* (1988), which included the hit single 'Birthday'. They were also part of the influential Reykjavík indie label Bad Taste *(Smekkleysa)*, which still champions Icelandic musicians, artists, poets and writers, and was an early ground for fostering Icelandic creative artists. You can visit its shop at Hjartatorg and Hverfisgata 32 in Reykjavík.

When The Sugarcubes disbanded in 1992, lead vocalist Björk spun off into a smashing solo career spanning a fecund range of styles from her platinum album *Debut* (1993) to her most recent, *Fossora* (2022). You'll hear historic roots in her song from *Fossora* called 'Sorrowful Soil', which is influenced by a 17th-century elegiac Icelandic hymn. Check out her bestselling *Gling Gló,* a collection of jazz standards and traditional Icelandic songs.

Sigur Rós

The wildly creative band Sigur Rós have followed Björk to international stardom. Their album *Ágætis byrjun* (A Good Beginning; 1999) brought them worldwide attention for lead singer Jónsi's unique vocals (usually sung in Icelandic or an improvised vocalisation they dub Volenska) and the band's bowed guitar techniques. Their biggest-selling album *Takk...* (Thanks...; 2005) garnered rave reviews around the world and firmly cemented them on the international stage. Seek out their concert film *Heima* (Home; 2007), a must-see for its blend of brilliant music and Icelandic settings captured during a series of free concerts they gave around the country upon returning from their 2006 concert tour.

One of their albums, *Route One* (2017), was assembled from music created while the band drove the entire Ring Road in midsummer 2016. And in 2023 they toured internationally with a full orchestra behind their latest album *Átta* (Eight; 2023), featuring a singing style reminiscent of early Icelandic devotional music. Lead singer Jónsi also had success with his joyful solo album Go (2010), and the music of Sigur Rós is used widely in film and television.

It's emblematic of the international reach of Icelandic composers in general, like Hildur Guðnadóttir, who won an Academy Award for her score to *Joker* (2019) and has collaborated with all manner of rock, metal and classical musicians.

Indie-Folk Stars

Understandably, with its rich folk-music history, indie-folk bands hit well in Iceland. Of Monsters and Men stormed the US charts in 2011 with their debut album, *My Head Is an Animal*. The track 'Little Talks' from that album reached number one on the Billboard US Alternative Songs chart. *Beneath the Skin* (2015) debuted at number three on the US Billboard 200, and their latest album is *All Is Love and Pain in the Mouse Parade* (2025).

Of Monsters and Men (p115)

KALEO, a popular blues-folk-rock band from Mosfellsbær, hit the international stage with a splash – the song 'No Good' from their 2016 studio album *A/B* garnered a Grammy Award nomination and the album peaked at 16 on the US Billboard 200. Their latest release is *Mixed Emotions* (2025).

Singer-songwriter Ásgeir Trausti, who records simply as Ásgeir, had a breakout hit with *In the Silence* (2014), sung mostly in moody English, and sells out concerts internationally. His latest albums are *Afterglow* (2017), *Bury the Moon/Sátt* (2020) and *Time on My Hands* (2022).

Seabear, an indie-folk band, has spawned several top music-makers like Sin Fang (try *Flowers* from 2013) and Sóley (*We Sink* from 2012). Árstíðir records minimalist indie-folk and had a 2013 Youtube viral hit when they sang a 13th-century Icelandic hymn a-cappella in a train station in Germany.

Troubadour Svavar Knútur draws influence from Icelandic folklore and his debut solo album *Kvöldvaka* – named for the Icelandic tradition of storytelling by the fire – was released to critical acclaim in 2009. His latest release *Ahoy! Side B* (2024) is a continued exploration of human emotions, including a richer soundscape than earlier albums.

The Scene

Reykjavík's flourishing music scene rocks with a constantly changing lineup of new bands and sounds – see *icelandmusic.is* for a sampling and check website/paper *Grapevine* for music news and performances. If your trip coincides with one of the country's many music festivals, go! Fabulous Iceland Airwaves (held in Reykjavík in November) showcases local and international acts. *Aldrei fór ég Suður* shakes up Ísafjörður every Easter, while the *Þjóðhátíð* (National Festival), in Vestmannaeyjar, attracts over 16,000 people for four days of music and debauchery in late July or early August.

Iceland and electronica go hand in hand, as demonstrated by Mosfellsbær-born and Grammy-nominated Ólafur Arnalds.

REYKJAVÍK'S FLOURISHING MUSIC SCENE ROCKS WITH A CONSTANTLY CHANGING LINEUP OF NEW BANDS AND SOUNDS.

Sóley
BADEN ROTH/IMAGESPACE/SHUTTERSTOCK

GusGus, a top pop-electronica act, has 11 studio albums, while Kiasmos is an Icelandic-Faroese duo which mixes moody, minimalist electronica – check out *Kiasmos* (2014) or EPs like the excellent *Blurred* (2017).

In September 2016, Sturla Atlas, the Icelandic hip-hop/R&B phenomenon, opened for Justin Bieber (whose video 'I'll Show You' was shot in Iceland). Other well-known Icelandic rappers include pioneering Quarashi, Gisli Pálmi, rap collective Reykjavíkurdætur (Daughters of Reykjavík), Cyber and Emmsjé Gauti.

Floating Harmonies, the 2016 debut album by Vestmannaeyjar Islands-born Júníus Meyvant, is a creative blend of beautifully orchestrated folk, funk, and soul. Idiosyncratic pop-meister and Eurovision star Daði Freyr rocketed to stardom with his 2020 'Think About Things'. His videos are a Dadaesque study in humour. Pop-country songstress Bríet made waves with her hit single 'Esjan' in 2020. Her debut album *Kveðja* (2020) was named best of the year at the 2021 Icelandic Music Awards.

Iceland's latest international star is jazz-pop artist Laufey, whose debut *Everything I Know About Love* (2022) reached third place on the US Jazz Album chart. *Bewitched* (2023) earned her a Grammy for Best Traditional Pop Vocal Album in 2024. Laufey has collaborated with artists such as Barbara Streisand and Norah Jones, and there are more exciting projects on the horizon – so stay tuned.

INDEX

> **ALPHABETICAL ORDER**
> The Icelandic letters þ/Þ and ð/Ð appear at the end of the alphabet after the letter Z.

A

accessible travel 361
accommodation 353, *see also individual locations*
activities 36-7, *see also individual activities*
Aðalstræti Settlement Exhibition 54-5
air travel 351
airplane crashes 139
airport buses 350
Akureyri 266-74, **267**
 accommodation 300
 beyond Akureyri 275-9
 drinking 270, 274
 food 268, 270, 274
 travel around Akureyri 275
 travel within Akureyri 266
 walking tour 269, **269**
Álftanes 95
animals 14-15, *see also individual species*
aquariums
 Beluga Whale Sanctuary 148
 Sudurnes Science & Learning Centre 115
archaeology, *see also* ruins
 Aðalstræti Settlement Exhibition 54-5
 Eiríksstaðir 210-11
 Reykholt 200-1
 Skriðuklaustur 306-7
 Stöng 135
 Stöð 315
 Þjórsárdalur Valley 135
Arctic foxes 241
 Arctic Fox Centre 242
Arctic Henge 296-7
Arnarfjörður 226-30, **227**

Map Pages **000**

accommodation 247
beyond Arnarfjörður 231-5
food 228
travel around Arnarfjörður 226, 231
Arnarson, Ingólfur 172
art 316, *see also* museums & galleries
 Sun Voyager 70
Askja Route 339-46, **340**
 accommodation 347
 travel within Askja Route 339
Ásmundarsafn 51
Ásmundarson, Grettir, *see* Grettir the Strong
ATV tours 90, 112, 124, 138, 147

B

Bakkafjörður 299
bank cards 352
Bárður 215
Básendar 115
beaches
 Borgarsandur 257
 Cape Ingólfshöfði 141
 clean-up 271
 Diamond Beach 181
 Djúpalónssandur 216-17
 Dyrhólaey 153
 Fellsfjara 181
 Héraðsflói 323
 Hringsdalur 229
 Jökulsárlón 180
 Minnibakki Beach 240
 Nauthólsvík 89
 Rauðisandur 231, 234
 Reynisfjara 123, 155
 Skarðsvík 217
 Sólheimasandur 139
 Stapavík 320
 Víkurfjara 155
beauty products 70
beer 34, 184, 259, *see also* breweries
bicycle travel, *see* cycling, mountain biking
Bieber, Justin 139, 362

Bifröst 198-9
birdwatching, *see also* gannets, puffins
 Krýsuvíkurberg Bird Cliffs 112-13
 Lake Mývatn 284
 Reykjanes Peninsula 112-13
 Reykjavík 81
 Seyðisfjörður 319-20
 Stöðvarfjörður 315
Bjarnarhöfn 212
Björk 33, 60, 72, 115, 128, 382
Blönduós 261
boat tours 81, 178, 180, 258
Bolungarvík 240-1
Book of Settlement, *see Íslendingabók*
books 33, *see also* sagas
 Dark Iceland 277
 Good Shepherd, The 307
 Stefánsson, Davíð 268
 Sveinsson, Jón 267
 Þórðarson, Þórbergur 184
Borgarfjörður Eystri 319-20
 accommodation 325
 food 320
Borgarnes 194-7, **195**
 accommodation 219
 beyond Borganes 198-204
 drinking 196
 food 197
 shopping 197
 travel around Borgarnes 194, 198
Breiðdalsvík 314
 shopping 314
breweries 34, 72, 184, 357, *see also* beer
 Breiðdalsvík 314
 Galdur Brewery 246
 Lady Brewery 79
Bridge Between Continents 110, 114
Brimketill 113
budgets 352, 353, 357
bus 351
business hours 363
Búðardalur 209-10
 shopping 210

C

calderas
 Askja 343
 Snæfellsjökull 217
 Stampar 110
campervans 353
camping 353
 highlands 332, 333, 337, 342
 southeast region 170
 southwest region 117, 121, 146, 147
canyons
 Ásbyrgi 290-1
 Brúarhlöð 123
 Fjaðrárgljúfur 141, 151, 176-7
 Hafrahvammagljúfur 311
 Nauthusagil 139, 142
 Stakkholtsgjá Canyon 143, 146
cathedrals, *see* churches & cathedrals
caves, *see also* ice caves
 Caves of Hella 140, 142
 Caves of Laugarvatn
 Hálsanefshellir 155
 Loftsalahellir 155
 Reykjavík 93
children, travel with, *see* family travel
Christmas 61, 285, 311
churches & cathedrals
 Akureyrarkirkja 268
 Dómkirkja 51, 57
 Grímsey 276
 Hallgrímskirkja 62-3
 Hólar cathedral 258
 Hvalsneskirkja 114
 Ingjaldshóll 218
 Nonnahús 267-8
 Raufarhafnarkirkja 296
 Saurbæjarkirkja 199, 279
 Skálholtsdómkirkja 125
 Skeggjastaðakirkja 299
 Stafkirkjan 148
 Víkurkirkja 155
cinemas 70
climate 30-1
climate change 358, 374-6

country code 363
craters, see also volcanoes
  Grábrók 198
  Kerið 128
  Landmannalaugar 146
  Rauðhólar 92
  Saxhóll 217
credit cards 352
culture 372-3
Culture Night 58
cycling 37, 38-9, 351, see also mountain biking
  Borgarfjörður Eystri 319
  Húsavík 282-3
  Ísafjörður 239
  Reykjavik Marathon 58
  Southwest Iceland 108
  Westfjords Way Challenge 227

Dalabyggð 212
Dalvík 275-6
dangers, see safe travel
Diamond Beach, see Fellsfjara
disabilities, travellers with 361
distilleries 72
  Kópavogur 93
  Old Harbour 79
  Reyka Vodka 196
diving & snorkelling
  Silfra fissure 122
  Strýtan 279
  Þingvellir National Park 122
Djúpivogur 314
  accommodation 325
  food 314
dolphins 81, 114, 246, 280-1, 282
drinking 357
drinks, see beer, breweries, distilleries
driving 351
driving tours, see road trips
ducks 113, 147, 284
Dýrafjörður 227

earthquakes 294, 355
East Iceland 302-25, see also individual locations
  accommodation 325
  activities 305
  Fljótsdalur 306-9, **307**
  itineraries 305
  Seyðisfjörður 316-18, **317**
  travel seasons 305
  travel within 304

Eddic poetry 380
Eggin í Gleðivík 314
Egil's Saga 194-5, 204
Egilsstaðir 312-13
  accommodation 325
  food 312
Eldhraun 175
electricity 363
emergency number 363
Erik the Red 210-11, 333, 369
Eskifjörður 321-2
etiquette 32, 71
EV charging 351
events, see festivals & events
Eyjafjarðarsveit 279
Eyrarbakki 133-4
  accommodation 161
  food 134
Eyvindur of the Mountains 343

F985 182
F roads 134, 351, 204
family travel 354
  Ljósafoss Power Station 116-17
  Reykjavík Zoo & Family Park 87
  Viking World 115
  Westfjords 238
Fáskrúðsfjörður 320-1
Fellsfjara 180-1
fermented shark meat, see *hákarl*
ferries 351
festivals & events 31, 35
  Á fætur í Fjarðabyggð 311
  Akureyri Art Summer 31, 257
  Aldrei fór ég suður 31, 238
  Árnarhóll 58
  Blue Church Summer Concert 316-17
  Bræðslan 31
  Brákarhátíð 195
  Culture Night 58
  Dagar myrkurs 311
  Dark Music Days 59
  DesignMarch 58
  Fisherman's Day 31
  Food & Fun 35, 58
  Great Forest Day 35
  Hafnarfjörður Viking Festival 95
  Humarhátíð 35, 186
  Iceland Airwaves 31, 59
  Innipúkinn Festival 59
  Jólakötturinn 311
  Landsmót Hestamanna 257
  List í ljósi festival 317

Lóa Festival 59
Múlakaffi 61
Mývatn Winter Festival 257
National Festival 31, 149
National Icelandic Horse Competition 255
Ormsteiti 311
Reykjavík Arts Festival 58
Reykjavík Culture Night 31
Reykjavík International Film Festival 58
Reykjavík International Literary Festival 58
Reykjavík Jazz Festival 31, 59
Reykjavík Pride 58, 360
Siglufjörður Folk Music Festival 257, 277
Ski Week 238
Skógardagurinn mikli 311
Sorcery Festival 245
Westfjords Way Challenge 227
Winter Lights Festival 58
Yule Lads' Bath 257
Þorrablót 35, 58, 61
films 33, 139
  Bíó Paradís 70
  Djöflaeyjan 382
  Eurovision Song Contest: The Story of Fire Saga 280, 368
  Gunnlaugsson, Harfn 86
  Heima 139, 382
Fishcher, Bobby 132
fish farming 235
  Westfjords 241
fishing 12, 13
  Faxafoss 125
  Flateyri 241-2
  Mývatn Winter Festival 257
  Reykjavík 81
  rules 127
  Snæfellsnes Peninsula 213
  Stykkishólmur 205
  Tunguflјót 125
  Veiðivötn 337
  Þingvellir National Park 122
Fjaðrárgljúfur 176-7
Fjallabaksleið Nyrðri 159
Flatey 209
Flateyri 241-2
flightseeing
  FlyOver Iceland 79
  Holuhraun 342
  Reykjavík 70-1
  Skaftafell 171
  Southwest Iceland 108
Fljótsdalur 306-9, **307**
  accommodation 325

beyond Fljótsdalur 310-15
  festivals 311
  food 308
  hiking 308
  travel around Fljótsdalur 310
  travel within Fljótsdalur 306
fjords, see individual fjords
Flóahreppur 132
Flúðir 125
  accommodation 160
FlyOver Iceland 79
food 34-5, 356-7, see also individual locations
  ethics 78
  geothermal bread 34, 59, 123, 130, 356
  hákarl 34, 35, 78, 211-2, 356
  ice cream 77, 117, 210, 279
  Múlakaffi 61
  saltfiskur 111
  skyr 34, 210, 357
  vegetarian & vegan 56
  Þorrablót 61
food trucks 57
forests 311-12
forts
  Skansinn 147, 148
Foss á Siðu 175

galleries, see museums & galleries
Game of Thrones 139, 201, 211, 285
gannets 80, 113, 295
  Skoruvík 299
gardens, see parks & gardens
Garður 115
gay travellers 58, 360
geothermal areas
  Eldfell 147
  Gunnuhver 113
  Landmannalaugar 146-7
  Reykjanesfólkvangur Wilderness Reserve 111
  Seltún 112
  Strýtan 279
geothermal energy 358
  Hellisheiði Geothermal Power Plant 131
  Þeistareykir Power Plant 286
geothermal pools 17, see also swimming pools
  Blue Lagoon 104-5
  Borgarnes Swimming Pool 196-7
  Forest Lagoon 268, 270
  Gamla Laugin 127

G–H

geothermal pools *continued*
GeoSea 283
Grettislaug 257-8
Guðrúnarlaug 210
Hrunalaug 127, 128
Hvammsvík Hot Springs 199
Hveradalir 131
Hveragarðurinn 130
Laugafell 338
Lýsulaugar 215
Pollurinn 234-5
Reykholtslaug 128
Secret Lagoon, 127
Sundlaugin Laugaskarði 131
Vesturbæjarlaug 82
Vígðalaug 117, 123
Vök Baths 312-13
West Iceland 201
geysers 124, 127
Geysir 124
 accommodation 160
glacial floods, *see jökulhlaup*
glacier hiking 37, *see also* hiking, hiking tours
 Fjallsárlón 178-9, 182
 Katla Geopark 150
 Skaftafell 169-70
 Vatnajökull 166, 168
glacier tours 108, 130
glaciers 18-19, 38-9, 354
 Eyjafjallajökull 143
 Falljökull 168
 Fláajökull 183
 Heinabergsjökull 183
 Hoffellsjökull 183
 Langjökull 129-30
 Mýrdalsjökull 143
 Skaftafellsjökull 166, 168
 Skálafellsjökull 183
 Sólheimajökull 140, 150
 Svínafellsjökull 168
 Tindfjallajökull 143, 151
goats 201, 270
Golden Circle 116-28, **118**
 beyond Golden Circle 129-35
 drinking 125
 Flúðir 125
 food 117, 125, 127
 Laugarás 125
 Reykholt 125

Selfoss 125
 shopping 128
 travel within Golden Circle 116
golf
 Geysir 124
 Ísafjörður 239
 Seltjarnarnes 83
 Vestarr 212
Grandi 74
greenhouses 356
Grenivík 278-9
Grettir the Strong 257, 258
Grímsey 276
 ferry 276
Grindavik 110, 111, **106**
 food 110
Grund 324
Grundarfjörður 211-12
guesthouses 353
guided tours 61, 108-9
 Akureyri Art Museum 268
 Caves of Laugarvatn 123
 Reykjavík Maritime Museum 77
 Snæfellsjökull National Park 217
 Southwest Iceland 108-9
Gullfoss 126
 accommodation 160
Gunnarsson, Gunnar 307, 309
Gunnlaugsson, Harfn 86

H

Hafnarhólmi 320
hákarl 34, 35, 78, 211-2, 356
Hallormsstaðaskógur 311-12
Handknitting Association of Iceland 68
Hauganes 275-6
Heimskautsgerðið, *see* Arctic Henge
Hellnar 215
herring 276-7
Highlands, the 327-47, **328**
 accommodation 347
 activities 329
 Askja Route 339-46, **340**
 driving tips 332
 hiking 337
 itineraries 329
 Kjölur Route 330-4, **331**
 Sprengisandur Route 335-8, **336**
 tours 338
 travel seasons 329
 travel within the Highlands 328
 highlights 8-19
hiking 36-7, 38-9, 114, *see also* glacier hiking, hiking tours

Ásbyrgi 290-1
Askja Trail 341
Borgarfjörður Eystri 319
Drekagil 341-2
Fimmvörðuháls 149, 152
Fjallsárlón 182
Hafnarfjall 196
Hengifoss 307-8
Herjólfsdalur 149
Hlíðarfjall 271
Höfn 187
Holuhraun 342
Húsavík 282-3
Jökulsárlón 182
Kirkjufjara 155
Kjölur Route 334
Lake Mývatn 285
Laki 176
Landmannalaugar 146-7
Mjóifjörður 322-3
Mt Esja 200
Naustavhilft 238
Nauthusagil 139, 142
Núpsstaðarskógar 174
Nýidalur 337
Rauðanes 298-9
Reykjadalur 130
Sandafell 228-9
Seven Peak Challenge 317-18
Skaftafell 169
Skaftafellsheiði Loop 169
Southern Highlands 143
Southwest Iceland 108
Spákonufell 256-7
Stapavík 320
Stóraklif 149
Tálknafjörður 235
Tvísöngur 316
hiking tours
 Canyon Trail 292-3, **293**
 Glymur 202-3, **203**
 Landmannalaugar to Þórsmörk 144-5, **145**
 Royal Horn 243, **243**
history, *see also* archaeology, sagas, vikings
 Árbær Open Air Museum 369
 Bíldudalur 228
 Eiríksstaðir 369-70
 Eyjafjallajökull 371
 Gásir 369
 Hallgrímskirkja 371
 Höfði House 86, 371
 Húsavík 368
 Íslendingabók 88
 Keflavík International Airport 370
 Kirkjubæjarklaustur 370
 Ocean of Memories 321
 Raufarhólshellir Lava Tunnel 370

Reykholt 369
Sauðárkrókur 257
Settlement Exhibition 371
Skaftafell 170
Skagafjörður 259
Skálholtsdómkirkja 369
Sturluson, Snorri 204
Vestmannaeyjar 370
Þingvellir National Park 121, 368-9
Þórdís 256-7
hitchhiking 351
Hlíðarendi 138
Höfn 141, 185-8, **186**
 accommodation 189
 food 185, 186, 187
 travel around Höfn 185
Hólar 176
Hólmavík 244-6, **245**
 accommodation 247
 food 246
 travel within Hólmavík 244
Hópsnes peninsula 110-11
horse riding
 Golden Circle 116, 132
 Hallormsstaðaskógur forest 309
 Hveragerði 131
 Kjölur Route 330, 332
 Laugarfell 311
 Rauðavatn 93
 Rauðhólar 92
 Skagafjörður 254-5
 Snæfellsnes 215
 Southwest Iceland 108
 tölt 309
 Víkurfjara 155
horses, wild 133
hotels 353
hot-pots, *see* geothermal pools
hot springs, *see* geothermal pools
hot-tubs, *see* geothermal pools
Hraunhafnartangi 295
Hrífunes 175
 accommodation 189
Hrísey 275
huldufólk 94-5
Húsavík 280-3, **281**
 accommodation 300-1
 beyond Húsavík 284-7
 food 282
 travel around Húsavík 284
 travel within Húsavík 280
Hvalfjörður 199-200
Hvammstangi 261
Hvannadalshnúkur 173
Hvanneyri 198
Hveragerði 130-1
 accommodation 160
 food 130

shopping 131
Hvolsvöllur 136-42, **137**
  accommodation 161
  beyond Hvolsvöllur 143-52
  food 138, 139, 142
  travel within Hvolsvöllur 136

ice caps
  Langjökull 204
  melting 374-6
  Snæfellsjökull 217
  Tungnafellsjökull 337
  Vatnajökull 166, 168, 170-1
ice caves 37, 38-9, 152, 157, 354, see also caves
  Fjallsárlón 179, 182
  Katla Ice Cave 151
  Skaftafell 171
ice caving 37
ice climbing
  Skaftafell 169-70
ice cream 77, 117, 210, 279
Icelandic Sea Monster Museum 230
Ingólfshöfði 172
insurance 134, 261, 330, 355
internet 363
Ísafjörður 236-9, **237**
  accommodation 247
  beyond Ísafjörður 240-3
  food 239
  history 236, 238
  travel around Ísafjörður 236, 240
Íslendingabók 188
itineraries 22-9, **23**, **24-5**, **27**, **29**, see also individual locations

jökulhlaup 158, 174, 175
Jökulsárgljúfur Canyon 288-93, **289**
  accommodation 301
  hiking trail 292-3, **293**
  travel within Jökulsárgljúfur Canyon 288
Jökulsárlón 180-1, **179**
  accommodation 189
  food 182, 184
  travel around Jökulsárlón 178
Jólahlaðborð 61
Jónsi 68, 382

Kaldidalur Valley 204
KALEO 383
Kárahnjúkar 310
Katla Geopark 150-1
kayaking 108
  Eyrarbakki 134
  Grenivík 278
  Heinabergslón 183
  Hvítá River 123, 125
  Ísafjörður 239
  Jökulsárlón 180
  Skagafjörður 260
  Stykkishólmur 205
  Varmahlíð 260
Keflavík 104, **106**
  food 114
Keflavík International Airport 350, 361, 370
Kerlingarfjöll 332-3
Kirkjubæjarklaustur 174-5
  accommodation 189
  food 174
Kjarval, Jóhannes 51, 87
Kjölur Route 330-4, **331**
  accommodation 347
  travel within Kjölur Route 330
knitting 68, 156, 261, 270
Kópasker 294-5, **295**
Kverkfjöll Route 343, 346

lagoons
  Fjallsárlón 178-9
  Fjállsárlón 141
Lake Mývatn 284-6
  food 286
lakes
  Askja 343
  Fagradalsfjall 110
  Grænavatn 112
  Kerið 129
  Kleifarvatn 111, 112
  Landmannalaugar 146
  Öskjuvatn 343
  Reykjanesfólkvangur Wilderness Reserve 111
  Systravatn 175
  Tjarnargígar Crater Lake 177
  Tjörnin 48
  Veiðivötn 337
  Þingvallavatn 122
Landbrotshólar 175
Langjökull 129-30
language 33, 364-5
Látrabjarg 234
Laugarás 125
  accommodation 160
Laugarfell 310-11

Laugarvatn 117, 123
  accommodation 160
laundry 59
lava fields
  Bárðarbunga 341
  Bifröst 198-9
  Eldhraun 175
  Elliðaárhraun 92
  Gjáin 135
  Holuhraun 342
  Hraunfossar 204
  Lakagígar 151
  Lake Mývatn 285
  Laki 176-7
  Landbrotshólar 175
  Mýrdalssandur 158-9
lava flows
  Gaujulundur 147
  Hellisgerði 94-5
  Landmannalaugar 146
  Lava Show 79, 82
  Öndverðarnes 217
  Valahnúkur 113-14
lava tubes
  Húsafell 204
  Raufarhólshellir 133
  Reykjavík 93
  Vatnshellir 217
lava tunnels, see lava tubes
Laxdæla Saga 207, 210
Leif the Lucky 114, 115
lesbian travellers 58, 360
LGBTIQ+ travellers 58, 360
lighthouses
  Digranes Lighthouse 299
  Dyrhólaey Lighthouse 153
  Garður Lighthouse 114
  Gaujulundur 147
  Grímsey 276
  Höfði Lighthouse 84
  Hópsnes Lighthouse 111
  Knarraros Lighthouse 134
  Langanesviti 299
  Malarrif Lighthouse 217
  Raufarhöfn 296
  Reykjanesviti Lighthouse 113-14
  Stórhöfðaviti lighthouse 147
  Svalvogar lighthouse 227
  Svörtuloft Lighthouse 217
Lón 187-8
longhouses 54, 210-11
lupine 282-3, 290, 376

Mælifell 158
Magnússon, Skúli 57
markets
  Christmas 311
  farmers 127

Kolaportið flea market 57, 59, 68
Ljómalind 197
measures 363
Melrakkaslétta Peninsula 294-7, **295**
  accommodation 301
  beyond Melrakkaslétta 298-9
  food 296
  travel around Melrakkaslétta Peninsula 294, 298
midges 374
milk 356
Mjóifjörður 322-3
money 352
Mosfellsbær 129
moss 139, 339, 359, 362
mountain biking 36, 37, 108, see also cycling
  Hlíðarfjall Bike Park 271
  Hveragerði 131
  Ísafjörður 239
mountains 314
  Herðubreið 341
  Kerlingarfjöll 332-3
  Kirkjufell 211
  Mt Kaldbakur 229, 278
  Sandafell 228-9
  Snæfell 310-11
  Spákonufell 256-7
museums & galleries
  1238 The Battle of Iceland 267
  Aðalstræti Settlement Exhibition 54-5
  Agricultural Museum of Iceland 198
  Akureyri Museum 266
  Akureyri Art Museum 268
  Árbær Open Air Museum 89
  Árnes Museum 256
  Ásmundarsafn 51
  Bjarnarhöfn Shark Museum 212-13
  Bobby Fischer Center 132
  Borgarfjörður Museum 197
  Bustarfell 324
  Davíð Stefánsson Writers' Museum 268
  Earthquake Centre 294
  Einar Jónsson Museum 63, 68
  Eldheimar 147
  French Museum 320
  Garðskagi Museum 114
  Gerðarsafn Art Museum 95
  Glaumbær Museum 260
  Gljúfrasteinn Laxness Museum 129

museums & galleries *continued*
Grenivík Fishing Museum 278
Hafnarborg Centre of Culture & Fine Art 95
Hafnarfjörður Museum Pakkhúsið 95
Hafnarhús 51
Herring Era Museum 277
Húsavík Museum 282
Húsið á Eyrarbakka 134
i8 gallery 51
Icelandic Aviation Museum 268
Icelandic Emigration Centre 259
Icelandic Folk Music Centre 277
Icelandic Horse History Centre 259
Icelandic Museum of Rock 'n' Roll 115
Icelandic Phallological Museum 59-60
Icelandic Punk Museum 60
Icelandic Seal Centre 261
Icelandic Sea Monster Museum 230
Icelandic Wartime Museum 321
Jón Sigurðsson Memorial Museum 228
Kjarvalsstaðir 87
Kling & Bang 78
Laufás Turf House Museum 278-9
Lava Centre 136
Library of Water 207
Listasafn Árnesinga 131
Marshall House 51, 77-8
Motorcycle Museum of Iceland 268
Museum of Design & Applied Art 95
Museum of Icelandic Sorcery & Witchcraft 244-5
Museum of Prophecies 256
National Gallery of Iceland 51, 69-70
National Museum 52-3
National Museum of Iceland 51
Natural History Museum of Kópavogur 95
Nýló 77-8
Ósvör Maritime Museum 241
Perlan 89
Petra's Stone & Mineral Collection 315
Recycled House 86
Reykjavík Art Museum 51
Reykjavík Maritime Museum 77
Reykjavík Museum of Photography 56
Saga Museum 82
Samúel Jónsson's Art Museum 229
Sauðaneshús museum 298
Settlement Centre 195-6
Sheep Farming Museum 246
Sigurgeir's Bird Museum 284
Sigurjón Ólafsson Museum 85
Skaftfellingur Museum 155
Skógar Museum 152
Snartarstaðir Folk Museum 294
Stúdíó Ólafur Elíasson 78
Sudurnes Science & Learning Center 115
Textile Museum 261
Toy Museum 268
Viking Park 159
Viking World 115
War & Peace Museum 200
Westfjords Heritage Museum 238
Whale Museum 282
Whales of Iceland 82
Þjóðveldisbærinn 135
Þórbergssetur 184
music 31, 33, 380-3
Björk 33, 60, 72, 115, 128, 382
Dark Music Days 59
Iceland Airwaves 59
Innipúkinn Festival 59
instruments 382
Lóa Festival 59
Of Monsters & Men 33, 115, 382
Reykjavík 73
Reykjavík Jazz Festival 31, 59
Sigur Rós 33, 115, 139, 380, 382
Sugarcubes, the 72, 382
Mýrdalssandur 158-9

National Museum 52-3
national parks & nature reserves 38-9, *see also* parks & gardens
Fjallabak Nature Reserve 146
Flói Nature Reserve 134
Heiðmörk Nature Reserve 92
Herðubreiðarlindir 339-40
Hornstrandir Nature Reserve 241
Ingólfshöfði 172
Reykjanesfólkvangur Wilderness Reserve 110, 111
Snæfellsjökull National Park 216-17
Vatnajökull National Park 168
Vestdalur Nature Reserve 318
Þingvellir National Park 120-2
Þórsmörk 143
nature reserves, *see* national parks & nature reserves
navigation
East Iceland 304
Highlands, the 328
North Iceland 250-1
Reykjavík 44-5
Southwest Iceland 100-1
Westfjords 222-3
West Iceland 192
necropants 246
Neskaupstaður 321-2
Nootka lupine, *see* lupine
Nordal, Ólöf 79
North Iceland 249-301
accommodation 300-1
activities 252-3
Akureyri 266-72, **267**
driving tours 262-5, 287, **263**, **287**
festivals 257
hiking trail 292-3, **293**
Húsavík 280-3, **280**
itineraries 252-3
Jökulsárgljúfur Canyon 288-93, **289**
Melrakkaslétta Peninsula 294-7, **295**
Skagafjörður 254-60, **255**
tours 277
travel seasons 252-3
travel within North Iceland 250-1
walking tour 269, **269**
Northern Lights 16, 272-3
Brimketill 113
Reykjavík 75-6, 77
notable buildings
Alþingi 51
Ásmundarsafn 51
Bæjarbíó 94
Bessastaðir 95
Harpa 56, 58
Höfði House 86
Landlyst 148
Langabúð 314
Ráðhús 48
Salurinn 94
Núpsstaður 173-4

Of Monsters and Men 33, 115, 382
Ólafsfjörður 278
opening hours 363
Orbis et Globus 276
Ósvífursdóttir, Guðrún 210

paragliding 36
parks & gardens, *see also* national parks & nature reserves
Austurvöllur 51
Hljómskálagarður 48
Klambratún Park 51
Reykjavík Botanic Garden 86-7
planning
clothes 32
etiquette 32
polar bears 242
population 363, 372-3
public holidays 363
puffins 149
Dyrhólaey 153
Ingólfshöfði 172
Látrabjarg Bird Cliffs 234
Rauðinúpur 295
Reykjavík 80-1
Seyðisfjörður 319-20
Snæfellsnes Peninsula 213, 215
Stykkishólmur 205-6
Vestmannaeyjar 147
tours 147

quad biking
Eyrarbakki 134
Hvolsvöllur 138
Reykjanes Peninsula 112
Reykjavík 90

Rauðe, Eiríkur see Erik the Red
Rauðisandur 231, 234
food 234
Raufarhöfn 295-6, **295**
record stores 72
reindeer 314
reserves, see national parks & nature reserves
respectful tourism 362
responsible travel 358-9
Reyðarfjörður 321-2
Reykholt 125, 200-1
accommodation 160, 219
Reykjanes Peninsula 104-15, **106-7**
accommodation 160
drinking 111
food 105, 110, 111, 114
hiking 105
travel within Reykjanes Peninsula 104
Reykjavík 42-97, **49**, **50**, **64-5**, **66-7**, **75**, **76**, **85**, **92**
accommodation 96-7
activities 47-8, 60-1
boat tours 81
drinking 60, 61, 70, 71, 72, 73, 77, 79, 84, 89
festivals & events 58, 59
flightseeing 70-1
food 51, 56, 58, 59, 60, 63, 68, 69, 77, 78, 82, 84, 89, 93, 94
guided tours 61
Hafnarfjörður 91-5, 92, **92**
Hlíðar 84-90, **85**
itineraries 46-7
Kópavogur 91-5, **92**
Laugardalur 84-90, **85**
Laugavegur 62-73, **64-5**, **66-7**
Miðborg 48-61, **49**, **50**
museums 95
music 73
nightlife 73
Old Harbour 74-83, **76**
shopping 59, 68-9, 70, 79
swimming pools 71-2
travel within Reykjavík 44-5, 48, 56, 62, 74, 84
Vesturbær 74-83, **75**

walking tours 57, 83, 88, **57**, **83**, **88**
winter 82
rideshares 351
Rif 218
Rifstangi 295
rivers 12-3
Brúará 123
Hvítá 123, 125
Tungufljót 125
Þórsmörk 143
road trips 8-9
Arctic Coast Way 262-5, **263**
Diamond Circle 287, **287**
South Coast 140-1, **141**
Westfjords Way 232-3, **233**
rock formations
Dyrhólaey 153
Reynisdrangar 155
Þakgil 158
ruins, see also archaeology
Aðalstræti Settlement Exhibition 54-5
Básendar 115
Dritvík 217
Helgafell 207
Þingvellir National Park 121
Þjórsárdalur Valley 135

S

safe travel 123, 157, 355
sagas
Egil's Saga 194-5, 204
Heimskringla 200
Helgafell 206-7
Icelandic Saga Data Base 258
Laxdæla Saga 207, 210
Njál's Saga 138, 153, 155
Saga Museum 82
Saga of Erik the Red 210-11
Saga of Grettir the Strong, The 257
Saga of the Greenlanders 211
Snæfellsáss Saga 215
Víglundar Saga 218
Samúelsson, Guðjón 63, 71, 96, 121, 268, 296
sandar 158
Skeiðarársandur 173, 175
Sandgerði 115
Sauðárkrókur 257
scuba diving 36, see also diving & snorkelling
sea stacks
Djúpalón Beach 216
Hvítserkur 263
Rauðinúpur 295
Reynisdrangar 155

seals
Borgarfjörður Eystri 319
Garður 114, 115
Hvammstangi 261
Hvítserkur 263
Illugastadir 262
Ísafjörður 239
Látrabjarg 234
Lón 187-8
Skjálfandi Bay 282
Stykkishólmur 205-6
Selfoss 125, 132-3
accommodation 160-1
food 133
Seyðisfjörður 316-18, **317**
accommodation 325
beyond Seyðisfjörður 319-24
food 318
shopping 317
travel around Seyðisfjörður 316, 319
sharks 275
Bjarnarhöfn 211-12
sheep 246, 256, 299
shipwrecks 112
Garðar BA 234
Hrafn Sveinbjarnarson III 110-11
Pourquois Pas? 115
Þorgeir GK 205
shopping, see markets, individual locations
Siglufjörður 276-8
drinking 278
food 277, 278
Sigur Rós 33, 115, 139, 380, 382
Sigurðsson, Jón 51, 57, 228
Skaftafell 166-72, **167**
accommodation 189
beyond Skaftafell 172-8, see also individual locations
food 171
travel around Skaftafell 166, 172
Skagafjörður 254-60, **255**
accommodation 300
beyond Skagafjörður 261-5, see also individual locations
food 256, 257, 258
laundry 259
travel around Skagafjörður 254, 261
Skaldic poetry 380
Skálholt 125
skiing 36, 38-9
Hlíðarfjall 270-1
Seyðisfjörður 317
Skógar 149, 152
accommodation 161
drinking 152
food 152

skuas 159
Breiðamerkursandur 182
Ingólfshöfði 172
skyr 34, 210, 357
sleeping-bag accommodation 353
smoking 363
Snæfellsjökull National Park 216-17
Snæfellsnes Peninsula 213-18, **214**
accommodation 219
food 215
travel around Snæfellsnes Peninsula 213
snorkelling, see diving & snorkelling
snowboarding 36, 38-9
snowmobiling 37
Kaldidalur Valley 204
Mýrdalsjökull 151
Vatnajökull 170-1
Sóley 383
Sólheimar Eco-Village 128
Southeast Iceland 162-89
accommodation 189
activities 165
drinking 184
Höfn 141, 185-8, **186**
itineraries 165
Jökulsárlón 180-1, **179**
Skaftafell 166-72, **167**
travel within Southeast Iceland 164
Southern Highlands 143, 146-7
shopping 147
Southwest Iceland 99-161
accommodation 117, 160-1
activities 102, 102-3
driving tour 142-3, **141**
events 102-3
festivals 102-3
Golden Circle 116-28, **118**
hiking tour 144-5, **145**
Hvolsvöllur 136-42, **137**
itineraries 22-3, 102-3, **23**
Reykjanes Peninsula 104-15, **106-7**
travel around Southwest Iceland 100-1, 104, 146
Vík 153-7, **154**
Spákonuhof 256
spas 17, see also geothermal pools
Blue Lagoon 104-5
Forest Lagoon 268-9
Hveragerði 130
Laugar Spa 86
Sprengisandur Route 335-8, **336**
accommodation 347

Southwest Iceland *continued*
travel within Sprengisandur Route 335
Stapavík 320
Stöðvarfjörður 315
Stokkseyri 134
 accommodation 161
Strýtan 279
Stuðlagil 324
Sturluson, Snorri 142, 200-1, 204
Stykkishólmur 205-8, **206**
 accommodation 219
 beyond Stykkishólmur 209-12
 food 206
 travel around Stykkishólmur 205
 walking tour 208, **208**
Sugarcubes, the 72, 382
Sun Voyager 70
super-Jeep tours 108
 Askja Route 339
 Kerlingarfjöll 333
 Laki 177
 Laugarfell 311
 Vatnajökull 170-1
 Vík 156
sustainability 128, 358-9
sustainable travel 113
Súðavík 242
Sveinsson 51
Sveinsson, Ásmundur 51, 56
swans 48, 113, 188
swimming pools, *see also* see also geothermal pools
 Brimketill 110
 etiquette 71
 Hofsós 259
 Húsavík Swimming Pool 283
 Landmannalaugar 146-7
 Laugarás Lagoon 127
 Laugardalslaug 86
 Laugarvatn Swimming Pool 123
 Seljavallalaug 140
 Stykkishólmur Swimming Pool 207
 Sundhöll Selfoss 132
 Sundlaug Akureyrar 270

Sundlaug Hafnar 187
Tálknafjörður Swimming Pool 235
Þórshöfn 298

Tálknafjörður 234-5
taxes 352, 353
tectonic plates 110
 Bridge Between Continents 114
time zone 363
tipping 352
Tjörnin 48
tölt 309
train 351
tours, *see* ATV tours, boat tours, glacier tours, hiking tours, super-Jeep tours, volcanoes, walking tours, *individual locations*
travel seasons 30-1
travel to/from Iceland 350
travel within Iceland 351
travelling with kids, *see* family travel
trolls 238-9
turf houses
 Íslenski Bærinn Turf House 133
 Keldur 142
 Núpsstaður 173
 Nýibær turf house 259
 Stekkjarkot 115

University of Iceland 51

Valahnúkur 110
Vallanes Organic Farm 313
Vatnajökull National Park 183
Vestmannaeyjar 147-9
 accommodation 161
 food 146
Vík 153-7, **154**
 accommodation 161
 beyond Vík 158-9, *see also individual locations*
 drinking 156
 food 155
 travel around Vík 153, 158
Vikings 133, 199
 Aðalstræti Settlement Exhibition 54-5
 Arnarson, Ingólfur 51, 159
 Búðardalur 210-11

Eiríksson, Leifur 63
Hafnarfjörður Viking Festival 95
Hjörleifshöfði 159
Hróðmarsson, Hjörleifur 159
 poetry 142
 Saga Museum 82
 Viking World 115
 Þjórsárdalur Valley 135
visas 350
volcanic eruptions 355, 377-9
 Askja 340
 Eyjafjallajökull 136
 Hekla volcano 135
 Laki 176
volcanoes 10-11, 94, 377-9, *see also* craters
 Askja 343
 Eyjafjallajökull 136
 Fagradalsfjall 110
 Heimaey 148
 Helgafell 147
 Hvannadalshnúkur 173
 Katla 150
 Leirhnjúkur 286
 tours 147
 Þríhnúkagígur 93
volleyball 86, 87, 90
Vopnafjörður 323-4

walking tours 57, *see also* hiking, hiking tours
 Akureyri 269, **269**
 Old Reykjavík 57, **57**
 Seltjarnarnes 83, **83**
 Stykkishólmur 208, **208**
 Viðey Island 88, **88**
water activities 12-13
waterfalls
 Ægissiðufoss 142
 Aldeyjarfoss 336
 Brúarfoss 123
 Búðarárfoss 321
 Dettifoss 288, 290
 Drifandi 138
 Dynjandi 226-7
 Fagrifoss 177
 Faxafoss 125
 Gljúfrabúi 139
 Gljúfursárfoss 324
 Gluggafoss 138
 Glymur 199
 Gufufoss 317
 Gullfoss 126
 Hafragilsfoss 288, 290
 Háifoss 135
 Heljarfoss 323-4
 Hengifoss 307-8
 Hjálparfoss 135
 Hlauptungufoss 123

 Hraunfossar 204
 Kirkjufellsfoss 211
 Kirkjufoss 310
 Klifbrekkufossar 323
 Kvernufoss 149
 Litlanesfoss 307-8
 Miðfoss 123
 Reykjafoss 131
 Selfoss 288, 290
 Seljalandsfoss 139
 Skógafoss 149
 Stuðlafoss 324
 Svartifoss 168
 Svöðufoss 218
 Systrafoss 175
 Vestdalsá 318
 Þórðarfoss 138
weather 30-1
weights 363
West Iceland 191-219
 accommodation 219
 activities 193
 Borgarnes 194-7, **195**
 hiking tour 202-3, **203**
 itineraries 28-9, 193, **29**
 Snæfellsnes Peninsula 213-18, **214**
 Stykkishólmur 205-8, **206**
 travel within West Iceland 192
Westfjords 220-47, **222-3**
 accommodation 227, 247
 activities 224-5
 Arnarfjörður 226-30, **227**
 driving tour 232-3, **233**
 hiking 229
 hiking tour 243, **243**
 Hólmavík 244-6, **245**
 Ísafjörður 236-9, **237**
 itineraries 224-5
 travel seasons 224-5
 travel within Westfjords 222-3
whale watching 14, 61, 147
 Reykjavík 80-1
 code of conduct 283
 Eyjafjörður 271, 274
 Hólmavík 246
 Húsavík 264, 354, 368
 Ólafsvík 218
 Öndverðarnes 217
 Skjálfandi Bay 280-1, 282
 Snæfellsnes Peninsula 213
whaling 81
white-water rafting 37
 Hvítá river 123, 125
 Hvítárvatn 332
 Skagafjörður 260
wi-fi 350
Wilderness Center 308-9
wool 131, 132, 156, 198, 199, 270

Yule Lads 285

ziplining
 Hveragerði 131
 Vík 156-7
zoos
 Reykjavík Zoo & Family
  Park 87

Þingeyri 227
Þingvellir National Park
 120-2
Þjórsárdalur
 accommodation 161
Þjórsárdalur Valley 135
Þór 206-7
Þorbjarnardóttir, Guðriður
 218
Þórshöfn 298-9
 food 299
Þúfa 78-9

"The first time I walked the coast in the Vestmannaeyjar islands (p147) watching puffins teeter into the ocean and return to their burrows."

ALEXIS AVERBUCK

"Standing at Raufarhöfn's Arctic Henge (p296) with views in all directions, imagining the ancient Icelandic sagas coming to life."

MARY FITZPATRICK

All rights reserved. No part of this publication may be copied, stored in a retrieval system, or transmitted in any form by any means, electronic, mechanical, recording or otherwise, except brief extracts for the purpose of review, and no part of this publication may be sold or hired, without the written permission of the publisher. Lonely Planet and the Lonely Planet logo are trademarks of Lonely Planet and are registered in the US Patent and Trademark Office and in other countries. Lonely Planet does not allow its name or logo to be appropriated by commercial establishments, such as retailers, restaurants or hotels. Please let us know of any misuses: lonelyplanet.com/legal/intellectual-property.

Mapping data sources:
© Lonely Planet
© OpenStreetMap http://openstreetmap.org/copyright

FROM LEFT: KORNEL_FILIPJAK/SHUTTERSTOCK, STEFANO RULLI/SHUTTERSTOCK

THIS BOOK

The 14th edition of Lonely Planet's *Iceland* guidebook was written and researched by Eygló Svala Arnarsdóttir, Alexis Averbuck, Jade Bremner, Mary Fitzpatrick and Anthony Ham. The previous edition was written by Eygló, Alexis, Egill Bjarnason and Meena Thiruvengadam. This guidebook was produced by the following:

Destination Editor
Amy Lynch

Production Editor
Robin Yule

Image Editor
Dominic Allen

Cartographer
Julie Dodkins

Assisting Cartographers
Chris Lee-ack, Bohumil Ptáček

Coordinating Editor
Andrea Dobbin

Assisting Editor
Paul Harding

Cover Researcher
Katelyn Perry

Thanks Janet Austin, Michelle Bennett, Soo Hamilton, Alison Killilea, Kate Mathews, James Smart

Paper in this book is certified against the Forest Stewardship Council™ standards. FSC™ promotes environmentally responsible, socially beneficial and economically viable management of the world's forests.

Published by Lonely Planet Global Limited
CRN 554153
14th edition – Apr 2026
ISBN 978 1 83869 799 0
© Lonely Planet 2026
10 9 8 7 6 5 4 3 2 1
Printed in China